Grosset's **UNIVERSAL** *Library*

Christ Stopped at Eboli by Carlo Levi (UL-1)

The Dance of Life by Havelock Ellis (UL-2)

The Good Society by Walter Lippmann (UL-3)

The Late George Apley by John P. Marquand (UL-4)

Man and His Gods by Homer Smith (UL-5)

The Measure of Man by Joseph Wood Krutch (UL-6)

Melbourne by Lord David Cecil (UL-7)

Oscar Wilde by Hesketh Pearson (UL-8)

The Puritan Oligarchy by Thomas Wertenbaker (UL-9)

Quackery in the Public Schools by Albert Lynd (UL-10)

Reveille in Washington by Margaret Leech (UL-11)

The Web and the Rock by Thomas Wolfe (UL-12)

The Ides of March by Thornton Wilder (UL-13)

Noble Essences by Sir Osbert Sitwell (UL-14)

Why Was Lincoln Murdered? by Otto Eisenschiml (UL-15)

You Can't Go Home Again by Thomas Wolfe (UL-16)

The Shock of Recognition *(Vol. I—The 19th Century),* edited by Edmund Wilson (UL-17)

The Shock of Recognition *(Vol. II—The 20th Century),* edited by Edmund Wilson (UL-18)

THE SHOCK OF RECOGNITION

THE DEVELOPMENT OF LITERATURE
IN THE UNITED STATES
RECORDED BY THE MEN
WHO MADE IT

EDITED BY
EDMUND WILSON

VOLUME II
THE TWENTIETH CENTURY

Grosset's UNIVERSAL *Library*

GROSSET & DUNLAP · NEW YORK

WITH ILLUSTRATIONS BY
ROBERT F. HALLOCK

LIBRARY OF CONGRESS CATALOG CARD NUMBER: 55-12140

PRINTED IN THE UNITED STATES OF AMERICA
BY ARRANGEMENT WITH FARRAR, STRAUS AND CUDAHY

For genius, all over the world, stands hand in hand, and one shock of recognition runs the whole circle round.

HERMAN MELVILLE

FOREWORD

THIS BOOK is not a critical anthology, but a collection of literary documents. It is an attempt to present a chronicle of the progress of literature in the United States as one finds it recorded by those who had some part in creating that literature.

But this statement requires qualification. I have had to exclude general discussions, even where these were interesting, of literary principles and tendencies, and to confine myself to pieces which deal with particular writers, because I should not have had space to cover both kinds of criticism in a manageable volume. The best way to understand the general is, in any case, to study the concrete; and in the course of these examinations of individual writers, one gets, though by glimpses, a fairly complete view of the larger backgrounds and movements. But even within these limitations I have restricted the scope further by excluding essays and reviews by professional literary critics. There would, of course, be a large field to choose from in this department, but a collection of critical essays would be quite another kind of anthology. I was aiming to show the effect on one another of the first-rate American figures; and these writers, though, like Poe or Howells, they have sometimes practiced criticism, have never simply been scholars or reviewers, but have always expressed themselves in literature in some more direct way. What I am trying to present, in fact, is the developing self-consciousness of the American genius from the moment in the middle of the last century when we first really had a literature worth talking about to the moment toward the end of the second decade of ours when it was plain that, following the cultural slump of the period after the Civil War, a new movement had got under way.

For this purpose I have brought together materials of the most varied shapes and styles: essays, monographs, memoirs, journals, letters, satires, dialogues, poems. And I have violated my American canon by admitting a few pieces by foreigners that show the repercussions of American books thrown back to us from abroad and the consciousness of Europe of *us*. I have also departed from the program suggested by my title of showing only the moments when genius becomes aware of its kin by including a few examples of the shock of recognition which occurs when the very good writer is confronted by the very bad. It requires gifts just as rare—since they are just the same gifts—to be fully aware of the bad as to be fully aware of the good.

As a hater of extracts and omissions, I have printed the whole of everything.

The following acknowledgments are due for permission to use copyrighted material: to Houghton Mifflin Company for letters from *The Life of James Russell Lowell* by Horace E. Scudder, letter and quotations from *Walt Whitman* by Bliss Perry, quotations from *My Own Story* by John Taylor Trowbridge, Emerson's *Journals* and *Whitman and Burroughs, Comrades* by Clara Barrus, and *A Critical Fable* by Amy Lowell; the Columbia University Press for Emerson letters and quotation from Mr. Rusk in *Letters of Ralph Waldo Emerson* edited by Ralph L. Rusk; Doubleday, Doran and Company, Inc., for quotations from *Walt Whitman in Camden* by Horace Traubel and selections from *Collected Prose Works* of Walt Whitman; The Macmillan Company for quotations from *Days with Walt Whitman* by Edward Carpenter; the Harvard University Press for a quotation from *Whitman's Workshop* by Clifton Joseph Furness and Mrs. Frank J. Sprague, who owns the original manuscript of this dialogue; for quotations from *Reminiscences of Walt Whitman* by W. S. Kennedy; Harper and Brothers for *The Literary Offenses of James Fenimore Cooper* by Mark Twain and a selection from *My Mark Twain* by William Dean Howells; Charles Scribner's Sons for *Emerson* by J. J. Chapman and essays on *William James* and *Josiah Royce* from *Character and Opinion in the United States* by George Santayana; Mr. H. G. Wells for *Stephen Crane from an English Standpoint;* Miss Mildred Howells for selections from *My Mark Twain* by William Dean Howells; Miss Elizabeth Lodge for *The Life of George Cabot Lodge* by Henry Adams; Mr. T. S. Eliot for his essays on Henry James; Viking Press, Inc., for *Studies in Classic American Literature* by D. H. Lawrence, copyright 1923 by Thomas Seltzer, Inc., 1951 by Frieda Lawrence; Alfred A. Knopf, Inc., for essays from *A Book of Prefaces and Prejudices, First* and *Fifth Series* by H. L. Mencken; Mr. Mencken and *The Nation* for *A Short View of Gamalielese;* Mr. John Dos Passos for his review of E. E. Cummings' *The Enormous Room;* and Mrs. Sherwood Anderson, Mr. Van Wyck Brooks and the editors of *Story* magazine for *Letters of Sherwood Anderson to Van Wyck Brooks.*

I have especially to thank the authorities of the Harvard University Library, who have greatly facilitated my researches; Mr. Clifton Joseph Furness of Cambridge, who has generously advised me out of his immense knowledge of Walt Whitman, and who has loaned me materials and allowed me to quote from his own unpublished manuscripts; Mr. Ferris Greenslet and Mr. R. N. Linscott of Houghton Mifflin, to whom I am indebted for loan of materials and help of other kinds; and Miss Helen Gould, who has worked with me with expert skill on the mechanical side of the book.

FOREWORD TO THE SECOND EDITION

I HAVE ADDED, in this new edition, with the permission of Harper and Brothers, a second section of Mark Twain's essay, *Fenimore Cooper's Literary Offenses,* discovered recently among the Mark Twain papers by Mr. Bernard De Voto and published in the *New England Quarterly.* I may also take this opportunity to mention another piece which I should have liked to include in *The Shock of Recognition* but for which I was unable to get permission: the essay called *Mark Twain: An Inquiry,* which stands as the last chapter of Howells' book *My Mark Twain* and which should stand here beside the personal memoir. This essay, which first appeared in the *North American Review* of February, 1901, was written to celebrate the occasion of Mark Twain's return to the United States, after his five years spent abroad, and of the first publication of his collected works. Mark Twain had left the States a popular humorist and had come back a great public figure, who had been praised and made much of in Europe, and who was now taken seriously at home by the younger generation as he had hardly ever been by his contemporaries. This essay is the most extensive critical study that Howells devoted to the work of his friend, and it has a unique interest in attempting to explain this work in terms of Mark Twain's Western origins, which Howells was in a position to understand so much better than the Eastern critics.

I should like to recommend, also, as supplementary reading, Thomas Beer's little book on Stephen Crane: *Stephen Crane: A Study in American Letters*—to which, on rereading it since *The Shock* was compiled, I have felt that I have done something less than justice in my introduction to the section on Crane. The more recent and scholarly writers on Crane complain that Beer is most unreliable, that his book is full of errors of fact; but it will serve to fill in, by its picture of Crane's period, a chapter of our literary history which I have otherwise rather slighted: the Bohemian "end of the century," when people like Stephen Crane and Harold Frederic and Henry Harland would begin as American realists, champions of Art and Truth, fighting the genteel tradition, and end up in Paris or London as journalists or fashionable novelists. Thomas Beer—not himself a writer on a level with the figures in this book—had a special relish for the nineties and the early nineteen hundreds and has given the sense of this moment of Mouquin's and *M'lle New York*, of Hearst papers and President McKinley, of *Yellow Book* writers and of young correspondents conducting themselves gallantly in minor wars, of efforts to grow in American soil the windblown seeds from Europe of Aestheticism and Naturalism, as no other non-contemporary has been able to give it.

I have taken the occasion, also, to correct a number of errors of the kind that can be easily corrected; but I shall have to explain here—to avoid more extensive changes in the plates—that Mr. Ferris Greenslet of Houghton, Mifflin has been able to set me right in my account, in the last paragraph of page 743, of the biography of John Hay that Herbert Croly was discouraged from writing by an interview with Henry Adams. It was the publishers, it seems, not the Hay family, who had selected Herbert Croly to do the biography of Hay, and he had actually signed a contract and been at work for some time on Hay's papers when his desolating meeting with Adams had the effect of making him throw up the job.

CONTENTS

Volume II — The Twentieth Century

CONTENTS

Note: Volume I of *The Shock of Recognition* is UL–17 in Grosset's Universal Library. It is devoted to nineteenth-century essays and includes pages 1–658.

THE SHOCK OF RECOGNITION

It has been difficult to find anything about Stephen Crane for the purposes of this book. Thomas Beer's *Stephen Crane* is valuable, but it is simply a sort of memoir written by one who did not know him; and though the collected edition of Crane includes prefaces by Amy Lowell, Willa Cather, Sherwood Anderson and Howells, these are brief and deal with special aspects. One has to go abroad for something better. There are three fine and moving pieces by Joseph Conrad: *Stephen Crane: A Note without Dates* in the volume called *Life and Letters;* and, in *Last Essays, Stephen Crane* and a review of *The Red Badge of Courage.* But these are well known and easily accessible, and it has seemed more appropriate to include this essay by Mr. Wells, which has never before been reprinted. It appeared in the *North American Review* of August 1900. Crane, who had been living in England for more than a year, had died of tuberculosis on June 4.

The end of the century was a moment when the literary migrants from America were beginning to impinge on the consciousness of literary England. The novelists, Harold Frederic and Henry Harland, had already gone to live in England, and Harland had been editor of *The Yellow Book.*

Henry James and Logan Pearsall Smith had been settled there since the eighties. The set of writers to which Crane belonged and which has been so entertainingly and stimulatingly described by the late Ford Madox Ford in his various books of reminiscences, was curiously cosmopolitan; Crane and Henry James were Americans; Conrad was a Pole; and Ford himself (then Hueffer) was part German. All were working in the English language with trained skill and anxious intensity, but they were all outside the English tradition. It seemed to Mr. Wells that Crane had got free of this English tradition as no American had ever done before.

H. G. WELLS

STEPHEN CRANE FROM AN ENGLISH STANDPOINT

THE UNTIMELY DEATH at thirty of Stephen Crane robs English literature of an interesting and significant figure, and the little world of those who write, of a stout friend and a pleasant comrade. For a year and more he had been ailing. The bitter hardships of his Cuban expedition had set its mark upon mind and body alike, and the slow darkling of the shadow upon him must have been evident to all who were not blinded by their confidence in what he was yet to do. Altogether, I knew Crane for less than a year, and I saw him for the last time hardly more than seven weeks ago. He was then in a hotel at Dover, lying still and comfortably wrapped about, before an open window and the calm and spacious sea. If you would figure him as I saw him, you must think of him as a face of a type very typically American, long and spare, with very straight hair and straight features and long, quiet hands and hollow eyes, moving slowly, smiling and speaking slowly, with that deliberate New Jersey manner he had, and lapsing from speech again into a quiet contemplation of his ancient enemy. For it was the sea that had taken his strength, the same sea that now shone, level waters beyond level waters, with here and there a minute, shining ship, warm and tranquil beneath the tranquil evening sky. Yet I felt scarcely a suspicion then that this was a last meeting. One might have seen it all, perhaps. He was thin and gaunt and wasted, too weak for more than a remembered jest and a greeting and good wishes. It did not seem to me in any way credible that he would reach his refuge in the Black Forest only to die at the journey's end. It will be a long time yet before I can fully realize that he is no longer a contemporary of mine; that the last I saw of him was, indeed, final and complete.

Though my personal acquaintance with Crane was so soon truncated, I have followed his work for all the four years it has been known in England. I have always been proud, and now I am glad, that, however obscurely, I also was in the first chorus of welcome that met his coming. It is, perhaps, no great distinction for me; he was abundantly praised; but, at least, I was early and willing to praise him when I was wont to be youthfully jealous of my praises. His success in England began with the *Red Badge of Courage,* which did, indeed, more completely than any other book has done for many years, take the reading public by storm. Its freshness of method, its vigor of imagination, its force of color and its essential freedom from many traditions that dominate this side of the Atlantic, came—in spite of the previous shock of Mr. Kipling—with a positive effect of impact. It was a new thing, in a new school. When one looked for sources, one thought at once of Tolstoy; but, though it was clear that Tolstoy had exerted a powerful influence upon the conception, if not the actual writing, of the book, there still remained something entirely original and novel. To a certain extent, of course, that was the new man as an individual; but, to at least an equal extent, it was the new man as a typical young American, free at last, as no generation of Americans have been free before, of any regard for English criticism, comment, or tradition, and applying to literary work the conception and theories of the cosmopolitan studio with a quite American directness and vigor. For the great influence of the studio on Crane cannot be ignored; in the persistent selection of the essential elements of an impression, in the ruthless exclusion of mere information, in the direct vigor with which the selected points are made, there is Whistler even more than there is Tolstoy in the *Red Badge of Courage*. And witness this, taken almost haphazard:

> At nightfall the column broke into regimental pieces, and the fragments went into the fields to camp. Tents sprang up like strange plants. Camp fires, like red, peculiar blossoms, dotted the night. . . . From this little distance the many fires, with the black forms of men passing to and fro before the crimson rays, made weird and satanic effects.

And here again; consider the daring departure from all academic requirements in this void countenance:

> A warm and strong hand clasped the youth's languid fingers for an instant, and then he heard a cheerful and audacious whistling as the man strode away. As he who had so befriended him was thus passing out of his life, it suddenly occurred to the youth that he had not once seen his face.

I do not propose to add anything here to the mass of criticism upon this remarkable book. Like everything else which has been abundantly praised, it has occasionally been praised "all wrong"; and I suppose that it must have been said hundreds of times that this book is a subjective study of the typical soldier in war. But Mr. George Wyndham, himself a soldier of experience, has pointed out in an admirable preface to a re-issue of this and other of Crane's war studies that the hero of the *Red Badge* is, and is intended to be, altogether a more sensitive and imaginative person than the ordinary man. He is the idealist, the dreamer of boastful things brought suddenly to the test of danger and swift occasions and the presence of death. To this theme Crane returned several times, and particularly in a story called *Death and the Child* that was written after the Greek war. That story is considered by very many of Crane's admirers as absolutely his best. I have carefully reread it in deference to opinions I am bound to respect, but I still find it inferior to the earlier work. The generalized application is, to my taste, a little too evidently underlined; there is just that touch of insistence that prevails so painfully at times in Victor Hugo's work, as of a writer not sure of his reader, not happy in his reader, and seeking to drive his implication (of which also he is not quite sure) home. The child is not a natural child; there is no happy touch to make it personally alive; it is THE CHILD, something unfalteringly big; a large, pink, generalized thing, I cannot help but see it, after the fashion of a Vatican cherub. The fugitive runs panting to where, all innocent of the battle about it, it plays; and he falls down breathless to be asked, "Are you a man?" One sees the intention clearly enough; but in the later story it seems to me there is a new ingredient that is absent from the earlier stories, an ingredient imposed on Crane's natural genius from without—a concession to the demands of a criticism it had been wiser, if less modest, in him to disregard—criticism that missed this quality of generalization and demanded it, even though it had to be artificially and deliberately introduced.

Following hard upon the appearance of the *Red Badge of Courage* in England came reprints of two books, *Maggie* and *George's Mother,* that had already appeared in America six years earlier. Their reception gave Crane his first taste of the peculiarities of the new public he had come upon. These stories seem to me in no way inferior to the *Red Badge;* and at times there are passages, the lament of Maggie's mother at the end of *Maggie,* for example, that it would be hard to beat by any passage from the later book. But on all hands came discouragement or tepid praise. The fact of it is, there had been almost an orgy of praise—for England, that is; and ideas and adjectives and phrases were exhausted. To write further long reviews on works displaying the same qualities as had been already amply discussed in the notices of the *Red Badge* would be difficult and laborious; while to admit an equal excellence and deny an equal prominence would be absurd. But to treat these stories as early work, to find them immature, dismiss them and proceed to fresher topics, was obvious and convenient. So it was, I uncharitably imagine, that these two tales have been overshadowed and are still comparatively unknown. Yet they are absolutely essential to a just understanding of Crane. In these stories, and in these alone, he achieved tenderness and a compulsion of sympathy for other than vehement emotions, qualities that the readers of *The Third Violet* and *On Active Service,* his later love stories, might well imagine beyond his reach.

And upon the appearance of these books in England came what, in my present mood, I cannot but consider as the great blunder and misfortune of Crane's life. It is a trait of the public we writers serve that to please it is to run the gravest risk of never writing again. Through a hundred channels and with a hundred varieties of seduction and compulsion, the public seeks to induce its favorite to do something else—to act, to lecture, to travel, to jump down volcanoes or perform in music halls, to do anything, rather than to possess his soul in peace and to pursue the work he was meant to do. Indeed, this modern public is as violently experimental with its writers as a little child with a kitten. It is animated, above all things, by an insatiable desire to plunge its victim into novel surroundings and watch how he feels. And since Crane had demonstrated, beyond all cavil, that he could sit at home and, with nothing but his wonderful brain and his wonderful induction from recorded things, build up the truest and most convincing picture of war; since he was a fastidious and careful worker, intensely subjective in his mental habit; since he was a man of fragile physique and of that unreasonable courage that will wreck the strongest physique; and since, moreover, he was habitually a bad traveler, losing trains and luggage and missing connections even in the orderly circumstances of peace, it was clearly the most reasonable thing in the world to propose, it was received with the applause of two hemispheres as a most right and proper thing, that he should go as a war correspondent, first to Greece and then to Cuba. Thereby, and for nothing but disappointment and bitterness, he utterly wrecked his health. He came into comparison with men as entirely his masters in this work as he was the master of all men in his own; and I read even in the most punctual of his obituary notices the admission of his journalistic failure. I have read, too, that he brought back nothing from these expeditions. But, indeed, even not counting his death, he brought back much. On his way home from Cuba he was wrecked, and he wrote the story of the nights and days that followed the sinking of the ship with a simplicity and vigor that even he cannot rival elsewhere.

The Open Boat is to my mind, beyond all question, the crown of all his work. It has all the stark power of the earlier stories, with a new element of restraint; the color is as full and strong as ever, fuller and stronger, indeed; but those chromatic splashes that at times deafen and confuse in the *Red Badge,* those images that astonish rather than enlighten, are disciplined and controlled. "That and *Flanagan,*" he told me, with a philosophical laugh, "was all I got out of Cuba." I cannot say whether they were worth the price, but I am convinced that these two things are as immortal as any work of any living man. And the way *The Open Boat* begins, no stress, plain—even a little gray and flattish:

> None of them knew the color of the sky. Their eyes glanced level, and were fastened upon the waves that swept toward them. These waves were of the hue of slate, save for the tops, which were of foaming white, and all of the men knew the color of the sea. The horizon narrowed and widened, and dipped and rose, and at all times its edge was jagged with waves that seemed thrust up in points like rocks.
>
> Many a man ought to have a bathtub larger than the boat which here rode upon the sea. These waves were most wrongfully and barbarously abrupt and tall, and each froth top was a problem in small-boat navigation.
>
> The cook squatted in the bottom, and looked with both eyes at the six inches of gunwale which separated him from the ocean. His sleeves were rolled over his fat forearms, and the two flaps of his unbuttoned vest dangled as he bent to bail out the boat. Often he said, "Gawd! That was a narrow clip." As he remarked it, he invariably gazed eastward over the broken sea.
>
> The oiler, steering with one of the two oars in the boat, sometimes raised himself suddenly to keep clear of the water that swirled in over the stern. It was a thin little oar and it seemed often ready to snap.
>
> The correspondent, pulling at the other oar, watched the waves and wondered why he was there.

From that beginning, the story mounts and mounts over the waves, wave frothing after wave, each wave a threat, and the men toil and toil and toil again; by insensible degrees the day lights the waves to green and olive, and the foam grows dazzling. Then as the long day draws out, they come toward the land.

"Look! There's a man on the shore!"
"Where?"
"There! See 'im?"
"Yes, sure! He's walking along."
"Now he's stopped. Look! He's facing us!"
"So he is, by thunder!"
"Ah, now we're all right! Now we're all right! There'll be a boat out here for us in half an hour."
"He's going on. He's running. He's going up to that house there."

The remote beach seemed lower than the sea, and it required a searching glance to discern the little black figure. The captain saw a floating stick and they rowed to it. A bath towel was by some weird chance in the boat, and, tying this on the stick, the captain waved it. The oarsman did not dare turn his head, so he was obliged to ask questions.

"What's he doing now?"
"He's standing still again. He's looking, I think. . . . There he goes again. Towards the house. Now he's stopped again."
"Is he waving at us?"
"No, not now! he was, though."
"Look! There comes another man!"
"He's running."

. . . .

"Well, I wish I could make something out of those signals. What do you suppose he means!"
"He don't mean anything. He's just playing."
"Well, if he'd just signal us to try the surf again, or to go to sea and wait, or go north, or go south, or go to hell—there would be some reason in it. But look at him. He just stands there and keeps his coat revolving like a wheel. The ass!"
"There come more people."
"Now there's quite a mob. Look! Isn't that a boat?"
"Where? Oh, I see where you mean. No, that's no boat."
"That fellow is still waving his coat."
"He must think we like to see him do that. Why don't he quit it? It don't mean anything."

"I don't know. I think he's trying to make us go north. It must be that there's a life saving station there somewhere."

"Say, he ain't tired yet. Look at 'im wave."

. . . .

"Holy smoke!" said one, allowing his voice to express his impious mood. "If we keep on monkeying out here! If we've got to flounder out here all night!"

"Oh, we'll never have to stay here all night! Don't you worry. They've seen us now, and it won't be long before they'll come chasing out after us."

The shore grew dusky. The man waving a coat blended gradually into this gloom, and it swallowed in the same manner the omnibus and the group of people. The spray, when it dashed uproariously over the side, made the voyagers shrink and swear like men who were being branded.

"I'd like to catch the chump who waved the coat. I feel like soaking him one, just for luck."

"Why? What did he do?"

. . . .

In the meantime the oiler rowed, and then the correspondent rowed, and then the oiler rowed. Gray-faced and bowed forward, they mechanically, turn by turn, plied the leaden oars. The form of the lighthouse had vanished from the southern horizon, but finally a pale star appeared, just lifting from the sea. The streaked saffron in the west passed before the all-merging darkness, and the sea to the east was black. The land had vanished, and was expressed only by the low and dread thunder of the surf.

The Open Boat gives its title to a volume containing, in addition to that and *Flanagan,* certain short pieces. One of these others, at least, is also to my mind a perfect thing, *The Wise Men.* It tells of the race between two bartenders in the city of Mexico, and I cannot imagine how it could possibly have been better told. And in this volume, too, is that other masterpiece—the one I deny—*Death and the Child.*

Now I do not know how Crane took the reception of this book, for he was not the man to babble of his wrongs; but I cannot conceive how it could have been anything but a grave disappointment to him. To use the silly phrase of the literary shopman, "the vogue of the short story" was already over; rubbish, pure rubbish, provided only it was lengthy, had resumed its former precedence again in the reviews, in the publishers' advertisements, and on the library and booksellers' counters. The book was taken as a trivial by-product, its author was exhorted to abandon this production of "brilliant fragments"—anything less than fifty thousand words is a fragment to the writer of literary columns—and to make that "sustained effort," that architectural undertaking, that alone impresses the commercial mind. Of course, the man who can call *The Open Boat* a brilliant fragment would reproach Rodin for not completing the edifice his brilliant fragments of statuary are presumably intended to adorn, and would sigh, with the late Mr. Ruskin, for the day when Mr. Whistler would "finish" his pictures. Moreover, he was strongly advised—just as they have advised Mr. Kipling—to embark upon a novel. And from other quarters, where a finer wisdom might have been displayed, he learned that the things he had written were not "short stories" at all; they were "sketches" perhaps, "anecdotes"—just as they call Mr. Kipling's short stories "anecdotes"; and it was insinuated that for him also the true, the ineffable "short story" was beyond his reach. I think it is indisputable that the quality of this reception, which a more self-satisfied or less sensitive man than Crane might have ignored, did react very unfavorably upon his work. They put him out of conceit with these brief intense efforts in which his peculiar strength was displayed.

It was probably such influence that led him to write *The Third Violet.* I do not know certainly, but I imagine, that the book was to be a demonstration, and it is not a successful demonstration, that Crane could write a charming love story. It is the very simple affair of an art student and a summer boarder, with the more superficial incidents of their petty encounters set forth in a forcible, objective manner that is curiously hard and unsympathetic. The characters act, and on reflection one admits they act, *true,* but the play of their emotions goes on behind the curtain of the style, and all the enrichments of imaginative appeal that make love beautiful are omitted. Yet, though the story as a whole fails to satisfy, there are many isolated portions of altogether happy effectiveness, a certain ride behind an ox cart, for example. Much more surely is *On Active Service* an effort, and in places a painful effort, to fit his peculiar gift to the uncongenial conditions of popular acceptance. It is the least capable and least satisfactory of all Crane's work.

While these later books were appearing, and right up to his last fatal illness, Crane continued to produce fresh war pictures that show little or no falling off in vigor of imagination and handling; and, in addition, he was experimenting with verse. In that little stone-blue volume, *War Is Kind,* and in the earlier *Black Riders,* the reader will find a series of acute and vivid impressions and many of the finer qualities of Crane's descriptive prose, but he will not find any novel delights of melody or cadence or any fresh aspects of Crane's personality. There remain some children's stories to be published and an unfinished romance. With that the tale of his published work ends, and the career of one of the most brilliant, most significant, and most distinctively American of all English writers comes to its unanticipated *finis.*

It would be absurd, here and now, to attempt to apportion any relativity of importance to Crane, to say that he was greater than A or less important than B. That class-list business is, indeed, best left forever to the newspaper plebiscite and the library statistician; among artists, whose sole, just claim to recognition and whose sole title to immortality must necessarily be the possession of unique qualities, that is to say, of unclassifiable factors, these gradations are absurd. Suffice it that, even before his death, Crane's right to be counted in the hierarchy of those who have made a permanent addition to the great and growing fabric of English letters was not only assured, but conceded. To define his position in time, however, and in relation to periods and modes of writing will be a more reasonable undertaking; and it seems to me that, when at last the true proportions can be seen, Crane will be found to occupy a position singularly cardinal. He was a New Englander of Puritan lineage,[1] and

[1]Stephen Crane was not a New Englander. He was born in Newark, New Jersey, and his family, says Thomas Beer, "was old in the State of New Jersey."—E. W.

the son of a long tradition of literature. There had been many Cranes who wrote before him. He has shown me a shelf of books, for the most part the pious and theological works of various antecedent Stephen Cranes. He had been at some pains to gather together these alien products of his kin. For the most part they seemed little, insignificant books, and one opened them to read the beaten *clichés,* the battered, outworn phrases, of a movement that has ebbed. Their very size and binding suggested a dying impulse, that very same impulse that in its prime had carried the magnificence of Milton's imagery and the pomp and splendors of Milton's prose. In Crane that impulse was altogether dead. He began stark—I find all through this brief notice I have been repeating that in a dozen disguises, "freedom from tradition," "absolute directness," and the like—as though he came into the world of letters without ever a predecessor. In style, in method, and in all that is distinctively *not* found in his books, he is sharply defined, the expression in literary art of certain enormous repudiations. Was ever a man before who wrote of battles so abundantly as he has done, and never had a word, never a word from first to last, of the purpose and justification of the war? And of the God of Battles, no more than the battered name; "Hully Gee!"—the lingering trace of the Deity! And of the sensuousness and tenderness of love, so much as one can find in *The Third Violet!* Any richness of allusion, any melody or balance of phrase, the half quotation that refracts and softens and enriches the statement, the momentary digression that opens like a window upon beautiful or distant things, are not merely absent, but obviously and sedulously avoided. It is as if the racial thought and tradition had been razed from his mind and its site plowed and salted. He is more than himself in this; he is the first expression of the opening mind of a new period, or, at least, the early emphatic phase of a new initiative—beginning, as a growing mind must needs begin, with the record of impressions, a record of a vigor and intensity beyond all precedent.

WILLIAM DEAN HOWELLS (1837–1920) presided over American literature through the half-century after the Civil War. He was our always tactful toastmaster, our clearing-house, our universal solvent, our respecter of the distinguished veteran, our encourager of the promising young. He had been the son of a printer in Ohio, an American consul in Venice, the editor of the *Atlantic Monthly* in Boston, an editor of *Harper's* in New York, and something of a publicist for social reform. He knew how to be discreet in Cambridge and was on excellent terms with Lowell and Aldrich; he was delighted to greet gifted Middle Westerners like Booth Tarkington and Hamlin Garland; he was on charming terms with John Hay and usually *persona grata* at the White House; he paid attention to the new plays of Clyde Fitch and George Ade; and he did his best for the realism of the end of the century, advising Henry B. Fuller to stick to Chicago, reviewing and praising Frank Norris' *McTeague,* and trying to persuade the New York bookdealers to handle Stephen Crane's *Maggie*. During Howells' later years one heard a great deal of complaint that his natural prudery and primness rather neutralized his advanced opinions. If one goes back over his criticism today, one does find it rather watery and uninteresting; yet one is brought to the realization that, all through that period of our history when letters were so far from enjoying their earlier exalted prestige, Howells did serve us pretty well. He did want to see good writing get published and read, no matter what it was about or who wrote it; and he cared little about conventional opinion. His instinctive respect for the proprieties and his deference to his feminine audience were a more serious handicap in his fiction than in the exercise of his literary taste.

Howells' most remarkable feat was to appreciate and remain on close terms with both the two great men of our letters who seemed, with their so different publics, antipodal and mutually repellent: Mark Twain and Henry James. Mark Twain till almost the end of his career was much under suspicion of "vulgarity": famous as a popular humorist and in demand as an after-dinner speaker, he was not generally accepted as a serious writer. But Howells had not only taken him seriously—reviewed his books and criticized his manuscripts; he had felt Clemens' strange superiority to even the revered masters of Boston. Mark Twain's disastrous *gaffe* at the Whittier dinner (described in the memoir that follows)—which must, however, have had behind it some real unconscious antagonism on Mark Twain's part—could embarrass Howells but could not scare him. *My Mark Twain,* written when Clemens died in 1910, is probably the best "character" of Mark Twain we have; and it is certainly one of the works of Howells in which he rises to something of intensity both of expression and of feeling.

WILLIAM DEAN HOWELLS

MY MARK TWAIN[1]

It was in the little office of James T. Fields, over the bookstore of Ticknor & Fields, at 124 Tremont Street, Boston, that I first met my friend of now forty-four years, Samuel L. Clemens. Mr. Fields was then the editor of the *Atlantic Monthly,* and I was his proud and glad assistant, with a pretty free hand as to manuscripts, and an unmanacled command of the book-notices at the end of the magazine. I wrote nearly all of them myself, and in 1869 I had written rather a long notice of a book just winning its way to universal favor. In this review I had intimated my reservations concerning the *Innocents Abroad,* but I had the luck, if not the sense, to recognize that it was such fun as we had not had before. I forget just what I said in praise of it, and it does not matter; it is enough that I praised it enough to satisfy the author. He now signified as much, and he stamped his gratitude into my memory with a story wonderfully allegorizing the situation, which the mock modesty of print forbids my repeating here. Throughout my long acquaintance with him his graphic touch was always allowing itself a freedom which I cannot bring my fainter pencil to illustrate. He had the Southwestern, the Lincolnian, the Elizabethan breadth of parlance, which I suppose one ought not to call coarse without calling one's self prudish; and I was often hiding away in discreet holes and corners the letters in which he had loosed his bold fancy to stoop on rank suggestion; I could not bear to burn them, and I could not, after the first reading, quite bear to look at them. I shall best give my feeling on this point by saying that in it he was Shakespearian, or if his ghost will not suffer me the word, then he was Baconian.

At the time of our first meeting, which must have been well toward the winter, Clemens (as I must call him instead of Mark Twain, which seemed always somehow to mask him from my personal sense) was wearing a sealskin coat, with the fur out, in the satisfaction of a caprice, or the love of strong effect which he was apt to indulge through life. I do not know what droll comment was in Fields's mind with respect to this garment, but probably he felt that here was an original who was not to be brought to any Bostonian book in the judgment of his vivid qualities. With his crest of dense red hair, and the wide sweep of his flaming mustache, Clemens was not discordantly clothed in that sealskin coat, which afterward, in spite of his own warmth in it, sent the cold chills through me when I once accompanied it down Broadway, and shared the immense publicity it won him. He had always a relish for personal effect, which expressed itself in the white suit of complete serge which he wore in his last years, and in the Oxford gown which he put on for every possible occasion, and said he would like to wear all the time. That was not vanity in him, but a keen feeling for costume which the severity of our modern tailoring forbids men, though it flatters women to every excess in it; yet he also enjoyed the shock, the offense, the pang which it gave the sensibilities of others. Then there were times he played these pranks for pure fun, and for the pleasure of the witness. Once I remember seeing him come into his drawing-room at Hartford in a pair of white cowskin slippers, with the hair out, and do a crippled colored uncle to the joy of all beholders. Or, I must not say all, for I remember also the dismay of Mrs. Clemens, and her low, despairing cry of, "Oh, Youth!" That was her name for him among their friends, and it fitted him as no other would, though I fancied with her it was a shrinking from his baptismal Samuel, or the vernacular Sam of his earlier companionships. He was a youth to the end of his days, the heart of a boy with the head of a sage; the heart of a good boy, or a bad boy, but always a wilful boy, and wilfulest to show himself out at every time for just the boy he was.

II

There is a gap in my recollections of Clemens, which I think is of a year or two, for the next thing I remember of him is meeting him at a lunch in Boston given us by that genius of hospitality, the tragically destined Ralph Keeler, author of one of the most unjustly forgotten books, *Vagabond Adventures,* a true bit of picaresque autobiography. Keeler never had any money, to the general knowledge, and he never borrowed, and he could not have had credit at the restaurant where he invited us to feast at his expense. There was T. B. Aldrich, there was J. T. Fields, much the oldest of our company, who had just freed himself from the trammels of the publishing business, and was feeling his freedom in every word; there was Bret Harte, who had lately come East in his princely progress from California; and there was Clemens. Nothing remains to me of the happy time but a sense of idle and aimless and joyful talk-play, beginning and ending nowhere, of eager laughter, of countless good stories from Fields, of a heat-lightning shimmer of wit from Aldrich, of an occasional concentration of our joint mockeries upon our host, who took it gladly; and amid the discourse, so little improving, but so full of good fellowship, Bret Hart's fleering dramatization of Clemens' mental attitude toward a symposium of Boston illuminates. "Why, fellows," he spluttered, "this is the dream of Mark's life," and I remember the glance from under Clemens' feathery eyebrows which betrayed his enjoyment of the fun. We had beefsteak with mushrooms, which in recognition of their shape Aldrich hailed as shoe-pegs, and to crown the feast we had an omelette soufflé, which the waiter brought in as flat as a pancake, amid our shouts of congratulations to poor Keeler, who took them with appreciative submission. It was in every way what a Boston literary lunch ought not to have been in the popular ideal which Harte attributed to Clemens.

Our next meeting was at Hartford, or, rather, at Springfield, where Clemens greeted us on the way to Hartford. Aldrich was going on to be his guest, and I was going to be Charles Dudley Warner's, but Clemens had come part way to welcome us both. In the good fellowship of that cordial neighborhood we had two such days as the aging sun no longer shines on in his round. There was constant running in and out of friendly houses where the lively hosts and guests called one another by their Christian names or nicknames, and no such vain ceremony as knocking or ringing at doors. Clemens was then building the stately mansion in which he satisfied his love of magnificence as if it had been another sealskin coat, and he was at the crest of the prosperity which enabled him to humor every whim or extravagance. The house was the design of that most original artist, Edward Potter, who once, when hard pressed by incompetent curiosity for the name of his style in a certain church, proposed that it should be called the English violet order of architecture; and this house was so absolutely suited to the owner's humor that I suppose there never was another house like it; but its character must be for recognition farther along in these reminiscenses. The vividest impression which Clemens gave us two ravenous young Boston authors was of the satisfying, the surfeiting nature of subscription publication. An army of agents was overrunning the country with the prospectuses of his books, and delivering them by the scores of thousands in completed sale. Of the *Innocents Abroad* he said, "It sells right along just like the Bible," and *Roughing It* was swiftly following, without perhaps ever quite overtaking it in popularity. But he lectured Aldrich and me on the folly of that mode of publication in the trade which we had thought it the highest success to achieve a chance in. "Anything but subscription publication is printing for private circulation," he maintained, and he so won upon our greed and hope that on the way back to Boston we planned the joint authorship of a volume adapted to subscription publication. We got a very good name for it, as we believed, in *Memorable Murders,* and we never got farther with it, but by the time we reached Boston we were rolling in wealth so deep that we could hardly walk home in the frugal fashion by which we still thought it best to spare carfare; carriage fare we did not dream of even in that opulence.

III

The visits to Hartford which had begun with this affluence continued without actual increase of riches for me, but now I went alone, and in Warner's European and Egyptian absences I formed the habit of going to Clemens. By this time he was in his new house, where he used to give me a royal chamber on the ground floor, and come in at night after I had gone to bed to take off the burglar alarm so that the family should not be roused if anybody tried to get in at my window. This would be after we had sat up late, he smoking the last of his innumerable cigars, and soothing his tense nerves with a mild hot Scotch, while we both talked and talked and talked, of everything in the heavens and on the earth, and the waters under the earth. After two days of this talk I would come away hollow, realizing myself best in the image of one of those locust-shells which you find sticking to the bark of trees at the end of summer. Once, after some such bout of brains, we went down to New York together, and sat facing each other in the Pullman smoker without passing a syllable till we had occasion to say, "Well, we're there." Then, with our installation in a now vanished hotel (the old Brunswick, to be specific), the talk began again with the inspiration of the novel environment, and went on and on. We wished to be asleep, but we could not stop, and he lounged through the rooms in the long nightgown which he always wore in preference to the pajamas which he despised, and told the story of his life, the inexhaustible, the fairy, the Arabian Nights story, which I could never tire of even when it began to be told over again. Or at times he would reason high—

> Of Providence, foreknowledge, will and fate,
> Fixed fate, free will, foreknowledge absolute,

walking up and down, and halting now and then, with a fine toss and slant of his shaggy head, as some bold thought or splendid joke struck him.

He was in those days a constant attendant at the church of his great friend, the Rev. Joseph H. Twichell, and at least tacitly far from the entire negation he came to at last. I should say he had hardly yet examined the grounds of his passive acceptance of his wife's belief, for it was hers and not his, and he held it unscanned in the beautiful and tender loyalty to her which was the most moving quality of his most faithful soul. I make bold to speak of the love between them, because without it I could not make him known to others as he was known to me. It was a greater part of him than the love of most men for their wives, and she merited all the worship he could give her, all the devotion, all the implicit obedience, by her surpassing force and beauty of character. She was in a way the loveliest person I have ever seen, the gentlest, the kindest, without a touch of weakness; she united wonderful tact with wonderful truth; and Clemens not only accepted her rule implicitly, but he rejoiced, he gloried in it. I am not sure that he noticed all her goodness in the actions that made it a heavenly vision to others, he so had the habit of her goodness; but if there was any forlorn and helpless creature in the room Mrs. Clemens was somehow promptly at his side or hers; she was always seeking occasion of kindness to those in her household or out of it; she loved to let her heart go beyond the reach of her hand, and imagined the whole hard and suffering world with compassion for its structural as well as incidental wrongs. I suppose she had her ladyhood limitations, her female fears of etiquette and convention, but she did not let them hamper the wild and splendid generosity with which Clemens rebelled against the social stupidities and cruelties. She had been a lifelong invalid when he met her, and he liked to tell the beautiful story of their courtship to each new friend whom he found capable of feeling its beauty or worthy of hearing it. Naturally, her father had hesitated to give her into the keeping of the young strange Westerner, who had risen up out of the unknown with his giant reputation of burlesque humorist, and demanded guaranties, demanded proofs. "He asked me," Clemens would say, "if I couldn't give him the names of people who knew me in California, and when it was time to hear from them I heard from him. 'Well, Mr. Clemens,' he said, 'nobody seems to have a very good word for you.' I hadn't referred him to people that I thought were going to whitewash me. I thought it was all up with me, but I was disappointed. 'So I guess I shall have to back you myself.'"

Whether this made him faithfuler to the trust put in him I cannot say, but probably not; it was always in him to be faithful to any trust, and in proportion as a trust of his own was betrayed he was ruthlessly and implacably resentful. But I wish now to speak of the happiness of that household in Hartford which responded so perfectly to the ideals of the mother when the three daughters, so lovely and so gifted, were yet little children. There had been a boy, and "Yes, *I* killed him," Clemens once said, with the unsparing self-blame in which he would wreak an unavailing regret. He meant that he had taken the child out imprudently, and the child had taken the cold which he died of, but it was by no means certain this was through its father's imprudence. I never heard him speak of his son except that once, but no doubt in his deep heart his loss was irreparably present. He was a very tender father and delighted in the minds of his children, but he was wise enough to leave their training altogether to the wisdom of their mother. He left them to that in everything, keeping for himself the pleasure of teaching them little scenes of drama, learning languages with them, and leading them in singing. They came to the table with their parents, and could have set him an example in behavior when, in moments of intense excitement, he used to leave his place and walk up and down the room, flying his napkin and talking and talking.

It was after his first English sojourn that I used to visit him, and he was then full of praise of everything English: the English personal independence and public spirit, and hospitality, and truth. He liked to tell stories in proof of their virtues, but he was not blind to the defects of their virtues: their submissive acceptance of caste, their callousness with strangers, their bluntness with one another. Mrs. Clemens had been in a way to suffer socially more than he, and she praised the English less. She had sat after dinner with ladies who snubbed and ignored one another, and left her to find her own amusement in the absence of the attention with which Americans perhaps cloy their guests, but which she could not help preferring. In their successive sojourns among them I believe he came to like the English less and she more; the fine delight of his first acceptance among them did not renew itself till his Oxford degree was given him; then it made his cup run over, and he was glad the whole world should see it.

His wife would not chill the ardor of his early Anglomania, and in this, as in everything, she wished to humor him to the utmost. No one could have realized more than she his essential fineness, his innate nobleness. Marriages are what the parties to them alone really know them to be, but from the outside I should say that this marriage was one of the most perfect. It lasted in his absolute devotion to the day of her death, that delayed long in cruel suffering, and that left one side of him in lasting night. From Florence there came to me heartbreaking letters from him about the torture she was undergoing, and at last a letter saying she was dead, with the simple-hearted cry, "I wish I was with Livy." I do not know why I have left saying till now that she was a very beautiful woman, classically regular in features, with black hair smooth over her forehead, and with tenderly peering, myopic eyes, always behind glasses, and a smile of angelic kindness. But this kindness went with a sense of humor which qualified her to appreciate the self-lawed genius of a man who will be remembered with the great humorists of all time, with Cervantes, with Swift, or with any others worthy his company; none of them was his equal in humanity.

IV

Clemens had appointed himself, with the architect's connivance, a luxurious study over the library in his new house, but as his children grew older this study, with its carved and cushioned armchairs, was given over to them for a schoolroom, and he took the room above his stable, which had been intended for his coachman. There we used to talk together, when we were not walking and talking together, until he discovered that he could make a more commodious use of the billiard room at the top of his house, for the purposes of literature and friendship. It was pretty cold up there in the early spring and late fall weather with which I chiefly associate the place, but by lighting up all the gas burners and kindling a reluctant fire on the hearth we could keep it well above freezing. Clemens could also push the balls about, and, without rivalry from me, who could no more play billiards than smoke, could win endless games of pool, while he carried points of argument against imaginable differers in opinion. Here he wrote many of his tales and sketches, and for anything I know some of his books. I particularly remember his reading me here his first rough sketch of *Captain Stormfield's Visit to Heaven,* with the real name of the captain, whom I knew already from his many stories about him.

We had a peculiar pleasure in looking off from the high windows on the pretty Hartford landscape, and down from them into the tops of the trees clothing the hillside by which his house stood. We agreed that there was a novel charm in trees seen from such a vantage, far surpassing that of the farther scenery. He had not been a country boy for nothing; rather he had been a country boy, or, still better, a village boy, for everything that Nature can offer the young of our species, and no aspect of her was lost on him. We were natives of the same vast Mississippi Valley; and Missouri was not so far from Ohio but that we were akin in our first knowledges of woods and fields as we were in our early parlance. I had outgrown the use of mine through my greater bookishness, but I gladly recognized the phrases which he employed for their lasting juiciness and the long-remembered savor they had on his mental palate.

I have elsewhere sufficiently spoken of his unsophisticated use of words, of the diction which forms the backbone of his manly style. If I mention my own greater bookishness, by which I mean his less quantitative reading, it is to give myself better occasion to note that he was always reading some vital book. It might be some out-of-the-way book, but it had the root of the human matter in it: a volume of great trials; one of the supreme autobiographies; a signal passage of history, a narrative of travel, a story of captivity, which gave him life at first-hand. As I remember, he did not care much for fiction, and in that sort he had certain distinct loathings; there were certain authors whose names he seemed not so much to pronounce as to spew out of his mouth. Goldsmith was one of these, but his prime abhorrence was my dear and honored prime favorite, Jane Austen. He once said to me, I suppose after he had been reading some of my unsparing praises of her—I am always praising her, "*You* seem to think that woman could write," and he forebore withering me with his scorn, apparently because we had been friends so long, and he more pitied than hated me for my bad taste. He seemed not to have any preferences among novelists; or at least I never heard him express any. He used to read the modern novels I praised, in or out of print; but I do not think he much liked reading fiction. As for plays, he detested the theater, and said he would as lief do a sum as follow a plot on the stage. He could not, or did not, give any reasons for his literary abhorrences, and perhaps he really had none. But he could have said very distinctly, if he had needed, why he liked the books he did. I was away at the time of his great Browning passion, and I know of it chiefly from hearsay; but at the time Tolstoy was doing what could be done to make me over Clemens wrote, "That man seems to have been to you what Browning was to me."

I do not know that he had other favorites among the poets, but he had favorite poems which he liked to read to you, and he read, of course, splendidly. I have forgotten what piece of John Hay's it was that he liked so much, but I remember how he fiercely reveled in the vengefulness of William Morris' *Sir Guy of the Dolorous Blast,* and how he especially exulted in the lines which tell of the supposed speaker's joy in slaying the murderer of his brother:

> I am threescore years and ten,
> And my hair is nigh turned gray,
> But I am glad to think of the moment when
> I took his life away.

Generally, I fancy his pleasure in poetry was not great, and I do not believe he cared much for the conventionally accepted masterpieces of literature. He liked to find out good things and great things for himself; sometimes he would discover these in a masterpiece new to him alone, and then, if you brought his ignorance home to him, he enjoyed it, and enjoyed it the more the more you rubbed it in.

Of all the literary men I have known he was the most unliterary in his make and manner. I do not know whether he had any acquaintance with Latin, but I believe not the least; German he knew pretty well, and Italian enough late in life to have fun with it; but he used English in all its alien derivations as if it were native to his own air, as if it had come up out of American, out of Missourian ground. His style was what we know, for good and for bad, but his manner, if I may difference the two, was as entirely his own as if no one had ever written before. I have noted before this how he was not enslaved to the consecutiveness in writing which the rest of us try to keep chained to. That is, he wrote as he thought, and as all men think, without sequence, without an eye to what went before or should come after. If something beyond or beside what he was saying occurred to him, he invited it into his page, and made it as much at home there as the nature of it would suffer him. Then, when he was through with the welcoming of this casual and unexpected guest, he would go back to the company he was entertaining, and keep on with what he had been talking about. He observed this manner in the construction of his sentences, and the arrangement of his chapters, and the ordering or disordering of his compilations. I helped him with a Library of Humor, which he once edited, and when I had done my work according to tradition, with authors, times, and topics carefully studied in due sequence, he tore it all apart, and "chucked" the pieces in wherever the fancy for them took him at the moment. He was right: we were not making a textbook, but a book for the pleasure rather than the instruction of the reader and he did not see why the principle on which he built his travels and reminiscences and tales and novels should not apply to it; and I do not now see, either, though at the time it confounded me. On minor points he was, beyond any author I have known, without favorite phrases or pet words. He utterly despised the avoidance of repetitions out of fear of tautology. If a word served his turn better than a substitute, he would use it as many times in a page as he chose.

V

At that time I had become editor of the *Atlantic Monthly,* and I had allegiances belonging to the conduct of what was and still remains the most scrupulously cultivated of our periodicals. When Clemens began to write for it he came willingly under its rules, for with all his wilfulness there never was a more biddable man in things you could show him a reason for. He never made the least of that trouble which so abounds for the hapless editor from narrower-minded contributors. If you wanted a thing changed, very good, he changed it; if you suggested that a word or a sentence or a paragraph had better be struck out, very good, he struck it out. His proof sheets came back each a veritable "mush of concession," as Emerson says. Now and then he would try a little stronger language than the *Atlantic* had stomach for, and once when I sent him a proof I made him observe that I had left out the profanity. He wrote back: "Mrs. Clemens opened that proof, and lit into the room with danger in her eye. What profanity? You see, when I read the manuscript to her I skipped that." It was part of his joke to pretend a violence in that gentlest creature which the more amusingly realized the situation to their friends.

I was always very glad of him and proud of him as a contributor, but I must not claim the whole merit, or the first merit of having him write for us. It was the publisher, the late H. O. Houghton, who felt the incongruity of his absence from the leading periodical of the country, and was always urging me to get him to write. I will take the credit of being eager for him, but it is to the publisher's credit that he tried, so far as the modest traditions of the *Atlantic* would permit, to meet the expectations in pay which the colossal profits of Clemens' books might naturally have bred in him. Whether he was really able to do this he never knew from Clemens himself, but probably twenty dollars a page did not surfeit the author of books that "sold right along just like the Bible."

We had several short contributions from Clemens first, all of capital quality, and then we had the series of papers which went mainly to the making of his great book, *Life on the Mississippi*. Upon the whole I have the notion that Clemens thought this his greatest book, and he was supported in his opinion by that of the *portier* in his hotel at Vienna, and that of the German Emperor, who, as he told me with equal respect for the preference of each, united in thinking it his best; with such far-sundered social poles approaching in its favor, he apparently found himself without standing for opposition. At any rate, the papers won instant appreciation from his editor and publisher, and from the readers of their periodical, which they expected to prosper beyond precedent in its circulation. But those were days of simpler acceptance of the popular rights of newspapers than these are, when magazines strictly guard their vested interests against them. The New York *Times* and the St. Louis *Democrat* profited by the advance copies of the magazine sent them to reprint the papers month by month. Together they covered nearly the whole reading territory of the Union, and the terms of their daily publication enabled them to anticipate the magazine in its own restricted field. Its subscription list was not enlarged in the slightest measure, and the *Atlantic Monthly* languished on the newsstands as undesired as ever.

VI

It was among my later visits to Hartford that we began to talk up the notion of collaborating a play, but we did not arrive at any clear intention, and it was a telegram out of the clear sky that one day summoned me from Boston to help with a continuation of *Colonel Sellers*. I had been a witness of the high joy of Clemens in the prodigious triumph of the first *Colonel Sellers,* which had been dramatized from the novel of *The Gilded Age*. This was the joint work of Clemens and Charles Dudley Warner, and the story had been put upon the stage by someone in Utah, whom Clemens first brought to book in the courts for violation of his copyright, and then indemnified for such rights as his adaptation of the book had given him. The structure of the play as John T. Raymond gave it was substantially the work of this unknown dramatist. Clemens never pretended, to me at any rate, that he had the least hand in it; he frankly owned that he was incapable of dramatization; yet the vital part was his, for the characters in the play were his as the book embodied them, and the success which it won with the public was justly his. This he shared equally with the actor, following the company with an agent, who counted out the author's share of the gate money, and sent him a note of the amount every day by postal card. The postals used to come about dinner-time, and Clemens would read them aloud to us in wild triumph. One hundred and fifty dollars—two hundred dollars—three hundred dollars were the gay figures which they bore, and which he flaunted in the air before he sat down at table, or rose from it to brandish, and then, flinging his napkin into his chair, walked up and down to exult in.

By and by the popularity of the play waned, and the time came when he sickened of the whole affair, and withdrew his agent, and took whatever gain from it the actor apportioned him. He was apt to have these sudden surceases, following upon the intensities of his earlier interest; though he seemed always to have the notion of making something more of *Colonel Sellers.* But when I arrived in Hartford in answer to his summons, I found him with no definite idea of what he wanted to do with him. I represented that we must have some sort of plan, and he agreed that we should both jot down a scenario overnight and compare our respective schemes the next morning. As the author of a large number of little plays which have been privately presented throughout the United States and in parts of the United Kingdom, without ever getting upon the public stage except for the noble ends of charity, and then promptly getting off it, I felt authorized to make him observe that his scheme was as nearly nothing as chaos could be. He agreed hilariously with me, and was willing to let it stand in proof of his entire dramatic inability. At the same time he liked my plot very much, which ultimated Sellers, according to Clemens' intention, as a man crazed by his own inventions and by his superstition that he was the rightful heir to an English earldom. The exuberant nature of Sellers and the vast range of his imagination served our purpose in other ways. Clemens made him a spiritualist, whose specialty in the occult was materialization; he became on impulse an ardent temperance reformer, and he headed a procession of temperance ladies after disinterestedly testing the deleterious effects of liquor upon himself until he could not walk straight; always he wore a marvelous fire-extinguisher strapped on his back, to give proof in any emergency of the effectiveness of his invention in that way.

We had a jubilant fortnight in working the particulars of these things out. It was not possible for Clemens to write like anybody else, but I could very easily write like Clemens, and we took the play scene and scene about, quite secure of coming out in temperamental agreement. The characters remained for the most part his, and I varied them only to make them more like his than, if possible, he could. Several years after, when I looked over a copy of the play, I could not always tell my work from his; I only knew that I had done certain scenes. We would work all day long at our several tasks, and then at night, before dinner, read them over to each other. No dramatists ever got greater joy out of their creations, and when I reflect that the public never had the chance of sharing our joy I pity the public from a full heart. I still believe that the play was immensely funny; I still believe that if it could once have got behind the footlights it would have continued to pack the house before them for an indefinite succession of nights. But this may be my fondness.

At any rate, it was not to be. Raymond had identified himself with Sellers in the playgoing imagination, and whether consciously or unconsciously we constantly worked with Raymond in our minds. But before this time bitter displeasures had risen between Clemens and Raymond, and Clemens was determined that Raymond should never have the play. He first offered it to several other actors, who eagerly caught at it, only to give it back with the despairing renunciation, "That is a Raymond play." We tried managers with it, but their only question was whether they could get Raymond to do it. In the meantime Raymond had provided himself with a play for the winter—a very good play, by Demarest Lloyd; and he was in no hurry for ours. Perhaps he did not really care for it; perhaps he knew when he heard of it that it must come to him in the end. In the end it did, from my hand, for Clemens would not meet him. I found him in a mood of sweet reasonableness, perhaps the more softened by one of those lunches which our publisher, the hospitable James R. Osgood, was always bringing people together over in Boston. He said that he could not do the play that winter, but he was sure that he should like it, and he had no doubt he would do it the next winter. So I gave him the manuscript, in spite of Clemens' charges, for his suspicions and rancors were such that he would not have had me leave it for a moment in the actor's hands. But it seemed a conclusion that involved success and fortune for us. In due time, but I do not remember how long after, Raymond declared himself delighted with the piece; he entered into a satisfactory agreement for it, and at the beginning of the next season he started with it to Buffalo, where he was to give a first production. At Rochester he paused long enough to return it, with the explanation that a friend had noted to him the fact that Colonel Sellers in the play was a lunatic, and insanity was so serious a thing that it could not be represented on the stage without outraging the sensibilities of the audience; or words to that effect. We were too far off to allege Hamlet to the contrary, or King Lear, or to instance the delight which generations of readers throughout the world had taken in the mad freaks of Don Quixote.

Whatever were the real reasons of Raymond for rejecting the play, we had to be content with those he gave, and to set about getting it into other hands. In this effort we failed even more signally than before, if that were possible. At last a clever and charming elocutionist, who had long wished to get himself on the stage, heard of it and asked to see it. We would have shown it to anyone by this time, and we very willingly showed it to him. He came to Hartford and did some scenes from it for us. I must say he did them very well, quite as well as Raymond could have done them, in whose manner he did them. But now, late toward spring, the question was where he could get an engagement with the play, and we ended by hiring a theater in New York for a week of trial performances.

Clemens came on with me to Boston, where we were going to make some changes in the piece, and where we made them to our satisfaction, but not to the effect of that high rapture which we had in the first draft. He went back to Hartford, and then the cold fit came upon me, and "in visions of the night, in slumberings upon the bed," ghastly forms of failure appalled me, and when I rose in the morning I wrote him: "Here is a play which every manager has put out-of-doors and which every actor known to us has refused, and now we go and give it to an elocutioner. We are fools." Whether Clemens agreed with me or not in my conclusion, he agreed with me in my premises, and we promptly bought our play off the stage at a cost of seven hundred dollars, which we shared between us. But Clemens was never a man to give up. I relinquished gratis all right and title I had in the play, and he paid its entire expenses for a week of one-night stands in the country. It never came to New York; and yet I think now that if it had come, it would have succeeded. So hard does the faith of the unsuccessful dramatist in his work die!

VII

There is an incident of this time so characteristic of both men that I will yield to the temptation of giving it here. After I had gone to Hartford in response to Clemens' telegram, Matthew Arnold arrived in Boston, and one of my family called on him, to explain why I was not at home to receive his introduction: I had gone to see Mark Twain. "Oh, but he doesn't like *that* sort of thing, does he?" "He likes Mr. Clemens very much," my representative answered, "and he thinks him one of the greatest men he ever knew." I was still Clemens' guest at Hartford when Arnold came there to lecture, and one night we went to meet him at a reception. While his hand laxly held mine in greeting, I saw his eyes fixed intensely on the other side of the room. "Who—who in the world is that?" I looked and said, "Oh, that is Mark Twain." I do not remember just how their instant encounter was contrived by Arnold's wish, but I have the impression that they were not parted for long during the evening, and the next night Arnold, as if still under the glamour of that potent presence, was at Clemens' house. I cannot say how they got on, or what they made of each other; if Clemens ever spoke of Arnold, I do not recall what he said, but Arnold had shown a sense of him from which the incredulous sniff of the polite world, now so universally exploded, had already perished. It might well have done so with his first dramatic vision of that prodigious head. Clemens was then hard upon fifty, and he had kept, as he did to the end, the slender figure of his youth, but the ashes of the burnt-out years were beginning to gray the fires of that splendid shock of red hair which he held to the height of a stature apparently greater than it was, and tilted from side to side in his undulating walk. He glimmered at you from the narrow slits of fine blue-greenish eyes, under branching brows, which with age grew more and more like a sort of plumage, and he was apt to smile into your face with a subtle but amiable perception, and yet with a sort of remote absence; you were all there for him, but he was not all there for you.

VIII

I shall not try to give chronological order to my recollections of him, but since I am just now with him in Hartford I will speak of him in association with the place. Once when I came on from Cambridge he followed me to my room to see that the water was not frozen in my bath, or something of the kind, for it was very cold weather, and then hospitably lingered. Not to lose time in banalities I began at once from the thread of thought in my mind. "I wonder why we hate the past so," and he responded from the depths of his own consciousness, "It's so damned humiliating," which is what any man would say of his past if he were honest; but honest men are few when it comes to themselves. Clemens was one of the few, and the first of them among all the people I have known. I have known, I suppose, men as truthful, but not so promptly, so absolutely, so positively, so almost aggressively truthful. He could lie, of course, and did to save others from grief or harm; he was not stupidly truthful; but his first impulse was to say out the thing and everything that was in him. To those who can understand it will not be contradictory of his sense of humiliation from the past that he was not ashamed for anything he ever did to the point of wishing to hide it. He could be, and he was, bitterly sorry for his errors, which he had enough of in his life, but he was not ashamed in that mean way. What he had done he owned to, good, bad, or indifferent, and if it was bad he was rather amused than troubled as to the effect in your mind. He would not obtrude the fact upon you, but if it were in the way of personal history he would not dream of withholding it, far less of hiding it.

He was the readiest of men to allow an error if he were found in it. In one of our walks about Hartford, when he was in the first fine flush of his agnosticism, he declared that Christianity had done nothing to improve morals and conditions, and that the world under the highest pagan civilization was as well off as it was under the highest Christian influences. I happened to be fresh from the reading of Charles Loring Brace's *Gesta Christi; or, History of Humane Progress,* and I could offer him abundant proofs that he was wrong. He did not like that evidently, but he instantly gave way, saying he had not known those things. Later he was more tolerant in his denials of Christianity, but just then he was feeling his freedom from it, and rejoicing in having broken what he felt to have been the shackles of belief worn so long. He greatly admired Robert Ingersoll, whom he called an angelic orator, and regarded as an evangel of a new gospel—the gospel of free thought. He took the warmest interest in the newspaper controversy raging at the time as to the existence of a hell; when the noes carried the day, I suppose that no enemy of perdition was more pleased. He still loved his old friend and pastor, Mr. Twichell, but he no longer went to hear him preach his sane and beautiful sermons, and was, I think, thereby the greater loser. Long before that I had asked him if he went regularly to church, and he groaned out: "Oh yes, I go. It 'most kills me, but I go," and I did not need his telling me to understand that he went because his wife wished it. He did tell me, after they both ceased to go, that it had finally come to her saying, "Well, if you are to be lost, I want to be lost with you." He could accept that willingness for supreme sacrifice and exult in it because of the supreme truth as he saw it. After they had both ceased to be formal Christians, she was still grieved by his denial of immortality, so grieved that he resolved upon one of those heroic lies, which for love's sake he held above even the truth, and he went to her, saying that he had been thinking the whole matter over, and now he was convinced that the soul did live after death. It was too late. Her keen vision pierced through his ruse, as it did when he brought the doctor who had diagnosticated her case as organic disease of the heart, and, after making him go over the facts of it again with her, made him declare it merely functional.

To make an end of these records as to Clemens' beliefs, so far as I knew them, I should say that he never went back to anything like faith in the Christian theology, or in the notion of life after death, or in a conscious divinity. It is best to be honest in this matter; he would have hated anything else, and I do not believe that the truth in it can hurt anyone. At one period he argued that there must have been a cause, a conscious source of things; that the universe could not have come by chance. I have heard also that in his last hours or moments he said, or his dearest ones hoped he had said, something about meeting again. But the expression, of which they could not be certain, was of the vaguest, and it was perhaps addressed to their tenderness out of his tenderness. All his expressions to me were of a courageous renunciation of any hope of living again, or elsewhere seeing those he had lost. He suffered terribly in their loss, and he was not fool enough to try ignoring his grief. He knew that for this there were but two medicines; that it would wear itself out with the years, and that meanwhile there was nothing for it but those respites in which the mourner forgets himself in slumber. I remember that in a black hour of my own when I was called down to see him, as he thought from sleep, he said with an infinite, an exquisite compassion, "Oh, did I wake you, did I *wake* you?" Nothing more, but the look, the voice, were everything; and while I live they cannot pass from my sense.

IX

He was the most caressing of men in his pity, but he had the fine instinct, which would have pleased Lowell, of never putting his hands on you—fine, delicate hands, with taper fingers, and pink nails, like a girl's, and sensitively quivering in moments of emotion; he did not paw you with them to show his affection, as so many of us Americans are apt to do. Among the half-dozen, or half-hundred, personalities that each of us becomes, I should say that Clemens' central and final personality was something exquisite. His casual acquaintance might know him, perhaps, from his fierce intensity, his wild pleasure in shocking people with his ribaldries and profanities, or from the mere need of loosing his rebellious spirit in that way, as anything but exquisite, and yet that was what in the last analysis he was. They might come away loathing or hating him, but one could not know him well without realizing him the most serious, the most humane, the most conscientious of men. He was Southwestern, and born amid the oppression of a race that had no rights as against ours, but I never saw a man more regardful of negroes. He had a yellow butler when I first began to know him, because he said he could not bear to order a white man about, but the terms of his ordering George were those of the softest entreaty which command ever wore. He loved to rely upon George, who was such a broken reed in some things, though so stanch in others, and the fervent Republican in politics that Clemens then liked him to be. He could interpret Clemens' meaning to the public without conveying his mood, and could render his roughest answer smooth to the person denied his presence. His general instructions were that this presence was to be denied all but personal friends, but the soft heart of George was sometimes touched by importunity, and once he came up into the billiard-room saying that Mr. Smith wished to see Clemens. Upon inquiry, Mr. Smith developed no ties of friendship, and Clemens said, "You go and tell Mr. Smith that I wouldn't come down to see the Twelve Apostles." George turned from the threshold where he had kept himself, and framed a paraphrase of this message which apparently sent Mr. Smith away content with himself and all the rest of the world.

The part of him that was Western in his Southwestern origin Clemens kept to the end, but he was the most de-southernized Southerner I ever knew. No man more perfectly sensed and more entirely abhorred slavery, and no one has ever poured such scorn upon the second-hand,

Walter-Scotticized, pseudo-chivalry of the Southern ideal. He held himself responsible for the wrong which the white race had done the black race in slavery, and he explained, in paying the way of a negro student through Yale, that he was doing it as his part of the reparation due from every white to every black man. He said he had never seen this student, nor ever wished to see him or know his name; it was quite enough that he was a negro. About that time a colored cadet was expelled from West Point for some point of conduct "unbecoming an officer and gentleman," and there was the usual shabby philosophy in a portion of the press to the effect that a negro could never feel the claim of honor. The man was fifteen parts white, but, "Oh yes," Clemens said, with bitter irony, "it was that one part black that undid him." It made him a "nigger" and incapable of being a gentleman. It was to blame for the whole thing. The fifteen parts white were guiltless.

Clemens was entirely satisfied with the result of the Civil War, and he was eager to have its facts and meanings brought out at once in history. He ridiculed the notion, held by many, that "it was not yet time" to philosophize the events of the great struggle; that we must "wait till its passions had cooled," and "the clouds of strife had cleared away." He maintained that the time would never come when we should see its motives and men and deeds more clearly, and that now, now, was the hour to ascertain them in lasting verity. Picturesquely and dramatically he portrayed the imbecility of deferring the inquiry at any point to the distance of future years when inevitably the facts would begin to put on fable.

He had powers of sarcasm and a relentless rancor in his contempt which those who knew him best appreciated most. The late Noah Brooks, who had been in California at the beginning of Clemens' career, and had witnessed the effect of his ridicule before he had learned to temper it, once said to me that he would rather have anyone else in the world down on him than Mark Twain. But as Clemens grew older he grew more merciful, not to the wrong, but to the men who were in it. The wrong was often the source of his wildest drolling. He considered it in such hopelessness of ever doing it justice that his despair broke in laughter.

X

I go back to that house in Hartford, where I was so often a happy guest, with tenderness for each of its endearing aspects. Over the chimney in the library which had been cured of smoking by so much art and science, Clemens had written in perennial brass the words of Emerson, "The ornament of a house is the friends who frequent it," and he gave his guests a welcome of the simplest and sweetest cordiality: but I must not go aside to them from my recollections of him, which will be of sufficient garrulity, if I give them as fully as I wish. The windows of the library looked northward from the hillside above which the house stood, and over the little valley with the stream in it, and they showed the leaves of the trees that almost brushed them as in a Claude Lorraine glass. To the eastward the dining-room opened amply, and to the south there was a wide hall, where the voices of friends made themselves heard as they entered without ceremony and answered his joyous hail. At the west was a little semicircular conservatory of a pattern invented by Mrs. Harriet Beecher Stowe, and adopted in most of the houses of her kindly neighborhood. The plants were set in the ground, and the flowering vines climbed up the sides and overhung the roof above the silent spray of a fountain companied by callas and other water-loving lilies. There, while we breakfasted, Patrick came in from the barn and sprinkled the pretty bower, which poured out its responsive perfume in the delicate accents of its varied blossoms. Breakfast was Clemens' best meal, and he sat longer at his steak and coffee than at the courses of his dinner; luncheon was nothing to him, unless, as might happen, he made it his dinner, and reserved the later repast as the occasion of walking up and down the room, and discoursing at large on anything that came into his head. Like most good talkers, he liked other people to have their say; he did not talk them down; he stopped instantly at another's remark and gladly or politely heard him through; he even made believe to find suggestion or inspiration in what was said. His children came to the table, as I have told, and after dinner he was apt to join his fine tenor to their trebles in singing.

Fully half our meetings were at my house in Cambridge, where he made himself as much at home as in Hartford. He would come ostensibly to stay at the Parker House, in Boston, and take a room, where he would light the gas and leave it burning, after dressing, while he drove out to Cambridge and stayed two or three days with us. Once, I suppose it was after a lecture, he came in evening dress and passed twenty-four hours with us in that guise, wearing an overcoat to hide it when we went for a walk. Sometimes he wore the slippers which he preferred to shoes at home, and if it was muddy, as it was wont to be in Cambridge, he would put a pair of rubbers over them for our rambles. He liked the lawlessness and our delight in allowing it, and he rejoiced in the confession of his hostess, after we had once almost worn ourselves out in our pleasure with the intense talk, with the stories and the laughing, that his coming almost killed her, but it was worth it.

In those days he was troubled with sleeplessness, or, rather, with reluctant sleepiness, and he had various specifics for promoting it. At first it had been champagne just before going to bed, and we provided that, but later he appeared from Boston with four bottles of lager beer under his arms; lager beer, he said now, was the only thing to make you go to sleep, and we provided that. Still later, on a visit I paid him at Hartford, I learned that hot Scotch was the only soporific worth considering, and Scotch whisky duly found its place on our sideboard. One day, very long afterward, I asked him if he were still taking hot Scotch to make him sleep. He said he was not taking anything. For a while he had found going to bed on the bathroom floor a soporific; then one night he went to rest in his own bed at ten o'clock, and had gone promptly to sleep without anything. He had done the like with the like effect ever since. Of course, it amused him; there were few experiences of life, grave or gay, which did not amuse him, even when they wronged him.

He came on to Cambridge in April 1875 to go with me to the centennial ceremonies at Concord in celebration of the battle of the Minute Men with the British troops a hundred years before. We both had special invitations, including passage from Boston; but I said, Why bother to go into Boston when we could just as well take the train for Concord at the Cambridge station? He equally decided that it would be absurd; so we breakfasted deliberately, and then walked to the station, reasoning of many things as usual. When the train stopped, we found it packed inside and out. People stood dense on the platforms of the cars; to our startled eyes they seemed to project from the windows, and unless memory betrays me they lay strewn upon the roofs like brakemen slain at the post of duty. Whether this was really so or not, it is certain that the train presented an impenetrable front even to our imagination, and we left it to go its way without the slightest effort to board. We remounted the fame-worn steps of Porter's Station, and began exploring North Cambridge for some means of transportation overland to Concord, for we were that far on the road by which the British went and came on the day of the battle. The liverymen whom we appealed to received us, some with compassion, some with derision, but in either mood convinced us that we could not have hired a cat to attempt our conveyance, much less a horse, or vehicle of any description. It was a raw, windy day, very unlike the exceptionally hot April day when the routed redcoats, pursued by the Colonials, fled panting back to Boston, with "their tongues hanging out like dogs," but we could not take due comfort in the vision of their discomfiture; we could almost envy them, for they had at least got to Concord. A swift procession of coaches, carriages, and buggies, all going to Concord, passed us, inert and helpless, on the sidewalk in the peculiarly cold mud of North Cambridge. We began to wonder if we might not stop one of them and bribe it to take us, but we had not the courage to try, and

Clemens seized the opportunity to begin suffering with an acute indigestion, which gave his humor a very dismal cast. I felt keenly the shame of defeat, and the guilt of responsibility for our failure, and when a gay party of students came toward us on the top of a tallyho, luxuriously empty inside, we felt that our chance had come, and our last chance. He said that if I would stop them and tell them who I was they would gladly, perhaps proudly, give us passage; I contended that if with his far vaster renown he would approach them, our success would be assured. While we stood, lost in this "contest of civilities," the coach passed us, with gay notes blown from the horns of the students, and then Clemens started in pursuit, encouraged with shouts from the merry party who could not imagine who was trying to run them down, to a rivalry in speed. The unequal match could end only in one way, and I am glad I cannot recall what he said when he came back to me. Since then I have often wondered at the grief which would have wrung those blithe young hearts if they could have known that they might have had the company of Mark Twain to Concord that day and did not.

We hung about, unavailingly, in the bitter wind a while longer, and then slowly, very slowly, made our way home. We wished to pass as much time as possible, in order to give probability to the deceit we intended to practice, for we could not bear to own ourselves baffled in our boasted wisdom of taking the train at Porter's Station, and had agreed to say that we had been to Concord and got back. Even after coming home to my house, we felt that our statement would be wanting in verisimilitude without further delay, and we crept quietly into my library, and made up a roaring fire on the hearth, and thawed ourselves out in the heat of it before we regained our courage for the undertaking. With all these precautions we failed, for when our statement was imparted to the proposed victim she instantly pronounced it unreliable, and we were left with it on our hands intact. I think the humor of this situation was finally a greater pleasure to Clemens than an actual visit to Concord would have been; only a few weeks before his death he laughed our defeat over with one of my family in Bermuda, and exulted in our prompt detection.

XI

From our joint experience in failing I argue that Clemens' affection for me must have been great to enable him to condone in me the final defection which was apt to be the end of our enterprises. I have fancied that I presented to him a surface of such entire trustworthiness that he could not imagine the depths of unreliability beneath it; and that never realizing it, he always broke through with fresh surprise but unimpaired faith. He liked, beyond all things, to push an affair to the bitter end, and the end was never too bitter unless it brought grief or harm to another. Once in a telegraph office at a railway station he was treated with such insolent neglect by the young lady in charge, who was preoccupied in a flirtation with a "gentleman friend," that emulous of the public spirit which he admired in the English, he told her he should report her to her superiors, and (probably to her astonishment) he did so. He went back to Hartford, and in due time the poor girl came to me in terror and in tears; for I had abetted Clemens in his action, and had joined my name to his in his appeal to the authorities. She was threatened with dismissal unless she made full apology to him and brought back assurance of its acceptance. I felt able to give this, and, of course, he eagerly approved; I think he telegraphed his approval. Another time, some years afterward, we sat down together in places near the end of a car, and a brakeman came in looking for his official note-book. Clemens found that he had sat down upon it, and handed it to him; the man scolded him very abusively, and came back again and again, still scolding him for having no more sense than to sit down on a note-book. The patience of Clemens in bearing it was so angelic that I saw fit to comment, "I suppose you will report this fellow." "Yes," he answered, slowly and sadly. "That's what I should have done once. But now I remember that he gets twenty dollars a month."

Nothing could have been wiser, nothing tenderer, and his humanity was not for humanity alone. He abhorred the dull and savage joy of the sportsman in a lucky shot, an unerring aim, and once when I met him in the country he had just been sickened by the success of a gunner in bringing down a blackbird, and he described the poor, stricken, glossy thing, how it lay throbbing its life out on the grass, with such pity as he might have given a wounded child. I find this a fit place to say that his mind and soul were with those who do the hard work of the world, in fear of those who give them a chance for their livelihoods and underpay them all they can. He never went so far in socialism as I have gone, if he went that way at all, but he was fascinated with *Looking Backward* and had Bellamy to visit him; and from the first he had a luminous vision of organized labor as the only present help for working-men. He would show that side with such clearness and such force that you could not say anything in hopeful contradiction; he saw with that relentless insight of his that in the unions was the working-man's only present hope of standing up like a man against money and the power of it. There was a time when I was afraid that his eyes were a little holden from the truth; but in the very last talk I heard from him I found that I was wrong, and that this great humorist was as great a humanist as ever. I wish that all the work-folk could know this, and could know him their friend in life as he was in literature; as he was in such a glorious gospel of equality as the *Connecticut Yankee in King Arthur's Court.*

XII

Whether I will or no I must let things come into my story thoughtwise, as he would have let them, for I cannot remember them in their order. One night, while we were giving a party, he suddenly stormed in with a friend of his and mine, Mr. Twichell, and immediately began to eat and drink of our supper, for they had come straight to our house from walking to Boston, or so great a part of the way as to be ahungered and athirst. I can see him now as he stood up in the midst of our friends, with his head thrown back, and in his hand a dish of those escalloped oysters without which no party in Cambridge was really a party, exulting in the tale of his adventure, which had abounded in the most original characters and amusing incidents at every mile of their progress. They had broken their journey with a night's rest, and they had helped themselves lavishly out by rail in the last half; but still it had been a mighty walk to do in two days. Clemens was a great walker in those years, and was always telling of his tramps with Mr. Twichell to Talcott's Tower, ten miles out of Hartford. As he walked of course he talked, and of course he smoked. Whenever he had been a few days with us, the whole house had to be aired, for he smoked all over it from breakfast to bedtime. He always went to bed with a cigar in his mouth, and sometimes, mindful of my fire insurance, I went up and took it away, still burning, after he had fallen asleep. I do not know how much a man may smoke and live, but apparently he smoked as much as a man could, for he smoked incessantly.

He did not care much to meet people, as I fancied, and we were greedy of him for ourselves; he was precious to us; and I would not have exposed him to the critical edge of that Cambridge acquaintance which might not have appreciated him at, say, his transatlantic value. In America his popularity was as instant as it was vast. But it must be acknowledged that for a much longer time here than in England polite learning hesitated his praise. In England rank, fashion, and culture rejoiced in him. Lord mayors, lord chief justices, and magnates of many kinds were his hosts; he was desired in country houses, and his bold genius captivated the favor of periodicals which spurned the rest of our nation. But in his own country it was different. In proportion as people thought themselves refined they questioned that quality which all recognize in him now, but which was then the inspired knowledge of the simple-hearted multitude. I went with him to see Longfellow, but I do not think Longfellow made much of him, and Lowell made less. He stopped as if with the long Semitic curve of

Clemens' nose, which in the indulgence of his passion for finding everyone more or less a Jew he pronounced unmistakably racial. It was two of my most fastidious Cambridge friends who accepted him with the English, the European entirety—namely, Charles Eliot Norton and Professor Francis J. Child. Norton was then newly back from a long sojourn abroad, and his judgments were delocalized. He met Clemens as if they had both been in England, and rejoiced in his bold freedom from environment, and in the rich variety and boundless reach of his talk. Child was of a personal liberty as great in its fastidious way as that of Clemens himself, and though he knew him only at second-hand, he exulted in the most audacious instance of his grotesquery, as I shall have to tell by and by, almost solely. I cannot say just why Clemens seemed not to hit the favor of our community of scribes and scholars, as Bret Harte had done, when he came on from California, and swept them before him, disrupting their dinners and delaying their lunches with impunity; but it is certain he did not, and I had better say so.

I am surprised to find from the bibliographical authorities that it was so late as 1875 when he came with the manuscript of *Tom Sawyer,* and asked me to read it, as a friend and critic, and not as an editor. I have an impression that this was at Mrs. Clemens' instance in his own uncertainty about printing it. She trusted me, I can say with a satisfaction few things now give me, to be her husband's true and cordial adviser, and I was so. I believe I never failed him in this part, though in so many of our enterprises and projects I was false as water through my temperamental love of backing out of any undertaking. I believe this never ceased to astonish him, and it has always astonished me; it appears to me quite out of character; though it is certain that an undertaking, when I have entered upon it, holds me rather than I it. But however this immaterial matter may be, I am glad to remember that I thoroughly liked *Tom Sawyer,* and said so with every possible amplification. Very likely, I also made my suggestions for its improvement; I could not have been a real critic without that; and I have no doubt they were gratefully accepted and, I hope, never acted upon. I went with him to the horse-car station in Harvard Square, as my frequent wont was, and put him aboard a car with his MS. in his hand, stayed and reassured, so far as I counted, concerning it. I do not know what his misgivings were; perhaps they were his wife's misgivings, for she wished him to be known not only for the wild and boundless humor that was in him, but for the beauty and tenderness and "natural piety"; and she would not have had him judged by a too close fidelity to the rude conditions of Tom Sawyer's life. This is the meaning that I read into the fact of his coming to me with those doubts.

XIII

Clemens had then and for many years the habit of writing to me about what he was doing, and still more of what he was experiencing. Nothing struck his imagination, in or out of the daily routine, but he wished to write me of it, and he wrote with the greatest fulness and a lavish dramatization, sometimes to the length of twenty or forty pages, so that I have now perhaps fifteen hundred pages of his letters. They will no doubt someday be published, but I am not even referring to them in these records, which I think had best come to the reader with an old man's falterings and uncertainties. With his frequent absences and my own abroad, and the intrusion of calamitous cares, the rich tide of his letters was more and more interrupted. At times it almost ceased, and then it would come again, a torrent. In the very last weeks of his life he burst forth, and, though too weak himself to write, he dictated his rage with me for recommending to him a certain author whose truthfulness he could not deny, but whom he hated for his truthfulness to sordid and ugly conditions. At heart Clemens was romantic, and he would have had the world of fiction stately and handsome and whatever the real world was not; but he was not romanticistic, and he was too helplessly an artist not to wish his own work to show life as he had seen it. I was preparing to rap him back for these letters when I read that he had got home to die; he would have liked the rapping back.

He liked coming to Boston, especially for those luncheons and dinners in which the fertile hospitality of our publisher, Osgood, abounded. He dwelt equidistant from Boston and New York, and he had special friends in New York, but he said he much preferred coming to Boston; of late years he never went there, and he had lost the habit of it long before he came home from Europe to live in New York. At these feasts, which were often of after-dinner-speaking measure, he could always be trusted for something of amazing delightfulness. Once, when Osgood could think of no other occasion for a dinner, he gave himself a birthday dinner, and asked his friends and authors. The beautiful and splendid trooperlike Waring was there, and I recall how in the long, rambling speech in which Clemens went round the table hitting every head at it, and especially visiting Osgood with thanks for his ingenious pretext for our entertainment, he congratulated Waring upon his engineering genius and his hypnotic control of municipal governments. He said that if there was a plan for draining a city at a cost of a million, by seeking the level of the water in the downhill course of the sewers, Waring would come with a plan to drain that town uphill at twice the cost and carry it through the Common Council without opposition. It is hard to say whether the time was gladder at these dinners, or at the small lunches at which Osgood and Aldrich and I foregathered with him and talked the afternoon away till well toward the winter twilight.

He was a great figure, and the principal figure, at one of the first of the now worn-out Authors' Readings, which was held in the Boston Museum to aid a Longfellow memorial. It was the late George Parsons Lathrop (everybody seems to be late in these sad days) who imagined the reading, but when it came to a price for seats I can always claim the glory of fixing it at five dollars. The price if not the occasion proved irresistible, and the museum was packed from the floor to the topmost gallery. Norton presided, and when it came Clemens' turn to read he introduced him with such exquisite praises as he best knew how to give, but before he closed he fell a prey to one of those lapses of tact which are the peculiar peril of people of the greatest tact. He was reminded of Darwin's delight in Mark Twain, and how when he came from his long day's exhausting study, and sank into bed at midnight, he took up a volume of Mark Twain, whose books he always kept on a table beside him, and whatever had been his tormenting problem, or excess of toil, he felt secure of a good night's rest from it. A sort of blank ensued which Clemens filled in the only possible way. He said he should always be glad that he had contributed to the repose of that great man, whom science owed so much, and then without waiting for the joy in every breast to burst forth, he began to read. It was curious to watch his triumph with the house. His carefully studied effects would reach the first rows in the orchestra first, and ripple in laughter back to the standees against the wall, and then with a fine resurgence come again to the rear orchestra seats, and so rise from gallery to gallery till it fell back, a cataract of applause from the topmost rows of seats. He was such a practiced speaker that he knew all the stops of that simple instrument man, and there is no doubt that these results were accurately intended from his unerring knowledge. He was the most consummate public performer I ever saw, and it was an incomparable pleasure to hear him lecture; on the platform he was the great and finished actor which he probably would not have been on the stage. He was fond of private theatricals, and liked to play in them with his children and their friends, in dramatizations of such stories of his as *The Prince and the Pauper;* but I never saw him in any of these scenes. When he read his manuscript to you, it was with a thorough, however involuntary, recognition of its dramatic qualities; he held that an actor added fully half to the character the author created. With my own hurried and half-hearted reading of passages which I wished to try on him from unprinted chapters (say, out of *The Undiscovered Country* or *A Modern Instance*) he said frankly that my reading could spoil anything. He was realistic, but he was essentially histrionic, and he was rightly so. What we have strongly conceived we ought to make others strongly imagine, and we ought to use every genuine art to that end.

XIV

There came a time when the lecturing which had been the joy of his prime became his loathing, loathing unutterable, and when he renounced it with indescribable violence. Yet he was always hankering for those fleshpots whose savor lingered on his palate and filled his nostrils after his withdrawal from the platform. The Authors' Readings when they had won their brief popularity abounded in suggestion for him. Reading from one's book was not so bad as giving a lecture written for a lecture's purpose, and he was willing at last to compromise. He had a magnificent scheme for touring the country with Aldrich and Mr. G. W. Cable and myself, in a private car, with a cook of our own, and every facility for living on the fat of the land. We should read only four times a week, in an entertainment that should not last more than an hour and a half. He would be the impresario, and would guarantee us others at least seventy-five dollars a day, and pay every expense of the enterprise, which he provisionally called the Circus, himself. But Aldrich and I were now no longer in those earlier thirties when we so cheerfully imagined *Memorable Murders* for subscription publication; we both abhorred public appearances, and, at any rate, I was going to Europe for a year. So the plan fell through except as regarded Mr. Cable, who, in his way, was as fine a performer as Clemens, and could both read and sing the matter of his books. On a far less stupendous scale they two made the rounds of the great lecturing circuit together. But I believe a famous lecture-manager had charge of them and traveled with them.

He was a most sanguine man, a most amiable person, and such a believer in fortune that Clemens used to say of him, as he said of one of his early publishers, that you could rely upon fifty per cent of everything he promised. I myself many years later became a follower of this hopeful prophet, and I can testify that in my case at least he was able to keep ninety-nine, and even a hundred, per cent of his word. It was I who was much nearer failing of mine, for I promptly began to lose sleep from the nervous stress of my lecturing and from the gratifying but killing receptions afterward, and I was truly in that state from insomnia which Clemens recognized in the brief letter I got from him in the Western city, after half-a-dozen wakeful nights. He sardonically congratulated me on having gone into "the lecture field," and then he said: "I know where you are *now*. You are in hell."

It was this perdition which he re-entered when he undertook that round-the-world lecturing tour for the payment of the debts left to him by the bankruptcy of his firm in the publishing business. It was not purely perdition for him, or, rather, it was perdition for only one half of him, the author half; for the actor half it was paradise. The author who takes up lecturing without the ability to give histrionic support to the literary reputation which he brings to the crude test of his reader's eyes and ears invokes a peril and a misery unknown to the lecturer who has made his first public from the platform. Clemens was victorious on the platform from the beginning, and it would be folly to pretend that he did not exult in his triumphs there. But I suppose, with the wearing nerves of middle life, he hated more and more the personal swarming of interest upon him, and all the inevitable clatter of the thing. Yet he faced it, and he labored round our tiresome globe that he might pay the uttermost farthing of debts which he had not knowingly contracted, the debts of his partners who had meant well and done ill, not because they were evil, but because they were unwise, and as unfit for their work as he was. "Pay what thou owest." That is right, even when thou owest it by the error of others, and even when thou owest it to a bank, which had not lent it from love of thee, but in the hard line of business and thy need.

Clemens' behavior in this matter redounded to his glory among the nations of the whole earth, and especially in this nation, so wrapped in commerce and so little used to honor among its many thieves. He had behaved like Walter Scott, as millions rejoiced to know, who had not known how Walter Scott had behaved till they knew it was like Clemens. No doubt it will be put to his credit in the books of the Recording Angel, but what the Judge of all the Earth will say of it at the Last Day there is no telling. I should not be surprised if He accounted it of less merit than some other things that Clemens did and was: less than his abhorrence of the Spanish War, and the destruction of the South-African republics, and our deceit of the Filipinos, and his hate of slavery, and his payment of his portion of our race's debt to the race of the colored student whom he saw through college, and his support of a poor artist for three years in Paris, and his loan of opportunity to the youth who became the most brilliant of our actor-dramatists, and his eager pardon of the thoughtless girl who was near paying the penalty of her impertinence with the loss of her place, and his remembering that the insolent brakeman got so few dollars a month, and his sympathy for working-men standing up to money in their unions, and even his pity for the wounded bird throbbing out its little life on the grass for the pleasure of the cruel fool who shot it. These and the thousand other charities and beneficences in which he abounded, openly or secretly, may avail him more than the discharge of his firm's liabilities with the Judge of all the Earth, who surely will do right, but whose measures and criterions no man knows, and I least of all men.

He made no great show of sympathy with people in their anxieties, but it never failed, and at a time when I lay sick for many weeks his letters were of comfort to those who feared I might not rise again. His hand was out in help for those who needed help, and in kindness for those who needed kindness. There remains in my mind the dreary sense of a long, long drive to the uttermost bounds of the South End at Boston, where he went to call upon some obscure person whose claim stretched in a lengthening chain from his early days in Missouri—a most inadequate person, in whose vacuity the gloom of the dull day deepened till it was almost too deep for tears. He bore the ordeal with grim heroism, and silently smoked away the sense of it, as we drove back to Cambridge, in his slippered feet, somberly musing, somberly swearing. But he knew he had done the right, the kind thing, and he was content. He came the whole way from Hartford to go with me to a friendless play of mine, which Alessandro Salvini was giving in a series of matinees to houses never enlarging themselves beyond the count of the grave two hundred who sat it through, and he stayed my fainting spirit with a cheer beyond flagons, joining me in my joke at the misery of it, and carrying the fun farther.

Before that he had come to witness the aesthetic suicide of Anna Dickinson, who had been a flaming light of the political platform in the war days, and had been left by them consuming in a hapless ambition for the theater. The poor girl had had a play written especially for her, and as Anne Boleyn she ranted and exhorted through the five acts, drawing ever nearer the utter defeat of the anticlimax. We could hardly look at each other for pity, Clemens sitting there in the box he had taken, with his shaggy head out over the corner and his slippered feet curled under him: he either went to a place in his slippers or he carried them with him, and put them on as soon as he could put off his boots. When it was so that we could not longer follow her failure and live, he began to talk of the absolute close of her career which the thing was, and how probably she had no conception that it was the end. He philosophized the mercifulness of the fact, and of the ignorance of most of us, when mortally sick or fatally wounded. We think it is not the end, because we have never ended before, and we do not see how we can end. Some can push by the awful hour and live again, but for Anna Dickinson there could be, and was, no such palingenesis. Of course we got that solemn joy out of reading her fate aright which is the compensation of the wise spectator in witnessing the inexorable doom of others.

XV

When Messrs. Houghton & Mifflin became owners of the *Atlantic Monthly,* Mr. Houghton fancied having some breakfasts and dinners, which should bring the publisher and the editor face to face with the contributors, who were bidden from far and near. Of course, the subtle fiend of advertising, who has now grown so unblushing bold, lurked under the covers at these banquets, and the junior partner and the young editor had their joint and separate fine anguishes of misgiving as to the taste and the principle of them; but they were really very simple-hearted and honestly meant hospitalities, and they prospered as they ought, and gave great pleasure and no pain. I forget some of the "emergent occasions," but I am sure of a birthday dinner most unexpectedly accepted by Whittier, and a birthday luncheon to Mrs. Stowe, and I think a birthday dinner to Longfellow; but the passing years have left me in the dark as to the pretext of that supper at which Clemens made his awful speech, and came so near being the death of us all. At the breakfasts and luncheons we had the pleasure of our lady contributors' company, but that night there were only men, and because of our great strength we survived.

I suppose the year was about 1879, but here the almanac is unimportant, and I can only say that it was after Clemens had become a very valued contributor of the magazine, where he found himself to his own great explicit satisfaction. He had jubilantly accepted our invitation, and had promised a speech, which it appeared afterward he had prepared with unusual care and confidence. It was his custom always to think out his speeches, mentally wording them, and then memorizing them by a peculiar system of mnemonics which he had invented. On the dinner-table a certain succession of knife, spoon, salt-cellar, and butter-plate symbolized a train of ideas, and on the billiard-table a ball, a cue, and a piece of chalk served the same purpose. With a diagram of these printed on the brain he had full command of the phrases which his excogitation had attached to them, and which embodied the ideas in perfect form. He believed he had been particularly fortunate in his notion for the speech of that evening, and he had worked it out in joyous self-reliance. It was the notion of three tramps, three dead-beats, visiting a California mining-camp, and imposing themselves upon the innocent miners as respectively Ralph Waldo Emerson, Henry Wadsworth Longfellow, and Oliver Wendell Holmes. The humor of the conception must prosper or must fail according to the mood of the hearer, but Clemens felt sure of compelling this to sympathy, and he looked forward to an unparalleled triumph.

But there were two things that he had not taken into account. One was the species of religious veneration in which these men were held by those nearest them, a thing that I should not be able to realize to people remote from them in time and place. They were men of extraordinary dignity, of the thing called *presence,* for want of some clearer word, so that no one could well approach them in a personally light or trifling spirit. I do not suppose that anybody more truly valued them or more piously loved them than Clemens himself, but the intoxication of his fancy carried him beyond the bounds of that regard, and emboldened him to the other thing which he had not taken into account —namely, the immense hazard of working his fancy out before their faces, and expecting them to enter into the delight of it. If neither Emerson, nor Longfellow, nor Holmes had been there, the scheme might possibly have carried, but even this is doubtful, for those who so devoutly honored them would have overcome their horror with difficulty, and perhaps would not have overcome it at all.

The publisher, with a modesty very ungrateful to me, had abdicated his office of host, and I was the hapless president, fulfilling the abhorred function of calling people to their feet and making them speak. When I came to Clemens I introduced him with the cordial admiring I had for him as one of my greatest contributors and dearest friends. Here, I said, in sum, was a humorist who never left you hanging your head for having enjoyed his joke; and then the amazing mistake, the bewildering blunder, the cruel catastrophe was upon us. I believe that after the scope of the burlesque made itself clear, there was no one there, including the burlesquer himself, who was not smitten with a desolating dismay. There fell a silence, weighing many tons to the square inch, which deepened from moment to moment, and was broken only by the hysterical and bloodcurdling laughter of a single guest, whose name shall not be handed down to infamy. Nobody knew whether to look at the speaker or down at his plate. I chose my plate as the least affliction, and so I do not know how Clemens looked, except when I stole a glance at him, and saw him standing solitary amid his appalled and appalling listeners, with his joke dead on his hands. From a first glance at the great three whom his jest had made its theme, I was aware of Longfellow sitting upright, and regarding the humorist with an air of pensive puzzle, of Holmes busily writing on his menu, with a well-feigned effect of preoccupation, and of Emerson, holding his elbows, and listening with a sort of Jovian oblivion of this nether world in that lapse of memory which saved him in those later years from so much bother. Clemens must have dragged his joke to the climax and left it there, but I cannot say this from any sense of the fact. Of what happened afterward at the table where the immense, the wholly innocent, the truly unimagined affront was offered, I have no longer the least remembrance. I next remember being in a room of the hotel, where Clemens was not to sleep, but to toss in despair, and Charles Dudley Warner's saying, in the gloom, "Well, Mark, *you're* a funny fellow." It was as well as anything else he could have said, but Clemens seemed unable to accept the tribute.

I stayed the night with him, and the next morning, after a haggard breakfast, we drove about and he made some purchases of bric-à-brac for his house in Hartford, with a soul as far away from bric-à-brac as ever the soul of man was. He went home by an early train, and he lost no time in writing back to the three divine personalities which he had so involuntarily seemed to flout. They all wrote back to him, making it as light for him as they could. I have heard that Emerson was a good deal mystified, and in his sublime forgetfulness asked, Who was this gentleman who appeared to think he had offered him some sort of annoyance? But I am not sure that this is accurate. What I am sure of is that Longfellow, a few days after, in my study, stopped before a photograph of Clemens and said, "Ah, he is a *wag!*" and nothing more. Holmes told me, with deep emotion, such as a brother humorist might well feel, that he had not lost an instant in replying to Clemens' letter, and assuring him that there had not been the least offense, and entreating him never to think of the matter again. "He said that he was a fool, but he was God's fool," Holmes quoted from the letter, with a true sense of the pathos and the humor of the self-abasement.

To me Clemens wrote a week later, "It doesn't get any better; it burns like fire." But now I understand that it was not shame that burnt, but rage for a blunder which he had so incredibly committed. That to have conceived of those men, the most dignified in our literature, our civilization, as impersonable by three hoboes, and then to have imagined that he could ask them personally to enjoy the monstrous travesty, was a break, he saw too late, for which there was no repair. Yet the time came, and not so very long afterward, when some mention was made of the incident as a mistake, and he said, with all his fierceness, "But I don't admit that it *was* a mistake," and it was not so in the minds of all witnesses at second hand. The morning after the dreadful dinner there came a glowing note from Professor Child, who had read the newspaper report of it, praising Clemens' burlesque as the richest piece of humor in the world, and betraying no sense of incongruity in its perpetration in the presence of its victims. I think it must always have ground in Clemens' soul that he was the prey of circumstances, and that if he had some more favoring occasion he could retrieve his loss in it by giving the thing the right setting. Not more than two or three years ago, he came to try me as to trying it again at a meeting of newspaper-men in Washington. I had to own my fears, while I alleged Child's note on the other hand, but in the end he did not try it with the newspaper-men. I do not know whether he has ever printed it or not, but since the thing happened I have often wondered how much offense there really was in it. I am not sure but the horror of the spectators read more indignation into the subjects of the hapless drolling than they felt. But it must have been difficult for them to bear it with equanimity. To be sure, they were not themselves mocked; the joke was, of course, beside them; nevertheless, their personality was trifled with, and I could only end by reflecting that if I had been in their place I should not have liked it myself. Clemens would have liked it himself, for he had the heart for that sort of wild play, and he so loved a joke that even if it took the form of a liberty, and was yet a good joke, he would have loved it. But perhaps this burlesque was not a good joke.

XVI

Clemens was oftenest at my house in Cambridge, but he was also sometimes at my house in Belmont; when, after a year in Europe, we went to live in Boston, he was more rarely with us. We could never be long together without something out of the common happening, and one day something far out of the common happened, which fortunately refused the nature of absolute tragedy, while remaining rather the saddest sort of comedy. We were looking out of my library window on that view of the Charles which I was so proud of sharing with my all-but-next-door neighbor, Doctor Holmes, when another friend who was with us called out with curiously impersonal interest, "Oh, see that woman getting into the water!" This would have excited curiosity and alarmed anxiety far less lively than ours, and Clemens and I rushed downstairs and out through my basement and back gate. At the same time a coachman came out of a stable next door, and grappled by the shoulders a woman who was somewhat deliberately getting down the steps to the water over the face of the embankment. Before we could reach them he had pulled her up to the driveway, and stood holding her there while she crazily grieved at her rescue. As soon as he saw us he went back into his stable, and left us with the poor wild creature on our hands. She was not very young and not very pretty, and we could not have flattered ourselves with the notion of anything romantic in her suicidal mania, but we could take her on the broad human level, and on, this we proposed to escort her up Beacon Street till we could give her into the keeping of one of those kindly policemen whom our neighborhood knew. Naturally there was no policeman known to us or unknown the whole way to the Public Garden. We had to circumvent our charge in her present design of drowning herself, and walk her past the streets crossing Beacon to the river. At these points it needed considerable reasoning to overcome her wish and some active maneuvering in both of us to enforce our arguments. Nobody else appeared to be interested, and though we did not court publicity in the performance of the duty so strangely laid upon us, still it was rather disappointing to be so entirely ignored.

There are some four or five crossings to the river between 302 Beacon Street and the Public Garden, and the suggestions at our command were pretty well exhausted by the time we reached it. Still the expected policeman was nowhere in sight; but a brilliant thought occurred to Clemens. He asked me where the nearest police station was, and when I told him, he started off at his highest speed, leaving me in sole charge of our hapless ward. All my powers of suasion were now taxed to the utmost, and I began attracting attention as a short, stout gentleman in early middle life endeavoring to distrain a respectable female of her personal liberty, when his accomplice had abandoned him to his wicked design. After a much longer time than I thought *I* should have taken to get a policeman from the station, Clemens reappeared in easy conversation with an officer who had probably realized that he was in the company of Mark Twain, and was in no hurry to end the interview. He took possession of our captive, and we saw her no more. I now wonder that with our joint instinct for failure we ever got rid of her; but I am sure we did, and few things in life have given me greater relief. When we got back to my house we found the friend we had left there quite unruffled and not much concerned to know the facts of our adventure. My impression is that he had been taking a nap on my lounge; he appeared refreshed and even gay; but if I am inexact in these details he is alive to refute me.

XVII

A little after this Clemens went abroad with his family, and lived several years in Germany. His letters still came, but at longer intervals, and the thread of our intimate relations was inevitably broken. He would write me when something I had written pleased him, or when something signal occurred to him, or some political or social outrage stirred him to wrath, and he wished to free his mind in pious profanity. During this sojourn he came near dying of pneumonia in Berlin, and he had slight relapses from it after coming home. In Berlin also he had the honor of dining with the German Emperor at the table of a cousin married to a high officer of the court. Clemens was a man to enjoy such a distinction; he knew how to take it as a delegated recognition from the German people; but as coming from a rather cockahoop sovereign who had as yet only his sovereignty to value himself upon, he was not very proud of it. He expressed a quiet disdain of the event as between the imperiality and himself, on whom it was supposed to confer such glory, crowning his life with the topmost leaf of laurel. He was in the same mood in his account of an English dinner many years before, where there was a "little Scotch lord" present, to whom the English tacitly referred Clemens' talk, and laughed when the lord laughed, and were grave when he failed to smile. Of all the men I have known he was the farthest from a snob, though he valued recognition, and liked the flattery of the fashionable fair when it came in his way. He would not go out of his way for it, but like most able and brilliant men he loved the minds of women, their wit, their agile cleverness, their sensitive perception, their humorous appreciation, the saucy things they would say, and their pretty, temerarious defiances. He had, of course, the keenest sense of what was truly dignified and truly undignified in people; but he was not really interested in what we call society affairs; they scarcely existed for him, though his books witness how he abhorred the dreadful fools who through some chance of birth or wealth hold themselves different from other men.

Commonly he did not keep things to himself, especially dislikes and condemnations. Upon most current events he had strong opinions, and he uttered them strongly. After a while he was silent in them, but if you tried him you found him in them still. He was tremendously worked up by a certain famous trial, as most of us were who lived in the time of it. He believed the accused guilty, but when we met some months after it was over, and I tempted him to speak his mind upon it, he would only say, The man had suffered enough; as if the man had expiated his wrong, and he was not going to do anything to renew his penalty. I found that very curious, very delicate. His continued blame could not come to the sufferer's knowledge, but he felt it his duty to forbear it.

He was apt to wear himself out in the vehemence of his resentments; or, he had so spent himself in uttering them that he had literally nothing more to say. You could offer Clemens offenses that would anger other men and he did not mind; he would account for them from human nature; but if he thought you had in any way played him false you were anathema and maranatha forever. Yet not forever, perhaps, for by and by, after years, he would be silent. There were two men, half a generation apart in their succession, whom he thought equally atrocious in their treason to him, and of whom he used to talk terrifyingly, even after they were out of the world. He went farther than Heine, who said that he forgave his enemies, but not till they were dead. Clemens did not forgive his dead enemies; their death seemed to deepen their crimes, like a base evasion, or a cowardly attempt to escape; he pursued them to the grave; he would like to dig them up and take vengeance upon their clay. So he said, but no doubt he would not have hurt them if he had had them living before him. He was generous without stint; he trusted without measure, but where his generosity was abused, or his trust betrayed, he was a fire of vengeance, a consuming flame of suspicion that no sprinkling of cool patience from others could quench; it had to burn itself out. He was eagerly and lavishly hospitable, but if a man seemed willing to batten on him, or in any way to lie down upon him, Clemens despised him unutterably. In his frenzies of resentment or suspicion he would not, and doubtless could not, listen to reason. But if between the paroxysms he were confronted with the facts he would own them, no matter how much they told against him. At one period he fancied that a certain newspaper was hounding him with biting censure and poisonous paragraphs, and he was filling himself up with wrath to be duly discharged on the editor's head. Later, he wrote me with a humorous joy in his mistake that Warner had advised him to have the paper watched for these injuries. He had done so, and how many mentions of him did I reckon he had found in three months? Just two, and they were rather indifferent than unfriendly. So the paper was acquitted, and the editor's life was spared. The wretch never knew how near he was to losing it, with incredible preliminaries of obloquy, and a subsequent devotion to lasting infamy.

XVIII

His memory for favors was as good as for injuries, and he liked to return your friendliness with as loud a band of music as could be bought or bribed for the occasion. All that you had to do was to signify that you wanted his help. When my father was consul at Toronto during Arthur's administration, he fancied that his place was in danger, and he appealed to me. In turn I appealed to Clemens, bethinking myself of his friendship with Grant and Grant's friendship with Arthur. I asked him to write to Grant in my father's behalf, but No, he answered me, I must come to Hartford, and we would go on to New York together and see Grant personally. This was before, and long before, Clemens became Grant's publisher and splendid benefactor, but the men liked each other as such men could not help doing. Clemens made the appointment, and we went to find Grant in his business office, that place where his business innocence was afterward so betrayed. He was very simple and very cordial, and I was instantly the more at home with him, because his voice was the soft, rounded, Ohio River accent to which my years were earliest used from my steamboating uncles, my earliest heroes. When I stated my business he merely said, Oh no; that must not be; he would write to Mr. Arthur; and he did so that day; and my father lived to lay down his office, when he tired of it, with no urgence from above.

It is not irrelevant to Clemens to say that Grant seemed to like finding himself in company with two literary men, one of whom at least he could make sure of, and unlike that silent man he was reputed, he talked constantly, and so far as he might he talked literature. At least he talked of John Phœnix, that delightfulest of the early Pacific Slope humorists, whom he had known under his real name of George H. Derby, when they were fellow-cadets at West Point. It was mighty pretty, as Pepys would say, to see the delicate deference Clemens paid our plain hero, and the manly respect with which he listened. While Grant talked, his luncheon was brought in from some unassuming restaurant near by, and he asked us to join him in the baked beans and coffee which were served us in a little room out of the office with about the same circumstance as at a railroad refreshment-counter. The baked beans and coffee were of about the railroad-refreshment quality; but eating them with Grant was like sitting down to baked beans and coffee with Julius Cæsar, or Alexander, or some other great Plutarchan captain.

One of the highest satisfactions of Clemens' often supremely satisfactory life was his relation to Grant. It was his proud joy to tell how he found Grant about to sign a contract for his book on certainly very good terms, and said to him that he would himself publish the book and give him a percentage three times as large. He said Grant seemed to doubt whether he could honorably withdraw from the negotiation at that point, but Clemens overbore his scruples, and it was his unparalleled privilege, his princely pleasure, to pay the author a far larger check for his work than had ever been paid to an author before. He valued even more than this splendid opportunity the sacred moments in which their business brought him into the presence of the slowly dying, heroically living man whom he was so befriending; and he told me in words which surely lost none of their simple pathos through his report how Grant described his suffering.

The prosperity of this venture was the beginning of Clemens' adversity, for it led to excesses of enterprise which were forms of dissipation. The young sculptor who had come back to him from Paris modeled a small bust of Grant, which Clemens multiplied in great numbers to his great loss, and the success of Grant's book tempted him to launch on publishing seas where his bark presently foundered. The first and greatest of his disasters was the *Life of Pope Leo XIII,* which he came to tell me of, when he had imagined it, in a sort of delirious exultation. He had no words in which to paint the magnificence of the project, or to forecast its colossal success. It would have a currency bounded only by the number of Catholics in Christendom. It would be translated into every language which was anywhere written or printed; it would be circulated literally in every country of the globe, and Clemens' book agents would carry the prospectuses and then the bound copies of the work to the ends of the whole earth. Not only would every Catholic buy it, but every Catholic must, as he was a good Catholic, as he hoped to be saved. It was a magnificent scheme, and it captivated me, as it had captivated Clemens; it dazzled us both, and neither of us saw the fatal defect in it. We did not consider how often Catholics could not read, how often when they could, they might not wish to read. The event proved that whether they could read or not the immeasurable majority did not wish to read the life of the Pope, though it was written by a dignitary of the Church and issued to the world with every sanction from the Vatican. The failure was incredible to Clemens; his sanguine soul was utterly confounded, and soon a silence fell upon it where it had been so exuberantly jubilant.

XIX

The occasions which brought us to New York together were not nearly so frequent as those which united us in Boston, but there was a dinner given him by a friend which remains memorable from the fatuity of two men present, so different in everything but their fatuity. One was the sweet old comedian Billy Florence, who was urging the unsuccessful dramatist across the table to write him a play about Oliver Cromwell, and giving the reasons why he thought himself peculiarly fitted to portray the character of Cromwell. The other was a modestly millioned rich man who was then only beginning to amass the moneys afterward heaped so high, and was still in the condition to be flattered by the condescension of a yet greater millionaire. His contribution to our gaiety was the verbatim report of a call he had made upon William H. Vanderbilt, whom he had found just about starting out of town, with his trunks actually in the front hall, but who had stayed to receive the narrator. He had, in fact, sat down on one of the trunks, and talked with the easiest friendliness, and quite, we were given to infer, like an ordinary human being. Clemens often kept on with some thread of the talk when we came away from a dinner, but now he was silent, as if "high sorrowful and cloyed"; and it was not till well afterward that I found he had noted the facts from the bitterness with which he mocked the rich man, and the pity he expressed for the actor.

He had begun before that to amass those evidences against mankind which eventuated with him in his theory of what he called "the damned human race." This was not an expression of piety, but of the kind contempt to which he was driven by our follies and iniquities as he had observed them in himself as well as in others. It was as mild a misanthropy, probably, as ever caressed the objects of its malediction. But I believe it was about the year 1900 that his sense of our perdition became insupportable and broke out in a mixed abhorrence and amusement which spared no occasion, so that I could quite understand why Mrs. Clemens should have found some compensation, when kept to her room by sickness, in the reflection that now she should not hear so much about "the damned human race." He told of that with the same wild joy that he told of overhearing her repetition of one of his most inclusive profanities, and her explanation that she meant him to hear it so that he might know how it sounded. The contrast of the lurid blasphemy with her heavenly whiteness should have been enough to cure anyone less grounded than he in what must be owned was as fixed a habit as smoking with him. When I first knew him he rarely vented his fury in that sort, and I fancy he was under a promise to her which he kept sacred till the wear and tear of his nerves with advancing years disabled him. Then it would be like him to struggle with himself till he could struggle no longer and to ask his promise back, and it would be like her to give it back. His profanity was the heritage of his boyhood and young manhood in social conditions and under the duress of exigencies in which everybody swore about as impersonally as he smoked. It is best to recognize the fact of it, and I do so the more readily because I cannot suppose the Recording Angel really minded it much more than that Guardian Angel of his. It probably grieved them about equally, but they could equally forgive it. Nothing came of his pose regarding "the damned human race" except his invention of the Human Race Luncheon Club. This was confined to four persons who were never all got together, and it soon perished of their indifference.

In the earlier days that I have more specially in mind one of the questions that we used to debate a good deal was whether every human motive was not selfish. We inquired as to every impulse, the noblest, the holiest in effect, and he found them in the last analysis of selfish origin. Pretty nearly the whole time of a certain railroad run from New York to Hartford was taken up with the scrutiny of the self-sacrifice of a mother for her child, of the abandon of the lover who dies in saving his mistress from fire or flood, of the hero's courage in the field and the martyr's at the stake. Each he found springing from the unconscious love of self and the dread of the greater pain which the self-sacrificer would suffer in forbearing the sacrifice. If we had any time left from this inquiry that day, he must have devoted it to a high regret that Napoleon did not carry out his purpose of invading England, for then he would have destroyed the feudal aristocracy, or "reformed the lords," as it might be called now. He thought that would have been an incalculable blessing to the English people and the world. Clemens was always beautifully and unfalteringly a republican. None of his occasional misgivings for America implicated a return to monarchy. Yet he felt passionately the splendor of the English monarchy, and there was a time when he gloried in that figurative poetry by which the king was phrased as "the Majesty of England." He rolled the words deep-throatedly out, and exulted in their beauty as if it were beyond any other glory of the world. He read, or read *at,* English history a great deal, and one of the by-products of his restless invention was a game of English Kings (like the game of Authors) for children. I do not know whether he ever perfected this, but I am quite sure it was not put upon the market. Very likely he brought it to a practicable stage, and then tired of it, as he was apt to do in the ultimation of his vehement undertakings.

XX

He satisfied the impassioned demand of his nature for incessant activities of every kind by taking a personal as well as a pecuniary interest in the inventions of others. At one moment "the damned human race" was almost to be redeemed by a process of founding brass without air bubbles in it; if this could once be accomplished, as I understood, or misunderstood, brass could be used in art-printing to a degree hitherto impossible. I dare say I have got it wrong, but I am not mistaken as to Clemens' enthusiasm for the process, and his heavy losses in paying its way to ultimate failure. He was simultaneously absorbed in the perfection of a type-setting machine, which he was paying the inventor a salary to bring to a perfection so expensive that it was practically impracticable. We were both printers by trade, and I could take the same interest in this wonderful piece of mechanism that he could; and it was so truly wonderful that it did everything but walk and talk. Its ingenious creator was so bent upon realizing the highest ideal in it that he produced a machine of quite unimpeachable efficiency. But it was so costly, when finished, that it could not be made for less than twenty thousand dollars, if the parts were made by hand. This sum was prohibitive of its introduction, unless the requisite capital could be found for making the parts by machinery, and Clemens spent many months in vainly trying to get this money together. In the meantime simpler machines had been invented and the market filled, and his investment of three hundred thousand dollars in the beautiful miracle remained permanent but not profitable. I once went with him to witness its performance, and it did seem to me the last word in its way, but it had been spoken too exquisitely, too fastidiously. I never heard him devote the inventor to the infernal gods, as he was apt to do with the geniuses he lost money by, and so I think he did not regard him as a traitor.

In these things, and in his other schemes for the *subiti guadagni* of the speculator and the "sudden making of splendid names" for the benefactors of our species, Clemens satisfied the Colonel Sellers nature in himself (from which he drew the picture of that wild and lovable figure), and perhaps made as good use of his money as he could. He did not care much for money in itself, but he luxuriated in the lavish use of it, and he was as generous with it as ever a man was. He liked giving it, but he commonly wearied of giving it himself, and wherever he lived he established an almoner, whom he fully trusted to keep his left hand ignorant of what his right hand was doing. I believe he felt no finality in charity, but did it because in its provisional way it was the only thing a man could do. I never heard him go really into any sociological inquiry, and I have a feeling that that sort of thing baffled and dispirited him. No one can read *The Connecticut Yankee* and not be aware of the length and breadth of his sympathies with poverty, but apparently he had not thought out any scheme for righting the economic wrongs we abound in. I cannot remember our ever getting quite down to a discussion of the matter; we came very near it once in the day of the vast wave of emotion sent over the world by *Looking Backward,* and again when we were all so troubled by the great coal strike in Pennsylvania; in considering that he seemed to be for the time doubtful of the justice of the working-man's cause. At all other times he seemed to know that whatever wrongs the working-man committed work was always in the right.

When Clemens returned to America with his family, after lecturing round the world, I again saw him in New York, where I so often saw him while he was shaping himself for that heroic enterprise. He would come to me, and talk sorrowfully over his financial ruin, and picture it to himself as the stuff of some unhappy dream, which, after long prosperity, had culminated the wrong way. It was very melancholy, very touching, but the sorrow to which he had come home from his long journey had not that forlorn bewilderment in it. He was looking wonderfully well, and when I wanted the name of his elixir, he said it was plasmon. He was apt, for a man who had put faith so decidedly away from him, to take it back and pin it to some superstition, usually of a hygienic sort. Once, when he was well on in years, he came to New York without glasses, and announced that he and all his family, so astigmatic and myopic and old-sighted, had, so to speak, burned their spectacles behind them upon the instruction of some sage who had found out that they were a delusion. The next time he came he wore spectacles freely, almost ostentatiously, and I heard from others that the whole Clemens family had been near losing their eyesight by the miracle worked in their behalf. Now, I was not surprised to learn that "the damned human race" was to be saved by plasmon, if anything, and that my first duty was to visit the plasmon agency with him, and procure enough plasmon to secure my family against the ills it was heir to forevermore. I did not immediately understand that plasmon was one of the investments which he had made from "the substance of things hoped for," and in the destiny of a disastrous disappointment. But after paying off the creditors of his late publishing firm, he had to do something with his money, and it was not his fault if he did not make a fortune out of plasmon.

XXI

For a time it was a question whether he should not go back with his family to their old home in Hartford. Perhaps the father's and mother's hearts drew them there all the more strongly because of the grief written ineffaceably over it, but for the younger ones it was no longer the measure of the world. It was easier for all to stay on indefinitely in New York, which is a sojourn without circumstance, and equally the home of exile and of indecision. The Clemenses took a pleasant, spacious house at Riverdale, on the Hudson, and there I began to see them again on something like the sweet old terms. They lived far more unpretentiously than they used, and I think with a notion of economy, which they had never very successfully practiced. I recall that at the end of a certain year in Hartford, when they had been saving and paying cash for everything, Clemens wrote, reminding me of their avowed experiment, and asking me to guess how many bills they had at New Year's; he hastened to say that a horse-car would not have held them. At Riverdale they kept no carriage, and there was a snowy night when I drove up to their handsome old mansion in the station carryall, which was crusted with mud as from the going down of the Deluge after transporting Noah and his family from the Ark to whatever point they decided to settle at provisionally. But the good talk, the rich talk, the talk that could never suffer poverty of mind or soul, was there, and we jubilantly found ourselves again in our middle youth. It was the mighty moment when Clemens was building his engines of war for the destruction of Christian

Science, which superstition nobody, and he least of all, expected to destroy. It would not be easy to say whether in his talk of it his disgust for the illiterate twaddle of Mrs. Eddy's book, or his admiration of her genius for organization was the greater. He believed that as a religious machine the Christian Science Church was as perfect as the Roman Church and destined to be more formidable in its control of the minds of men. He looked for its spread over the whole of Christendom, and throughout the winter he spent at Riverdale he was ready to meet all listeners more than halfway with his convictions of its powerful grasp of the average human desire to get something for nothing. The vacuous vulgarity of its texts was a perpetual joy to him, while he bowed with serious respect to the sagacity which built so securely upon the everlasting rock of human credulity and folly.

An interesting phase of his psychology in this business was not only his admiration for the masterly policy of the Christian Science hierarchy, but his willingness to allow the miracles of its healers to be tried on his friends and family, if they wished it. He had a tender heart for the whole generation of empirics, as well as the newer sorts of scientitians, but he seemed to base his faith in them largely upon the failure of the regulars rather than upon their own successes, which also he believed in. He was recurrently, but not insistently, desirous that you should try their strange magics when you were going to try the familiar medicines.

XXII

The order of my acquaintance, or call it intimacy, with Clemens was this: our first meeting in Boston, my visits to him in Hartford, his visits to me in Cambridge, in Belmont, and in Boston, our briefer and less frequent meetings in Paris and New York, all with repeated interruptions through my absences in Europe, and his sojourns in London, Berlin, Vienna, and Florence, and his flights to the many ends, and odds and ends, of the earth. I will not try to follow the events, if they were not rather the subjective experiences, of those different periods and points of time which I must not fail to make include his summer at York Harbor, and his divers residences in New York, on Tenth Street and on Fifth Avenue, at Riverdale, and at Stormfield, which his daughter has told me he loved best of all his houses and hoped to make his home for long years.

Not much remains to me of the week or so that we had together in Paris early in the summer of 1904. The first thing I got at my bankers was a cable message announcing that my father was stricken with paralysis, but urging my stay for further intelligence, and I went about, till the final summons came, with my head in a mist of care and dread. Clemens was very kind and brotherly through it all. He was living greatly to his mind in one of those arcaded little hotels in the Rue de Rivoli, and he was free from all household duties to range with me. We drove together to make calls of digestion at many houses where he had got indigestion through his reluctance from their hospitality, for he hated dining out. But, as he explained, his wife wanted him to make these visits, and he did it, as he did everything she wanted. At one place, some suburban villa, he could get no answer to his ring, and he "hove" his cards over the gate just as it opened, and he had the shame of explaining in his unexplanatory French to the man picking them up. He was excruciatingly helpless with his cabmen, but by very cordially smiling and casting himself on the drivers' mercy he always managed to get where he wanted. The family was on the verge of their many moves, and he was doing some small errands; he said that the others did the main things, and left him to do what the cat might.

It was with that return upon the buoyant billow of plasmon, renewed in look and limb, that Clemens' universally pervasive popularity began in his own country. He had hitherto been more intelligently accepted or more largely imagined in Europe, and I suppose it was my sense of this that inspired the stupidity of my saying to him when we came to consider "the state of polite learning" among us, "You mustn't expect people to keep it up here as they do in England." But it appeared that his countrymen were only wanting the chance, and they kept it up in honor of him past all precedent. One does not go into a catalogue of dinners, receptions, meetings, speeches, and the like, when there are more vital things to speak of. He loved these obvious joys, and he eagerly strove with the occasions they gave him for the brilliancy which seemed so exhaustless and was so exhausting. His friends saw that he was wearing himself out, and it was not because of Mrs. Clemens' health alone that they were glad to have him take refuge at Riverdale. The family lived there two happy, hopeless years, and then it was ordered that they should change for his wife's sake to some less exacting climate. Clemens was not eager to go to Florence, but his imagination was taken as it would have been in the old-young days by the notion of packing his furniture into flexible steel cages from his house in Hartford and unpacking it from them untouched at his villa in Fiesole. He got what pleasure any man could out of that triumph of mind over matter, but the shadow was creeping up his life. One sunny afternoon we sat on the grass before the mansion, after his wife had begun to get well enough for removal, and we looked up toward a balcony where by and by that lovely presence made itself visible, as if it had stooped there from a cloud. A hand frailly waved a handkerchief; Clemens ran over the lawn toward it, calling tenderly: "What? What?" as if it might be an asking for him instead of the greeting it really was for me. It was the last time I saw her, if indeed I can be said to have seen her then, and long afterward when I said how beautiful we all thought her, how good, how wise, how wonderfully perfect in every relation of life, he cried out in a breaking voice: "Oh, why didn't you ever tell her? She thought you didn't like her." What a pang it was then not to have told her, but how could we have told her? His unreason endeared him to me more than all his wisdom.

To that Riverdale sojourn belong my impressions of his most violent anti-Christian Science rages, which began with the postponement of his book, and softened into acceptance of the delay till he had well nigh forgotten his wrath when it came out. There was also one of those joint episodes of ours, which, strangely enough, did not eventuate in entire failure, as most of our joint episodes did. He wrote furiously to me of a wrong which had been done to one of the most helpless and one of the most helped of our literary brethren, asking me to join with him in recovering the money paid over by that brother's publisher to a false friend who had withheld it and would not give any account of it. Our hapless brother had appealed to Clemens, as he had to me, with the facts, but not asking our help, probably because he knew he need not ask; and Clemens enclosed to me a very taking-by-the-throat message which he proposed sending to the false friend. For once I had some sense, and answered that this would never do, for we had really no power in the matter, and I contrived a letter to the recreant so softly diplomatic that I shall always think of it with pride when my honesties no longer give me satisfaction, saying that this incident had come to our knowledge, and suggesting that we felt sure he would not finally wish to withhold the money. Nothing more, practically, than that, but that was enough; there came promptly back a letter of justification, covering a very substantial check, which we hilariously forwarded to our beneficiary. But the helpless man who was so used to being helped did not answer with the gladness I, at least, expected of him. He acknowledged the check as he would any ordinary payment, and then he made us observe that there was still a large sum due him out of the moneys withheld. At this point I proposed to Clemens that we should let the nonchalant victim collect the remnant himself. Clouds of sorrow had gathered about the bowed head of the delinquent since we began on him, and my fickle sympathies were turning his way from the victim who was really to blame for leaving his affairs so unguardedly to him in the first place. Clemens made some sort of grim assent, and we dropped the matter. He was more used to ingratitude from those he helped than I was, who found being lain down upon not so amusing as he found my revolt. He reckoned I was right, he said, and after that I think we never recurred to the incident. It was not ingratitude that he ever minded; it was treachery that really maddened him past forgiveness.

XXIII

During the summer he spent at York Harbor I was only forty minutes away at Kittery Point, and we saw each other often; but this was before the last time at Riverdale. He had a wide, low cottage in a pine grove overlooking York River, and we used to sit at a corner of the veranda farthest away from Mrs. Clemens' window, where we could read our manuscripts to each other, and tell our stories, and laugh our hearts out without disturbing her. At first she had been about the house, and there was one gentle afternoon when she made tea for us in the parlor, but that was the last time I spoke with her. After that it was really a question of how soonest and easiest she could be got back to Riverdale; but, of course, there were specious delays in which she seemed no worse and seemed a little better, and Clemens could work at a novel he had begun. He had taken a room in the house of a friend and neighbor, a fisherman and boatman; there was a table where he could write, and a bed where he could lie down and read; and there, unless my memory has played me one of those constructive tricks that people's memories indulge in, he read me the first chapters of an admirable story. The scene was laid in a Missouri town, and the characters such as he had known in boyhood; but often as I tried to make him own it, he denied having written any such story; it is possible that I dreamed it, but I hope the MS. will yet be found.

XXIV

I cannot say whether or not he believed that his wife would recover; he fought the fear of her death to the end; for her life was far more largely his than the lives of most men's wives are theirs. For his own life I believe he would never have much cared, if I may trust a saying of one who was so absolutely without pose as he was. He said that he never saw a dead man whom he did not envy for having had it over and being done with it. Life had always amused him, and in the resurgence of its interests after his sorrow had ebbed away he was again deeply interested in the world and in the human race, which, though damned, abounded in subjects of curious inquiry. When the time came for his wife's removal from York Harbor I went with him to Boston, where he wished to look up the best means of her conveyance to New York. The inquiry absorbed him: the sort of invalid-car he could get; how she could be carried to the village station; how the car could be detached from the Eastern train at Boston and carried round to the Southern train on the other side of the city, and then how it could be attached to the Hudson River train at New York and left at Riverdale. There was no particular of the business which he did not scrutinize and master, not only with his poignant concern for her welfare, but with his strong curiosity as to how these unusual things were done with the usual means. With the inertness that grows upon an aging man he had been used to delegating more and more things, but of that thing I perceived that he would not delegate the least detail.

He had meant never to go abroad again, but when it came time to go he did not look forward to returning; he expected to live in Florence always after that; they were used to the life and they had been happy there some years earlier before he went with his wife for the cure of Nauheim. But when he came home again it was for good and all. It was natural that he should wish to live in New York, where they had already had a pleasant year in Tenth Street. I used to see him there in an upper room, looking south over a quiet open space of back yards where we fought our battles in behalf of the Filipinos and the Boers, and he carried on his campaign against the missionaries in China. He had not yet formed his habit of lying for whole days in bed and reading and writing there, yet he was a good deal in bed, from weakness, I suppose, and for the mere comfort of it.

My perspectives are not very clear, and in the foreshortening of events which always takes place in our review of the past I may not always time things aright. But I believe it was not until he had taken his house at 21 Fifth Avenue that he began to talk to me of writing his autobiography. He meant that it should be a perfectly veracious record of his life and period; for the first time in literature there should be a true history of a man and a true presentation of the men the man had known. As we talked it over the scheme enlarged itself in our riotous fancy. We said it should be not only a book, it should be a library, not only a library, but a literature. It should make good the world's loss through Omar's barbarity at Alexandria; there was no image so grotesque, so extravagant that we did not play with it; and the work so far as he carried it was really done on a colossal scale. But one day he said that as to veracity it was a failure; he had begun to lie, and that if no man ever yet told the truth about himself it was because no man ever could. How far he had carried his autobiography I cannot say; he dictated the matter several hours each day; and the public has already seen long passages from it, and can judge, probably, of the make and matter of the whole from these. It is immensely inclusive, and it observes no order or sequence. Whether now, after his death, it will be published soon or late I have no means of knowing. Once or twice he said in a vague way that it was not to be published for twenty years, so that the discomfort of publicity might be minimized for all the survivors. Suddenly he told me he was not working at it; but I did not understand whether he had finished it or merely dropped it; I never asked.

We lived in the same city, but for old men rather far apart, he at Tenth Street and I at Seventieth, and with our colds and other disabilities we did not see each other often. He expected me to come to him, and I would not without some return of my visits, but we never ceased to be friends, and good friends, so far as I know. I joked him once as to how I was going to come out in his autobiography, and he gave me some sort of joking reassurance. There was one incident, however, that brought us very frequently and actively together. He came one Sunday afternoon to have me call with him on Maxim Gorky, who was staying at a hotel a few streets above mine. We were both interested in Gorky, Clemens rather more as a revolutionist and I as a realist, though I too wished the Russian Tsar ill, and the novelist well in his mission to the Russian sympathizers in this republic. But I had lived through the episode of Kossuth's visit to us and his vain endeavor to raise funds for the Hungarian cause in 1851, when we were a younger and nobler nation than now, with hearts if not hands opener to the "oppressed of Europe"; the oppressed of America, the four or five millions of slaves, we did not count. I did not believe that Gorky could get the money for the cause of freedom in Russia which he had come to get; as I told a valued friend of his and mine, I did not believe he could get twenty-five hundred dollars, and I think now I set the figure too high. I had already refused to sign the sort of general appeal his friends were making to our principles and pockets because I felt it so wholly idle, and when the paper was produced in Gorky's presence and Clemens put his name to it I still refused. The next day Gorky was expelled from his hotel with the woman who was not his wife, but who, I am bound to say, did not look as if she were not, at least to me, who am, however, not versed in those aspects of human nature.

I might have escaped unnoted, but Clemens' familiar head gave us away to the reporters waiting at the elevator's mouth for all who went to see Gorky. As it was, a hunt of interviewers ensued for us severally and jointly. I could remain aloof in my hotel apartment, returning answer to such guardians of the public right to know everything that I had nothing to say of Gorky's domestic affairs; for the public interest had now strayed far from the revolution, and centered entirely upon these. But with Clemens it was different; he lived in a house with a street door kept by a single butler, and he was constantly rung for. I forget how long the siege lasted, but long enough for us to have fun with it. That was the moment of the great Vesuvian eruption, and we figured ourselves in easy reach of a volcano which was every now and then "blowing a cone off," as the telegraphic phrase was. The roof of the great market in Naples had just broken in under its load of ashes and cinders, and crushed hundreds of people; and we asked each other if we were not sorry we had not been there, where the pressure would have been far less terrific than it was with us in Fifth Avenue. The forbidden butler came up with a message that there were some gentlemen below who wanted to see Clemens.

"How many?" he demanded.

"Five," the butler faltered.

"Reporters?"

The butler feigned uncertainty.

"What would you do?" he asked me.

"I wouldn't see them," I said, and then Clemens went directly down to them. How or by what means he appeased their voracity I cannot say, but I fancy it was by the confession of the exact truth, which was harmless enough. They went away joyfully, and he came back in radiant satisfaction with having seen them. Of course he was right and I wrong, and he was right as to the point at issue between Gorky and those who had helplessly treated him with such cruel ignominy. In America it is not the convention for men to live openly in hotels with women who are not their wives. Gorky had violated this convention and he had to pay the penalty; and concerning the destruction of his efficiency as an emissary of the revolution, his blunder was worse than a crime.

XXV

To the period of Clemens' residence in Fifth Avenue belongs his efflorescence in white serge. He was always rather aggressively indifferent about dress, and at a very early date in our acquaintance Aldrich and I attempted his reform by clubbing to buy him a cravat. But he would not put away his stiff little black bow, and until he imagined the suit of white serge, he wore always a suit of black serge, truly deplorable in the cut of the sagging frock. After his measure had once been taken he refused to make his clothes the occasion of personal interviews with his tailor; he sent the stuff by the kind elderly woman who had been in the service of the family from the earliest days of his marriage, and accepted the result without criticism. But the white serge was an inspiration which few men would have had the courage to act upon. The first time I saw him wear it was at the authors' hearing before the Congressional Committee on Copyright in Washington. Nothing could have been more dramatic than the gesture with which he flung off his long loose overcoat, and stood forth in white from his feet to the crown of his silvery head. It was a magnificent *coup,* and he dearly loved a *coup;* but the magnificent speech which he made, tearing to shreds the venerable farrago of nonsense about non-property in ideas which had formed the basis of all copyright legislation, made you forget even his spectacularity.

It is well known how proud he was of his Oxford gown, not merely because it symbolized the honor in which he was held by the highest literary body in the world, but because it was so rich and so beautiful. The red and the lavender of the cloth flattered his eyes as the silken black of the same degree of Doctor of Letters, given him years before at Yale, could not do. His frank, defiant happiness in it, mixed with a due sense of burlesque, was something that those lacking his poet-soul could never imagine; they accounted it vain, weak; but that would not have mattered to him if he had known it. In his London sojourn he had formed the top-hat habit, and for a while he lounged splendidly up and down Fifth Avenue in that society emblem; but he seemed to tire of it, and to return kindly to the soft hat of his Southwestern tradition.

He disliked clubs; I don't know whether he belonged to any in New York, but I never met him in one. As I have told, he himself had formed the Human Race Club, but as he never could get it together it hardly counted. There was to have been a meeting of it the time of my only visit to Stormfield in April of last year; but of three who were to have come I alone came. We got on very well without the absentees, after finding them in the wrong, as usual, and the visit was like those I used to have with him so many years before in Hartford, but there was not the old ferment of subjects. Many things had been discussed and put away for good, but we had our old fondness for nature and for each other, who were so differently parts of it. He showed his absolute content with his house, and that was the greater pleasure for me because it was my son who designed it. The architect had been so fortunate as to be able to plan it where a natural avenue of savins, the close-knit, slender, cypresslike cedars of New England, led away from the rear of the villa to the little level of a pergola, meant someday to be wreathed and roofed with vines. But in the early spring days all the landscape was in the beautiful nakedness of the Northern winter. It opened in the surpassing loveliness of wooded and meadowed uplands, under skies that were the first days blue, and the last gray over a rainy and then a snowy floor. We walked up and down, up and down, between the villa terrace and the pergola, and talked with the melancholy amusement, the sad tolerance of age for the sort of men and things that used to excite us or enrage us; now we were far past turbulence or anger. Once we took a walk together across the yellow pastures to a chasmal creek on his grounds, where the ice still knit the clayey banks together like crystal mosses; and the stream far down clashed through and over the stones and the shards of ice. Clemens pointed out the scenery he had bought to give himself elbow-room, and showed me the lot he was going to have me build on. The next day we came again with the geologist he had asked up to Stormfield to analyze its rocks. Truly he loved the place, though he had been so weary of change and so indifferent to it that he never saw it till he came to live in it. He left it all to the architect whom he had known from a child in the intimacy which bound our families together, though we bodily lived far enough apart. I loved his little ones and he was sweet to mine and was their delighted-in and wondered-at friend. Once and once again, and yet again and again, the black shadow that shall never be lifted where it falls, fell in his house and in mine, during the forty years and more that we were friends, and endeared us the more to each other.

XXVI

My visit at Stormfield came to an end with tender relucting on his part and on mine. Every morning before I dressed I heard him sounding my name through the house for the fun of it and I know for the fondness; and if I looked out of my door, there he was in his long nightgown swaying up and down the corridor, and wagging his great white head like a boy that leaves his bed and comes out in the hope of frolic with someone. The last morning a soft sugar-snow had fallen and was falling, and I drove through it down to the station in the carriage which had been given him by his wife's father when they were first married, and been kept all those intervening years in honorable retirement for this final use. Its springs had not grown yielding with time; it had rather the stiffness and severity of age; but for him it must have swung low like the sweet chariot of the Negro "spiritual" which I heard him sing with such fervor, when those wonderful hymns of the slaves began to make their way northward. *Go Down, Daniel,* was one in which I can hear his quavering tenor now. He was a lover of the things he liked, and full of a passion for them which satisfied itself in reading them matchlessly aloud. No one could read *Uncle Remus* like him; his voice echoed the voices of the Negro nurses who told his childhood the wonderful tales. I remember especially his rapture with Mr. Cable's *Old Creole Days,* and the thrilling force with which he gave the forbidding of the leper's brother when the city's survey ran the course of an avenue through the cottage where the leper lived in hiding: "Strit must not pass!"

Out of a nature rich and fertile beyond any I have known, the material given him by the Mystery that makes a man and then leaves him to make himself over, he wrought a character of high nobility upon a foundation of clear and solid truth. At the last day he will not have to confess anything, for all his life was the free knowledge of anyone who would ask him of it. The Searcher of hearts will not bring him to shame at that day, for he did not try to hide any of the things for which he was often so bitterly sorry. He knew where the Responsibility lay, and he took a man's share of it bravely; but not the less fearlessly he left the rest of the answer to the God who had imagined men.

It is in vain that I try to give a notion of the intensity with which he pierced to the heart of life, and the breadth of vision with which he compassed the whole world, and tried for the reason of things, and then left trying. We had other meetings, insignificantly sad and brief; but the last time I saw him alive was made memorable to me by the kind clear judicial sense with which he explained and justified the labor unions as the sole present help of the weak against the strong.

Next I saw him dead, lying in his coffin amid those flowers with which we garland our despair in that pitiless hour. After the voice of his old friend Twichell had been lifted in the prayer which it wailed through in broken-hearted supplication, I looked a moment at the face I knew so well; and it was patient with the patience I had so often seen in it: something of puzzle, a great silent dignity, an assent to what must be from the depths of a nature whose tragical seriousness broke in the laughter which the unwise took for the whole of him. Emerson, Longfellow, Lowell, Holmes—I knew them all and all the rest of our sages, poets, seers, critics, humorists; they were like one another and like other literary men; but Clemens was sole, incomparable, the Lincoln of our literature.

George cabot lodge (1873–1907) belonged to a generation of poets, born in the late sixties or seventies, that never really accomplished its work. Almost all were born in New England and went to Harvard. Many of them died young. William Vaughn Moody, who died at forty-three, is still to some extent read. Trumbull Stickney, who died at thirty, was a more authentic poet, and some of his best pieces survive in anthologies. Edwin Arlington Robinson alone both was a poet of the first rank and completed a life's work. Outliving so many of his coevals, he became the real spokesman for all these men. Though he had moved from New England to New York, he wrote much of the twilight of New England, and he celebrated the dignity of failure. The typical hero of Robinson is the man who has failed but who has "followed the gleam."

In the work of George Cabot Lodge, though he expended in the writing of his verse a good deal of intellectual energy, the gleam does not glow very brilliantly. One cannot say that he was a bad poet: he was hardly a poet at all—though he did some service to poetry in rescuing the work of Stickney. Edith Wharton, who knew him, says in *A Backward Glance* that "he had a naturally scholarly mind, and might have turned in the end to history and archaeology; unless, indeed, he was simply intended to be the most sensitive of contemplators, as he was the most sensitive and dazzling of talkers." The sole interest of Lodge today is a sad typicality which lends itself to the purposes of historians and critics. Santayana, in a letter to William Lyon Phelps on the subject of his novel, *The Last Puritan,* writes that "an important element in the tragedy of 'his hero' is drawn from the fate of a whole string of Harvard poets in the 1880's and 1890's—Sanborn, Philip Savage, Hugh McCulloch, Trumbull Stickney, and Cabot Lodge. . . . Now, all those friends of mine . . . were visibly killed by the lack of air to breathe. People individually were kind and appreciative to them, as they were to me, but the system was deadly, and they hadn't any alternative tradition (as I had) to fall back upon; and of course . . . they hadn't the strength of a great intellectual hero who can stand alone."

But there would, of course, be no point in including a memoir of Lodge in this volume if Henry Adams had not written about him. Anatole France was once demonstrating in a salon that Jesus could never have existed, and Marcel Proust was listening with serious attention, watching the face of the speaker. France noticed this and stopped and asked his opinion of the matter. "It is not Jesus, monsieur," said Proust, "who interests me in this conversation, but Anatole France."

The late Herbert Croly told a curious story about an interview with Henry Adams. Croly had published in 1912 a biography of Mark Hanna; and the family of John Hay, then in search of a biographer for Hay, thought Croly was a possible man. They had been prompted perhaps by Adams: it was at any rate Adams whom Croly saw. He talked, Croly said, with an air of the great world which exercised a certain spell, but the occasion was deeply chilling. By the time he left Adams' presence, Croly had been made to feel that he would not for anything in the world undertake that biography of Hay. Though Adams' ostensible role had been that of a friend of the family who was trying to provide a memorial for an old and valued friend, he had constantly betrayed this purpose by intimating in backhanded but unmistakable fashion his conviction that Hay was a mediocre person, that it would be impossible to write truthfully about him and to satisfy the family at the same time, and that no self-respecting writer ought to think of taking on the job.

Adams had at that time himself just written, at the request of the family of another old friend, Henry Cabot Lodge, the life of Lodge's son; and he had let down the younger Lodge just as he had let down Hay and just as he was to let down Henry Cabot in *The Education of Henry Adams.* This dreary and cold little book—published in 1911, when Adams was seventy-three—is perhaps the most uncanny example of Adams' equivocal attitude in relation to the social world of Boston and to the official world of Washington out of which he had come and to which he had inevitably reverted, but with which he never ceased to express his extreme dissatisfaction. He assumes that Lodge, as a Lodge and the son of a friend of Adams, is worth taking seriously and writing about; but he turns the poor young man into a shadow, and withers up his verse with a wintry pinch.

It is possible to check Henry Adams' account by the portrait left by Edith Wharton. Mrs. Wharton says, for example, that Lodge was "brilliant and exuberant"—which is the kind of fact one does not get from Adams; and her description of the atmosphere of loving protection with which young Lodge was surrounded is strikingly at variance with Adams' picture of a violator of convention and a contender against the times.

His fate [she writes] was the reverse of mine, for he grew up in a hothouse of intensive culture, and was one of the most complete examples I have ever known of the young genius before whom an adoring family unites in smoothing the way. This kept him out of the struggle of life, and consequently out of its experiences, and to the end his intellectual precocity was combined with a boyishness of spirit at once delightful and pathetic. He had always lived in Washington, where, at the time when he was growing up, his father, Henry Adams, John

Hay, and the eccentric Sturgis Bigelow of Boston, whose erudition so far exceeded his mental capacity, formed a close group of intimates. Until Theodore Roosevelt came to Washington theirs were almost the only houses where one breathed a cosmopolitan air, and where such men as Sir Cecil Spring-Rice, J. J. Jusserand, and Lord Bryce felt themselves immediately at home. But Washington, even then, save for the politician and the government official, was a place to retire to, not to be young in; and Bay [as Lodge was called] often complained of the lack of friends of his own age. Even more than from the narrowness of his opportunities he suffered from the slightly rarefied atmosphere of mutual admiration and disdain of the rest of the world that prevailed in his immediate surroundings. John Hay was by nature the most open-minded of the group, and his diplomatic years in London had enlarged his outlook; but the dominating spirits were Henry Adams and Cabot Lodge, and though they were extremely kind to me, and my pleasantest hours in Washington were spent at their houses, I always felt that the influences prevailing there kept Bay in a state of brilliant immaturity.

Lodge, then, was kept under glass, and he dried up from "lack of air to breathe"; and Adams himself was a part of the stifling. He composes for his young friend an epitaph which buries his aspirations with him. The stealthy and elusive malice which lies in *The Education* here colors what is meant as a tribute with an irony so ready and pervasive that it is hardly aware of itself. J. P. Marquand could not do so well: the dismal comments on Lodge's *Wanderjahre*—"At best, the atmosphere of Paris in December lacks gaiety except for Parisians. . . . One founders through it as one best can." . . . "A winter in Berlin is, under the best of circumstances, a grave strain on the least pessimistic temper" . . . ; the chapter called *War and Love,* with its remark that if poets may be judged by the excellence of the women they are attached to, "young Lodge would take rank among the strongest"; the irony of the final picture—how far is it deliberate on Adams' part?—of poor Lodge arriving back in Boston, weighted down with family, nurses and baggage and in a panic for fear he has lost his manuscripts in the confusion of the North Station; and Henry Adams' own gingerly justification of the element of violence in Greek tragedy: "The better informed and the more accomplished the critic may be, who reads the *Herakles* for the first time, knowing nothing of the author, the more disconcerted he is likely to be in reading it a second time. His first doubts of the poet's knowledge or merits will be followed by doubts of his own."

This double-edged doubt, so characteristic of Adams—the doubt that peeled the gilt off the Gilded Age yet despaired of Adams' strength to stand up to it, the doubt which, in envying the faith that had erected the cathedral at Chartres, yet found in the weakness of the church's foundations a symbol for its own painful fears—this doubt is all through the life of Lodge, the last of Adams' published books. One feels that he dislikes Lodge's poetry. He would like to see something in it; but he shrinks—from what?—from finding in the younger man the reflection of his own sterility or from the disquieting possibility that Lodge may have really been a poet and hence have lived in some richer way than Adams had ever known? He wants to think that Lodge was a nonconformist as he imagines himself to have been; yet he meets in him all the old round of the life-cycle of people from Boston, of people like oneself; and he cannot repress a shiver. We people all come to nothing—not, of course, that we aren't better than the others.

With all this, there is even here that candor in dubiety and impotence which has the accents of a kind of strength; and the rare sensitive-cynical Adams who is himself a kind of poet, as it were, signs the little memoir with the passage at the end of the seventh chapter in which he tells of the solitary writer weaving secret enchantments at night like a drug-merchant or a magician.

HENRY ADAMS

THE LIFE OF GEORGE CABOT LODGE

I. Childhood

POETS ARE PROVERBIALLY BORN, not made; and, because they have been born rarely, the conditions of their birth are singularly interesting. One imagines that the conditions surrounding the birth of New England poets can have varied little, yet, in shades, these conditions differ deeply enough to perplex an artist who does not know where to look for them. Especially the society of Boston has always believed itself to have had, from the start, a certain complexity—certain rather refined *nuances*—which gave it an avowed right to stand apart; a right which its members never hesitated to assert, if it pleased them to do so, and which no one thought of questioning. One of the best-known and most strongly marked of these numerous families, was—and still is—that of the Cabots, whose early story has been told by Henry Cabot Lodge in his life of the best-known member of the family, his great-grandfather, George Cabot, Senator of the United States.

George Cabot's son Henry married Anna Blake, and had a daughter, Anna Sophia Cabot, who married John Ellerton Lodge. The Lodges were new arrivals in Boston. Giles Lodge, the grandfather, having narrowly escaped with his life from the San Domingo massacre, arrived, a young Englishman and a stranger, in Boston in 1791. There he established himself in business and married Mary Langdon, daughter of John Langdon, an officer of the Continental Army and cousin of President Langdon of Harvard College, who prayed for the troops on the eve of Bunker Hill. Through his mother John Lodge was descended from the Walleys and Brattles and other Puritan families of Boston, now for the most part extinct and forgotten. But despite the paternal grandmother, Henry Cabot Lodge, the only son of John Ellerton Lodge and Anna Cabot, felt himself Bostonian chiefly on the mother's side, as an offshoot of the prolific stock of the Cabots, who were really all of Essex County origin. He marked the point by making for himself a world-wide reputation under the double name of Cabot Lodge. Of him the public needs no biography, since he became a familiar figure to millions of his fellow-citizens from somewhat early youth to a fairly advanced age; and, from the conspicuous stage of the United States Senate, offered a far more conspicuous presence than his great-grandfather, George Cabot, had ever done.

To Bostonians, in general, the Cabots altogether are a stock too strong, too rich, too varied in their family characteristics, to need explanation. Volumes might be written on them, without exhausting the varieties of the strain.

That such a family should produce a poet was not matter for surprise; but as though to make such a product quite natural and normal, Henry Cabot Lodge, who was born May 12, 1850, married, on June 29, 1871, into another Massachusetts family with history and characteristics as marked as those of the Cabots themselves.

The Plymouth Colony produced Davises as freely as the north shore produced Cabots. Daniel Davis, of the Barnstaple stock, was Solicitor-General of Massachusetts in the days, about 1800, when the Reverend James Freeman was the Unitarian minister of King's Chapel; and Daniel Davis married Lois Freeman, who bore him thirteen children. The oldest, Louisa, married William Minot, of a family more thoroughly Bostonian, if possible, than all the rest. The youngest, Charles Henry Davis, born January 16, 1807, in Somerset Street, Boston, and, in due course, sent to Harvard College, left the college, in 1823, to enter the navy as midshipman, in order to cruise in the old frigate, the *United States,* in the Pacific, under the command of his friend and patron, Commodore Isaac Hull.

The life of Admiral Davis has been admirably told elsewhere, and his victories at Hilton Head, in November 1861, at Fort Pillow, in May 1862, at Memphis and Vicksburg, afterwards, rank among the most decisive of the Civil War, as they rank also among the earliest to give some share of hope or confidence to the national government and to the loyal voters; but his brilliant career in the navy concerns his grandson-poet less than the domestic event of his marriage, in 1842, to Harriette Blake Mills, daughter of still another United States Senator, Elijah Hunt Mills, of Northampton, Massachusetts, who was also a conspicuous figure in his day.

The complications of this alliance were curious, and among them was the chance that another daughter of Senator Mills married Benjamin Peirce, the famous Professor of Mathematics at Harvard College, so that the children of Admiral Davis became first cousins of the great mathematician Charles Peirce and his brothers. Among these children of Admiral Davis was a daughter, Anna Cabot Mills Davis, who grew up to girlhood in Cambridge, under the shadow of Harvard College, where her father, the Admiral, lived while not in active service; and when, after his appointment to the Naval Observatory, he transferred his residence to Washington, she made her home there until her marriage, in June 1871, to Henry Cabot Lodge.

Her second child, George Cabot Lodge, the subject of this story, was born in Boston, October 10, 1873.

A poet, born in Boston, in 1873, saw about him a society which commonly bred refined tastes, and often did refined work, but seldom betrayed strong emotions. The excitements of war had long passed; its ideals were forgotten, and no other great ideal had followed. The twenty-five years between 1873 and 1898—years of astonishing scientific and mechanical activity—were marked by a steady decline of literary and artistic intensity, and especially of the feeling for poetry, which, at best, had never been the favorite form of Boston expression. The only poet who could be called strictly Bostonian by birth—Ralph Waldo Emerson—died in the year 1882, before young Lodge was ten years old. Longfellow, who always belonged to Cambridge rather than to Boston, died in the same year. James Russell Lowell survived till 1891, but was also in no strict social sense a Bostonian. Young men growing up on Beacon Hill or the Back Bay never met such characters unless by a rare chance; and as the city became busier and more crowded, the chances became rarer still.

Not the society, therefore, could have inspired a taste for poetry. Such an instinct must have been innate, like his cousin's mathematics. Society could strike him only as the absence of all that he might have supposed it to be, as he read of it in the history and poetry of the past. Even since the youth of R. W. Emerson, the sense of poetry had weakened like the sense of religion. Boston differed little from other American towns with less reputation for intellect, where, as a rule, not many persons entered their neighbors' houses, and these were members of the family. A stranger was unknown.

The classic and promiscuous turmoil of the forum, the theater, or the bath, which trained the Greeks and the Romans, or the narrower contact of the church and the coffee-house, which bred the polished standards of Dryden and Racine, were unknown in America, and nearly extinct in Paris and London. An American boy scarcely conceived of getting social education from contact with his elders. In previous generations he had been taught to get it from books, but the young American of this period was neither a bookish nor a social animal. Climate and custom combined to narrow his horizon.

Commonly the boy was well pleased to have it so; he asked only to play with his fellows, and to escape contact with the world; but the Boston child of the Cabot type was apt to feel himself alone even as a child. Unless singularly fortunate in finding and retaining sympathetic companions, his strong individuality rebelled against its surroundings. Boys are naturally sensitive and shy. Even as men, a certain proportion of society showed, from the time of the Puritans, a marked reserve, so that one could never be quite sure in State Street, more than in Concord, that the lawyer or banker whom one consulted about drawing a deed or negotiating a loan might not be unconsciously immersed in introspection, as his ancestors, two centuries before, had been absorbed in their chances of salvation. The latent contrasts of character were full of interest, and so well understood that any old Bostonian, familiar with family histories, could recall by scores the comedies and tragedies which had been due to a conscious or unconscious revolt against the suppression of instinct and imagination.

Poetry was a suppressed instinct: and except where, as in Longfellow, it kept the old character of ornament, it became a reaction against society, as in Emerson and the Concord school, or, further away and more roughly, in Walt Whitman. Less and less it appeared, as in earlier ages, the natural, favorite expression of society itself. In the last half of the nineteenth century, the poet became everywhere a rebel against his surroundings. What had been begun by Wordsworth, Byron, and Shelley, was carried on by Algernon Swinburne in London or Paul Verlaine in Paris or Walt Whitman in Washington, by a common instinct of revolt. Even the atmosphere of Beacon Street was at times faintly redolent of Schopenhauer.

The tendency of Bostonians to break away from conventional society was fostered by the harshness of the climate, but was vastly helped by the neighborhood of the ocean. Snow and ice and fierce northwest gales shut up society within doors during three months of winter; while equally fierce heat drove society to camp within tide-water during three months of summer. There the ocean was the closest of friends. Everyone knows the little finger of granite that points oceanward, some ten miles north of Boston, as though directing the Bostonian homeward. The spot is almost an island, connected with Lynn by a long, narrow strip of sand-beach; but on the island a small township called Nahant has long existed, and the end of this point of Nahant was bought by the grandfather, John Ellerton Lodge, as a country place for summer residence.

The whole coast, for five hundred miles in either direction, has since been seized for summer residence, but Nahant alone seems to be actually the ocean itself, as though it were a ship quitting port, or, better, just stranded on the rocky coast of Cape Ann. There the winds and waves are alone really at home, and man can never by day or night escape their company. At the best of times, and in their most seductive temper, their restlessness carries a suggestion of change, —a warning of latent passion,—a threat of storm. One looks out forever to an infinite horizon of shoreless and shifting ocean.

The sea is apt to revive some primitive instinct in boys, as though in a far-off past they had been fishes, and had never quite forgotten their home. The least robust can feel the repulsion, even when they cannot feel the physical attraction, of the waves playing with the rocks like children never quite sure of their temper; but the Lodge boy, like most other boys of his class and breed, felt the sea as an echo or double of himself. Commonly this instinct of unity with nature dies early in American life; but young Lodge's nature was itself as elementary and simple as the salt water. Throughout life, the more widely his character spread in circumference, the more simply he thought, and even when trying to grow complex—as was inevitable since it was to grow in Boston—the mind itself was never complex, and the complexities merely gathered on it, as something outside, like the sea-weeds gathering and swaying about the rocks. Robust in figure, healthy in appetite, careless of consequences, he could feel complex and introspective only as his ideal, the Norse faun, might feel astonished and angry at finding nature perverse and unintelligible in a tropical jungle. Since nature could not be immoral or futile, the immorality and futility must be in the mind that conceived it. Man became an outrage; society an artificial device for the distortion of truth; civilization a wrong. Many millions of simple natures have thought, and still think, the same thing, and the more complex have never quite made up their minds whether to agree with them or not; but the thought that was simple and sufficient for the Norseman exploring the tropics, or for an exuberant young savage sailing his boat off the rude shores of Gloucester and Cape Ann, could not long survive in the atmosphere of State Street. Commonly the poet dies young.

The Nahant life was intensely home, with only a father and mother for companions, an elder sister, a younger brother, cousins, or boy friends at hazard, and boundless sea and sky. As the boy passed his tenth year, his father—possibly inspired by the same spirit of restlessness—turned much of his time and attention to politics, and the mother became all the more the companion and resource of the children. From the earliest forms of mammal life, the mothers of fauns have been more in love with their offspring than with all else in existence; and when the mother has had the genius of love and sympathy, the passion of altruism, the instinct of taste and high breeding, besides the commoner resources of intelligence and education, the faun returns the love, and is molded by it into shape.

These were the elements of his youth, and the same elements will be found recurring in all that he thought and said during his thirty-six years of life. He was himself, both in fact and in imagination, *The Wave,* whose song he began his literary career by composing:

This is the song of the wave, that died in the fullness of life.
The prodigal this, that lavished its largess of strength
In the lust of achievement.
Aiming at things for Heaven too high,
Sure in the pride of life, in the richness of strength.
So tried it the impossible height, till the end was found,
Where ends the soul that yearns for the fillet of morning stars,
The soul in the toils of the journeying worlds,
Whose eye is filled with the image of God,
    And the end is Death.

Had the *Song of the Wave* been written after death instead of before the beginning of life, the figure could not have been more exact. The young man felt the image as he felt the act; his thought offered itself to him as a wave. From first to last he identified himself with the energies of nature, as the story will show; he did not invent images for amusement, but described himself in describing the energy. Even the figure of the Norse faun was his own figure, and, like the Wave, with which it belongs, was an effort at the first avowal of himself to himself; for these things were of his youth, felt and not feigned:

These are the men!
The North has given them name,
The children of God who dare. . . .
These are the men!
In their youth without memory
They were glad, for they might not see
The lies that the world has wrought
On the parchment of God. The tree
Yielded them ships, and the sky
Flamed as the waters fought;
But they knew that death was a lie,
That the life of man was as nought,
And they dwelt in the truth of the sea.
These are the men.

In conditions of life less intimate than those of Boston, such a way of conceiving one's own existence seems natural; indeed almost normal for Wordsworths and Byrons, Victor Hugos and Walter Savage Landors, Algernon Swinburnes, and Robert Louis Stevensons; but to the Bostonian absorbed in the extremely practical problem of effecting some sort of working arrangement between Beacon Street and the universe, the attitude of revolt seemed unnatural and artificial. He could not even understand it. For centuries the Bostonian had done little but wrestle with nature for a bare existence, and his foothold was not so secure, nor had it been so easily acquired, nor was it so victoriously sufficient for his wants, as to make him care to invite the ice or the ocean once more to cover it or himself; while, even more keenly than the Scotchman or Norseman, he felt that he ought not to be reproached for the lies that the world, including himself, had wrought, under compulsion, on the exceedingly rough and scanty parchment of God.

Therefore the gap between the poet and the citizen was so wide as to be impassable in Boston, but it was not a division of society into hostile camps, as it had been in England with Shelley and Keats, or in Boston itself, half a century before, with the anti-slavery outbursts of Emerson and Whittier, Longfellow and Lowell, which shook the foundations of the State. The Bostonian of 1900 differed from his parents and grandparents of 1850, in owning nothing the value of which, in the market, could be affected by the poet. Indeed, to him, the poet's pose of hostility to actual conditions of society was itself mercantile,—a form of drama,—a thing to sell, rather than a serious revolt. Society could safely adopt it as a form of industry, as it adopted other forms of bookmaking.

Therefore, while, for young Lodge and other protestants of his age and type, the contrast between Nahant and Beacon Street was a real one, even a vital one, life in both places was normal, healthy, and quite free from bitterness or social strain. Society was not disposed to defend itself from criticism or attack. Indeed, the most fatal part of the situation for the poet in revolt, the paralyzing drug that made him helpless, was that society no longer seemed sincerely to believe in itself or anything else; it resented nothing, not even praise. The young poet grew up without being able to find an enemy. With a splendid physique, a warmly affectionate nature, a simple but magnificent appetite for all that life could give, a robust indifference or defiance of consequences, a social position unconscious of dispute or doubt, and a large, insatiable ambition to achieve ideals—with these ample endowments and energies, in full consciousness of what he was about to attempt, the young man entered deliberately upon what he was to call his Great Adventure.

II. Cambridge and Paris

To ALL YOUNG BOSTONIANS of a certain age and social position Harvard College opens its doors so genially as to impose itself almost as a necessary path into the simple problems of Boston life; and it has the rather unusual additional merit of offering as much help as the student is willing to accept towards dealing with the more complex problems of life in a wider sense. Like most of his friends and family, young Lodge, at eighteen years old, went to the University, and profited by it in his own way, which was rarely, with Bostonians of his type, precisely the way which the actual standards of American life required or much approved. The first two years seldom profit young men of this class at all, but with the third year, their tastes, if they have any, begin to show themselves, and their minds grope for objects that offer them attraction, or for supports that the young tendrils can grasp. Every instructor has seen this rather blind process going on in generation after generation of students, and is seldom able to lend much help to it; but if he is so fortunate as to teach some subject that attracts the student's fancy, he can have influence. Owing to some innate sympathies, which were apparently not due to inheritance or conditions, Lodge seemed to care less for English than for French or Italian or classic standards; and it happened that the French department was then directed by Professor Bôcher, who took a fancy to the young man, and not only helped him to an acquaintance with the language, but still more with the literature and the thought of France, a subject in which Professor Bôcher was an admirable judge and critic.

At first, the student made the usual conscientious effort to do what did not amuse him. "I am going to acquire the faculty of not minding applying myself to uninteresting subjects, if I can, and I am sure that it is possible," he wrote to his mother, March 21, 1893; and then, pursuing the usual course which started most Harvard students on literary careers, he fell at once into the arms of Thomas Carlyle. "I am making a study of the religious and philosophical side of Carlyle, with a view to writing a book on the same; and it is a most absorbing subject," he wrote on May 6, 1893. "My head is full of ideas which I want to let out in that book. I propose to devote my summer to it. Even if it isn't a success, it is better than doing nothing, and it is profoundly interesting. I have read attentively almost everything he ever wrote except *Cromwell,* and I am taking notes on all the more philosophical ones, like *Sartor Resartus;* and I am also reading and studying conjointly the French philosophers, Descartes, Malebranche, and Spinoza, and the German Schopenhauer and Fichte, and also Plato, so that I shall get an idea of his relations to the celebrated philosophies. I am going to read Froude's life of him." The door by which a student enters the vast field of philosophy matters little, for, whatever it is, the student cannot stay long in it; but for one of such wide views, Carlyle could serve a very short time as the central interest.

"Today Bourget came out here to a lecture in French 7 by Sumichrast, and Sumichrast got him to talk, which he did most charmingly. I have been taking a course of Bourget, among other things, *Mensonges;* and I feel as if I had been living in the mire. Never have I read books whose atmosphere was so unhealthy and fetid." This was written to his mother, December 12, 1893, when he was barely twenty years old, and marks the steady tide of French influence that was carrying him on to its usual stage of restlessness and depression. On February 28, 1894, he wrote again, announcing that he had fairly reached the moral chaos which belonged to his temperament and years: "I am in very good health and very bad spirits, and I am feeling pretty cynical. It is a constant struggle for me to prevent myself from becoming cynical, and when I feel blue and depressed, the dykes break and it all comes to the surface. I suppose I have seen more of the evil and mean side of men and things than most men of my age, which accounts for my having naturally a pessimistic turn. Really, though, I hate cynicism, —it is a compilation of cheap aphorisms that any fool can learn to repeat,—and yet the world does seem a bad place."

A common place rather than a bad place was the next natural and cheap aphorism which every imaginative young man could look with confidence to reach, but the process of reaching it varies greatly with the temperament of the men. In Lodge it soon took the form of philosophic depression accompanied by intense ambition. The combination, at the age of twenty, is familiar in Europeans, but not so common among Americans, who are apt to feel, or to show, diffidence in their own powers. Lodge's letters will reveal himself fully on that side, but what they show still better is the immense appetite of the young man for his intellectual food, once he had found the food he liked.

"Since I got back [to Cambridge]," he wrote to his mother on March 14, 1894, "I have been reading an immense quantity from variegated authors, Balzac especially; also Flaubert, Alfred de Vigny, Leconte de Lisle, and Musset, Hugo, Renan (whom I am going to write a long French theme about), Schopenhauer, and then the Upanishads, etc. Next time French literature is discussed, ask them what living poet equals Sully Prudhomme." He was already in a region where Boston society—or indeed, any other society except perhaps that of Paris—would have been puzzled to answer his questions; but the sense of reaching new regions excited him. "I am beginning to get beautifully into harness now," he wrote on November 16, 1894, "and find that, outside my College work, I can read from one hundred and fifty to two hundred pages a day. . . . If I were living in Gobi or Sahara, with the British Museum next door and the Louvre round the corner, I think I could do almost anything. When I work I have to fill myself full of my subject, and then write everything down without referring to any books. If I am interrupted in the agonies of composition, it takes me some time to get into the vein." The passion for reading passed naturally into the passion for writing, and every new volume read reflected itself in a volume to be written. The last term of college began and ended in this frame of mind. He wrote on January 17, 1895: "I have a scheme of writing essays on Schopenhauer, Swift, Molière, Poe, Leconte de Lisle, Carlyle, Alfred de Vigny, Balzac, Thackeray (perhaps), and any others I may think of, and entitling the collection *Studies in Pessimism,* or some such title, and treat them all, of course, from that point of view. I could write them all except Swift and Thackeray and Balzac with very little preparation; and even with those three I should not need much. I wish you would ask papa what he thinks of my idea. Last night Max Scull and I took Brun (the French teacher) to dinner and the theater afterwards. He was quite entertaining, and I improved my French considerably, as we spoke nothing else. I told him I was going to France next summer, and he told me to write to him and *qu'il me montrerait Paris à fond.* I have been working on my wretched story, and have gone over it about eight times. It now seems to me to be quite valueless. Also I have burst into song several times—rather lamely, I fear."

Then began, still in college, the invariable, never-ending effort of the artist to master his art,—to attain the sureness of hand and the quality of expression which should be himself. Lodge plunged into the difficulties with the same appetite which he felt for the facilities of expression, and felt at once where his personal difficulties were likely to be greatest, in his own exuberance. "I find I cannot polish my verses to any great extent," he continued on March 20, 1895; "I write when I feel in the mood, and then they are done—badly or well, as the case may be. If badly, they must either be all written over, or else burnt, and a new one written, generally the most appropriate fate for most of them. However, I am indeed very glad that you and papa think I am improving, however slightly. I enclose three efforts in a more lyrical strain. I find it rather a relief to be less trammeled, and unfettered to so concrete and absolute a form as the Petrarchan sonnet,—which is the only kind I write now. I have been looking over the few sonnets Shelley wrote. He had no form at all in them. He seems to have built them up with no preconceived idea of form whatever. Take *Ozymandias,* for instance, which I admire intensely, and one finds no structure at all. Yet of course we know that the whole, as read, is superb. I wonder if most people notice the form of a sonnet. I know I didn't, before I began to scribble myself. Still, I do think, other things being equal, that the Petrarchan form adds a dignity and beauty to a sonnet which no other form possesses. The contour is much more harmonious and symmetrical."

Thus the young man had plunged headlong into the higher problems of literary art before he was fairly acquainted with the commoner standards. Whether he ever framed to himself a reason for pursuing one form rather than another, might be a curious question. Why should not Shakespeare and the Elizabethans have appealed to him first? Was it because the Petrarchan form was more perfect, or because it was less English? Whatever the answer to this question may be, the fact is that, throughout life, he turned away from the English models, and seemed often indifferent to their existence. The trait was not wholly peculiar to him, for even in England itself the later Victorian poets, with Algernon Swinburne at their head, showed a marked disposition to break rather abruptly with the early Victorian poets, and to wander away after classical or mediaeval standards; but their example was hardly the influence that affected Lodge. With him, the English tradition possibly represented a restraint,—a convention,—a chain that needed to be broken, —that jarred on his intense ambition.

"Oh, I am devoured by ambition," he wrote in the last days of his college life, to his mother: "I do so want to do something that will last,—some man's work in the world,—that I am constantly depressed by an awful dread that perhaps I shan't be able to. I am never satisfied with what I do,—never contented with my expression of what I wish to express, and yet I hope and sometimes feel that it is possible I may do something permanent in value. I have got at last a scheme for the future which I think it probable you will like, and papa also; but I shall be better able to tell you when I see you. I have read nothing lately outside my work except the *Theologia Germanica* which Mrs. Wintie [Chanler] sent me, and which has many beautiful things in it. I have written even less,—just a few scraps of verse (one of which, a sonnet, is coming out in the next *Monthly* by the way), and that article on Shakespeare which went to papa. I am anxious to know what he thinks of it."

With this, the college life closed, having given, liberally and sympathetically, all it could give, leaving its graduates free, and fairly fitted, to turn where they chose for their further food; which meant, for young Lodge, as his letters have told, the immediate turning to Paris. The choice showed the definite determination of his thought. England, Germany, Italy, did not, at that stage, offer the kind of education he wanted. He meant to make himself a literary artist, and in Paris alone he could expect to find the technical practice of the literary arts. In Paris alone, a few men survived who talked their language, wrote prose, and constructed drama, as they modeled a statue or planned a structure.

Thus far, as commonly happens even to ambitious young men, the path was easy, and the outlook clear; but the illusion of ease and horizon seldom lasts long in Paris. A few days completely dispel it. Almost instantly the future becomes desperately difficult. Especially to an American, the processes and machinery of a French education are hard to apply in his home work. The French mind thinks differently and expresses its thought differently, so that the American, though he may actually think in French, will express his thought according to an American formula. Merely the language profits him little; the arts not much more; the history not at all; the poetry is ill suited to the genius of the English tongue; the drama alone is capable of direct application; in sum, it is the whole—the combination of tradition, mental habit, association of ideas, labor of technique, criticism, instinct—that makes a school, and the school, once mastered, is of only indirect use to an American. The secret of French literary art is a secret of its own which does not exist in America. Indeed, the American soon begins to doubt whether America has any secrets, either in literary or any other art.

Within a few weeks all these doubts and difficulties had risen in young Lodge's face, and he found himself reduced to the usual helplessness of the art-student in Paris, working without definite purpose in several unrelated directions. At best, the atmosphere of Paris in December lacks gaiety except for Parisians, or such as have made themselves by time and temperament more or less Parisian. One flounders through it as one best can; but in Lodge's case, the strain was violently aggravated by the political storm suddenly roused by President Cleveland's Venezuela message, and sympathy with his father's political responsibilities in the Senate.

PARIS, *December 26, 1895*

The study here is wholly different from anything I have been accustomed to and I am in some ways much alone. It seems to me here as if I was losing my grip, my aggressiveness, my force of mind, and it is a feeling that has been gradually coming over me, and that Venezuela has brought to a crisis. I don't do anything here, nothing tangible. I work five hours a day or six, and what on—a miserable little poetaster. I want to get home and get some place on a newspaper or anything of that kind, and really do something. I spend more money than is necessary, and altogether don't seem to lead a very profitable life. For me, loafing is not fun except in a recognized vacation. I never realized this until now. I thought I should like to take it easy for a while and *soi-disant* amuse myself. I am wretched. I want something real to do. I don't want to become a mere Teutonic grind, and it's necessary to do that if you are going to take degrees here. Both you and papa told me to feel no hesitation in coming home if I wanted to, and so now that I have been here long enough to see I have made an error, I write as I do. I am always slow of comprehension, and if it has taken me a long time to find this out, it's just that I am getting experience—rather slowly and stupidly. I have not yet absolutely decided. If this appears to you hasty or ill-advised, please let me know in the shortest way possible.

Venezuela excites me horribly and my poor mind is rather torn, as you may see by this somewhat incoherent letter.

PARIS, *January 6, 1896*

Since I last wrote you I have quieted down a good deal more. I feel as if I had been through three hideous weeks of madness and were become on a sudden sane. You see the Venezuela affair came on me on a sudden and filled me with such a longing for home that I lost all pleasure in things over here. So my poor mind whirled round and round from one thing to another till I almost went mad. Now Venezuela seems to be a danger only in the future if at all, and I am realizing how much I am getting here.

If papa is willing I should stay I can come back with a good knowledge of German, Italian, and Spanish, and of Romance Philology and Middle Age Literature—all of which things I very much need.

The thing which tore me worst in all this mental struggle I have been going through was the continual thought of money and my crying inability to adapt myself to my time and to become a money-maker. I felt as if it was almost cowardly of me not to turn in and leave all the things I love and the world doesn't, behind, and to adjust myself to my age, and try to take its ideals and live strongly and wholly in its spirit. It seems so useless being an eternal malcontent. Unless one is a Carlyle, to scream on paper generally ends in a thin squeak, and I fought and fought to try to be more a man of my age so that I might work with the tide and not against it. But it's no use, I cannot stifle my own self or alter it in that way. I said to myself that I ought to go home in order to get into the tide of American life if for nothing else; that I oughtn't to be dreaming and shrieking inside and poetizing and laboring on literature here in Paris, supported by my father, and that I ought to go home and live very hard making money. I said to myself that I knew I could not be very quick at money-making, but that at any rate in the eyes of men I should lead a self-respecting life and my hideous, utter failure would only be for myself and you, who understand. But somehow all the while my soul refused to believe the plain facts and illogically clung to the belief that I might do some good in creative work in the world after all, and so I struggled with the facts and my faiths and loves and there was the Devil of a row inside me and I most wretched. Now it seems to me that my staying here can do no harm, as I can just as well begin to be nineteenth century next year as this, and I shall have a very happy winter and acquire some knowledge and much experience. And so now my mind is comparatively calm and I am becoming happy again and seeing things a little more in their proper perspective.

Now like Marcus Aurelius I have come home to my own soul and found there, I am glad to say, sufficient strength and resource and calm to reëstablish my equilibrium, and make me see how cowardly it is not to have enough self-reliance to bear such things as these with a tolerably good grace. . . .

I might entitle this letter: "Of the entering, passing through, and coming out of, the madness of George Cabot Lodge." I really feel as if the past two weeks were a great black hole in my life, in which all my landmarks were blurred, and I have just found them again.

Paris, *January 16, 1896*

I am now working principally on Romance Philology, Spanish, and Italian. I usually go to the Bibliothèque in the morning and work on Spanish. I am studying the history of the literature and trying to read the most important things as I go along. It is hard work reading the old Spanish of the twelfth to fifteenth centuries, but I am convinced it is the only way to know the language or literature really thoroughly. I also work on my Spanish courses. In Italian I am reading Tiraboschi, *Storia della litteratura Italiana,* which of course is the great history of the Italian literature. I also work a good deal on Petrarch: he is one of my courses, you know. Mr. Stickney sent to Italy for me for a good edition of Dante, and when it comes I shall begin the study of it. In the afternoon I go to courses, and sometimes of course in the morning, too, and play billiards as a rule about five with Joe, and in the evening work on my Romance Philology. I have procured by good fortune a very good dictionary of the old French.

Thus, you see, my work now is concentrated on the Romance Languages and Literature, especially before the sixteenth century. I shall keep on principally on them, because I am sure by so doing I can come home with a more or less thorough knowledge of the Latin tongues and a little more than a smattering of their literature. The Latin languages attract me and I shall work hard on them. As for German, I shall learn it if I can find time, but I don't know. . . . I see now that I must do the best in me if I can; and if there is a best to do; and at any rate I haven't the force or the weakness to renounce everything without having one glorious fight for what I want to do and believe is best to do. It is this realization of my own self that has done me most good, I think.

I went to the Français last night. It was the birthday of Molière and they gave the *École des Femmes* and the *Malade Imaginaire,* and afterwards the ceremony of crowning the bust by all the *Sociétaires* and *pensionnaires* of the Théâtre. It was most interesting. I think the best night of theater I ever had.

PARIS, *January 27, 1896*

My languages get on very well. Italian and Spanish I am really getting very smart in and read with perfect ease, and I am sure when I come back I shall know a good deal about the Romance Languages. My German I am working on, and of course it comes more slowly, but I think I can do it all right.

PARIS, *February 21, 1896*

I have just lived through the Carnival here, which began on Saturday night with the *bal de l'opéra* (third of the name) and continued until Wednesday morning. I took it in with considerable thoroughness. There was the procession of the Bœuf Gras—the first time this has occurred since the Franco-German war. It was very pretty and the crowds in the street tremendous—all throwing paper confetti and long rolls of paper, which one might throw across the boulevards. Now the trees are all covered with long ribbons of papers of all colors. It was a very pretty sight and most amusing. I never imagined such a good-tempered crowd, and one so bound to have a good time. I send by this mail a sort of program with an amusing picture by Caran D'Ache. I was glad of the Carnival. I think one gets into terrible ruts and little habits close around one, and one gets dull and mechanical. The Carnival just broke all that up for me, and for three days I led a wholly irregular life, that had a certain splendor in the unexpectedness of everything I did. . . .

C. and P. both wrote me very nice things about my poems. I have just read over a lot and become drearily conscious that they are far from deserving any praise, so that it rather worries me to have people so kind about them, as it seems as if I could never live up to what they think I ought to do. However, I have become an excellent critic of my own work and diligently weed out from time to time all that seems flat, so that I may someday have something really poetry.

PARIS, *April 5, 1896*

Here it's Easter Sunday and I haven't had a happier day for a long time. The skies have been bright blue and the sun pure gold, and the trees all timidly "uttering leaves" everywhere, and so I want to write to you. Early this morning Joe and I went and rode horses in the Bois, which we had already done last Sunday, and are going to do more often. It was most marvelous—all the little fresh greening things looking out of the earth, and the early sunlight coming wet and mild through the trees, and the rare fresh air, and the sense of physical glow and exercise.

I found an alley with about a dozen jumps in it and whisked my old hired horse over the entire lot, with the surprising result that he jumped rather well, except the water-jump, into which he flatly jumped, managing, however, to stand up. Then I came home and read Petrarch and Ronsard, and in the afternoon took a boat down a bright blue Seine with white bridges spanning it and a Louvre, etc., on either hand. I got off at the Ile St. Louis, and for the pure dramatic effect went into the "Doric little morgue" and saw two terrible dead old women with the lower jaw dropped on the withered breast and the green of decomposition beginning about the open eyes. Then I came out into the broad sunshine, with that blessed Cathedral Apse in front of me, and its little sun-filled garden with the old Gothic fountain running pure water, and felt it was very good to live. Then I went in and heard a splendid mass, with the great organ rolling up by the front rose window, and saw the Host raised and the church full (really full) of people fall on their knees, and the thick incense come slowly out, and felt alas! how far away I was from the substance of the shadow of splendor I was feeling. But I was very happy for all that, and wandered around some more in the sunlight, and then came home, where I am now writing to you.

This winter I have been realizing a copy-book commonplace, which is at the same time a metaphysical profundity, viz.: that the present is all that *is* and it is not. One of the crowning metaphysical paradoxes. Of course the present is not. While you are uttering "now," it is fled—it never existed. It is like a geometrical point, non-existent. And the past—that's the cruel thing, the killing memories. Memories of yesterday, of the moment just fled, which are as hopelessly dead, as impossibly distant as memories of ten years gone. The past is like a great pit, and the present like a frittered edge which is continually crumbling and falling utterly down into the pit. . . . For me—my past is all *amoncelé,* nothing nearer, nothing farther. I have a more vivid memory of Sister with long hair, driving old Rab up the sidewalk by the Gibsons' at Nahant on a gray autumn day, than of most things happened within the year. And my memories are all sad—sad with an infinite hopeless regret; that one of Sister, for example, has almost made me cry. And then the present is the past so facilely, so quickly, and I find myself sometimes when I am not doing anything—talking perhaps or sitting idle or even reading, in fact *un peu toujours*—suddenly turning sick and cold and saying to myself, "See, your life goes, goes, goes. Every day you get more memories to dwell about you like mourning creatures, and still nothing done—with your youth, your strength, and every minute the memories thickening and the pain of them increasing, and still nothing done. Man! Man! Your life is very short, already twenty and two years; as many again, and you will be hardened into your mold, and the mold yet unmade! Up, up and do something!"

And the future—it is the veriest of commonplaces to say the future doesn't exist. It is nothing but a probability—at best a hope. And then did it ever occur to you that the present is like a piece of paper on which experience writes in invisible ink, and that only when the heat of the pain of memory and regret blows upon it, do the characters come out and you know how intensely alive, how happy, or at any rate how miserable, or at least how unbored, you *had been.*

It seems to me all the happiness (except, of course, physical) which we get is only the more or less incomplete suggestion or partial realization of some remembered happiness. For instance, the slant of the western sun through green leaves sometimes brings back one perfectly unimportant afternoon when I was very small, and Sister sat on the grass under those willows, behind the little toolhouse in front of Mr. Locke's, and read a story aloud to me.

She left off in the middle, and I can distinctly remember the last words she said. Now when I can get a vivid suggestion of something intensely happy in my memory, infinitely richer and more happy than I had any idea of when it occurred, it makes me more happy than anything. Happiness is a continual thinking backward or forward, memory or expectation.

This may all sound rather rhetorical, but I assure you it is unintentional. If you knew how intensely I have been feeling all this and much more that I cannot express, you would know that this isn't rhetoric, but pure crying out of the soul—such as I could only say to you.

Thousands of young people, of both sexes, pass through the same experience in their efforts to obtain education, in Paris or elsewhere, and are surprised to find at the end that their education consists chiefly in whatever many-colored impressions they have accidentally or unconsciously absorbed. In these their stock or capital of experience is apt to consist, over and above such general training as is the common stock of modern society; but most of them would find themselves puzzled to say in what particular class of impression their gain was greatest. Lodge would have said at once that his gain was greatest in the friendship with young Stickney, to which the letters allude.

Joseph Trumbull Stickney, who was then preparing his

thesis for the unusual distinction of doctorate at the Sorbonne—the University of France—was a European in the variety and extent of his education and the purest of Americans by blood, as his name proclaimed. Nearly of Lodge's age, almost identical in tastes and convictions, and looking forward to much the same career, he and his companionship were among those rare fortunes that sometimes bless unusually favored youth when it needs, more than all else, the constant contact with its kind.

III. The Song of the Wave

Early in his college course, the young man had acquired a taste for Schopenhauer. The charm of Schopenhauer is due greatly to his clearness of thought and his excellence of style,—merits rare among German philosophers,—but another of his literary attractions is the strong bent of his thought towards oriental and especially Buddhistic ideals and methods. At about the same time it happened that Sturgis Bigelow returned to Boston from a long residence in Japan, and brought with him an atmosphere of Buddhistic training and esoteric culture quite new to the realities of Boston and Cambridge. The mystical side of religion had vanished from the Boston mind, if it ever existed there, which could have been at best only in a most attenuated form; and Boston was as fresh wax to new impressions. The oriental ideas were full of charm, and the oriental training was full of promise. Young Lodge, tormented by the old problems of philosophy and religion, felt the influence of Sturgis Bigelow deeply, for Bigelow was the closest intimate of the family, and during the summer his island of Tuckanuck, near Nantucket, was the favorite refuge and resource for the Lodges. As time went on, more and more of the young man's letters were addressed to Bigelow.

Returning home after the winter of 1895–96 in Paris, he found himself more than ever harrowed by the conflict of interests and tastes. He went to Newport in August, for a few days, and rebelled against all its standards. "I hate the philistine-plutocrat atmosphere of this place, and it tends not to diminish my views anent modern civilization and the money power. I sincerely thank God I shall never be a rich man, and never will I, if my strength holds. The world cannot be fought with its own weapons; David fought Goliath with a sling, and the only way to kill the world is to fight it with one's own toy sword or sling, and deny strenuously contact with, or participation in, the power it cherishes. Much more of the same nature is yearning to be said, but I will spare you. . . . If I haven't it in me to write a poem, what a sordid farce my life will be!" The expression is strong, but in reality the young man had fairly reached the point where his life was staked on literary success. The bent of his energy was fixed beyond change, and as though he meant deliberately to make change impossible, he returned to Europe, to pass the next winter, 1896–97, in Berlin.

A winter in Berlin is, under the best of circumstances, a grave strain on the least pessimistic temper, but to a young poet of twenty-two, fresh from Paris, and exuberant with the full sense of life and health, Berlin required a conscientious sense of duty amounting to self-sacrifice, in order to make it endurable. Socially it was complete solitude except for the presence of Cecil Spring-Rice, an old Washington intimate then in the British Embassy. As a matter of education in art or literature, the study of German had never been thought essential to poets, or even to prose writers, in the English language; and although, at about the middle of the century, many of the best English and French authors, and some American, had insisted that no trained student could afford to be ignorant of so important a branch of human effort, none had ever imposed it on their pupils as a standard of expression. In that respect, a serious devotion to the language was likely to do more harm than good.

The New England conscience is responsible for much that seems alien to the New England nature. Naturally, young Lodge would have gone to Rome to study his art, and no doubt he would have greatly preferred it. He needed to fill out his education on that side,—not on the side of Germany,—and his future work suffered for want of the experience. If he went to Berlin, he did it because in some vague way he hoped that Germany might lead to practical work. His letters show the strenuous conscientiousness with which he labored through the task.

TO HIS MOTHER

BERLIN, *January 1897*

It's a week now since I wrote you and I've not much more news than I had. I am very well off here. All German bedrooms are bad and mine no worse than the rest, I imagine—large enough for a bed and two tables for my books and papers, a porcelain stove and bureau, washstand, etc. To be sure, it has but one window, through which, by leaning uncomfortably to one side, one can perceive the withered corner of a gray garden, but otherwise facing a dirty wall of brick. But, as I say, it seems this is a chronic malady of German bedrooms, and besides I have the use of a very pleasant front room where I work in the morning, and afternoon, too, sometimes. The people here are very nice, and eager to make me comfortable; otherwise all my news is contained in the word work. Nearer ten hours than eight of this have I done every day—written translations from German, reading of German Grammar, reading Schiller with the man or his Frau, talking, going to the theater,—*Faust, The Winter's Tale,* very good, and a translation of the *Dindon,* etc. All German, you observe, and in fact it seemed best at first to let Greek and everything go, and devote every energy to the acquisition of this tongue—infernally hard it is too. I found, right off, I didn't know anything about it, and since then have really made a good deal of progress.

It's wonderful how the soul clears itself up in this sort of solitude in which I am living—picks up all the raveled threads and weaves them carefully together again, and gradually simplifies and straightens itself out. All my life since last April I have been going over, as I have some of my poems, forcing the events into sequence and building a sort of soul-history, fibrous and coherent. It's a wonderful clearing out of refuse, and I feel strong and self-reliant as I never did before. I have acquired the ability to write over poetry and work it into shape, which is a great step forward, I believe, and several of my poems have I been over in this way with much advantage. And so I am almost childishly contented at getting back to an existence of sleep and food at a minimum and work at a maximum, and I really think I have never worked harder or lived more utterly simply. And oh! It is good with the entire spiritual solitude and mental solitude that I abide in.

BERLIN, *January 17, 1897*

I am now, after infinite pains and vast expense, matriculate at the University here, with several large and most beautiful diplomas certifying in Latin that I am in fact matriculate. The diplomas alone are worth the price of admission. It was heavy, though—four solid mornings' work and about 75 marks. First I went with the man I am living with, and found I couldn't hear any lectures at all unless I did matriculate and that to matriculate I had to have my degree from Cambridge, which I had carefully left at home. Then the next day I went to the Embassy and found Mr. Jackson, who had very kindly written me a letter already, saying he hoped I would come to see him when I wanted to. Well, Mr. Jackson gave me a letter certifying that I had a degree, and with this and my passport I went again to the University, and found I was too late that day and must come the next. So the next—this time alone—I went and passed—oh, such a morning! First I sat in a room while the Rector went over my papers; then I and two Germans were called in to the Rector and he gave us handsome degrees and swore us to obedience to all the rules of the University, and then we shook hands with him. Then someone said, "Go to room 4." So I and the two Germans went, and there they wrote my name and birthplace and papa's business, which I tried to explain and failed, and so he is registered in the Berlin University as anything from a coal-heaver up.

All this time my nerves were rasping like taxed wires for fear I shouldn't understand what was said to me.

And then I wrote my own name, birthplace, etc., in my

own sweet hand in another big book, and then was given a little card where I wrote my name again, and a huge card filled with questions. When I understood them I answered; when not, I put *ja* and *nein* alternately. Then they said, "Go to room 15." So I went and gave a man my filled-out card and he wrote something which he gave me and said, "Go to room 4 *zurück*"; so I went. There I got a book and another card—the last one—and then I filled out all sorts of things in the book and finally went to room 2, where I paid out vast sums, got some receipts, and—left, a shattered man in mind and soul. The strain of trying to understand and write correctly and being always afraid you won't is really terrible. Then today I had to go again to see the Dean of the Philosophical Department in which I matriculated, and he gave me another beautiful degree. And now it's all over. I am an *academischer Bürger,* and if the police try to arrest me all I've got to do is to show my card and they can't touch me. . . .

This place is gray, gray, gray. I have done a constant stream of work, which has flowed in a steady and almost uninterrupted course, with six hours' sleep interval in the twenty-four. I have been theater-going a lot. I have seen a good deal of Shakespeare, Schiller, and Sudermann.

BERLIN, *January 26, 1897*

It is for the best my being here, of that rest assured. I am entirely convinced that it was and is the very best thing possible for me in the circumstances, and I find sufficient content and interest, and especially work, to keep me far from stagnant. As I wrote you, I feel a sense of increased strength and reliance, which I don't explain and don't try to. Sufficient that so it is. Much of my life have I overlooked and condemned and profited by in this solitude and I finally begin to feel a certain strength that I trust will urge into expression fit and simple and sufficient one day, and not be trampled under in this awful struggle to acquire a financial independence which I see is inevitable for me. Writing prose is the only utterly depressing thing I have done, and that, D. V., I shall learn by mere gritting of teeth.

I've this moment got back from Dresden, where I've been since Friday with Springy[1]—a little vacation. It's very pretty and the gallery very wonderful. Naturally there I spent my days, and twice I went to the opera.

BERLIN, *February 9, 1897*

I have written some new verse and written over with much time and labor a good deal more old. It's with the greatest difficulty that I can take any other form of literary endeavor seriously; and put my heart in it, I can't. I live and breathe in an atmosphere of imagination and verse here, all alone when I am not a working-machine, and it's all around me like a garment. It's hard to express what I mean—but the other day I went early to the University and saw a radiant sunrise through the snowy Thiergarten and sort of sang inside all the rest of the day—odd rhythms with here and there a word. I was so content I didn't even want to write down anything. I wonder if you have ever had the feeling—I suppose you have—of having a beautiful thing compose the scatteredness of your mind into an order, a rhythm, so that you think and feel everything rhythmically. My expression is weak, but if you've had it you'll know what I mean.

I saw the whole of *Wallenstein* the other day—or rather in two successive evenings—first the *Lager* and the *Piccolomini,* and second evening the *Tod,* which is certainly very fine—both dramatically and poetically,—quite the biggest German play I've seen. I'm reading *Faust* with my teacher here, and admiring very much of it.

BERLIN, *February 1897*

I have been reading over some of Schopenhauer and Kant in the German and enjoying it immensely. I think the study and pursuit of pure metaphysical thought makes a man more contentedly, peacefully happy than any other thing. There

[1]Cecil Spring-Rice.

is a white purity consisting in its utter lack of connection to the particular, in its entire devotion to the pure, synthetical ideas which never touch the feeling, individual world, which makes metaphysics the nearest approach to will-lessness, to pure intellectual contemplation, that I know. And of course, as all suffering is willful (in its essential meaning) and emotional, pure intellectual contemplation must be that privation of suffering in which happiness consists—for I become more than ever convinced that in this world of evil and separation happiness is only the privation of pain as good is the privation of evil. 'Tis only the transcendent emotion that you get in poetry or in great passions such as pity and love, that can be called positive happiness. Pity or love, I mean, so aggrandized that the sense of individuality is lost in the feeling of union with the whole where there is no space or time or separation. That is, that only morally and esthetically can one be positively happy—all other happiness must be simply the denial of pain. Metaphysics is the completest expression of such a denial, I think, and also with an almost esthetic poetic value sometimes—in some metaphysicians an undoubted poetic value, as for instance in Plato and Schopenhauer. But it seems I am writing you an essay on metaphysics, so I will stop.

BERLIN, *February, late, 1897*

I am gradually digging a way into the language, and you'd be surprised at my fluent inaccuracy in the German tongue, and I can write it pretty well, too. Reading is thoroughly acquired, and I am more than satisfied with my progress. I have heard a good deal of music which always does me good, though, as Joe tells me, I don't in the least understand it. I saw the Emperor the other day for the first time, and rather a fine strong face he has.

I really believe that nothing I ever did benefited me as much as has this short time here. I have grown more rigid and surer of myself, and withal have acquired a certain capacity and love of a great deal of work, which I never had before, and which is only surpassed by my love of not doing work after I have done a great deal. My poetry, I think, shows that—I have tried to hope so. Please tell me if you think any of the things I sent you show a clearer, firmer touch than before. As I say, I try to think so and almost feel sometimes as if it really was in me after all to speak a strong, sincere word clearly for men to hear; but then, on the other hand, whiles I think I am going to dry up, and in my perfectly lucid moments, I see with a ghostly distinctness how far short all my work falls of what I seem sometimes to know as an ideal.

The dear Springy came to see me yesterday and I had a good talk with him and subsequently dined with him. I've seen very little of him this month, as society has been on the rampage, and he has rampaged with it perforce. He went to London for a week today, but when he comes back, the world will be quiet and I expect to see a great deal of him.

The German experience added little or nothing to his artistic education, for Schopenhauer can be studied anywhere, and neither Goethe nor Schiller needs to be read in Berlin; but his letters show that his enforced, solitary labor during this winter threw him back upon himself, and led him to publish his work before he fairly knew in what direction his strength lay. During these three years of post-graduate education he had toiled, with sure instinct, to learn the use of his tools, and chiefly of his tongue. All art-students must go through this labor, and probably the reason why so many young poets begin by writing sonnets is that the sonnet is the mode of expression best adapted for practice; it insists on high perfection in form; any defect or weakness betrays itself, and the eye can cover fourteen lines at once without too great an effort. Lodge liked the labor of sonnet-writing, and it taught him the intricacies of language and the refinements of expression which every literary artist must try at least to understand, even when he does not choose to practice them; but, at heart, Lodge was less a poet than a dramatist, though he did not yet know it; and the dramatic art is the highest and most exacting in all literature. The crown of genius belongs only to the very rare poets who have written successful plays. They alone win the blue ribbon of literature. This was the prize to which Lodge, perhaps unconsciously, aspired, and his labor in sonnet-writing, however useful as training in verse, was no great advantage for his real purpose, even though he had Shakespeare for his model.

On the other hand, the lack of society in a manner compels the artist to publish before he is ready. The artist, living in a vacuum without connection with free air, is forced by mere want of breath to cry out against the solitude that stifles him; and the louder he cries, the better is his chance of attracting notice. The public resents the outcry, but remembers the name. A few—very few—readers appreciate the work, if it is good, on its merits; but the poet himself gets little satisfaction from it, and, ten years afterwards, will probably think of it only as a premature effort of his youth.

To this rule a few exceptions exist, like Swinburne's *Poems and Ballads,* where the poet, at the first breath, struck a note so strong and so new as to overpower protest; but, as a rule, recognition is slow, and the torpor of the public serves only to discourage the artist, who would have saved his strength and energy had he waited. When young Lodge returned from Germany in the summer of 1897, he felt himself unpleasantly placed between these two needs,—that of justifying his existence, on the one hand, and that of challenging premature recognition, on the other. He chose boldly to assert his claims to literary rank, and justified his challenge by publishing, in the spring of 1898, the volume of a hundred and thirty-five pages, called *The Song of the Wave.*

Here are some eighty short poems, one half of which are sonnets, and all of which reflect the long, tentative, formative effort of the past five years. Most of them have a personal character, like *The Song of the Wave* itself, which has been already quoted. From a simple, vigorous nature like Lodge's, one would have expected, in a first effort, some vehement or even violent outburst of self-assertion; some extravagance, or some furious protest against the age he lived in; but such an attitude is hardly more than indicated by the dedication to Leopardi. The exordium, "Speak, said my soul!" expresses rather his own need of strength and the solitude of his ambitions:

Speak! thou art lonely in thy chilly mind,
With all this desperate solitude of wind,
The solitude of tears that make thee blind,
    Of wild and causeless tears.
Speak! thou hast need of me, heart, hand, and head,
Speak, if it be an echo of thy dread,
A dirge of hope, of young illusions dead,—
    Perchance God hears!

Most of these poems are echoes of early youth, of the ocean, of nature: simple and vigorous expressions of physical force, with an occasional recurrence to Schopenhauer and Leopardi; but the verses that most concern the artist are those which show his effort for mastery of his art, and his progress in power of expression. He scattered such verses here and there, for their own sake, on nearly every page, as most young poets do, or try to do, and such verses are more or less a measure, not only of his correctness of ear, but of his patient labor. Take, for instance, the first half-dozen lines of *The Gates of Life,* which happens to be written in a familiar meter:

Held in the bosom of night, large to the limits of wonder,
Close where the refluent seas wrinkle the wandering sands,
Where, with a tenderness torn from the secrets of sorrow, and under
The pale pure spaces of night felt like ineffable hands,
The weak strange pressure of winds moved with the moving of waters,
Vast with their solitude, sad with their silences, strange with their sound,
Comes like a sigh from the sleep . . .

This meter seems to call for excessive elaboration of phrase; a few pages further, the poet has tried another meter which repels all such refinements; it is called *Age,* and begins:

Art thou not cold?
Brother, alone tonight on God's great earth?

The two last stanzas run:

Shalt thou not die,
Brother? the chill is fearful on thy life,
Shalt thou not die?
Is this a lie?
This threadbare hope—of death?
A lie, like God, and human love, and strife
For pride, and fame,—this soiled and withered wreath.

Art thou not cold?
Brother? alone on God's great earth tonight;
Art thou not cold?
Art thou not old
And dying and forlorn?
Art thou not choking in the last stern fight
While in divine indifference glows the morn?

The sonnet, again, offers a different temptation. The verses tend of their own accord to group themselves about the favorite verse. The first sonnet in this series begins with what Mrs. Wharton calls the magnificent apostrophe to Silence:

Lord of the deserts, 'twixt a million spheres,

and need go no further; the rest of the lines infallibly group themselves to sustain the level of the first. So, the sonnet to his own Essex begins with the singularly happy line,—

Thy hills are kneeling in the tardy spring,

which leads to an echo in the last verse:

We know how wanton and how little worth
Are all the passions of our bleeding heart
That vex the awful patience of the earth.

The sonnet to his friend Stickney, after reading the twelfth-century Roman of *Amis and Amile,* begins:

And were they friends as thou and I art friends,

in order to work out the personal touch of their common ambition:

Ah, they who walked the sunshine of the world,
And heard grave angels speaking through a dream,
Had never their unlaureled brows defiled,
Nor strove to stem the world's enormous stream.

The form of the sonnet tends to carry such verbal or personal refinements to excess; they become labored; perhaps particularly so in denunciation, like the sonnet, *Aux Modernes,* which begins:

Only an empty platitude for God;

and ends with the line,

The hard, gray, tacit distances of dawn.

Such work marks the steps of study and attainment rather than attainment itself, as the second *Nirvana* marks effort:

TO W. STURGIS BIGELOW

December 10, 1897

I will trouble you with this poem, which here I send to you. I wrote it without correction in half an hour before dinner, and I feel of it, as I have felt of so many of my things, that no one will understand it except you; also I know it's my fault and not theirs that no one will understand it—my implements are still so rude—my ideas seem luminous and limpid while they are wordless, and, I think, owing to practice, most ideas come to me now wordless—but in words they become crude, misty, and imperfect; whiles I feel quite hopeless. But you have been there, have seen vividly all I've half perceived, and you can supply my lapses in coherency. This was, I think, the result of an hour's practice last night. Certainly if it has a merit, it is that I have not been economical in this poem, every word seems to me now over-full with meaning. My soul has gone into the writing of it and, good Lord, it's melancholy to feel how it might have been said—luminously and unavoidably—and how it is said—Well! perhaps, someday! . . . if I could only be with you to try to tell you all I have endeavored to say in these fourteen lines!

NIRVANA

Woof of the scenic sense, large monotone
  Where life's diverse inceptions, Death and Birth,
  Where all the gaudy overflow of Earth
  Die—they the manifold, and thou the one.
Increate, complete, when the stars are gone
  In cinders down the void, when yesterday
  No longer spurs desire starvation-gray,
  When God grows mortal in men's hearts of stone;
As each pulsation of the heart divine
  Peoples the chaos, or with falling breath
  Beggars creation, still the soul is thine!
And still, untortured by the world's increase,
  Thy wide harmonic silences of death,
  And last—thy white, uncovered breast of peace!

I will now, as did Michael Angelo, add a commentary:

Nirvana is the woof on which sense traces its scenic patterns; it is the one, the monotone upon which death and birth, both inceptions, in that death is merely the beginning of changed conditions of life, and "the gaudy overflow of earth"—that is, all finite things and emotions—sing their perishable songs and, as rockets disperse their million sparks which die on the universal night blackness, so they die and leave the constant unchanging monotone. Nirvana is increate because never created, and of course complete. Yesterday spurs desire to a state of starvation-grayness because desire and hope look back on every yesterday as a renewed disappointment. The phrase meant life. "When God grows mortal in men's hearts of stone," has two meanings, first that when men grow unbelieving God perishes—God being the creature of belief; and second that Nirvana endureth when God himself perishes. The next three lines are an embodiment of the idea that with every beat of the heart divine a cosmos swells into existence, and with every subsiding of this heart it sinks, perishes into nothingness. Also from line five to line eleven means that after everything and through everything the soul is still Nirvana's, if I can so express myself; thus reiterating the idea suggested in the first quatrain, that the condition of the finite is separateness and of the spiritual, unity; and that all life, though clothed in diverse forms, holds in it the identical soul which is Nirvana's, attained or potential. The world's increase is of course the cycle of life and death in its largest sense. This is of course a mere shadowing forth of the ideas I had in writing the poem. You will see their possible amplifications.

January 1898

Poetry is an absolute necessity for me, but when I think of dumping a volume of verse that nobody will read on to a gorged world, I say to myself: *"A quoi bon?"* The foolish publisher will have to be found first, however, so I don't worry. Does the enclosed (*The Wind of Twilight—Tuckanuck*) say anything to you? The long things (Oh, be thankful) are too long to send, so I send this. I've done several of these sorts of things lately.

To the cold critic, this stage of an artist's life is the most sympathetic, and the one over which he would most gladly linger. He loves the youthful freshness, the candor, the honest workmanship, the naïf self-abandonment of the artist, in proportion as he is weary of the air of attainment, of cleverness, of certainty and completion. He would, for his own amusement, go on quoting verse after verse to show how the artist approaches each problem of his art, what he gains; what he sacrifices; but this is the alphabet of criticism, and can be practiced on Eginetan marbles or early Rembrandts better than on youthful lyrics. The interested reader has only to read for himself.

IV. War and Love

In January 1898 young Lodge was in Washington, acting as secretary to his father, varying between office-work all day and composition the greater part of the night. The outbreak of the Spanish War drew him at once into the government service, and he obtained a position as cadet on board his uncle Captain Davis's ship, the *Dixie*. During the three summer months that this war in the tropics lasted, he had other things than poems to think about, and his letters convey an idea that perhaps the life of a naval officer actually suited his inherited instincts best.

TO HIS MOTHER

FORTRESS MONROE, *May 1898*

Here I am and here I rest until Saturday, when the ship will probably sail. I am, and feel like, a perfect fool. Everybody knows everything and I don't know anything; but they are kind and I guess I shall get on when the thing gets fairly started. I went over and saw the ship today and she is fine —at any rate while I am here in this business, I am going to learn all I can.

NEWPORT NEWS, *May 20, 1898*

I am getting on as well as possible and learning a good deal all the time. There is plenty of room for learning. These great golden days go over me, and it seems as if all the real imaginative side of me was under lock and key. The practical things occupy me entirely.

FORTRESS MONROE, *June 2, 1898*

We have been taking on coal all day, and before it's all aboard we shall be chock-full. Uncle Harry has got orders to be ready to sail at a moment's notice, and he is going to telegraph tonight that he is all ready. I hope it may mean that we are to be moved out of here very soon toward the scene of action. A day or two ago we went out for thirty-six hours and fired all the big guns. I fired both mine myself, and was surprised to find the shock not at all serious. The whole process was very interesting, and I shall try to remember it all and be able to tell you all about it when I get back. I get on pretty well. There is one thing I am convinced of and that is that I can make my gun crews fight and my guns effective, and that is after all the principal thing.

The internal condition of Spain makes me believe that the war must end soon. I only hope it will last long enough to insure our possession of Cuba, Puerto Rico, and the Philippines, and give me one fight for my money.

OFF CIENFUEGOS, CUBA, *June 25, 1898*

We reached the squadron the day after I wrote from Mole St. Nicolas, and were immediately sent down here to patrol. In fact, the Admiral gave Uncle Harry discretion to do pretty much what he pleased. We came down and on our way destroyed two blockhouses which were at the southern end of the Trocha. The next day we engaged a battery at a place called Trinidad, and yesterday we engaged the same battery, a gunboat in the harbor, and a gunboat that came out at us, and used them up pretty badly. So you see I am in it. Nothing very serious so far, but still we have been under fire and have killed a good many Spaniards. It is a most beautiful coast all along here, great splendid hills close to the water's edge, and splendid vegetation. The weather has been hot, but very fine and to me excessively pleasant, and I am quite happy to be on the scene of action and in the way of seeing all that's going. My two guns have behaved very well and I have had several very nice compliments from the First Lieutenant. We relieved the *Yankee* here and she goes today to Key West for coal, which gives me a chance to send this letter. I really enjoy the life immensely, far more than I thought I should—the work interests me, and I am learning a good deal every day. Last night Uncle Harry and I dined with Captain Brownson on the *Yankee* and it was very interesting.

August 1898

Many thanks for your letter which I have just got today. I am more than delighted we are going to Spain. We came up from Cape Cruz on the sixth and saw the wrecks of the Spanish fleet lying up on the beach below Santiago—a great sight. It's a great business to be here and see the wheels go round and be a wheel one's self, even if not a very big one. I am very glad on the whole I came as a cadet and not as an ensign, for as a cadet I am not supposed to know anything, which puts me in a true position and not a false one. None of these militia officers know any more than I do, and they are in false positions. Anyway, I do a lot of work and I think accomplish something. It hardly seems as if the war could last now, and I only hope it will hang on long enough to give us a whack at Camara and the Spanish coast.

Yesterday we got the first ice we have had since June 15, and today the first mail since we left Old Point.

U. S. S. "DIXIE," *August 5, 1898*

We left Guantanamo after having coaled, and went to Puerto Rico with the troops. On the way we were detached from the convoy and sent all round the island to hunt up transports, and so we did not get to Guanica until after the army had landed. We got there in the morning, and that afternoon we were sent with the *Annapolis* and the *Wasp*—Uncle Harry[1] being the senior officer—down to Ponce, Puerto Rico. We got there about four and went peacefully into the harbor. Then Uncle Harry sent Mr. Merriam[2] in to demand the surrender of the place, and I went along. We landed under a flag of truce, and found that there was a Spanish Colonel with about 300 men, who said he would "die at his post." He was back in the town, which is about two miles inland. However, during the night delegates came off and surrendered the town, on condition that the troops be allowed to withdraw, which we granted, and at six o'clock the next morning we went in again and I myself raised the flag over the office of the Captain of the Port, amid immense enthusiasm of the populace. Haines,[3] the marine

[1]Captain Davis, commanding the *Dixie*. H. A.

[2]Lieutenant and executive officer of the *Dixie*. H. A.

[3]Lieutenant of Marines on the *Dixie*. H. A.

officer, was put in charge with a file of Marines, and put guards and sentries on the Customs House and other public places; and then two other officers and I got into a carriage, with a Puerto Rican friend, and drove up to the town.

It was most picturesque. The town had been deserted fearing a bombardment, and from every nook and corner crowds appeared cheering and crying, *"Viva los conquistadores Americanos"*; *"Viva el Puerto Rico libre."* We drove through the town, the crowd and enthusiasm increasing always, and finally returned and got Haines, who had formally delivered the town to General Miles when he landed. . . . We then went back to Ponce with Haines. We were taken to the club and to the headquarters of the fire-brigade—everywhere amid yelling mobs. While we were there I heard that there were some political prisoners confined in the City Hall. I told Haines, who was senior officer, and he went over to see about liberating them.

Ponce is the largest town in Puerto Rico, about 40,000 people. The City Hall stands at one end of a great square—about as large as Lafayette Square. In it is the Mayor's office and the courtroom, with a dais and throne where the judges sat. There Haines liberated sixteen political prisoners; for the army, though supposed to be in possession of the town, had not taken the City Hall. Finding this to be the case, I got an American flag and told Haines I was going to raise it over the City Hall. I then went onto the roof where the flag-staff was, taking with me the Mayor of Ponce. There with great solemnity, the Mayor and I bareheaded, I raised the flag. The whole square was swaying with people, and as the flag went up they cheered—such a noise as I never heard. Then the Mayor and I went below and the Mayor presented me with his staff of office, the Spanish flag which flew over the City Hall, and the banner of Ponce, and formally delivered over to me his authority. I sent to the barracks where were our soldiers, and got some over to occupy the City Hall. I then, with great ceremony, gave back to the Mayor his badge of office and the town of Ponce. Shortly after we left.

GUANTANAMO BAY, CUBA, *August 10, 1898*

I got your letter just a day or two ago, and mighty glad I was to get it. The flagship has just signaled "Associated Press dispatch states that peace protocol has been arranged." I suppose this is the end. If so, if hostilities cease and peace is eventually certain, I wish you would find out if the *Dixie* is to be put out of commission. I suppose it will take three or four months to patch up the treaty and have it ratified, and if the *Dixie* is to lie here or convoy transports during that time, I should like very much to be detached and ordered home on waiting orders, until my resignation is sent in and accepted. I suppose there would be no trouble about this. I came for the war, and as this isn't and never will be my life when the war is over, I want to get home as soon as possible, and pick up life again where I left off. Of course if the *Dixie* is to be put right out of commission, I should much prefer to go out of active service with the ship, and I should think that the Department would not wish to keep these auxiliary ships, manned with militia, in service any longer than was absolutely necessary. Well, I have learned a good deal and I am mighty glad I came. I haven't seen as much fighting as some, but I have had my share of the fun, I think, and anyway one does one's best and takes the chances of war. I really think I have made myself useful, and at least have not encumbered or hurt the service by coming, and that's as much as an amateur can hope for. Anyway I've worked hard. I shall have a great story to tell you about Ponce, of which *"Magna pars fui,"* and I have got some splendid trophies. I have had a good time and am happy now; but as peace grows more certain I long to get home and see you all again. It seems an enormous stretch of time since I left you.

EXTRACT FROM A LETTER OF CAPTAIN DAVIS TO H. C. L.

July 20, 1898

. . . He [G. C. L.] shows unbounded zeal and unflagging industry, and a great aptitude for the profession. He has already developed the real sailor's trick of being always the first on hand. No one has ever been known to say, "Where is Mr. Lodge?" This is not the encomium of a fond uncle. I see very little of him on duty except in working ship, when his station is near mine. He is a daily companion to me in hours of leisure, but on duty he is the First Lieutenant's man, and I notice he is always called on for duty where promptness and intelligence are required. I could give you a much higher estimate of his usefulness if I quoted Merriam, than in recording my own observation.

Brought back again to the chronic divergence between paths of life, the young man struggled as he best could to assert his mastery over his own fate, and developed a persistence of will that amounted to primitive instinct rather than to reasoning process. Constantly he threw himself with all his energy in the direction which led away from the regular paths of modern activity. He was familiar with them all, if only as Secretary of a Senate Committee, and he read science quite as seriously as poetry, but when he came to action he always widened the gap between himself and his world. *The Song of the Wave* was his first public act of divorce. Only the difficulty of finding a publisher prevented him from taking a tone much more hostile to society in novels which he wrote and burned one after another, because they failed to satisfy him. His letters to his early friend, Marjorie Nott, have much to say of this phase of mind. On September 12, 1899, he wrote from Tuckanuck:

TO MISS MARJORIE NOTT

Why do your letters make me so needlessly happy! I think it's because you believe in so much and because I do, too, and need to have someone to tell me that it is so. Not that I doubt,—what would my life be if I doubted! No, it's only that pretty much everybody believes I'm a crank or a fool, or asks when I'm going to begin to do something; to which question, by the way, I invariably respond—never! and oh! it's so good not to be on the defensive, not to feel the good anger rising in you, and step on it because you know they won't understand; not to suffer with the desire to insult the whole world; to lay its ugliness naked; to say: "There, there! don't you see all the dust and ashes that we're all admiring? don't you see? don't you understand?" And then not say it, because you know they can't see, and they won't understand. Ah, yes! it's so good to sit here, and write all this rot to you, and think that you'll know, that you'll understand. Isn't it horrible to get your mind twisted into cheap cynicisms while the tears are falling in your heart? and it's what we have to do—*nous autres!* I shall certainly end in publishing my book if I can find a bold enough publisher. The temptation is too immense. I know they won't understand, and yet I'm young enough to hope they will. Do you remember the book I talked to you of last winter? Well, that's it! I've done it over again, and—well! I don't know! I don't know why I write all this. I am here so calm, with my brother the sun and my sister the sea—by the way, Tuckanuck—and I feel as if I was anywhere except in the hither end of the nineteenth century; and my book, I don't think of it at all here. I write verse now—nothing else.

Naturally, since man or bird began to sing, he has sung to the woman,—or the female. The male is seldom a sympathetic listener; he prefers to do his own singing, or not to sing at all. He is not much to blame, but his indifference commonly ends by stifling the song, and the male singer has to turn to the female, or perish. In America, the male is not only a bad listener, but also, for poetry, a distinctly hostile audience; he thinks poorly of poetry and poets, so that the singer has no choice but to appeal to the woman. That young Lodge should have done so with an intensity proportioned to the repression of his instinct for sympathy and encouragement elsewhere was inevitable. Poets have always done it, but they have not shown by any means the surest instinct of poetry in their affairs of love, so that perhaps a woman who should criticize their work might feel tempted to use this test as the surest proof of force or failure in their instinct for art. By such a test, young Lodge would take rank among the strongest. Little credit is due to any man for yielding to altogether extraordinary beauty and charm in the perfection of feminine ideals,—although few men do it,—but it is far from being a rule that young men who rebel against the world's standards, and with infinite effort set up a standard of private war on the world, and maintain it with long and exhausting endurance, should go directly into the heart of the society they are denouncing, and carry off a woman whom lovers less sensitive to beauty, and less youthful in temperament, than poets or artists, might be excused for adoring.

Elizabeth Davis—another survival of rare American stock: Davis of Plymouth, Frelinghuysen of New Jersey, Griswold of Connecticut, with the usual leash of Senators, Cabinet officers, and other such ornaments, in her ancestry—was in truth altogether the highest flight of young Lodge's poetry, as he constantly told her when her own self-confidence naturally hesitated to believe it; and since his letters to her strike a note which rises high above the level of art or education, they cannot be wholly left out of his life. The man or woman who claims to be a poet at all must prove poetry to the heart, and neither Shakespeare nor Shelley can be exempted from the proof,—neither Dante nor Petrarch,—whatever their society might think about it.

Lodge's letters began in March 1899, when he was starting with his father and mother on a trip to Europe, which led to Sicily. From New York he wrote to bid good-by; the engagement was not yet avowed. And from Rome, a month later:

TO MISS DAVIS

I saw the grave of Keats the other day, and also of Shelley. It was a very keen sensation—more living, I think, than anything I have felt since you. My life is happy here, but my soul is very dolorous and strenuous. In life nothing resolves itself well. If a good issue is to come to anything, so much must be struggled with and sacrificed, so much confusion and distress, before serenity comes! When one is very young, it doesn't seem fitting. One wants so much! Heaven and

Earth is hardly enough for the large desire of youth, and the gates of possible expansion close one by one, until at last one runs through the last one just closing, without perhaps its being the right one. The period of choice is very short; then comes the short, sharp stab of necessity, and then —one has made one's bed, and one must lie in it. It's all very eager and restless, and perhaps better for being so.

From Rome in April he wrote:

"One makes oneself so very largely, and to make oneself greater or better, one must believe. Apply your religion: 'Thy faith has made thee whole!' That's the most wonderful thing Christ ever said, and it applies everywhere in life. Believe in yourself! it should be so easy for you. I do it, and it is of course far harder for me, for I've less to believe in."

The young people had much need to believe in themselves, for, in a worldly point of view, they had not much else to believe in. He wrote in July:

TO HIS MOTHER

BOSTON, *July 1899*

I am almost crazed with the desire to be independent, and yet I won't do anything that I don't approve and I won't give up my writing, God willing. I must keep at it and accomplish what I can in my own way. I feel sure it's the only way for me, and I know my intention is not low, whatever my performance may be. I feel desperate sometimes that it all comes so slowly and that I do no better; but I grit my teeth and keep at it. The agony of getting a thought into adequate expression is enormous. However, I feel so much resolution that I take heart, and now, too, I see my path clearer ahead of me. I must write and write, and as I say, I believe my purposes are good.

TUCKANUCK, *September 1899*

I haven't written for a long time, I am afraid, but since I have been here—the last ten days—I have been so happy in the sun and sea that I haven't written to anyone at all and have hardly done any work. I have just lived very happily. I have begun to write a tragedy in verse, and it's terrible work and not very encouraging. However, I get along—I have in my head also a plot for a prose play, very good, I think, and some other things besides. Indeed my mind is quite fertile, and physically I am in splendid condition. I got a letter from Mr. Stedman this morning, who is preparing an anthology of American poets and wants to put me in it. *J'apporte un bagage assez mince,* but still if he can find anything he wants to print he is welcome to it.

A few days afterwards, he wrote from Boston:

TO MISS DAVIS

To get away, very far from all this greasy gossip, this world of little motives and little desires! We must do it very soon. Only men who live in the constant strain of feeling alone against the world are forced to concentrate their passions on an object that seems to them above the world.

V. Marriage

NATURALLY, life cannot be lived in heroics. The man who places himself out of line with the current of society sees most the ridiculous or grotesque features of his surroundings, and finds most in them to laugh at. The conviction that either he or society is insane—or perhaps both—becomes a fixed idea, with many humorous sides; and though the humor tends to irony and somewhat cruel satire, it is often genial and sometimes playful. Young Lodge laughed with the rest, at the world or himself by turns. When Bigelow rebelled at his anarchic handwriting, he replied:

TO W. STURGIS BIGELOW

Ballade d'ung excellent poète au Sieur Bigelow au sujet d'ung certain plaint dudit Sieur Bigelow à luy addressé.

Ballade

I

I like to see the phrases flow
So smooth in writing round and plain—
Pooh! Hang the time and trouble! Though
It gave me fever on the brain
And caused intolerable pain
In hand and wrist—you set at nought
The beautiful, and still maintain
That writing must be slave to thought.

II

I wrote for beauty and I know
That beauty is its own best gain;
"Art for art's sake," I cried, and so
My unintelligible train
Of words was writ—you grew insane
Trying to read them, for you sought
A meaning and you swore again
That writing must be slave to thought.

III

You held the sheet above, below
Your head, and every nerve did strain
To read, and from your lips did go
Grim curses manifold as rain.
You should have known your toil was vain;
For Art's sole sake my writing wrought;
I scorned the axiom with disdain
That writing must be slave to thought.

IV

Prince, speak! Does anything remain
Now art is gone? No sense you've caught!
Then tell not me, the pure inane,
That writing must be slave to thought.

Fin de la Ballade d'ung excellent poète au Sieur Bigelow. Composée et mise en escript ce neuvième Décembre. A. D. MDCCCXCIX.

From Washington, on April 28, he wrote again to Bigelow:

"Well! the point is here! one should learn that it is not life that should be taken seriously, but living. In that way, one gets pleasure if not happiness. I wish I was going to Tuckanuck with you right off; but I'm not, and I have yards and miles of drudgery that maketh the heart sick. I've got to write another play before June. I have written several this winter, all on a steadily decreasing scale of merit, and I hope this one will be bad enough to be successful. The trees are full of leaves, and the air full of sun, and only I am vile. I wish I could pretend it was all somebody else's fault, but I can't. *Voilà!*"

A successful play needs not only to be fairly bad in a literary sense, but bad in a peculiar way which had no relation with any standard of badness that Lodge could reach. He toiled in vain.

When one is twenty-six years old, splendid in health and strength, and still more splendid in love, one enjoys the exuberant energy of complaint with a Gargantuan appetite:

TO W. STURGIS BIGELOW

WASHINGTON, *May 16, 1900*

Here it has been as high as 106°—Why don't you go to Tuckanuck? I would if I could, Gawd knows. It is of course self-evident to you as it is to me, that in the event of one's absence the world will cease to function,—but then who the Devil cares whether it functions or not? Not you, nor yet I. I would willingly barter the tattered remnants of a devilish tried soul to be under one of the great waves on the outside beach and, please Heaven, I soon shall be doing it. Meanwhile I grovel along in the living heat which I like, and do all the work that's in me—but after these months of it, the supply is running a little short, I'm afraid. I suppose I am here for about three weeks more—and then, with your permission, kind Sir! surf, Sir! and sun, Sir! and nakedness! —Oh, Lord! how I want to get my clothes off—alone in natural solitudes. In this heavy springtime I grow to feel exquisitely pagan, and worship the implacable Aphrodite, and read Sappho (with considerable difficulty) in the Greek.

From the beginnings of life, the poet and artist have gone on, surprising themselves always afresh by the discovery that their highest flights of poetry and art end in some simple and primitive emotion; but the credit of seeing and feeling it is the best proof of the poet. In his next volume of Poems, published in 1902, two years afterwards, he put these emotions into verse—"for E. L."—no longer Elizabeth Davis but Elizabeth Lodge.

She moves in the dusk of my mind, like a bell with the sweetness of singing
In a twilight of summer fulfilled with the joy of the sadness of tears;
And the calm of her face, and the splendid, slow smile are as memories clinging
Of songs and of silences filling the distance of passionate years.

She moves in the twilight of life like a prayer in a heart that is grieving,
And her youth is essential and old as the spring and the freshness of spring;
And her eyes watch the world and the little low ways of the sons of the living,
As the seraph might watch from the golden grave height of his heaven-spread wing.

The variations on this oldest of themes are endless, and yet are eternally new to someone who discovers them afresh; so that very slight differences of expression have artistic value. So, for example, the sonnet beginning:

Why are you gone? I grope to find your hand.
Why are you gone? The large winds seaward-bound,
Tell of long journeying in the endless void.
Why are you gone? I strain to catch the sound
Of footsteps, watch to see the dark destroyed
Before your lustrous fingers that would creep
Over my eyes, and give me strength to sleep.

One does not venture to suggest a famous line of a great poet for the sake of imitating the art, but one does it readily for the sake of rivaling the feeling. "You and I have gone behind the scenes and beyond, where all is light. I say, grip my hand always, for it is always laid in yours. Get from me some of the joy you give—some of the light and strength. I am overflowing with love, which is force, and you must take from me for my sake. Everywhere there is love, vast treasures of love, that people deny and conceal, but cannot kill, and in the earth and sea also. I am there for you, and love is there!"

All this is the purest sentiment, and yet young Lodge was not sentimental, and especially disliked sentimentality in literature. He would have ruthlessly burned any verse that offered to him the suggestion of sentimentalism. His idyl was intense because it was as old and instinctive as nature itself, and as simple. If he ever approached a sentimental expression, it was in the relation between parent and child, not between lover and mistress. Love was to him a passion, and a very real one, not capable of dilution or disguise. Such passions generally have their own way, and force everything to yield. The marriage took place in Boston, August 18, 1900. True to his instinct of shrinking from close and serious contact with the forms and conventions of a society which was to him neither a close nor a serious relation, he was married without previous notice, and without other than the necessary witnesses, at the Church of the Advent. The officiating clergyman is said to have remarked that he had never seen a more beautiful wedding; but he was the only person present to appreciate its beauty.

They went off to Concord to pass the honeymoon, and thence to Tuckanuck. All the practical difficulties in their way were ignored, and remained ignored through life, without interfering with the young couple's happiness. The world is still kind to those who are young, and handsome, and in love, and who trample on respectability. Naturally, as soon as the winter came, they set off for Paris.

TO HIS MOTHER

PARIS, *January 1901*

We have found a most charming little apartment, furnished—with only the indispensable, thank Heaven! The superfluous in a furnished apartment of modest price is horrible—and for only two hundred francs a month. We took it. It is 46 Rue du Bac. The house is an old palace of the days when the Rue du Bac was a fashionable street. It is built on three sides of an enormous court as wide as Massachusetts Avenue without the sidewalks. At the back of the court are large greenhouses of a florist—very pretty. Our apartment is on the court, on a southwest corner, filled with sun and very nice for us. It is at the top of the house. The staircase is really splendid—very large, with three great windows on every landing and fine wrought-iron railing, the first flight in stone, the other two in bricks. The apartment itself is the funniest, nicest place you ever saw, a sort of *Vie de Bohême* poetry about it, and sun and air to waste. The walls are very thick, so that the place is full of closets and the windows are all in deep recesses. Some of the floors are stone, others hard wood. We are delighted with it. The Rue du Bac runs up from the Pont Royal, if you remember, and 46 is near the river, and in fact within striking distance of everywhere. Well, we got the apartment, and you may imagine we have been busy, and Mrs. Cameron has been kindness itself, lending us things to cover the walls, etc. We are having a bully time getting installed and altogether I never had such fun in my life.

And there's for the practical side of things. I haven't got round to the absorbing psychological problems surrounding me, nor to the theaters we've seen, nor the work I've done, —a good deal,—nor the thoughts we've thought.

TO HIS FATHER

PARIS, *1901*

We live quite alone and see hardly anyone. I am hard at work on one or two things. The law against religious associations has at last passed and all socialists are happy. The next move is to confiscate Rothschild, then the manufacturers, then the other bourgeois, and so on to socialism. There are one or two new things here which would interest you, I think—such as casts of some of the things found at Delphi, the new bridge over the Seine, Pont Alexandre III, which is really very good, and some other things too.

PARIS, *1901*

I have sent the Louis to Bourgouin, and I will at once attend to the books. The socialists here have started a *"librairie socialiste."* How it differs from an ordinary bookshop neither they nor I know; but as I live more or less among socialists, I find myself obliged to get my books there and yours will be sent from there. Curiously enough it is an excellent shop. I was very glad to hear that you expect to get through without an extra session. I had been afraid that Cuba and the Philippines might delay you and produce discord. You know, however, how difficult it is to know what is happening *de par le monde* in this most provincial capital. The New York *Herald* has become merely a vulgar sort of *Town Topics,* published every day, and has, I really think, less news than the best French papers. In which connection I should like extremely to know the truth about the row Sampson has got himself into. I saw that Allen attacked him in his usual polished way in the Senate, which, coupled with the fact that I greatly admire Sampson, warmed my heart for him. But it seems impossible to find out what it was all about.

Here the whole of France is shaken over the pending bill confiscating the property of the religious orders. It is going to pass and the Church is pretty sick. The debate has produced one interesting piece of statistics: that there are three times as many monks in France now as there were in 1789, whereas the population has not quite doubled. My friend, Hubert, says, *"C'est curieux, ça démontre que nous retournions à la barbarie."* B—— saw some American colonist lady the other day, who told her that Porter was a very bad ambassador. *B——*. Why?—*American colonist lady*. Because he is pro-Boer.—*B——*. But I thought that was popular in France.—*American colonist lady*. Oh, no, all the Americans here are pro-English.—This strikes me as a very characteristic expression of the American colonist point of view.

We see very few people and no society, and less than no American colony, and we are very happy indeed. We are looking forward very much to your advent on the scene. There are some new plays and things which may amuse you. Also they have at last arranged the great series of Rubenses in the Louvre, as decorations, which is what they are meant to be. I am writing a good deal and studying the rest of the time. Please give my love to Theodore when he takes the veil. I hope it will be a fine day for him.

PARIS, *1901*

I am so glad you got through the session so well, and I hope you are not worn out. I was very much interested to see that England had refused our treaty, and I wonder what is coming next. Is the sentiment strong to abrogate the Clayton-Bulwer treaty by resolution? I hope so. This refusal really makes one believe that those whom the Gods wish to destroy they first make mad.

PARIS, *Spring 1901*

Many, many thanks for your kind letter, and for all the trouble you have taken about my novel and my play. I am very glad indeed to have R. S.'s criticism, and I think that dramatically you and he are pretty nearly right. Indeed I think the action in *Villon* is really too subjective for the stage. It is far more the presentation of an idea than of an action, and I doubt very much if it can be fitted for acting. I should be very glad, however, if you would bring it over when you come. I have so much on my hands now that I could not attend to it before then.

The other night I went to hear Jaurès, the Socialist, speak. He is, I think, a very remarkable orator and a very sincere man.

The salon is open here and I have been through it once. There are seven kilometers of canvas, I think, and it's altogether a pretty poor showing, so it seems to me. There are, however, one or two good things, especially in the sculpture, and many clever things.

I hope you will succeed in getting the Bayreuth tickets. We are all very much looking forward to going.

TO HIS MOTHER

PARIS, *Spring 1901*

Day before yesterday Hubert took us to St. Germain, where he is "*attaché au Musée.*" It was very interesting and we had a drive in the forest—superb. Hubert is the nicest little man in the world—sympathetic, gentle, bright, and with a preposterous amount of learning. He insists he is going to make me collaborate in some scientific magazine on an Egyptian topic. I hope not. However, I am tolerably strong in Egyptian now. I can read the texts with considerable fluency and the inscriptions on tombs, etc., become very intelligible. It is certainly a useless accomplishment, but excessively interesting. At the same time I have been reading up Chaldea and Syria, Babylonia, etc., so that I have a pretty good idea of the classic Orient. It's a point of departure I have always lacked and needed. Meanwhile, I have written considerably. I enclose a couple of things you may like to see. I am very glad the *Atlantic* and *Century* received me so well. I have just received Papa's letter with the letter from Gilder, and shall answer it at once. Gissing has gone away, I am sorry to say. I should have been glad to see more of him. He is a real man.

VI. Cain

THE EUROPEAN PART of the idyl ended with a week at Bayreuth and the return home in August 1901. Thenceforward, the life at Washington in winter, and at Nahant or Tuckanuck in summer—the life of husband and father—becomes only the background for literary work, and the work alone remains to tell of the life. The poet's education was finished; what the poet could do with it remains to be shown.

The first result appeared in the volume already mentioned, entitled *Poems (1899–1902)*, which appeared in the winter of 1902–3. The next was *Cain*, published in November 1904. The first volume, of one hundred and fifty pages, consisted of the short efforts of the poet's youth. The second volume is a single, sustained effort of drama, and claimed attention less for its poetic than for its dramatic qualities.

Like all the poets of the same school, Lodge conceded nothing to mere decoration or ornament. The vigorous standards of this severe Academy regarded a popular or conventional flower as a blot. Every verse must have its stress, or strain, and every thought its intensity. This preliminary condition is something not to be discussed, but to be accepted or rejected in advance, like the conditions of a color scheme, or an architectural or musical composition; and, since few readers are trained to such technical appreciation, at a moment when the public refuses to make any mental effort that it can avoid, the poet's audience is very small. In reality the mental effort of reading is much less than that of listening to Wagner or Debussy; but the poet numbers his audience by scores, while the musician, if he gets any audience at all, numbers it by thousands. These restraints are a part of the given situation under which the dramatic poet works; conditions which he cannot change; they are in reality far more severe and paralyzing than the conditions imposed by the old unities. They must be kept in mind by the reader, unless his reading is to be waste of time.

So, too, the dramatic idea is a condition given beforehand, to be accepted or refused as a whole. The poet does not want an audience that looks for gems,—that selects a pretty song or verse, and rejects the whole,—the unity. He has some one great tragic motive, which he tries to work out in a way he thinks his own, and he wants to be judged by his dramatic effect, as an actor is judged by his power of holding an audience. Properly he would ask, not whether his drama is liked, but whether it is dramatic; not whether the reader was pleased, but whether he was bored.

Lodge's dramatic motive was always the same, whether in *Cain,* or in *Herakles,* or in the minor poems. It was that of Schopenhauer, of Buddhism, of oriental thought everywhere,—the idea of Will, making the universe, but existing only as subject. The Will is God; it is nature; it is all that is; but it is knowable only as ourself. Thus the sole tragic action of humanity is the Ego,—the Me,—always maddened by the necessity of self-sacrifice, the superhuman effort of lifting himself and the universe by sacrifice, and, of course, by destroying the attachments which are most vital, in order to attain. The idea is a part of the most primitive stock of religious and philosophical motives, worked out in many forms, as Prometheus, as Herakles, as Christ, as Buddha,—to mention only the most familiar,—but, in our modern conception of life, impossible to realize except as a form of insanity. All Saviors were anarchists, but Christian anarchists, tortured by the self-contradictions of their role. All were insane, because their problem was self-contradictory, and because, in order to raise the universe in oneself to its highest power, its negative powers must be paralyzed or destroyed. In reality, nothing was destroyed; only the Will —or what we now call Energy—was freed and perfected.

This idea, which probably seemed simpler than shower or sunshine to a Hindoo baby two thousand years ago, has never taken root in the western mind except as a form of mysticism, and need not be labored further. It was what the French call the *donnée* of Lodge's drama,—the condition to be granted from the start; and it had, for a dramatist, the supreme merit of being the most universal tragic motive in the whole possible range of thought. Again and again, from varied points of view, Lodge treated it in varied moods and tempers; but his two dramas, *Cain* and *Herakles,* were elaborately developed expansions of the theme.

The general reader, who reads a Greek drama in the same spirit in which he reads the morning newspaper, can scarcely get beyond the first half-dozen pages of such a theme; and, in fact, the subject was never intended for him. The more serious student, who reads further, can seldom escape a sense of discomfort from the excessive insistence on the motive,—the violence with which it is—over and over again—thrust before his eyes in its crudest form; and, in fact, Lodge has what the French call the faults of his qualities; he is exuberant, and exuberance passes the bounds of *mesure*. Nature herself is apt to exaggerate in the same way. We must take it—or reject it—as we take a thunderstorm or a flood; it may be unnecessary, but is it dramatic?

Every just critic will leave the reader to answer this question for himself. Taste is a matter about which the Gods themselves are at odds. American taste is shocked by every form of paradox except its own. Greek taste was lavish of paradox, especially about the Gods. Saturn ate his children, and Zeus dethroned his father. Questions of taste! while Lodge's paradox, as developed in *Cain,* was a question rather of logic,—even almost of mathematics. Step by step, like a demonstration in geometry, the primitive man is forced into the attitude of submission to destiny or assertion of self, and Lodge develops each step as a necessary sequence, in the nature of the Greek fate, but a result of conscious Will. The paradox that Cain killed Abel because, from the beginning, man had no choice but to make himself slave of nature or its master, is, after all, nothing like so paradoxical as the philanthropist idea that man has gone on killing himself since the world began, without any reason at all.

This, then, is the paradox of Cain which Lodge undertook to work out, as Byron had worked it out before him, in one of his strongest dramas; and the readers who take it in this sense can hardly fail to find it dramatic. They may not like the drama, but they will probably not toss it aside. They will admit its force. They may even, if particularly sensitive to this oldest of emotional motives, follow the poet himself to the end.

> Captain, my Soul, despair is not for thee!
> Thou shalt behold the seals of darkness lift,
> Weather the wrathful tempest and at last,
> Resolute, onward, headlong, dazed and scarred,
> Reel through the gates of Truth's enormous dawn!

To develop this idea in its dramatic form, Lodge took as his text the words of *Genesis,* and allowed himself only the four characters, Adam, Eve, Cain, and Abel. He gave himself no favors; he introduced no light tones; on his somber background the figures move in no more light than is strictly necessary to see them move at all; they follow the rules of the mediaeval Mystery Play, rather than those of the Greek drama. Yet any sympathetic workman of literary effect will probably admit that they do move, and even that at certain moments their movement is highly dramatic; so much so as to be genuinely emotional.

So also with the characters themselves! If there is a character hard to deal with in the whole range of dramatic effort, Adam is he! No artist has succeeded in making Adam sympathetic, and very few indeed have tried to do so. "The woman tempted me and I did eat" has been his sentence of condemnation as a figure of drama, since drama was acted. Such a figure could not be heroic, and only with difficulty could be saved from being ridiculous on the stage. Even the twelfth-century *Mystery of Adam's Fall* dwelt only on his weakness and abject submission to Eve on one side, and to God on the other. Lodge accepted the traditional figure, and made the best of it.

> Though my life is bruised with sore affliction
> And dire repentance blast my happiness;
> Though in remembrance Paradise forever
> Blooms with fresh light and flowers ineffable,
> Clear pieties and peaceful innocence,
> Against the gloom of this grieved sentience
> Of violence and starvation, yet I bear,
> Scornful of tears, the grief and scorn of life!
> Faith is the stern, austere acknowledgment
> And dumb obedience to the will of God:
> Such faith my soul has kept inviolable!
> What though he crush me, is not He the Lord!

The drama permitted little development of Adam's character: he scarcely appears after the first act, leaving the stage to the two brothers to work out their inevitable antagonism and their contradictory conceptions of duty.

Although Cain's character necessarily had to be developed to the point of insanity, it was a logical insanity; while Abel's character remained also true to its logical conditions of submission to a force or will not its own. The two brothers represented two churches, and the strife ended as such strife in history has commonly ended,—in the destruction of one or the other, the victory of faith or free will.

The character which Lodge developed with evident sympathy was not masculine but feminine. Cain might be himself, but Eve was the mother, a nature far more to his liking. Upon her was thrown the whole burden and stress of the men's weakness or insanity. The drama opens upon her, bearing the alternate reproaches and entreaties of Adam, and trying to infuse into him a share of her own courage and endurance; Adam implores her:

> "Hold me—I need thy tenderness, I need
> Thy calm and pitiful hands to comfort me."

Eve answers:

> "Be still a little; all will be well, I know."

A total inversion of roles! and it is carried through consistently to the end. All the men appeal to Eve, and then refuse to listen to her. In the vehement dispute at the end of the first act, Adam at last turns to Eve, and bids her to lecture her son:

> And thou, Eve, Woman, most perilously wandered
> In weak delusion, now I charge thee speak—
> Lest thou should fall again in deathless sin,—
> Of God and man,—God's all, man's nothingness!

EVE

> Dear son, we are God's creatures every one—

CAIN

> Mother!

EVE

> I'll speak no more!—

Except perhaps the somewhat undeveloped figure of Abel, all these characters are personally felt,—to the dramatist they were real and living figures,—but that of Eve is the most personal of all. As the drama opens on the wife bearing the reproaches and supporting the weakness of the husband, so it ends by the mother assuming the insanities of the son. After the traditional development of the mediaeval drama, Eve is reproduced in the Virgin. Lodge adhered closely to the mediaeval scheme except in transposing the roles of the brothers and intensifying the role of the mother. As, in the mediaeval conception, the role of the Virgin almost effaced the role of Christ, the drama of *Cain* ends by almost effacing Cain in the loftier self-sacrifice of the woman:

"Go forth, go forth, lonely and godlike man!
My heart will follow tho' my feet must stay.
Yet in thy solitude shall there be a woman
To care for thee through the incessant days,
To lie beside thee in the desolate nights,
To love thee as thy soul shall love the truth!
In her thy generation shall conceive
Passionate daughters, strong and fierce-eyed sons,
To lift the light and bear the labor of truth
Whereof the spark is mine, the fire is thine."

Perhaps some readers would find more meaning and higher taste in the drama had Lodge called it *Eve* instead of calling it *Cain;* but here the dramatist was developing his theme in philosophy rather than in poetry, and the two motives almost invariably stand in each other's light. The maternal theme is the more poetic and dramatic, but without the philosophy the poem and the drama have no reason to exist. The reader must take it as it is given, or must throw it aside altogether, and compose a drama of his own, with a totally different *donnée.* In either case, he will search long, and probably in vain, through American literature, for another dramatic effort as vigorous and sustained as that of *Cain,* and, if he finds what he seeks, it is somewhat more than likely that he will end by finding it in *Herakles.*

VII. The Great Adventure

Composition, and especially dramatic composition, is an absorbing task. Night passes rapidly in shaping a single phrase, and dawn brings a harsh light to witness putting it in the fire. Lodge worked habitually by night, and destroyed as freely as he composed. Meanwhile life went on, with such pleasures and pains as American life offers; but, in narrative, the pains take the larger place, and the pleasures are to be understood as a background. The most serious loss to Lodge's life was the illness and death of his friend, Trumbull Stickney, whose companionship had beer. his best support since the early days of Paris and the Latin Quarter. Stickney owned a nature of singular refinement, and his literary work promised to take rank at the head of the work done by his generation of Americans; but he had hardly come home to begin it at Harvard College when he was struck down by fatal disease. Lodge's letters had much to say of the tragedy, and of the volume of verses which he helped to publish afterwards in order to save what relics remained of Stickney's poetry.

From Boston in August 1904 he wrote his wife: "Just after I wrote to you, John called me up on the telephone and told me that Joe [Stickney] was very seriously ill at the Victoria. I went down there at once and saw Lisel, the doctor, and Lucy, and I write to you now, in the greatest agony of mind. Joe has got a tumor on the brain. For ten days he has had almost constant terrific pains in his head. They brought him to Boston last Thursday. You can imagine how dreadful a shock it was to get this frightful news when I had hoped to take Joe to Tuckanuck with us. I am completely unnerved. . . . The doctor told me I should certainly not be able to see him—no one can. . . . I feel at present utterly prostrated. Somehow I have never conceived of Joe's dying."

From Tuckanuck, September 1: "You can imagine better than I can tell you, with what a tense and anxious hope I cling to the possibility that Joe will be saved, and returned to life a well man. I feel almost heartbroken when I think of him, and my mind goes back through all the immense days and ways of life that we have seen together. . . . Doc [Sturgis Bigelow] is, as you may guess, the best and dearest companion in this twilight of grief and anxiety in which I have my present being, and this place is of course more soothing than anywhere else to me. . . ."

From Nahant, November 1904: "Don't get carried away with the idea that Joe's death has set the term to youth or is really the end of anything. Life—our life, his life, the life of the human soul—is quite continuous, I'm convinced: one thing with another, big and little, sad and gay, real and false, and the whole business just life, which is its own punishment and reward, its own beginning and end. . . ."

From Nahant, November 1904: "I've finished rereading the *Republic,* and it is one of the few books in which my sons shall be thoroughly educated if I can manage it. There are not more than a very few books from which every man can catch a glimpse of the Great Idea, for there are only a very few great torchbearers. But the *Republic* is one, and much more accessible than any other, except the *Leaves of Grass;* for Christ is deeply hidden in the rubbish of the Church, and Buddha and Lao Tze are very far removed from the processes of our minds."

From Boston, January 1905: "I've had the most warm and vivid delight in Dok's [Sturgis Bigelow's] company, which has been constantly with me since I came here. He has surpassed himself in kindness and clear, warm, wise sympathy and comprehensiveness. Tonight I have passed a long and superb evening with him, in which we have together, in a manner of speaking, *fait le tour* on the parapets of thought. It has renewed and inspired me, given me, as it were, a new departure and a new vista. . . . I hate to leave tomorrow, for he seems so glad to have me, and I, the Gods know, get everything from being with him. He does, as you might say, continually see me through,—through confusion, and through mistakes and desperations,—in fact, through life. It's immense, what he has done and does for me. In short, after two days of him I feel all straightened out, and you, you best know how badly I needed this beneficent process. Last night we saw Réjane in *L'Hirondelle,* a play not at all superior, not of any brilliancy of merit or originality of human criticism, but so, after all, interesting by virtue of a certain apparent and immense genuine reality, —so 'written,' with such glitter of word and phrase and epigram, and so acted, above all, that we both passed an evening of immense, contented, uncritical delight."

From Mrs. Wharton's, New York, January 1905: "I left Boston rather sadly, for my days there had been marvelous. A real readjustment and recoherence of all the immense pressure of great experience which has, as you know, kept me struggling and a little breathless since Joe's death. With Dok I really found my footing, brushed the night from my eyes, and took a long glance forward. . . . Mrs. Wharton was really glad to see me, and I to see her, and we have had a good deal of the swift, lucid, elliptical conversation which is so perfect and so stimulating and so neatly defined in its range. . . . It is a great delight to be with her, as I am a good deal, and to be clear and orderly and correct in one's thought and speech, as far as one goes. It's good for one, and vastly agreeable besides,—indeed, it is to me a kind of gymnastic excitement, very stimulating."

As these letters show, the death of Stickney threw Lodge rather violently back on himself and his personal surroundings, and he stretched out his hands painfully for intellectual allies. A stroke of rare good fortune threw a new friend in his way, to fill the void in his life that Stickney had left. Langdon Mitchell, another poet and dramatist, with much the same ideals and difficulties, but with ten years' more experience, brought him help and counsel of infinite value, as his letters show:

TO LANGDON MITCHELL

NAHANT (*July 1903*)

DEAR MITCHELL,—Before receiving your letter and in an ecstasy of good manners, I wrote to your wife to ask her if

I might come to you on the seventeenth. I can't very well come earlier for I am by way of seeing my parents off to Europe, where my dad is going to assist in despoiling the virtuous Briton, for whom the wrathful tears of the State Department abundantly flow, of what neither is nor ought to be his except on the theory that everything of value should belong to that people who, when pressed, will blushingly confess that they are the chosen of God. My father starts, then, on this engaging mission[1] on the seventeenth, and after having given him my blessing and those counsels gained only by inexperience, without which no child with any sense of responsibility should take leave of his father, having in fact done all my duty, I shall at once turn myself to pleasure and embark with a mind wholly vague as to direction, you-ward. It's mighty good of you, dear Mitchell, and of your wife too to want me for a few days, and I can't tell you with how great pleasure I look forward to seeing you. We'll have some great days.

1925 F St., *October 1903*

Dear Mitchell,—Good! You understand Baudelaire as I do; indeed you say things about him which make me realize as never before my own comprehension of him. I am doubtful about French poetry being, like Latin, "City poetry." Think of Ronsard and his crowd, or Victor Hugo or Leconte de Lisle—but Baudelaire, like Villon, like Verlaine, is certainly a city poet. And why not? The civilization of an old society is, I am certain, the fair material of poems. The best is that Baudelaire has given you pleasure, and I feel that you have appreciated as I do that he is, in his best moments, really a great poet, one of the torchbearers. "*Allons!* after the great companions and to belong to them!" Ah! let us go and be of them if we can, dear Mitchell. At least we can follow on the "great road of the Universe." Which reminds me that I have been reading your verses again and again and I shall have, for what they're worth, some remarks to make when we next meet.

[1]The Alaskan Boundary Tribunal, which met in London in the summer of 1903 and of which his father was a member. H. A.

1925 F St., *Spring, 1904*

Dear Mitchell,—I largely agree with what you say of Viele's book, though to my mind you rate it a little too high. His delight in words seems to me far his strongest trick. He says not very much. Of course keep *Cain* till April 1st or as long as you wish. As you may imagine, all that you say about it in your letter is deeply interesting to me. As I've said to you, you are the only person from whom I expect genuine criticism and get it. As regards the stage directions I'll say this: Although the thing has no quality of a real play, nevertheless the action—that is, the main points of the action—are essential to the expression of the idea, and therefore it is necessary that there should be some environment indicated, and that the characters should perform certain motions (as few as possible, of course). The question, then, is merely this: whether the poem is more or less interrupted and the reader subjected to more or less of a jar, by having environment and action indicated as briefly and technically as possible, in brackets, or by having them introduced as verse into the body of the poem. It seemed to me, despite the obvious absurdities, the former was the method most frank and honest, and least likely to mar the poetic and intellectual integrity of the whole. Of course the mere technicalities could be eliminated if they seriously jarred. Thank you—I wish I could—for all that you say, which I find very just and of the utmost assistance to me in clarifying and enlightening my own criticism; and thank you, above all, for your interest, which is valuable to me beyond words.

I'm mighty sorry but not very greatly surprised to hear your news of the condition of the stage. It's depressing beyond measure to know that the American theater is reserved exclusively, either for importations, or the worthless manufactures of almost illiterate Americans who regard plays merely as merchandise, and who would manufacture boots with equal enjoyment and success. Indeed it's most depressing; and what is to be done? Your assertion that the American public will take good plays as well as bad is I believe quite correct, but unfortunately it doesn't help as long as they'll take bad plays as well as good. The stage situation is to me merely another sign of the intellectual, moral, and spiritual childishness of the American. Indeed was there ever such an anomaly as the American man? In practical affairs his cynicism, energy, and capacity are simply stupefying, and in every other respect he is a sentimental idiot possessing neither the interest, the capacity, nor the desire for even the most elementary processes of independent thought. Consider for one moment his position as a domestic animal as it was fifty years ago and as it is today. Then he was the unquestioned head of his family, the master of his house, the father of as many children as he wanted to have. His wife's business was to bear his children and manage his household to suit him, and she never questioned it. Today he is absolutely dethroned. A woman rules in his stead. His wife finds him so sexually inapt that she refuses to bear him children and so driveling in every way except as a money-getter that she compels him to expend his energies solely in that direction while she leads a discontented, sterile, stunted life, not because she genuinely prefers it but because she cannot find a first-rate *man* to make her desire to be the mother of his children and to live seriously and happily. I speak of course only of the well-to-do classes, which as a matter of fact comprise most real Americans, and of which the average number of children per family is under two. We are, dear Mitchell, a dying race, as every race must be of which the men are, as men and not accumulators, third-rate. American women don't fall in love with the American men (I mean, really) and they're quite right; only a woman won't have children by a man she's not really in love with, and when you think of the travail and the peril of death can you blame her? It's an odd situation; we are a dying race and really we've never lived.

Forgive this long dissertation. I got started and could not stop.

1925 F St., *April 1904*

Dear Mitchell,—I'm nearly in a position now to answer the question which we discussed—perhaps you remember—

last summer at Tuckanuck: namely whether or not Jesus Christ appeared as the logical outcome of the Jewish religious tradition. You remember I contended he was wholly sporadic and attached to nothing. I begin now to see I was in a measure quite wrong, and perhaps to a small extent right. I am very anxious to talk it over with you when you return here, and also to discuss with you the whole state of thought and feeling in Judaea at the time of Christ's appearance. All this, you will guess, is the result of work I've been doing in preparation for writing the Christ-play of which I spoke to you and which, to my immense delight, you seem to approve —at least the idea—in your last letter. I've already gone far enough to realize that no subject could be more fascinating or more interesting. Jesus Christ and his teachings, which are neglected and unknown, form a background against which the dark threads of the lives and passions and thoughts of worldly men should stand out like the black bars on the solar spectrum. I have reread Renan's *Vie de Jésus* and it's interesting in many ways and a *"beau livre"*; but, dear Mitchell, can you imagine a man spending ten years on the study of Jesus Christ and at last summing up his appreciation of the man in this phrase: *"C'est un charmeur!"* It's staggering.

1925 F St. (*Spring of 1904*)

Dear Mitchell,—I imagine what you say of solitude is very true. *"Tout se paie"*—in one form or another. Certainly you have kept singularly balanced, singularly vital and sane —in the true sense. What I shall be in ten years there's no guessing. One stakes one's life on the chance of ransoming "one lost moment with a rhyme" and the wheel turns——

Of course keep *Cain* as long as you want. I really feel ashamed to bother you with it when you are so busy, but it's vastly important to me to know precisely what you think; whether, in your deliberate opinion, it's the real thing in any degree whatever, and not merely and utterly—literature! But don't, I beg you, look at it until it's convenient. I shan't write another long thing in verse for some time. Since publishing *Cain* I've had a time of horrible reaction and *"abatte-*

ment"—the sort of thing we all go through occasionally. This has become a drearily egotistical and dull letter. . . .

My days in New York were glorious, the only good days I've had since finishing that poem. I need hardly say how deeply I hope you will dispose of your plays to your satisfaction—for your sake and for the sake of the stage.

1925 F St., Washington
(*Spring, 1904*)

I think, dear Mitchell, that we really about agree as to the Sonnet. The first-rate ones are terribly few and in diverse forms. Witness Baudelaire.

. . . .

My dear man, I've got hold of such a splendid thing to write—immense. I'm shutting down on Society, in which we've been wandering this winter to the detriment of all I value in life, and I'm getting to work—God be praised. I wish I could have a talk with you about this and so many other things. One gets glimpses, such glimpses, of incredible, tremendous things. I wish you were by so we might share them. I feel always tempted to run over for a day to see you, but I'm afraid it's quite impossible now. Still if the desire pushes me too hard I'll turn up some afternoon. Spring-Rice has been here for a week and I had one splendid talk with him and wished more than ever you were here. There's a man who does, really, keep up wonderfully and by a very peculiar faculty he has of remaining, *au fond,* quite detached from his own circumstances and experience. He left tonight, alas! He goes back to Russia, about which he had absorbing things to say. Now that he's gone, once more the "void weighs on us,"—the dreadful, blank, mild nothingness of this nice, agreeable, easy, spacious vacuity (comp. James). And here I am again alone beyond belief, but, fortunately, with a very interesting thing to do, so I'm very well off.

Nahant, Mass., *October 1904*

Dear Mitchell,—I was extremely glad to get your note and I would have answered it before had not events compelled me. On the eleventh my friend Stickney died—quite suddenly at the last. On the fourteenth we buried him. He was thirty years old—by far the most promising man I have known, his best work still and surely to come. Under the terrible test of a mortal disease his mind and character rose to higher levels than they had ever touched before. He died, really, at the height of his powers. The future held nothing for him but suffering, mental and physical. He is very well out of it. Dear Mitchell, what a life it is!—what a life! I am having an undoubtedly hard time. So, it must be said, are other people.

I wish I could get to New York now and see you. I feel more deeply than ever how invaluable your friendship is to me and how incalculably better than anything else in life such friendship as I think you and I share together is in the last analysis. I would come if I had the energy, but I am pretty well done up morally and physically. I shall be in New York, though, from November ninth for some days. Couldn't you be there then too? It would be to me so true a happiness to see you again.

Naturally, too, in the social and literary sequence, young Lodge fell under the charm of Henry James:

TO HIS MOTHER

WASHINGTON, *May 1905*

To this even existence of mine there has been one delightful interruption, namely the lecture and subsequent visions of Henry James. The lecture was profoundly, and to one who writes himself, wonderfully interesting; so many splendid things which had been long at home in my own consciousness and which I first heard then, perfectly and irresistibly expressed. The amiable Miss T—— had asked us to tea for the next day; where I went and found, besides James, old Mrs. ——, a most original and charming and distinguished person, conveying, through all her rather stiff but flattering courtesy, the vivid impression that she might be, on occasion, equally original and the reverse of charming. There were besides some unremarkable people who all left, leaving me the chance to talk with James, which I did with the greatest delight then and also the next morning when, at his invitation, I went with him to the Capitol and the Library for two most interesting hours. This, I believe, can be said of James, though it is not the most obvious remark to make of him, and is, at the same time, the rarest and most important compliment that can be paid to any creative artist—namely, that he is, in matters of art, incorruptibly honest, and in consequence hugely expensive. He is, I mean, as an artist, built through and through of the same material—which you like or not according to your fancy. His very style—again whether you like it or not—bears by its mere tortuous originality, if by no other sign, infallible witness that he has, at immense expenditure, done all the work—artistically and intellectually—and that all the work is his own. In ideas and art he lives in a palace built of his own time and thought, while the usual, you might say the ubiquitous, average person and literary prostitute lives contentedly in one of an interminable row of hovels, built, so to speak, on an endless contract from bare material stolen from Time's intellectual scrap-heap. What it all amounts to is that, whether you like James or not, whether you think he is all on the wrong track or not, you are bound to respect him, for if you do not, whom, in this age of universal machine-made cheapness, whom more than James with his immense talent and industry *and* his small sales, are you going to respect?

This is a long, garrulous, egotistical (to a degree), and perhaps you will say, rather incoherent letter. So I will spare you any further palpitating details of my obscure life.

WASHINGTON, *June 1905*

Indeed, I wish I might have been with you, but on the other hand I have done an immense deal by being quietly [?] and in much long solitude just now at this time. I have lived high most of my working hours, and in consequence my volume of sonnets—*The Great Adventure,* I call it, which is,

I think, a good title—lies before me all but finished—seventy-five sonnets or more, with which I am pretty well pleased. I feel lonely, as I always do when I am hard at work, but I also feel much exhilaration. These are my great years. Well, I am sure I must have said all this before to you. My interest in myself is so poignant that I elude it with difficulty.

Joe's volume represents for me a good deal of work and an experience of grief that neither gives nor receives consolation, which has left its indelible mark upon me—which is good. For I believe there are but two ways with real grief: get rid of it if you can; but if you can't, then take all you can get of it, live in it, work in it, experience it as far as you are capable of experiencing anything. Let it nourish you! as it will, as anything will that is real, and in direct proportion to its reality and significance. I'll tell you that I sent my volume of sonnets to Houghton & Mifflin, who wrote me that they held my work in high consideration; which, I suppose, indicates that some people they have seen think well of *Cain*. Also, perhaps you have seen *Moriturus* (by me) in the July *Scribner*.

The Great Adventure was published in October,—a small volume of ninety pages, of which nearly one third were devoted to the memory of Stickney:

He said: "We are the Great Adventurers;
This is the Great Adventure: thus to be
Alive, and, on the universal sea
Of being, lone yet dauntless mariners.

. . . .

This is the Great Adventure!" All of us
Who saw his dead, deep-visioned eyes, could see,
After the Great Adventure, immanent,
Splendid and strange, the Great Discovery.

Love and Death were the two themes of these sonnets, almost as personal as the *Song of the Wave*. Underneath the phrases and motives of each lay almost always the sense of striving against the elements, like Odysseus, or against the mysteries, like Plato:

"At least," he said, "we spent with Socrates
Some memorable days, and in our youth
Were curious and respectful of the Truth,
Thrilled with perfections and discoveries,
And with the everlasting mysteries
We were irreverent and unsatisfied,—
And so we are!" he said . . .

The irreverence mattered little, since it was mostly the mere effervescence of youth and health; but the dissatisfaction went deep, and made a serious strain on his energy,—a strain which Stickney's death first made vital. The verses began to suggest discouragement:

In Time's cathedral, Memory, like a ghost,
Crouched in the narrow twilight of the nave,
Fumbles with thin pathetic hands to save
Relics of all things lived and loved and lost.
Life fares and feasts, and Memory counts the cost
With unrelenting lips that dare confess
Life's secret failures, sins and loneliness,
And life's exalted hopes, defiled and crossed.

The Great Adventure probably marked the instant when life did, in fact, hover between the two motives,—the beginning and the end,—Love and Death. Both were, for the moment, in full view, equally near, and equally intense, with the same background of the unknown:

In the shadow of the Mystery
We watched for light with sleepless vigilance,
Yet still, how far soever we climbed above
The nether levels, always, like a knife,
We felt the chill of fear's blind bitter breath;
For still a secret crazed the heart of Love,
An endless question blurred the eyes of Life,
A baffling silence sealed the lips of Death.

Meanwhile life went on with what most people would, at least in retrospect, regard as altogether exceptional happiness.

The small circle of sympathetic companions was immensely strengthened by the addition of Edith Wharton, whose unerring taste and finished workmanship served as a corrective to his youthful passion for license. Her fine appreciation felt this quality as the most insistent mark of his nature:

"Abundance,—that is the word which comes to me whenever I try to describe him. During the twelve years of our friendship,—and from the day that it began,—I had, whenever we were together, the sense of his being a creature as profusely as he was finely endowed. There was an exceptional delicacy in his abundance, and an extraordinary volume in his delicacy."

Life is not wholly thrown away on ideals, if only a single artist's touch catches like this the life and movement of a portrait. Such a picture needs no proof; it is itself convincing.

"The man must have had a sort of aura about him. Perhaps he was one of those who walk on the outer rim of the world, aware of the jumping-off place; which seems the only way to walk—but few take it. Odd that your article should have appealed so much to me, when I know so little of the subject!"

The more competent the reader,—and this reader, though unnamed, was among the most competent,—the more complete is the conviction; and the same simple quality of the truest art runs through the whole of Mrs. Wharton's painting, to which the critic was alluding. Every touch of her hand takes the place of proof.

"All this," she continues, "on the day when he was first brought to see me,—a spring afternoon of the year 1898, in Washington,—was lit up by a beautiful boyish freshness, which, as the years passed, somehow contrived to ripen without fading. In the first five minutes of our talk, he *gave* himself with the characteristic wholeness that made him so rare a friend; showing me all the sides of his varied nature; the grave sense of beauty, the flashing contempt of meanness, and that large spring of kindly laughter that comes to many only as a result of the long tolerance of life. It was one of his gifts thus to brush aside the preliminaries of acquaintance, and enter at once, with a kind of royal ease, on the rights and privileges of friendship; as though—one might think—with a foreboding of the short time given him to enjoy them.

"Aside from this, however, there was nothing of the pathetically predestined in the young Cabot Lodge. Then—and to the end—he lived every moment to the full, and the first impression he made was of a joyous physical life. His sweet smile, his easy strength, his deep eyes full of laughter and visions,—these struck one even before his look of intellectual power. I have seldom seen anyone in whom the natural man was so wholesomely blent with the reflecting intelligence; and it was not the least of his charms that he sent such stout roots into the earth, and had such a hearty love for all he drew from it. Nothing was common or unclean to him but the vulgar, the base, and the insincere, and his youthful impatience at the littleness of human nature was tempered by an unusually mature sense of its humors."

While young Lodge, or any other young artist, might find it the most natural thing in the world to give himself without thought or hesitation to another artist, like Mrs. Wharton, it by no means followed that he could give himself to men or women who had not her gifts, or standards, or sympathies. He could no more do this than he could write doggerel. However much he tried, and the more he tried, to lessen the gap between himself—his group of personal friends—and the public, the gap grew steadily wider; the circle of sympathies enlarged itself not at all, or with desperate slowness; and this consciousness of losing ground,—of failure to find a larger horizon of friendship beyond his intimacy;—the growing fear that, beyond this narrow range, no friends existed in the immense void of society,—or could exist, in the form of society which he lived in,—the suffocating sense of talking and singing in a vacuum that allowed no echo to return, grew more and more oppressive with each effort to overcome it. The experience is common among artists, and has often led to violent outbursts of egotism, of self-assertion, of vanity; but the New England temper distrusts itself as well as the world it lives in, and rarely yields to eccentricities of conduct. Emerson himself, protesting against every usual tendency of society, respected in practice all its standards.

"One is accustomed," continued Mrs. Wharton, "in enjoying the comradeship of young minds, to allow in them for a measure of passing egotism, often the more marked in proportion to their sensitiveness to impressions; but it was Cabot Lodge's special grace to possess the sensitiveness without the egotism. Always as free from pedantry as from conceit, he understood from the first the give and take of good talk, and was not only quick to see the other side of an argument, but ready to reinforce it by his sympathetic interpretation. And because of this responsiveness of mind, and of the liberating, vivifying nature from which it sprang, he must always, to his friends, remain first of all, and most incomparably, a Friend."

This quality was strongly felt by others. One who knew him intimately when he was Secretary of the British Embassy in Washington and later when they were together in Berlin, Sir Cecil Spring-Rice, now Minister of Great Britain in Stockholm, wrote of him after his death:

"The first time I saw him was at Nahant when the children were all there together; and since then I have always seemed to know him closely and intimately. We bathed together there, and I remember so well the immense joy he had in jumping into the water, and then lying out in the sun till he was all browned—as strong and healthy a human creature as I have ever seen, and exulting in his life. Then we rode together at Washington, and I can see him now galloping along in the woody country near Rock Creek. It didn't strike me then that he was anything but a strong healthy boy, absolutely straight, sincere, and natural.

"It wasn't till I saw a good deal of him in Berlin that I realized what a rare and extraordinary mind he had. He was then studying hard at philosophy. In an extraordinarily quick time he learnt German and seemed to take naturally to the most difficult books—just as he had done to the sea, without any conscious effort. We had many talks then, and his talk was most inspiring. He constantly lived face to face with immense problems, which he thought out thoroughly and earnestly,—things men often read and study in order to pass examinations or achieve distinction; but I am quite sure with him there was no object except just the attainment and the presence of truth. He had a most living mind, and a character absolutely independent; resolved on finding out things by himself, and living by his own lights and thinking out his own problems. Nothing would have stopped him or interfered with him. In all my experience of people about the world, I never knew anyone so 'detached,' deaf to the usual voices of the world; and so determined to live in the light of Truth, taking nothing for granted till he had proved it by his own original thought. He had greatly developed when I last saw him in Washington, during the few days I spent there. I had two long talks with him in his house. I think he was the sort of stuff that in the middle ages would have made a great saint or a great heresiarch—I dare say we have no use for such people now; I wonder if he found he was born out of his time, and that ours was not a world for him. I am not thinking of what he wrote or what he said, but of the atmosphere in which he lived, and the surroundings of his own soul—what his thoughts lived and moved in.

"In that detachment and independence and courage I have never known anyone like him. Yet it was hardly courage: for he didn't give the enemy a thought.

"I wonder if one often meets a man in these times who is literally capable of standing alone, to whom the noises and sights of the world, which to most people are everything, are nothing, absolutely nothing—the state of mind of someone who is madly in love, but with him it seemed normal and natural, an everyday habit of being.

"It was only last week I had a long think as I was walking about through these lonely woods here, and I was wondering whether I should see you all soon again, and I was saying to myself: At any rate Bay will have grown—he won't disappoint me: he is the sort of man who is bound to get bigger every day—and he is younger and stronger than I and he will last. And about how many men of his age could one say *that* with certainty, that time would surely improve and perfect him, and that with every new meeting one could gain something new?

"And that is how I thought of him naturally."

Like most of the clever young men of his time—Oscar Wilde, Bernard Shaw, Gilbert Chesterton—he loved a good paradox, and liked to chase it into its burrow. "When you are accustomed to anything, you are estranged from it"; and his supreme gift for liking was never to get accustomed to things or people. By way of a historical paradox he maintained that the Church was devised as a protection against the direct rays of Christ's spirit, which, undimmed, would compel to action and change of character. By way of a poetical paradox he loved Walt Whitman to fanaticism, and quoted, as his favorite description of the world, Walt's "little plentiful manikins skipping about in collars and tailcoats." Yet he sometimes declared that his favorite line in poetry was Swinburne's:

Out of the golden remote wild west where the sea without shore
 is,
Full of the sunset, and sad, if at all, with the fullness of joy.

Perhaps, too, if he had chosen a verse of poetry to suggest his own nature, after the description of Mrs. Wharton he might have found it in another line of Swinburne's:

Some dim derision of mysterious laughter.

However remote he thought himself from his world, he was, in fact, very much of his literary time,—and would not have been recognized at all by any other. Like most of his young contemporaries in literature, he loved his paradoxes chiefly because they served as arrows for him to practice his art on the social conventions which served for a target; and the essence of his natural simplemindedness showed itself in his love for this boy's-play of fresh life which he tired of only too soon, as he will himself tell in his *Noctambulist.* He knew, at bottom, that the world he complained of had as little faith in its conventions as he had; but, apart from the fun and easy practice of paradox, Lodge's most marked trait of mind lay in his instinctive love of logic, which he was probably not even aware of, although often—as is seen everywhere in the *Cain* and *Herakles*—the reasoning is as close and continuous as it might be in Plato or Schopenhauer.

This contrast of purposes disconcerted most readers. The usual reader finds the effort of following a single train of thought too severe for him; but even professional critics rebel against a paradox almost in the degree that it is logical, and find the Greek severity of Prometheus, in its motive, a worse fault than what they call the "excess of loveliness," which, in Shelley, "militates against the awful character of the drama." In modern society, the Greek drama is a paradox; which has not prevented most of the greatest nineteenth-century poets from putting their greatest poetry into that form; and Lodge loved it because of its rigorous logic even more than for its unequaled situations. Lodge could be exuberant enough when he pleased, but what he exacted from his readers was chiefly mind.

With this preamble, such readers as care for intellectual poetry can now take up his work of the years 1906 and 1907, published under the titles, *The Soul's Inheritance* and *Herakles. The Soul's Inheritance* appeared only after his death, but in the natural order of criticism it comes first. Although the vigor of his verse was greater, there were already signs that his physical strength was less, and that he was conscious of it. His health had begun to cause uneasiness; his heart warned him against strains; but he scorned warnings, and insisted that his health was never better. Submission to an obnoxious fact came hard to him, at all times; but the insidious weakness of literary workmen lies chiefly in their inability to realize that quiet work like theirs, which calls for no physical effort, may be a stimulant more exhausting than alcohol, and as morbid as morphine. The fascination of the silent midnight, the veiled lamp, the smoldering fire, the white paper asking to be covered with elusive words; the thoughts grouping themselves into architectural forms, and slowly rising into dreamy structures, constantly changing, shifting, beautifying their outlines,—this is the subtlest of solitary temptations, and the loftiest of the intoxications of genius.

VIII. Herakles

"The soul's inheritance" was a poem delivered before the Phi Beta Kappa Society at Cambridge in 1906, and in delivering it, Lodge discovered in himself a new power that would probably have led him in time into a new field, where he could put himself into closer relations with the world. His delivery was good, his voice admirable, and his power over his audience was evident. He was probably an orator by right of inheritance, though he had never cared to assert the claim, preferring to rest his distinction on his poetry.

In this poem he reiterated his life-long theme that the Soul, or Will, is the supreme energy of life:

> That here and now, no less for each of us,
> That inward voice, cogent as revelation,
> That trance of truth's sublime discovery,
> Which in the soul of Socrates wrought out
> Gold from the gross ore of humanity,
> Still speak, still hold, still work their alchemy;
> That here and now and in the soul's advance,
> And by the soul's perfection, we may feel
> The thought of Buddha in our mortal brain,
> The human heart of Jesus in our breast,
> And in our will the strength of Hercules!

Again, as always in his poetry, he recurred to the sense of struggle, of—

> The multitudinous menace of the night,

and the soul's need to stand out,—

> Importunate and undissuadable,

over the utmost verge of venture:

> There in our hearts the burning lamp of love,
> There in our sense the rhythm and amplitude,
> And startled splendor of the seas of song.

This last verse—the "startled splendor of the seas of song" —was one of the kind in which he delighted, and which he had a rare power of framing, but the thought was ever the same: the Soul of Man was the Soul of God; and it was repeated in various forms in the three sonnets attached to the blank verse:

> Strangely, inviolably aloof, alone,
> Once shall it hardly come to pass that we,
> As with his Cross, as up his Calvary,
> Burdened and blind, ascend and share his throne.

Again it was repeated in the poem called *Pilgrims,* delivered at the annual dinner of the New England Society, in New York, December 1906. The theme, on such an occasion and before such an audience, in the fumes of dinner and tobacco, was adventurous, but Lodge adhered to it bravely, and insisted all the more on its value,

> Lest we grow tired and tame and temperate.

He boldly asserted: "We *are* the Pilgrims," and proved it by attaching to the blank verse three sonnets, as beautiful as he ever wrote:

> They are gone. . . . They have all left us, one by one:
> Swiftly, with undissuadable strong tread,
> Cuirassed in song, with wisdom helmeted,
> They are gone before us, into the dark, alone. . . .
> Upward their wings rushed radiant to the sun;
> Seaward the ships of their emprise are sped;
> Onward their starlight of desire is shed;
> Their trumpet-call is forward;—they are gone!
> Let us take thought and go!—we know not why
> Nor whence nor where,—let us take wings and fly!
> Let us take ship and sail, take heart and dare!
> Let us deserve at last, as they have done,
> To say of all men living and dead who share
> The soul's supreme adventure,—*We* are gone!

These verses appeared in print only after his death, as though he had intended them for his epitaph; and perhaps he did, for he continued in the same tone:

> Let us go hence!—however dark the way,
> Haste!—lest we lose the clear, ambitious sense
> Of what is ours to gain and to gainsay.
> Let us go hence, lest dreadfully we die!

Two poems cast in the same form followed: *Life in Love* and *Love in Life;* which return to the intensely personal theme. Readers who feel the theme will probably feel the poetry as the highest he ever reached in feeling. Again the three sonnets follow, with their studied beauties of expression:

> Her voice is pure and grave as song;
>   Her lips are flushed as sunset skies;
>   The power, the myth, the mysteries
>   Of life and death in silence throng
> The secret of her silences;
>   Her face is sumptuous and strong,
>   And twilights far within prolong
>   The spacious glory of her eyes.

On these themes of Love and Life Lodge had dwelt without interruption from the start; and now, suddenly, without apparent steps of transition, he passed to a new motive,—Doubt! *The Noctambulist* suggests some change, physical or moral; some new influence or ripened growth, or fading youth. Perhaps he would himself have traced the influence and the change, to the death of Stickney. Mrs. Wharton says that "in its harmony of thought and form, it remains perhaps the completest product" of his art; and it is certainly the saddest. The note is struck in the first line:

> That night of tempest and tremendous gloom,

when,—

> Across the table, for—it seemed to us—
> An age of silence, in the dim-lit room,
> Tenantless of all humans save ourselves
> Yet seeming haunted, as old taverns are,
> With the spent mirth of unremembered men,
> He mused at us. . . . And then, "I know! . . . " he said,
> "I know! O Youth! . . . I too have seen the world
> At sunrise, candid as the candid dew;
>   . . . You look abroad,
> And see the new adventure wait for you,
> Splendid with wars and victories; for you

Trust the masked face of Destiny. But I!
I've turned the Cosmos inside out!" he said;
And on his lips the shadow of a smile
Looked hardly human. . . .

Some two hundred lines of unbroken disillusionment follow, which should not be torn to pieces to make easy quotations; but the passages that here and there suggest autobiography may serve as excuse for cutting up such a poem into fragments which now and then resemble the letters in their spontaneous outbursts.

Yes! and I feel anew the splendid zest
Of youth's brave service in truth's ancient cause,
When, with the self-same thunders that you use,
Edged with a wit—at no time Greek!—I too
Most pleasurably assailed and tumbled down,
With a fine sense of conquest and release,
The poor, one, old, enfeebled, cheerless God
Left to us of our much be-Deitied
And more be-Deviled past . . .
And all's well done I doubt not; though the times
Of life may well seem all too brief to waste!
But this comes later, when we learn,—as learn
We must, if we go forward still from strength
To strength incessantly,—to wage no more
With phantoms of the past fortunate wars;
To die no longer on the barricades
For the true faith; to spend no more the rich
And insufficient days and powers of life
Striving to shape the world and force the facts,
Tame the strong heart, and stultify the soul,
To fit some creed, some purpose, some design
Ingeniously contrived to spare the weak,
Protect the timid and delude the fools.—
The time must come
When we can deal in partialities
No more, if truth shall prosper; for we stand
Awfully face to face with just the whole
Secret,—our unrestricted Universe,
Spirit and sense! . . . And then, abruptly then
Swift as a passion, brutal as a blow,
The dark shuts down!

Whether he felt the dark already shutting down, brutal as a blow, or only divined it from the fate of Stickney, one need not know. The verses prove that he felt it personally, for he repeated it again and again:

> In the strict silence, while he spoke no more,
> We heard the tumult of our hearts, and feared
> Almost as men fear death, and know not why,
> We feared, . . . until at last, while at the closed
> Windows the wind cried like a frenzied soul,
> He said: "I too have tried, of mortal life,
> The daily brief excursions; . . .
>   and I have felt the one
> Utterly loosed and loving woman's heart,
> There where the twilight failed and night came on,
> Thrill to life's inmost secret on my breast;
> And I have known the whole of life and been
> The whole of man! The Night is best!"

The letters will show that the *Noctambulist* was meant as "a really new and large and valid departure," which, if followed in its natural direction, should have led to dramatic lyrics and problems more or less in the feeling of *Men and Women;* but, immediately, the *Noctambulist* abuts on *Herakles,* which properly closes the cycle. In the *Herakles,* the poet exhausted, once for all, the whole range of thought and expression with which his life had begun; it was an immense effort; and in approaching the analysis of this drama, which, in bulk, is nearly equal to all the rest of the poet's writings together, and in sustained stress stands beyond comparison with them, the critic or biographer is embarrassed, like the poet himself, by the very magnitude of the scheme.

Although no reader can be now safely supposed to know anything of the Greek drama, he must be assumed to have an acquaintance with Æschylus and Euripides at least. Something must be taken for granted, even though it be only the bare agreement that Shelley's *Prometheus Unbound* does not interfere with *Empedocles on Etna* and that neither of these Greek revivals jostles against *Atalanta in Calydon.*

Here are five or six of the greatest masterpieces of literature with which a reader must be supposed to be acquainted; and perhaps he would do well to keep in mind that, in bulk, Browning's *The Ring and the Book* is large enough to contain them all, and the *Herakles* too; while the methods and merits of all are as distinct and personal as the poets.

The reader, too, who takes up the *Herakles* for the first time, must be supposed to know that the plot of the drama is not of the poet's making: it is given,—imposed; and the dramatist has taken care to quote at the outset the words of the historian, Diodorus, whose story he meant to follow. Herakles and Creon and Megara are familiar characters in history as well as on the stage, and as real as historians can make them. Herakles did marry Megara, the daughter of Creon, King of Thebes; he did refuse to obey the orders of Eurystheus, King of Argos; he was actually—according to the historian—seized with frenzy, and pierced his children with arrows; he submitted to the will of God, performed his miracles, freed Prometheus, and became immortal. All this is fact, which the Greeks accepted, as they afterwards accepted the facts of the Christ's life and death, his miracles and immortality; and for the same reasons: for both were Saviors, Pathfinders, and Sacrifices.

Lodge took up this dramatic motive,—the greatest in human experience,—as it was given him; and so the reader must take it,—or leave it,—since he has nothing to do with the argument of the play once he has accepted it. His interest is in the dramatic development of the action and the philosophic development of the thought. As for the thought, something has already been said; but the reader must be assumed to know that it is the oldest thought that seems to have been known to the human mind, and, in the Christian religion, is the substantial fact which every Catholic sees realized before his eyes whenever he goes to mass. The God who sacrifices himself is one with the victim. The reader who does not already know this general law of religion which confounds all the different elements that enter into ordinary sacrifice, can know neither poetry nor religion. Christ carries the whole of humanity in his person. The identification of subject and object, of thought and matter, of will and universe, is a part of the alphabet of philosophy. The conception of a God sacrificing himself for a world of which he is himself a part, may be a mystery,—a confusion of ideas,—a contradiction of terms,—but it has been the most familiar and the highest expression of the highest—and perhaps also of the lowest—civilizations.

The reader's whole concern lies therefore not in the poem's motive but in its action,—the stages of its movement,—the skill and power with which the theme is developed,—the copiousness of the poet's resources,—the art and scope of his presentation. The critic can do no more than sketch an outline of the difficulties; he cannot attempt to discuss the solutions. Scholars seem inclined to think that Euripides himself failed in his treatment of this theme; that Æschylus scarcely rose quite to its level; and that Shelley used it chiefly as a field on which to embroider beauties wholly his own. Where three of the greatest poets that ever lived have found their highest powers taxed to the utmost, a critic can afford to keep silence.

The play opens at Thebes in the empty agora, at sunset, by a dialogue between the eternal poet and the eternal woman, who serve here in the place of the Greek chorus, each seeking, after the way of poet or woman, for something, —the light,—and so introducing the action, which begins abruptly by a feast in the palace of Creon, the king, who has called his people together to witness his abdication in favor of his son-in-law, Herakles.

Creon is a new creation in Lodge's poetry,—a deliberate effort at character-drawing till now unattempted. Creon is the man of the world, the administrator, the humorist and sage, who has accepted all the phases of life, and has reached the end, which he also accepts, whether as a fact or a phantasm,—whatever the world will,—but which has no more value to him than as being the end, neither comprehended nor comprehensible, but human. Perhaps it is only a coincidence that Æschylus vaguely suggested such a critic in

Okeanos, who appears early in the *Prometheus*. Creon speaks, "in an even, clear, quiet voice":

> I am your King; and I am old,—and wise.
>
> . . . .
>
> And I can now afford your censure! Yes,
> I can afford at last expensive things
> Which cost a man the kingdoms of the world,
> And all their glory! I have lived my life;
> —You cannot bribe me now by any threat
> Of ruin to my life's high edifice,
> Or any dazzled prospect of ambition. . . .
> I think despite these skeptical strange words,
> You will respect me,—for I am your King,
> And I have proved myself among you all
> An architect. Therefore you will not say,
> "This is the voice of failure!"—Yet I know
> That you will find some other things to say
> Not half so true! For, when a man is old,
> He knows at least how utterly himself
> Has failed! But say what things of me you will
> And be assured I sympathize! Indeed,
> A voice like mine is no-wise terrible,
> As might be the tremendous voice of truth
> Should it find speech that you could understand.
> Yet it may vex and dreadfully distress
> Reflective men,—if such indeed there be
> Among you all,—and therefore be assured,
> I sympathize!

With that, Creon names Herakles as his successor, and the crowd departs, leaving the family surrounding Herakles and congratulating him, until Herakles, breaking away, turns fiercely on the king with passionate reproaches for sacrificing him to selfish politics:

> Is this your wisdom, Sire? and is it wise,
> Lightly, and thus with calm complacency,
> Now to believe that I, that Herakles
> Should hold himself so cheaply as your price?

The unshaped, mystical consciousness of a destiny to become the Savior, not the Servant,—the creator, not the economist,—the source itself, not the conduit for "these safe human mediocrities,"—forces Herakles to reject the crown. He will be fettered by none of these ties to common, casual supremacies:

> Sire, I will not serve the Gods or you!
> Sire, I will not rule by grace of God
> Or by your grace! I will be Lord of none,
> And thus unto myself be Lord and Law!

Therewith the inexorable, tragic succession of sacrifices, insanities, begins. The dramatist follows up each step in the rising intensities of the theme, with almost as much care as though he were a professional alienist. He builds his climax from the ground,—that is to say, from the family, which is always the first sacrifice in these mystical ideals of the Savior. The first of the scenes is laid at night before the house of Herakles, who listens to Megara within, singing her children to sleep:

> My children sleep, whose lives fulfil
> The soul's tranquillity and trust;
> While clothed in life's immortal dust
> The patient earth lies dark and still.
>
> All night they lie against my breast
> And sleep, whose dream of life begins;
> Before the time of strife and sins,
> Of tears and truth, they take their rest.

The next scene is laid before a tavern door, at dawn, where Herakles, in his sleepless wandering, stops to listen to the men and women carousing within. The poet is heard singing:

> I know not what it is appears
> To us so worth the tragic task—
> I know beneath his ribald masque
> Man's sightless face is gray with tears!

This tavern scene, to readers who know their drama of sacrifice and redemption, "is gray with tears"; and the more because, true to tradition, it is the woman who first recognizes the Savior, and putting an end to his anguish of doubt and self-distrust, draws him on to his fated duty of self-immolation. The messenger from Eurystheus arrives, while Herakles is parting from his wife and children, bringing the order to submit to the King of Argos and the gods, to perform the imposed labors, and to remain a subject man; but the action of the drama is interrupted here by a discussion between Creon and the poet, of the drama itself,—the dilemma of Herakles,—a discussion which is, in a way, more dramatic than the drama because it broadens the interest to embrace humanity altogether. Like the chorus of Okeanids in Æschylus, Creon sees the hero, and admires him, but doubts what good will come of him to man. He lays down the law, as a King and a Judge must:

> Crowds are but numbers; and at last I see
> There are not merely players of the game;
> There is not, high or low, only the one
> Sensible and substantial prize, to which
> The fiat of the world gives currency,
> And which, in various ways, is always won!
> There is, besides, the one, estranged, rare man,
> Whose light of life is splendid in the soul,
> Burns with a kind of glory in his strength,
> And gives such special grandeur to ambition
> That he will make no terms with fortune. . . .

Creon's reply to this "estranged, rare man," is that "all men living are not ever free," and that, if not pliant, they are broken. In a dozen lines, as terse as those of Æschylus, he sums up the law of life:

> Life, like a candle in a starless night,
> Brightens and burns, or flutters and is spent,
> As man's wise weakness spares the guarded flame,
> Or man's rash strength resolves in all despite
> To lift his torch into the spacious winds,
> To blaze his path across the darknesses,
> And force the elements to his own undoing . . .
> Only the strong go forward—and are slain!

Only the strong, defenseless, dare—and die!
Only the strong, free, fain, and fearless—fail!
Remember this! lest a worse thing than mere
Passion and ecstasy of poems befall you!

"Listen to me," says Mercury to Prometheus, at the close of the same dispute in Æschylus; "When misfortune overwhelms you, do not accuse fate; do not upbraid Zeus for striking you an unfair blow! Accuse no one but yourself! You know what threatens you! No surprise! No artifice! Your own folly alone entangles you in these meshes of misery which never release their prey." Creon, as a wise judge, was bound to repeat this warning, and the Poet—in the poem—makes but an unconvincing answer to it,—in fact, loses his temper altogether, until both parties end, as usual, by becoming abusive, in spite of Creon's self-control.

The action of the play repeats the motive of the dialogue. Herakles is exasperated by the insolence of the messenger to the point of striking him, and threatening to destroy his master. Then, overwhelmed by the mortification of having yielded to a degraded human passion, and of having sunk to the level of the servitude against which he had rebelled, he sets out, in fury and despair, to challenge the oracle of the God at Delphi.

The scene in the temple of Apollo at Delphi follows, where Herakles drags the Pythia from her shrine, and finds himself suddenly saluted as the God.

THE PYTHIA

Yours is the resurrection and the life!

HERAKLES

I am the God!

THE PYTHIA

There is no God but I!
I am whatever is!
I am despair and hope and love and hate,
Freedom and fate,

Life's plangent cry, Death's stagnant silences!
I am the earth and sea and sky,
The race, the runner and the goal;—
There is no thought nor thing but I!

To the ecstasy of the Pythia, the chorus responds in the deepest tones of despair:

Have we not learned in bitterness to know
It matters nothing what we deem or do,
Whether we find the false or seek the true,
The profit of our lives is vain and small?
Have we not found, whatever price is paid,
Man is forever cheated and betrayed?
So shall the soul at last be cheated after all!

"Coward and weak and abject," is the rejoinder of Herakles, who rises at last to the full consciousness of his divine mission and of the price he must pay for it:

I am resolved! And I will stand apart,
Naked and perfect in my solitude
Aloft in the clear light perpetually,
Having afforded to the uttermost
The blood-stained, tear-drenched ransom of the soul!
Having by sacrifice, by sacrifice
Severed his bondage and redeemed the God!
The God I am indeed! For man is slain,
And in his death is God illustrious
And lives!

Then follows the Tenth Scene, the killing of the children. On this, the poet has naturally thrown his greatest effort, and his rank and standing as a dramatist must finally rest on it. The reader had best read it for himself; it is hardly suited to extracts or criticism; but perhaps, for his own convenience, he had better read first the same scene as Euripides rendered it. This is one of the rare moments of the dramatic art where more depends on the audience than on the poet, for the violence of the dramatic motive—the Sacrifice—carries the action to a climax beyond expression in words. The ordinary reader shrinks from it; the tension of the Greek drama over-strains him; he is shocked at the sight of an insane man killing his children with arrows, and refuses to forgive the dramatist for putting such a sight before him. Insanity has always been the most violent of tragic motives, and the insanity of Herakles surpassed all other insanities, as the Crucifixion of Christ surpassed all other crucifixions. Naturally, the person who objects to the Crucifixion as a *donnée* of the drama is quite right in staying away from Oberammergau; but if he goes to Oberammergau, he must at least try to understand what the drama means to the audience, which feels—or should feel—itself englobed and incarnated in it. The better-informed and the more accomplished the critic may be, who reads the *Herakles* for the first time, knowing nothing of the author, the more disconcerted he is likely to be in reading it a second time. His first doubts of the poet's knowledge or merits will be followed by doubts of his own.

In one respect at least, as a question of dramatic construction, the doubt is well founded. Critics object to the *Herakles* of Euripides that it consists of two separate dramas. The same objection applies to the myth itself. The Savior—whether Greek, or Christian, or Buddhist—always represents two distinct motives—the dramatic and the philosophic. The dramatic climax in the Christian version is reached in the Crucifixion; the philosophic climax, in the Resurrection and Ascension; but the same personal ties connect the whole action, and give it unity. This is not the case either with Herakles or Buddha. The climax of the Greek version is reached in the killing of the children, so far as the climax is dramatic; while the philosophic climax—the attainment—is proved by the freeing of Prometheus; and these two *données* are dramatically wide apart,—in fact, totally unconnected. Critics are Creons, and object to being tossed from one motive to another, with an impatient sense of wrong. As drama, one idea was capable of treatment; the other was not.

Probably the ordinary reader might find an advantage in reading the Twelfth Scene of *Herakles*,—the Prometheus,—as a separate poem. After the violent action of killing the children, the freeing of Prometheus seems cold and unconvincing; much less dramatic than the raising of Lazarus or even the Ascension. The Greek solution of this difficulty seems to be known only through fragments of the lost *Prometheus Unbound* of Æschylus, which are attached to most good editions of the poet. Lodge's solution is the necessary outcome of his philosophy, and is worth noting, if for no other reason, because it is personal to him,—or, more exactly, to his oriental and Schopenhauer idealism. Possibly—perhaps one might almost say probably—it is—both as logic and as history—the more correct solution; but on that point historians and metaphysicians are the proper sources of authority. Literature has no right to interfere, least of all to decide a question disputed since the origin of thought.

The *Prometheus Unbound*—the Twelfth Scene of *Herakles*—opens, then, upon the Attainment. Herakles has, by self-sacrifice, made himself—and the whole of humanity within him—one with the infinite Will which causes and maintains the universe. He has submitted to God by merging himself in God; he has, by his so-called labors, or miracles, raised humanity to the divine level. Æschylus puts in the mouth of Prometheus the claim to have freed man from the terrors of death and inspired him with blind hopes: "And a precious gift it is that you have given them," responds the chorus! Lodge puts the claim into the mouth of Herakles, and with it his own deification:

> Not in vain, out of the night of Hell,
> I drew the Hound of Hell, the ravening Death,
> Into the light of life, and held him forth
> Where the soul's Sun shed lightnings in his eyes,
> And he was like a thing of little meaning,
> Powerless and vain and nowise terrible.—
> While with my inmost heart I laughed aloud
> Into the blind and vacant face of Death,
> And cast him from me, so he fled away
> Screaming into the darkness whence he came!
> Nothing is vain of all that I have done!
> I have prevailed by labors, and subdued
> All that man is below his utmost truth,
> His inmost virtue, his essential strength,
> His soul's transcendent, one pre-eminence!

Yea, I have brought into the soul's dominion
All that I am!—and in the Master's House
There is no strength of all my mortal being
That does not serve him now; there is no aim,
There is no secret which He does not know;
There is no will save one, which is the Lord's!

The Church had said the same thing from the beginning; and the Greek, or oriental, or German philosophy changed the idea only in order to merge the universe in man instead of merging man in the universe. The Man attained, not by absorption of himself in the infinite, but by absorbing the infinite and finite together, in himself, as his own Thought,—his Will,—

Giving to phases of the senseless flux,
One after one, the soul's identity;

so that the philosophic climax of the *Prometheus Unbound* suddenly developed itself as a Prometheus bound in fetters only forged by himself; fetters of his own creation which never existed outside his own thought; and which fell from his limbs at once when he attained the force to will it. Prometheus is as much astonished at his own energy as though he were Creon, and, in a dazed and helpless way, asks what he is to do with it:

I stand in the beginning, stand and weep.
Here in the new, bleak light of liberty . . .
And who am I, and what is liberty?

The answer to this question is that liberty, in itself, is the end,—the sufficient purpose of the will. This simple abstract of the simple thought is the theme of the last speech of Herakles on the last page of the drama:

When the long life of all men's endless lives,
Its gradual pregnancies, its pangs and throes,
Its countless multitudes of perished Gods
And outworn forms and spent humanities—
When all the cosmic process of the past
Stands in the immediate compass of our minds;
When all is present to us, and all is known,

Even to the least, even to the uttermost,
Even to the first and last,—when, over all,
The widening circles of our thought expand
To infinite horizons everywhere,—
Then, tenoned in our foothold on the still,
Supernal, central pinnacle of being,
Shall we not look abroad and look within,
Over the total Universe, the vast,
Complex, and vital sum of force and form
And say in one, sufficient utterance,
The single, whole, transcendent Truth,—"I am!"

Not only philosophers, but also, and particularly, society itself, for many thousands of years, have waged bloody wars over these two solutions of the problem, as Prometheus and Herakles, Buddha and Christ, struggled with them in turn: but while neither solution has ever been universally accepted as convincing, that of Herakles has at least the advantage of being as old as the oldest, and as new as the newest philosophy,—as familiar as the drama of the Savior in all his innumerable forms,—as dramatic as it is familiar,—as poetic as it is dramatic,—and as simple as sacrifice. Paradox for paradox, the only alternative—Creon's human solution—is on the whole rather more paradoxical, and certainly less logical, than the superhuman solution of Herakles.

IX. The End

THIS is the whole story! What other efforts Lodge might have made, if he had lived into another phase of life, the effort he had made in this first phase was fatal and final. He rebelled against admitting it,—refused to see it,—yet was conscious that something hung over him which would have some tragic end. Possibly the encouragement of great literary success might have helped and stimulated the action of the heart, but he steeled himself against the illusion of success, and bore with apparent and outward indifference the total indifference of the public. As early as September 30, 1907, he wrote to Marjorie Nott: "I am, for one thing,—and to open a subject too vast to be even properly hinted at here—drawing to the close of the immense piece of work which has held and compelled me for a year past. The end looms large in my prospect and I am doing my best,—as you shall one day see. You, in fact, will be one of only a half-dozen, at best, who will see it. Which is, I imagine, all to my credit; and certainly as much as I reasonably want. What I have learned in the last year, through the work and the days, I shall never live to express; which is, I take it, illustrative—as so much else is—of the radical inferiority of writing your truth instead of being and living it,—namely, that by writing you can never, at all, keep abreast of it, but inevitably fall more and more behind as your pace betters. So I shall eventually perish having consciously failed, with (like Esmé) 'all my epigrams in me.' I wonder if Jesus consciously failed; I don't mean, of course, his total, obvious, practical failure, which the world for so long has so loudly recorded in blood and misery and ruin; I mean, did he have that consciousness of personal, solitary failure, which one can hardly, with one's utmost imagination, dissociate from the religious being of the soul of man? I believe he did,—though perhaps his mind was too simple and single,—as, to some extent, apparently, was the mind of Socrates. I sometimes think that the peasant of genius is, perhaps, more outside our comprehension than any other type of man. I perceive that I moon, vaguely moon,—and I shall soon be boring you."

In June 1908 he went abroad with his mother and father, for change and rest, but his letters show a growing sense of fatigue and effort. To his wife he wrote from the steamer, before landing in England:

"Our own voyage has come so warmly, so beautifully, back to me in these tranquil sea-days, our own so clear and fine and high adventure into strange new ways, our great adventure which is still in the making. It seems to me, that gay glad beginning, so alone and so one as we were, as something, now, inexpressibly candid and lovely, and humanly brave. And since then, how much, how really much of our young, our confident, and defiant boast,—flung, at that time, so happily, and so, after all, grandly, at large,—has been proved and greatened and amplified!"

From London, in July: "London has given me a new sense of itself, a flavor of romance and adventure, and the pervading sense of a great, dingy charm. Yes! it's all been quite new to me, and wonderfully pleasant; which just satisfactorily means, I surmise, that I come all new to it,—unimpeded by unimportant prejudices, and prepared vastly more than I was, for life in all its varieties and interests."

Later, from Paris: "I've lunched and dined everywhere; I've been to what theater there is, and chiefly I've drifted about the streets. And I find essentially that I seem to demand much more of life than I ever did, and in consequence take it all here with a less perfect gaiety and a more intense reflection. I feel matured to an incredible degree,—as if I did now quite know the whole of life; and when one's matured, really matured, there is, I imagine, not much ahead except work. So, back to you and to work I'm coming soon."

In August, again from Paris: "This whole Paris experience has been queer and wonderful. Joe and you have been with me in all the familiar streets and places, and my youth has appeared to me in colors richer and more comprehensible than ever before. . . ."

He came home, and brought out *Herakles* in November. In reply to a letter of congratulation from Marjorie Nott, he wrote to her, on December 17: "Thank you! You know that I write for myself, of course, and then, as things are in fact, just for you and so few others. Which is enough! and sees me, so to speak, admirably through. Well! I'm glad you like it, and if you ever have anything more to say of it, you know, my dear, that I want to hear it. You'll find it, of course, long; and you'll strike, I guess, sandy places. Perhaps, though, there are some secrets in it, and some liberties. . . ."

Six months afterwards he took up the theme again, in the last few days of his life, making Marjorie Nott his confidante, as he had done since childhood.

He wrote from Nahant July 31, 1909:

"Before all else I must thank you, my dear, for the grave and deep emotions roused within me by your letter with its fine, clear note of serious trust and loving favor towards me.

Than just that, there isn't for me anything better to be had. I derive from it precisely the intimate encouragement which one so perpetually wants and so exceptionally gets. Moreover, in all your letter I don't find a word with which I can possibly disagree. It occurs to me that there may have been, in my pages to you, some note of complaint, which, in sober truth, I didn't intend and don't feel. Every man of us has the Gods to complain of; every man of us, sooner or later, in some shape, experiences the tragedy of life. But that, too obviously, is nothing to cry about, for the tragedy of life is one thing, and my tragedy or yours, his or hers, is another. All of us must suffer in the general human fate, and some must suffer of private wrongs. I've none such to complain of. At all events, I don't, as I said before, disagree with a word of your letter, but I do, my dear, find it dreadfully vague. You surely can't doubt that I deeply realize the value of human communion of any sort; but that doesn't take me far toward getting it. As I understand your letter it says to me: 'Well! you might get more and better if you tried more and better!' Perhaps! at any rate, goodness knows I do try—and more and more—as best I can. And surely I don't complain of the solitude, which has, of course, its high value; but I do, inevitably, well know it's there. I'll spare you more."

His letters to Langdon Mitchell expressed the same ideas, with such slight difference of form as one naturally uses in writing to a man rather than to a woman:

TO LANGDON MITCHELL

WASHINGTON (*Spring, 1906*)

Thank you, my dear Langdon, for your kind and so welcome letters. I want to thank you for your generous offer of help should I try my hand at a play. . . .

I should have but one personal advantage in writing a play, namely a genuine indifference as to its being played or being successful if played. I call this an advantage because it eliminates the possibility of my mind being disturbed and my powers consequently impaired by any influences external to myself. I become so increasingly convinced that precisely as perfection of being consists in a perfectly transparent reality, so artistic perfection depends upon the degree to which the artist speaks his own words in his own voice and is unhampered by the vocabulary of convention and the megaphone of oratory—which exists and could exist only on the theory of an omnipresent multitude. Let any man speak his own word and he is as original as Shakespeare and as permanently interesting as Plato. The whole core of the struggle, for ourselves and for art, is to emerge from the envelope of thoughts and words and deeds which are not our own, but the laws and conventions and traditions formed of a kind of composite of other men's ideas and emotions and prejudices. Excuse this dissertation! . . .

Your first letter interested me profoundly, for my winter has been curiously similar to yours as you describe it. I have had very poignantly the same sense of growth, of a revelation and of a consequent observable process of maturity. When shall we meet and make some exchange of thoughts? It seems absurd that so great a majority of my life should be spent without you.

I've been asked (peals of Homeric and scornful laughter from Mitchell) to deliver the poem at the Phi Beta Kappa in Cambridge this spring—June. (Mitchell chokes with mirth and shows symptoms of strangulation. Is patted on the back and recovers. Lodge then good-naturedly continues:) You observe how low I've sunk and for a punishment for your superior sneers I'm going to send you my poem for the occasion to read and criticize. (Mitchell sourly admits that the joke is not entirely on Lodge.) I shall send it soon, in fact it may arrive any day. So I hope that your condition of health is improved.

WASHINGTON, 2346 MASSACHUSETTS AVE.
(*Winter, 1908*)

MY DEAR, DEAR LANGDON,—I shall never have words and ways enough to thank you for your letter. What it meant, what it means to me—the encouragement, the life, the hope—and above all the high felicities of friendship—all these things and other and more things, which you, my dear friend, of your abundance so liberally afford, have enriched and fortified me beyond expression. . . .

My *Herakles* is done to the last three scenes and hastens somewhat to its end. I won't write you about it, for there is too much to say and finally you'll have to read it—however much it's long and dull.

It's too, too bad you should have been having such a devil's time with this world. But, good heavens, I know what it is to wait; how intolerable it may become sometimes just holding on. But the muscles of patience and that true daily courage which patience implies are fine muscles to have well developed even at some cost—isn't this so, dear man? The living bread and the consecrated wine must be earned and eaten day by day and day by day; we are not made free of perfection by any sudden moment's violence of virtue; the key of the gate of Paradise is not purchased in any single payment, however heavy; the travail of God's nativity within us is gradual and slow and laborious. It is the sustained courage, the long stern patience, the intensest daily labor, the clear, perpetual vigilance of thought, the great resolve, tranquil and faithful in its strength,—it is these things, it is the work, in short, the wonderful slow work of man about the soul's business, which accomplishes constantly—as we both know so well—some real thing which makes us, however gradually, other and nobler and greater than we are, because precisely it makes us more than we are. All of which you know better than I, for better than I you do the work and reap the result. But it's a truth nonetheless which takes time to learn—if it is ever learned at all—for the temptation to think that the reward, the advance is tomorrow, and that Paradise is in the next county, and that both can be got by some adventurous extravagance, some single, tense deed of excellence, is very great, I imagine, to us all. We never realize quite at once that only patience can see us through, and that if the moment is not eternity and the place not Paradise it must be just because we are busy about what is not, in the true strict test, our real concern.

WASHINGTON, 2346 MASSACHUSETTS AVE.
(*Spring, 1908*)

O! MY DEAR LANGDON,—Your letter thrilled and moved me beyond expression. If I do not thank you for it, it is because it has roused within me emotions nobler and more profound than gratitude; and it is in the glamor and power of these emotions—which will remain permanently interfused with all that I am—that I now write to you. I tried to read your letter aloud to B. but it moved me so much and to such depths that I was unable to continue. This may seem strange to you, for you will not have thought of all that it means to me; you will not have been aware of the bare fact that, apart from the immense inward satisfaction which the effort of expression must always bring, your letter is just all of real value I shall get for *Herakles*. And it is more, my dear friend, far more than enough! That is certain. I speak to you with an open heart and mind, which your letter has liberated, restored, revived, nourished and sustained. You know as well as I how passionately we have understanding and sympathy for what is best and noblest within us. The conception of God the Father, I believe, came from this longing in the human heart. But the habit of solitude and silence, which in this queer country, we perforce assume, ends by making us less attentive to the heart's need, and it is only when we are fed that we realize how consuming was our hunger. For all that is not what we at best and most truly are, we find recognition enough, but the very soul within us is like a solitary stranger in a strange land—and your letter was to me like a friendly voice speaking the words of my own tongue and like the lights of welcome. It is perhaps your criticisms that I rejoice in most, for I know them to be valid and just. I feel the faults you find as you feel them, I believe; and I keep alive the hope that I may learn to feel them with sufficient force and clearness to correct them. It would be of infinite advantage to me if you would, someday, go over the whole thing with me in detail. Nothing could so much improve my chances of better work in the future. In fact it would be to me the most essential assistance that I could possibly receive; for if I had you there to put your finger on the dreadful Saharas and other undeniable shortcomings, it would illuminate my understanding as nothing else could do. . . .

Just one thing more. It was a noble act of friendship for you to write me that letter amid all the labors of your present days. Thanks for that with all my heart.

With this single condition, the happy life went on, filled with affection and humor to the end, as his last letters tell:

TO HIS MOTHER

NAHANT, *June 13, 1909*

Our train was seven hours late to Boston, which fact, when in the East River, after four hours of open sea, at 6:30 A.M., and by the dull glare of the hot sun through a white fog, it first gradually and at last with agonizing completeness possessed my mind, produced in that sensitive organ emotions too vivid to be here described.

I had retired to rest reconciled, or at least steeled, to the thought of a two hours' delay in our journey; and when, on waking (abysmal moment!) in the squalor of my berth I found that the fog had changed the two hours' delay to seven, I felt in the first shock other emotions besides surprise. . . . Before emerging in unwashed squalor from my section, I had determined, however, in view of everything, to suppress my feelings and to be, for my poor good children and their nurses, just the requisite hope, cheer, and comfort—and this determination (it was the one consoling event of the dreadful day) I did, to the end, successfully carry out. Well, when at last from that dreadful boat we were jerkily drawn once more onto firm land, we fell of course inevitably into the mean hands of the N. Y., N. H., and H. R. R., which characteristically decided that it would, of course, be both cheaper and easier, to give us, instead of the dining car to which—Heaven knows—we seemed entitled, a "fifteen minutes for refreshments" at New Haven; and there, at ten o'clock, in the heartbreaking, dingy dreadfulness of the waiting-room, we—that is the passengers of that luckless train—thronged four deep round a vastly rectangular barrier like a shop-counter, girdled, for the public, by high, greasy, "fixed" stools, covered with inedible pseudo-foods under fly-blown glass bells, and defended, so to speak, by an insufficient and driven horde of waiters and waitresses. You can imagine what chance there was *dans cette galère* for the babes! Fräulein and the nurse secured, by prodigious exertions, and wonderfully drank, cups of a dim gray fluid which they believed to be coffee, while I and the children got back to the train with some apples, oranges, and sinister sandwiches, which all, later, and with every accompanying degradation of drip and slop and grease, all mixed with car dirt, we did devour,—to avoid starvation. I was still further, however, to be in a position to appreciate the exquisite benefits of a railroad monopoly, for when at last our interminable journey did end at Boston, we found, of course, no porters! And with a heavy microscope, book, coat, and cane, my three poor unceasingly good, weary, and toy-laden children, and my two weary and child-laden nurses, were, perforce, obliged to leave our four bags on the platform, in charge of the well-feed train porter, to be immediately "called for" by Moore's man. Which man, young Moore himself, I duly found and straitly charged about the four bags, as well as about my seven pieces in the "van." Then, somewhat cheered, and having renewed to Moore (who, as you will presently perceive, I have come to regard as an abysmal though quite well-intentioned young ass) my charge as to the four bags, I drove off to the North Station, stopping *en route* merely to reward my lambs for their exemplary conduct by a rubber toy apiece. Well! at that point I think you will agree with me that the wariest might have been lulled into a sense that the worst was over and plain sailing ahead. Such at least was my condition of confidence, and though in the North Station waiting-room our bedraggled, dirty, wornout company waited a full hour for Moore and the trunks, I just put it down as evidence that the benefits of the railroad we had just left were still accumulating, and hoped on. And then Moore arrived—arrived, having just merely forgotten the four bags—having in short left them—one of them containing Uncle Henry's manuscript and all of mine, both irreplaceable—just there on the platform where I couldn't have not left them. Well! for a moment I didn't "keep up" a bit and addressed to Moore a few—how inadequate!—"feeling words." I then dispatched him back to recover the bags, packed my poor babes into the 3:20 for Lynn,—trusting, as I had to, to Fräulein's ability to get them out at Lynn,—and remained myself at the North Station, where I waited for Moore for exactly one hour and fifteen minutes. My state of mind I won't describe. At the end of that vigil, however, I mounted—always with microscope, book, coat, and cane—in a taxicab, went to the South Station, found Moore, and after an interval of almost panic, when I thought all the manuscripts were lost for good, did, by dint of energy at last—thank Heaven—find the bags. . . . Well! I felt then a little "gone" and went therefore to the Club, had a drink and a sandwich, just in time, and got, at last, to Nahant, at about seven o'clock, to find that, by some mistake, they had given me, for the nurse's bag, the bag of a total stranger. In the nurse's bag was, beside her own effects, some of Helena's, including a silver mug; and so as I lay, at last, in my bath, I heard, strangely concordant with my whole horrible day's experience, Fräulein and Hedwig mourning, in shrill German, the loss. So Monday I go to town to do some errands and to find if possible the damned bag. The children are none the worse for the journey and are already benefited by the good air. The house is incredibly clean and charming and we are delighted with it.

TUCKANUCK, *July 1909*

I am having the most beautiful days—endless air and sea and sun and beauty, and best of all with Langdon's splendid companionship. It's all just what I've wanted and needed for so long. I have shown Langdon my latest work,—*The Noctambulist,* etc.,—what I read to you in Washington,—and he is most splendidly encouraging. He feels as strongly as I could wish that I have made, both in thought and form, a really new and large and valid departure. Which endlessly cheers me, as you will believe. We talk together of everything first and last, off and on, but chiefly on, all day and night with the exception of many hours of sleep. I do no work and just take easily all my present blessings as greedily as I can.

Langdon Mitchell was one of the half-dozen readers, as he said, for whose approbation he wrote, and this last companionship with him at Tuckanuck in July gave Lodge keen pleasure. On returning to Nahant he wrote to Sturgis Bigelow, who was then ill in Paris:

"I've just returned home from Tuckanuck, browned to the most beautiful color by ten glorious days of sun. Langdon and I went together, and except for one day of warm, sweet rain, and one morning of fog,—which cleared splendidly in time for the bath,—we had weather of uninterrupted magnificence. Immeasurable sky and sea and sun, warm water, hot clean sand, clear light, transparent air,—Tuckanuck at its perfect best. I've returned made over in mind and body, feeling better in every way than I've felt since I can remember. For this I have to thank you, for Tuckanuck,—and Langdon for his wonderful, interesting, vital companionship. Together—with every variety of the best talk, the finest communion—we lived all day and night long immersed in the beneficent elements, the prodigious light and air, the sounding, sparkling, flowing sea; and the bathing was different and better every day. The sea showed us all its loveliest moods. On one day it was stretched and smooth to the horizon, drawn away from the shore, on a light north wind, in endless fine blue wrinkles, with just the merest crisp, small ripple on the beach. Another day, fresh southwest wind, with a fine, high, lively, light surf. And even on one day the biggest waves of the season—too big for comfort. Well! it was all glorious;—you will understand; we have had it just like that so often together. Indeed your presence was the one thing we longed for, and didn't have, throughout our whole visit. There was hardly an hour down there when I didn't think of you and long for you. . . . Never had I more needed the restorative magic of nature and companionship than when I set forth for that blessed island, and never did it more wonderfully work upon me its beneficent spell. To judge by the way I feel now, I haven't known what it was to be really rested and well since I finished *Herakles*. I feel pages more of enthusiasm at the end of my pen, but I will spare you. I took down to the island with me my winter's work, which has taken the shape of a volume of poems ready for publication, and read it to Langdon, who, thank goodness, felt high praise for them—more enthusiastic approval, indeed, than I had dared to hope for."

Langdon Mitchell's encouragement and sympathy were pathetically grateful to him, so rare was the voice of an impartial and competent judge. He wrote to his wife in the warmest appreciation of it.

"I have been having such good days! Langdon is of course the utmost delight to me, and the presence of companionship day by day is fresh and wonderful to me beyond measure. Also the weather in general has been glorious, and the whole spectacle of the world clothed in light and beauty. I lead a sane and hygienic life. We go to bed before twelve, and sleep all we can. We breakfast, read, write perhaps an occasional letter, talk for long, fine, clear stretches of thought, and, regardless of time, play silly but active games on the grass, swim, bask in the sun, sail, and talk, and read aloud, and read to ourselves, and talk, and talk. . . . I'm getting into splendid condition."

When his father, fagged by the long fatigues of the tariff session, returned North, they went back to Tuckanuck together in August, and there he had the pleasure of a visit from a new and enthusiastic admirer, Mr. Alfred Brown, lecturer and critic, who brought him for the first time a sense of possible appreciation beyond his personal friends.

He never alluded to his own symptoms. Even his father, though on the watch, noticed only that he spared himself, and took more frequent rests. To Sturgis Bigelow he wrote of his anxiety about both Bigelow and his father, whom, he said, he was helping to "get his much-needed rest and recuperation, and I think he is getting them, both, good and plenty, but the knowledge that you will probably not get here this season makes the dear island seem singularly deserted. . . . It's all doing him good, and what is more, he thinks it is. . . . I read a good deal, and take my swim, and an occasional sail. Also, after a month's vacation during which I haven't written a line, I've now begun again, and write and meditate for four or five hours every day . . . so that life flows evenly and quietly and cheerfully. Still, lacking the stimulus of your prospective arrival, I shan't be sorry to get back to my Pussy and my babes."

This seems to have been one of the last letters he wrote. It was mailed at Nantucket, August 18, and on the nineteenth he was seized at night by violent indigestion, probably due to some ptomaine poison. The next day he was better. The distress returned on the night of the twentieth. Twenty-four hours of suffering ensued; then the heart suddenly failed and the end came.

THESE PAPERS on Henry James by T. S. Eliot appeared in *The Little Review* of August 1918, and have never been reprinted by Mr. Eliot. The whole number was devoted to James, who had died in 1916.

At this time it still seemed natural for some of the most gifted of American writers to prefer to live in Europe, and Henry James, who had been there since the eighties, was of special interest to them. Ezra Pound—who also contributed to this number of *The Little Review*—had gone abroad in 1908 and remained; and T. S. Eliot went in 1914 and eventually became a British citizen.

T. S. ELIOT

HENRY JAMES

I. In Memory

HENRY JAMES has been dead for some time. The current of English literature was not appreciably altered by his work during his lifetime; and James will probably continue to be regarded as the extraordinarily clever but negligible curiosity. The current hardly matters; it hardly matters that very few people will read James. The "influence" of James hardly matters: to be influenced by a writer is to have a chance inspiration from him; or to take what one wants; or to see things one has overlooked; there will always be a few intelligent people to understand James, and to be understood by a few intelligent people is all the influence a man requires. What matters least of all is his place in such a Lord Mayor's show as Mr. Chesterton's procession of Victorian Literature. The point to be made is that James has an importance which has nothing to do with what came before him or what may happen after him; an importance which has been overlooked on both sides of the Atlantic.

I do not suppose that anyone who is not an American can *properly* appreciate James. James's best American figures in the novels, in spite of their trim, definite outlines, the economy of strokes, have a fullness of existence and an external ramification of relationship which a European reader might not easily suspect. The Bellegarde family, for instance, are merely good outline sketches by an intelligent foreigner; when more is expected of them, in the latter part of the story, they jerk themselves into only melodramatic violence. In all appearance Tom Tristram is an even slighter sketch. Europeans can recognize him; they have seen him, known him, have even penetrated the Occidental Club; but no European has the Tom Tristram element in his composition, has anything of Tristram from his first visit to the Louvre to his final remark that Paris is the only place where a white man can live. It is the final perfection, the consummation of an American to become, not an Englishman, but a European—something which no born European, no person of any European nationality, can become. Tom is one of the failures, one of nature's misfortunes, in this process. Even General Packard, C. P. Hatch, and Miss Kitty Upjohn have a reality which Claire de Cintré misses. Noémie, of course, is perfect, but Noémie is a result of the intelligent eye; her existence is a triumph of the intelligence, and it does not extend beyond the frame of the picture.

For the English reader, much of James's criticism of America must merely be something taken for granted. English readers can appreciate it for what it has in common with criticism everywhere, with Flaubert in France and Turgenev in Russia. Still, it should have for the English an importance beyond the work of these writers. There is no English equivalent for James, and at least he writes in this language. As a critic, no novelist in our language can approach James; there is not even any large part of the reading public which knows what the word "critic" means. (The usual definition of a critic is a writer who cannot "create"—perhaps a reviewer of books.) James was emphatically not a successful *literary* critic. His criticism of books and writers is feeble. In writing of a novelist, he occasionally produces a valuable sentence out of his own experience rather than in judgment of the subject. The rest is charming talk, or gentle commendation. Even in handling men whom he could, one supposes, have carved joint from joint—Emerson, or Norton—his touch is uncertain;

there is a desire to be generous, a political motive, an admission (in dealing with American writers) that under the circumstances this was the best possible, or that it has fine qualities. His father was here keener than he. Henry was not a literary critic.

He was a critic who preyed not upon ideas, but upon living beings. It is criticism which is in a very high sense creative. The characters, the best of them, are each a distinct success of creation: Daisy Miller's small brother is one of these. Done in a clean, flat drawing, each is extracted out of a reality of its own, substantial enough; everything given is true for that individual; but what is given is chosen with great art for its place in a general scheme. The general scheme is not one character, nor a group of characters in a plot or merely in a crowd. The focus is a situation, a relation, an atmosphere, to which the characters pay tribute, but being allowed to give only what the writer wants. The real hero, in any of James's stories, is a social entity of which men and women are constituents. It is, in *The Europeans,* that particular conjunction of people at the Wentworth house, a situation in which several memorable scenes are merely timeless parts, only occurring necessarily in succession. In this aspect, you can say that James is dramatic; as what Pinero and Mr. Jones used to do for a large public, James does for the intelligent. It is in the chemistry of these subtle substances, these curious precipitates and explosive gases which are suddenly formed by the contact of mind with mind, that James is unequaled. Compared with James's, other novelists' characters seem to be only accidentally in the same book. Naturally, there is something terrible, as disconcerting as a quicksand, in this discovery, though it only becomes absolutely dominant in such stories as *The Turn of the Screw.* It is partly foretold in Hawthorne, but James carried it much farther. And it makes the reader, as well as the personae, uneasily the victim of a merciless clairvoyance.

James's critical genius comes out most tellingly in his mastery over, his baffling escape from, Ideas; a mastery and an escape which are perhaps the last test of a superior intelligence. He had a mind so fine that no idea could violate it.

Englishmen, with their uncritical admiration (in the present age) for France, like to refer to France as the Home of Ideas; a phrase which, if we could twist it into truth, or at least a compliment, ought to mean that in France ideas are very severely looked after; not allowed to stray, but preserved for the inspection of civic pride in a Jardin des Plantes, and frugally dispatched on occasions of public necessity. England, on the other hand, if it is not the Home of Ideas, has at least become infested with them in about the space of time within which Australia has been overrun by rabbits. In England ideas run wild and pasture on the emotions; instead of thinking with our feelings (a very different thing) we corrupt our feelings with ideas; we produce the political, the emotional idea, evading sensation and thought. George Meredith (the disciple of Carlyle) was fertile in ideas; his epigrams are a facile substitute for observation and inference. Mr. Chesterton's brain swarms with ideas; I see no evidence that it thinks. James in his novels is like the best French critics in maintaining a point of view, a viewpoint untouched by the parasite idea. He is the most intelligent man of his generation.

The fact of being everywhere a foreigner was probably an assistance to his native wit. Since Byron and Landor, no Englishman appears to have profited much from living abroad. We have had Birmingham seen from Chelsea, but not Chelsea seen (really *seen*) from Baden or Rome. There are advantages, indeed, in coming from a large flat country which no one wants to visit: advantages which both Turgenev and James enjoyed. These advantages have not won them recognition. Europeans have preferred to take their notion of the Russian from Dostoevsky and their notion of the American from, let us say, Frank Norris if not O. Henry. Thus, they fail to note that there are many kinds of their fellow-countrymen, and that most of these kinds, similarly to the kinds of *their* fellow-countrymen, are stupid; likewise with Americans. Americans also have encouraged this fiction of a general type, a formula or idea, usually the predaceous square-jawed or thin-lipped. They like to be told that they are a race of commercial buccaneers. It gives them something easily escaped from, moreover, when they wish to reject America. Thus the novels of Frank Norris have succeeded in both countries; though it is curious that the most valuable part of *The Pit* is its satire (quite unconscious, I believe; Norris was simply representing faithfully the life he knew) of Chicago society after business hours. All this show of commercialism which Americans like to present to the foreign eye James quietly waves aside; and in pouncing upon his fellow-countryman after the stock exchange has closed, in tracking down his vices and absurdities across the Atlantic, and exposing them in their highest flights of dignity or culture, James may be guilty of what will seem to most Americans scandalously improper behavior. It is too much to expect them to be grateful. And the British public, had it been more aware, would hardly have been more comfortable confronted with a smile which was so far from breaking into the British laugh. Henry James's death, if it had been more taken note of, should have given considerable relief "on both sides of the Atlantic," and cemented the Anglo-American Entente.

II. The Hawthorne Aspect

My object is not to discuss critically even one phase or period of James, but merely to provide a note, *Beitrage,* toward any attempt to determine his antecedents, affinities, and "place." Presumed that James's relation to Balzac, to Turgenev, to anyone else on the continent is known and measured—I refer to Mr. Hueffer's book and to Mr. Pound's article—and presumed that his relation to the Victorian novel is negligible, it is not concluded that James was simply a clever young man who came to Europe and improved himself, but that the soil of his origin contributed a flavor discriminable after transplantation in his latest fruit. We may even draw the instructive conclusion that this flavor was precisely improved and given its chance, not worked off, by transplantation. If there is this strong native taste, there will probably be some relation to Hawthorne; and if there is any relation to Hawthorne, it will probably help us to analyze the flavor of which I speak.

When we say that James is "American," we must mean that this "flavor" of his, and also more exactly definable qualities, are more or less diffused throughout the vast continent rather than anywhere else; but we cannot mean that this flavor and these qualities have found literary expression throughout the nation, or that they permeate the work of Mr. Frank Norris or Mr. Booth Tarkington. The point is that James is positively a continuator of the New England genius; that there is a New England genius, which has discovered itself only in a very small number of people in the middle of the nineteenth century—and which is *not* significantly present in the writings of Miss Sara Orne Jewett, Miss Eliza White, or the Bard of Appledore, whose name I forget. I mean whatever we associate with certain purlieus of Boston, with Concord, Salem, and Cambridge, Mass.: notably Emerson, Thoreau, Hawthorne, and Lowell. None of these men, with the exception of Hawthorne, is individually very important; they all can, and perhaps ought to be made to look very foolish; but there is a "something" there, a dignity, about Emerson, for example, which persists after we have perceived the taint of commonness about some English contemporary, as, for instance, the more intelligent, better-educated, more alert Matthew Arnold. Omitting such men as Bryant and Whittier as absolutely plebeian, we can still perceive this halo of dignity around the men I have named, and also Longfellow, Margaret Fuller and her crew, Bancroft and Motley, the faces of (later) Norton and Child pleasantly shaded by the Harvard elms. One distinguishing mark of this distinguished world was very certainly leisure; and importantly not in all cases a leisure given by money, but insisted upon. There seems no easy reason why Emerson or Thoreau or Hawthorne should have been men of leisure; it seems odd that the New England conscience should have allowed them leisure; yet they *would* have it, sooner or later. That is really one of the finest things about them, and sets a bold frontier between them and a world which will at any price avoid leisure, a world in which Theodore Roosevelt is a patron of the arts. An interesting document of this latter world is the *Letters* of a nimbly dull poet of a younger generation, of Henry James's generation, Richard Watson Gilder, Civil Service Reform, Tenement House Commission, Municipal Politics.

Of course leisure in a metropolis, with a civilized society (the society of Boston was and is quite uncivilized but refined beyond the point of civilization), with exchange of ideas and critical standards, would have been better; but these men could not provide the metropolis, and were right in taking the leisure under possible conditions.

Precisely this leisure, this dignity, this literary aristocracy, this unique character of a society in which the men of letters were also of the best people, clings to Henry James. It is some consciousness of this kinship which makes him so tender and gentle in his appreciations of Emerson, Norton, and the beloved Ambassador. With Hawthorne, as much the most important of these people in any question of literary art, his relation is more personal; but no more in the case of Hawthorne than with any of the other figures of the background is there any consideration of influence. James owes little, very little, to anyone; there are certain writers whom he consciously studied, of whom Hawthorne was not one; but in any case his relation to Hawthorne is on another plane from his relation to Balzac, for example. The influence of Balzac, not on the whole a good influence, is perfectly evident in some of the earlier novels; the influence of Turgenev is vaguer, but more useful. That James was, at a certain period, more moved by Balzac, that he followed him with more concentrated admiration, is clear from the tone of his criticism of that writer compared with the tone of his criticism of either Turgenev or Hawthorne. In *French Poets and Novelists,* though an early work, James's attitude toward Balzac is exactly that of having been very much attracted from his orbit, perhaps very wholesomely stimulated at an age when almost any foreign stimulus may be good, and having afterwards reacted from Balzac, though not to the point of injustice. He handles Balzac shrewdly and fairly. From the essay on Turgenev there is on the other hand very little to be got but a touching sense of appreciation; from the essay on Flaubert even less. The charming study of Hawthorne is quite different from any of these. The first conspicuous quality in it is tenderness, the tenderness of a man who had escaped too early from an environment to be warped or thwarted by it, who had escaped so effectually that he could afford the gift of affection. At the same time he places his finger, now and then, very gently, on some of Hawthorne's more serious defects as well as his limitations.

"The best things come, as a general thing, from the talents that are members of a group; every man works better when he has companions working in the same line, and yielding the stimulus of suggestion, comparison, emulation." Though when he says that "there was manifestly a strain of generous indolence in his [Hawthorne's] composition" he is understating the fault of laziness for which Hawthorne can chiefly be blamed. But gentleness is needed in criticizing Hawthorne, a necessary thing to remember about whom is precisely the difficult fact that the soil which produced him with his essential flavor is the soil which produced, just as inevitably, the environment which stunted him.

In one thing alone Hawthorne is more solid than James: he had a very acute historical sense. His erudition in the small field of American colonial history was extensive, and he made most fortunate use of it. Both men had that sense of the past which is peculiarly American, but in Hawthorne this sense exercised itself in a grip on the past itself; in James it is a sense of the sense. This, however, need not be dwelt upon here. The really vital thing, in finding any personal kinship between Hawthorne and James, is what James touches lightly when he says that "the fine thing in Hawthorne is that he cared for the deeper psychology, and that, in his way, he tried to become familiar with it." There are other points of resemblance, not directly included under this, but this one is of the first importance. It is, in fact, almost enough to ally the two novelists, in comparison with whom almost all others may be accused of either superficiality or aridity. I am not saying that this "deeper psychology" is essential, or that it can always be had without loss of other qualities, or that a novel need be any the less a work of art without it. It is a definition; and it separates the two novelists at once from the English contemporaries of either. Neither Dickens nor Thackeray, certainly, had the smallest notion of the "deeper psychology"; George Eliot had a kind of heavy intellect for it (Tito) but all her genuine feeling went into the visual realism of *Amos Barton.* On the continent it is known; but the method of Stendhal or of Flaubert is quite other. A situation is for Stendhal something deliberately constructed, often an illustration. There is a bleakness about it, vitalized by force rather than feeling, and its presentation is definitely visual. Hawthorne and James have a kind of sense, a receptive medium, which is not of sight. Not that they fail to make you *see,* so far as necessary, but sight is not the essential sense. They perceive by antennae; and the "deeper psychology" is here. The deeper psychology indeed led Hawthorne to some of his absurdest and most characteristic excesses; it was forever tailing off into the fanciful, even the allegorical, which is a lazy substitute for profundity. The fancifulness is the "strain of generous indolence," the attempt to get the artistic effect by meretricious means. On this side a critic might seize hold of *The Turn of the Screw,* a tale about which I have many doubts; but the actual working out of this is different from Hawthorne's, and we are not interested in approximation of the two men on the side of their weakness. The point is that Hawthorne was acutely sensitive to the situation; that he did grasp character through the relation of two or more persons to each other; and this is what no one else, except James, has done. Furthermore, he does establish, as James establishes, a solid atmosphere, and he does, in his quaint way, get New England, as James gets a larger part of America, and as none of their respective contemporaries get anything above a village or two, or a jungle. Compare, with anything that any English contemporary could do, the situation which Hawthorne sets up in the relation of Dimmesdale and Chillingworth. Judge Pyncheon and Clifford, Hepzibah and Phoebe, are similarly achieved by their relation to each other; Clifford, for one, being simply the intersection of a relation to three other characters. The only dimension in which Hawthorne could expand was the past, his present being so narrowly barren. It is a great pity, with his remarkable gift of observation, that the present did not offer him more to observe. But he is the one English-writing predecessor of James whose characters are *aware* of each other, the one whose novels were in any deep sense a criticism of even a slight civilization; and here is something more definite and closer than any derivation we can trace from Richardson or Marivaux.

The fact that the sympathy with Hawthorne is most felt in the last of James's novels, *The Sense of the Past,* makes me the more certain of its genuineness. In the meantime, James has been through a much more elaborate development than poor Hawthorne ever knew. Hawthorne, with his very limited culture, was not exposed to any bewildering variety of influences. James, in his astonishing career of self-improvement, touches Hawthorne most evidently at the beginning and end of his course; at the beginning, simply as a young New Englander of letters[1]; at the end, with almost a gesture of approach. *Roderick Hudson* is the novel of a clever and expanding young New Englander; immature, but just coming out to a self-consciousness where Hawthorne never arrived at all. Compared with *Daisy Miller* or *The Europeans* or *The American* its critical spirit is very crude. But *The Marble Faun (Transformation)*, the only European novel of Hawthorne, is of Cimmerian opacity; the mind of its author was closed to new impressions though with all its Walter Scott-Mysteries of Udolpho upholstery the old man does establish a kind of solid moral atmosphere which the young James does not get. James in *Roderick Hudson* does very little better with Rome than Hawthorne, and as he confesses in the later preface, rather fails with Northampton.[2]

[1]The James family came from Albany, and Henry James was born in New York City. His residence in New England, which was broken by trips abroad, was mostly confined to the years between 1860 and 1875, when James was, however, in the formative period between seventeen and thirty-two. E. W.

[2]Was Hawthorne at all in his mind here? In criticizing the *House of the Seven Gables* he says "it renders, to an initiated reader, the impression of a summer afternoon in an elm-shaded New England

He does in the later edition tone down the absurdities of Roderick's sculpture a little, the pathetic Thirst and the gigantic Adam; Mr. Striker remains a failure, the judgment of a young man consciously humorizing, too suggestive of *Martin Chuzzlewit.* The generic resemblance to Hawthorne is in the occasional heavy facetiousness of the style, the tedious whimsicality how different from the exactitude of *The American Scene,* the verbalism. He too much identifies himself with Rowland, does not see through the solemnity he has created in that character, commits the cardinal sin of failing to "detect" one of his own characters. The failure to create a situation is evident: with Christina and Mary, each nicely adjusted, but never quite set in relation to each other. The interest of the book for our present purpose is what he does *not* do in the Hawthorne way, in the instinctive attempt to get at something larger, which will bring him to the same success with much besides.

The interest in the "deeper psychology," the observation, and the sense for situation, developed from book to book, culminate in *The Sense of the Past* (by no means saying that this is his best), uniting with other qualities both personal and racial. James's greatness is apparent both in his capacity for development as an artist and his capacity for keeping his mind alive to the changes in the world during twenty-five years. It is remarkable (for the mastery of a span of American history) that the man who did the Wentworth family in the eighties could do the Bradhams in the hundreds. In *The Sense of the Past* the Midmores belong to the same generation as the Bradhams; Ralph belongs to the same race as the Wentworths, indeed as the Pyncheons. Compare the book with *The House of the Seven Gables* (Hawthorne's best novel after all); the situation, the "shrinkage and extinction of a family" is rather more complex, on the surface, than James's with (so far as the book was done) fewer character relations. But James's real situation here, to which Ralph's mounting the step is the key, as Hepzibah's opening

town," and in the preface to *Roderick Hudson* he says "what the early chapters of the book most 'render' to me today is not the umbrageous air of their New England town." T. S. E.

of her shop, is a situation of different states of mind. James's situation is the shrinkage and extinction of an idea. The Pyncheon tragedy is simple; the "curse" upon the family a matter of the simplest fairy mechanics. James has taken Hawthorne's ghost-sense and given it substance. At the same time making the tragedy much more ethereal: the tragedy of that "Sense," the hypertrophy, in Ralph, of a partial civilization; the vulgar vitality of the Midmores in their financial decay contrasted with the decay of Ralph in his financial prosperity, when they precisely should have been the civilization he had come to seek. All this watched over by the absent but conscious Aurora. I do not want to insist upon the Hawthorneness of the confrontation of the portrait, the importance of the opening of a door. We need surely not insist that this book is the most important, most substantial sort of thing that James did; perhaps there is more solid wear even in that other unfinished *Ivory Tower*. But I consider that it was an excursion which we could well permit him, after a lifetime in which he had taken talents similar to Hawthorne's and made them yield far greater returns than poor Hawthorne could harvest from his granite soil; a permissible exercise, in which we may by a legitimately cognate fancy seem to detect Hawthorne coming to a mediumistic existence again, to remind a younger and incredulous generation of what he really was, had he had the opportunity, and to attest his satisfaction that that opportunity had been given to James.

THESE ESSAYS by George Santayana on William James and Josiah Royce appeared in 1920 in *Character and Opinion in the United States.*

This book, with *Egotism in German Philosophy,* which came out a few years before it, was evidently provoked by World War I, which had stimulated Mr. Santayana to think of the issues of the war in terms of national points of view. Both books are examples of an art of which Santayana is a master but for which he is not much praised or known. In these essays he is able to derive his subjects from their social and geographical backgrounds and to paint them in their local colors as would only be possible for an interested observer of how men actually live and grow; but this spectacle does not absorb him: he confidently and quietly passes on to criticize their philosophical positions in an arena where all minds meet.

George Santayana was born in Madrid, the child of Spanish parents, but was brought to the United States at nine and remained here for forty years. He graduated from Harvard and returned to teach there in the philosophy department from 1888 to 1912. In 1912 he resigned and went permanently to live in Europe.

GEORGE SANTAYANA

I. WILLIAM JAMES

William James enjoyed in his youth what are called advantages: he lived among cultivated people, traveled, had teachers of various nationalities. His father was one of those somewhat obscure sages whom early America produced: mystics of independent mind, hermits in the desert of business, and heretics in the churches. They were intense individuals, full of veneration for the free souls of their children, and convinced that everyone should paddle his own canoe, especially on the high seas. Williams James accordingly enjoyed a stimulating if slightly irregular education: he never acquired that reposeful mastery of particular authors and those safe ways of feeling and judging which are fostered in great schools and universities. In consequence he showed an almost physical horror of club sentiment and of the stifling atmosphere of all officialdom. He had a knack for drawing, and rather the temperament of the artist; but the unlovely secrets of nature and the troubles of man preoccupied him, and he chose medicine for his profession. Instead of practicing, however, he turned to teaching physiology, and from that passed gradually to psychology and philosophy.

In his earlier years he retained some traces of polyglot student days at Paris, Bonn, Vienna, or Geneva; he slipped sometimes into foreign phrases, uttered in their full vernacular; and there was an occasional afterglow of Bohemia about him, in the bright stripe of a shirt or the exuberance of a tie. On points of art or medicine he retained a professional touch and an unconscious ease which he hardly acquired in metaphysics. I suspect he had heartily admired some of his masters in those other subjects, but had never seen a philosopher whom he would have cared to resemble. Of course there was nothing of the artist in William James, as the artist is sometimes conceived in England, nothing of the aesthete, nothing affected or limp. In person he was short rather than tall, erect, brisk, bearded, intensely masculine. While he shone in expression and would have wished his style to be noble if it could also be strong, he preferred in the end to be spontaneous, and to leave it at that; he tolerated slang in himself rather than primness. The rough, homely, picturesque phrase, whatever was graphic and racy, recommended itself to him; and his conversation outdid his writing in this respect. He believed in improvisation, even in thought; his lectures were not minutely prepared. Know your subject thoroughly, he used to say, and trust to luck for the rest. There was a deep sense of insecurity in him, a mixture of humility with romanticism: we were likely to be more or less wrong anyhow, but we might be wholly sincere. One moment should respect the insight of another, without trying to establish too regimental a uniformity. If you corrected yourself tartly, how could you know that the correction was not the worse mistake? All our opinions were born free and equal, all children of the Lord, and if they were not consistent that was the Lord's business, not theirs. In reality, James was consistent enough, as even Emerson (more extreme in this sort of irresponsibility) was too. Inspiration has its limits, sometimes very narrow ones. But James was not consecutive, not insistent; he turned to a subject afresh, without egotism or pedantry; he dropped his old points, sometimes very good ones; and he modestly looked for light from others, who had less light than himself.

His excursions into philosophy were accordingly in the nature of raids, and it is easy for those who are attracted by one part of his work to ignore other parts, in themselves perhaps more valuable. I think that in fact his popularity does not rest on his best achievements. His popularity rests on three somewhat incidental books, *The Will to Believe, Pragmatism,* and *The Varieties of Religious Experience,* whereas, as it seems to me, his best achievement is his *Principles of Psychology*. In this book he surveys, in a way which for him is very systematic, a subject made to his hand. In its ostensible outlook it is a treatise like any other, but what distinguishes it is the author's gift for evoking vividly the very life of the mind. This is a work of imagination; and the subject as he conceived it, which is the flux of immediate experience in men in general, requires imagination to read it at all. It is a literary subject, like autobiography or psychological fiction, and can be treated only poetically; and in this sense Shakespeare is a better psychologist than Locke or Kant. Yet this gift of imagination is not merely literary; it is not useless in divining the truths of science, and it is invaluable in throwing off prejudice and scientific shams. The fresh imagination and vitality of William James led him to break through many a false convention. He saw that experience, as we endure it, is not a mosaic of distinct sensations, nor the expression of separate hostile faculties, such as reason and the passions, or sense and the categories; it is rather a flow of mental discourse, like a dream, in which all divisions and units are vague and shifting, and the whole is continually merging together and drifting apart. It fades gradually in the rear, like the wake of a ship, and bites into the future, like the bow cutting the water. For the candid psychologist, carried bodily on this voyage of discovery, the past is but a questionable report, and the future wholly indeterminate; everything is simply what it is experienced as being.

At the same time, psychology is supposed to be a science, a claim which would tend to confine it to the natural history of man, or the study of behavior, as is actually proposed by Auguste Comte and by some of James's own disciples, more jejune if more clear-headed than he. As matters now stand, however, psychology as a whole is not a science, but a branch of philosophy; it brings together the literary description of mental discourse and the scientific description of material life, in order to consider the relation between them, which is the nexus of human nature.

What was James's position on this crucial question? It is impossible to reply unequivocally. He approached philosophy as mankind originally approached it, without having a philosophy, and he lent himself to various hypotheses in various directions. He professed to begin his study on the assumptions of common sense, that there is a material world which the animals that live in it are able to perceive and to think about. He gave a congruous extension to this view in his theory that emotion is purely bodily sensation, and also in his habit of conceiving the mind as a total shifting sensibility. To pursue this path, however, would have led him to admit that nature was automatic and mind simply cognitive, conclusions from which every instinct in him recoiled. He preferred to believe that mind and matter had independent energies and could lend one another a hand, matter operating by motion and mind by intention. This dramatic, amphibious way of picturing causation is natural to common sense, and might be defended if it were clearly defined; but James was insensibly carried away from it by a subtle implication of his method. This implication was that experience or mental discourse not only constituted a set of substantive facts, but the *only* substantive facts; all else, even that material world which his psychology had postulated, could be nothing but a verbal or fantastic symbol for sensations in their experienced order. So that while nominally the door was kept open to any hypothesis regarding the conditions of the psychological flux, in truth the question was prejudged. The hypotheses, which were parts of this psychological flux, could have no object save other parts of it. That flux itself, therefore, which he could picture so vividly, was the fundamental existence. The *sense* of bounding over the waves, the *sense* of being on an adventurous voyage, was the living fact; the rest was dead reckoning. Where one's gift is, there will one's faith be also; and to this poet appearance was the only reality.

This sentiment, which always lay at the back of his mind,

reached something like formal expression in his latest writings, where he sketched what he called radical empiricism. The word experience is like a shrapnel shell, and bursts into a thousand meanings. Here we must no longer think of its setting, its discoveries, or its march; to treat it radically we must abstract its immediate objects and reduce it to pure data. It is obvious (and the sequel has already proved) that experience so understood would lose its romantic signification, as a personal adventure or a response to the shocks of fortune. "Experience" would turn into a cosmic dance of absolute entities created and destroyed *in vacuo* according to universal laws, or perhaps by chance. No minds would gather this experience, and no material agencies would impose it; but the immediate objects present to anyone would simply be parts of the universal fireworks, continuous with the rest, and all the parts, even if not present to anybody, would have the same status. Experience would then not at all resemble what Shakespeare reports or what James himself had described in his psychology. If it could be experienced as it flows in its entirety (which is fortunately impracticable), it would be a perpetual mathematical nightmare. Every whirling atom, every changing relation, and every incidental perspective would be a part of it. I am far from wishing to deny for a moment the scientific value of such a cosmic system, if it can be worked out; physics and mathematics seem to me to plunge far deeper than literary psychology into the groundwork of this world; but human experience is the stuff of literary psychology; we cannot reach the stuff of physics and mathematics except by arresting or even hypostatizing some elements of appearance, and expanding them on an abstracted and hypothetical plane of their own. Experience, as memory and literature rehearse it, remains nearer to us than that: it is something dreamful, passionate, dramatic, and significative.

Certainly this personal human experience, expressible in literature and in talk, and no cosmic system however profound, was what James knew best and trusted most. Had he seen the developments of his radical empiricism, I cannot help thinking he would have marveled that such logical mechanisms should have been hatched out of that egg. The principal problems and aspirations that haunted him all his life long would lose their meaning in that cosmic atmosphere. The pragmatic nature of truth, for instance, would never suggest itself in the presence of pure data; but a romantic mind soaked in agnosticism, conscious of its own habits and assuming an environment the exact structure of which can never be observed, may well convince itself that, for experience, truth is nothing but a happy use of signs—which is indeed the truth of literature. But if we once accept *any* system of the universe as literally true, the value of convenient signs to prepare us for such experience as is yet absent cannot be called truth: it is plainly nothing but a necessary inaccuracy. So, too, with the question of the survival of the human individual after death. For radical empiricism a human individual is simply a certain cycle or complex of terms, like any other natural fact; that some echoes of his mind should recur after the regular chimes have ceased, would have nothing paradoxical about it. A mathematical world is a good deal like music, with its repetitions and transpositions, and a little trill, which you might call a person, might well peep up here and there all over a vast composition. Something of that sort may be the truth of spiritualism; but it is not what the spiritualists imagine. Their whole interest lies not in the experiences they have, but in the interpretation they give to them, assigning them to troubled spirits in another world; but both another world and a spirit are notions repugnant to a radical empiricism.

I think it is important to remember, if we are not to misunderstand William James, that his radical empiricism and pragmatism were in his own mind only methods; his doctrine, if he may be said to have had one, was agnosticism. And just because he was an agnostic (feeling instinctively that beliefs and opinions, if they had any objective beyond themselves, could never be sure they had attained it), he seemed in one sense so favorable to credulity. He was not credulous himself, far from it; he was well aware that the trust he put in people or ideas might betray him. For that very reason he was respectful and pitiful to the trustfulness of others. Doubtless they were wrong, but who were we to say so? In his own person he was ready enough to face the mystery of things, and whatever the womb of time might bring forth; but until the curtain was rung down on the last act of the drama (and it might have no last act!) he wished the intellectual cripples and the moral hunchbacks not to be jeered at; perhaps they might turn out to be the heroes of the play. Who could tell what heavenly influences might not pierce to these sensitive, half-flayed creatures, which are lost on the thick-skinned, the sane, and the duly goggled? We must not suppose, however, that James meant these contrite and romantic suggestions dogmatically. The agnostic, as well as the physician and neurologist in him, was never quite eclipsed. The hope that some new revelation might come from the lowly and weak could never mean to him what it meant to the early Christians. For him it was only a right conceded to them to experiment with their special faiths; he did not expect such faiths to be discoveries of absolute fact, which everybody else might be constrained to recognize. If anyone had made such a claim, and had seemed to have some chance of imposing it universally, James would have been the first to turn against him; not, of course, on the ground that it was *impossible* that such an orthodoxy should be true, but with a profound conviction that it was to be feared and distrusted. No: the degree of authority and honor to be accorded to various human faiths was a moral question, not a theoretical one. All faiths were what they were experienced as being, in their capacity of faiths; these faiths, not their objects, were the hard facts we must respect. We cannot pass, except under the illusion of the moment, to anything firmer or on a deeper level. There was accordingly no sense of security, no joy, in James's apology for personal religion. He did not really believe; he merely believed in the right of believing that you might be right if you believed.

It is this underlying agnosticism that explains an incoherence which we might find in his popular works, where the story and the moral do not seem to hang together. Professedly they are works of psychological observation; but the tendency and suasion in them seems to run to disintegrating the idea of truth, recommending belief without reason, and encouraging superstition. A psychologist who was not an agnostic would have indicated, as far as possible, whether the beliefs and experiences he was describing were instances of delusion or of rare and fine perception, or in what measure they were a mixture of both. But James—and this is what gives such romantic warmth to these writings of his—disclaims all antecedent or superior knowledge, listens to the testimony of each witness in turn, and only by accident allows us to feel that he is swayed by the eloquence and vehemence of some of them rather than of others. This method is modest, generous, and impartial; but if James intended, as I think he did, to picture the *drama* of human belief, with its risks and triumphs, the method was inadequate. Dramatists never hesitate to assume, and to let the audience perceive, who is good and who bad, who wise and who foolish, in their pieces; otherwise their work would be as impotent dramatically as scientifically. The tragedy and comedy of life lie precisely in the contrast between the illusions or passions of the characters and their true condition and fate, hidden from them at first, but evident to the author and the public. If in our diffidence and scrupulous fairness we refuse to take this judicial attitude, we shall be led to strange conclusions. The navigator, for instance, trusting his "experience" (which here, as in the case of religious people, means his imagination and his art), insists on believing that the earth is spherical; he has sailed round it. That is to say, he has seemed to himself to steer westward and westward, and has seemed to get home again. But how should he know that home is now where it was before, or that his past and present impressions of it come from the same, or from any, material object? How should he know that space is as trim and tri-dimensional as the discredited Euclidians used to say it was? If, on the contrary, my worthy aunt, trusting to her longer and less ambiguous experience of her garden, insists that the earth is flat, and observes that the theory that it is round, which is only a theory, is much less often tested and found useful than her own perception of its flatness, and that moreover that theory is pedantic, intellectualistic, and a product of academies, and a rash dogma to impose on mankind for ever and ever, it might seem that on James's principle we ought to agree with her. But no; on James's real principles we need not agree with her, nor with the navigator either. Radical empiricism, which is radical agnosticism, delivers us from so benighted a choice. For the quarrel becomes unmeaning when we remember that the earth is *both* flat and round, if it is experienced as being both. The substantive fact is not a single object on which both the perception and the theory are expected to converge; the substantive facts are the theory and the perception themselves. And we may note in passing that empiricism, when it ceases to value experience as a means of discovering external things, can give up its ancient prejudice in favor of sense as against imagination, for imagination and thought are immediate experiences as much as sensation is: they are therefore, for absolute empiricism, no less actual ingredients of reality.

In *The Varieties of Religious Experience* we find the same apologetic intention running through a vivid account of what seems for the most part (as James acknowledged) religious disease. Normal religious experience is hardly described in it. Religious experience, for the great mass of mankind, consists in simple faith in the truth and benefit of their religious traditions. But to James something so conventional and rationalistic seemed hardly experience and hardly religious; he was thinking only of irruptive visions and feelings as interpreted by the mystics who had them. These interpretations he ostensibly presents, with more or less wistful sympathy, for what they were worth; but emotionally he wished to champion them. The religions that had sprung up in America spontaneously—communistic, hysterical, spiritistic, or medicinal—were despised by select and superior people. You might inquire into them, as you might go slumming, but they remained suspect and distasteful. This picking up of genteel skirts on the part of his acquaintance prompted William James to roll up his sleeves—not for a knockout blow, but for a thorough clinical demonstration. He would tenderly vivisect the experiences in question, to show how living they were, though of course he could not guarantee, more than other surgeons do, that the patient would survive the operation. An operation that eventually kills may be technically successful, and the man may die cured; and so a description of religion that showed it to be madness might first show how real and how warm it was, so that if it perished, at least it would perish understood.

I never observed in William James any personal anxiety or enthusiasm for any of these dubious tenets. His conception even of such a thing as free will, which he always ardently defended, remained vague; he avoided defining even what he conceived to be desirable in such matters. But he wished to protect the weak against the strong, and what he hated beyond everything was the *non possumus* of any constituted authority. Philosophy for him had a Polish constitution; so long as a single vote was cast against the majority, nothing could pass. The suspense of judgment, which he had imposed on himself as a duty, became almost a necessity. I think it would have depressed him if he had had to confess that any important question was finally settled. He would still have hoped that something might turn up on the other side, and that just as the scientific hangman was about to dispatch the poor convicted prisoner, an unexpected witness would ride up in hot haste, and prove him innocent. Experience seems to most of us to lead to conclusions, but empiricism has sworn never to draw them.

In the discourse on *The Energies of Men,* certain physiological marvels are recorded, as if to suggest that the resources of our minds and bodies are infinite, or can be infinitely enlarged by divine grace. Yet James would not, I am sure, have accepted that inference. He would, under pressure, have drawn in his mystical horns under his scientific shell; but he was not naturalist enough to feel instinctively that the wonderful and the natural are all of a piece, and that only our degree of habituation distinguishes them. A nucleus, which we may poetically call the soul, certainly lies within us, by which our bodies and minds are generated and controlled, like an army by a government. In this nucleus, since nature in a small compass has room for anything, vast quantities of energy may well be stored up, which may be tapped on occasion, or which may serve like an electric spark to let loose energy previously existing in the grosser parts. But the absolute autocracy of this central power, or its success in imposing extraordinary trials on its subjects, is not an obvious good. Perhaps, like a democratic government, the soul is at its best when it merely collects and co-ordinates the impulses coming from the senses. The inner man is at times a tyrant, parasitical, wasteful, and voluptuous. At other times he is fanatical and mad. When he asks for and obtains violent exertions from the body, the question often is, as with the exploits of conquerors and conjurers, whether the impulse to do such prodigious things was not gratuitous, and the things nugatory. Who would wish to be a mystic? James himself, who by nature was a spirited rather than a spiritual man, had no liking for sanctimonious transcendentalists, visionaries, or ascetics; he hated minds that run thin. But he hastened to correct this manly impulse, lest it should be unjust, and forced himself to overcome his repugnance. This was made easier when the unearthly phenomenon had a healing or saving function in the everyday material world; miracle then reëstablished its ancient identity with medicine, and both of them were humanized. Even when this union was not attained, James was reconciled to the miracle-workers partly by his great charity, and partly by his hunter's instinct to follow a scent, for he believed discoveries to be imminent. Besides, a philosopher who is a teacher of youth is more concerned to give people a right start than a right conclusion. James fell in with the hortatory tradition of college sages; he turned his psychology, whenever he could do so honestly, to purposes of edification; and his little sermons on habit, on will, on faith, and this on the latent capacities of men, were fine and stirring, and just the sermons to preach to the young Christian soldier. He was much less skeptical in morals than in science. He seems to have felt sure that certain thoughts and hopes—those familiar to a liberal

Protestantism—were every man's true friends in life. This assumption would have been hard to defend if he or those he habitually addressed had ever questioned it; yet his whole argument for voluntarily cultivating these beliefs rests on this assumption, that they are beneficent. Since, whether we will or no, we cannot escape the risk of error, and must succumb to some human or pathological bias, at least we might do so gracefully and in the form that would profit us most, by clinging to those prejudices which help us to lead what we all feel is a good life. But what is a good life? Had William James, had the people about him, had modern philosophers anywhere, any notion of that? I cannot think so. They had much experience of personal goodness, and love of it; they had standards of character and right conduct; but as to what might render human existence good, excellent, beautiful, happy, and worth having as a whole, their notions were utterly thin and barbarous. They had forgotten the Greeks, or never known them.

This argument accordingly suffers from the same weakness as the similar argument of Pascal in favor of Catholic orthodoxy. You should force yourself to believe in it, he said, because if you do so and are right you win heaven, while if you are wrong you lose nothing. What would Protestants, Mohammedans, and Hindus say to that? Those alternatives of Pascal's are not the sole nor the true alternatives; such a wager—betting on the improbable because you are offered big odds—is an unworthy parody of the real choice between wisdom and folly. There is no heaven to be won in such a spirit, and if there was, a philosopher would despise it. So William James would have us bet on immortality, or bet on our power to succeed, because if we win the wager we can live to congratulate ourselves on our true instinct, while we lose nothing if we have made a mistake; for unless you have the satisfaction of finding that you have been right, the dignity of having been right is apparently nothing. Or if the argument is rather that these beliefs, whether true or false, make life better in this world, the thing is simply false. To be boosted by an illusion is not to live better than to live in harmony with the truth; it is not nearly so safe, not nearly so sweet, and not nearly so fruitful. These refusals to part with a decayed illusion are really an infection to the mind. Believe, certainly; we cannot help believing; but believe rationally, holding what seems certain for certain, what seems probable for probable, what seems desirable for desirable, and what seems false for false.

In this matter, as usual, James had a true psychological fact and a generous instinct behind his confused moral suggestions. It is a psychological fact that men are influenced in their beliefs by their will and desires; indeed, I think we can go further and say that in its essence belief is an expression of impulse, of readiness to act. It is only peripherally, as our action is gradually adjusted to things, and our impulses to our possible or necessary action, that our ideas begin to hug the facts, and to acquire a true, if still a symbolic, significance. We do not need a will to believe; we only need a will to study the object in which we are inevitably believing. But James was thinking less of belief in what we find than of belief in what we hope for: a belief which is not at all clear and not at all necessary in the life of mortals. Like most Americans, however, only more lyrically, James felt the call of the future and the assurance that it could be made far better, totally other, than the past. The pictures that religion had painted of heaven or the millennium were not what he prized, although his Swedenborgian connection might have made him tender to them, as perhaps it did to familiar spirits. It was the moral succor offered by religion, its open spaces, the possibility of miracles *in extremis,* that must be retained. If we recoiled at the thought of being dupes (which is perhaps what nature intended us to be), were we less likely to be dupes in disbelieving these sustaining truths than in believing them? Faith was needed to bring about the reform of faith itself, as well as all other reforms.

In some cases faith in success could nerve us to bring success about, and so justify itself by its own operation. This is a thought typical of James at his worst—a worst in which there is always a good side. Here again psychological observation is used with the best intentions to hearten oneself and other people; but the fact observed is not at all understood, and a moral twist is given to it which (besides being morally questionable) almost amounts to falsifying the fact itself. Why does belief that you can jump a ditch help you to jump it? Because it is a symptom of the fact that you *could* jump it, that your legs were fit and that the ditch was two yards wide and not twenty. A rapid and just appreciation of these facts has given you your confidence, or at least has made it reasonable, manly, and prophetic; otherwise you would have been a fool and got a ducking for it. Assurance is contemptible and fatal unless it is self-knowledge. If you had been rattled you might have failed, because that would have been a symptom of the fact that you were out of gear; you would have been afraid because you trembled, as James at his best proclaimed. You would never have quailed if your system had been reacting smoothly to its opportunities, any more than you would totter and see double if you were not intoxicated. Fear is a sensation of actual nervousness and disarray, and confidence a sensation of actual readiness; they are not disembodied feelings, existing for no reason, the devil Funk and the angel Courage, one or the other of whom may come down arbitrarily into your body, and revolutionize it. That is childish mythology, which survives innocently enough as a figure of speech, until a philosopher is found to take that figure of speech seriously. Nor is the moral suggestion here less unsound. What is good is not the presumption of power, but the possession of it: a clear head, aware of its resources, not a fuddled optimism, calling up spirits from the vasty deep. Courage is not a virtue, said Socrates, unless it is also wisdom. Could anything be truer both of courage in doing and of courage in believing? But it takes tenacity, it takes *reasonable* courage, to stick to scientific insights such as this of Socrates or that of James about the emotions; it is easier to lapse into the traditional manner, to search natural philosophy for miracles and moral lessons, and in morals proper, in the reasoned expression of preference, to splash about without a philosophy.

William James shared the passions of liberalism. He belonged to the left, which, as they say in Spain, is the side of the heart, as the right is that of the liver; at any rate there was much blood and no gall in his philosophy. He was one of those elder Americans still disquieted by the ghost of tyranny, social and ecclesiastical. Even the beauties of the past troubled him; he had a puritan feeling that they were tainted. They had been cruel and frivolous, and must have suppressed far better things. But what, we may ask, might these better things be? It may do for a revolutionary politician to say: "I may not know what I want—except office—but I know what I don't want"; it will never do for a philosopher. Aversions and fears imply principles of preference, goods acknowledged; and it is the philosopher's business to make these goods explicit. Liberty is not an art, liberty must be used to bring some natural art to fruition. Shall it be simply eating and drinking and wondering what will happen next? If there is some deep and settled need in the heart of man, to give direction to his efforts, what else should a philosopher do but discover and announce what that need is?

There is a sense in which James was not a philosopher at all. He once said to me: "What a curse philosophy would be if we couldn't forget all about it!" In other words, philosophy was not to him what it has been to so many, a consolation and sanctuary in a life which would have been unsatisfying without it. It would be incongruous, therefore, to expect of him that he should build a philosophy like an edifice to go and live in for good. Philosophy to him was rather like a maze in which he happened to find himself wandering, and what he was looking for was the way out. In the presence of theories of any sort he was attentive, puzzled, suspicious, with a certain inner prompting to disregard them. He lived all his life among them, as a child lives among grown-up people; what a relief to turn from those stolid giants, with their prohibitions and exactions and tiresome talk, to another real child or a nice animal! Of course grown-up people are useful, and so James considered that theories might be; but in themselves, to live with, they were rather in the way, and at bottom our natural enemies. It was well to challenge one or another of them when you got a chance; perhaps that challenge might break some spell, transform the strange landscape, and simplify life. A theory while you were creating or using it was like a story you were telling yourself or a game you were playing; it was a warm, self-justifying thing then; but when the glow of creation or expectation was over, a theory was a phantom, like a ghost, or like the minds of other people. To all other people, even to ghosts, William James was the soul of courtesy; and he was civil to most theories as well, as to more or less interesting strangers that invaded him. Nobody ever recognized more heartily the chance that others had of being right, and the right they had to be different. Yet when it came to understanding what they meant, whether they were theories or persons, his intuition outran his patience; he made some brilliant impressionistic sketch in his fancy and called it by their name. This sketch was as often flattered as distorted, and he was at times the dupe of his desire to be appreciative and give the devil his due; he was too impulsive for exact sympathy; too subjective, too romantic, to be just. Love is very penetrating, but it penetrates to possibilities rather than to facts. The logic of opinions, as well as the exact opinions themselves, were not things James saw easily, or traced with pleasure. He liked to take things one by one, rather than to put two and two together. He was a mystic, a mystic in love with life. He was comparable to Rousseau and to Walt Whitman; he expressed a generous and tender sensibility, rebelling against sophistication, and preferring daily sights and sounds, and a vague but indomitable faith in fortune, to any settled intellectual tradition calling itself science or philosophy.

A prophet is not without honor save in his own country; and until the return wave of James's reputation reached America from Europe, his pupils and friends were hardly aware that he was such a distinguished man. Everybody liked him, and delighted in him for his generous, gullible nature and brilliant sallies. He was a sort of Irishman among the Brahmins, and seemed hardly imposing enough for a great man. They laughed at his erratic views and his undisguised limitations. Of course a conscientious professor ought to know everything he professes to know, but then, they thought, a dignified professor ought to seem to know everything. The precise theologians and panoplied idealists, who exist even in America, shook their heads. What sound philosophy, said they to themselves, could be expected from an irresponsible doctor, who was not even a college graduate, a crude empiricist, and vivisector of frogs? On the other hand, the solid men of business were not entirely reassured concerning a teacher of youth who seemed to have no system in particular—the ignorant rather demand that the learned should have a system in store, to be applied at a pinch; and they could not quite swallow a private gentleman who dabbled in hypnotism, frequented mediums, didn't talk like a book, and didn't write like a book, except like one of his own. Even his pupils, attached as they invariably were to his person, felt some doubts about the profundity of one who was so very natural, and who after some interruption during a lecture—and he said life was a series of interruptions—would slap his forehead and ask the man in the front row, "What *was* I talking about?" Perhaps in the first years of his teaching he felt a little in the professor's chair as a military man might feel when obliged to read the prayers at a funeral. He probably conceived what he said more deeply than a more scholastic mind might have conceived it; yet he would have been more comfortable if someone else had said it for him. He liked to open the window, and look out for a moment. I think he was glad when the bell rang, and he could be himself again until the next day. But in the midst of this routine of the class-room the spirit would sometimes come upon him, and, leaning his head on his hand, he would let fall golden words, picturesque, fresh from the heart, full of the knowledge of good and evil. Incidentally there would crop up some humorous characterization, some candid confession of doubt or of instinctive preference, some pungent scrap of learning; radicalisms plunging sometimes into the sub-soil of all human philosophies; and, on occasion, thoughts of simple wisdom and wistful piety, the most unfeigned and manly that anybody ever had.

II. JOSIAH ROYCE

MEANTIME the mantle of philosophical authority had fallen at Harvard upon other shoulders. A young Californian, Josiah Royce, had come back from Germany with a reputation for wisdom; and even without knowing that he had already produced a new proof of the existence of God, merely to look at him you would have felt that he was a philosopher; his great head seemed too heavy for his small body, and his portentous brow, crowned with thick red hair, seemed to crush the lower part of his face. "Royce," said William James of him, "has an indecent exposure of forehead." There was a suggestion about him of the benevolent ogre or the old child, in whom a preternatural sharpness of insight lurked beneath a grotesque mask. If you gave him any cue, or even without one, he could discourse broadly on any subject; you never caught him napping. Whatever the textbooks and encyclopaedias could tell him, he knew; and if the impression he left on your mind was vague, that was partly because, in spite of his comprehensiveness, he seemed to view everything in relation to something else that remained untold. His approach to anything was oblique; he began a long way off, perhaps with the American preface of a funny story; and when the point came in sight, it was at once enveloped again in a cloud of qualifications, in the parliamentary jargon of philosophy. The tap once turned on, out flowed the stream of systematic disquisition, one hour, two hours, three hours of it, according to demand or opportunity. The voice, too, was merciless and harsh. You felt the overworked, standardized, academic engine, creaking and thumping on at the call of duty or of habit, with no thought of sparing itself or anyone else. Yet a sprightlier soul behind this performing soul seemed to watch and laugh at the process. Sometimes a merry light would twinkle in the little eyes, and a bashful smile would creep over the uncompromising mouth. A sense of the paradox, the irony, the inconclusiveness of the whole argument would pierce to the surface, like a white-cap bursting here and there on the heavy swell of the sea.

His procedure was first to gather and digest whatever the sciences or the devil might have to say. He had an evident sly pleasure in the degustation and savor of difficulties; biblical criticism, the struggle for life, the latest German theory of sexual insanity, had no terrors for him; it was all grist for the mill, and woe to any tender thing, any beauty or any illusion, that should get between that upper and that nether millstone! He seemed to say: If I were not Alexander how gladly would I be Diogenes, and if I had not a system to defend, how easily I might tell you the truth. But after the skeptic had ambled quizzically over the ground, the prophet would mount the pulpit to survey it. He would then prove that in spite of all those horrors and contradictions, or rather because of them, the universe was absolutely perfect. For behind that mocking soul in him there was yet another, a devout and heroic soul. Royce was heir to the Calvinistic tradition; piety, to his mind, consisted in trusting divine providence and justice, while emphasizing the most terrifying truths about one's own depravity and the sinister holiness of God. He accordingly addressed himself, in his chief writings, to showing that all lives were parts of a single divine life in which all problems were solved and all evils justified.

It is characteristic of Royce that in his proof of something sublime, like the existence of God, his premiss should be something sad and troublesome, the existence of error. Error exists, he tells us, and common sense will readily agree, although the fact is not unquestionable, and pure mystics and pure sensualists deny it. But if error exists, Royce continues, there must be a truth from which it differs; and the existence of truth (according to the principle of idealism, that nothing can exist except for a mind that knows it) implies that someone knows the truth; but as to know the truth thoroughly, and supply the corrective to every possible error, involves omniscience, we have proved the existence of an omniscient mind or universal thought; and this is almost, if not quite, equivalent to the existence of God.

What carried Royce over the evident chasms and assumptions in this argument was his earnestness and passionate eloquence. He passed for an eminent logician, because he was dialectical and fearless in argument and delighted in the play of formal relations; he was devoted to chess, music, and mathematics; but all this show of logic was but a screen for his heart, and in his heart there was no clearness. His reasoning was not pure logic or pure observation; it was always secretly enthusiastic or malicious, and the result it arrived at had been presupposed. Here, for instance, no unprejudiced thinker, not to speak of a pure logician, would have dreamt of using the existence of error to found the being of truth upon. Error is a biological accident which may any day cease to exist, say at the extinction of the human race; whereas the being of truth or fact is involved indefeasibly and eternally in the existence of anything whatever, past, present, or future; every event of itself renders true or false any proposition that refers to it. No one would conceive of such a thing as error or suspect its presence, unless he had already found or assumed many a truth; nor could anything be an error actually unless the truth was definite and real. All this Royce of course recognized, and it was in some sense the heart of what he meant to assert and to prove; but it does not need proving and hardly asserting. What needed proof was something else, of less logical importance but far greater romantic interest, namely, that the truth was hovering over us and about to descend into our hearts; and this Royce was not disinclined to confuse with the being of truth, so as to bring it within the range of logical argument. He was tormented by the suspicion that he might be himself in the toils of error, and fervently aspired to escape from it. Error to him was no natural, and in itself harmless, incident of finitude; it was a sort of sin, as finitude was too. It was a part of the problem of evil; a terrible and urgent problem when your first postulate or dogma is that moral distinctions and moral experience are the substance of the world, and not merely an incident in it. The mere being of truth, which is all a logician needs, would not help him in this wrestling for personal salvation; as he keenly felt and often said, the truth is like the stars, always laughing at us. Nothing would help him but *possession* of the truth, something eventual and terribly problematic. He longed to believe that all his troubles and questions, someday and somewhere, must find their solution and quietus; if not in his own mind, in some kindred spirit that he could, to that extent, identify with himself. There must be not only cold truth, not even cold truth personified, but victorious *knowledge* of the truth, breaking like a sunburst through the clouds of error. The nerve of his argument was not logical at all; it was a confession of religious experience, in which the agonized consciousness of error led to a strong imaginative conviction that the truth would be found at last.

The truth, as here conceived, meant the whole truth about everything; and certainly, if any plausible evidence for such a conclusion could be adduced, it would be interesting to learn that we are destined to become omniscient, or are secretly omniscient already. Nevertheless, the aspiration of all religious minds does not run that way. Aristotle tells us that there are many things it is better not to know; and his sublime deity is happily ignorant of our errors and of our very existence; more emphatically so the even sublimer deities of Plotinus and the Indians. The omniscience which our religion attributes to God as the searcher of hearts and the judge of conduct has a moral function rather than a logical one; it prevents us from hiding our sins or being unrecognized in our merits; it is not conceived to be requisite in order that it may be true that those sins or merits have existed. Atheists admit the facts, but they are content or perhaps relieved that they should pass unobserved. But here again Royce slipped into a romantic equivocation which a strict logician would not have tolerated. Knowledge of the truth, a passing psychological possession, was substituted for the truth known, and this at the cost of rather serious ultimate confusions. It is the truth itself, the facts in their actual relations, that honest opinion appeals to, not to another opinion or instance of knowledge; and if, in your dream of warm sympathy and public corroboration, you lay up your treasure in some instance of knowledge, which time and doubt might corrupt, you have not laid up your treasure in heaven. In striving to prove the being of truth, the young Royce absurdly treated it as doubtful, setting a bad example to the pragmatists; while in striving to lend a psychological quality to this truth and turning it into a problematical instance of knowledge, he unwittingly deprived it of all authority and sublimity. To personify the truth is to care less for truth than for the corroboration and sympathy which the truth, become human, might bring to our opinions. It is to set up another thinker, ourself enlarged, to vindicate us; without considering that this second thinker would be shut up, like us, in his own opinions, and would need to look to the truth beyond him as much as we do.

To the old problem of evil Royce could only give an old answer, although he rediscovered and repeated it for himself in many ways, since it was the core of his whole system. Good, he said, is essentially the struggle with evil and the victory over it; so that if evil did not exist, good would be impossible. I do not think this answer set him at rest; he could hardly help feeling that all goods are not of that bellicose description, and that not all evils produce a healthy reaction or are swallowed up in victory; yet the fact that the most specious solution to this problem of evil left it unsolved was in its way appropriate; for if the problem had been really solved, the struggle to find a solution and the faith that there was one would come to an end; yet perhaps this faith and this struggle are themselves the supreme good. Accordingly the true solution of this problem, which we may all accept, is that no solution can ever be found.

Here is an example of the difference between the being of truth and the ultimate solution of all our problems. There is certainly a truth about evil, and in this case not an unknown truth; yet it is no solution to the "problem" which laid the indomitable Royce on the rack. If a younger son asks why he was not born before his elder brother, that question may represent an intelligible state of his feelings; but there is no answer to it, because it is a childish question. So the question why it is right that there should be any evil is itself perverse and raised by false presumptions. To an unsophisticated mortal the existence of evil presents a task, never a problem. Evil, like error, is an incident of animal life, inevitable in a crowded and unsettled world, where one spontaneous movement is likely to thwart another, and all to run up against material impossibilities. While life lasts this task is recurrent, and every creature, in proportion to the vitality and integrity of his nature, strives to remove or abate those evils of which he is sensible. When the case is urgent and he is helpless, he will cry out for divine aid; and (if he does not perish first) he will soon see this aid coming to him through some shift in the circumstances that renders his situation endurable. Positive religion takes a naturalistic view of things, and requires it. It parts company with a scientific naturalism only in accepting the authority of instinct or revelation in deciding certain questions of fact, such as immortality or miracles. It rouses itself to crush evil, without asking why evil exists. What could be more intelligible than that a deity like Jehovah, a giant inhabitant of the natural world, should be confronted with rivals, enemies, and rebellious children? What could be more intelligible than that the inertia of matter, or pure chance, or some contrary purpose, should mar the expression of any platonic idea exercising its magic influence over the world? For the Greek as for the Jew the task of morals is the same: to subdue nature as far as possible to the uses of the soul, by whatever agencies material or spiritual may be at hand; and when a limit is reached in that direction, to harden and cauterize the heart in the face of inevitable evils, opening it wide at the same time to every sweet influence that may descend to it from heaven. Never for a moment was positive religion entangled in a sophistical optimism. Never did it conceive that the most complete final deliverance and triumph would *justify* the evils which they abolished. As William James put it, in his picturesque manner, if at the last day all creation was shouting hallelujah and there remained one cockroach with an unrequited love, *that* would spoil the universal harmony; it would spoil it, he meant, in truth and for the tender philosopher, but probably not for those excited saints. James was thinking chiefly of the present and future, but the same scrupulous charity has its application to the past.

To remove an evil is not to remove the fact that it has existed. The tears that have been shed were shed in bitterness, even if a remorseful hand afterwards wipes them away. To be patted on the back and given a sugar plum does not reconcile even a child to a past injustice. And the case is much worse if we are expected to make our heaven out of the foolish and cruel pleasures of contrast, or out of the pathetic offuscation produced by a great relief. Such a heaven would be a lie, like the sardonic heavens of Calvin and Hegel. The existence of any evil anywhere at any time absolutely ruins a total optimism.

Nevertheless philosophers have always had a royal road to complete satisfaction. One of the purest of pleasures, which they cultivate above all others, is the pleasure of understanding. Now, as playwrights and novelists know, the intellect is no less readily or agreeably employed in understanding evil than in understanding good—more so, in fact, if in the intellectual man, besides his intelligence, there is a strain of coarseness, irony, or desire to belittle the good things others possess and he himself has missed. Sometimes the philosopher, even when above all meanness, becomes so devoted a naturalist that he is ashamed to remain a moralist, although this is what he probably was in the beginning; and where all is one vast cataract of events, he feels it would be impertinent of him to divide them censoriously into things that ought to be and things that ought not to be. He may even go one step farther. Awestruck and humbled before the universe, he may insensibly transform his understanding and admiration of it into the assertion that the existence of evil is no evil at all, but that the order of the universe is in every detail necessary and perfect, so that the mere mention of the word evil is blind and blasphemous.

This sentiment, which as much as any other deserves the name of pantheism, is often expressed incoherently and with a false afflatus; but when rationally conceived, as it was by Spinoza, it amounts to this: that good and evil are relations which things bear to the living beings they affect. In itself nothing—much less this whole mixed universe—can be either good or bad; but the universe wears the aspect of a good in so far as it feeds, delights, or otherwise fosters any creature within it. If we define the intellect as the power to see things as they are, it is clear that in so far as the philosopher is a pure intellect the universe will be a pure good to the philosopher; everything in it will give play to his exclusive passion. Wisdom counsels us therefore to become philosophers and to concentrate our lives as much as possible in pure intelligence, that we may be led by it into the ways of peace. Not that the universe will be proved thereby to be intrinsically good (although in the heat of their intellectual egotism philosophers are sometimes betrayed into saying so), but that it will have become in that measure a good to us, and we shall be better able to live happily and freely in it. If intelligibility appears in things, it does so like beauty or use, because the mind of man, in so far as it is adapted to them, finds its just exercise in their society.

This is an ancient, shrewd, and inexpugnable position. If Royce had been able to adhere to it consistently, he would have avoided his gratuitous problem of evil without, I think, doing violence to the sanest element in his natural piety, which was joy in the hard truth, with a touch of humor and scorn in respect to mortal illusions. There was an observant and docile side to him; and as a child likes to see things work, he liked to see processions of facts marching on ironically, whatever we might say about it. This was his sense of the power of God. It attached him at first to Spinoza and later to mathematical logic. No small part of his life-long allegiance to the Absolute responded to this sentiment.

The outlook, however, was complicated and half reversed for him by the transcendental theory of knowledge which he had adopted. This theory regards all objects, including the universe, as merely terms posited by the will of the thinker, according to a definite grammar of thought native to his mind. In order that his thoughts may be addressed to any particular object, he must first choose and create it of his own accord; otherwise his opinions, not being directed upon any object in particular within his ken, cannot be either true or false, whatever picture they may frame. What anything external may happen to be, when we do not mean to speak of it, is irrelevant to our discourse. If, for instance, the real Royce were not a denizen and product of my mind—of my deeper self—I could not so much as have a wrong idea of him. The need of this initial relevance in our judgments seems to the transcendentalist to drive all possible objects into the fold of his secret thoughts, so that he has two minds, one that seeks the facts and another that already possesses or rather constitutes them.

Pantheism, when this new philosophy of knowledge is adopted, seems at first to lose its foundations. There is no longer an external universe to which to bow; no little corner left for us in the infinite where, after making the great sacrifice, we may build a safe nest. The intellect to which we had proudly reduced ourselves has lost its pre-eminence; it can no longer be called the faculty of seeing things as they are. It has become what psychological critics of intellectualism, such as William James, understand by it: a mass of human propensities to abstraction, construction, belief, or inference, by which imaginary things and truths are posited in the service of life. It is therefore on the same plane exactly as passion, music, or aesthetic taste: a mental complication which may be an index to other psychological facts connected with it genetically, but which has no valid intent, no ideal transcendence, no assertive or cognitive function. Intelligence so conceived understands nothing: it is a buzzing labor in the fancy which, by some obscure causation, helps us to live on.

To discredit the intellect, to throw off the incubus of an external reality or truth, was one of the boons which transcendentalism in its beginnings brought to the romantic soul. But although at first the sense of relief (to Fichte, for instance) was most exhilarating, the freedom achieved soon proved illusory: the terrible Absolute had been simply transplanted into the self. You were your own master, and omnipotent; but you were no less dark, hostile, and inexorable to yourself than the gods of Calvin or of Spinoza had been before. Since every detail of this mock world was your secret work, you were not only wiser but also more criminal than you knew. You were stifled, even more than formerly, in the arms of nature, in the toils of your own unaccountable character, which made your destiny. Royce never recoiled from paradox or from bitter fact; and he used to say that a mouse, when tormented and torn to pieces by a cat, was realizing his own deepest will, since he had subconsciously chosen to be a mouse in a world that should have cats in it. The mouse really, in his deeper self, wanted to be terrified, clawed, and devoured. Royce was superficially a rationalist, with no tenderness for superstition in detail and not much sympathy with civilized religions; but we see here that in his heart he was loyal to the aboriginal principle of all superstition: reverence for what hurts. He said to himself that in so far as God was the devil—as daily experience and Hegelian logic proved was largely the case—devil-worship was true religion.

A protest, however, arose in his own mind against this doctrine. Strong early bonds attached him to moralism—to the opinion of the Stoics and of Kant that virtue is the only good. Yet if virtue were conceived after their manner, as a heroic and sublimated attitude of the will, of which the world hardly afforded any example, how should the whole whirligig of life be good also? How should moralism, that frowns on this wicked world, be reconciled with pantheism and optimism, that hug it to their bosom? By the ingenious if rather melodramatic notion that we should hug it with a bear's hug, that virtue consisted (as Royce often put it) in holding evil by the throat; so that the world was good because it was a good world to strangle, and if we only managed to do so, the more it deserved strangling the better world it was. But this Herculean feat must not be considered as something to accomplish once for all; the labors of Hercules must be not twelve but infinite, since his virtue consisted in performing them, and if he ever rested or was received into Olympus he would have left virtue—the only good—behind. The wickedness of the world was no reason for quitting it; on the contrary, it invited us to plunge into all its depths and live through every phase of it; virtue was severe but not squeamish. It lived by endless effort, turbid vitality, and *Sturm und Drang*. Moralism and an apology for evil could thus be reconciled and merged in the praises of tragic experience.

This had been the burden of Hegel's philosophy of life, which Royce admired and adopted. Hegel and his followers seem to be fond of imagining that they are moving in a tragedy. But because Aeschylus and Sophocles were great poets, does it follow that life would be cheap if it did not resemble their fables? The life of tragic heroes is not good; it is misguided, unnecessary, and absurd. Yet that is what romantic philosophy would condemn us to; we must all strut and roar. We must lend ourselves to the partisan earnestness of persons and nations calling their rivals villains and themselves heroes; but this earnestness will be of the histrionic German sort, made to order and transferable at short notice from one object to another, since what truly matters is not that we should achieve our ostensible aim (which Hegel contemptuously called ideal) but that we should carry on perpetually, if possible with a *crescendo,* the strenuous experience of living in a gloriously bad world, and always working to reform it, with the comforting speculative assurance that we never can succeed. We never can succeed, I mean, in rendering reform less necessary or life happier; but of course in any specific reform we may succeed half the time, thereby sowing the seeds of new and higher evils, to keep the edge of virtue keen. And in reality we, or the Absolute in us, are succeeding all the time; the play is always going on, and the play's the thing.

It was inevitable that Royce should have been at home only in this circle of Protestant and German intuitions; a more refined existence would have seemed to him to elude moral experience. Although he was born in California he had never got used to the sunshine; he had never tasted peace. His spirit was that of courage and labor. He was tender in a bashful way, as if in tenderness there was something pathological, as indeed to his sense there was, since he conceived love and loyalty to be divine obsessions refusing to be rationalized; he saw their essence in the child who clings to an old battered doll rather than accept a new and better one. Following orthodox tradition in philosophy, he insisted on seeing reason at the bottom of things as well as at the top, so that he never could understand either the root or the flower of anything. He watched the movement of events as if they were mysterious music, and instead of their causes and potentialities he tried to divine their *motif*. On current affairs his judgments were highly seasoned and laboriously wise. If anything escaped him, it was only the simplicity of what is best. His reward was that he became a prophet to a whole class of earnest, troubled people who, having discarded doctrinal religion, wished to think their life worth living when, to look at what it contained, it might not have seemed so; it reassured them to learn that a strained and joyless existence was not their unlucky lot, or a consequence of their solemn folly, but was the necessary fate of all good men and angels. Royce had always experienced and seen about him a groping, burdened, mediocre life; he had observed how fortune is continually lying in ambush for us, in order to bring good out of evil and evil out of good. In his age and country all was change, preparation, hurry, material achievement; nothing was an old and sufficient possession; nowhere, or very much in the background, any leisure, simplicity, security, or harmony. The whole scene was filled with arts and virtues which were merely useful or remedial. The most pressing arts, like war and forced labor, presuppose evil, work immense havoc, and take the place of greater possible goods. The most indispensable virtues, like courage and industry, do likewise. But these seemed in Royce's world the only honorable things, and he took them to be typical of all art and virtue—a tremendous error. It is very true, however, that in the welter of material existence no concrete thing can be good or evil in every respect; and so long as our rough arts and virtues do more good than harm we give them honorable names, such as unselfishness, patriotism, or religion; and it remains a mark of good breeding among us to practice them instinctively. But an absolute love of such forced arts and impure virtues is itself a vice; it is, as the case may be, barbarous, vain, or fanatical. It mistakes something specific—some habit or emotion which may be or may have been good in some respect, or under some circumstances the lesser of two evils—for the very principle of excellence. But good and evil, like light and shade, are ethereal; all things, events, persons, and conventional virtues are in themselves utterly valueless, save as an immaterial harmony (of which mind is an expression) plays about them on occasion, when their natures meet propitiously, and bathes them in some tint of happiness or beauty. This immaterial harmony may be made more and more perfect; the difficulties in the way of perfection, either in man, in society, or in universal nature, are physical not logical. Worship of barbarous virtue is the blackest conservatism; it shuts the gate of heaven, and surrenders existence to perpetual follies and crimes. Moralism itself is a superstition. In its abstract form it is moral, too moral; it adores the conventional conscience, or perhaps a morbid one. In its romantic form, moralism becomes barbarous and actually immoral; it obstinately craves action and stress for their own sake, experience in the gross, and a good-and-bad way of living.

Royce sometimes conceded that there might be some pure goods, music, for instance, or mathematics; but the impure moral goods were better and could not be spared. Such a concession, however, if it had been taken to heart, would have ruined his whole moral philosophy. The romanticist must maintain that *only* what is painful can be noble and *only* what is lurid bright. A taste for turbid and contrasted values would soon seem perverse when once anything perfect had been seen and loved. Would it not have been better to leave out the worst of the crimes and plagues that have heightened the tragic value of the world? But if so, why stop before we had deleted them all? We should presently be horrified at the mere thought of passions that before had been found necessary by the barbarous tragedian to keep his audience awake; and the ear at the same time would become sensitive to a thousand harmonies that had been inaudible in the hurly-burly of romanticism. The romanticist thinks he has life by virtue of his confusion and torment, whereas in truth that torment and confusion are his incipient death, and it is only the modicum of harmony he has achieved in his separate faculties that keeps him alive at all. As Aristotle taught, unmixed harmony would be intensest life. The spheres might make a sweet and perpetual music, and a happy God is at least possible.

It was not in this direction, however, that Royce broke away on occasion from his Hegelian ethics; he did so in the direction of ethical dogmatism and downright sincerity. The deepest thing in him personally was conscience, firm recognition of duty, and the democratic and American spirit of service. He could not adopt a moral bias histrionically, after the manner of Hegel or Nietzsche. To those hardened professionals any role was acceptable, the more commanding the better; but the good Royce was like a sensitive amateur, refusing the role of villain, however brilliant and necessary to the play. In contempt of his own speculative insight, or in an obedience to it which forgot it for the time being, he lost himself in his part, and felt that it was infinitely important to be cast only for the most virtuous of characters. He retained inconsistently the Jewish allegiance to a God essentially the vindicator of only one of the combatants, not in this world often the victor; he could not stomach the providential scoundrels which the bad taste of Germany, and of Carlyle and Browning, was wont to glorify. The last notable act of his life was an illustration of this, when he uttered a ringing public denunciation of the sinking of the *Lusitania*. Orthodox Hegelians might well have urged that here, if anywhere, was a plain case of the providential function of what, from a finite merely moral point of view, was an evil in order to make a higher good possible—the virtue of German self-assertion and of American self-assertion in antithesis to it, synthesized in the concrete good of war and victory, or in the perhaps more blessed good of defeat. What could be more unphilosophical and *gedankenlos* than the intrusion of mere morality into the higher idea of world-development? Was not the Universal Spirit compelled to bifurcate into just such Germans and just such Americans, in order to attain self-consciousness by hating, fighting against, and vanquishing itself? Certainly it was American duty to be angry, as it was German duty to be ruthless. The Idea liked to see its fighting-cocks at it in earnest, since that was what it had bred them for; but both were good cocks. Villains, as Hegel had observed in describing Greek tragedy, were not less self-justified than heroes; they were simply the heroes of a lower stage of culture. America and England remained at the stage of individualism; Germany had advanced to the higher stage of organization. Perhaps this necessary war was destined, through the apparent defeat of Germany, to bring England and America up to the German level. Of course; and yet somehow, on this occasion, Royce passed over these profound considerations, which life-long habit must have brought to his lips. A Socratic demon whispered No, No in his ear; it would have been better for such things never to be. The murder of those thousand passengers was not a providential act, requisite to spread abroad a vitalizing war; it was a crime to execrate altogether. It would have been better for Hegel, or whoever was responsible for it, if a millstone had been hanged about his neck and he, and not those little ones, had been drowned at the bottom of the sea. Of this terrestrial cock-pit Royce was willing to accept the agony, but not the ignominy. The other cock was a wicked bird.

This honest lapse from his logic was habitual with him at the sight of sin, and sin in his eyes was a fearful reality. His conscience spoiled the pantheistic serenity of his system; and what was worse (for he was perfectly aware of the contradiction) it added a deep, almost remorseful unrest to his hard life. What calm could there be in the double assurance that it was really right that things should be wrong, but that it was really wrong not to strive to right them? There was no conflict, he once observed, between science and religion, but the real conflict was between religion and morality. There could indeed be no conflict in his mind between faith and science, because his faith began by accepting all facts and all scientific probabilities in order to face them religiously. But there was an invincible conflict between religion as he conceived it and morality, because morality takes sides and regards one sort of motive and one kind of result as better than another, whereas religion according to him gloried in everything, even in the evil, as fulfilling the will of God.

Of course the practice of virtue was not excluded; it was just as needful as evil was in the scheme of the whole; but while the effort of morality was requisite, the judgments of morality were absurd. Now I think we may say that a man who finds himself in such a position has a divided mind, and that while he has wrestled with the deepest questions like a young giant, he has not won the fight. I mean, he has not seen his way to any one of the various possibilities about the nature of things, but has remained entangled, sincerely, nobly, and pathetically, in contrary traditions stronger than himself. In the goodly company of philosophers he is an intrepid martyr.

In metaphysics as in morals Royce perpetually labored the same points, yet they never became clear; they covered a natural complexity in the facts which his idealism could not disentangle. There was a voluminous confusion in his thought; some clear principles and ultimate possibilities turned up in it, now presenting one face and now another, like chips carried down a swollen stream; but the most powerful currents were below the surface, and the whole movement was hard to trace. He had borrowed from Hegel a way of conceiving systems of philosophy, and also the elements of his own thought, which did not tend to clarify them. He did not think of correcting what incoherence there might remain in any view, and then holding it in reserve, as one of the possibilities, until facts should enable us to decide whether it was true or not. Instead he clung to the incoherence as if it had been the heart of the position, in order to be driven by it to some other position altogether, so that while every view seemed to be considered, criticized, and in a measure retained (since the argument continued on the same lines, however ill-chosen they might have been originally), yet justice was never done to it; it was never clarified, made consistent with itself, and then accepted or rejected in view of the evidence. Hence a vicious and perplexing suggestion that philosophies are bred out of philosophies, not out of men in the presence of things. Hence too a sophistical effort to find everything self-contradictory, and in some disquieting way both true and false, as if there were not an infinite number of perfectly consistent systems which the world might have illustrated.

Consider, for instance, his chief and most puzzling contention, that all minds are parts of one mind. It is easy, according to the meaning we give to the word mind, to render this assertion clear and true, or clear and false, or clear and doubtful (because touching unknown facts), or utterly absurd. It is obvious that all minds are parts of one flux or system of experiences, as all bodies are parts of one system of bodies. Again, if mind is identified with its objects, and people are said to be "of one mind" when they are thinking of the same thing, it is certain that many minds are often identical in part, and they would all be identical with portions of an omniscient mind that should perceive all that they severally experienced. The question becomes doubtful if what we mean by oneness of mind is unity of type; our information or plausible guesses cannot assure us how many sorts of experience may exist, or to what extent their development (when they develop) follows the same lines of evolution. The animals would have to be consulted, and the other planets, and the infinite recesses of time. The strait-jacket which German idealism has provided is certainly far too narrow even for the varieties of human imagination. Finally, the assertion becomes absurd when it is understood to suggest that an actual instance of thinking, in which something, say the existence of America, is absent or denied, can be part of another actual instance of thinking in which it is present and asserted. But this whole method of treating the matter—and we might add anything that observation might warrant us in adding about multiple personalities—would leave out the problem that agitated Royce and that bewildered his readers. He wanted all minds to be one in some way which should be logically and morally necessary, and which yet, as he could not help feeling, was morally and logically impossible.

For pure transcendentalism, which was Royce's technical method, the question does not arise at all. Transcendentalism is an attitude or a point of view rather than a system. Its Absolute is thinking "as such," wherever thought may exert itself. The notion that there are separate instances of thought is excluded, because space, time, and number belong to the visionary world posited by thought, not to the function of thinking; individuals are figments of constructive fancy, as are material objects. The stress of moral being is the same wherever it may fall, and there are no finite selves, or relations between thinkers; also no infinite self, because on this principle the Absolute is not an existent being, a psychological monster, but a station or office; its essence is a task. Actual thinking is therefore never a part of the Absolute, but always the Absolute itself. Thinkers, finite or infinite, would be existing persons or masses of feelings; such things are dreamt of only. *Any* system of existences, *any* truth or matter of fact waiting to be recognized, contradicts the transcendental insight and stultifies it. The all-inclusive mind is my mind as I think, mind in its living function, and beyond that philosophy cannot go.

Royce, however, while often reasoning on this principle, was incapable of not going beyond it, or of always remembering it. He could not help believing that constructive fancy not only feigns individuals and instances of thought, but is actually seated in them. The Absolute, for instance, must be not merely the abstract subject or transcendental self in all of us (although it was that too), but an actual synthetic universal mind, the God of Aristotle and of Christian theology. Nor was it easy for Royce, a sincere soul and a friend of William James, not to be a social realist; I mean, not to admit that there are many collateral human minds, in temporal existential relations to one another, any of which may influence another, but never supplant it nor materially include it. Finite experience was not a mere element in infinite experience; it was a tragic totality in itself. I was not God looking at myself, I was myself looking for God. Yet this strain was utterly incompatible with the principles of transcendentalism; it turned philosophy into a simple anticipation of science, if not into an indulgence in literary psychology. Knowledge would then have been only faith leaping across the chasm of coexistence and guessing the presence and nature of what surrounds us by some hint of material influence or brotherly affinity. Both the credulity and the finality which such naturalism implies were offensive to Royce, and contrary to his skeptical and mystical instincts. Was there some middle course?

The audience in a theater stand in a transcendental relation to the persons and events in the play. The performance may take place today and last one hour, while the fable transports us to some heroic epoch or to an age that never existed, and stretches through days and perhaps years of fancied time. Just so transcendental thinking, while actually timeless and not distributed among persons, might survey infinite time and rehearse the passions and thoughts of a thousand characters. Thought, after all, needs objects, however fictitious and ideal they may be; it could not think if it thought nothing. This indispensable world of appearance is far more interesting than the reality that evokes it; the qualities and divisions found in the appearance diversify the monotonous function of pure thinking and render it concrete. Instances of thought and particular minds may thus be introduced consistently into a transcendental system, provided they are distinguished not by their own times and places, but only by their themes. The transcendental mind would be a pure poet, with no earthly life, but living only in his works, and in the times and persons of his fable. This view, firmly and consistently held, would deserve the name of absolute idealism, which Royce liked to give to his own system. But he struggled to fuse it with social realism, with which it is radically incompatible. Particular minds and the whole process of time, for absolute idealism, are *ideas* only; they are thought of and surveyed, they never think or lapse actually. For this reason genuine idealists can speak so glibly of the mind of a nation or an age. It is just as real and unreal to them as the mind of an individual; for within the human individual they can trace unities that run through and beyond him, so that parts of him, identical with parts of other people, form units as living as himself; for it is all a web of themes, not a concourse of existences. This is the very essence and pride of idealism, that knowledge is not knowledge of the world but is the world itself, and that the units of discourse, which are interwoven and crossed units, are the only individuals in being. You may call them persons, because "person" means a mask; but you cannot call them souls. They are knots in the web of history. They are words in their context, and the only spirit in them is the sense they have for me.

Royce, however, in saying all this, also wished not to say it, and his two thick volumes on *The World and the Individual* leave their subject wrapped in utter obscurity. Perceiving the fact when he had finished, he very characteristically added a "Supplementary Essay" of a hundred more pages, in finer print, in which to come to the point. Imagine, he said, an absolutely exhaustive map of England spread out upon English soil. The map would be a part of England, yet would reproduce every feature of England, including itself; so that the map would reappear on a smaller scale within itself an infinite number of times, like a mirror reflected in a mirror. In this way we might be individuals within a larger individual, and no less actual and complete than he. Does this solve the problem? If we take the illustration as it stands, there is still only one individual in existence, the material England, all the maps being parts of its single surface; nor will it at all resemble the maps, since it will be washed by the sea and surrounded by foreign nations, and not, like the maps, by other Englands enveloping it. If, on the contrary, we equalize the status of all the members of the series, by making it infinite in both directions, then there would be no England at all, but only map within map of England. There would be no absolute mind inclusive but not included, and the Absolute would be the series as a whole, utterly different from any of its members. It would be a series while they were maps, a truth while they were minds; and if the Absolute from the beginning had been regarded as a truth only, there never would have been any difficulty in the existence of individuals under it. Moreover, if the individuals are all exactly alike, does not their exact similarity defeat the whole purpose of the speculation, which was to vindicate the equal reality of the whole and of its *limited* parts? And if each of us, living through infinite time, goes through precisely the same experiences as everyone else, why this vain repetition? Is it not enough for this insatiable world to live its life once? Why not admit solipsism and be true to the transcendental method? Because of conscience and good sense? But then the infinite series of maps is useless, England is herself again, and the prospect opens before us of an infinite number of supplementary essays.

Royce sometimes felt that he might have turned his hand to other things than philosophy. He once wrote a novel, and its want of success was a silent disappointment to him. Perhaps he might have been a great musician. Complexity, repetitions, vagueness, endlessness are hardly virtues in writing or thinking, but in music they might have swelled and swelled into a real sublimity, all the more that he was patient, had a voluminous meandering memory, and loved technical devices. But rather than a musician—for he was no artist—he resembled some great-hearted mediaeval peasant visited by mystical promptings, whom the monks should have adopted and allowed to browse among their theological folios; a Duns Scotus earnest and studious to a fault, not having the lightness of soul to despise those elaborate sophistries, yet minded to ferret out their secret for himself and walk by his inward light. His was a gothic and scholastic spirit, intent on devising and solving puzzles, and honoring God in systematic works, like the coral insect or the spider; eventually creating a fabric that in its homely intricacy and fullness arrested and moved the heart, the web of it was so vast, and so full of mystery and yearning.

THE MIGRATION of Americans to Europe began to give way during the twenties to a movement of Europeans toward America. D. H. Lawrence's *Studies in Classic American Literature* did not appear in book-form till 1922; but he had begun them during World War I. In a letter of February 1, 1919, to Harriet Monroe, the editor of the Chicago magazine *Poetry,* he wrote: "I have worked at them for more than four years—hard work. They may not look it."

In September 1922, Lawrence came to America, and he remained here, with one brief visit to England, till October 1925. The instincts and thoughts that appear in these essays are reflected in his letters of this period. "The sense of doom deepens inside me," he wrote to J. Middleton Murry on August 13, 1923, "at the thought of the old world which I loved—and the new world means nothing to me." But he liked the Southwest and Mexico, because they seemed to bring him close to the primitive "dark gods" from which he tended to think the white race was cutting itself off in abstraction. He spent very little time in the East and lived mostly in the country in New Mexico. "I must say I am glad," he wrote Harriet Monroe from Taos, April 8, 1924, "to be out here in the Southwest of America—there is the pristine something, unbroken, unbreakable, and not to be got under even by us awful whites with our machines—for which I thank whatever gods there be."

He tried to formulate his opinion of America in a letter to Gilbert Seldes of February 25, 1923, from Del Monte Ranch, Questa, New Mexico:

> No, I am not disappointed in America. I said I was coming to Europe this spring. But I don't want to. We leave in a fortnight for old Mexico. Perhaps I shall came back here. . . .
>
> But I feel about U.S.A., as I vaguely felt a long time ago: that there is a vast unreal intermediary thing intervening between the real thing which was Europe and the next real thing, which will probably be America, but which isn't yet, at all. Seems to me a vast death-happening must come first. But probably it is here, in America (I don't say just U.S.A.), that the quick will keep alive and come through.

The *Studies in Classic American Literature* have shots that do not hit the mark and moments that are quite hysterical; but they remain one of the few first-rate books that have ever been written on the subject. To an American, American literature is a part of his native landscape, and so veiled with associations that he cannot always see what the author is really saying. D. H. Lawrence has here tried to do what it would be difficult for an American to do: read our books for their meaning in the life of the western world as a whole.

And his *Studies* mark the moment when Europe first begins to look toward America, not merely for freedom, not merely for money, not merely from curiosity, but with a desperate need for new ideals to sustain European civilization.

D. H. LAWRENCE

STUDIES IN CLASSIC AMERICAN LITERATURE

I. The Spirit of Place

WE LIKE TO THINK of the old-fashioned American classics as children's books. Just childishness, on our part. The old American art speech contains an alien quality, which belongs to the American continent and to nowhere else. But, of course, so long as we insist on reading the books as children's tales, we miss all that.

One wonders what the proper high-brow Romans of the third and fourth or later centuries read into the strange utterances of Lucretius or Apuleius or Tertullian, Augustine or Athanasius. The uncanny voice of Iberian Spain, the weirdness of old Carthage, the passion of Libya and North Africa; you may bet the proper old Romans never heard these at all. They read old Latin inference over the top of it, as we read old European inference over the top of Poe or Hawthorne.

It is hard to hear a new voice, as hard as it is to listen to an unknown language. We just don't listen. There is a new voice in the old American classics. The world has declined to hear it, and has babbled about children's stories.

Why?—Out of fear. The world fears a new experience

more than it fears anything. Because a new experience displaces so many old experiences. And it is like trying to use muscles that have perhaps never been used, or that have been going stiff for ages. It hurts horribly.

The world doesn't fear a new idea. It can pigeonhole any idea. But it can't pigeonhole a real new experience. It can only dodge. The world is a great dodger, and the Americans the greatest. Because they dodge their own very selves.

There is a new feeling in the old American books, far more than there is in the modern American books, which are pretty empty of any feeling, and proud of it. There is a "different" feeling in the old American classics. It is the shifting over from the old psyche to something new, a displacement. And displacements hurt. This hurts. So we try to tie it up, like a cut finger. Put a rag round it.

It is a cut too. Cutting away the old emotions and consciousness. Don't ask what is left.

Art speech is the only truth. An artist is usually a damned liar, but his art, if it be art, will tell you the truth of his day. And that is all that matters. Away with eternal truth. Truth lives from day to day, and the marvelous Plato of yesterday is chiefly bosh today.

The old American artists were hopeless liars. But they were artists, in spite of themselves. Which is more than you can say of most living practitioners.

And you can please yourself, when you read *The Scarlet Letter,* whether you accept what that sugary, blue-eyed little darling of a Hawthorne has to say for himself, false as all darlings are, or whether you read the impeccable truth of his art speech.

The curious thing about art speech is that it prevaricates so terribly, I mean it tells such lies. I suppose because we always all the time tell ourselves lies. And out of a pattern of lies art weaves the truth. Like Dostoevsky posing as a sort of Jesus, but most truthfully revealing himself all the while as a little horror.

Truly art is a sort of subterfuge. But thank God for it, we can see through the subterfuge if we choose. Art has two great functions. First, it provides an emotional experience.

And then, if we have the courage of our own feelings, it becomes a mine of practical truth. We have had the feelings *ad nauseam.* But we've never dared dig the actual truth out of them, the truth that concerns us, whether it concerns our grandchildren or not.

The artist usually sets out—or used to—to point a moral and adorn a tale. The tale, however, points the other way, as a rule. Two blankly opposing morals, the artist's and the tale's. Never trust the artist. Trust the tale. The proper function of a critic is to save the tale from the artist who created it.

Now we know our business in these studies; saving the American tale from the American artist.

Let us look at this American artist first. How did he ever get to America, to start with? Why isn't he a European still, like his father before him?

Now listen to me, don't listen to him. He'll tell you the lie you expect. Which is partly your fault for expecting it.

He didn't come in search of freedom of worship. England had more freedom of worship in the year 1700 than America had. Won by Englishmen who wanted freedom, and so stopped at home and fought for it. And got it. Freedom of worship? Read the history of New England during the first century of its existence.

Freedom anyhow? The land of the free! This the land of the free! Why, if I say anything that displeases them, the free mob will lynch me, and that's my freedom. Free? Why, I have never been in any country where the individual has such an abject fear of his fellow-countrymen. Because, as I say, they are free to lynch him the moment he shows he is not one of them.

No, no, if you're so fond of the truth about Queen Victoria, try a little about yourself.

Those Pilgrim Fathers and their successors never came here for freedom of worship. What did they set up when they got here? Freedom, would you call it?

They didn't come for freedom. Or if they did, they sadly went back on themselves.

All right then, what did they come for? For lots of reasons.

Perhaps least of all in search of freedom of any sort: positive freedom, that is.

They came largely to get *away*—that most simple of motives. To get away. Away from what? In the long run, away from themselves. Away from everything. That's why most people have come to America, and still do come. To get away from everything they are and have been.

"Henceforth be masterless."

Which is all very well, but it isn't freedom. Rather the reverse. A hopeless sort of constraint. It is never freedom till you find something you really *positively want to be*. And people in America have always been shouting about the things they are *not*. Unless, of course, they are millionaires, made or in the making.

And after all there is a positive side to the movement. All that vast flood of human life that has flowed over the Atlantic in ships from Europe to America has not flowed over simply on a tide of revulsion from Europe and from the confinements of the European ways of life. This revulsion was, and still is, I believe, the prime motive in emigration. But there was some cause, even for the revulsion.

It seems as if at times man had a frenzy for getting away from any control of any sort. In Europe the old Christianity was the real master. The Church and the true aristocracy bore the responsibility for the working out of the Christian ideals: a little irregularly, maybe, but responsible nevertheless.

Mastery, kingship, fatherhood had their power destroyed at the time of the Renaissance.

And it was precisely at this moment that the great drift over the Atlantic started. What were men drifting away from? The old authority of Europe? Were they breaking the bonds of authority, and escaping to a new more absolute unrestrainedness? Maybe. But there was more to it.

Liberty is all very well, but men cannot live without masters. There is always a master. And men either live in glad obedience to the master they believe in, or they live in a frictional opposition to the master they wish to undermine. In America this frictional opposition has been the vital factor. It has given the Yankee his kick. Only the continual influx of more servile Europeans has provided America with an obedient laboring class. The true obedience never outlasting the first generation.

But there sits the old master, over in Europe. Like a parent. Somewhere deep in every American heart lies a rebellion against the old parenthood of Europe. Yet no American feels he has completely escaped its mastery. Hence the slow, smoldering patience of American opposition. The slow, smoldering, corrosive obedience to the old master Europe, the unwilling subject, the unremitting opposition.

Whatever else you are, be masterless.

Ca Ca Caliban
Get a new master, be a new man.

Escaped slaves, we might say, people the republics of Liberia or Haiti. Liberia enough! Are we to look at America in the same way? A vast republic of escaped slaves. When you consider the hordes from eastern Europe, you might well say it: a vast republic of escaped slaves. But one dare not say this of the Pilgrim Fathers, and the great old body of idealist Americans, the modern Americans tortured with thought. A vast republic of escaped slaves. Look out, America! And a minority of earnest, self-tortured people.

The masterless.

Ca Ca Caliban
Get a new master, be a new man.

What did the Pilgrim Fathers come for, then, when they came so gruesomely over the black sea? Oh, it was in a black spirit. A black revulsion from Europe, from the old authority of Europe, from kings and bishops and popes. And more. When you look into it, more. They were black, masterful men, they wanted something else. No kings, no bishops maybe. Even no God Almighty. But also, no more of this new "humanity" which followed the Renaissance. None of this new liberty which was to be so pretty in Europe. Something grimmer, by no means free-and-easy.

America has never been easy, and is not easy today. Americans have always been at a certain tension. Their liberty is a thing of sheer will, sheer tension: a liberty of THOU SHALT NOT. And it has been so from the first. The land of THOU SHALT NOT. Only the first commandment is: THOU SHALT NOT PRESUME TO BE A MASTER. Hence democracy.

"We are the masterless." That is what the American Eagle shrieks. It's a Hen-Eagle.

The Spaniards refused the post-Renaissance liberty of Europe. And the Spaniards filled most of America. The Yankees, too, refused, refused the post-Renaissance humanism of Europe. First and foremost, they hated masters. But under that, they hated the flowing ease of humor in Europe. At the bottom of the American soul was always a dark suspense, at the bottom of the Spanish-American soul the same. And this dark suspense hated and hates the old European spontaneity, watches it collapse with satisfaction.

Every continent has its own great spirit of place. Every people is polarized in some particular locality, which is home, the homeland. Different places on the face of the earth have different vital effluence, different vibration, different chemical exhalation, different polarity with different stars: call it what you like. But the spirit of place is a great reality. The Nile valley produced not only the corn, but the terrific religions of Egypt. China produces the Chinese, and will go on doing so. The Chinese in San Francisco will in time cease to be Chinese, for America is a great melting pot.

There was a tremendous polarity in Italy, in the city of Rome. And this seems to have died. For even places die. The Island of Great Britain had a wonderful terrestrial magnetism or polarity of its own, which made the British people. For the moment, this polarity seems to be breaking. Can England die? And what if England dies?

Men are less free than they imagine; ah, far less free. The freest are perhaps least free.

Men are free when they are in a living homeland, not when they are straying and breaking away. Men are free when they are obeying some deep, inward voice of religious belief. Obeying from within. Men are free when they belong to a living, organic, *believing* community, active in fulfilling some unfulfilled, perhaps unrealized purpose. Not when they are escaping to some wild west. The most unfree souls go west, and shout of freedom. Men are freest when they are most unconscious of freedom. The shout is a rattling of chains, always was.

Men are not free when they are doing just what they like. The moment you can do just what you like, there is nothing you care about doing. Men are only free when they are doing what the deepest self likes.

And there is getting down to the deepest self! It takes some diving.

Because the deepest self is way down, and the conscious self is an obstinate monkey. But of one thing we may be sure. If one wants to be free, one has to give up the illusion of doing what one likes, and seek what IT wishes done.

But before you can do what IT likes, you must first break the spell of the old mastery, the old IT.

Perhaps at the Renaissance, when kinship and fatherhood fell, Europe drifted into a very dangerous half-truth: of liberty and equality. Perhaps the men who went to America felt this, and so repudiated the old world altogether. Went one better than Europe. Liberty in America has meant so far the breaking away from *all* dominion. The true liberty will only begin when Americans discover IT, and proceed possibly to fulfill IT. IT being the deepest *whole* self of man, the self in its wholeness, not idealistic halfness.

That's why the Pilgrim Fathers came to America, then; and that's why we come. Driven by IT. We cannot see that invisible winds carry us, as they carry swarms of locusts, that invisible magnetism brings us as it brings the migrating birds to their unforeknown goal. But it is so. We are not the marvelous choosers and deciders we think we are. IT chooses for us, and decides for us. Unless, of course, we are just escaped slaves, vulgarly cocksure of our ready-made destiny. But if we are living people, in touch with the source, IT drives us and decides us. We are free only so long as we obey. When we run counter, and think we will do as we like, we just flee around like Orestes pursued by the Eumenides.

And still, when the great day begins, when Americans have at last discovered America and their own wholeness, still there will be the vast number of escaped slaves to reckon with, those who have no cocksure, ready-made destinies.

Which will win in America, the escaped slaves, or the new whole men?

The real American day hasn't begun yet. Or at least, not yet sunrise. So far it has been the false dawn. That is, in the progressive American consciousness there has been the one dominant desire, to do away with the old thing. Do away with masters, exalt the will of the people. The will of the people being nothing but a figment, the exalting doesn't count for much. So, in the name of the will of the people, get rid of masters. When you have got rid of masters, you are left with this mere phrase of the will of the people. Then you pause and bethink yourself, and try to recover your own wholeness.

So much for the conscious American motive, and for democracy over here. Democracy in America is just the tool with which the old master of Europe, the European spirit, is undermined. Europe destroyed potentially, American democracy will evaporate. America will begin.

American consciousness has so far been a false dawn. The negative ideal of democracy. But underneath, and contrary to this open ideal, the first hints and revelations of IT. IT, the American whole soul.

You have got to pull the democratic and idealistic clothes off American utterance, and see what you can of the dusky body of IT underneath.

"Henceforth be masterless."

Henceforth be mastered.

II. Benjamin Franklin

THE Perfectibility of Man! Ah heaven, what a dreary theme! The perfectibility of the Ford car! The perfectibility of which man? I am many men. Which of them are you going to perfect? I am not a mechanical contrivance.

Education! Which of the various me's do you propose to educate, and which do you propose to suppress?

Anyhow, I defy you. I defy you, oh society, to educate me or to suppress me, according to your dummy standards.

The ideal man! And which is he, if you please? Benjamin Franklin or Abraham Lincoln? The ideal man! Roosevelt or Porfirio Diaz?

There are other men in me, besides this patient ass who sits here in a tweed jacket. What am I doing, playing the patient ass in a tweed jacket? Who am I talking to? Who are you, at the other end of this patience?

Who are you? How many selves have you? And which of these selves do you want to be?

Is Yale College going to educate the self that is the dark of you, or Harvard College?

The ideal self! Oh, but I have a strange and fugitive self shut out and howling like a wolf or a coyote under the ideal windows. See his red eyes in the dark? This is the self who is coming into his own.

The perfectibility of man, dear God! When every man as long as he remains alive is in himself a multitude of conflicting men. Which of these do you choose to perfect, at the expense of every other?

Old Daddy Franklin will tell you. He'll rig him up for you, the pattern American. Oh, Franklin was the first downright American. He knew what he was about, the sharp little man. He set up the first dummy American.

At the beginning of his career this cunning little Benjamin drew up for himself a creed that should "satisfy the professors of every religion, but shock none."

Now wasn't that a real American thing to do?

"That there is One God, who made all things."

(But Benjamin made Him.)

"That He governs the world by His Providence."

(Benjamin knowing all about Providence.)

"That He ought to be worshiped with adoration, prayer, and thanksgiving."

(Which cost nothing.)

"But——" But me no buts, Benjamin, saith the Lord.

"But that the most acceptable service of God is doing good to men."

(God having no choice in the matter.)

"That the soul is immortal."

(You'll see why, in the next clause.)

"And that God will certainly reward virtue and punish vice, either here or hereafter."

Now if Mr. Andrew Carnegie, or any other millionaire, had wished to invent a God to suit his ends, he could not have done better. Benjamin did it for him in the eighteenth century. God is the supreme servant of men who want to get on, to *produce*. Providence. The provider. The heavenly storekeeper. The everlasting Wanamaker.

And this is all the God the grandsons of the Pilgrim Fathers had left. Aloft on a pillar of dollars.

"That the soul is immortal."

The trite way Benjamin says it!

But man has a soul, though you can't locate it either in his purse or his pocket-book or his heart or his stomach or his head. The *wholeness* of a man is his soul. Not merely that nice little comfortable bit which Benjamin marks out.

It's a queer thing is a man's soul. It is the whole of him. Which means it is the unknown him, as well as the known. It seems to me just funny, professors and Benjamins fixing the functions of the soul. Why the soul of man is a vast forest, and all Benjamin intended was a neat back garden. And we've all got to fit into his kitchen-garden scheme of things. Hail Columbia!

The soul of man is a dark forest. The Hercynian Wood that scared the Romans so, and out of which came the white-skinned hordes of the next civilization.

Who knows what will come out of the soul of man? The soul of man is a dark vast forest, with wild life in it. Think of Benjamin fencing it off!

Oh, but Benjamin fenced a little tract that he called the soul of man, and proceeded to get it into cultivation. Providence, forsooth! And they think that bit of barbed wire is going to keep us in pound forever? More fools they.

This is Benjamin's barbed-wire fence. He made himself a list of virtues, which he trotted inside like a gray nag in a paddock.

1
TEMPERANCE

Eat not to fullness; drink not to elevation.

2
SILENCE

Speak not but what may benefit others or yourself; avoid trifling conversation.

3
ORDER

Let all your things have their places; let each part of your business have its time.

4
RESOLUTION

Resolve to perform what you ought; perform without fail what you resolve.

5
FRUGALITY

Make no expense but to do good to others or yourself—i.e., waste nothing.

6
INDUSTRY

Lose no time, be always employed in something useful; cut off all unnecessary action.

7
SINCERITY

Use no hurtful deceit; think innocently and justly, and, if you speak, speak accordingly.

8
JUSTICE

Wrong none by doing injuries, or omitting the benefits that are your duty.

9
MODERATION

Avoid extremes, forbear resenting injuries as much as you think they deserve.

10
CLEANLINESS

Tolerate no uncleanliness in body, clothes, or habitation.

11
TRANQUILLITY

Be not disturbed at trifles, or at accidents common or unavoidable.

12
CHASTITY

Rarely use venery but for health and offspring, never to dullness, weakness, or the injury of your own or another's peace or reputation.

13
HUMILITY

Imitate Jesus and Socrates.

A Quaker friend told Franklin that he, Benjamin, was generally considered proud, so Benjamin put in the Humility touch as an afterthought. The amusing part is the sort of humility it displays. "Imitate Jesus and Socrates," and mind you don't outshine either of these two. One can just imagine Socrates and Alcibiades roaring in their cups over Philadelphian Benjamin, and Jesus looking at him a little puzzled, and murmuring: "Aren't you wise in your own conceit, Ben?"

"Henceforth be masterless," retorts Ben. "Be ye each one his own master unto himself, and don't let even the Lord put His spoke in." "Each man his own master" is but a puffing up of masterlessness.

Well, the first of Americans practiced this enticing list with assiduity, setting a national example. He had the virtues in columns, and gave himself good and bad marks according as he thought his behavior deserved. Pity these conduct charts are lost to us. He only remarks that Order was his stumbling block. He could not learn to be neat and tidy.

Isn't it nice to have nothing worse to confess?

He was a little model, was Benjamin. Doctor Franklin. Snuff-colored little man! Immortal soul and all!

The immortal soul part was a sort of cheap insurance policy.

Benjamin had no concern, really, with the immortal soul. He was too busy with social man.

1. He swept and lighted the streets of young Philadelphia.

2. He invented electrical appliances.

3. He was the center of a moralizing club in Philadelphia, and he wrote the moral humorisms of Poor Richard.

4. He was a member of all the important councils of Philadelphia, and then of the American colonies.

5. He won the cause of American Independence at the French Court, and was the economic father of the United States.

Now what more can you want of a man? And yet he is *infra dig.*, even in Philadelphia.

I admire him. I admire his sturdy courage first of all, then his sagacity, then his glimpsing into the thunders of electricity, then his common-sense humor. All the qualities of a great man, and never more than a great citizen. Middle-sized, sturdy, snuff-colored Doctor Franklin, one of the soundest citizens that ever trod or "used venery."

I do not like him.

And, by the way, I always thought books of Venery were about hunting deer.

There is a certain earnest naïveté about him. Like a child. And like a little old man. He has again become as a little child, always as wise as his grandfather, or wiser.

Perhaps, as I say, the most complete citizen that ever "used venery."

Printer, philosopher, scientist, author and patriot, impeccable husband and citizen, why isn't he an archetype?

Pioneer, Oh, Pioneers! Benjamin was one of the greatest pioneers of the United States. Yet we just can't do with him.

What's wrong with him then? Or what's wrong with us?

I can remember, when I was a little boy, my father used to buy a scrubby yearly almanac with the sun and moon and stars on the cover. And it used to prophesy bloodshed and famine. But also crammed in corners it had little anecdotes and humorisms, with a moral tag. And I used to have my little priggish laugh at the woman who counted her chickens before they were hatched and so forth, and I was convinced that honesty was the best policy, also a little priggishly. The author of these bits was Poor Richard, and Poor Richard was Benjamin Franklin, writing in Philadelphia well over a hundred years before.

And probably I haven't got over those Poor Richard tags yet. I rankle still with them. They are thorns in young flesh.

Because, although I still believe that honesty is the best policy, I dislike policy altogether; though it is just as well not to count your chickens before they are hatched, it's still more hateful to count them with gloating when they *are* hatched. It has taken me many years and countless smarts to get out of that barbed-wire moral enclosure that Poor Richard rigged up. Here am I now in tatters and scratched to ribbons, sitting in the middle of Benjamin's America looking at the barbed wire, and the fat sheep crawling under the fence to get fat outside, and the watchdogs yelling at the gate lest by chance anyone should get out by the proper exit. Oh, America! Oh, Benjamin! And I just utter a long, loud curse against Benjamin and the American corral.

Moral America! Most moral Benjamin. Sound, satisfied Ben!

He had to go to the frontiers of his State to settle some disturbance among the Indians. On this occasion he writes:

> We found that they had made a great bonfire in the middle of the square; they were all drunk, men and women quarreling and fighting. Their dark-colored bodies, half naked, seen only by the gloomy light of the bonfire, running after and beating one another with firebrands, accompanied by their horrid yellings, formed a scene the most resembling our ideas of hell that could well be imagined. There was no appeasing the tumult,

and we retired to our lodging. At midnight a number of them came thundering at our door, demanding more rum, of which we took no notice.

The next day, sensible they had misbehaved in giving us that disturbance, they sent three of their counselors to make their apology. The orator acknowledged the fault, but laid it upon the rum, and then endeavored to excuse the rum by saying: "The Great Spirit, who made all things, made everything for some use; and whatever he designed anything for, that use it should always be put to. Now, when he had made the rum, he said: 'Let this be for the Indians to get drunk with.' And it must be so."

And, indeed, if it be the design of Providence to extirpate these savages in order to make room for the cultivators of the earth, it seems not improbable that rum may be the appointed means. It has already annihilated all the tribes who formerly inhabited all the seacoast. . . .

This, from the good doctor with such suave complacency, is a little disenchanting. Almost too good to be true.

But there you are! The barbed-wire fence. "Extirpate these savages in order to make room for the cultivators of the earth." Oh, Benjamin Franklin! He even "used venery" as a cultivator of seed.

Cultivate the earth, ye gods! The Indians did that, as much as they needed. And they left off there. Who built Chicago? Who cultivated the earth until it spawned Pittsburgh, Pa.?

The moral issue! Just look at it! Cultivation included. If it's a mere choice of Kultur or cultivation, I give it up.

Which brings us right back to our question, what's wrong with Benjamin, that we can't stand him? Or else, what's wrong with us, that we find fault with such a paragon?

Man is a moral animal. All right. I am a moral animal. And I'm going to remain such. I'm not going to be turned into a virtuous little automaton as Benjamin would have me. "This is good, that is bad. Turn the little handle and let the good tap flow," saith Benjamin, and all America with him. "But first of all extirpate those savages who are always turning on the bad tap."

I am a moral animal. But I am not a moral machine. I

don't work with a little set of handles or levers. The Temperance-silence-order-resolution-frugality-industry-sincerity-justice-moderation-cleanliness-tranquillity-chastity-humility keyboard is not going to get me going. I'm really not just an automatic piano with a moral Benjamin getting tunes out of me.

Here's my creed, against Benjamin's. This is what I believe:

That I am I.

That my soul is a dark forest.

That my known self will never be more than a little clearing in the forest.

That gods, strange gods, come forth from the forest into the clearing of my known self, and then go back.

That I must have the courage to let them come and go.

That I will never let mankind put anything over me, but that I will try always to recognize and submit to the gods in me and the gods in other men and women.

There is my creed. He who runs may read. He who prefers to crawl, or to go by gasoline, can call it rot.

Then for a "list." It is rather fun to play at Benjamin.

1

TEMPERANCE

Eat and carouse with Bacchus, or munch dry bread with Jesus, but don't sit down without one of the gods.

2

SILENCE

Be still when you have nothing to say; when genuine passion moves you, say what you've got to say, and say it hot.

3

ORDER

Know that you are responsible to the gods inside you and to the men in whom the gods are manifest. Recognize your superiors and your inferiors, according to the gods. This is the root of all order.

4

Resolution

Resolve to abide by your own deepest promptings, and to sacrifice the smaller thing to the greater. Kill when you must, and be killed the same: the *must* coming from the gods inside you, or from the men in whom you recognize the Holy Ghost.

5

Frugality

Demand nothing; accept what you see fit. Don't waste your pride or squander your emotion.

6

Industry

Lose no time with ideals; serve the Holy Ghost; never serve mankind.

7

Sincerity

To be sincere is to remember that I am I, and that the other man is not me.

8

Justice

The only justice is to follow the sincere intuition of the soul, angry or gentle. Anger is just, and pity is just, but judgment is never just.

9

Moderation

Beware of absolutes. There are many gods.

10

Cleanliness

Don't be too clean. It impoverishes the blood.

11

Tranquillity

The soul has many motions, many gods come and go. Try and find your deepest issue, in every confusion, and abide by that. Obey the man in whom you recognize the Holy Ghost; command when your honor comes to command.

12

Chastity

Never "use" venery at all. Follow your passional impulse, if it be answered in the other being; but never have any motive in mind, neither offspring nor health nor even pleasure, nor even service. Only know that "venery" is of the great gods. An offering-up of yourself to the very great gods, the dark ones, and nothing else.

13

Humility

See all men and women according to the Holy Ghost that is within them. Never yield before the barren.

There's my list. I have been trying dimly to realize it for a long time, and only America and old Benjamin have at last goaded me into trying to formulate it.

And now I, at least, know why I can't stand Benjamin. He tries to take away my wholeness and my dark forest, my freedom. For how can any man be free, without an illimitable background? And Benjamin tries to shove me into a barbed-wire paddock and make me grow potatoes or Chicagoes.

And how can I be free, without gods that come and go? But Benjamin won't let anything exist except my useful fellow-men, and I'm sick of them; as for his Godhead, his Providence, He is Head of nothing except a vast heavenly store that keeps every imaginable line of goods, from victrolas to cat-o'-nine tails.

And how can any man be free without a soul of his own, that he believes in and won't sell at any price? But Benjamin doesn't let me have a soul of my own. He says I am nothing but a servant of mankind—galley-slave I call it—and if I don't get my wages here below—that is, if Mr. Pierpont Morgan or Mr. Nosey Hebrew or the grand United States Government, the great US, US OR SOMEOFUS, manages to scoop in my bit, along with their lump—why, never mind, I shall get my wages HEREAFTER.

Oh, Benjamin! Oh, Binjum! You do NOT suck me in any longer.

And why, oh, why should the snuff-colored little trap have wanted to take us all in? Why did he do it?

Out of sheer human cussedness, in the first place. We do all like to get things inside a barbed-wire corral. Especially our fellow-men. We love to round them up inside the barbed-wire enclosure of FREEDOM, and make 'em work. *"Work, you free jewel,* WORK!" shouts the liberator, cracking his whip. Benjamin, I will not work. I do not choose to be a free democrat. I am absolutely a servant of my own Holy Ghost.

Sheer cussedness! But there was as well the salt of a subtler purpose. Benjamin was just in his eyeholes—to use an English vulgarism, meaning he was just delighted—when he was at Paris judiciously milking money out of the French monarchy for the overthrow of all monarchy. If you want to ride your horse to somewhere you must put a bit in his mouth. And Benjamin wanted to ride his horse so that it would upset the whole apple-cart of the old masters. He wanted the whole European apple-cart upset. So he had to put a strong bit in the mouth of his ass.

"Henceforth be masterless."

That is, he had to break in the human ass completely, so that much more might be broken, in the long run. For the moment it was the British Government that had to have a hole knocked in it. The first real hole it ever had: the breach of the American rebellion.

Benjamin, in his sagacity, knew that the breaking of the old world was a long process. In the depths of his own under-consciousness he hated England, he hated Europe, he hated the whole corpus of the European being. He wanted to be American. But you can't change your nature and mode of consciousness like changing your shoes. It is a gradual shedding. Years must go by, and centuries must elapse before you have finished. Like a son escaping from the domination of his parents. The escape is not just one rupture. It is a long and half-secret process.

So with the American. He was a European when he first went over the Atlantic. He is in the main a recreant European still. From Benjamin Franklin to Woodrow Wilson may be a long stride, but it is a stride along the same road. There is no new road. The same old road, become dreary and futile. Theoretic and materialistic.

Why then did Benjamin set up this dummy of a perfect citizen as a pattern to America? Of course, he did it in perfect good faith, as far as he knew. He thought it simply was the true ideal. But what we *think* we do is not very important. We never really know what we are doing. Either we are materialistic instruments, like Benjamin, or we move in the gesture of creation, from our deepest self, usually unconscious. We are only the actors, we are never wholly the authors of our own deeds or works. IT is the author, the unknown inside us or outside us. The best we can do is to try to hold ourselves in unison with the deeps which are inside us. And the worst we can do is to try to have things our own way, when we run counter to IT, and in the long run get our knuckles rapped for our presumption.

So Benjamin contriving money out of the Court of France. He was contriving the first steps of the overthrow of all Europe, France included. You can never have a new thing without breaking an old. Europe happens to be the old thing. America, unless the people in America assert themselves too much in opposition to the inner gods, should be the new thing. The new thing is the death of the old. But you can't cut the throat of an epoch. You've got to steal the life from it through several centuries.

And Benjamin worked for this both directly and indirectly. Directly, at the Court of France, making a small but very dangerous hole in the side of England, through which hole Europe has by now almost bled to death. And indirectly in Philadelphia, setting up this unlovely, snuff-colored little ideal, or automaton, of a pattern American. The pattern American, this dry, moral, utilitarian little democrat, has done more to ruin the old Europe than any Russian nihilist. He has done it by slow attrition, like a son who has stayed at home and obeyed his parents, all the while silently hating their authority, and silently, in his soul, destroying not only their authority but their whole existence. For the American spiritually stayed at home in Europe. The spiritual home of

America was, and still is, Europe. This is the galling bondage, in spite of several billions of heaped-up gold. Your heaps of gold are only so many muck-heaps, America, and will remain so till you become a reality to yourselves.

All this Americanizing and mechanizing has been for the purpose of overthrowing the past. And now look at America, tangled in her own barbed wire, and mastered by her own machines. Absolutely got down by her own barbed wire of shalt-nots, and shut up fast in her own "productive" machines like millions of squirrels running in millions of cages. It is just a farce.

Now is your chance, Europe. Now let Hell loose and get your own back, and paddle your own canoe on a new sea, while clever America lies on her muck-heaps of gold, strangled in her own barbed wire of shalt-not ideals and shalt-not moralisms. While she goes out to work like millions of squirrels in millions of cages. Production!

Let Hell loose, and get your own back, Europe!

III. Hector St. John de Crèvecœur

CRÈVECŒUR was born in France, at Caen, in the year 1735. As a boy he was sent over to England and received part of his education there. He went to Canada as a young man, served for a time with Montcalm in the war against the English, and later passed over into the United States, to become an exuberant American. He married a New England girl, and settled on the frontier. During the period of his "cultivating the earth" he wrote the *Letters from an American Farmer,* which enjoyed great vogue in their day, in England especially, among the new reformers like Godwin and Tom Paine.

But Crèvecœur was not a mere cultivator of the earth. That was his best stunt, shall we say. He himself was more concerned with a perfect society and his own manipulation thereof, than with growing carrots. Behold him, then, trotting off importantly and idealistically to France, leaving his farm in the wilds to be burnt by the Indians, and his wife to shift as best she might. This was during the American

War of Independence, when the Noble Red Man took to behaving like his own old self. On his return to America, the American Farmer entered into public affairs and into commerce. Again tripping to France, he enjoyed himself as a *littérateur* Child-of-Nature-sweet-and-pure, was a friend of old Benjamin Franklin in Paris, and quite a favorite with Jean Jacques Rousseau's Madame d'Houdetot, that literary soul.

Hazlitt, Godwin, Shelley, Coleridge, the English romanticists, were, of course, thrilled by the *Letters from an American Farmer*. A new world, a world of the Noble Savage and Pristine Nature and Paradisal Simplicity and all that gorgeousness that flows out of the unsullied fount of the ink-bottle. Lucky Coleridge, who got no farther than Bristol. Some of us have gone all the way.

I think this wild and noble America is the thing that I have pined for most ever since I read Fenimore Cooper, as a boy. Now I've got it.

Franklin is the real *practical* prototype of the American. Crèvecœur is the emotional. To the European, the American is first and foremost a dollar-fiend. We tend to forget the emotional heritage of Hector St. John de Crèvecœur. We tend to disbelieve, for example, in Woodrow Wilson's wrung heart and wet hanky. Yet surely these are real enough. Aren't they?

It wasn't to be expected that the dry little snuff-colored Doctor should have it all his own way. The new Americans might use venery for health or offspring, and their time for cultivating potatoes and Chicagoes, but they had got *some* sap in their veins after all. They had got to get a bit of luscious emotion somewhere.

NATURE.

I wish I could write it larger than that.

N A T U R E.

Benjamin overlooked NATURE. But the French Crèvecœur spotted it long before Thoreau and Emerson worked it up. Absolutely the safest thing to get your emotional reactions over is NATURE.

Crèvecœur's *Letters* are written in a spirit of touching

simplicity, almost better than Chateaubriand. You'd think neither of them would ever know how many beans make five. This American Farmer tells of the joys of creating a home in the wilderness, and of cultivating the virgin soil. Poor virgin, prostituted from the very start.

The Farmer had an Amiable Spouse and an Infant Son, his progeny. He took the Infant Son—who enjoys no other name than this—

What is thy name?
I have no name.
I am the Infant Son——

to the fields with him, and seated the same I. S. on the shafts of the plow whilst he, the American Farmer, plowed the potato patch. He also, the A. F., helped his Neighbors, whom no doubt he loved as himself, to build a barn, and they labored together in the Innocent Simplicity of one of Nature's Communities. Meanwhile the Amiable Spouse, who likewise in Blakean simplicity has No Name, cooked the doughnuts or the pie, though these are not mentioned. No doubt she was a deep-breasted daughter of America, though she may equally well have been a flat-bosomed Methodist. She would have been an Amiable Spouse in either case, and the American Farmer asked no more. I don't know whether her name was Lizzie or Ahoolibah, and probably Crèvecœur didn't. Spouse was enough for him. "Spouse, hand me the carving knife."

The Infant Son developed into Healthy Offspring as more appeared: no doubt Crèvecœur had used venery as directed. And so these Children of Nature toiled in the Wilds at Simple Toil with a little Honest Sweat now and then. You have the complete picture, dear reader. The American Farmer made his own Family Picture, and it is still on view. Of course the Amiable Spouse put on her best apron to be *Im Bild,* for all the world to see and admire.

I used to admire my head off: before I tiptoed into the Wilds and saw the shacks of the Homesteaders. Particularly the Amiable Spouse, poor thing. No wonder *she* never sang the song of Simple Toil in the Innocent Wilds. Poor haggard drudge, like a ghost wailing in the wilderness, nine times out of ten.

Hector St. John, you have lied to me. You lied even more scurrilously to yourself. Hector St. John, you are an emotional liar.

Jean Jacques, Bernardin de St. Pierre, Chateaubriand, exquisite François Le Vaillant, you lying little lot, with your Nature-Sweet-and-Pure! Marie Antoinette got her head off for playing dairymaid, and nobody even dusted the seats of your pants, till now, for all the lies you put over us.

But Crèvecœur was an artist as well as a liar, otherwise we would not have bothered with him. He wanted to put NATURE in his pocket, as Benjamin put the Human Being. Between them, they wanted the whole scheme of things in their pockets, and the things themselves as well. Once you've got the scheme of things in your pocket, you can do as you like with it, even make money out of it, if you can't find in your heart to destroy it, as was your first intention. So H. St. J. de C. tried to put Nature-Sweet-and-Pure in his pocket. But nature wasn't having any, she poked her head out and baa-ed.

This Nature-sweet-and-pure business is only another effort at intellectualizing. Just an attempt to make all nature succumb to a few laws of the human mind. The sweet-and-pure sort of laws. Nature seemed to be behaving quite nicely, for a while. She has left off.

That's why you get the purest intellectuals in a Garden Suburb or a Brook Farm experiment. You bet, Robinson Crusoe was a highbrow of highbrows.

You can idealize or intellectualize. Or, on the contrary, you can let the dark soul in you see for itself. An artist usually intellectualizes on top, and his dark under-consciousness goes on contradicting him beneath. This is almost laughably the case with most American artists. Crèvecœur is the first example. He is something of an artist, Franklin isn't anything.

Crèvecœur the idealist puts over us a lot of stuff about nature and the noble savage and the innocence of toil, etc.,

etc. Blarney! But Crèvecœur the artist gives us glimpses of actual nature, not writ large.

Curious that his vision sees only the lowest forms of natural life. Insects, snakes, and birds he glimpses in their own mystery, their own pristine being. And straightway gives the lie to Innocent Nature.

"I am astonished to see," he writes quite early in the *Letters,* "that nothing exists but what has its enemy, one species pursue and live upon another: unfortunately our king-birds are the destroyers of those industrious insects (the bees); but on the other hand, these birds preserve our fields from the depredations of the crows, which they pursue on the wing with great vigilance and astonishing dexterity."

This is a sad blow to the sweet-and-pureness of Nature. But it is the voice of the artist in contrast to the voice of the ideal turtle. It is the rudimentary American vision. The glimpsing of the king-birds in winged hostility and pride is no doubt the aboriginal Indian vision carrying over. The Eagle symbol in human consciousness. Dark, swinging wings of hawk-beaked destiny, that one cannot help but feel, beating here above the wild center of America. You look round in vain for the "One being Who made all things, and governs the world by His Providence."

"One species pursue and live upon another."

Reconcile the two statements if you like. But, in America, act on Crèvecœur's observation.

The horse, however, says Hector, is the friend of man, and man is the friend of the horse. But then we leave the horse no choice. And I don't see much *friend,* exactly, in my sly old Indian pony, though he is quite a decent old bird.

Man, too, says Hector, is the friend of man. Whereupon the Indians burnt his farm; so he refrains from mentioning it in the *Letters,* for fear of invalidating his premises.

Some great hornets have fixed their nest on the ceiling of the living-room of the American Farmer, and these tiger-striped animals fly round the heads of the Healthy Offspring and the Amiable Spouse, to the gratification of the American Farmer. He liked their buzz and their tiger waspishness. Also, on the utilitarian plane, they kept the house free of flies.

So Hector says. Therefore Benjamin would have approved. But of the feelings of the Amiable S., on this matter, we are not told, and after all, it was she who had to make the jam.

Another anecdote. Swallows built their nest on the veranda of the American Farm. Wrens took a fancy to the nest of the swallows. They pugnaciously (I like the word pugnaciously, it is so American) attacked the harbingers of spring, and drove them away from their nice adobe nest. The swallows returned upon opportunity. But the wrens, coming home, violently drove them forth again. Which continued until the gentle swallows patiently set about to build another nest, while the wrens sat in triumph in the usurped home. The American Farmer watched this contest with delight, and no doubt loudly applauded those little rascals of wrens. For in the Land of the Free, the greatest delight of every man is in getting the better of the other man.

Crèvecœur says he shot a king-bird that had been devouring his bees. He opened the craw and took out a vast number of bees, which little democrats, after they had lain a minute or two stunned, in the sun roused, revived, preened their wings and walked off debonair, like Jonah up the seashore; or like true Yanks escaped from the craw of the kingbird of Europe.

I don't care whether it's true or not. I like the picture, and see in it a parable of the American resurrection.

The humming-bird.

Its bill is as long and as sharp as a coarse sewing needle; like the Bee, Nature has taught it to find out in the calyx of flowers and blossoms those mellifluous particles that can serve it for sufficient food; and yet it seems to leave them untouched, undeprived of anything that the eye can possibly distinguish. Where it feeds it appears as if immovable, though continually on the wing: and sometimes, from what motives I know not, it will tear and lacerate flowers into a hundred pieces; for, strange to tell, they are the most irascible of the feathered tribe. Where do passions find room in so diminutive a body? They often fight with the fury of lions, until one of the combatants falls a sacrifice and dies. When fatigued, it has often perched within a few feet of me, and on such favorable opportunities I have surveyed it with the most minute attention. Its little eyes appear like diamonds, reflecting light on every side; most elegantly finished in all parts, it is a miniature work of our Great Parent, who seems to have formed it smallest, and at the same time most beautiful, of the winged species.

A regular little Tartar, too. Lions no bigger than ink-spots! I have read about humming-birds elsewhere, in Bates and W. H. Hudson, for example. But it is left to the American Farmer to show me the real little raging lion. Birds are evidently no angels in America, or to the true American. He sees how they start and flash their wings like little devils, and stab each other with egoistic sharp bills. But he sees also the reserved, tender shyness of the wild creature, upon occasion. Quails in winter, for instance.

"Often, in the angles of the fences, where the motion of the wind prevents the snow from settling, I carry them both chaff and grain; the one to feed them, the other to prevent their tender feet from freezing fast to the earth, as I have frequently observed them to do."

This is beautiful, and blood-knowledge. Crèvecœur knows the touch of birds' feet, as if they had stood with their vibrating, sharp, cold-cleaving balance, naked-footed on his naked hand. It is a beautiful, barbaric tenderness of the blood. He doesn't after all turn them into "little sisters of the air," like St. Francis, or start preaching to them. He knows them as strange, shy, hot-blooded concentrations of bird presence.

The *Letter* about snakes and humming-birds is a fine essay, in its primal, dark veracity. The description of the fight between two snakes, a great water-snake and a large black serpent, follows the description of the humming-bird: "Strange was this to behold; two great snakes strongly adhering to the ground, mutually fastened together by means of the writhings which lashed them to each other, and stretched at their full length, they pulled, but pulled in vain; and in the moments of greatest exertions that part of their bodies which was entwined seemed extremely small, while the rest appeared inflated, and now and then convulsed with strong undulations, rapidly following each other. Their eyes seemed on fire, and ready to start out of their heads; at one time the conflict seemed decided; the water-snake bent itself into two great folds, and by that operation rendered the other more than commonly outstretched. The next minute the new struggles of the black one gained an unexpected superiority; it acquired two great folds likewise, which necessarily extended the body of its adversary in proportion as it had contracted its own."

This fight, which Crèvecœur describes to a finish, he calls a sight "uncommon and beautiful." He forgets the sweet-and-pureness of Nature, and is for the time a sheer ophiolater, and his chapter is as handsome a piece of ophiolatry, perhaps, as that coiled Aztec rattlesnake carved in stone.

And yet the real Crèvecœur is, in the issue, neither farmer, nor child of Nature, nor ophiolater. He goes back to France, and figures in the literary salons, and is a friend of Rousseau's Madame d'Houdetot. Also he is a good business man, and arranges a line of shipping between France and America. It all ends in materialism, really. But the *Letters* tell us nothing about this.

We are left to imagine him retiring in grief to dwell with his Red Brothers under the wigwams. For the War of Independence has broken out, and the Indians are armed by the adversaries; they do dreadful work on the frontiers. While Crèvecœur is away in France his farm is destroyed, his family rendered homeless. So that the last letter laments bitterly over the war, and man's folly and inhumanity to man.

But Crèvecœur ends his lament on a note of resolution. With his amiable spouse, and his healthy offspring, now rising in stature, he will leave the civilized coasts, where man is sophisticated, and therefore inclined to be vile, and he will go to live with the Children of Nature, the Red Men, under the wigwam. No doubt, in actual life, Crèvecœur made some distinction between the Indians who drank rum à la Franklin, and who burnt homesteads and massacred families, and those Indians, the noble Children of Nature, who peopled his own predetermined fancy. Whatever he did in actual life, in his innermost self he would not give up this self-made world, where the natural man was an object of undefiled brotherliness. Touchingly and vividly he describes his tented home near the Indian village, how he breaks the aboriginal earth to produce a little maize, while his wife weaves within the wigwam. And his imaginary efforts to save his tender offspring from the brutishness of unchristian darkness are touching and puzzling, for how can Nature, so sweet and pure under the greenwood tree, how can it have any contaminating effect?

But it is all a swindle. Crèvecœur was off to France in high-heeled shoes and embroidered waistcoat, to pose as a literary man, and to prosper in the world. We, however, must perforce follow him into the backwoods, where the simple natural life shall be perfected, near the tented village of the Red Man.

He wanted, of course, to imagine the dark, savage way of life, to get it all off pat in his head. He wanted to know as the Indians and savages know, darkly, and in terms of otherness. He was simply crazy, as the Americans say, for this. Crazy enough! For at the same time he was absolutely determined that Nature is sweet and pure, that all men are brothers, and equal, and that they love one another like so many cooing doves. He was determined to have life according to his own prescription. Therefore, he wisely kept away from any too close contact with Nature, and took refuge in commerce and the material world. But yet, he was determined to know the savage way of life, to his own *mind's* satisfaction. So he just faked us the last *Letters*. A sort of wish-fulfillment.

For the animals and savages are isolate, each one in its own pristine self. The animal lifts its head, sniffs, and knows within the dark, passionate belly. It knows at once, in dark mindlessness. And at once it flees in immediate recoil; or it crouches predatory, in the mysterious storm of exultant anticipation of seizing a victim; or it lowers its head in blank indifference again; or it advances in the insatiable wild curiosity, insatiable passion to approach that which is unspeakably strange and incalculable; or it draws near in the slow trust of wild, sensual love.

Crèvecœur wanted this kind of knowledge. But comfortably, in his head, along with his other ideas and ideals. He didn't go too near the wigwam. Because he must have suspected that the moment he saw as the savages saw, all his fraternity and equality would go up in smoke, and his ideal world of pure sweet goodness along with it. And still worse than this, he would have to give up his own will, which insists that the world is so, because it would be nicest if it were so. Therefore he trotted back to France in high-heeled shoes, and imagined America in Paris.

He wanted his ideal state. At the same time he wanted to know the other state, the dark, savage mind. He wanted both.

Can't be done, Hector. The one is the death of the other.

Best turn to commerce, where you may get things your own way.

He hates the dark, pre-mental life, really. He hates the true sensual mystery. But he wants to "know." To KNOW. Oh, insatiable American curiosity!

He's a liar.

But if he won't risk knowing in flesh and blood, he'll risk all the imagination you like.

It is amusing to see him staying away and calculating the dangers of the step which he takes so luxuriously, in his fancy, alone. He tickles his palate with a taste of true wildness, as men are so fond nowadays of tickling their palates with a taste of imaginary wickedness—just self-provoked.

"I must tell you," he says, "that there is something in the proximity of the woods which is very singular. It is with men as it is with the plants and animals that live in the forests; they are entirely different from those that live in the plains. I will candidly tell you all my thoughts, but you are not to expect that I shall advance any reasons. By living in or near the woods, their actions are regulated by the wildness of the neighborhood. The deer often come to eat their grain, the wolves destroy their sheep, the bears kill their hogs, the foxes catch their poultry. This surrounding hostility immediately puts the gun into their hands; they watch these animals, they kill some; and thus by defending their property they soon become professed hunters; this is the progress; once hunters, farewell to the plow. The chase renders them ferocious, gloomy, unsociable; a hunter wants no neighbors, he rather hates them, because he dreads the competition. . . . Eating of wild meat, whatever you may think, tends to alter their temper. . . ."

Crèvecœur, of course, had never intended to return as a *hunter* to the bosom of Nature, only as a husbandman. The hunter is a killer. The husbandman, on the other hand, brings about the birth and increase. But even the husbandman strains in dark mastery over the unwilling earth and beast; he struggles to win forth substance, he must master the soil and the strong cattle, he must have the heavy blood-knowledge, and the slow, but deep, mastery. There is no equality or selfless humility. The toiling blood swamps the idea, inevitably. For this reason the most idealist nations invent most machines. America simply teems with mechanical inventions, because nobody in America ever wants to *do* anything. They are idealists. Let a machine do the doing.

Again, Crèvecœur dwells on "the apprehension lest my younger children should be caught by that singular charm, so dangerous to their tender years"—meaning the charm of savage life. So he goes on: "By what power does it come to pass that children who have been adopted when young among these people (the Indians) can never be prevailed upon to readopt European manners? Many an anxious parent have I seen last war who, at the return of peace, went to the Indian villages where they knew their children to have been carried in captivity, when to their inexpressible sorrow they found them so perfectly Indianized that many knew them no longer, and those whose more advanced ages permitted them to recollect their fathers and mothers, absolutely refused to follow them, and ran to their adopted parents to protect them against the effusions of love their unhappy real parents lavished on them! Incredible as this may appear, I have heard it asserted in a thousand instances, among persons of credit.

"There must be something in their (the Indians') social bond singularly captivating, and far superior to anything to be boasted of among us; for thousands of Europeans are

Indians, and we have no examples of even one of those aborigines having from choice become Europeans. . . ."

Our cat and another, Hector.

I like the picture of thousands of obdurate offspring, with faces averted from their natural white father and mother, turning resolutely to the Indians of their adoption.

I have seen some Indians whom you really couldn't tell from white men. And I have never seen a white man who looked really like an Indian. So Hector is again a liar.

But Crèvecœur wanted to be an *intellectual* savage, like a great many more we have met. Sweet children of Nature. Savage and bloodthirsty children of Nature.

White Americans do try hard to intellectualize themselves. Especially white women Americans. And the latest stunt is this "savage" stunt again.

White savages, with motor-cars, telephones, incomes, and ideals! Savages fast inside the machine; yet savage enough, ye gods!

IV. Fenimore Cooper's White Novels

BENJAMIN FRANKLIN had a specious little equation in providential mathemathics:

$$\text{Rum} + \text{Savage} = 0.$$

Awfully nice! You might add up the universe to nought, if you kept on.

Rum plus Savage may equal a dead savage. But is a dead savage nought? Can you make a land virgin by killing off its aborigines?

The Aztec is gone, and the Incas. The Red Indian, the Esquimo, the Patagonian are reduced to negligible numbers.

Où sont les neiges d'antan?

My dear, wherever they are, they will come down again next winter, sure as houses.

Not that the Red Indian will ever possess the broad lands of America. At least I presume not. But his ghost will.

The Red Man died hating the white man. What remnant of him lives, lives hating the white man. Go near the Indians, and you just feel it. As far as we are concerned, the

Red Man is subtly and unremittingly diabolic. Even when he doesn't know it. He is dispossessed in life, and unforgiving. He doesn't believe in us and our civilization, and so is our mystic enemy, for we push him off the face of the earth.

Belief is a mysterious thing. It is the only healer of the soul's wounds. There is no belief in the world.

The Red Man is dead, disbelieving in us. He is dead and unappeased. Do not imagine him happy in his Happy Hunting Ground. No. Only those that die in belief die happy. Those that are pushed out of life in chagrin come back unappeased, for revenge.

A curious thing about the Spirit of Place is the fact that no place exerts its full influence upon a newcomer until the old inhabitant is dead or absorbed. So America. While the Red Indian existed in fairly large numbers, the new colonials were in a great measure immune from the daimon, or demon, of America. The moment the last nuclei of Red life break up in America, then the white men will have to reckon with the full force of the demon of the continent. At present the demon of the place and the unappeased ghosts of the dead Indians act within the unconscious or under-conscious soul of the white American, causing the great American grouch, the Orestes-like frenzy of restlessness in the Yankee soul, the inner malaise which amounts almost to madness, sometimes. The Mexican is macabre and disintegrated in his own way. Up till now, the unexpressed spirit of America has worked covertly in the American, the white American soul. But within the present generation the surviving Red Indians are due to merge in the great white swamp. Then the Daimon of America will work overtly, and we shall see real changes.

There has been all the time, in the white American soul, a dual feeling about the Indian. First was Franklin's feeling, that a wise Providence no doubt intended the extirpation of these savages. Then came Crèvecœur's contradictory feeling about the noble Red Man and the innocent life of the wigwam. Now we hate to subscribe to Benjamin's belief in a Providence that wisely extirpates the Indian to make room for "cultivators of the soil." In Crèvecœur we meet a sentimental desire for the glorification of the savages. Absolutely sentimental. Hector pops over to Paris to enthuse about the wigwam.

The desire to extirpate the Indian. And the contradictory desire to glorify him. Both are rampant still, today.

The bulk of the white people who live in contact with the Indian today would like to see this Red brother exterminated; not only for the sake of grabbing his land, but because of the silent, invisible, but deadly hostility between the spirit of the two races. The minority of whites intellectualize the Red Man and laud him to the skies. But this minority of whites is mostly a high-brow minority with a big grouch against its own whiteness. So there you are.

I doubt if there is possible any real reconciliation, in the flesh, between the white and the red. For instance, a Red Indian girl who is servant in the white man's home, if she is treated with natural consideration, will probably serve well, even happily. She is happy with the new power over the white woman's kitchen. The white world makes her feel prouder, so long as she is free to go back to her own people at the given times. But she is happy because she is playing at being a white woman. There are other Indian women who would never serve the white people, and who would rather die than have a white man for a lover.

In either case, there is no reconciliation. There is no mystic conjunction between the spirit of the two races. The Indian girl who happily serves white people leaves out her own race-consideration, for the time being.

Supposing a white man goes out hunting in the mountains with an Indian. The two will probably get on like brothers. But let the same white man go alone with two Indians, and there will start a most subtle persecution of the unsuspecting white. If they, the Indians, discover that he has a natural fear of steep places, then over every precipice in the country will the trail lead. And so on. Malice! That is the basic feeling in the Indian heart towards the white. It may even be purely unconscious.

Supposing an Indian loves a white woman, and lives with her. He will probably be very proud of it, for he will be a big man among his own people, especially if the white mistress has money. He will never get over the feeling of pride at dining in a white dining-room and smoking in a white drawing-room. But at the same time he will subtly jeer at his white mistress, try to destroy her white pride. He will submit to her, if he is forced to, with a kind of false, unwilling childishness, and even love her with the same childlike gentleness, sometimes beautiful. But at the bottom of his heart he is gibing, gibing, gibing at her. Not only is it the sex resistance, but the race resistance as well.

There seems to be no reconciliation in the flesh.

That leaves us only expiation, and then reconciliation in the soul. Some strange atonement: expiation and oneing.

Fenimore Cooper has probably done more than any writer to present the Red Man to the white man. But Cooper's presentment is indeed a wish-fulfillment. That is why Fenimore is such a success still.

Modern critics begrudge Cooper his success. I think I resent it a little myself. This popular wish-fulfillment stuff makes it so hard for the real thing to come through, later.

Cooper was a rich American of good family. His father founded Cooperstown, by Lake Champlain. And Fenimore was a gentleman of culture. No denying it.

It is amazing how cultured these Americans of the first half of the eighteenth century were. Most intensely so. Austin Dobson and Andrew Lang are flea-bites in comparison. Volumes of very *raffiné* light verse and finely drawn familiar literature will prove it to anyone who cares to commit himself to these elderly books. The English and French writers of the same period were clumsy and hoydenish, judged by the same standards.

Truly, European decadence was anticipated in America; and American influence passed over to Europe, was assimilated there, and then returned to this land of innocence as something purplish in its modernity and a little wicked. So absurd things are.

Cooper quotes a Frenchman, who says, *"L'Amérique est pourrie avant d'être mûre."* And there is a great deal in it. America was not taught by France—by Baudelaire, for example. Baudelaire learned his lesson from America.

Cooper's novels fall into two classes: his white novels, such as *Homeward Bound, Eve Effingham, The Spy, The Pilot,* and then the *Leatherstocking Series.* Let us look at the white novels first.

The Effinghams are three extremely refined, genteel Americans who are "Homeward Bound" from England to the States. Their party consists of father, daughter, and uncle, and faithful nurse. The daughter has just finished her education in Europe. She has, indeed, skimmed the cream off Europe. England, France, Italy, and Germany have nothing more to teach her. She is bright and charming, admirable creature; a real modern heroine; intrepid, calm, and self-collected, yet admirably impulsive, always in perfectly good taste; clever and assured in her speech, like a man, but withal charmingly deferential and modest before the stronger sex. It is the perfection of the ideal female. We have learned to shudder at her, but Cooper still admired.

On board is the other type of American, the parvenu, the demagogue, who has "done" Europe and put it in his breeches pocket, in a month. Oh, Septimus Dodge, if a European had drawn you, that European would never have been forgiven by America. But an American drew you, so Americans wisely ignore you.

Septimus is the American self-made man. God had no hand in his make-up. He made himself. He has been to Europe, no doubt seen everything, including the Venus de Milo. "What, is *that* the Venus de Milo?" And he turns his back on the lady. He's seen her. He's got her. She's a fish he has hooked, and he's off to America with her, leaving the scum of a statue standing in the Louvre.

That is one American way of Vandalism. The original Vandals would have given the complacent dame a knock with a battle-ax, and ended her. The insatiable American looks at her. "Is *that* the Venus de Milo?—come on!" And the Venus de Milo stands there like a naked slave in a market-place, whom someone has spat on. Spat on!

I have often thought, hearing American tourists in Europe—in the Bargello in Florence, for example, or in the Piazza di San Marco in Venice—exclaiming, "Isn't that just too cunning!" or else, "Aren't you perfectly crazy about Saint Mark's! Don't you think those cupolas are like the loveliest *turnips* upside down, you know"—as if the beautiful things of Europe were just having their guts pulled out by these American admirers. They admire so wholesale. Sometimes they even seem to grovel. But the golden cupolas of St. Mark's in Venice are turnips upside down in a stale stew, after enough American tourists have looked at them. Turnips upside down in a stale stew. Poor Europe!

And there you are. When a few German bombs fell upon Rheims Cathedral up went a howl of execration. But there are more ways than one of vandalism. I should think the American admiration of five-minutes' tourists has done more to kill the sacredness of old European beauty and aspiration than multitudes of bombs would have done.

But there you are. Europe has got a fall, and peace hath her victories.

Behold then Mr. Septimus Dodge returning to Dodgetown victorious. Not crowned with laurel, it is true, but wreathed in lists of things he has seen and sucked dry. Seen and sucked dry, you know: Venus de Milo, the Rhine, or the Coliseum: swallowed like so many clams, and left the shells.

Now the aristocratic Effinghams, Homeward Bound from Europe to America, are at the mercy of Mr. Dodge: Septimus. He is their compatriot, so they may not disown him. Had they been English, of course, they would never once have let themselves become aware of his existence. But no. They are American democrats, and therefore, if Mr. Dodge marches up and says: "Mr. Effingham? Pleased to meet you, Mr. Effingham"—why, then Mr. Effingham is *forced* to reply: "Pleased to meet you, Mr. Dodge." If he didn't, he would have the terrible hounds of democracy on his heels and at his throat, the moment he landed in the Land of the Free. An Englishman is free to continue unaware of the existence of a fellow-countryman, if the looks of that fellow-countryman are distasteful. But every American citizen is free to force his presence upon you, no matter how unwilling you may be.

Freedom!

The Effinghams detest Mr. Dodge. They abhor him. They loathe and despise him. They have an unmitigated contempt for him. Everything he is, says, and does, seems to them too vulgar, too despicable. Yet they are forced to answer, when he presents himself: "Pleased to meet you, Mr. Dodge."

Freedom!

Mr. Dodge, of Dodge-town, alternately fawns and intrudes, cringes and bullies. And the Effinghams, terribly "superior" in a land of equality, writhe helpless. They would fain snub Septimus out of existence. But Septimus is not to be snubbed. As a true democrat, he is unsnubbable. As a true democrat, he has right on his side. And right is might.

Right is might. It is the old struggle for power.

Septimus, as a true democrat, is the equal of any man. As a true democrat with a full pocket, he is, by the amount that fills his pocket, so much the superior of the democrats with empty pockets. Because, though all men are born equal and die equal, you will not get anybody to admit that ten dollars equal ten thousand dollars. No, no, there's a difference there, however far you may push equality.

Septimus has the Effinghams on the hip. He has them fast, and they will not escape. What tortures await them at home, in the Land of the Free, at the hands of the hideously affable Dodge, we do not care to disclose. What was the persecution of a haughty Lord or a marauding Baron or an inquisitorial Abbot compared to the persecution of a million Dodges? The proud Effinghams are like men buried naked to the chin in ant-heaps, to be bitten into extinction by a myriad of ants. Stoically, as good democrats and idealists, they writhe and endure, without making too much moan.

They writhe and endure. There is no escape. Not from that time to this. No escape. They writhed on the horns of the Dodge dilemma.

Since then Ford has gone one worse.

Through these white novels of Cooper runs this acid of ant bites, the formic acid of democratic poisoning. The

Effinghams feel superior. Cooper felt superior. Mrs. Cooper felt superior too. And bitten.

For they were democrats. They didn't believe in kings, or lords, or masters, or real superiority of any sort. Before God, of course. In the sight of God, of course, all men were equal. This they believed. And therefore, though they *felt* terribly superior to Mr. Dodge, yet, since they were his equals in the sight of God, they could not feel free to say to him: "Mr. Dodge, please go to the devil." They had to say: "Pleased to meet you."

What a lie to tell! Democratic lies.

What a dilemma! To feel so superior. To *know* you are superior. And yet to believe that, in the sight of God, you are equal. Can't help yourself.

Why couldn't they let the Lord Almighty look after the equality, since it seems to happen specifically in His sight, and stick themselves to their own superiority? Why couldn't they?

Somehow they daren't.

They were Americans, idealists. How dare they balance a mere intense feeling against an IDEA and an IDEAL?

Ideally—i.e., in the sight of God, Mr. Dodge was their equal.

What a low opinion they held of the Almighty's faculty for discrimination.

But it was so. The IDEAL of EQUALITY.

Pleased to meet you, Mr. Dodge.

We are equal in the sight of God, of course. But er——

Very glad to meet you, Miss Effingham. Did you say—*er?* Well now, I think my bank balance will bear it.

Poor Eve Effingham.

Eve! Think of it. Eve! And birds of paradise. And apples.

And Mr. Dodge.

This is where apples of knowledge get you, Miss Eve. You should leave 'em alone.

"Mr. Dodge, you are a hopeless and insufferable inferior."

Why couldn't she say it? She felt it. And she was a heroine.

Alas, she was an American heroine. She was an EDUCATED

WOMAN. She KNEW all about IDEALS. She swallowed the IDEAL of EQUALITY with her first mouthful of KNOWLEDGE. Alas for her and that apple of Sodom that looked so rosy. Alas for all her knowing.

Mr. Dodge (in check knickerbockers): Well, feeling a little uncomfortable below the belt, are you, Miss Effingham?

Miss Effingham (with difficulty withdrawing her gaze from the INFINITE OCEAN): Good morning, Mr. Dodge. I was admiring the dark blue distance.

Mr. Dodge: Say, couldn't you admire something a bit nearer.

Think how easy it would have been for her to say "Go away!" or "Leave me, varlet!"—or "Hence, base-born knave!" Or just to turn her back on him.

But then he would simply have marched round to the other side of her.

Was she his superior, or wasn't she?

Why surely, intrinsically, she *was*. Intrinsically Fenimore Cooper was the superior of the Dodges of his day. He felt it. But he felt he ought not to feel it. And he never had it out with himself.

That is why one rather gets impatient with him. He feels he is superior, and feels he ought *not* to feel so, and is therefore rather snobbish, and at the same time a little apologetic. Which is surely tiresome.

If a man feels superior, he should have it out with himself. "Do I feel superior because I *am* superior? Or is it just the snobbishness of class, or education, or money?"

Class, education, money won't make a man superior. But if he's just *born* superior, in himself, there it is. Why deny it?

It is a nasty sight to see the Effinghams putting themselves at the mercy of a Dodge, just because of a mere idea or ideal. Fools. They ruin more than they know. Because at the same time they are snobbish.

Septimus at the Court of King Arthur.

Septimus: Hello, Arthur! Pleased to meet you. By the way, what's all that great long sword about?

Arthur: This is Excalibur, the sword of my knighthood and my kingship.

Septimus: That so! We're all equal in the sight of God, you know, Arthur.

Arthur: Yes.

Septimus: Then I guess it's about time I had that yard-and-a-half of Excalibur to play with. Don't you think so? We're equal in the sight of God, and you've had it for quite a while.

Arthur: Yes, I agree. (Hands him Excalibur.)

Septimus (prodding Arthur with Excalibur): Say, Art, which is your fifth rib?

Superiority is a sword. Hand it over to Septimus, and you'll get it back between your ribs.—The whole moral of democracy.

But there you are. Eve Effingham had pinned herself down on the *Contrat Social,* and she was prouder of that pin through her body than of any mortal thing else. Her IDEAL. Her IDEAL of DEMOCRACY.

When America set out to destroy Kings and Lords and Masters, and the whole paraphernalia of European superiority, it pushed a pin right through its own body, and on that pin it still flaps and buzzes and twists in misery. The pin of democratic equality. Freedom.

There'll never be any life in America till you pull the pin out and admit natural inequality. Natural superiority, natural inferiority. Till such time, Americans just buzz round like various sorts of propellers, pinned down by their freedom and equality.

That's why these white novels of Fenimore Cooper are only historically and sardonically interesting. The people are all pinned down by some social pin, and buzzing away in social importance or friction, round and round on the pin. Never real human beings. Always things pinned down, choosing to be pinned down, transfixed by the idea or ideal of equality and democracy, on which they turn loudly and importantly, like propellers propelling. These States. Humanly, it is boring. As a historic phenomenon, it is amazing, ludicrous, and irritating.

If you don't pull the pin out in time, you'll never be able to pull it out. You must turn on it forever, or bleed to death.

> Naked to the waist was I,
> And deep within my breast did lie,
> Though no man any blood could spy,
> The truncheon of a spear——

Is it already too late?

Oh God, the democratic pin!

Freedom, Equality, Equal Opportunity, Education, Rights of Man.

The pin! The pin!

Well, there buzzes Eve Effingham, snobbishly, impaled. She is a perfect American heroine, and I'm sure she wore the first smartly-tailored "suit" that ever woman wore. I'm sure she spoke several languages. I'm sure she was hopelessly competent. I'm sure she "adored" her husband, and spent masses of his money, and divorced him because he didn't understand LOVE.

American women in their perfect "suits." American men in their imperfect coats and skirts!

I feel I'm the superior of most men I meet. Not in birth, because I never had a great-grandfather. Not in money, because I've got none. Not in education, because I'm merely scrappy. And certainly not in beauty or in manly strength.

Well, what then?

Just in myself.

When I'm challenged, I do feel myself superior to most of the men I meet. Just a natural superiority.

But not till there enters an element of challenge.

When I meet another man, and he is just himself—even if he is an ignorant Mexican pitted with small-pox—then there is no question between us of superiority or inferiority. He is a man and I am a man. We are ourselves. There is no question between us.

But let a question arise, let there be a challenge, and then I feel he should do reverence to the gods in me, because they are more than the gods in him. And he should give reverence to the very me, because it is more at one with the gods than is his very self.

If this is conceit, I am sorry. But it's the gods in me that matter. And in other men.

As for me, I am so glad to salute the brave, reckless gods in another man. So glad to meet a man who will abide by his very self.

Ideas! Ideals! All this paper between us. What a weariness.

If only people would meet in their very selves, without wanting to put some idea over one another, or some ideal.

Damn all ideas and all ideals. Damn all the false stress, and the pins.

I am I. Here am I. Where are you?

Ah, there you are! Now, damn the consequences, we have met.

That's my idea of democracy, if you can call it an idea.

V. Fenimore Cooper's Leatherstocking Novels

In his Leatherstocking books Fenimore is off on another track. He is no longer concerned with social white Americans that buzz with pins through them, buzz loudly against every mortal thing except the pin itself. The pin of the Great Ideal.

One gets irritated with Cooper because he never for once snarls at the Great Ideal Pin which transfixes him. No, indeed. Rather he tries to push it through the very heart of the Continent.

But I have loved the Leatherstocking books so dearly. Wish-fulfillment!

Anyhow, one is not supposed to take Love seriously in these books. Eve Effingham, impaled on the social pin, conscious all the time of her own ego and of nothing else, suddenly fluttering in throes of love: no, it makes me sick. Love is never Love until it has a pin pushed through it and becomes an Ideal. The ego, turning on a pin, is wildly In Love, always. Because that's the thing to be.

Cooper was a Gentleman, in the worst sense of the word.

In the nineteenth-century sense of the word. A correct, clockwork man.

Not altogether, of course.

The great national Grouch was grinding inside him. Probably he called it COSMIC URGE. Americans usually do: in capital letters.

Best stick to National Grouch. The great American grouch.

Cooper had it, gentleman that he was. That is why he flitted round Europe so uneasily. Of course, in Europe he could be, and was, a gentleman to his heart's content.

"In short," he says in one of his letters, "we were at table two counts, one monsignore, an English lord, an ambassador, and my humble self."

Were we really!

How nice it must have been to know that oneself, at least, was humble.

And he felt the democratic American tomahawk wheeling over his uncomfortable scalp all the time.

The great American grouch.

Two monsters loomed on Cooper's horizon.

MRS. COOPER	MY WORK
MY WORK	MY WIFE
MY WIFE	MY WORK

THE DEAR CHILDREN
MY WORK!!!

There you have the essential keyboard of Cooper's soul.

If there is one thing that annoys me more than a businessman and his BUSINESS, it is an artist, a writer, painter, musician, and MY WORK. When an artist says MY WORK, the flesh goes tired on my bones. When he says MY WIFE, I want to hit him.

Cooper grizzled about his work. Oh, heaven, he cared so much whether it was good or bad, and what the French thought, and what Mr. Snippy Knowall said, and how Mrs. Cooper took it. The pin, the pin!

But he was truly an artist: then an American: then a gentleman.

And the grouch grouched inside him, through all.

They seem to have been specially fertile in imagining themselves "under the wigwam," do these Americans, just when their knees were comfortably under the mahogany, in Paris, along with the knees of

4 Counts
2 Cardinals
1 Milord
5 Cocottes
1 Humble self

You bet, though, that when the cocottes were being raffled off, Fenimore went home to his WIFE.

Wish-Fulfillment		*Actuality*
THE WIGWAM	*vs.*	MY HOTEL
CHINGACHGOOK	*vs.*	MY WIFE
NATTY BUMPPO	*vs.*	MY HUMBLE SELF

Fenimore, lying in his Louis Quatorze hotel in Paris, passionately musing about Natty Bumppo and the pathless forest, and mixing his imagination with the Cupids and Butterflies on the painted ceiling, while Mrs. Cooper was struggling with her latest gown in the next room, and the *déjeuner* was with the Countess at eleven. . . .

Men live by lies.

In actuality, Fenimore loved the genteel continent of Europe, and waited gasping for the newspapers to praise his WORK.

In another actuality he loved the tomahawking continent of America, and imagined himself Natty Bumppo.

His actual desire was to be: *Monsieur Fenimore Cooper, le grand écrivain américain.*

His innermost wish was to be: Natty Bumppo.

Now Natty and Fenimore, arm in arm, are an old couple.

You can see Fenimore: blue coat, silver buttons, silver-and-diamond buckle shoes, ruffles.

You see Natty Bumppo: a grizzled, uncouth old renegade, with gaps in his old teeth and a drop on the end of his nose.

But Natty was Fenimore's great wish: his wish-fulfillment.

"It was a matter of course," says Mrs. Cooper, "that he should dwell on the better traits of the picture rather than on the coarser and more revolting, though more common points. Like West, he could see Apollo in the young Mohawk."

The coarser and more revolting, though more common points.

You see now why he depended so absolutely on MY WIFE. She had to look things in the face for him. The coarser and more revolting, and certainly more common points, she had to see.

He himself did so love seeing pretty-pretty, with the thrill of a red scalp now and then.

Fenimore, in his imagination, wanted to be Natty Bumppo, who, I am sure, belched after he had eaten his dinner. At the same time Mr. Cooper was nothing if not a gentleman. So he decided to stay in France and have it all his own way.

In France, Natty would not belch after eating, and Chingachgook could be all the Apollo he liked.

As if ever any Indian was like Apollo. The Indians, with their curious female quality, their archaic figures, with high shoulders and deep, archaic waists, like a sort of woman! And their natural devilishness, their natural insidiousness.

But men see what they want to see: especially if they look from a long distance, across the ocean, for example.

Yet the Leatherstocking books are lovely. Lovely half-lies.

They form a sort of American Odyssey, with Natty Bumppo for Odysseus.

Only, in the original Odyssey, there is plenty of devil, Circes and swine and all. And Ithacus is devil enough to outwit the devils. But Natty is a saint with a gun, and the Indians are gentlemen through and through, though they may take an occasional scalp.

There are five Leatherstocking novels: a *decrescendo* of reality, and a crescendo of beauty.

1. *Pioneers:* A raw frontier village on Lake Champlain, at the end of the eighteenth century. Must be a picture of Cooper's

home, as he knew it when a boy. A very lovely book. Natty Bumppo an old man, an old hunter half civilized.

2. *The Last of the Mohicans:* A historical fight between the British and the French, with Indians on both sides, at a fort by Lake Champlain. Romantic flight of the British general's two daughters, conducted by the scout, Natty, who is in the prime of life; romantic death of the last of the Delawares.

3. *The Prairie:* A wagon of some huge, sinister Kentuckians trekking west into the unbroken prairie. Prairie Indians, and Natty, an old, old man; he dies seated on a chair on the Rocky Mountains, looking east.

4. *The Pathfinder:* The Great Lakes. Natty, a man of about thirty-five, makes an abortive proposal to a bouncing damsel, daughter of the Sergeant at the Fort.

5. *Deerslayer:* Natty and Hurry Harry, both quite young, are hunting in the virgin wild. They meet two white women. Lake Champlain again.

These are the five Leatherstocking books: Natty Bumppo being Leatherstocking, Pathfinder, Deerslayer, according to his ages.

Now let me put aside my impatience at the unreality of this vision, and accept it as a wish-fulfillment vision, a kind of yearning myth. Because it seems to me that the things in Cooper that make one so savage, when one compares them with actuality, are perhaps, when one considers them as presentations of a deep subjective desire, real in their way, and almost prophetic.

The passionate love for America, for the soil of America, for example. As I say, it is perhaps easier to love America passionately, when you look at it through the wrong end of the telescope, across all the Atlantic water, as Cooper did so often, than when you are right there. When you are actually *in* America, America hurts, because it has a powerful disintegrative influence upon the white psyche. It is full of grinning, unappeased aboriginal demons, too, ghosts, and it persecutes the white men, like some Eumenides, until the white men give up their absolute whiteness. America is tense with latent violence and resistance. The very common sense of white Americans has a tinge of helplessness in it, and deep fear of what might be if they were not common-sensical.

Yet one day the demons of America must be placated, the ghosts must be appeased, the Spirit of Place atoned for. Then the true passionate love for American Soil will appear. As yet, there is too much menace in the landscape.

But probably one day America will be as beautiful in actuality as it is in Cooper. Not yet, however. When the factories have fallen down again.

And again, this perpetual blood-brother theme of the Leatherstocking novels, Natty and Chingachgook, the Great Serpent. At present it is a sheer myth. The Red Man and the White Man are not blood-brothers: even when they are most friendly. When they are most friendly, it is as a rule the one betraying his race-spirit to the other. In the white man—rather high-brow—who "loves" the Indian, one feels the white man betraying his own race. There is something unproud, underhand in it. Renegade. The same with the Americanized Indian who believes absolutely in the white mode. It is a betrayal. Renegade again.

In the actual flesh, it seems to me the white man and the red man cause a feeling of oppression, the one to the other, no matter what the good will. The red life flows in a different direction from the white life. You can't make two streams that flow in opposite directions meet and mingle soothingly.

Certainly, if Cooper had had to spend his whole life in the backwoods, side by side with a Noble Red Brother, he would have screamed with the oppression of suffocation. He had to have Mrs. Cooper, a straight strong pillar of society, to hang on to. And he had to have the culture of France to turn back to, or he would just have been stifled. The Noble Red Brother would have smothered him and driven him mad.

So that the Natty and Chingachgook myth must remain a myth. It is a wish-fulfillment, an evasion of actuality. As we have said before, the folds of the Great Serpent would have been heavy, very heavy, too heavy, on any white man. Unless the white man were a true renegade, hating himself and his own race spirit, as sometimes happens.

It seems there can be no fusion in the flesh. But the spirit can change. The white man's spirit can never become as the red man's spirit. It doesn't want to. But it can cease to be the opposite and the negative of the red man's spirit. It can open out a new great area of consciousness, in which there is room for the red spirit too.

To open out a new wide area of consciousness means to slough the old consciousness. The old consciousness has become a tight-fitting prison to us, in which we are going rotten.

You can't have a new, easy skin before you have sloughed the old, tight skin.

You can't.

And you just can't, so you may as well leave off pretending.

Now the essential history of the people of the United States seems to me just this: At the Renaissance the old consciousness was becoming a little tight. Europe sloughed her last skin, and started a new, final phase.

But some Europeans recoiled from the last final phase. They wouldn't enter the *cul de sac* of post-Renaissance, "liberal" Europe. They came to America.

They came to America for two reasons:

1. To slough the old European consciousness completely.
2. To grow a new skin underneath, a new form. This second is a hidden process.

The two processes go on, of course, simultaneously. The slow forming of the new skin underneath is the slow sloughing of the old skin. And sometimes this immortal serpent feels very happy, feeling a new golden glow of a strangely-patterned skin envelop him: and sometimes he feels very sick, as if his very entrails were being torn out of him, as he wrenches once more at his old skin, to get out of it.

Out! Out! he cries, in all kinds of euphemisms.

He's got to have his new skin on him before ever he can get out.

And he's got to get out before his new skin can ever be his own skin.

So there he is, a torn, divided monster.

The true American, who writhes and writhes like a snake that is long in sloughing.

Sometimes snakes can't slough. They can't burst their old skin. Then they go sick and die inside the old skin, and nobody ever sees the new pattern.

It needs a real desperate recklessness to burst your old skin at last. You simply don't care what happens to you, if you rip yourself in two, so long as you do get out.

It also needs a real belief in the new skin. Otherwise you are likely never to make the effort. Then you gradually sicken and go rotten and die in the old skin.

Now Fenimore stayed very safe inside the old skin: a gentleman, almost a European, as proper as proper can be. And, safe inside the old skin, he *imagined* the gorgeous American pattern of a new skin.

He hated democracy. So he evaded it, and had a nice dream of something beyond democracy. But he belonged to democracy all the while.

Evasion!—Yet even that doesn't make the dream worthless.

Democracy in America was never the same as Liberty in Europe. In Europe Liberty was a great life throb. But in America Democracy was always something anti-life. The greatest democrats, like Abraham Lincoln, had always a sacrificial, self-murdering note in their voices. American Democracy was a form of self-murder, always. Or of murdering somebody else.

Necessarily. It was a *pis aller*. It was the *pis aller* to European Liberty. It was a cruel form of sloughing. Men murdered themselves into this democracy. Democracy is the utter hardening of the old skin, the old form, the old psyche. It hardens till it is tight and fixed and inorganic. Then it *must* burst, like a chrysalis shell. And out must come the soft grub, or the soft damp butterfly of the American-at-last.

America has gone the *pis aller* of her democracy. Now she must slough even that, chiefly that, indeed.

What did Cooper dream beyond democracy? Why, in his immortal friendship of Chingachgook and Natty Bumppo he dreamed the nucleus of a new society. That is, he dreamed a new human relationship. A stark, stripped human relationship of two men, deeper than the deeps of sex. Deeper than property, deeper than fatherhood, deeper than marriage, deeper than love. So deep that it is loveless. The stark, loveless, wordless unison of two men who have come to the bottom of themselves. This is the new nucleus of a new society, the clue to a new world-epoch. It asks for a great and cruel sloughing first of all. Then it finds a great release into a new world, a new moral, a new landscape.

Natty and the Great Serpent are neither equals nor unequals. Each obeys the other when the moment arrives. And each is stark and dumb in the other's presence, starkly himself, without illusion created. Each is just the crude pillar of a man, the crude living column of his own manhood. And each knows the godhead of this crude column of manhood. A new relationship.

The Leatherstocking novels create the myth of this new relation. And they go backwards, from old age to golden youth. That is the true myth of America. She starts old, old, wrinkled and writhing in an old skin. And there is a gradual sloughing of the old skin, towards a new youth. It is the myth of America.

You start with actuality. *Pioneers* is no doubt Cooperstown, when Cooperstown was in the stage of inception: a village of one wild street of log cabins under the forest hills by Lake Champlain: a village of crude, wild frontiersmen, reacting against civilization.

Towards this frontier village in the wintertime, a Negro slave drives a sledge through the mountains, over deep snow. In the sledge sits a fair damsel, Miss Temple, with her handsome pioneer father, Judge Temple. They hear a shot in the trees. It is the old hunter and backwoodsman, Natty Bumppo, long and lean and uncouth, with a long rifle and gaps in his teeth.

Judge Temple is "squire" of the village, and he has a ridiculous, commodious "hall" for his residence. It is still the old English form. Miss Temple is a pattern young lady, like Eve Effingham: in fact, she gets a young and very genteel but impoverished Effingham for a husband. The old world holding its own on the edge of the wild. A bit tiresomely, too, with rather more prunes and prisms than one can digest. Too romantic.

Against the "hall" and the gentry, the real frontiers-folk, the rebels. The two groups meet at the village inn, and at the frozen church, and at the Christmas sports, and on the ice of the lake, and at the great pigeon shoot. It is a beautiful, resplendent picture of life. Fenimore puts in only the glamour.

Perhaps my taste is childish, but these scenes in *Pioneers* seem to me marvelously beautiful. The raw village street, with woodfires blinking through the unglazed window-chinks, on a winter's night. The inn, with the rough woodsman and the drunken Indian John; the church, with the snowy congregation crowding to the fire. Then the lavish abundance of Christmas cheer, and turkey shooting in the snow. Spring coming, forests all green, maple-sugar taken from the trees: and clouds of pigeons flying from the south, myriads of pigeons, shot in heaps; and night-fishing on the teeming, virgin lake; and deer hunting.

Pictures! Some of the loveliest, most glamorous pictures in all literature.

Alas, without the cruel iron of reality. It is all real enough. Except that one realizes that Fenimore was writing from a safe distance, where he would idealize and have his wish-fulfillment.

Because, when one comes to America, one finds that there is always a certain slightly devilish resistance in the American landscape, and a certain slightly bitter resistance in the white man's heart. Hawthorne gives this. But Cooper glosses it over.

The American landscape has never been at one with the white man. Never. And white men have probably never felt so bitter anywhere, as here in America, where the very landscape, in its very beauty, seems a bit devilish and grinning, opposed to us.

Cooper, however, glosses over this resistance, which in actuality can never quite be glossed over. He *wants* the landscape to be at one with him. So he goes away to Europe and sees it as such. It is a sort of vision.

And, nevertheless, the oneing will surely take place—someday.

The myth is the story of Natty. The old, lean hunter and backwoodsman lives with his friend, the gray-haired Indian John, an old Delaware chief, in a hut within reach of the village. The Delaware is christianized and bears the Christian name of John. He is tribeless and lost. He humiliates his gray hairs in drunkenness, and dies, thankful to be dead, in a forest fire, passing back to the fire whence he derived.

And this is Chingachgook, the splendid Great Serpent of the later novels.

No doubt Cooper, as a boy, knew both Natty and the Indian John. No doubt they fired his imagination even then. When he is a man, crystallized in society and sheltering behind the safe pillar of Mrs. Cooper, these two old fellows become a myth to his soul. He traces himself to a new youth in them.

As for the story: Judge Temple has just been instrumental in passing the wise game laws. But Natty has lived by his gun all his life in the wild woods, and simply childishly cannot understand how he can be poaching on the Judge's land among the pine trees. He shoots a deer in the close season. The Judge is all sympathy, but the law *must* be enforced. Bewildered Natty, an old man of seventy, is put in stocks and in prison. They release him as soon as possible. But the thing was done.

The letter killeth.

Natty's last connection with his own race is broken. John, the Indian, is dead. The old hunter disappears, lonely and severed, into the forest, away, away from his race.

In the new epoch that is coming, there will be no letter of the Law.

Chronologically, *The Last of the Mohicans* follows *Pioneers*. But in the myth, *The Prairie* comes next.

Cooper of course knew his own America. He traveled west and saw the prairies, and camped with the Indians of the prairie.

The Prairie, like *Pioneers,* bears a good deal the stamp of actuality. It is a strange, splendid book, full of the sense of doom. The figures of the great Kentuckian men, with their wolf-women, loom colossal on the vast prairie, as they camp with their wagons. These are different pioneers from Judge Temple. Lurid, brutal, tinged with the sinisterness of crime; these are the gaunt white men who push West, push on and on against the natural opposition of the continent. On towards a doom. Great wings of vengeful doom seem spread over the West, grim against the intruder. You feel them again in Frank Norris' novel, *The Octopus*. While in the West of Bret Harte there is a very devil in the air, and beneath him are sentimental, self-conscious people being wicked and goody by evasion.

In *The Prairie* there is a shadow of violence and dark cruelty flickering in the air. It is the aboriginal demon hovering over the core of the continent. It hovers still, and the dread is still there.

Into such a prairie enters the huge figure of Ishmael, ponderous, pariah-like Ishmael and his huge sons and his werewolf wife. With their wagons they roll on from the frontiers of Kentucky, like Cyclops into the savage wilderness. Day after day they seem to force their way into oblivion. But their force of penetration ebbs. They are brought to a stop. They recoil in the throes of murder and entrench themselves in isolation on a hillock in the midst of the prairie. There they hold out like demigods against the elements and the subtle Indian.

The pioneering brute invasion of the West, crime-tinged!

And into this setting, as a sort of minister of peace, enters the old, old hunter Natty, and his suave, horse-riding Sioux Indians. But he seems like a shadow.

The hills rise softly west, to the Rockies. There seems a new peace: or is it only suspense, abstraction, waiting? Is it only a sort of beyond?

Natty lives in these hills, in a village of the suave, horse-riding Sioux. They revere him as an old wise father.

In these hills he dies, sitting in his chair and looking far east, to the forest and great sweet waters, whence he came. He dies gently, in physical peace with the land and the Indians. He is an old, old man.

Cooper could see no further than the foothills where Natty died, beyond the prairie.

The other novels bring us back East.

The Last of the Mohicans is divided between real historical narrative and true "romance." For myself, I prefer the romance. It has a myth meaning, whereas the narrative is chiefly record.

For the first time we get actual women: the dark, handsome Cora and her frail sister, the White Lily. The good old division, the dark sensual woman and the clinging, submissive little blonde, who is so "pure."

These sisters are fugitives through the forest, under the protection of a Major Heyward, a young American officer and Englishman. He is just a "white" man, very good and brave and generous, etc., but limited, most definitely *borné*. He would probably love Cora, if he dared, but he finds it safer to adore the clinging White Lily of a younger sister.

This trio is escorted by Natty, now Leatherstocking, a hunter and scout in the prime of life, accompanied by his inseparable friend Chingachgook, and the Delaware's beautiful son—Adonis rather than Apollo—Uncas, the last of the Mohicans.

There is also a "wicked" Indian, Magua, handsome and injured incarnation of evil.

Cora is the scarlet flower of womanhood, fierce, passionate offspring of some mysterious union between the British officer and a Creole woman in the West Indies. Cora loves Uncas, Uncas loves Cora. But Magua also desires Cora, violently desires her. A lurid little circle of sensual fire. So Fenimore kills them all off, Cora, Uncas, and Magua, and leaves the White Lily to carry on the race. She will breed plenty of white children to Major Heyward. These tiresome "lilies that fester," of our day.

Evidently Cooper—or the artist in him—has decided that there can be no blood-mixing of the two races, white and red. He kills 'em off.

Beyond all this heartbeating stand the figures of Natty and Chingachgook: the two childless, womanless men, of opposite races. They are the abiding thing. Each of them is alone, and final in his race. And they stand side by side, stark, abstract, beyond emotion, yet eternally together. All the other loves seem frivolous. This is the new great thing, the clue, the inception of a new humanity.

And Natty, what sort of a white man is he? Why, he is a man with a gun. He is a killer, a slayer. Patient and gentle as he is, he is a slayer. Self-effacing, self-forgetting, still he is a killer.

Twice, in the book, he brings an enemy down hurtling in death through the air, downwards. Once it is the beautiful, wicked Magua—shot from a height, and hurtling down ghastly through space, into death.

This is Natty, the white forerunner. A killer. As in *Deerslayer,* he shoots the bird that flies in the high, high sky, so that the bird falls out of the invisible into the visible, dead, he symbolizes himself. He will bring the bird of the spirit out of the high air. He is the stoic American killer of the old great life. But he kills, as he says, only to live.

Pathfinder takes us to the Great Lakes, and the glamour and beauty of sailing the great sweet waters. Natty is now called Pathfinder. He is about thirty-five years old, and he falls in love. The damsel is Mabel Dunham, daughter of Sergeant Dunham of the Fort garrison. She is blonde and in all things admirable. No doubt Mrs. Cooper was very much like Mabel.

And Pathfinder doesn't marry her. She won't have him. She wisely prefers a more comfortable Jasper. So Natty goes off to grouch, and to end by thanking his stars. When he had got right clear, and sat by the campfire with Chingachgook, in the forest, didn't he just thank his stars! A lucky escape!

Men of an uncertain age are liable to these infatuations. They aren't always lucky enough to be rejected.

Whatever would poor Mabel have done, had she been Mrs. Bumppo?

Natty had no business marrying. His mission was elsewhere.

The most fascinating Leatherstocking book is the last, *Deerslayer*. Natty is now a fresh youth, called Deerslayer.

But the kind of silent prim youth who is never quite young, but reserves himself for different things.

It is a gem of a book. Or a bit of perfect paste. And myself, I like a bit of perfect paste in a perfect setting, so long as I am not fooled by pretense of reality. And the setting of *Deerslayer could* not be more exquisite. Lake Champlain again.

Of course it never rains: it is never cold and muddy and dreary: no one has wet feet or toothache: no one ever feels filthy, when they can't wash for a week. God knows what the women would really have looked like, for they fled through the wilds without soap, comb, or towel. They breakfasted off a chunk of meat, or nothing, lunched the same, and supped the same.

Yet at every moment they are elegant, perfect ladies, in correct toilet.

Which isn't quite fair. You need only go camping for a week, and you'll see.

But it is a myth, not a realistic tale. Read it as a lovely myth. Lake Glimmerglass.

Deerslayer, the youth with the long rifle, is found in the woods with a big, handsome, blond-bearded backwoodsman called Hurry Harry. Deerslayer seems to have been born under a hemlock tree out of a pine-cone: a young man of the woods. He is silent, simple, philosophic, moralistic, and an unerring shot. His simplicity is the simplicity of age rather than of youth. He is race-old. All his reactions and impulses are fixed, static. Almost he is sexless, so race-old. Yet intelligent, hardy, dauntless.

Hurry Harry is a big blusterer, just the opposite of Deerslayer. Deerslayer keeps the center of his own consciousness steady and unperturbed. Hurry Harry is one of those floundering people who bluster from one emotion to another, very self-conscious, without any center to them.

These two young men are making their way to a lovely, smallish lake, Lake Glimmerglass. On this water the Hutter family has established itself. Old Hutter, it is suggested, has a criminal, coarse, buccaneering past, and is a sort of fugitive from justice. But he is a good enough father to his two grown-up girls. The family lives in a log hut "castle," built on piles in the water, and the old man has also constructed an "ark," a sort of houseboat, in which he can take his daughters when he goes on his rounds to trap the beaver.

The two girls are the inevitable dark and light. Judith, dark, fearless, passionate, a little lurid with sin, is the scarlet-and-black blossom. Hetty, the younger, blonde, frail and innocent, is the white lily again. But alas, the lily has begun to fester. She is slightly imbecile.

The two hunters arrive at the lake among the woods just as war has been declared. The Hutters are unaware of the fact. And hostile Indians are on the lake already. So, the story of thrills and perils.

Thomas Hardy's inevitable division of women into dark and fair, sinful and innocent, sensual and pure, is Cooper's division too. It is indicative of the desire in the man. He wants sensuality and sin, and he wants purity and "innocence." If the innocence goes a little rotten, slightly imbecile, bad luck!

Hurry Harry, of course, like a handsome, impetuous meat-fly, at once wants Judith, the lurid poppy blossom. Judith rejects him with scorn.

Judith, the sensual woman, at once wants the quiet, reserved, unmastered Deerslayer. She wants to master him. And Deerslayer is half tempted, but never more than half. He is not going to be mastered. A philosophic old soul, he does not give much for the temptations of sex. Probably he dies virgin.

And he is right of it. Rather than be dragged into a false heat of deliberate sensuality, he will remain alone. His soul is alone, forever alone. So he will preserve his integrity, and remain alone in the flesh. It is a stoicism which is honest and fearless, and from which Deerslayer never lapses, except when, approaching middle age, he proposes to the buxom Mabel.

He lets his consciousness penetrate in loneliness into the new continent. His contacts are not human. He wrestles with the spirits of the forest and the American wild, as a hermit wrestles with God and Satan. His one meeting is with Chingachgook, and this meeting is silent, reserved, across an unpassable distance.

Hetty, the White Lily, being imbecile, although full of vaporous religion and the dear, good God, "who governs all things by his providence," is hopelessly infatuated with Hurry Harry. Being innocence gone imbecile, like Dostoevsky's Idiot, she longs to give herself to the handsome meat-fly. Of course he doesn't want her.

And so nothing happens: in that direction. Deerslayer goes off to meet Chingachgook, and help him woo an Indian maid. Vicarious.

It is the miserable story of the collapse of the white psyche. The white man's mind and soul are divided between these two things: innocence and lust, the Spirit and Sensuality. Sensuality always carries a stigma, and is therefore more deeply desired, or lusted after. But spirituality alone gives the sense of uplift, exaltation, and "winged life," with the inevitable reaction into sin and spite. So the white man is divided against himself. He plays off one side of himself against the other side, till it is really a tale told by an idiot, and nauseating.

Against this, one is forced to admire the stark, enduring figure of Deerslayer. He is neither spiritual nor sensual. He is a moralizer, but he always tries to moralize from actual experience, not from theory. He says: "Hurt nothing unless you're forced to." Yet he gets his deepest thrill of gratification, perhaps, when he puts a bullet through the heart of a beautiful buck, as it stoops to drink at the lake. Or when he brings the invisible bird fluttering down in death, out of the high blue. "Hurt nothing unless you're forced to." And yet he lives by death, by killing the wild things of the air and earth.

It's not good enough.

But you have there the myth of the essential white America. All the other stuff, the love, the democracy, the floundering into lust, is a sort of by-play. The essential American soul is hard, isolate, stoic, and a killer. It has never yet melted.

Of course, the soul often breaks down into disintegration,

and you have lurid sin and Judith, imbecile innocence lusting in Hetty, and bluster, bragging, and self-conscious strength in Harry. But there are the disintegration products.

What true myth concerns itself with is not the disintegration product. True myth concerns itself centrally with the onward adventure of the integral soul. And this, for America, is Deerslayer. A man who turns his back on white society. A man who keeps his moral integrity hard and intact. An isolate, almost selfless, stoic, enduring man, who lives by death, by killing, but who is pure white.

This is the very intrinsic-most American. He is at the core of all the other flux and fluff. And when *this* man breaks from his static isolation, and makes a new move, then look out, something will be happening.

VI. Edgar Allan Poe

Poe has no truck with Indians or Nature. He makes no bones about Red Brothers and Wigwams.

He is absolutely concerned with the disintegration-processes of his own psyche. As we have said, the rhythm of American art-activity is dual.

1. A disintegrating and sloughing of the old consciousness.

2. The forming of a new consciousness underneath.

Fenimore Cooper has the two vibrations going on together. Poe has only one, only the disintegrative vibration. This makes him almost more a scientist than an artist.

Moralists have always wondered helplessly why Poe's "morbid" tales need have been written. They need to be written because old things need to die and disintegrate, because the old white psyche has to be gradually broken down before anything else can come to pass.

Man must be stripped even of himself. And it is a painful, sometimes a ghastly process.

Poe had a pretty bitter doom. Doomed to seethe down his soul in a great continuous convulsion of disintegration, and doomed to register the process. And then doomed to be abused for it, when he had performed some of the bitterest tasks of human experience, that can be asked of a man. Necessary tasks, too. For the human soul must suffer its own disintegration, *consciously,* if ever it is to survive.

But Poe is rather a scientist than an artist. He is reducing his own self as a scientist reduces a salt in a crucible. It is an almost chemical analysis of the soul and consciousness. Whereas in true art there is always the double rhythm of creating and destroying.

This is why Poe calls his things "tales." They are a concatenation of cause and effect.

His best pieces, however, are not tales. They are more. They are ghastly stories of the human soul in its disruptive throes.

Moreover, they are "love" stories.

Ligeia and *The Fall of the House of Usher* are really love stories.

Love is the mysterious vital attraction which draws things together, closer, closer together. For this reason sex is the actual crisis of love. For in sex the two blood-systems, in the male and female, concentrate and come into contact, the merest film intervening. Yet if the intervening film breaks down, it is death.

So there you are. There is a limit to everything. There is a limit to love.

The central law of all organic life is that each organism is intrinsically isolate and single in itself.

The moment its isolation breaks down, and there comes an actual mixing and confusion, death sets in.

This is true of every individual organism, from man to amœba.

But the secondary law of all organic life is that each organism only lives through contact with other matter, assimilation, and contact with other life, which means assimilation of new vibrations, non-material. Each individual organism is vivified by intimate contact with fellow organisms: up to a certain point.

So man. He breathes the air into him, he swallows food and water. But more than this. He takes into him the life of his fellow-men, with whom he comes into contact, and he gives back life to them. This contact draws nearer and nearer, as the intimacy increases. When it is a whole contact, we call it love. Men live by food, but die if they eat too much. Men live by love, but die, or cause death, if they love too much.

There are two loves: sacred and profane, spiritual and sensual.

In sensual love, it is the two blood-systems, the man's and the woman's, which sweep up into pure contact, and *almost* fuse. Almost mingle. Never quite. There is always the finest imaginable wall between the two blood-waves, through which pass unknown vibrations, forces, but through which the blood itself must never break, or it means bleeding.

In spiritual love, the contact is purely nervous. The nerves in the lovers are set vibrating in unison like two instruments. The pitch can rise higher and higher. But carry this too far, and the nerves begin to break, to bleed, as it were, and a form of death sets in.

The trouble about man is that he insists on being master of his own fate, and he insists on *oneness*. For instance, having discovered the ecstasy of spiritual love, he insists that he shall have this all the time, and nothing but this, for this is life. It is what he calls "heightening" life. He wants his nerves to be set vibrating in the intense and exhilarating unison with the nerves of another being, and by this means he acquires an ecstasy of vision, he finds himself in glowing unison with all the universe.

But as a matter of fact this glowing unison is only a temporary thing, because the first law of life is that each organism is isolate in itself, it must return to its own isolation.

Yet man has tried the glow of unison, called love, and he *likes* it. It gives him his highest gratification. He wants it. He wants it all the time. He wants it and he will have it. He doesn't want to return to his own isolation. Or if he must, it is only as a prowling beast returns to its lair to rest and set out again.

This brings us to Edgar Allan Poe. The clue to him lies

in the motto he chose for *Ligeia,* a quotation from the mystic Joseph Glanville: "And the will therein lieth, which dieth not. Who knoweth the mysteries of the will, with its vigor? For God is but a great Will pervading all things by nature of its intentness. Man doth not yield himself to the angels, nor unto death utterly, save only through the weakness of his feeble will."

It is a profound saying: and a deadly one.

Because if God is a great will, then the universe is but an instrument.

I don't know what God is. But He is not simply a will. That is too simple. Too anthropomorphic. Because a man wants his own will, and nothing but his will, he needn't say that God is the same will, magnified *ad infinitum.*

For me, there may be one God, but He is nameless and unknowable.

For me, there are also many gods, that come into me and leave me again. And they have very various wills, I must say.

But the point is Poe.

Poe had experienced the ecstasies of extreme spiritual love. And he wanted those ecstasies and nothing but those ecstasies. He wanted that great gratification, the sense of flowing, the sense of unison, the sense of heightening of life. He had experienced this gratification. He was told on every hand that this ecstasy of spiritual, nervous love was the greatest thing in life, was life itself. And he had tried it for himself, he knew that for him it *was* life itself. So he wanted it. And he *would have* it. He set up his will against the whole of the limitations of nature.

This is a brave man, acting on his own belief and his own experience. But it is also an arrogant man, and a fool.

Poe was going to get the ecstasy and the heightening, cost what it might. He went on in a frenzy, as characteristic American women nowadays go on in a frenzy, after the very same thing: the heightening, the flow, the ecstasy. Poe tried alcohol, and any drug he could lay his hand on. He also tried any human being he could lay his hands on.

His grand attempt and achievement was with his wife;

his cousin, a girl with a singing voice. With her he went in for the intensest flow, the heightening, the prismatic shades of ecstasy. It was the intensest nervous vibration of unison, pressed higher and higher in pitch, till the blood-vessels of the girl broke, and the blood began to flow out loose. It was love. If you call it love.

Love can be terribly obscene.

It is love that causes the neuroticism of the day. It is love that is the prime cause of tuberculosis.

The nerves that vibrate most intensely in spiritual unisons are the sympathetic ganglia of the breast, of the throat, and the hind brain. Drive this vibration overintensely, and you weaken the sympathetic tissues of the chest—the lungs—or of the throat, or of the lower brain, and the tubercles are given a ripe field.

But Poe drove the vibrations beyond any human pitch of endurance.

Being his cousin, she was more easily keyed to him.

Ligeia is the chief story. Ligeia! A mental-derived name. To him the woman, his wife, was not Lucy. She was Ligeia. No doubt she even preferred it thus.

Ligeia is Poe's love story, and its very fantasy makes it more truly his own story.

It is a tale of love pushed over a verge. And love pushed to extremes is a battle of wills between the lovers.

Love is become a battle of wills.

Which shall first destroy the other, of the lovers? Which can hold out longest against the other?

Ligeia is still the old-fashioned woman. Her will is still to submit. She wills to submit to the vampire of her husband's consciousness. Even death.

"In stature she was tall, somewhat slender, and, in her later days, even emaciated. I would in vain attempt to portray the majesty, the quiet ease, of her demeanor, or the incomprehensible lightness and elasticity of her footfall. I was never made aware of her entrance into my closed study save by the dear music of her low, sweet voice, as she placed her marble hand on my shoulder."

Poe has been so praised for his style. But it seems to me

a meretricious affair. "Her marble hand" and "the elasticity of her footfall" seem more like chair springs and mantelpieces than a human creature. She never was quite a human creature to him. She was an instrument from which he got his extremes of sensation. His *machine à plaisir,* as somebody says.

All Poe's style, moreover, has this mechanical quality, as his poetry has a mechanical rhythm. He never sees anything in terms of life, almost always in terms of matter, jewels, marble, etc.—or in terms of force, scientific. And his cadences are all managed mechanically. This is what is called "having a style."

What he wants to do with Ligeia is to analyze her, till he knows all her component parts, till he has got her all in his consciousness. She is some strange chemical salt which he must analyze out in the test tubes of his brain, and then—when he's finished the analysis—*E finita la commedia!*

But she won't be quite analyzed out. There is something, something he can't get. Writing of her eyes, he says: "They were, I must believe, far larger than the ordinary eyes of our race"—as if anybody would want eyes "far larger" than other folks'. "They were even fuller than the fullest of the gazelle eyes of the tribe of Nourjahad"—which is blarney. "The hue of the orbs was the most brilliant of black and, far over them, hung jetty lashes of great length"—suggests a whip-lash. "The brows, slightly irregular in outline, had the same tint. The *strangeness,* which I found in the eyes, was of a nature distinct from the formation, or the color, or the brilliancy of the features, and must, after all, be referred to as the *expression."*—Sounds like an anatomist anatomizing a cat. "Ah, word of no meaning! behind whose vast latitude of sound we entrench our ignorance of so much of the spiritual. The expression of the eyes of Ligeia! How for long hours have I pondered upon it! How have I, through the whole of a midsummer night, struggled to fathom it! What was it—that something more profound than the well of Democritus—which lay far within the pupils of my beloved? What *was* it? I was possessed with a passion to discover. . . ."

It is easy to see why each man kills the thing he loves. To *know* a living thing is to kill it. You have to kill a thing to know it satisfactorily. For this reason, the desirous consciousness, the SPIRIT, is a vampire.

One should be sufficiently intelligent and interested to know a good deal *about* any person one comes into close contact with. *About* her. Or *about* him.

But to try to *know* any living being is to try to suck the life out of that being.

Above all things, with the woman one loves. Every sacred instinct teaches one that one must leave her unknown. You know your woman darkly, in the blood. To try to *know* her mentally is to try to kill her. Beware, oh, woman, of the man who wants to *find out what you are*. And, oh, men, beware a thousand times more of the woman who wants to *know* you, or *get* you, what you are.

It is the temptation of a vampire fiend, is this knowledge.

Man does so horribly want to master the secret of life and of individuality *with his mind*. It is like the analysis of protoplasm. You can only analyze *dead* protoplasm, and know its constituents. It is a death process.

Keep KNOWLEDGE for the world of matter, force, and function. It has got nothing to do with being.

But Poe wanted to know—wanted to know what was the strangeness in the eyes of Ligeia. She might have told him it was horror at his probing, horror at being vamped by his consciousness.

But she wanted to be vamped. She wanted to be probed by his consciousness, to be KNOWN. She paid for wanting it, too.

Nowadays it is usually the man who wants to be vamped, to be KNOWN.

Edgar Allan probed and probed. So often he seemed on the verge. But she went over the verge of death before he came over the verge of knowledge. And it is always so.

He decided, therefore, that the clue to the strangeness lay in the mystery of will. "And the will therein lieth, which dieth not . . ."

Ligeia had a "gigantic volition." . . . "An intensity in

thought, action, or speech was possibly, in her, a result, or at least an index" (he really meant indication) "of that gigantic volition which, during our long intercourse, failed to give other and more immediate evidence of its existence."

I should have thought her long submission to him was chief and ample "other evidence."

"Of all the women whom I have ever known, she, the outwardly calm, the ever-placid Ligeia, was the most violently a prey to the tumultuous vultures of stern passion. And of such passion I could form no estimate, save by the miraculous expansion of those eyes which at once so delighted and appalled me—by the almost magical melody, modulation, distinctness, and placidity of her very low voice—and by the fierce energy (rendered doubly effective by contrast with her manner of utterance) of the wild words which she habitually uttered."

Poor Poe, he had caught a bird of the same feather as himself. One of those terrible cravers, who crave the further sensation. Crave to madness or death. "Vultures of stern passion" indeed! Condors.

But having recognized that the clue was in her gigantic volition, he should have realized that the process of this loving, this craving, this knowing, was a struggle of wills. But Ligeia, true to the great tradition and mode of womanly love, by her will kept herself submissive, recipient. She is the passive body who is explored and analyzed into death. And yet, at times, her great female will must have revolted. "Vultures of stern passion!" With a convulsion of desire she desired his further probing and exploring. To any lengths. But then, "tumultuous vultures of stern passion." She had to fight with herself.

But Ligeia wanted to go on and on with the craving, with the love, with the sensation, with the probing, with the knowing, on and on to the end.

There is no end. There is only the rupture of death. That's where men, and women, are "had." Man is always sold, in his search for final KNOWLEDGE.

"That she loved me I should not have doubted; and I might have been easily aware that, in a bosom such as hers, love would have reigned no ordinary passion. But in death only was I fully impressed with the strength of her affection. For long hours, detaining my hand, would she pour out before me the overflowing of a heart whose more than passionate devotion amounted to idolatry." (Oh, the indecency of all this endless intimate talk!) "How had I deserved to be blessed by such confessions?" (Another man would have felt himself cursed.) "How had I deserved to be cursed with the removal of my beloved in the hour of her making them? But upon this subject I cannot bear to dilate. Let me say only that in Ligeia's more than womanly abandonment to a love, alas! unmerited, all unworthily bestowed, I at length recognized the principle of her longing with so wildly earnest a desire for the life which was fleeing so rapidly away. It is this wild longing–it is this vehement desire for life–*but* for life–that I have no power to portray–no utterance capable of expressing."

Well, that is ghastly enough, in all conscience.

"And from them that have not shall be taken away even that which they have."

"To him that hath life shall be given life, and from him that hath not life shall be taken away even that life which he hath."

Or her either.

These terribly conscious birds, like Poe and his Ligeia, deny the very life that is in them; they want to turn it all into talk, into *knowing*. And so life, which will *not* be known, leaves them.

But poor Ligeia, how could she help it. It was her doom. All the centuries of the SPIRIT, all the years of American rebellion against the Holy Ghost, had done it to her.

She dies, when she would rather do anything than die. And when she dies the clue, which he only lived to grasp, dies with her.

Foiled!

Foiled!

No wonder she shrieks with her last breath.

On the last day Ligeia dictates to her husband a poem. As poems go, it is rather false, meretricious. But put yourself in Ligeia's place, and it is real enough, and ghastly beyond bearing.

Out, out are all the lights—out all! 17½
  And over each quivering form
The curtain, a funeral pall,
  Comes down with the rush of a storm,
And the angels, all pallid and wan,
  Uprising, unveiling, affirm
That the play is the tragedy "Man,"
  And its hero the Conqueror Worm.

Which is the American equivalent for a William Blake poem. For Blake, too, was one of these ghastly, obscene "Knowers."

"'O God!' half shrieked Ligeia, leaping to her feet and extending her arms aloft with a spasmodic movement, as I made an end of these lines. 'O God! O Divine Father!—shall these things be undeviatingly so? Shall this conqueror be not once conquered? Are we not part and parcel in Thee? Who—who knoweth the mysteries of the angels, *nor unto death utterly,* save only through the weakness of his feeble will.'"

So Ligeia dies. And yields to death at least partly. *Anche troppo.*

As for her cry to God—has not God said that those who sin against the Holy Ghost shall not be forgiven?

And the Holy Ghost is within us. It is the thing that prompts us to be real, not to push our own cravings too far, not to submit to stunts and highfalutin, above all, not to be too egoistic and willful in our conscious self, but to change as the spirit inside us bids us change, and leave off when it bids us leave off, and laugh when we must laugh, particularly at ourselves, for in deadly earnestness there is always something a bit ridiculous. The Holy Ghost bids us never be too deadly in our earnestness, always to laugh in time, at ourselves and everything. Particularly at our sublimities. Everything has its hour of ridicule—everything.

Now Poe and Ligeia, alas, couldn't laugh. They were frenziedly earnest. And frenziedly they pushed on this vibration of consciousness and unison in consciousness. They sinned against the Holy Ghost that bids us all laugh and forget, bids us know our own limits. And they weren't forgiven.

Ligeia needn't blame God. She had only her own will, her "gigantic volition" to thank, lusting after more consciousness, more beastly KNOWING.

Ligeia dies. The husband goes to England, vulgarly buys or rents a gloomy, grand old abbey, puts it into some sort of repair, and furnishes it with exotic, mysterious, theatrical splendor. Never anything open and real. This theatrical "volition" of his. The bad taste of sensationalism.

Then he marries the fair-haired, blue-eyed Lady Rowena Trevanion, of Tremaine. That is, she would be a sort of Saxon-Cornish blue-blood damsel. Poor Poe!

"In halls such as these—in a bridal chamber such as this—I passed, with the Lady of Tremaine, the unhallowed hours of the first month of our marriage—passed them with but little disquietude. That my wife dreaded the fierce moodiness of my temper—that she shunned and loved me but little—I could not help perceiving, but it gave me rather pleasure than otherwise. I loathed her with a hatred belonging rather to a demon than a man. My memory flew back (Oh, with what intensity of regret!) to Ligeia, the beloved, the august, the entombed. I reveled in recollections of her purity . . ." etc.

Now the vampire lust is consciously such.

In the second month of the marriage the Lady Rowena fell ill. It is the shadow of Ligeia hangs over her. It is the ghostly Ligeia who pours poison into Rowena's cup. It is the spirit of Ligeia, leagued with the spirit of the husband, that now lusts in the slow destruction of Rowena. The two vampires, dead wife and living husband.

For Ligeia has not yielded unto death *utterly*. Her fixed, frustrated will comes back in vindictiveness. She could not have her way in life. So she, too, will find victims in life. And the husband, all the time, only uses Rowena as a living body on which to wreak his vengeance for his being thwarted with Ligeia. Thwarted from the final KNOWING her.

And at last from the corpse of Rowena, Ligeia rises. Out

of her death, through the door of a corpse they have destroyed between them, reappears Ligeia, still trying to have her will, to have more love and knowledge, the final gratification which is never final, with her husband.

For it is true, as William James and Conan Doyle and the rest allow, that a spirit can persist in the after-death. Persist by its own volition. But usually the evil persistence of a thwarted will, returning for vengeance on life. Lemures, vampires.

It is a ghastly story of the assertion of the human will, the will-to-love and the will-to-consciousness, asserted against death itself. The pride of human conceit in KNOWLEDGE.

There are terrible spirits, ghosts, in the air of America.

Eleanora, the next story, is a fantasy revealing the sensational delights of the man in his early marriage with the young and tender bride. They dwelt, he, his cousin and her mother, in the sequestered Valley of Many-colored Grass, the valley of prismatic sensation, where everything seems spectrum colored. They looked down at their *own images* in the River of Silence, and drew the god Eros from that wave: out of their own self-consciousness, that is. This is a description of the life of introspection and of the love which is begotten by the self in the self, the self-made love. The trees are like serpents worshiping the sun. That is, they represent the phallic passion in its poisonous or mental activity. Everything runs to consciousness: serpents worshiping the sun. The embrace of love, which should bring darkness and oblivion, would with these lovers be a daytime thing bringing more heightened consciousness, visions, spectrum-visions, prismatic. The evil thing that daytime love-making is, and all sex palaver.

In *Berenice* the man must go down to the sepulcher of his beloved and pull out her thirty-two small white teeth, which he carries in a box with him. It is repulsive and gloating. The teeth are the instruments of biting, of resistance, of antagonism. They often become symbols of opposition, little instruments or entities of crushing and destroying. Hence the dragon's teeth in the myth. Hence the man in *Berenice* must take possession of the irreducible part of his mistress.

"Toutes ses dents étaient des idées," he says. Then they are little fixed ideas of mordant hate, of which he possesses himself.

The other great story linking up with this group is *The Fall of the House of Usher.* Here the love is between brother and sister. When the self is broken, and the mystery of the recognition of *otherness* fails, then the longing for identification with the beloved becomes a lust. And it is this longing for identification, utter merging, which is at the base of the incest problem. In psychoanalysis almost every trouble in the psyche is traced to an incest-desire. But it won't do. Incest-desire is only one of the modes by which men strive to get their gratification of the intensest vibration of the spiritual nerves, without any resistance. In the family, the natural vibration is most nearly in unison. With a stranger, there is greater resistance. Incest is the getting of gratification and the avoiding of resistance.

The root of all evil is that we all want this spiritual gratification, this flow, this apparent heightening of life, this knowledge, this valley of many-colored grass, even grass and light prismatically decomposed, giving ecstasy. We want all this *without resistance*. We want it continually. And this is the root of all evil in us.

We ought to pray to be resisted, and resisted to the bitter end. We ought to decide to have done at last with craving.

The motto to *The Fall of the House of Usher* is a couple of lines from Béranger.

> *Son cœur est un luth suspendu;*
> *Sitôt qu'on le touche il résonne.*

We have all the trappings of Poe's rather overdone, vulgar fantasy. "I reined my horse to the precipitous brink of a black and lurid tarn that lay in unruffled luster by the dwelling, and gazed down—but with a shudder even more thrilling than before—upon the remodeled and inverted images of the gray sedge, and the ghastly tree stems, and the vacant and eyelike windows." The House of Usher, both dwelling and family, was very old. Minute fungi overspread the exterior of the house, hanging in festoons from the eaves. Gothic archways, a valet of stealthy step, somber tapestries, ebon black floors, a profusion of tattered and antique furniture, feeble gleams of encrimsoned light through latticed panes, and over all "an air of stern, deep, irredeemable gloom"—this makes up the interior.

The inmates of the house, Roderick and Madeline Usher, are the last remnants of their incomparably ancient and decayed race. Roderick has the same large, luminous eye, the same slightly arched nose of delicate Hebrew model, as characterized Ligeia. He is ill with the nervous malady of his family. It is he whose nerves are so strung that they vibrate to the unknown quiverings of the ether. He, too, has lost his self, his living soul, and become a sensitized instrument of the external influences; his nerves are verily like an æolian harp which must vibrate. He lives in "some struggle with the grim phantasm, Fear," for he is only the physical, post-mortem reality of a living being.

It is a question how much, once the true centrality of the self is broken, the instrumental consciousness of man can register. When man becomes selfless, wafting instrumental like a harp in an open window, how much can his elemental consciousness express? The blood as it runs has its own sympathies and responses to the material world, quite apart from seeing. And the nerves we know vibrate all the while to unseen presences, unseen forces. So Roderick Usher quivers on the edge of material existence.

It is this mechanical consciousness which gives "the fervid facility of his impromptus." It is the same thing that gives Poe his extraordinary facility in versification. The absence of real central or impulsive being in himself leaves him inordinately, mechanically sensitive to sounds and effects, associations of sounds, associations of rhyme, for example—mechanical, facile, having no root in any passion. It is all a secondary, meretricious process. So we get Roderick Usher's poem, *The Haunted Palace,* with its swift yet mechanical subtleties of rhyme and rhythm, its vulgarity of epithet. It is all a sort of dream-process, where the association between parts is mechanical, accidental as far as passional meaning goes.

Usher thought that all vegetable things had sentience. Surely all material things have a *form* of sentience, even the inorganic: surely they all exist in some subtle and complicated tension of vibration which makes them sensitive to external influence and causes them to have an influence on other external objects, irrespective of contact. It is of this vibration or inorganic consciousness that Poe is master: the sleep consciousness. Thus Roderick Usher was convinced that his whole surroundings, the stones of the house, the fungi, the water in the tarn, the very reflected image of the whole, was woven into a physical oneness with the family, condensed, as it were, into one atmosphere—the special atmosphere in which alone the Ushers could live. And it was this atmosphere which had molded the destinies of his family.

But while ever the soul remains alive, it is the molder and not the molded. It is the souls of living men that subtly impregnate stones, houses, mountains, continents, and give these their subtlest form. People only become subject to stones after having lost their integral souls.

In the human realm, Roderick had one connection: his sister Madeline. She, too, was dying of a mysterious disorder, nervous, cataleptic. The brother and sister loved each other passionately and exclusively. They were twins, almost identical in looks. It was the same absorbing love between them, this process of unison in nerve-vibration, resulting in more and more extreme exaltation and a sort of consciousness, and a gradual breakdown into death. The exquisitely sensitive Roger, vibrating without resistance with his sister Madeline, more and more exquisitely, and gradually devouring her, sucking her life like a vampire in his anguish of extreme love. And she asking to be sucked.

Madeline died and was carried down by her brother into the deep vaults of the house. But she was not dead. Her brother roamed about in incipient madness—a madness of unspeakable terror and guilt. After eight days they were suddenly startled by a clash of metal, then a distinct, hollow metallic, and clangorous, yet apparently muffled, reverberation. Then Roderick Usher, gibbering, began to express himself: *"We have put her living into the tomb!* Said I not that my senses were acute? I *now* tell you that I heard her first feeble movements in the hollow coffin. I heard them—many, many days ago—yet I dared not—*I dared not speak."*

It is the same old theme of "each man kills the thing he loves." He knew his love had killed her. He knew she died at last, like Ligeia, unwilling and unappeased. So, she rose again upon him. "But then without those doors there *did* stand the lofty and enshrouded figure of the Lady Madeline of Usher. There was blood upon her white robes, and the evidence of some bitter struggle upon every portion of her emaciated frame. For a moment she remained trembling and reeling to and fro upon the threshold, then, with a low moaning cry, fell heavily inward upon the person of her brother, and in her violent and now final death-agonies bore him to the floor a corpse, and a victim to the terrors he had anticipated."

It is lurid and melodramatic, but it is true. It is a ghastly psychological truth of what happens in the last stages of this beloved love, which cannot be separate, cannot be isolate, cannot listen in isolation to the isolate Holy Ghost. For it is the Holy Ghost we must live by. The next era is the era of the Holy Ghost. And the Holy Ghost speaks individually inside each individual: always, forever a ghost. There is no manifestation to the general world. Each isolate individual listening in isolation to the Holy Ghost within him.

The Ushers, brother and sister, betrayed the Holy Ghost in themselves. They would love, love, love, without resistance. They would love, they would merge, they would be as one thing. So they dragged each other down into death. For the Holy Ghost says you must *not* be as one thing with another being. Each must abide by itself, and correspond only within certain limits.

The best tales all have the same burden. Hate is as inordinate as love, and as slowly consuming, as secret, as underground, as subtle. All this underground vault business in Poe only symbolizes that which takes place *beneath* the consciousness. On top, all is fair-spoken. Beneath, there is awful murderous extremity of burying alive. Fortunato, in *The Cask of Amontillado,* is buried alive out of perfect hatred, as the Lady Madeline of Usher is buried alive out of love. The lust of hate is the inordinate desire to consume and unspeakably possess the soul of the hated one, just as the lust of love is the desire to possess, or to be possessed by, the beloved, utterly. But in either case the result is the dissolution of both souls, each losing itself in transgressing its own bounds.

The lust of Montresor is to devour utterly the soul of Fortunato. It would be no use killing him outright. If a man is killed outright his soul remains integral, free to return into the bosom of some beloved, where it can enact itself. In walling up his enemy in the vault, Montresor seeks to bring about the indescribable capitulation of the man's soul, so that he, the victor, can possess himself of the very being of the vanquished. Perhaps this can actually be done. Perhaps, in the attempt, the victor breaks the bonds of his own identity, and collapses into nothingness, or into the infinite. Becomes a monster.

What holds good for inordinate hate holds good for inordinate love. The motto, *Nemo me impune lacessit,* might just as well be *Nemo me impune amat.*

In *William Wilson* we are given a rather unsubtle account of the attempt of a man to kill his own soul. William Wilson the mechanical, lustful ego succeeds in killing William Wilson the living self. The lustful ego lives on, gradually reducing itself towards the dust of the infinite.

In the *Murders in the Rue Morgue* and *The Gold Bug* we have those mechanical tales where the interest lies in the following out of a subtle chain of cause and effect. The interest is scientific rather than artistic, a study in psychologic reactions.

The fascination of murder itself is curious. Murder is not just killing. Murder is a lust to get at the very quick of life itself, and kill it—hence the stealth and the frequent morbid dismemberment of the corpse, the attempt to get at the very quick of the murdered being, to find the quick and to possess it. It is curious that the two men fascinated by the art of murder, though in different ways, should have been De Quincey and Poe, men so different in ways of life, yet perhaps not so widely different in nature. In each of them is traceable that strange lust for extreme love and extreme hate, possession by mystic violence of the other soul, or violent deathly surrender of the soul in the self: an absence of manly virtue, which stands alone and accepts limits.

Inquisition and torture are akin to murder: the same lust. It is a combat between inquisitor and victim as to whether the inquisitor shall get at the quick of life itself, and pierce it. Pierce the very quick of the soul. The evil will of man tries to do this. The brave soul of man refuses to have the life-quick pierced in him. It is strange: but just as the thwarted will can persist evilly, after death, so can the brave spirit preserve, even through torture and death, the quick of life and truth. Nowadays society is evil. It finds subtle ways of torture, to destroy the life-quick, to get at the life-quick in a man. Every possible form. And still a man can hold out, if he can laugh and listen to the Holy Ghost.—But society is evil, evil, and love is evil. And evil breeds evil, more and more.

So the mystery goes on. La Bruyère says that all our human unhappiness *viennent de ne pouvoir être seuls*. As long as man lives he will be subject to the yearning of love or the burning of hate, which is only inverted love.

But he is subject to something more than this. If we do not live to eat, we do not live to love either.

We live to stand alone, and listen to the Holy Ghost. The Holy Ghost, who is inside us, and who is many gods. Many gods come and go, some say one thing and some say another, and we have to obey the God of the innermost hour. It is the multiplicity of gods within us make up the Holy Ghost.

But Poe knew only love, love, love, intense vibrations and heightened consciousness. Drugs, women, self-destruction, but anyhow the prismatic ecstasy of heightened consciousness and sense of love, of flow. The human soul in him was beside itself. But it was not lost. He told us plainly how it was, so that we should know.

He was an adventurer into vaults and cellars and horrible underground passages of the human soul. He sounded the horror and the warning of his own doom.

Doomed he was. He died wanting more love, and love killed him. A ghastly disease, love. Poe telling us of his disease: trying even to make his desease fair and attractive. Even succeeding.

Which is the inevitable falseness, duplicity of art, American art in particular.

VII. Nathaniel Hawthorne and The Scarlet Letter

NATHANIEL HAWTHORNE writes romance.

And what's romance? Usually, a nice little tale where you have everything As You Like It, where rain never wets your jacket and gnats never bite your nose and it's always daisy-time. *As You Like It* and *Forest Lovers,* etc. *Morte D'Arthur.*

Hawthorne obviously isn't this kind of romanticist: though nobody has muddy boots in *The Scarlet Letter,* either.

But there is more to it. *The Scarlet Letter* isn't a pleasant, pretty romance. It is a sort of parable, an earthly story with a hellish meaning.

All the time there is this split in the American art and art-consciousness. On the top it is as nice as pie, goody-goody and lovey-dovey. Like Hawthorne being such a blue-eyed darling, in life, and Longfellow and the rest such sucking-doves. Hawthorne's wife said she "never saw him in time," which doesn't mean she saw him too late. But always in the "frail effulgence of eternity."

Serpents they were. Look at the inner meaning of their art and see what demons they were.

You *must* look through the surface of American art, and see the inner diabolism of the symbolic meaning. Otherwise it is all mere childishness.

That blue-eyed darling Nathaniel knew disagreeable things in his inner soul. He was careful to send them out in disguise.

Always the same. The deliberate consciousness of Americans so fair and smooth-spoken, and the under-consciousness so devilish. *Destroy! destroy! destroy!* hums the under-consciousness. *Love and produce! Love and produce!* cackles the upper consciousness. And the world hears only the love-and-produce cackle. Refuses to hear the hum of destruction underneath. Until such time as it will *have* to hear.

The American has got to destroy. It is his destiny. It is his destiny to destroy the whole corpus of the white psyche, the white consciousness. And he's got to do it secretly. As the growing of a dragonfly inside a chrysalis or cocoon destroys the larva grub, secretly.

Though many a dragonfly never gets out of the chrysalis case: dies inside. As America might.

So the secret chrysalis of *The Scarlet Letter*, diabolically destroying the old psyche inside.

Be good! Be good! warbles Nathaniel. *Be good, and never sin! Be sure your sins will find you out.*

So convincingly that his wife never saw him "as in time."

Then listen to the diabolic undertone of *The Scarlet Letter.*

Man ate of the tree of knowledge, and became ashamed of himself.

Do you imagine Adam had never lived with Eve before that apple episode? Yes, he had. As a wild animal with his mate.

It didn't become "sin" till the knowledge-poison entered. That apple of Sodom.

We are divided in ourselves, against ourselves. And that is the meaning of the cross symbol.

In the first place, Adam knew Eve as a wild animal knows its mate, momentaneously, but vitally, in blood-knowledge. Blood-knowledge, not mind-knowledge. Blood-knowledge, that seems utterly to forget, but doesn't. Blood-knowledge, instinct, intuition, all the vast vital flux of knowing that goes on in the dark, antecedent to the mind.

Then came that beastly apple, and the other sort of knowledge started.

Adam began to look at himself. "My hat!" he said.

"What's this? My Lord! What the deuce!—And Eve! I wonder about Eve."

Thus starts KNOWING. Which shortly runs to UNDERSTANDING, when the devil gets his own.

When Adam went and took Eve, *after* the apple, he didn't do any more than he had done many a time before, in act. But in consciousness he did something very different. So did Eve. Each of them kept an eye on what they were doing, they watched what was happening to them. They wanted to KNOW. And that was the birth of sin. Not *doing* it, but KNOWING about it. Before the apple, they had shut their eyes and their minds had gone dark. Now, they peeped and pried and imagined. They watched themselves. And they felt uncomfortable after. They felt self-conscious. So they said, "The *act* is sin. Let's hide. We've sinned."

No wonder the Lord kicked them out of the Garden. Dirty hypocrites.

The sin was the self-watching, self-consciousness. The sin, and the doom. Dirty understanding.

Nowadays men do hate the idea of dualism. It's no good, dual we are. The cross. If we accept the symbol, then, virtually, we accept the fact. We are divided against ourselves.

For instance, the blood *hates* being KNOWN by the mind. It feels itself destroyed when it is KNOWN. Hence the profound instinct of privacy.

And on the other hand, the mind and the spiritual consciousness of man simply *hates* the dark potency of blood-acts: hates the genuine dark sensual orgasms, which do, for the time being, actually obliterate the mind and the spiritual consciousness, plunge them in a suffocating flood of darkness.

You can't get away from this.

Blood-consciousness overwhelms, obliterates, and annuls mind-consciousness.

Mind-consciousness extinguishes blood-consciousness, and consumes the blood.

We are all of us conscious in both ways. And the two ways are antagonistic in us.

They will always remain so.

That is our cross.

The antagonism is so obvious, and so far-reaching, that it extends to the smallest thing. The cultured, highly-conscious person of today *loathes* any form of physical, "menial" work: such as washing dishes or sweeping a floor or chopping wood. This menial work is an insult to the spirit. "When I see men carrying heavy loads, doing brutal work, it always makes me want to cry," said a beautiful, cultured woman to me.

"When you say that, it makes me want to beat you," said I, in reply. "When I see you with your beautiful head pondering heavy thoughts, I just want to hit you. It outrages me."

My father hated books, hated the sight of anyone reading or writing.

My mother hated the thought that any of her sons should be condemned to manual labor. Her sons must have something higher than that.

She won. But she died first.

He laughs longest who laughs last.

There is a basic hostility in all of us between the physical and the mental, the blood and the spirit. The mind is "ashamed" of the blood. And the blood is destroyed by the mind, actually. Hence pale-faces.

At present the mind-consciousness and the so-called spirit triumphs. In America supremely. In America, nobody does anything from the blood. Always from the nerves, if not from the mind. The blood is chemically reduced by the nerves, in American activity.

When an Italian laborer labors, his mind and nerves sleep, his blood acts ponderously.

Americans, when they are *doing* things, never seem really to be doing them. They are "busy about" it. They are always busy "about" something. But truly *immersed* in *doing* something, with the deep blood-consciousness active, that they never are.

They *admire* the blood-conscious spontaneity. And they want to get it in their heads. "Live from the body," they shriek. It is their last mental shriek. *Co-ordinate.*

It is a further attempt still to rationalize the body and blood. "Think about such and such a muscle," they say, "and relax there."

And every time you "conquer" the body with the mind (you can say "heal" it, if you like) you cause a deeper, more dangerous complex or tension somewhere else.

Ghastly Americans, with their blood no longer blood. A yellow spiritual fluid.

The Fall.

There have been lots of Falls.

We *fell* into *knowledge* when Eve bit the apple. Self-conscious knowledge. For the first time the mind put up a fight against the blood. Wanting to UNDERSTAND. That is to intellectualize the blood.

The blood must be *shed,* says Jesus.

Shed on the cross of our own divided psyche.

Shed the blood, and you become mind-conscious. Eat the body and drink the blood, self-cannibalizing, and you become extremely conscious, like Americans and some Hindus. Devour yourself, and God knows what a lot you'll know, what a lot you'll be conscious of.

Mind you don't choke yourself.

For a long time men *believed* that they could be perfected through the mind, through the spirit. They believed, passionately. They had their ecstasy in pure consciousness. They *believed* in purity, chastity, and the wings of the spirit.

America soon plucked the bird of the spirit. America soon killed the *belief* in the spirit. But not the practice. The practice continued with a sarcastic vehemence. America, with a perfect inner contempt for the spirit and the consciousness of man, practices the same spirituality and universal love and KNOWING all the time, incessantly, like a drug habit. And inwardly gives not a fig for it. Only for the *sensation.* The pretty-pretty *sensation* of love, loving all the world. And the nice fluttering aeroplane *sensation* of knowing, knowing, knowing. Then the prettiest of all sensations, the sensation of UNDERSTANDING. Oh, what a lot they understand, the darlings! *So* good at the trick, they are. Just a trick of self-conceit.

The Scarlet Letter gives the show away.

You have your pure-pure young parson Dimmesdale.

You have the beautiful Puritan Hester at his feet.

And the first thing she does is to seduce him.

And the first thing he does is to be seduced.

And the second thing they do is to hug their sin in secret, and gloat over it, and try to understand.

Which is the myth of New England.

Deerslayer refused to be seduced by Judith Hutter. At least the Sodom apple of sin didn't fetch him.

But Dimmesdale was seduced gloatingly. Oh, luscious Sin!

He was such a pure young man.

That he had to make a fool of purity.

The American psyche.

Of course, the best part of the game lay in keeping up pure appearances.

The greatest triumph a woman can have, especially an American woman, is the triumph of seducing a man: especially if he is pure.

And he gets the greatest thrill of all, in falling.—"Seduce me, Mrs. Hercules."

And the pair of them share the subtlest delight in keeping up pure appearances, when everybody knows all the while. But the power of pure appearances is something to exult in. All America gives in to it. *Look* pure!

To seduce a man. To have everybody know. To keep up appearances of purity. Pure!

This is the great triumph of woman.

A. The Scarlet Letter. Adulteress! The great Alpha, Alpha! Adulteress! The new Adam and Adama! American!

A. Adulteress! Stitched with gold thread, glittering upon the bosom. The proudest insignia.

Put her upon the scaffold and worship her there. Worship her there. The Woman, the Magna Mater. *A*. Adulteress! Abel!

Abel! Abel! Abel! Admirable!

It becomes a farce.

The fiery heart. *A*. Mary of the Bleeding Heart. Mater

Adolerata! *A*. Capital *A*. Adulteress. Glittering with gold thread. Abel! Adultery. Admirable!

It is, perhaps, the most colossal satire ever penned. *The Scarlet Letter*. And by a blue-eyed darling of a Nathaniel.

Not Bumppo, however.

The human spirit, fixed in a lie, adhering to a lie, giving itself perpetually the lie.

All begins with *A*.

Adulteress. Alpha. Abel, Adam. *A*. America.

The Scarlet Letter.

"Had there been a Papist among the crowd of Puritans, he might have seen in this beautiful woman, so picturesque in her attire and mien, and with the infant at her bosom, an object to remind him of the image of Divine Maternity, which so many illustrious painters have vied with one another to represent; something which should remind him, indeed, but only by contrast, of that sacred image of sinless Motherhood, whose infant was to redeem the world."

Whose infant was to redeem the world indeed! It will be a startling redemption the world will get from the American infant.

"Here was a taint of deepest sin in the most sacred quality of human life, working such effect that the world was only the darker for this woman's beauty, and more lost for the infant she had borne."

Just listen to the darling. Isn't he a master of apology?

Of symbols, too.

His pious blame is a chuckle of praise all the while.

Oh, Hester, you are a demon. A man *must* be pure, just that you can seduce him to a fall. Because the greatest thrill in life is to bring down the Sacred Saint with a flop into the mud. Then when you've brought him down, humbly wipe off the mud with your hair, another Magdalen. And then go home and dance a witch's jig of triumph, and stitch yourself a Scarlet Letter with gold thread, as duchesses used to stitch themselves coronets. And then stand meek on the scaffold and fool the world. Who will all be envying you your sin, and beating you because you've stolen an advantage over them.

Hester Prynne is the great nemesis of woman. She is the KNOWING Ligeia risen diabolic from the grave. Having her own back. UNDERSTANDING.

This time it is Mr. Dimmesdale who dies. She lives on and is Abel.

His spiritual love was a lie. And prostituting the woman to his spiritual love, as popular clergymen do, in his preachings and loftiness, was a tall white lie. Which came flop.

We are so pure in spirit. Hi-tiddly-i-ty!

Till she tickled him in the right place, and he fell.

Flop.

Flop goes spiritual love.

But keep up the game. Keep up appearances. Pure are the pure. To the pure all things, etc.

Look out, Mister, for the Female Devotee. Whatever you do, don't let her start tickling you. She knows your weak spot. Mind your Purity.

When Hester Prynne seduced Arthur Dimmesdale it was the beginning of the end. But from the beginning of the end to the end of the end is a hundred years or two.

Mr. Dimmesdale also wasn't at the end of his resources. Previously, he had lived by governing his body, ruling it, in the interests of his spirit. Now he has a good time all by himself torturing his body, whipping it, piercing it with thorns, macerating himself. It's a form of masturbation. He wants to get a mental grip on his body. And since he can't quite manage it with the mind, witness his fall—he will give it what for, with whips. His will shall *lash* his body. And he enjoys his pains. Wallows in them. To the pure all things are pure.

It is the old self-mutilation process, gone rotten. The mind wanting to get its teeth in the blood and flesh. The ego exulting in the tortures of the mutinous flesh. I, the ego, I *will* triumph over my own flesh. Lash! Lash! I am a grand free spirit. *Lash!* I am the master of my soul! *Lash! Lash!* I am the captain of my soul. *Lash!* Hurray! "In the fell clutch of circumstance," etc., etc.

Good-by Arthur. He depended on women for his Spiritual Devotees, spiritual brides. So, the woman just touched him in his weak spot, his Achilles Heel of the flesh. Look out for the spiritual bride. She's after the weak spot.

It is the battle of wills.

"For the will therein lieth, which dieth not——"

The Scarlet Woman becomes a Sister of Mercy. Didn't she just, in the late war. Oh, Prophet Nathaniel!

Hester urges Dimmesdale to go away with her, to a new country, to a new life. He isn't having any.

He knows there is no new country, no new life on the globe today. It is the same old thing, in different degrees, everywhere. *Plus ça change, plus c'est la même chose.*

Hester thinks, with Dimmesdale for her husband, and Pearl for her child, in Australia, maybe, she'd have been perfect.

But she wouldn't. Dimmesdale had already fallen from his integrity as a minister of the Gospel of the Spirit. He had lost his manliness. He didn't see the point of just leaving himself between the hands of a woman and going away to a "new country," to be her thing entirely. She'd only have despised him more, as every woman despises a man who has "fallen" to her; despises him with her tenderest lust.

He stood for nothing any more. So let him stay where he was and dree out his weird.

She had dished him and his spirituality, so he hated her. As Angel Clare was dished, and hated Tess. As Jude in the end hated Sue: or should have done. The women make fools of them, the spiritual men. And when, as men, they've gone flop in their spirituality, they can't pick themselves up whole any more. So they just crawl, and die detesting the female, or the females, who made them fall.

The saintly minister gets a bit of his own back, at the last minute, by making public confession from the very scaffold where she was exposed. Then he dodges into death. But he's had a bit of his own back, on everybody.

"Shall we not meet again?" whispered she, bending her face down close to him. "Shall we not spend our immortal life together? Surely, surely we have ransomed one another with all this woe! Thou lookest far into eternity with those bright dying eyes. Tell me what thou seest!"

"Hush, Hester—hush," said he, with tremulous solemnity. "The law we broke!—the sin here so awfully revealed! Let these alone be in thy thoughts. I fear! I fear!"

So he dies, throwing the "sin" in her teeth, and escaping into death.

The law we broke, indeed. You bet!

Whose law?

But it is truly a law, that man must either stick to the belief he has grounded himself on, and obey the laws of that belief, or he must admit the belief itself to be inadequate, and prepare himself for a new thing.

There was no change in belief, either in Hester or in Dimmesdale or in Hawthorne or in America. The same old treacherous belief, which was really cunning disbelief, in the Spirit, in Purity, in Selfless Love, and in Pure Consciousness. They would go on following this belief, for the sake of the sensationalism of it. But they would make a fool of it all the time. Like Woodrow Wilson, and the rest of modern Believers. The rest of modern Saviors.

If you meet a Savior today, be sure he is trying to make an innermost fool of you. Especially if the savior be an UNDERSTANDING WOMAN, offering her love.

Hester lives on, pious as pie, being a public nurse. She becomes at last an acknowledged saint, Abel of the Scarlet Letter.

She would, being a woman. She has had her triumph over the individual man, so she quite loves subscribing to the whole spiritual life of society. She will make herself as false as hell, for society's sake, once she's had her real triumph over Saint Arthur.

Blossoms out into a Sister-of-Mercy Saint.

But it's a long time before she really takes anybody in. People kept on thinking her a witch, which she was.

As a matter of fact, unless a woman is held, by man, safe within the bounds of belief, she becomes inevitably a destructive force. She can't help herself. A woman is almost always vulnerable to pity. She can't bear to see anything *physically* hurt. But let a woman loose from the bounds and restraints of man's fierce belief, in his gods and in himself, and she becomes a gentle devil. She becomes subtly diabolic. The colossal evil of the united spirit of Woman. WOMAN, German woman or American woman, or every other sort of woman, in the last war, was something frightening. As every *man* knows.

Woman becomes a helpless, would-be-loving demon. She is helpless. Her very love is a subtle poison.

Unless a man believes in himself and his gods, *genuinely:* unless he fiercely obeys his own Holy Ghost: his woman will destroy him. Woman is the nemesis of doubting man. She can't help it.

And with Hester, after Ligeia, woman becomes a nemesis to man. She bolsters him up from the outside, she destroys him from the inside. And he dies hating her, as Dimmesdale did.

Dimmesdale's spirituality had gone on too long, too far. It had become a false thing. He found his nemesis in woman. And he was done for.

Woman is a strange and rather terrible phenomenon, to man. When the subconscious soul of woman recoils from its creative union with man, it becomes a destructive force. It exerts, willy-nilly, an invisible destructive influence. The woman herself may be as nice as milk, to all appearance, like Ligeia. But she is sending out waves of silent destruction of the faltering spirit in men, all the same. She doesn't know it. She can't even help it. But she does it. The devil is in her.

The very women who are most busy saving the bodies of men, and saving the children: these women doctors, these nurses, these educationalists, these public-spirited women, these female saviors: they are all, from the inside, sending out waves of destructive malevolence which eat out the inner life of a man, like a cancer. It is so, it will be so, till men realize it and react to save themselves.

God won't save us. The women are so devilish godly.

Men must save themselves in this strait, and by no sugary means either.

A woman can use her sex in sheer malevolence and poison, while she is *behaving* as meek and good as gold. Dear darling, she is really snow-white in her blamelessness. And all the while she is using her sex as a she-devil, for the endless hurt of her man. She doesn't know it. She will never believe it if you tell her. And if you give her a slap in the face for her fiendishness, she will rush to the first magistrate, in indignation. She is so *absolutely* blameless, the she-devil, the dear, dutiful creature.

Give her the great slap, just the same, just when she is being most angelic. Just when she is bearing her cross most meekly.

Oh, woman out of bounds is a devil. But it is man's fault. Woman never *asked,* in the first place, to be cast out of her bit of an Eden of belief and trust. It is man's business to bear the responsibility of belief. If he becomes a spiritual fornicator and liar, like Ligeia's husband and Arthur Dimmesdale, how *can* a woman believe in him? Belief doesn't go by choice. And if a woman doesn't believe in a *man,* she believes, essentially, in nothing. She becomes, willy-nilly, a devil.

A devil she is, and a devil she will be. And most men will succumb to her devilishness.

Hester Prynne was a devil. Even when she was so meekly going round as a sick-nurse. Poor Hester. Part of her wanted to be saved from her own devilishness. And another part wanted to go on and on in devilishness, for revenge. Revenge! REVENGE! It is this that fills the unconscious spirit of woman today. Revenge against man, and against the spirit of man, which has betrayed her into unbelief. Even when she is most sweet and a salvationist, she is her most devilish, is woman. She gives her man the sugar-plum of her own submissive sweetness. And when he's taken this sugar-plum in his mouth, a scorpion comes out of it. After he's taken this Eve to his bosom, oh, so loving, she destroys him inch by inch. Woman and her revenge! She will have it, and go on having it, for decades and decades, unless she's stopped. And to stop her you've got to believe in yourself and your gods, your own Holy Ghost, Sir Man; and then you've got to fight her, and never give in. She's a devil. But in the long run she is conquerable. And just a tiny bit of her wants to be conquered. You've got to fight three quarters of her, in absolute hell, to get at the final quarter of her that wants a release, at last, from the hell of her own revenge. But it's a long last. And not yet.

"She had in her nature a rich, voluptuous, oriental characteristic—a taste for the gorgeously beautiful." This is Hester. This is American. But she repressed her nature in the above direction. She would not even allow herself the luxury of laboring at fine, delicate stitching. Only she dressed her little sin-child Pearl vividly, and the scarlet letter was gorgeously embroidered. Her Hecate and Astarte insignia.

"A voluptuous, oriental characteristic——" That lies waiting in American women. It is probable that the Mormons are the forerunners of the coming real America. It is probable that men will have more than one wife, in the coming America. That you will have again a half-Oriental womanhood, and a polygamy.

The gray nurse, Hester. The Hecate, the hell-cat. The slowly evolving, voluptuous female of the new era, with a whole new submissiveness to the dark, phallic principle.

But it takes time. Generation after generation of nurses and political women and salvationists. And in the end, the dark erection of the images of sex-worship once more, and the newly submissive women. That kind of depth. Deep women in that respect. When we have at last broken this insanity of mental-spiritual consciousness. And the women *choose* to experience again the great submission.

"The poor, whom she sought out to be the objects of her bounty, often reviled the hand that was stretched to succor them."

Naturally. The poor hate a salvationist. They smell the devil underneath.

"She was patient—a martyr indeed—but she forbore to

pray for her enemies, lest, in spite of her forgiving aspirations, the words of the blessing should stubbornly twist themselves into a curse."

So much honesty, at least. No wonder the old witch-lady Mistress Hibbins claimed her for another witch.

"She grew to have a dread of children; for they had imbibed from their parents a vague idea of something horrible in this dreary woman gliding silently through the town, with never any companion but only one child."

"A vague idea!" Can't you see her "gliding silently"? It's not a question of a vague idea imbibed, but a definite feeling directly received.

"But sometimes, once in many days, or perchance in many months, she felt an eye—a human eye—upon the ignominious brand, that seemed to give a momentary relief, as if half her agony were shared. The next instant, back it all rushed again, with a still deeper throb of pain; for in that brief interval she had sinned again. Had Hester sinned alone?"

Of course not. As for sinning again, she would go on all her life silently, changelessly "sinning." She never repented. Not she. Why should she? She had brought down Arthur Dimmesdale, that too-too snow-white bird, and that was her life-work.

As for sinning again when she met two dark eyes in a crowd, why of course. Somebody who understood as she understood.

I always remember meeting the eyes of a gipsy woman, for one moment, in a crowd, in England. She knew; and I knew. What did we know? I was not able to make out. But we knew.

Probably the same fathomless hate of this spiritual-conscious society in which the outcast woman and I both roamed like meek-looking wolves. Tame wolves waiting to shake off their tameness. Never able to.

And again, that "voluptuous, oriental" characteristic that knows the mystery of the ithyphallic gods. She would not betray the ithyphallic gods to this white, leprous-white society of "lovers." Neither will I, if I can help it. These leprous-white, seducing, spiritual women, who "understand" so much. One has been too often seduced, and "understood." "I can read him like a book," said my first lover of me. The book is in several volumes, dear. And more and more comes back to me the gulf of dark hate and *other* understanding, in the eyes of the gipsy woman. So different from the hateful white light of understanding which floats like scum on the eyes of white, oh, so white English and American women, with their understanding voices and their deep, sad words, and their profound, *good* spirits. Pfui!

Hester was scared only of one result of her sin: Pearl. Pearl, the scarlet letter incarnate. The little girl. When women bear children, they produce either devils or sons with gods in them. And it is an evolutionary process. The devil in Hester produced a purer devil in Pearl. And the devil in Pearl will produce—she married an Italian count—a piece of purer devilishness still.

And so from hour to hour we ripe and ripe.

And then from hour to hour we rot and rot.

There was that in the child "which often impelled Hester to ask in bitterness of heart, whether it were for good or ill that the poor little creature had been born at all."

For ill, Hester. But don't worry. Ill is as necessary as good. Malevolence is as necessary as benevolence. If you have brought forth, spawned, a young malevolence, be sure there is a rampant falseness in the world against which this malevolence must be turned. Falseness has to be bitten and bitten, till it is bitten to death. Hence Pearl.

Pearl. Her own mother compares her to the demon of plague, or scarlet fever, in her red dress. But then, plague is necessary to destroy a rotten, false humanity.

Pearl, the devilish girl-child, who can be so tender and loving and *understanding,* and then, when she has understood, will give you a hit across the mouth, and turn on you with a grin of sheer diabolic jeering.

Serves you right, you shouldn't be *understood.* That is your vice. You shouldn't want to be loved, and then you'd not get hit across the mouth. Pearl will love you: marvelously. And she'll hit you across the mouth: oh, so neatly. And serves you right.

Pearl is perhaps the most modern child in all literature.

Old-fashioned Nathaniel, with his little-boy charm, he'll tell you what's what. But he'll cover it with smarm.

Hester simply *hates* her child, from one part of herself. And from another, she cherishes her child as her one precious treasure. For Pearl is the continuing of her female revenge on life. But female revenge hits both ways. Hits back at its own mother. The female revenge in Pearl hits back at Hester, the mother, and Hester is simply livid with fury and "sadness," which is rather amusing.

"The child could not be made amenable to rules. In giving her existence a great law had been broken; and the result was a being whose elements were perhaps beautiful and brilliant, but all in disorder, or with an order peculiar to themselves, amidst which the point of variety and arrangement was difficult or impossible to discover."

Of course, the order is peculiar to themselves. But the point of variety is this: "Draw out the loving, sweet soul, draw it out with marvelous understanding; and then spit in its eye."

Hester, of course, didn't at all like it when her sweet child drew out her motherly soul, with yearning and deep understanding: and then spit in the motherly eye, with a grin. But it was a process the mother had started.

Pearl had a peculiar look in her eyes: "a look so intelligent, yet so inexplicable, so perverse, sometimes so malicious, but generally accompanied by a wild flow of spirits, that Hester could not help questioning at such moments whether Pearl was a human child."

A little demon! But her mother, and the saintly Dimmesdale, had borne her. And Pearl, by the very openness of her perversity, was more straightforward than her parents. She flatly refuses any Heavenly Father, seeing the earthly one such a fraud. And she has the pietistic Dimmesdale on toast, spits right in his eye: in both his eyes.

Poor, brave, tormented little soul, always in a state of recoil, she'll be a devil to men when she grows up. But the men deserve it. If they'll let themselves be "drawn" by her loving understanding, they deserve that she shall slap them across the mouth the moment they *are* drawn. The chickens! Drawn and trussed.

Poor little phenomenon of a modern child, she'll grow up into the devil of a modern woman. The nemesis of weak-kneed modern men, craving to be love-drawn.

The third person in the diabolic trinity, or triangle, of the Scarlet Letter, is Hester's first husband, Roger Chillingworth. He is an old Elizabethan physician, with a gray beard and a long-furred coat and a twisted shoulder. Another healer. But something of an alchemist, a magician. He is a magician on the verge of modern science, like Francis Bacon.

Roger Chillingworth is of the old order of intellect, in direct line from the mediaeval Roger Bacon alchemists. He has an old, intellectual belief in the dark sciences, the Hermetic philosophies. He is no Christian, no selfless aspirer. He is not an aspirer. He is the old authoritarian in man. The old male authority. But without passional belief. Only intellectual belief in himself and his male authority.

Shakespeare's whole tragic wail is because of the downfall of the true male authority, the ithyphallic authority and masterhood. It fell with Elizabeth. It was trodden underfoot with Victoria.

But Chillingworth keeps on the *intellectual* tradition. He hates the new spiritual aspirers, like Dimmesdale, with a black, crippled hate. He is the old male authority, in intellectual tradition.

You can't keep a wife by force of an intellectual tradition. So Hester took to seducing Dimmesdale.

Yet her only marriage, and her last oath, is with the old Roger. He and she are accomplices in pulling down the spiritual saint.

"Why dost thou smile so at me?" she says to her old, vengeful husband. "Art thou not like the Black Man that haunts the forest around us? Hast thou not enticed me into a bond which will prove the ruin of my soul?"

"Not thy soul!" he answered with another smile. "No, not thy soul!"

It is the soul of the pure preacher, that false thing, which they are after. And the crippled physician—this other healer—blackly vengeful in his old, distorted male authority, and the "loving" woman, they bring down the saint between them.

A black and complementary hatred, akin to love, is what Chillingworth feels for the young, saintly parson. And Dimmesdale responds, in a hideous kind of love. Slowly the saint's life is poisoned. But the black old physician smiles, and tries to keep him alive. Dimmesdale goes in for self-torture, self-lashing, lashing his own white, thin, spiritual savior's body. The dark old Chillingworth listens outside the door and laughs, and prepares another medicine, so that the game can go on longer. And the saint's very soul goes rotten. Which is the supreme triumph. Yet he keeps up appearances still.

The black, vengeful soul of the crippled, masterful male, still dark in his authority: and the white ghastliness of the fallen saint! The two halves of manhood mutually destroying one another.

Dimmesdale has a "*coup*" in the very end. He gives the whole show away by confessing publicly on the scaffold, and dodging into death, leaving Hester dished, and Roger, as it were, doubly cuckolded. It is a neat last revenge.

Down comes the curtain, as in Ligeia's poem.

But the child Pearl will be on in the next act, with her Italian count and a new brood of vipers. And Hester grayly Abelling, in the shadows, after her rebelling.

It is a marvelous allegory. It is to me one of the greatest allegories in all literature, *The Scarlet Letter*. Its marvelous under-meaning! And its perfect duplicity.

The absolute duplicity of that blue-eyed *Wunderkind* of a Nathaniel. The American wonder-child, with his magical allegorical insight.

But even wonder-children have to grow up in a generation or two.

And even SIN becomes stale.

VIII. *Hawthorne's* Blithedale Romance

No other book of Nathaniel Hawthorne is so deep, so dual, and so complete as *The Scarlet Letter:* this great allegory of the triumph of sin.

Sin is a queer thing. It isn't the breaking of divine commandments. It is the breaking of one's own integrity.

For instance, the sin in Hester and Arthur Dimmesdale's case was a sin because they did what they *thought* it *wrong* to do. If they had really *wanted* to be lovers, and if they had had the honest courage of their own passion, there would have been no sin, even had the desire been only momentary.

But if there had been no sin, they would have lost half the fun, or more, of the game.

It was this very doing of the thing that *they themselves* believed to be wrong, that constituted the chief charm of the act. Man invents sin, in order to enjoy the feeling of being naughty. Also, in order to shift the responsibility for his own acts. A Divine Father tells him what to do. And man is naughty and doesn't obey. And then shiveringly, ignoble man lets down his pants for a flogging.

If the Divine Father doesn't bring on the flogging, in this life, then Sinful Man shiveringly awaits his whipping in the afterlife.

Bah, the Divine Father, like so many other Crowned Heads, has abdicated his authority. Man can sin as much as he likes.

There is only one penalty: the loss of his own integrity. Man should *never* do the thing he believes to be wrong. Because if he does, he loses his own singleness, wholeness, natural honor.

If you want to do a thing, you've either got to believe, sincerely, that it's your true nature to do this thing—or else you've got to let it alone.

Believe in your own Holy Ghost. Or else, if you doubt, abstain.

A thing that you sincerely believe in cannot be wrong, because belief does not come at will. It comes only from the

Holy Ghost within. Therefore a thing you truly believe in cannot be wrong.

But there is such a thing as spurious belief. There is such a thing as *evil* belief: a belief that one *cannot do wrong.* There is also such a thing as a half-spurious belief. And this is rottenest of all. The devil lurking behind the cross.

So there you are. Between genuine belief, and spurious belief, and half-genuine belief, you're as likely as not to be in a pickle. And the half-genuine belief is much the dirtiest and most deceptive thing in life.

Hester and Dimmesdale believed in the Divine Father, and almost gloatingly sinned against Him. The Allegory of Sin.

Pearl no longer believes in the Divine Father. She says so. She has no Divine Father. Disowns Papa both big and little.

So she can't sin against him.

What will she do, then, if she's got no god to sin against? Why, of course, she'll not be able to sin at all. She'll go her own way gaily, and do as she likes, and she'll say, afterwards, when she's made a mess: "Yes, I did it. But I acted for the best, and therefore I am blameless. It's the other person's fault. Or else it's Its fault."

She will be blameless, will Pearl, come what may.

And the world is simply a string of Pearls today. And America is a whole rope of these absolutely immaculate Pearls, who can't sin, let them do what they may, because they've no god to sin against. Mere men, one after another. Men with no ghost to their name.

Pearls!

Oh, the irony, the bitter, bitter irony of the name! Oh, Nathaniel, you great man! Oh, America, you Pearl, you Pearl without a blemish!

How *can* Pearl have a blemish, when there's no one but herself to judge Herself? Of course she'll be immaculate, even if, like Cleopatra, she drowns a lover a night in her dirty Nile. The Nilus Flux of her love.

Candida!

By Hawthorne's day it was already Pearl. Before swine,

of course. There never yet was a Pearl that wasn't cast before swine.

It's part of her game, part of her pearldom.

Because when Circe lies with a man, *he's* a swine after it, if he wasn't one before. Not *she*. Circe is the great white impeccable Pearl.

And yet, oh, Pearl, there's a Nemesis even for you.

There's a Doom, Pearl.

Doom! What a beautiful northern word. Doom.

The doom of the Pearl.

Who will write that Allegory?

Here's what the Doom is, anyhow.

When you don't have a Divine Father to sin against; and when you don't sin against the Son; which the Pearls don't, because they all are very strong on LOVE, stronger on LOVE than on anything: then there's nothing left for you to sin against except the Holy Ghost.

Now, Pearl, come, let's drop you in the vinegar.

And it's a ticklish thing sinning against the Holy Ghost. *"It shall not be forgiven him."*

Didn't I tell you there was Doom.

It shall not be forgiven her.

The Father forgives; the Son forgives; but the Holy Ghost does *not* forgive. So take that.

The Holy Ghost doesn't forgive because the Holy Ghost is within you. The Holy Ghost *is* you: your very You. So if, in your conceit of your ego, you make a break in your own YOU, in your own integrity, how can you be forgiven? You might as well make a rip in your own bowels. You *know* if you rip your own bowels they will go rotten and *you* will go rotten. And there's an end of you, in the body.

The same if you make a breach with your own Holy Ghost. You go soul-rotten. Like the Pearls.

These dear Pearls, they do anything they like, and remain pure. Oh, purity!

But they can't stop themselves from going rotten inside. Rotten Pearls, fair outside. Their *souls* smell, because their souls are putrefying inside them.

The sin against the Holy Ghost.

And gradually, from within outwards, they rot. Some form of dementia. A thing disintegrating. A decomposing psyche. Dementia.

Quos vult perdere Deus, dementat prius.

Watch these Pearls, these Pearls of modern women. Particularly American women. Battening on love. And fluttering in the first batlike throes of dementia.

You *can* have your cake and eat it. But my God, it will go rotten inside you.

Hawthorne's other books are nothing compared to *The Scarlet Letter.*

But there are good parables, and wonderful dark glimpses of early Puritan America, in *Twice-Told Tales.*

The House of the Seven Gables has "atmosphere." The passing of the old order of the proud, bearded, black-browed Father: an order which is slowly ousted from life, and lingeringly haunts the old dark places. But comes a new generation to sweep out even the ghosts, with these new vacuum cleaners. No ghost could stand up against a vacuum cleaner.

The new generation is having no ghosts or cobwebs. It is setting up in the photography line, and is just going to make a sound financial thing out of it. For this purpose all old hates and old glooms, that belong to the antique order of Haughty Fathers, all these are swept up in the vacuum cleaner, and the vendetta-born young couple effect a perfect understanding under the black cloth of a camera and prosperity. *Vivat Industria!*

Oh, Nathaniel, you savage ironist! Ugh, how you'd have *hated* it if you'd had nothing but the prosperous, "dear" young couple to write about! If you'd lived to the day when America was nothing but a Main Street.

The Dark Old Fathers.

The Beloved Wishy-Washy Sons.

The Photography Business.

? ? ?

Hawthorne came nearest to actuality in the *Blithedale Romance.* This novel is a sort of picture of the notorious

Brook Farm experiment. There the famous idealists and transcendentalists of America met to till the soil and hew the timber in the sweat of their own brows, thinking high thoughts the while, and breathing an atmosphere of communal love, and tingling in tune with the Oversoul, like so many strings of a super-celestial harp. An old twang of the Crèvecœur instrument.

Of course they fell out like cats and dogs. Couldn't stand one another. And all the music they made was the music of their quarreling.

You *can't* idealize hard work. Which is why America invents so many machines and contrivances of all sort: so that they need do no physical work.

And that's why the idealists left off brookfarming and took to bookfarming.

You *can't* idealize the essential brute blood-activity, the brute blood desires, the basic, sardonic blood-knowledge.

That you *can't* idealize.

And you can't eliminate it.

So there's the end of ideal man.

Man is made up of a dual consciousness, of which the two halves are most of the time in opposition to one another—and will be so as long as time lasts.

You've got to learn to change from one consciousness to the other, turn and about. Not to try to make either absolute, or dominant. The Holy Ghost tells you the how and when.

Never did Nathaniel feel himself more spectral—of course he went brookfarming—than when he was winding the horn in the morning to summon the transcendental laborers to their tasks, or than when marching off with a hoe ideally to hoe the turnips, "Never did I feel more spectral," says Nathaniel.

Never did I feel such a fool, would have been more to the point.

Farcical fools, trying to idealize labor. You'll never succeed in idealizing hard work. Before you can dig mother earth you've got to take off your ideal jacket. The harder a man works, at brute labor, the thinner becomes his idealism, the darker his mind. And the harder a man works at mental labor, at idealism, at transcendental occupations, the thinner becomes his blood, and the more brittle his nerves.

Oh, the brittle-nerved brookfarmers!

You've got to be able to do both: the mental work, and the brute work. But be prepared to step from one pair of shoes into another. Don't try and make it all one pair of shoes.

The attempt to idealize the blood!

Nathaniel knew he was a fool, attempting it.

He went home to his amiable spouse and his sanctum sanctorum of a study.

Nathaniel!

But the *Blithedale Romance*. It has a beautiful, wintry-evening farm-kitchen sort of opening.

Dramatis Personæ

1. *I.*—The narrator: whom we will call Nathaniel. A wisp of a sensitive, withal deep, literary young man no longer so very young.

2. *Zenobia:* a dark, proudly voluptuous clever woman with a tropical flower in her hair. Said to be sketched from Margaret Fuller, in whom Hawthorne saw some "evil nature." Nathaniel was more aware of Zenobia's voluptuousness than of her "mind."

3. *Hollingsworth:* a black-bearded blacksmith with a deep-voiced lust for saving criminals. Wants to build a great Home for these unfortunates.

4. *Priscilla:* a sort of White Lily, a clinging little mediumistic sempstress who has been made use of in public seances. A sort of prostitute soul.

5. *Zenobia's Husband:* an unpleasant decayed person with magnetic powers and teeth full of gold—or set in gold. It is he who has given public spiritualist demonstrations, with Priscilla for the medium. He is of the dark, sensual, decayed-handsome sort, and comes in unexpectedly by the back door.

Plot I.—I, Nathaniel, at once catch cold, and have to be put to bed. Am nursed with inordinate tenderness by the blacksmith, whose great hands are gentler than a woman's, etc.

The two men love one another with a love surpassing

the love of women, so long as the healing-and-salvation business lasts. When Nathaniel wants to get well and have a soul of his own, he turns with hate to this black-bearded, booming salvationist, Hephæstos of the underworld. Hates him for tyrannous monomaniac.

Plot II.—Zenobia, that clever lustrous woman, is fascinated by the criminal-saving blacksmith, and would have him at any price. Meanwhile she has the subtlest current of understanding with the frail but deep Nathaniel. And she takes the White Lily half pityingly, half contemptuously under a rich and glossy dark wing.

Plot III.—The blacksmith is after Zenobia, to get her money for his criminal asylum: of which, of course, he will be the first inmate.

Plot IV.—Nathaniel also feels his mouth watering for the dark-luscious Zenobia.

Plot V.—The White Lily, Priscilla, vaporously festering, turns out to be the famous Veiled Lady of public spiritualist shows: she whom the undesirable Husband, called the Professor, has used as a medium. Also she is Zenobia's half-sister.

Débâcle

Nobody wants Zenobia in the end. She goes off without her flower. The blacksmith marries Priscilla. Nathaniel dribblingly confesses that he, too, has loved Prissy all the while. Boo-hoo!

Conclusion

A few years after, Nathaniel meets the blacksmith in a country lane near a humble cottage, leaning totteringly on the arm of the frail but fervent Priscilla. Gone are all dreams of asylums, and the savior of criminals can't even save himself from his own Veiled Lady.

There you have a nice little bunch of idealists, transcendentalists, brookfarmers, and disintegrated gentry. All going slightly rotten.

Two Pearls: a white Pearl and a black Pearl: the latter more expensive, lurid with money.

The white Pearl, the little medium, Priscilla, the imitation pearl, has truly some "supernormal" powers. She could drain the blacksmith of his blackness and his smith-strength.

Priscilla, the little psychic prostitute. The degenerate descendant of Ligeia. The absolutely yielding, "loving" woman, who abandons herself utterly to her lover. Or even to a gold-toothed "professor" of spiritualism.

Is it all bunkum, this spiritualism? Is it just rot, this Veiled Lady?

Not quite. Apart even from telepathy, the apparatus of human consciousness is the most wonderful message-receiver in existence. Beats a wireless station to nothing.

Put Prissy under the tablecloth then. Miaow!

What happens? Prissy under the tablecloth, like a canary when you cover his cage, goes into a "sleep," a trance.

A trance, not a sleep. A trance means that all her *individual* personal intelligence goes to sleep, like a hen with her head under her wing. But the *apparatus* of consciousness remains working. Without a soul in it.

And what can this apparatus of consciousness do when it works? Why surely something. A wireless apparatus goes tick-tick-tick, taking down messages. So does your human apparatus. All kinds of messages. Only the soul, or the under-consciousness, deals with these messages in the dark, in the under-conscious. Which is the natural course of events.

But what sorts of messages? All sorts. Vibrations from the stars, vibrations from unknown magnetos, vibrations from unknown people, unknown passions. The human apparatus receives them all and they are all dealt with in the under-conscious.

There are also vibrations of thought, many, many. Necessary to get the two human instruments in key.

There may even be vibrations of ghosts in the air. Ghosts being dead *wills,* mind you, not dead souls. The soul has nothing to do with these dodges.

But some unit of force may persist for a time, after the death of an individual—some associations of vibrations may linger like little clouds in the etheric atmosphere after the death of a human being, or an animal. And these little clots of vibration may transfer themselves to the conscious-apparatus of the medium. So that the dead son of a disconsolate widow may send a message to his mourning mother to tell her that he owes Bill Jackson seven dollars: or that Uncle Sam's will is in the back of the bureau: and cheer up, Mother, I'm all right.

There is never much worth in these "messages," because they are never more than fragmentary items of dead, disintegrated consciousness. And the medium has, and always will have, a hopeless job, trying to disentangle the muddle of messages.

Again, coming events *may* cast their shadow before. The oracle may receive on her conscious-apparatus material vibrations to say that the next great war will break out in 1925. And in so far as the realm of cause-and-effect is master of the living soul, in so far as events are mechanically maturing, the forecast may be true.

But the living souls of men may upset the *mechanical* march of events at any moment.

Rien de certain.

Vibrations of subtlest matter. Concatenations of vibrations and shocks! Spiritualism.

And what then? It is all just materialistic, and a good deal is, and always will be, charlatanry.

Because the real human soul, the Holy Ghost, has its own deep prescience, which will not be put into figures, but flows on dark, a stream of prescience.

And the real human soul is too proud, and too sincere in its belief in the Holy Ghost that is within, to stoop to the practices of these spiritualist and other psychic tricks of material vibrations.

Because the first part of reverence is the acceptance of the fact that the Holy Ghost will never materialize: will never be anything but a ghost.

And the second part of reverence is the watchful observance of the motions, the comings and goings within us, of the Holy Ghost, and of the many gods that make up the Holy Ghost.

The Father had his day, and fell.

The Son has had his day, and fell.

It is the day of the Holy Ghost.

But when souls fall corrupt, into disintegration, they have no more day. They have sinned against the Holy Ghost.

These people in *Blithedale Romance* have sinned against the Holy Ghost, and corruption has set in.

All, perhaps, except the I, Nathaniel. He is still a sad, integral consciousness.

But not excepting Zenobia. The Black Pearl is rotting down. Fast. The cleverer she is, the faster she rots.

And they are all disintegrating, so they take to psychic tricks. It is a certain sign of the disintegration of the psyche in a man, and much more so in a woman, when she takes to spiritualism, and table-rapping, and occult messages, or witchcraft and supernatural powers of that sort. When men want to be supernatural, be sure that something has gone wrong in their natural stuff. More so, even, with a woman.

And yet the soul has its own profound subtleties of knowing. And the blood has its strange omniscience.

But this isn't impudent and materialistic, like spiritualism and magic and all that range of pretentious supernaturalism.

IX. Dana's Two Years Before the Mast

You CAN'T IDEALIZE brute labor. That is to say, you can't idealize brute labor, without coming undone, as an idealist.

The soil! The great ideal of the soil. Novels like Thomas Hardy's and pictures like the Frenchman Millet's. The soil.

What happens when you idealize the soil, the mother earth, and really go back to it? Then with overwhelming conviction it is borne in upon you, as it was upon Thomas Hardy, that the whole scheme of things is against you. The whole massive rolling of natural fate is coming down on you like a slow glacier, to crush you to extinction. As an idealist.

Thomas Hardy's pessimism is an absolutely true finding. It is the absolutely true statement of the idealist's last realization, as he wrestles with the bitter soil of beloved mother-earth. He loves her, loves her, loves her. And she just entangles and crushes him like a slow Laocoön snake. The idealist must perish, says mother-earth. Then let him perish.

The great imaginative love of the soil itself! Tolstoy had it, and Thomas Hardy. And both are driven to a kind of fanatic denial of life, as a result.

You can't idealize mother-earth. You can try. You can even succeed. But succeeding, you succumb. She will have no pure idealist sons. None.

If you are a child of mother-earth, you must learn to discard your ideal self, in season, as you discard your clothes at night.

Americans have never loved the soil of America as Europeans have loved the soil of Europe. America has never been a blood-homeland. Only an ideal homeland. The homeland of the idea, of the *spirit*. And of the pocket. Not of the blood.

That has yet to come, when the idea and the spirit have collapsed from their false tyranny.

Europe has been loved with a blood love. That has made it beautiful.

In America, you have Fenimore Cooper's beautiful landscape: but that is wish-fulfillment, done from a distance. And you have Thoreau in Concord. But Thoreau sort of isolated his own bit of locality and put it under a lens, to examine it. He almost anatomized it, with his admiration.

America isn't a blood-homeland. For every American, the blood-homeland is Europe. The spirit-homeland is America.

Transcendentalism. Transcend this homeland business, exalt the idea of These States till you have made it a universal idea, says the true American. The oversoul is a world-soul, not a local thing.

So, in the next great move of imaginative conquest, Americans turned to the sea. Not to the land. Earth is too specific, too particular. Besides, the blood of white men is wine of no American soil. No, no.

But the blood of all men is ocean-born. We have our material universality, our blood-oneness, in the sea. The salt water.

You can't idealize the soil. But you've got to try. And

trying, you reap a great imaginative reward. And the greatest reward is failure. To know you have failed, that you *must* fail. That is the greatest comfort of all, at last.

Tolstoy failed with the soil; Thomas Hardy, too; and Giovanni Verga: the three greatest.

The further extreme, the greatest mother, is the sea. Love the great mother of the sea, the Magna Mater. And see how bitter it is. And see how you must fail to win her to your ideal: forever fail. Absolutely fail.

Swinburne tried in England. But the Americans made the greatest trial. The most vivid failure.

At a certain point, human life becomes uninteresting to men. What then? They turn to some universal.

The greatest material mother of us all is the sea.

Dana's eyes failed him when he was studying at Harvard. And suddenly he turned to the sea, the naked Mother. He went to sea as a common sailor before the mast.

You can't idealize brute labor. Yet you can. You can go through with brute labor, and *know* what it means. You can even meet and match the sea, and KNOW her.

This is what Dana wanted: a naked fighting experience with the sea.

KNOW THYSELF. That means, know the earth that is in your blood. Know the sea that is in your blood. The great elementals.

But we must repeat: KNOWING and BEING are opposite, antagonistic states. The more you know, exactly, the less you *are*. The more you *are*, in being, the less you know.

This is the great cross of man, his dualism. The blood-self, and the nerve-brain self.

Knowing, then, is the slow death of being. Man has his epochs of being, his epochs of knowing. It will always be a great oscillation. The goal is to know how not-to-know.

Dana took another great step in knowing: knowing the mother sea. But it was a step also in his own undoing. It was a new phase of dissolution of his own being. Afterwards, he would be a less human thing. He would be a knower: but more near to mechanism than before. That is our cross, our doom.

And so he writes, in his first days at sea, in winter, on the Atlantic:

> Nothing can compare with the *early breaking of day* upon the wide, sad ocean. There is something in the first gray streaks stretching along the eastern horizon, and throwing an indistinct light upon the face of the deep, which creates a feeling of loneliness, of dread, and of melancholy foreboding, which nothing else in nature can give.

So he ventures wakeful and alone into the great naked watery universe of the end of life, the twilight place where integral being lapses, and warm life begins to give out. It is man moving on into the face of death, the great adventure, the great undoing, the strange extension of the consciousness. The same in his vision of the albatross. "But one of the finest sights that I have ever seen was an albatross asleep upon the water, off Cape Horn, when a heavy sea was running. There being no breeze, the surface of the water was unbroken, but a long, heavy swell was rolling, and we saw the fellow, all white, directly ahead of us, asleep upon the waves, with his head under his wing; now rising upon the top of a huge billow, and then falling slowly until he was lost in the hollow between. He was undisturbed for some time, until the noise of our bows, gradually approaching, roused him; when lifting his head, he stared upon us for a moment, and then spread his wide wings, and took his flight."

We must give Dana credit for a profound mystic vision. The best Americans are mystics by instinct. Simple and bare as his narrative is, it is deep with profound emotion and stark comprehension. He sees the last light-loving incarnation of life exposed upon the eternal waters: a speck, solitary upon the verge of the two naked principles, aerial and watery. And his own soul is as the soul of the albatross.

It is a storm-bird. And so is Dana. He has gone down to fight with the sea. It is a metaphysical, actual struggle of an integral soul with the vast, non-living, yet potent element. Dana never forgets, never ceases to watch. If Hawthorne was a specter on the land, how much more is

Dana a specter at sea. But he must watch, he must know, he must conquer the sea in his consciousness. This is the poignant difference between him and the common sailor. The common sailor lapses from consciousness, becomes elemental like a seal, a creature. Tiny and alone Dana watches the great seas mount round his own small body. If he is swept away, some other man will have to take up what he has begun. For the sea must be mastered by the human consciousness, in the great fight of the human soul for mastery over life and death, in KNOWLEDGE. It is the last bitter necessity of the Tree. The Cross. Impartial, Dana beholds himself among the elements, calm and fatal. His style is great and hopeless, the style of a perfect tragic recorder.

> Between five and six the cry of "All starbowlines ahoy!" summoned our watch on deck, and immediately all hands were called. A great cloud of a dark slate-color was driving on us from the southwest; and we did our best to take in sail before we were in the midst of it. We had got the light sails furled, the courses hauled up, and the topsail reef tackles hauled out, and were just mounting the forerigging when the storm struck us. In an instant the sea, which had been comparatively quiet, was running higher and higher; and it became almost as dark as night. The hail and sleet were harder than I had yet felt them, seeming almost to pin us down to the rigging.

It is in the dispassionate statement of plain material facts that Dana achieves his greatness. Dana writes from the remoter, non-emotional centers of being—not from the passional emotional self.

So the ship battles on, round Cape Horn, then into quieter seas. The island of Juan Fernandez, Crusoe's island, rises like a dream from the sea, like a green cloud, and like a ghost Dana watches it, feeling only a faint, ghostly pang of regret for the life that was.

But the strain of the long sea-voyage begins to tell. The sea is a great disintegrative force. Its tonic quality is its disintegrative quality. It burns down the tissue, liberates energy. And after a long time, this burning-down is destructive. The psyche becomes destroyed, irritable, frayed, almost dehumanized.

So there is trouble on board the ship, irritating discontent, friction unbearable, and at last a flogging. This flogging rouses Dana for the first and last time to human and ideal passion.

> Sam was by this time seized up—that is, placed against the shrouds, with his wrists made fast to the shrouds, his jacket off, and his back exposed. The captain stood on the break of the deck, a few feet from him, and a little raised, so as to have a good swing at him, and held in his hand a light, thick rope. The officers stood round, and the crew grouped together in the waist. All these preparations made me feel sick and faint, angry and excited as I was. A man—a human being made in God's likeness—fastened up and flogged like a beast! The first and almost uncontrollable impulse was resistance. But what could be done?—The time for it had gone by——

So Mr. Dana couldn't act. He could only lean over the side of the ship and spew.

Whatever made him vomit?

Why shall man not be whipped?

As long as man has a bottom, he must surely be whipped. It is as if the Lord intended it so.

Why? For lots of reasons.

Man doth not live by bread alone, to absorb it and to evacuate it.

What is the breath of life? My dear, it is the strange current of interchange that flows between men and men, and men and women, and men and things. A constant current of interflow, a constant vibrating interchange. That is the breath of life.

And this interflow, this electric vibration is polarized. There is a positive and a negative polarity. This is a law of life, of vitalism.

Only ideas are final, finite, static, and single.

All life-interchange is a polarized communication. A circuit.

There are lots of circuits. Male and female, for example, and master and servant. The idea, the IDEA, that fixed gorgon monster, and the IDEAL, that great stationary engine, these two gods-of-the-machine have been busy destroying all *natural* reciprocity and *natural* circuits, for centuries. IDEAS have played the very old Harry with sex relationship, that is, with the great circuit of man and woman. Turned the thing into a wheel on which the human being in both is broken. And the IDEAL has mangled the blood-reciprocity of master and servant into an abstract horror.

Master and servant—or master and man relationship is, essentially, a polarized flow, like love. It is a circuit of vitalism which flows between master and man and forms a very precious nourishment to each, and keeps both in a state of subtle, quivering, vital equilibrium. Deny it as you like, it is so. But once you *abstract* both master and man, and make them both serve an *idea:* production, wage, efficiency, and so on: so that each looks on himself as an instrument performing a certain repeated evolution, then you have changed the vital, quivering circuit of master and man into a mechanical machine unison. Just another way of life: or anti-life.

You could never quite do this on a sailing ship. A master had to be master, or it was hell. That is, there had to be this strange interflow of master-and-man, the strange reciprocity of command and obedience.

The reciprocity of command and obedience is a state of unstable vital equilibrium. Everything vital, or natural, is unstable, thank God.

The ship had been at sea many weeks. A great strain on master and men. An increasing callous indifference in the men, an increasing irritability in the master.

And then what?

A storm.

Don't expect me to say *why* storms must be. They just are. Storms in the air, storms in the water, storms of thunder, storms of anger. Storms just are.

Storms are a sort of violent readjustment in some polarized flow. You have a polarized circuit, a circuit of unstable equilibrium. The instability increases till there is a crash. Everything seems to break down. Thunder roars, lightning flashes. The master roars, the whip whizzes. The sky sends down sweet rain. The ship knows a new strange stillness, a readjustment, a refinding of equilibrium.

Ask the Lord Almighty why it is so. I don't know. I know it is so.

But flogging? Why flogging? Why not use reason or take away jam for tea?

Why not? Why not ask the thunder please to abstain from this physical violence of crashing and thumping, please to swale away like thawing snow.

Sometimes the thunder *does* swale away like thawing snow, and then you hate it. Muggy, sluggish, inert, dreary sky.

Flogging.

You have a Sam, a fat slow fellow, who has got slower and more slovenly as the weeks wear on. You have a master who has grown more irritable in his authority. Till Sam becomes simply wallowing in his slackness, makes your gorge rise. And the master is on red-hot iron.

Now these two men, Captain and Sam, are there in a very unsteady equilibrium of command and obedience. A polarized flow. Definitely polarized.

The poles of will are the great ganglia of the voluntary nerve system, located beside the spinal column, in the back. From the poles of will in the backbone of the Captain, to the ganglia of will in the back of the sloucher Sam, runs a frazzled, jagged current, a staggering circuit of vital electricity. This circuit gets one jolt too many, and there is an explosion.

"Tie up that lousy swine!" roars the enraged Captain.

And whack! Whack! down on the bare back of that sloucher Sam comes the cat.

What does it do? By Jove, it goes like ice-cold water into his spine. Down those lashes runs the current of the Captain's rage, right into the blood and into the toneless ganglia of Sam's voluntary system. Crash! Crash! runs the lightning flame, right into the cores of the living nerves.

And the living nerves respond. They start to vibrate. They brace up. The blood begins to go quicker. The nerves begin to recover their vividness. It is their tonic. The man Sam has a new clear day of intelligence, and a smarty back. The

Captain has a new relief, a new ease in his authority, and a sore heart.

There is a new equilibrium, and a fresh start. The *physical* intelligence of a Sam is restored, the turgidity is relieved from the veins of the Captain.

It is a natural form of human coition, interchange.

It is good for Sam to be flogged. It is good, on this occasion, for the Captain to have Sam flogged. I say so. Because they were both in that physical condition.

Spare the rod and spoil the *physical* child.

Use the rod and spoil the *ideal* child.

There you are.

Dana, as an idealist, refusing the blood-contact of life, leaned over the side of the ship powerless, and vomited: or wanted to. His solar plexus was getting a bit of its own back. To him, Sam was an "ideal" being, who should have been approached through the mind, the reason, and the spirit. That lump of a Sam!

But there was another idealist on board, the seaman John, a Swede. He wasn't named John for nothing, this Jack-tar of the Logos. John felt himself called upon to play Mediator, Interceder, Savior, on this occasion. The popular Paraclete.

"Why are you whipping this man, sir?"

But the Captain had got his dander up. He wasn't going to have his natural passion judged and interfered with by these long-nosed salvationist Johannuses. So he had nosey John hauled up and whipped as well.

For which I am very glad.

Alas, however, the Captain got the worst of it in the end. He smirks longest who smirks last. The Captain wasn't wary enough. Natural anger, natural passion has its unremitting enemy in the idealist. And the ship was already tainted with idealism. A good deal more so, apparently, than Herman Melville's ships were.

Which reminds us that Melville was once going to be flogged. In *White Jacket*. And he, too, would have taken it as the last insult.

In my opinion there are worse insults than floggings. I would rather be flogged than have most people "like" me.

Melville, too, had an Interceder: a quiet, self-respecting man, not a savior. The man spoke in the name of Justice. Melville was to be unjustly whipped. The man spoke honestly and quietly. Not in any salvationist spirit. And the whipping did not take place.

Justice is a great and manly thing. Saviorism is a despicable thing.

Sam was justly whipped. It was a passional justice.

But Melville's whipping would have been a cold, disciplinary injustice. A foul thing. Mechanical *justice* even is a foul thing. For true justice makes the heart's fibers quiver. You can't be cold in a matter of real justice.

Already in those days it was no fun to be a captain. You had to learn already to abstract yourself into a machine-part, exerting machine-control. And it is a good deal bitterer to exert machine-control, selfless, ideal control, than it is to have to obey, mechanically. Because the idealists who mechanically obey almost always hate the *man* who must give the orders. Their idealism rarely allows them to exonerate the man for the office.

Dana's captain was one of the real old-fashioned sort. He gave himself away terribly. He should have been more wary, knowing he confronted a shipful of enemies and at least two cold and deadly idealists, who hated all "masters" on principle.

As he went on, his passion increased, and he danced about on the deck, calling out as he swung the rope, "If you want to know what I flog you for, I'll tell you. It's because I like to do it!—Because I like to do it!—It suits me. That's what I do it for!"

The man writhed under the pain. My blood ran cold, I could look no longer. Disgusted, sick, and horror-stricken, I turned away and leaned over the rail and looked down in the water. A few rapid thoughts of my own situation, and the prospect of future revenge, crossed my mind; but the falling of the blows, and the cries of the man called me back at once. At length they ceased, and, turning round, I found that the Mate, at a signal from the Captain, had cut him down.

After all, it was not so terrible. The Captain evidently did not exceed the ordinary measure. Sam got no more than he asked for. It was a natural event. All would have been well, save for the *moral* verdict. And this came from theoretic idealists like Dana and the seaman John, rather than from the sailors themselves. The sailors understood spontaneous *passional* morality, not the artificial ethical. They respected the violent readjustments of the naked force, in man as in nature.

The flogging was seldom, if ever, alluded to by us in the forecastle. If anyone was inclined to talk about it, the other, with a delicacy which I hardly expected to find among them, always stopped him, or turned the subject.

Two men had been flogged: the second and the elder, John, for interfering and asking the Captain why he flogged Sam. It is while flogging John that the Captain shouts, "If you want to know what I flog you for, I'll tell you——"

But the behavior of the two men who were flogged [Dana continues] toward one another, showed a delicacy and a sense of honor which would have been worthy of admiration in the highest walks of life. Sam knew that the other had suffered solely on his account, and in all his complaints he said that if he alone had been flogged it would have been nothing, but that he could never see that man without thinking that he had been the means of bringing that disgrace upon him; and John never, by word or deed, let anything escape him to remind the other that it was by interfering to save his shipmate that he had suffered.

As a matter of fact, it was John who ought to have been ashamed for bringing confusion and false feeling into a clear issue. Conventional morality apart, John is the reprehensible party, not Sam or the Captain. The case was one of passional readjustment, nothing abnormal. And who was the sententious Johannus, that he should interfere in this? And if Mr. Dana had a weak stomach, as well as weak eyes, let him have it. But let this pair of idealists abstain from making all the other men feel uncomfortable and fuzzy about a thing they would have left to its natural course, if they had been allowed. No, your Johannuses and your Danas have to be creating "public opinion," and mugging up the life-issues with their sententiousness. O idealism!

The vessel arrives at the Pacific coast, and the swell of the rollers falls in our blood—the weary coast stretches wonderful, on the brink of the unknown.

Not a human being but ourselves for miles—the steep hill rising like a wall, and cutting us off from all the world—but the "world of waters." I separated myself from the rest, and sat down on a rock, just where the sea ran in and formed a fine spouting horn. Compared with the dull, plain sand beach of the rest of the coast, this grandeur was as refreshing as a great rock in a weary land. It was almost the first time I had been positively alone. . . . My better nature returned strong upon me. I experienced a glow of pleasure at finding that what of poetry and romance I had ever had in me had not been entirely deadened in the laborious life I had been lately leading. Nearly an hour did I sit, almost lost in the luxury of this entire new scene of the play in which I was acting, when I was aroused by the distant shouts of my companions.

So Dana sits and Hamletizes by the Pacific—chief actor in the play of his own existence. But in him, self-consciousness is almost nearing the mark of scientific indifference to self.

He gives us a pretty picture of the then wild, unknown bay of San Francisco—"The tide leaving us, we came to anchor near the mouth of the bay, under a high and beautifully sloping hill, upon which herds of hundreds of red deer and the stag with his high-branching antlers were bounding about, looking at us for a moment, and then starting off affrighted at the noises we made for the purpose of seeing the variety of their beautiful attitudes and motions——"

Think of it now, and the Presidio! The idiotic guns.

Two moments of strong human emotion Dana experiences: one moment of strong but impotent hate for the captain, one strong impulse of pitying love for the Kanaka boy,

Hope—a beautiful South Sea Islander sick of a white man's disease, phthisis or syphilis. Of him Dana writes:

> But the other, who was my friend, and aikane—Hope—was the most dreadful object I had ever seen in my life; his hands looking like claws; a dreadful cough, which seemed to rack his whole shattered system; a hollow, whispering voice, and an entire inability to move himself. There he lay, upon a mat on the ground, which was the only floor of the oven, with no medicine, no comforts, and no one to care for or help him but a few Kanakas, who were willing enough, but could do nothing. The sight of him made me sick and faint. Poor fellow! During the four months that I lived upon the beach we were continually together, both in work and in our excursions in the woods and upon the water. I really felt a strong affection for him, and preferred him to any of my own countrymen there. When I came into the oven he looked at me, held out his hand, and said in a low voice, but with a delightful smile, "*Aloha,* Aikane! *Aloha nui!*" I comforted him as well as I could, and promised to ask the captain to help him from the medicine chest.

We have felt the pulse of hate for the Captain—now the pulse of Savior-like love for the bright-eyed man of the Pacific, a real child of the ocean, full of the mystery-being of that great sea. Hope is for a moment to Dana what Chingachgook is to Cooper—the hearts-brother, the answerer. But only for an ephemeral moment. And even then his love was largely pity, tinged with philanthropy. The inevitable saviorism. The ideal being.

Dana was mad to leave the California coast, to be back in the civilized East. Yet he feels the poignancy of departure when at last the ship draws off. The Pacific is his glamour world: the Eastern states his world of actuality, scientific, materially real. He is a servant of civilization, an idealist, a democrat, a hater of master, a KNOWER. Conscious and self-conscious, without ever forgetting.

> When all sail had been set and the decks cleared up the *California* was a speck in the horizon, and the coast lay like a low cloud along the northeast. At sunset they were both out of sight, and we were once more upon the ocean, where sky and water meet.

The description of the voyage home is wonderful. It is as if the sea rose up to prevent the escape of this subtle explorer. Dana seems to pass into another world, another life, not of this earth. There is first the sense of apprehension, then the passing right into the black deeps. Then the waters almost swallow him up, with his triumphant consciousness.

The days became shorter and shorter, the sun running lower in its course each day, and giving less and less heat, and the nights so cold as to prevent our sleeping on deck; the Magellan Clouds in sight of a clear night; the skies looking cold and angry; and at times a long, heavy, ugly sea, setting in from the southward, told us what we were coming to.

They were approaching Cape Horn, in the southern winter, passing into the strange, dread regions of the violent waters.

And there lay, floating in the ocean, several miles off, an immense irregular mass, its top and points covered with snow, its center a deep indigo. This was an iceberg, and of the largest size. As far as the eye could reach the sea in every direction was of a deep blue color, the waves running high and fresh, and sparkling in the light; and in the midst lay this immense mountain island, its cavities and valleys thrown into deep shade, and its points and pinnacles glittering in the sun. But no description can give any idea of the strangeness, splendor, and, really, the sublimity of the sight. Its great size—for it must have been two or three miles in circumference, and several hundred feet in height; its slow motion, as its base rose and sunk in the water and its points nodded against the clouds; the lashing of the waves upon it, which, breaking high with foam, lined its base with a white crust; and the thundering sound of the cracking of the mass, and the breaking and the tumbling down of huge pieces; together with its nearness and approach, which added a slight element of fear—all combined to give it the character of true sublimity——

But as the ship ran further and further into trouble, Dana became ill. First it is a slight toothache. Ice and exposure cause the pains to take hold of all his head and face. And then the face so swelled that he could not open his mouth to eat, and was in danger of lockjaw. In this state he was forced to keep his bunk for three or four days.

At the end of the third day, the ice was very thick; a complete fog-bank covered the ship. It blew a tremendous gale from the eastward, with sleet and snow, and there was every promise of a dangerous and fatiguing night. At dark, the captain called the hands aft, and told them that not a man was to leave the deck that night; that the ship was in the greatest danger; any cake of ice might knock a hole in her, or she might run on an island and go to pieces. The lookouts were then set, and every man was put in his station. When I heard what was the state of things, I began to put on my things, to stand it out with the rest of them, when the mate came below, and looking at my face ordered me back to my berth, saying if we went down we should all go down together, but if I went on deck I might lay myself up for life. In obedience to the mate's orders, I went back to my berth; but a more miserable night I never wish to spend.

It is the story of a man pitted in conflict against the sea, the vast, almost omnipotent element. In contest with this cosmic enemy, man finds his further ratification, his further ideal vindication. He comes out victorious, but not till the sea has tortured his living, integral body, and made him pay something for his triumph in consciousness.

The horrific struggle round Cape Horn, homewards, is the crisis of the Dana history. It is an entry into chaos, a heaven of sleet and black ice-rain, a sea of ice and ironlike water. Man fights the element in all its roused, mystic hostility to conscious life. This fight is the inward crisis and triumph of Dana's soul. He goes through it all consciously, enduring, *knowing*. It is not a mere overcoming of obstacles. It is a pitting of the deliberate consciousness against all the roused, hostile, anti-life waters of the Pole.

After this fight, Dana has achieved his success. He knows. He knows what the sea is. He knows what the Cape Horn is. He knows what work is, work before the mast. He knows, he knows a great deal. He has carried his consciousness open-eyed through it all. He has won through. The ideal being.

And from his book we know, too. He has lived this great experience for us; we owe him homage.

The ship passes through the strait, strikes the polar death mystery, and turns northward, home. She seems to fly with new strong plumage, free.

> Every rope yarn seemed stretched to the utmost, and every thread of the canvas; and with this sail added to her the ship sprang through the water like a thing possessed. The sail being nearly all forward, it lifted her out of the water, and she seemed actually to jump from sea to sea.

Beautifully the sailing ship nodalizes the forces of sea and wind, converting them to her purpose. There is no violation, as in a steamship, only a winged centrality. It is this perfect adjusting of ourselves to the elements, the perfect equipoise between them and us, which gives us a great part of our life-joy. The more we intervene machinery between us and the naked forces the more we numb and atrophy our own senses. Every time we turn on a tap to have water, every time we turn a handle to have fire or light, we deny ourselves and annul our being. The great elements, the earth, air, fire, water, are there like some great mistress whom we woo and struggle with, whom we heave and wrestle with. And all our appliances do but deny us these fine embraces, take the miracle of life away from us. The machine is the great neuter. It is the eunuch of eunuchs. In the end it emasculates us all. When we balance the sticks and kindle a fire, we partake of the mysteries. But when we turn on an electric tap there is, as it were, a wad between us and the dynamic universe. We do not know what we lose by all our labor-saving appliances. Of the two evils it would be much the lesser to lose all machinery, every bit, rather than to have, as we have, hopelessly too much.

When we study the pagan gods, we find they have now one meaning, now another. Now they belong to the creative essence, and now to the material-dynamic world. First they have one aspect, then another. The greatest god has both aspects. First he is the source of life. Then he is mystic dynamic lord of the elemental physical forces. So Zeus is Father, and Thunderer.

Nations that worship the material-dynamic world, as all nations do in their decadence, seem to come inevitably to worship the Thunderer. He is Ammon, Zeus, Wotan and Thor, Shango of the West Africans. As the creator of man himself, the Father is greatest in the creative world, the Thunderer is greatest in the material world. He is the god of force and of earthly blessing, the god of the bolt and of sweet rain.

So that electricity seems to be the first, intrinsic principle among the Forces. It has a mystic power of readjustment. It seems to be the overlord of the two naked elements, fire and water, capable of mysteriously enchaining them, and of mysteriously sundering them from their connections. When the two great elements become hopelessly clogged, entangled, the sword of the lightning can separate them. The crash of thunder is really not the clapping together of waves of air. Thunder is the noise of the explosion which takes place when the waters are loosed from the elemental fire, when old vapors are suddenly decomposed in the upper air by the electric force. Then fire flies fluid, and the waters roll off in purity. It is the liberation of the elements from hopeless conjunction. Thunder, the electric force, is the counterpart in the material-dynamic world of the life-force, the creative mystery, itself, in the creative world.

Dana gives a wonderful description of a tropical thunderstorm.

When our watch came on deck at twelve o'clock it was as black as Erebus; not a breath was stirring; the sails hung heavy and motionless from the yards; and the perfect stillness, and the darkness, which was almost palpable, were truly appalling. Not a word was spoken, but everyone stood as though waiting for something to happen. In a few minutes the mate came forward, and in a low tone which was almost a whisper, gave the command to haul down the jib. When we got down we found all hands looking aloft, and then, directly over where we had been standing, upon the main topgallant masthead, was a ball of light, which the sailors name a corposant (*corpus sancti*).

They were all watching it carefully, for sailors have a notion that if the corposant rises in the rigging, it is a sign of fair weather; but if it comes lower down, there will be a storm. Unfortunately, as an omen, it came down and showed itself on the topgallant yard.

In a few minutes it disappeared and showed itself again on the fore topgallant yard, and, after playing about for some time, disappeared again, when the man on the forecastle pointed to it upon the flying-jib-boom-end. But our attention was drawn from watching this by the falling of some drops of rain. In a few minutes low growling thunder was heard, and some random flashes of lightning came from the southwest. Every sail was taken in but the topsail. A few puffs lifted the topsails, but they fell again to the mast, and all was as still as ever. A minute more, and a terrific flash and peal broke simultaneously upon us, and a cloud appeared to open directly over our heads and let down the water in one body like a falling ocean. We stood motionless and almost stupefied, yet nothing had been struck. Peal after peal rattled over our heads with a sound which actually seemed to stop the breath in the body. The violent fall of the rain lasted but a few minutes, and was succeeded by occasional drops and showers; but the lightning continued incessant for several hours, breaking the midnight darkness with irregular and blinding flashes.

During all this time hardly a word was spoken, no bell was struck, and the wheel was silently relieved. The rain fell at intervals in heavy showers, and we stood drenched through, and blinded by the flashes, which broke the Egyptian darkness with a brightness which seemed almost malignant, while the thunder rolled in peals, the concussion of which appeared to shake the very ocean. A ship is not often injured by lightning, for the electricity is separated by the great number of points she presents, and the quality of iron which she has scattered in various parts. The electric fluid ran over our anchors, topsail-sheets and ties; yet no harm was done to us. We went below at four o'clock, leaving things in the same state.

Dana is wonderful at relating these mechanical, or dynamic-physical events. He could not tell about the being of men: only about the forces. He gives another curious instance of the process of recreation, as it takes place within the very corpuscles of the blood. It is *salt* this time which arrests the life-activity, causing a static arrest in Matter, after a certain sundering of water from the fire of the warm-substantial body.

The scurvy had begun to show itself on board. One man had it so badly as to be disabled and off duty; and the English lad, Ben, was in a dreadful state, and was gradually growing worse. His legs swelled and pained him so that he could not walk; his flesh lost its elasticity, so that if it were pressed in, it would not return to its shape; and his gums swelled until he could not open his mouth. His breath, too, became very offensive; he lost all strength and spirit; could eat nothing; grew worse every day; and, in fact, unless something was done for him, would be a dead man in a week at the rate at which he was sinking. The medicines were all gone, or nearly all gone; and if we had had a chestful they would have been of no use; for nothing but fresh provisions and terra firma has any effect upon the scurvy.

However, a boat-load of potatoes and onions was obtained from a passing ship. These the men ate raw.

The freshness and crispness of the raw onion, with the earthy state, give it a great relish to one who has been a long time on salt provisions. We were perfectly ravenous after them. We ate them at every meal, by the dozen; and filled our pockets with them, to eat on the watch on deck. The chief use, however, of the fresh provisions was for the men with the scurvy. One was able to eat, and he soon brought himself to by gnawing upon raw potatoes; but the other, by this time, was hardly able to open his mouth; and the cook took the potatoes raw, pounded them in a mortar, and gave him the juice to suck. The strong earthy taste and smell of this extract of the raw potatoes at first produced a shuddering through his whole frame, and after drinking it, an acute pain, which ran through all parts of his body; but knowing by this that it was taking strong hold, he persevered, drinking a spoonful every hour or so, until, by the effect of this drink, and of his own restored hope, he became so well as to be able to move about, and open his mouth enough to eat the raw potatoes and onions pounded into a soft pulp. This course soon restored his appetite and strength; and ten days after we spoke the *Solon,* so rapid was his recovery that, from lying helpless and almost hopeless in his berth, he was at the masthead, furling a royal.

This is the strange result of the disintegrating effect of the sea, and of salt food. We are all sea-born, science tells us. The moon, and the sea, and salt, and phosphorus, and us: it is a long chain of connection. And then the earth: mother-earth. Dana talks of the relish which the *earthy* taste of the onion gives. The taste of created juice, the living milk of Gea. And limes, which taste of the sun.

How much stranger is the interplay of *life* among the elements than any chemical interplay among the elements themselves. Life—and salt—and phosphorus—and the sea—and the moon. Life—and sulphur—and carbon—and volcanoes—and the sun. The way up, and the way down. The strange ways of life.

But Dana went home, to be a lawyer, and a rather dull and distinguished citizen. He was once almost an ambassador. And pre-eminently respectable.

He had been. He KNEW. He had even told us. It is a great achievement.

And then what?—Why, nothing. The old vulgar humdrum. That's the worst of knowledge. It leaves one only the more lifeless. Dana lived his bit in two years, and knew, and drummed out the rest. Dreary lawyer's years, afterwards.

We know enough. We know too much. We know nothing.

Let us smash something. Ourselves included. But the machine above all.

Dana's small book is a very great book: contains a great extreme of knowledge, knowledge of the great element.

And after all, we have to know all before we can know that knowing is nothing.

Imaginatively, we have to know all: even the elemental waters. And know and know on, until knowledge suddenly shrivels and we know that forever we don't know.

Then there is a sort of peace, and we can start afresh, knowing we don't know.

X. *Herman Melville's* Typee and Omoo

THE GREATEST SEER and poet of the sea for me is Melville. His vision is more real than Swinburne's, because he doesn't personify the sea, and far sounder than Joseph Conrad's, because Melville doesn't sentimentalize the ocean and the sea's unfortunates. Snivel in a wet hanky like Lord Jim.

Melville has the strange, uncanny magic of sea-creatures, and some of their repulsiveness. He isn't quite a land animal. There is something slithery about him. Something always half-seas-over. In his life they said he was mad—or crazy. He was neither mad nor crazy. But he was over the border. He was half a water animal, like those terrible yellow-bearded Vikings who broke out of the waves in beaked ships.

He was a modern Viking. There is something curious about real blue-eyed people. They are never quite human, in the good classic sense, human as brown-eyed people are human: the human of the living humus. About a real blue-eyed person there is usually something abstract, elemental. Brown-eyed people are, as it were, like the earth, which is tissue of bygone life, organic, compound. In blue eyes there is sun and rain and abstract, uncreate element, water, ice, air, space, but not humanity. Brown-eyed people are people of the old, old world: *Allzu menschlich.* Blue-eyed people tend to be too keen and abstract.

Melville is like a Viking going home to the sea, encumbered with age and memories, and a sort of accomplished despair, almost madness. For he cannot accept humanity. He can't belong to humanity. Cannot.

The great Northern cycle of which he is the returning unit has almost completed its round, accomplished itself. Balder the beautiful is mystically dead, and by this time he stinketh. Forget-me-nots and sea-poppies fall into water. The man who came from the sea to live among men can stand it no longer. He hears the horror of the cracked church bell, and goes back down the shore, back into the ocean again, home, into the salt water. Human life won't do. He turns back to the elements. And all the vast sun-and-wheat consciousness of his day he plunges back into the deeps, burying the flame in the deep, self-conscious and deliberate. As blue flax and sea-poppies fall into the waters and give back their created sun-stuff to the dissolution of the flood.

The sea-born people, who can meet and mingle no longer: who turn away from life, to the abstract, to the elements: the sea receives her own.

Let life come asunder, they say. Let water conceive no more with fire. Let mating finish. Let the elements leave off kissing, and turn their backs on one another. Let the merman turn away from his human wife and children, let the seal-woman forget the world of men, remembering only the waters.

So they go down to the sea, the sea-born people. The Vikings are wandering again. Homes are broken up. Cross the seas, cross the seas, urges the heart. Leave love and home. Leave love and home. Love and home are a deadly illusion. Woman, what have I to do with thee? It is finished. *Consummatum est.* The crucifixion into humanity is over. Let us go back to the fierce, uncanny elements: the corrosive vast sea. Or Fire.

Basta! It is enough. It is enough of life. Let us have the vast elements. Let us get out of this loathsome complication of living humanly with humans. Let the sea wash us clean of the leprosy of our humanity and humanness.

Melville was a northerner, sea-born. So the sea claimed him. We are most of us, who use the English language, water-people, sea-derived.

Melville went back to the oldest of all the oceans, to the Pacific. *Der grosse oder stille Ozean.*

Without doubt the Pacific Ocean is æons older than the Atlantic or the Indian Oceans. When we say older, we mean it has not come to any modern consciousness. Strange convulsions have convulsed the Atlantic and Mediterranean peoples into phase after phase of consciousness, while the Pacific and the Pacific peoples have slept. To sleep is to dream: you can't stay unconscious. And, oh, heaven, for how many thousands of years has the true Pacific been dreaming, turning over in its sleep and dreaming again: idyls: nightmares.

The Maoris, the Tongans, the Marquesans, the Fijians, the Polynesians: holy God, how long have they been turning over in the same sleep, with varying dreams? Perhaps, to a sensitive imagination, those islands in the middle of the Pacific are the most unbearable places on earth. It simply stops the heart, to be translated there, unknown ages back, back into that life, that pulse, that rhythm. The scientists say the South Sea Islanders belong to the Stone Age. It seems absurd to class people according to their implements. And yet there is something in it. The heart of the Pacific is still the Stone Age; in spite of steamers. The heart of the Pacific seems like a vast vacuum, in which, mirage-like, continues the life of myriads of ages back. It is a phantom-persistence of human beings who should have died, by our chronology, in the Stone Age. It is a phantom, illusion-like trick of reality: the glamorous South Seas.

Even Japan and China have been turning over in their sleep for countless centuries. Their blood is the old blood, their tissue the old soft tissue. Their busy day was myriads of years ago, when the world was a softer place, more moisture in the air, more warm mud on the face of the earth, and the lotus was always in flower. The great bygone world, before Egypt. And Japan and China have been turning over in their sleep, while we have "advanced." And now they are starting up into nightmare.

The world isn't what it seems.

The Pacific Ocean holds the dream of immemorial centuries. It is the great blue twilight of the vastest of all evenings: perhaps of the most wonderful of all dawns. Who knows?

It must once have been a vast basin of soft, lotus-warm civilization, the Pacific. Never was such a huge man-day swung down into slow disintegration, as here. And now the waters are blue and ghostly with the end of immemorial peoples. And phantomlike the islands rise out of it, illusions of the glamorous Stone Age.

To this phantom Melville returned. Back, back, away from

life. Never man instinctively hated human life, our human life, as we have it, more than Melville did. And never was a man so passionately filled with the sense of vastness and mystery of life which is non-human. He was mad to look over our horizons. Anywhere, anywhere out of *our* world. To get away. To get away, out!

To get away, out of our life. To cross a horizon into another life. No matter what life, so long as it is another life.

Away, away from humanity. To the sea. The naked, salt, elemental sea. To go to sea, to escape humanity.

The human heart gets into a frenzy at last, in its desire to dehumanize itself.

So he finds himself in the middle of the Pacific. Truly over a horizon. In another world. In another epoch. Back, far back, in the days of palm trees and lizards and stone implements. The sunny Stone Age.

Samoa, Tahiti, Raratonga, Nukuheva: the very names are a sleep and a forgetting. The sleep-forgotten past magnificence of human history. "Trailing clouds of glory."

Melville hated the world: was born hating it. But he was looking for heaven. That is, choosingly. Choosingly, he was looking for paradise. Unchoosingly, he was mad with hatred of the world.

Well, the world is hateful. It is as hateful as Melville found it. He was not wrong in hating the world. *Delenda est Chicago.* He hated it to a pitch of madness, and not without reason.

But it's no good *persisting* in looking for paradise "regained."

Melville at his best invariably wrote from a sort of dream-self, so that events which he relates as actual fact have indeed a far deeper reference to his own soul, his own inner life.

So in *Typee* when he tells of his entry into the valley of the dread cannibals of Nukuheva. Down this narrow, steep, horrible dark gorge he slides and struggles as we struggle in a dream, or in the act of birth, to emerge in the green Eden of the Golden Age, the valley of the cannibal savages. This is a bit of birth-myth, or rebirth myth, on Melville's part—

unconscious, no doubt, because his running under-consciousness was always mystical and symbolical. He wasn't aware that he was being mystical.

There he is then, in Typee, among the dreaded cannibal savages. And they are gentle and generous with him, and he is truly in a sort of Eden.

Here at last is Rousseau's Child of Nature and Chateaubriand's Noble Savage called upon and found at home. Yes, Melville loves his savage hosts. He finds them gentle, laughing lambs compared to the ravening wolves of his white brothers, left behind in America and on an American whaleship.

The ugliest beast on earth is the white man, says Melville.

In short, Herman found in Typee the paradise he was looking for. It is true, the Marquesans were "immoral," but he rather liked that. Morality was too white a trick to take him in. Then again, they were cannibals. And it filled him with horror even to think of this. But the savages were very private and even fiercely reserved in their cannibalism, and he might have spared himself his shudder. No doubt he had partaken of the Christian Sacraments many a time. "This is my body, take and eat. This is my blood. Drink it in remembrance of me." And if the savages liked to partake of their sacrament without raising the transubstantiation quibble, and if they liked to say, directly: "This is thy body, which I take from thee and eat. This is thy blood, which I sip in annihilation of thee," why surely their sacred ceremony was as awe-inspiring as the one Jesus substituted. But Herman chose to be horrified. I confess, I am not horrified; though, of course, I am not on the spot. But the savage sacrament seems to me more valid than the Christian: less sidetracking about it. Thirdly, he was shocked by their wild methods of warfare. He died before the great European war, so his shock was comfortable.

Three little quibbles: morality, cannibal sacrament, and stone axes. You must have a fly even in Paradisal ointment. And the first was a ladybird.

But Paradise. He insists on it. Paradise. He could even go stark naked, as before the Apple episode. And his Fayaway, a laughing little Eve, naked with him, and hankering after no apple of knowledge, so long as he would just love her when he felt like it. Plenty to eat, needing no clothes to wear, sunny, happy people, sweet water to swim in: everything a man can want. Then why wasn't he happy along with the savages?

Because he wasn't.

He grizzled in secret, and wanted to escape.

He even pined for Home and Mother, the two things he had run away from as far as ships would carry him. HOME and MOTHER. The two things that were his damnation.

There on the island, where the golden-green great palm-trees chinked in the sun, and the elegant reed houses let the sea breeze through, and people went naked and laughed a great deal, and Fayaway put flowers in his hair for him—great red hibiscus flowers, and frangipani—O God, why wasn't he happy? Why wasn't he?

Because he wasn't.

Well, it's hard to make a man happy.

But I should not have been happy either. One's soul seems under a vacuum, in the South Seas.

The truth of the matter is, one cannot go back. Some men can: renegade. But Melville couldn't go back: and Gauguin couldn't really go back: and I know now that I could never go back. Back towards the past, savage life. One cannot go back. It is one's destiny inside one.

There are these peoples, these "savages." One does not despise them. One does not feel superior. But there is a gulf. There is a gulf in time and being. I cannot commingle my being with theirs.

There they are, these South Sea Islanders, beautiful big men with their golden limbs and their laughing, graceful laziness. And they will call you brother, choose you as a brother. But why cannot one truly be brother?

There is an invisible hand grasps my heart and prevents it opening too much to these strangers. They are beautiful, they are like children, they are generous: but they are more than this. They are far off, and in their eyes is an easy darkness of the soft, uncreate past. In a way, they are uncreate.

Far be it from me to assume any "white" superiority. But they are savages. They are gentle and laughing and physically very handsome. But it seems to me that in living so far, through all our bitter centuries of civilization, we have still been living onwards, forwards. God knows it looks like a *cul de sac* now. But turn to the first Negro, and then listen to your own soul. And your own soul will tell you that however false and foul our forms and systems are now, still, through the many centuries since Egypt, we have been living and struggling forwards along some road that is no road, and yet is a great life-development. We have struggled on, and on we must still go. We may have to smash things. Then let us smash. And our road may have to take a great swerve, that seems a retrogression.

But we can't go back. Whatever else the South Sea Islander is, he is centuries and centuries behind us in the life struggle, the consciousness-struggle, the struggle of the soul into fullness. There is his woman, with her knotted hair and her dark, inchoate, slightly sardonic eyes. I like her, she is nice. But I would never want to touch her. I could not go back on myself so far. Back to their uncreate condition.

She has soft warm flesh, like warm mud. Nearer the reptile, the Saurian age. *Noli me tangere.*

We can't go back. We can't go back to the savages: not a stride. We can be in sympathy with them. We can take a great curve in their direction, onwards. But we cannot turn the current of our life backwards, back towards their soft warm twilight and uncreate mud. Not for a moment. If we do it for a moment, it makes us sick.

We can only do it when we are renegade. The renegade hates life itself. He wants the death of life. So these many "reformers" and "idealists" who glorify the savages in America. They are death-birds, life-haters. Renegades.

We can't go back, and Melville couldn't. Much as he hated the civilized humanity he knew. He couldn't go back to the savages; he wanted to, he tried to, and he couldn't.

Because, in the first place, it made him sick; it made him physically ill. He had something wrong with his leg, and this would not heal. It got worse and worse, during his four months on the island. When he escaped, he was in a deplorable condition—sick and miserable, ill, very ill.

Paradise!

But there you are. Try to go back to the savages, and you feel as if your very soul was decomposing inside you. That is what you feel in the South Seas, anyhow: as if your soul was decomposing inside you. And with any savages the same, if you try to go their way, take their current of sympathy.

Yet, as I say, we must make a great swerve in our onward-going life-course now, to gather up again the savage mysteries. But this does not mean going back on ourselves.

Going back to the savages made Melville sicker than anything. It made him feel as if he were decomposing. Worse even than Home and Mother.

And that is what really happens. If you prostitute your psyche by returning to the savages, you gradually go to pieces. Before you can go back, you *have* to decompose. And a white man decomposing is a ghastly sight. Even Melville in Typee.

We have to go on, on, on, even if we must smash a way ahead.

So Melville escaped, and threw a boathook full in the throat of one of his dearest savage friends, and sank him, because that savage was swimming in pursuit. That's how he felt about the savages when they wanted to detain him. He'd have murdered them one and all, vividly, rather than be kept from escaping. Away from them—he must get away from them—at any price.

And once he has escaped, immediately he begins to sigh and pine for the "Paradise"—Home and Mother being at the other end even of a whaling voyage.

When he really was Home with Mother, he found it Purgatory. But Typee must have been even worse than Purgatory, a soft hell, judging from the murderous frenzy which possessed him to escape.

But once aboard the whaler that carried him off from Nukuheva, he looked back and sighed for the Paradise he had just escaped from in such a fever.

Poor Melville! He was determined Paradise existed. So he was always in Purgatory.

He was born for Purgatory. Some souls are purgatorial by destiny.

The very freedom of his Typee was a torture to him. Its ease was slowly horrible to him. This time *he* was the fly in the odorous tropical ointment.

He needed to fight. It was no good to him, the relaxation of the non-moral tropics. He didn't really want Eden. He wanted to fight. Like every American. To fight. But with weapons of the spirit, not the flesh.

That was the top and bottom of it. His soul was in revolt, writhing forever in revolt. When he had something definite to rebel against—like the bad conditions on a whaling ship—then he was much happier in his miseries. The mills of God were grinding inside him, and they needed something to grind on.

When they could grind on the injustice and folly of missionaries, or of brutal sea-captains, or of governments, he was easier. The mills of God were grinding inside him.

They are grinding inside every American. And they grind exceeding small.

Why? Heaven knows. But we've got to grind down our old forms, our old selves, grind them very very small, to nothingness. Whether a new somethingness will ever start, who knows? Meanwhile the mills of God grind on, in American Melville, and it was himself he ground small: himself and his wife, when he was married. For the present, the South Seas.

He escapes on to the craziest, most impossible of whaling ships. Lucky for us Melville makes it fantastic. It must have been pretty sordid.

And anyhow, on the crazy *Julia,* his leg, that would never heal in the paradise of Typee, began quickly to get well. His life was falling into its normal pulse. The drain back into past centuries was over.

Yet, oh, as he sails away from Nukuheva, on the voyage that will ultimately take him to America, oh, the acute and intolerable nostalgia he feels for the island he has left.

The past, the Golden Age of the past—what a nostalgia we all feel for it. Yet we don't want it when we get it. Try the South Seas.

Melville had to fight, fight against the existing world, against his own very self. Only he would never quite put the knife in the heart of his paradisal ideal. Somehow, somewhere, somewhen, love should be a fulfillment, and life should be a thing of bliss. That was his fixed ideal. Fata Morgana.

That was the pin he tortured himself on, like a pinned-down butterfly.

Love is never a fulfillment. Life is never a thing of continuous bliss. There is no paradise. Fight and laugh and feel bitter and feel bliss: and fight again. Fight, fight. That is life.

Why pin ourselves down on a paradisal ideal? It is only ourselves we torture.

Melville did have one great experience, getting way from humanity: the experience of the sea.

The South Sea Islands were not his great experience. They were a glamorous world outside New England. Outside. But it was the sea that was both outside and inside: the universal experience.

The book that follows on from *Typee* is *Omoo*.

Omoo is a fascinating book; picaresque, rascally, roving. Melville, as a bit of a beachcomber. The crazy ship *Julia* sails to Tahiti, and the mutinous crew are put ashore. Put in the Tahitian prison. It is good reading.

Perhaps Melville is at his best, his happiest, in *Omoo*. For once he is really reckless. For once he takes life as it comes. For once he is the gallant rascally epicurean, eating the world like a snipe, dirt and all baked into one *bonne bouche*.

For once he is really careless, roving with that scamp, Doctor Long Ghost. For once he is careless of his actions, careless of his morals, careless of his ideals: ironic, as the epicurean must be. The deep irony of your real scamp: your real epicurean of the moment.

But it was under the influence of the Long Doctor. This long and bony Scotsman was not a mere ne'er-do-well. He was a man of humorous desperation, throwing his life ironically away. Not a mere loose-kneed loafer, such as the South Seas seem to attract.

That is good about Melville: he never repents. Whatever he did, in Typee or in Doctor Long Ghost's wicked society, he never repented. If he ate his snipe, dirt and all, and enjoyed it at the time, he didn't have bilious bouts afterwards, which is good.

But it wasn't enough. The Long Doctor was really knocking about in a sort of despair. He let his ship drift rudderless.

Melville couldn't do this. For a time, yes. For a time, in this Long Doctor's company, he was rudderless and reckless. Good as an experience. But a man who will not abandon himself to despair or indifference cannot keep it up.

Melville would never abandon himself either to despair or indifference. He always cared. He always cared enough to hate missionaries, and to be touched by a real act of kindness. He always cared.

When he saw a white man really "gone savage," a white man with a blue shark tattooed over his brow, gone over to the savages, then Herman's whole being revolted. He couldn't bear it. He could not bear a renegade.

He enlisted at last on an American man-of-war. You have the record in *White Jacket*. He was back in civilization, but still at sea. He was in America, yet loose in the seas. Good regular days, after Doctor Long Ghost and the *Julia*.

As a matter of fact, a long thin chain was round Melville's ankle all the time, binding him to America, to civilization, to democracy, to the ideal world. It was a long chain, and it never broke. It pulled him back.

By the time he was twenty-five his wild oats were sown; his reckless wanderings were over. At the age of twenty-five he came back to Home and Mother, to fight it out at close quarters. For you can't fight it out by running away. When you have run a long way from Home and Mother, then you realize that the earth is round, and if you keep on running you'll be back on the same old doorstep—like a fatality.

Melville came home to face out the long rest of his life. He married and had an ecstasy of a courtship and fifty years of disillusion.

He had just furnished his home with disillusions. No more Typees. No more paradises. No more Fayaways. A mother: a gorgon. A home: a torture box. A wife: a thing with clay feet. Life: a sort of disgrace. Fame: another disgrace, being patronized by common snobs who just know how to read.

The whole shameful business just making a man writhe.

Melville writhed for eighty years.

In his soul he was proud and savage.

But in his mind and will he wanted the perfect fulfillment of love; he wanted the lovey-doveyness of perfect mutual understanding.

A proud savage-souled man doesn't really want any perfect lovey-dovey fulfillment in love: no such nonsense. A mountain lion doesn't mate with a Persian cat; and when a grizzly bear roars after a mate, it is a she-grizzly he roars after—not after a silky sheep.

But Melville stuck to his ideal. He wrote *Pierre* to show that the more you try to be good the more you make a mess of things: that following righteousness is just disastrous. The better you are, the worse things turn out with you. The better you try to be, the bigger mess you make. Your very striving after righteousness only causes your own slow degeneration.

Well, it is true. No men are so evil today as the idealists, and no women half so evil as your earnest woman, who feels herself a power for good. It is inevitable. After a certain point, the ideal goes dead and rotten. The old pure ideal becomes in itself an impure thing of evil. Charity becomes pernicious, the spirit itself becomes foul. The meek are evil. The pure in heart have base, subtle revulsions: like Dostoevsky's Idiot. The whole Sermon on the Mount becomes a litany of white vice.

What then?

It's our own fault. It was *we* who set up the ideals. And if we are such fools, that we aren't able to kick over our ideals in time, the worse for us.

Look at Melville's eighty long years of writhing. And to the end he writhed on the ideal pin.

From the "perfect woman lover" he passed on to the "perfect friend." He looked and looked for the perfect man friend.

Couldn't find him.

Marriage was a ghastly disillusion to him, because he looked for perfect marriage.

Friendship never even made a real start in him—save perhaps his half-sentimental love for Jack Chase, in *White Jacket.*

Yet to the end he pined for this: a perfect relationship; perfect mating; perfect mutual understanding. A perfect friend.

Right to the end he could never accept the fact that *perfect* relationships cannot be. Each soul is alone, and the aloneness of each soul is a double barrier to perfect relationship between two beings.

Each soul *should* be alone. And in the end the desire for a "perfect relationship" is just a vicious, unmanly craving. *"Tous nos malheurs viennent de ne pouvoir être seuls."*

Melville, however, refused to draw his conclusion. *Life* was wrong, he said. He refused Life. But he stuck to his ideal of perfect relationship, possible perfect love. The world *ought* to be a harmonious loving place. And it *can't* be. So life itself is wrong.

It is silly arguing. Because, after all, only temporary man sets up the "oughts."

The world ought *not* to be a harmonious loving place. It ought to be a place of fierce discord and intermittent harmonies: which it is.

Love ought *not* to be perfect. It ought to have perfect moments, and wildernesses of thorn bushes—which it has.

A "perfect" relationship ought *not* to be possible. Every relationship should have its absolute limits, its absolute reserves, essential to the singleness of the soul in each person. A truly perfect relationship is one in which each party leaves great tracts unknown in the other party.

No two persons can meet at more than a few points, consciously. If two people can just be together fairly often, so that the presence of each is a sort of balance to the other, that is the basis of perfect relationship. There must be true separatenesses as well.

Melville was, at the core, a mystic and an idealist.

Perhaps, so am I.

And he stuck to his ideal guns.

I abandon mine.

He was a mystic who raved because the old ideal guns shot havoc. The guns of the "noble spirit." Of "ideal love."

I say, let the old guns rot.

Get new ones, and shoot straight.

XI. Herman Melville's Moby Dick

Moby Dick, or the White Whale.

A hunt. The last great hunt.

For what?

For Moby Dick, the huge white sperm whale: who is old, hoary, monstrous, and swims alone; who is unspeakably terrible in his wrath, having so often been attacked; and snow-white.

Of course he is a symbol.

Of what?

I doubt if even Melville knew exactly. That's the best of it.

He is warm-blooded, he is lovable. He is lonely Leviathan, not a Hobbes sort. Or is he?

But he is warm-blooded and lovable. The South Sea Islanders, and Polynesians, and Malays, who worship shark, or crocodile, or weave endless frigate-bird distortions, why did they never worship the whale? So big!

Because the whale is not wicked. He doesn't bite. And their gods had to bite.

He's not a dragon. He is Leviathan. He never coils like the Chinese dragon of the sun. He's not a serpent of the waters. He is warm-blooded, a mammal. And hunted, hunted down.

It is a great book.

At first you are put off by the style. It reads like journalism. It seems spurious. You feel Melville is trying to put something over you. It won't do.

And Melville really is a bit sententious: aware of himself, self-conscious, putting something over even himself. But then it's not easy to get into the swing of a piece of deep mysticism when you just set out with a story.

Nobody can be more clownish, more clumsy and sententiously in bad taste, than Herman Melville, even in a great book like *Moby Dick*. He preaches and holds forth because he's not sure of himself. And he holds forth, often, so amateurishly.

The artist was so *much* greater than the man. The man is rather a tiresome New Englander of the ethical mystical-transcendentalist sort: Emerson, Longfellow, Hawthorne, etc. So unrelieved, the solemn ass even in humor. So hopelessly *au grand serieux*, you feel like saying: Good God, what does it matter? If life is a tragedy, or a farce, or a disaster, or anything else, what do I care! Let life be what it likes. Give me a drink, that's what I want just now.

For my part, life is so many things I don't care what it is. It's not my affair to sum it up. Just now it's a cup of tea. This morning it was wormwood and gall. Hand me the sugar.

One wearies of the *grand serieux*. There's something false about it. And that's Melville. Oh dear, when the solemn ass brays! brays! brays!

But he was a deep, great artist, even if he was rather a sententious man. He was a real American in that he always felt his audience in front of him. But when he ceases to be American, when he forgets all audience, and gives us his sheer apprehension of the world, then he is wonderful, his book commands a stillness in the soul, an awe.

In his "human" self, Melville is almost dead. That is, he hardly reacts to human contacts any more; or only ideally: or just for a moment. His human-emotional self is almost played out. He is abstract, self-analytical, and abstracted. And he is more spellbound by the strange slidings and collidings of Matter than bv the things men do. In this he is like Dana. It is the material elements he really has to do with. His drama is with them. He was a futurist long before futurism found paint. The sheer naked slidings of the elements. And the human soul experiencing it all. So often, it is almost over the border: psychiatry. Almost spurious. Yet so great.

It is the same old thing as in all Americans. They keep their old-fashioned ideal frock-coat on, and an old-fashioned silk hat, while they do the most impossible things. There you are: you see Melville hugged in bed by a huge tattooed South Sea Islander, and solemnly offering burnt offering to this savage's little idol, and his ideal frock-coat just hides his shirt-tails and prevents us from seeing his bare posterior as he salaams, while his ethical silk hat sits correctly over his brow the while. That is so typically American: doing the most impossible things without taking off their spiritual get-up. Their ideals are like armor which has rusted in, and will never more come off. And meanwhile in Melville his bodily knowledge moves naked, a living quick among the stark elements. For with sheer physical vibrational sensitiveness, like a marvelous wireless station, he registers the effects of the outer world. And he records also, almost beyond pain or pleasure, the extreme transitions of the isolated, far-driven soul, the soul which is now alone, without any real human contact.

The first days in New Bedford introduce the only human being who really enters into the book, namely, Ishmael, the "I" of the book. And then the moment's hearts-brother, Queequeg, the tattooed, powerful South Sea harpooner, whom Melville loves as Dana loves "Hope." The advent of Ishmael's bedmate is amusing and unforgettable. But later the two swear "marriage," in the language of the savages. For Queequeg has opened again the flood-gates of love and human connection in Ishmael.

As I sat there in that now lonely room, the fire burning low, in that mild stage when, after its first intensity has warmed the air, it then only glows to be looked at; the evening shades and phantoms gathering round the casements, and peering in upon us silent, solitary twain: I began to be sensible of strange feelings. I felt a melting in me. No more my splintered hand and maddened heart was turned against the wolfish world. This soothing savage had redeemed it. There he sat, his very indifference speaking a nature in which there lurked no civilized hypocrisies and bland deceits. Wild he was; a very sight of sights to see; yet I began to feel myself mysteriously drawn towards him.

So they smoked together, and are clasped in each other's arms. The friendship is finally sealed when Ishmael offers sacrifice to Queequeg's little idol, Gogo.

I was a good Christian, born and bred in the bosom of the infallible Presbyterian Church. How then could I unite with the idolater in worshiping his piece of wood? But what is worship?—to do the will of God—*that* is worship. And what is the will of God?—to do to my fellow-man what I would have my fellow-man do to me—*that* is the will of God. [Which sounds like Benjamin Franklin, and is hopelessly bad theology. But it is real American logic.] Now Queequeg is my fellow-man. And what do I wish that this Queequeg would do to me? Why, unite with me in my particular Presbyterian form of worship. Consequently, I must unite with him; ergo, I must turn idolater. So I kindled the shavings; helped prop up the innocent little idol; offered him burnt biscuit with Queequeg; salaamed before him twice or thrice; kissed his nose; and that done, we undressed and went to bed, at peace with our own consciences and all the world. But we did not go to sleep without some little chat. How it is I know not; but there is no place like bed for confidential disclosures between friends. Man and wife, they say, open the very bottom of their souls to each other; and some old couples often lie and chat over old times till nearly morning. Thus, then, lay I and Queequeg—a cozy, loving pair——

You would think this relation with Queequeg meant something to Ishmael. But no. Queequeg is forgotten like yesterday's newspaper. Human things are only momentary excitements or amusements to the American Ishmael. Ishmael, the hunted. But much more Ishmael, the hunter. What's a Queequeg? What's a wife? The white whale must be hunted down. Queequeg must be just "KNOWN," then dropped into oblivion.

And what in the name of fortune is the white whale?

Elsewhere Ishmael says he loved Queequeg's eyes: "large, deep eyes, fiery black and bold." No doubt, like Poe, he wanted to get the "clue" to them. That was all.

The two men go over from New Bedford to Nantucket, and there sign on to the Quaker whaling ship, the *Pequod.* It is all strangely fantastic, phantasmagoric. The voyage of the soul. Yet curiously a real whaling voyage, too. We pass on into the midst of the sea with this strange ship and its incredible crew. The Argonauts were mild lambs in comparison. And Ulysses went *defeating* the Circes and overcoming the wicked hussies of the isles. But the *Pequod's* crew is a collection of maniacs fanatically hunting down a lonely, harmless white whale.

As a soul history, it makes one angry. As a sea yarn, it is marvelous: there is always something a bit over the mark in sea yarns. Should be. Then again the masking up of actual seaman's experience with sonorous mysticism sometimes gets on one's nerves. And again, as a revelation of destiny the book is too deep even for sorrow. Profound beyond feeling.

You are some time before you are allowed to see the captain, Ahab: the mysterious Quaker. Oh, it is a God-fearing Quaker ship.

Ahab, the captain. The captain of the soul.

> I am the master of my fate,
> I am the captain of my soul!

Ahab!

"Oh, captain, my captain, our fearful trip is done."

The gaunt Ahab, Quaker, mysterious person, only shows himself after some days at sea. There's a secret about him! What?

Oh, he's a portentous person. He stumps about on an ivory stump, made from sea-ivory. Moby Dick, the great white whale, tore off Ahab's leg at the knee, when Ahab was attacking him.

Quite right, too. Should have torn off both his legs, and a bit more besides.

But Ahab doesn't think so. Ahab is now a monomaniac.

Moby Dick is his monomania. Moby Dick must DIE, or Ahab can't live any longer. Ahab is atheist by this.

All right.

This *Pequod,* ship of the American soul, has three mates.

1. Starbuck: Quaker, Nantucketer, a good responsible man of reason, forethought, intrepidity, what is called a dependable man. At the bottom, *afraid.*

2. Stubb: "Fearless as fire, and as mechanical." Insists on being reckless and jolly on every occasion. Must be afraid, too, really.

3. Flask: Stubborn, obstinate, without imagination. To him "the wondrous whale was but a species of magnified mouse or water-rat——"

There you have them: a maniac captain and his three mates, three splendid seamen, admirable whalemen, first-class men at their job.

America!

It is rather like Mr. Wilson and his admirable, "efficient" crew at the Peace Conference. Except that none of the Pequodders took their wives along.

A maniac captain of the soul, and three eminently practical mates.

America!

Then such a crew. Renegades, castaways, cannibals: Ishmael, Quakers.

America!

Three giant harpooners, to spear the great white whale.

1. Queequeg, the South Sea Islander, all tattooed, big and powerful.

2. Tashtego, the Red Indian of the sea-coast, where the Indian meets the sea.

3. Daggoo, the huge black Negro.

There you have them, three savage races, under the American flag, the maniac captain, with their great keen harpoons, ready to spear the white whale.

And only after many days at sea does Ahab's own boat-crew appear on deck. Strange, silent, secret, black-garbed Malays, fire-worshiping Parsees. These are to man Ahab's boat, when it leaps in pursuit of that whale.

What do you think of the ship *Pequod,* the ship of the soul of an American?

Many races, many peoples, many nations, under the Stars and Stripes. Beaten with many stripes.

Seeing stars sometimes.

And in a mad ship, under a mad captain, in a mad, fanatic's hunt.

For what?

For Moby Dick, the great white whale.

But splendidly handled. Three splendid mates. The whole thing practical, eminently practical in its working. American industry!

And all this practicality in the service of a mad, mad chase.

Melville manages to keep it a real whaling ship, on a real cruise, in spite of all fantastics. A wonderful, wonderful voyage. And a beauty that is so surpassing only because of the author's awful flounderings in mystical waters. He wanted to get metaphysically deep. And he got deeper than metaphysics. It is a surpassingly beautiful book, with an awful meaning, and bad jolts.

It is interesting to compare Melville with Dana, about the albatross—Melville a bit sententious.

I remember the first albatross I ever saw. It was during a prolonged gale in waters hard upon the Antarctic seas. From my forenoon watch below I ascended to the overcrowded deck, and there, lashed upon the main hatches, I saw a regal feathered thing of unspotted whiteness, and with a hooked Roman bill sublime. At intervals it arched forth its vast, archangel wings—wondrous throbbings and flutterings shook it. Though bodily unharmed, it uttered cries, as some King's ghost in supernatural distress. Through its inexpressible strange eyes methought I peeped to secrets not below the heavens—the white thing was so white, its wings so wide, and in those forever exiled waters I had lost the miserable warping memories of traditions and of towns. I assert, then, that in the wondrous bodily whiteness of the bird chiefly lurks the secret of the spell——

Melville's albatross is a prisoner, caught by a bait on a hook.

Well, I have seen an albatross, too: following us in waters hard upon the Antarctic, too, south of Australia. And in the Southern winter. And the ship, a P. and O. boat, nearly empty. And the lascar crew shivering.

The bird with its long, long wings following, then leaving us. No one knows till they have tried, how lost, how lonely those Southern waters are. And glimpses of the Australian coast.

It makes one feel that our day is only a day. That in the dark of the night ahead other days stir fecund, when we have lapsed from existence.

Who knows how utterly we shall lapse.

But Melville keeps up his disquisition about "whiteness." The great abstract fascinated him. The abstract where we end, and cease to be. White or black. Our white, abstract end!

Then again it is lovely to be at sea on the *Pequod,* with never a grain of earth to us.

It was a cloudy, sultry afternoon; the seamen were lazily lounging about the decks, or vacantly gazing over into the lead-coloured waters. Queequeg and I were mildly employed weaving what is called a sword-mat, for an additional lashing to our boat. So still and subdued, and yet somehow preluding was all the scene, and such an incantation of reverie lurked in the air that each silent sailor seemed resolved into his own invisible self——

In the midst of this preluding silence came the first cry:

There she blows! there! there! there! She blows!

And then comes the first chase, a marvelous piece of true sea-writing, the sea, and sheer sea-beings on the chase, sea-creatures chased. There is scarcely a taint of earth—pure sea-motion.

"Give way, men," whispered Starbuck, drawing still further aft the sheet of his sail; "there is time to kill fish yet before the squall comes. There's white water again!—Close to!—Spring!" Soon after, two cries in quick succession on each side of us denoted that the other boats had got fast; but hardly were they overheard, when with a lightninglike hurtling whisper Starbuck said: "Stand up!" and Queequeg, harpoon in hand, sprang to his feet.—Though not one of the oarsmen was then facing the life and death peril so close to them ahead, yet their eyes on the intense countenance of the mate in the stern of the boat, they knew that the imminent instant had come; they heard, too, an enormous wallowing sound, as of fifty elephants stirring in their litter. Meanwhile the boat was still booming through the mist, the waves curbing and hissing around us like the erected crests of enraged serpents.

"That's his hump. *There! There,* give it to him!" whispered Starbuck.—A short rushing sound leapt out of the boat; it was the darted iron of Queequeg. Then all in one welded motion came a push from astern, while forward the boat seemed striking on a ledge; the sail collapsed and exploded; a gush of scalding vapor shot up near by; something rolled and tumbled like an earthquake beneath us. The whole crew were half suffocated as they were tossed helter-skelter into the white curling cream of the squall. Squall, whale, and harpoon had all blended together; and the whale, merely grazed by the iron, escaped——

Melville is a master of violent, chaotic physical motion; he can keep up a whole wild chase without a flaw. He is as perfect at creating stillness. The ship is cruising on the Carrol Ground, south of St. Helena:

It was while gliding through these latter waters that one serene and moonlight night, when all the waves rolled by like scrolls of silver; and by their soft, suffusing seethings, made what seemed a silvery silence, not a solitude; on such a silent night a silvery jet was seen far in advance of the white bubbles at the bow——

Then there is the description of Brit:

Steering northeastward from the Crozello we fell in with vast meadows of brit, the minute, yellow substance upon which the right whale largely feeds. For leagues and leagues it undulated round us, so that we seemed to be sailing through boundless fields of ripe and golden wheat. On the second day, numbers of right whales were seen, secure from the attack of a sperm whaler like the *Pequod.* With open jaws they sluggishly swam through the brit, which, adhering to the fringed fibers of that wondrous Venetian blind in their mouths, was in that manner separated from the water that escaped at the lip. As moving mowers who, side by side, slowly and seethingly advance their scythes through the long wet grass of the marshy meads; even so these monsters swam, making a strange, grassy, cutting sound; and leaving behind them endless swaths of blue on the yellow sea. But it was only the sound they made as they parted the brit which at all reminded one of mowers. Seen from the mastheads, especially when they paused and were stationary for a while, their vast black forms looked more like masses of rock than anything else——

This beautiful passage brings us to the apparition of the squid:

Slowly wading through the meadows of brit, the *Pequod* still held her way northeastward towards the island of Java; a gentle air impelling her keel, so that in the surrounding serenity her three tall, tapering masts mildly waved to that languid breeze, as three mild palms on a plain. And still, at wide intervals, in the silvery night, that lonely, alluring jet would be seen.

But one transparent-blue morning, when a stillness almost preternatural spread over the sea, however unattended with any stagnant calm; when the long burnished sunglade on the waters seemed a golden finger laid across them, enjoining secrecy; when all the slippered waves whispered together as they softly ran on; in this profound hush of the visible sphere a strange specter was seen by Daggoo from the mainmast head.

In the distance, a great white mass lazily rose, and rising higher and higher, and disentangling itself from the azure, at last gleamed before our prow like a snow-slide, new slid from the hills. Thus glistening for a moment, as slowly it subsided, and sank. Then once more arose, and silently gleamed. It seemed not a whale; and yet, is this Moby Dick? thought Daggoo——

The boats were lowered and pulled to the scene.

In the same spot where it sank, once more it slowly rose. Almost forgetting for the moment all thoughts of Moby Dick, we now gazed at the most wondrous phenomenon which the secret seas have hitherto revealed to mankind. A vast pulpy mass, furlongs in length and breadth, of a glancing cream color, lay floating on the water, innumerable long arms radiating from its center, and curling and twisting like a nest of anacondas, as if blindly to clutch at any hapless object within reach. No perceptible face or front did it have; no conceivable token of either sensation or instinct; but undulated there on the billows, an unearthly, formless, chance-like apparition of life. And with a low sucking it slowly disappeared again.

The following chapters, with their account of whale hunts, the killing, the stripping, the cutting up, are magnificent records of actual happening. Then comes the queer tale of the meeting of the *Jeroboam,* a whaler met at sea, all of whose men were under the domination of a religious maniac, one of the ship's hands. There are detailed descriptions of the actual taking of the sperm oil from a whale's head. Dilating on the smallness of the brain of a sperm whale, Melville significantly remarks—

for I believe that much of a man's character will be found betokened in his backbone. I would rather feel your spine than your skull, whoever you are——

And of the whale, he adds:

For, viewed in this light, the wonderful comparative smallness of his brain proper is more than compensated by the wonderful comparative magnitude of his spinal cord.

In among the rush of terrible, awful hunts, come touches of pure beauty.

As the three boats lay there on that gently rolling sea, gazing down into its eternal blue noon; and as not a single groan or cry of any sort, nay not so much as a ripple or a thought, came up from its depths; what landsman would have thought that beneath all that silence and placidity the utmost monster of the seas was writhing and wrenching in agony!

Perhaps the most stupendous chapter is the one called *The Grand Armada,* at the beginning of Volume III. The *Pequod* was drawing through the Sunda Straits towards Java when she came upon a vast host of sperm whales.

Broad on both bows, at a distance of two or three miles, and forming a great semicircle embracing one half of the level horizon, a continuous chain of whale jets were up-playing and sparkling in the noonday air.

Chasing this great herd, past the Straits of Sunda, themselves chased by Javan pirates, the whalers race on. Then the boats are lowered. At last that curious state of inert irresolution came over the whalers, when they were, as the seamen say, gallied. Instead of forging ahead in huge martial array they swam violently hither and thither, a surging sea of whales, no longer moving on. Starbuck's boat, made fast to a whale, is towed in amongst this howling Leviathan chaos. In mad career it cockles through the boiling surge of monsters, till it is brought into a clear lagoon in the very center of the vast, mad, terrified herd. There a sleek, pure calm reigns. There the females swam in peace, and the young whales came snuffing tamely at the boat, like dogs. And there the astonished seamen watched the love-making of these amazing monsters, mammals, now in rut far down in the sea—

But far beneath this wondrous world upon the surface, another and still stranger world met our eyes, as we gazed over the side. For, suspended in these watery vaults, floated the forms of the nursing mothers of the whales, and those that by their enormous girth seemed shortly to become mothers. The lake, as I have hinted, was to a considerable depth exceedingly transparent; and as human infants while sucking will calmly and fixedly gaze away from the breast, as if leading two different lives at a time; and while yet drawing moral nourishment, be still spiritually feasting upon some unearthly reminiscence, even so did the young of these whales seem looking up towards us, but not at us, as if we were but a bit of gulf weed in their new-born sight. Floating on their sides, the mothers also seemed quietly eying us.—Some of the subtlest secrets of the seas seemed divulged to us in this enchanted pond. We saw young Leviathan amours in the deep. And thus, though surrounded by circle upon circle of consternation and affrights, did these inscrutable creatures at the center freely and fearlessly indulge in all peaceful concernments; yea, serenely reveled in dalliance and delight——

There is something really overwhelming in these whale-hunts, almost superhuman or inhuman, bigger than life, more terrific than human activity. The same with the chapter on ambergris: it is so curious, so real, yet so unearthly. And again in the chapter called *The Cassock*—surely the oldest piece of phallicism in all the world's literature.

After this comes the amazing account of the Try-works, when the ship is turned into the sooty, oily factory in mid-ocean, and the oil is extracted from the blubber. In the light of the red furnace burning on deck, at sea, Melville has his startling experience of reversion. He is at the helm, but has turned to watch the fire: when suddenly he feels the ship rushing backward from him, in mystic reversion—

> Uppermost was the impression, that whatever swift, rushing thing I stood on was not so much bound to any haven ahead, as rushing from all havens astern. A stark bewildering feeling, as of death, came over me. Convulsively my hands grasped the tiller, but with the crazy conceit that the tiller was, somehow, in some enchanted way, inverted. My God! What is the matter with me, I thought!

This dream-experience is a real soul-experience. He ends with an injunction to all men, not to gaze on the red fire when its redness makes all things look ghastly. It seems to him that his gazing on fire has evoked this horror of reversion, undoing.

Perhaps it had. He was water-born.

After some unhealthy work on the ship, Queequeg caught a fever and was like to die.

> How he wasted and wasted in those few, long-lingering days, till there seemed but little left of him but his frame and tattooing. But as all else in him thinned, and his cheek-bones grew sharper, his eyes, nevertheless, seemed growing fuller and fuller; they took on a strangeness of luster; and mildly but deeply looked out at you there from his sickness, a wondrous testimony to that immortal health in him which could not die, or be weakened. And like circles on the water, which as they grow fainter, expand; so his eyes seemed rounding and rounding, like the circles of Eternity. An awe that cannot be named

would steal over you as you sat by the side of this waning savage——

But Queequeg did not die—and the *Pequod* emerges from the Eastern Straits, into the full Pacific.

To my meditative Magian rover, this serene Pacific once beheld, must ever after be the sea of his adoption. It rolls the utmost waters of the world——

In this Pacific the fights go on:

It was far down the afternoon, and when all the spearings of the crimson fight were done, and floating in the lovely sunset sea and sky, sun and whale both died stilly together; then such a sweetness and such a plaintiveness, such inwreathing orisons curled up in that rosy air, that it almost seemed as if far over from the deep green convent valleys of the Manila isles, the Spanish land breeze had gone to sea, freighted with these vesper hymns. Soothed again, but only soothed to deeper gloom, Ahab, who has steered off from the whale, sat intently watching his final wanings from the now tranquil boat. For that strange spectacle, observable in all sperm whales dying—the turning of the head sunwards, and so expiring—that strange spectacle, beheld of such a placid evening, somehow to Ahab conveyed wondrousness unknown before. "He turns and turns him to it; how slowly, but how steadfastly, his home-rendering and invoking brow, with his last dying motions. He, too, worships fire . . ."

So Ahab soliloquizes: and so the warm-blooded whale turns for the last time to the sun, which begot him in the waters.

But as we see in the next chapter, it is the Thunder-fire which Ahab really worships: that living, sundering fire of which he bears the brand, from head to foot; it is storm, the electric storm of the *Pequod,* when the corposants burn in high, tapering flames of supernatural pallor upon the masthead, and when the compass is reversed. After this all is fatality. Life itself seems mystically reversed. In these hunters of Moby Dick there is nothing but madness and possession. The captain, Ahab, moves hand in hand with the poor imbecile Negro boy, Pip, who has been so cruelly demented, left swimming alone in the vast sea. It is the imbecile child of the sun hand in hand with the northern monomaniac, captain and master.

The voyage surges on. They meet one ship, then another. It is all ordinary day-routine, and yet all is a tension of pure madness and horror, the approaching horror of the last fight.

> Hither and thither, on high, glided the snow-white wings of small unspecked birds; these were the gentle thoughts of the feminine air; but to and fro in the deeps, far down in the bottomless blue, rushed mighty leviathans, sword-fish and sharks; and these were the strong, troubled, murderous thinkings of the masculine sea——

On this day Ahab confesses his weariness, the weariness of his burden.

> "But do I look very old, so very, very old, Starbuck? I feel deadly faint, and bowed, and humped, as though I were Adam staggering beneath the piled centuries since Paradise——"

It is the Gethsemane of Ahab, before the last fight: the Gethsemane of the human soul seeking the last self-conquest, the last attainment of extended consciousness—infinite consciousness.

At last they sight the whale. Ahab sees him from his hoisted perch at the masthead:

> From this height the whale was now seen some mile or so ahead, at every roll of the sea revealing his high, sparkling hump, and regularly jetting his silent spout into the air.

The boats are lowered, to draw near the white whale.

> At length the breathless hunter came so nigh his seemingly unsuspectful prey that his entire dazzling hump was distinctly visible, sliding along the sea as if an isolated thing, and continually set in a revolving ring of finest, fleecy, greenish foam. He saw the vast involved wrinkles of the slightly projecting head, beyond. Before it, far out on the soft, Turkish rugged waters, went the glistening white shadow from his broad, milky forehead, a musical rippling playfully accompanying the shade; and behind, the blue waters interchangeably flowed over the

moving valley of his steady wake; and on either side bright bubbles arose and danced by his side. But these were broken again by the light toes of hundreds of gay fowl softly feathering the sea, alternate with their fitful flight; and like to some flag-staff rising from the pointed hull of an argosy, the tall but shattered pole of a recent lance projected from the white whale's back; and at intervals one of the clouds of soft-toed fowls hovering, and to and fro shimmering like a canopy over the fish, silently perched and rocked on this pole, the long tail-feathers streaming like pennons.

A gentle joyousness—a mighty mildness of repose in swiftness, invested the gliding whale——

The fight with the whale is too wonderful, and too awful, to be quoted apart from the book. It lasted three days. The fearful sight, on the third day, of the torn body of the Parsee harpooner, lost on the previous day, now seen lashed on to the flanks of the white whale by the tangle of harpoon lines, has a mystic dream-horror. The awful and infuriated whale turns upon the ship, symbol of this civilized world of ours. He smites her with a fearful shock. And a few minutes later, from the last of the fighting whale-boats comes the cry:

"The ship! Great God, where is the ship?" Soon they, through the dim, bewildering mediums, saw her sidelong fading phantom, as in the gaseous Fata Morgana; only the uppermost masts out of the water; while fixed by infatuation, or fidelity, or fate, to their once lofty perches, the pagan harpooners still maintained their sinking lookouts on the sea. And now concentric circles seized the lone boat itself, and all its crew, and each floating oar, and every lance-pole, and spinning, animate and inanimate, all round and round in one vortex, carried the smallest chip of the *Pequod* out of sight——

The bird of heaven, the eagle, St. John's bird, the Red Indian bird, the American, goes down with the ship, nailed by Tashtego's hammer, the hammer of the American Indian. The eagle of the spirit. Sunk!

Now small fowls flew screaming over the yet yawning gulf; a sullen white surf beat against its steep sides; then all collapsed; and then the great shroud of the sea rolled on as it rolled five thousand years ago.

So ends one of the strangest and most wonderful books in the world, closing up its mystery and its tortured symbolism. It is an epic of the sea such as no man has equaled; and it is a book of exoteric symbolism of profound significance, and of considerable tiresomeness.

But it is a great book, a very great book, the greatest book of the sea ever written. It moves awe in the soul.

The terrible fatality.

Fatality.

Doom.

Doom! Doom! Doom! Something seems to whisper it in the very dark trees of America. Doom!

Doom of what?

Doom of our white day. We are doomed, doomed. And the doom is in America. The doom of our white day.

Ah, well, if my day is doomed, and I am doomed with my day, it is something greater than I which dooms me, so I accept my doom as a sign of the greatness which is more than I am.

Melville knew. He knew his race was doomed. His white soul, doomed. His great white epoch, doomed. Himself, doomed. The idealist, doomed. The spirit, doomed.

The reversion. "Not so much bound to any haven ahead, as rushing from all havens astern."

That great horror of ours! It is our civilization rushing from all havens astern.

The last ghastly hunt. The White Whale.

What then is Moby Dick? He is the deepest blood-being of the white race; he is our deepest blood-nature.

And he is hunted, hunted, hunted by the maniacal fanaticism of our white mental consciousness. We want to hunt him down. To subject him to our will. And in this maniacal conscious hunt of ourselves we get dark races and pale to help us, red, yellow, and black, east and west, Quaker and fire-worshiper, we get them all to help us in this ghastly maniacal hunt which is our doom and our suicide.

The last phallic being of the white man. Hunted into the death of upper consciousness and the ideal will. Our blood-self subjected to our will. Our blood-consciousness sapped by a parasitic mental or ideal consciousness.

Hot-blooded, sea-born Moby Dick. Hunted by monomaniacs of the idea.

Oh God, Oh God, what next, when the *Pequod* has sunk?

She sank in the war, and we are all flotsam.

Now what next?

Who knows? *Quien sabe? Quien sabe, señor?*

Neither Spanish nor Saxon America has any answer.

The *Pequod* went down. And the *Pequod* was the ship of the white American soul. She sank, taking with her Negro and Indian and Polynesian, Asiatic and Quaker and good, businesslike Yankees and Ishmael: she sank all the lot of them.

Boom! as Vachel Lindsay would say.

To use the words of Jesus, IT IS FINISHED.

Consummatum est!

But *Moby Dick* was first published in 1851. If the Great White Whale sank the ship of the Great White Soul in 1851, what's been happening ever since?

Post-mortem effects, presumably.

Because, in the first centuries, Jesus was Cetus, the Whale. And the Christians were the little fishes. Jesus, the Redeemer, was Cetus, Leviathan. And all the Christians all his little fishes.

XII. Whitman

POST-MORTEM effects?

But what of Walt Whitman?

The "good gray poet."

Was he a ghost, with all his physicality?

The good gray poet.

Post-mortem effects. Ghosts.

A certain ghoulish insistency. A certain horrible pottage of human parts. A certain stridency and portentousness. A luridness about his beatitudes.

DEMOCRACY! THESE STATES! EIDOLONS! LOVERS, ENDLESS LOVERS!

One Identity!

One Identity!

I am he that aches with Amorous Love.

Do you believe me, when I say post-mortem effects?

When the *Pequod* went down, she left many a rank and dirty steamboat still fussing in the seas. The *Pequod* sinks with all her souls, but their bodies rise again to man innumerable tramp steamers and ocean-crossing liners. Corpses.

What we mean is that people may go on, keep on, and rush on, without souls. They have their ego and their will; that is enough to keep them going.

So that you see, the sinking of the *Pequod* was only a metaphysical tragedy after all. The world goes on just the same. The ship of the *soul* is sunk. But the machine-manipulating body works just the same: digests, chews gum, admires Botticelli and aches with amorous love.

I am he that aches with Amorous Love.

What do you make of that? I am he that aches. First generalization. First uncomfortable universalization. With amorous love! O God! Better a bellyache. A bellyache is at least specific. But the ache of Amorous Love!

Think of having that under your skin. All that!

I am he that aches with Amorous Love.

Walter, leave off. You are not he. You are just a limited Walter. And your ache doesn't include all Amorous Love, by any means. If you ache you only ache with a small bit of amorous love, and there's so much more stays outside the cover of your ache, that you might be a bit milder about it.

I am he that aches with Amorous Love.

Chuff! chuff! chuff!

Chu-chu-chu-chu-chuff!

Reminds one of a steam-engine. A locomotive. They're the only things that seem to me to ache with amorous love. All that steam inside them. Forty million foot-pounds pressure. The ache of Amorous Love. Steam-pressure. Chuff!

An ordinary man aches with love for Belinda, or his Native Land, or the Ocean, or the Stars, or the Oversoul: if he feels that an ache is in the fashion.

It takes a steam-engine to ache with Amorous Love. All of it.

Walt was really too superhuman. The danger of the superman is that he is mechanical.

They talk of his "splendid animality." Well, he'd got it on the brain, if that's the place for animality.

I am he that aches with amorous love:
Does the earth gravitate, does not all matter, aching, attract all matter?
So the body of me to all I meet or know.

What can be more mechanical? The difference between life and matter is that life, living things, living creatures, have the instinct of turning right away from *some* matter, and of blissfully ignoring the bulk of most matter, and of turning towards only some certain bits of specially selected matter. As for living creatures all helplessly hurtling together into one great snowball, why, most very living creatures spend the greater part of their time getting out of the sight, smell, or sound of the rest of living creatures. Even bees only cluster on their own queen. And that is sickening enough. Fancy all white humanity clustering on one another like a lump of bees.

No, Walt, you give yourself away. Matter *does* gravitate, helplessly. But men are tricky-tricksy, and they shy all sorts of ways.

Matter gravitates because it *is* helpless and mechanical.

And if you gravitate the same, if the body of you gravitates to all you meet or know, why, something must have gone seriously wrong with you. You must have broken your mainspring.

You must have fallen also into mechanization.

Your Moby Dick must be really dead. That lonely phallic monster of the individual you. Dead mentalized.

I only know that my body doesn't by any means gravitate to all I meet or know. I find I can shake hands with a few people. But most I wouldn't touch with a long prop.

Your mainspring is broken, Walt Whitman. The mainspring of your own individuality. And so you run down with a great whirr, merging with everything.

You have killed your isolate Moby Dick. You have mentalized your deep sensual body, and that's the death of it.

I am everything and everything is me and so we're all One in One Identity, like the Mundane Egg, which has been addled quite a while.

> Whoever you are, to endless announcements——
> And of these one and all I weave the song of myself.

Do you? Well then, it just shows you haven't *got* any self. It's a mush, not a woven thing. A hotch-potch, not a tissue. Your self.

Oh, Walter, Walter, what have you done with it? What have you done with yourself? With your own individual self? For it sounds as if it had all leaked out of you, leaked into the universe.

Post-mortem effects. The individuality had leaked out of him.

No, no, don't lay this down to poetry. These are post-mortem effects. And Walt's great poems are really huge fat tomb-plants, great rank graveyard growths.

All that false exuberance. All those lists of things boiled in one pudding-cloth! No, no!

I don't want all those things inside me, thank you.

"I reject nothing," says Walt.

If that is so, one must be a pipe open at both ends, so everything runs through.

Post-mortem effects.

"I embrace ALL," says Whitman. "I weave all things into myself."

Do you really! There can't be much left of *you* when you've done. When you've cooked the awful pudding of One Identity.

"And whoever walks a furlong without sympathy walks to his own funeral dressed in his own shroud."

Take off your hat then, my funeral procession of one is passing.

This awful Whitman. This post-mortem poet. This poet with the private soul leaking out of him all the time. All his privacy leaking out in a sort of dribble, oozing into the universe.

Walt becomes in his own person the whole world, the whole universe, the whole eternity of time, as far as his rather sketchy knowledge of history will carry him, that is. Because to *be* a thing he had to know it. In order to assume the identity of a thing he had to know that thing. He was not able to assume one identity with Charlie Chaplin, for example, because Walt didn't know Charlie. What a pity! He'd have done poems, pæans and what not, Chants, Songs of Cinematernity.

> Oh, Charlie, my Charlie, another film is done——

As soon as Walt *knew* a thing, he assumed a One Identity with it. If he knew that an Eskimo sat in a kyak, immediately there was Walt being little and yellow and greasy, sitting in a kyak.

Now will you tell me exactly what a kyak is?

Who is he that demands petty definition? Let him behold me *sitting in a kyak*.

I behold no such thing. I behold a rather fat old man full of a rather senile, self-conscious sensuosity.

DEMOCRACY. EN MASSE. ONE IDENTITY.

The universe, in short, adds up to ONE.

ONE.

I.

Which is Walt.

His poems, *Democracy, En Masse, One Identity,* they are long sums in addition and multiplication, of which the answer is invariably MYSELF.

He reaches the state of ALLNESS.

And what then? It's all empty. Just an empty Allness. An addled egg.

Walt wasn't an Eskimo. A little, yellow, sly, cunning, greasy little Eskimo. And when Walt blandly assumed Allness, including Eskimoness, unto himself, he was just sucking the wind out of a blown egg-shell, no more. Eskimos are not minor little Walts. They are something that I am not, I know that. Outside the egg of my Allness chuckles the greasy little Eskimo. Outside the egg of Whitman's Allness too.

But Walt wouldn't have it. He was everything and everything was in him. He drove an automobile with a very fierce headlight, along the track of a fixed idea, through the darkness of this world. And he saw everything that way. Just as a motorist does in the night.

I, who happen to be asleep under the bushes in the dark, hoping a snake won't crawl into my neck; I, seeing Walt go by in his great fierce poetic machine, think to myself: What a funny world that fellow sees!

ONE DIRECTION! toots Walt in the car, whizzing along it.

Whereas there are myriads of ways in the dark, not to mention trackless wildernesses, as anyone will know who cares to come off the road—even the Open Road.

ONE DIRECTION! whoops America, and sets off also in an automobile.

ALLNESS! shrieks Walt at a cross-road, going whizz over an unwary Red Indian.

ONE IDENTITY! chants democratic En Masse, pelting behind in motor-cars, oblivious of the corpses under the wheels.

God save me, I feel like creeping down a rabbit hole, to get away from all these automobiles rushing down the ONE IDENTITY track to the goal of ALLNESS.

A woman waits for me——

He might as well have said: "The femaleness waits for my maleness." Oh, beautiful generalization and abstraction! Oh, biological function.

"Athletic mothers of these States——" Muscles and wombs. They needn't have had faces at all.

As I see myself reflected in Nature,
As I see through a mist, One with inexpressible completeness, sanity, beauty,
See the bent head, and arms folded over the breast, the Female I see.

Everything was female to him: even himself. Nature just one great function.

This is the nucleus—after the child is born of woman, man is born of woman,
This is the bath of birth, the merge of small and large, and the outlet again——

"The Female I see——"

If I'd been one of his women, I'd have given him Female, with a flea in his ear.

Always wanting to merge himself into the womb of something or other.

"The Female I see——"

Anything, so long as he could merge himself.

Just a horror. A sort of white flux.

Post-mortem effects.

He found, as all men find, that you can't really merge in a woman, though you may go a long way. You can't manage the last bit. So you have to give it up, and try elsewhere if you *insist* on merging.

In *Calamus* he changes his tune. He doesn't shout and thump and exult any more. He begins to hesitate, reluctant, wistful.

The strange calamus has its pink-tinged root by the pond, and it sends up its leaves of comradeship, comrades from one root, without the intervention of woman, the female.

So he sings of the mystery of manly love, the love of comrades. Over and over he says the same thing: the new world will be built on the love of comrades, the new great dynamic of life will be manly love. Out of this manly love will come the inspiration for the future.

Will it though? Will it?

Comradeship! Comrades! This is to be the new Democracy of Comrades. This is the new cohering principle in the world: Comradeship.

Is it? Are you sure?

It is the cohering principle of true soldiery, we are told in *Drum Taps*. It is the cohering principle in the new unison for creative activity. And it is extreme and alone, touching the confines of death. Something terrible to bear, terrible to be responsible for. Even Walt Whitman felt it. The soul's last and most poignant responsibility, the responsibility of comradeship, of manly love.

Yet you are beautiful to me, you faint-tinged roots, you make
me think of death.
Death is beautiful from you (what indeed is finally beautiful
except death and love?)
I think it is not for life I am chanting here my chant of lovers,
I think it must be for death,
For how calm, how solemn it grows to ascend to the atmosphere
of lovers,
Death or life, I am then indifferent, my soul declines to prefer
(I am not sure but the high soul of lovers welcomes death most)
Indeed, O death, I think now these leaves mean precisely the
same as you mean——

This is strange, from the exultant Walt.

Death!

Death is now his chant! Death!

Merging! And Death! Which is the final merge.

The great merge into the womb. Woman.

And after that, the merge of comrades: man-for-man love.

And almost immediately with this, death, the final merge of death.

There you have the progression of merging. For the great mergers, woman at last becomes inadequate. For those who love to extremes. Woman is inadequate for the last merging. So the next step is the merging of man-for-man love. And this is on the brink of death. It slides over into death.

David and Jonathan. And the death of Jonathan.

It always slides into death.

The love of comrades.

Merging.

So that if the new Democracy is to be based on the love of comrades, it will be based on death too. It will slip so soon into death.

The last merging. The last Democracy. The last love. The love of comrades.

Fatality. And fatality.

Whitman would not have been the great poet he is if he had not taken the last steps and looked over into death. Death, the last merging, that was the goal of his manhood.

To the mergers, there remains the brief love of comrades, and then Death.

Whereto answering, the sea
Delaying not, hurrying not
Whispered me through the night, very plainly before daybreak,
Lisp'd to me the low and delicious word death,
And again death, death, death, death.
Hissing melodions, neither like the bird nor like my arous'd
    child's heart,
But edging near as privately for me rustling at my feet,
Creeping thence steadily up to my ears and laving me softly all
    over,
Death, death, death, death, death——

Whitman is a very great poet, of the end of life. A very great post-mortem poet, of the transitions of the soul as it loses its integrity. The poet of the soul's last shout and shriek, on the confines of death. *Après moi le déluge.*

But we have all got to die, and disintegrate.

We have got to die in life, too, and disintegrate while we live.

But even then the goal is not death.

Something else will come.

Out of the cradle endlessly rocking.

We've got to die first, anyhow. And disintegrate while we still live.

Only we know this much: Death is not the *goal.* And Love, and merging, are now only part of the death-process. Comradeship—part of the death-process. Democracy—part of the death-process. The new Democracy—the brink of death. One Identity—death itself.

We have died, and we are still disintegrating.

But IT IS FINISHED.

Consummatum est.

Whitman, the great poet, has meant so much to me. Whitman, the one man breaking a way ahead. Whitman, the one pioneer. And only Whitman. No English pioneers, no French. No European pioneer-poets. In Europe the would-be pioneers are mere innovators. The same in America. Ahead of Whitman, nothing. Ahead of all poets, pioneering into the wilderness of unopened life, Whitman. Beyond him, none. His wide, strange camp at the end of the great high-road. And lots of new little poets camping on Whitman's camping ground now. But none going really beyond. Because Whitman's camp is at the end of the road, and on the edge of a great precipice. Over the precipice, blue distances, and the blue hollow of the future. But there is no way down. It is a dead end.

Pisgah. Pisgah sights. And Death. Whitman like a strange, modern, American Moses. Fearfully mistaken. And yet the great leader.

The essential function of art is moral. Not aesthetic, not decorative, not pastime and recreation. But moral. The essential function of art is moral.

But a passionate, implicit morality, not didactic. A morality which changes the blood, rather than the mind. Changes the blood first. The mind follows later, in the wake.

Now Whitman was a great moralist. He was a great leader. He was a great changer of the blood in the veins of men.

Surely it is especially true of American art, that it is all essentially moral. Hawthorne, Poe, Longfellow, Emerson, Melville: it is the moral issue which engages them. They all feel uneasy about the old morality. Sensuously, passionally, they all attack the old morality. But they know nothing better, mentally. Therefore they give tight mental allegiance to a morality which all their passion goes to destroy. Hence the duplicity which is the fatal flaw in them: most fatal in the most perfect American work of art, *The Scarlet Letter*. Tight mental allegiance given to a morality which the passional self repudiates.

Whitman was the first to break the mental allegiance. He

was the first to smash the old moral conception that the soul of man is something "superior" and "above" the flesh. Even Emerson still maintained this tiresome "superiority" of the soul. Even Melville could not get over it. Whitman was the first heroic seer to seize the soul by the scruff of her neck and plant her down among the potsherds.

"There!" he said to the soul. "Stay there!"

Stay there. Stay in the flesh. Stay in the limbs and lips and in the belly. Stay in the breast and womb. Stay there, O Soul, where you belong.

Stay in the dark limbs of Negroes. Stay in the body of the prostitute. Stay in the sick flesh of the syphilitic. Stay in the marsh where the calamus grows. Stay there, Soul, where you belong.

The Open Road. The great home of the Soul is the open road. Not heaven, not paradise. Not "above." Not even "within." The soul is neither "above" nor "within." It is a wayfarer down the open road.

Not by meditating. Not by fasting. Not by exploring heaven after heaven, inwardly, in the manner of the great mystics. Not by exaltation. Not by ecstasy. Not by any of these ways does the soul come into her own.

Only by taking the open road.

Not through charity. Not through sacrifice. Not even through love. Not through good works. Not through these does the soul accomplish herself.

Only through the journey down the open road.

The journey itself, down the open road. Exposed to full contact. On two slow feet. Meeting whatever comes down the open road. In company with those that drift in the same measure along the same way. Towards no goal. Always the open road.

Having no known direction even. Only the soul remaining true to herself in her going.

Meeting all the other wayfarers along the road. And how? How meet them, and how pass? With sympathy, says Whitman. Sympathy. He does not say love. He says sympathy. Feeling with. Feel with them as they feel with themselves. Catching the vibration of their soul and flesh as we pass.

It is a new great doctrine. A doctrine of life. A new great morality. A morality of actual living, not of salvation. Europe has never got beyond the morality of salvation. America to this day is deathly sick with saviorism. But Whitman, the greatest and the first and the only American teacher, was no Savior. His morality was no morality of salvation. His was a morality of the soul living her life, not saving herself. Accepting the contact with other souls along the open way, as they lived their lives. Never trying to save them. As leave try to arrest them and throw them in jail. The soul living her life along the incarnate mystery of the open road.

This was Whitman. And the true rhythm of the American continent speaking out in him. He is the first white aboriginal.

"In my Father's house are many mansions."

"No," said Whitman. "Keep out of mansions. A mansion may be heaven on earth, but you might as well be dead. Strictly avoid mansions. The soul is herself when she is going on foot down the open road."

It is the American heroic message. The soul is not to pile up defenses round herself. She is not to withdraw and seek her heavens inwardly, in mystical ecstasies. She is not to cry to some God beyond, for salvation. She is to go down the open road, as the road opens, into the unknown, keeping company with those whose soul draws them near to her, accomplishing nothing save the journey, and the works incident to the journey, in the long life-travel into the unknown, the soul in her subtle sympathies accomplishing herself by the way.

This is Whitman's essential message. The heroic message of the American future. It is the inspiration of thousands of Americans today, the best souls of today, men and women. And it is a message that only in America can be fully understood, finally accepted.

Then Whitman's mistake. The mistake of his interpretation of his watchword: Sympathy. The mystery of SYMPATHY. He still confounded it with Jesus' LOVE, and with Paul's CHARITY. Whitman, like all the rest of us, was at the end of the great emotional highway of Love. And because he couldn't help himself, he carried on his Open Road as a prolongation of the emotional highway of Love, beyond Calvary. The highway of Love ends at the foot of the Cross. There is no beyond. It was a hopeless attempt to prolong the highway of love.

He didn't follow his Sympathy. Try as he might, he kept on automatically interpreting it as Love, as Charity. Merging!

This merging, *en masse,* One Identity, Myself monomania was a carry-over from the old Love idea. It was carrying the idea of Love to its logical physical conclusion. Like Flaubert and the leper. The decree of unqualified Charity, as the soul's one means of salvation, still in force.

Now Whitman wanted his soul to save itself; *he* didn't want to save it. Therefore he did not need the great Christian receipt for saving the soul. He needed to supersede the Christian Charity, the Christian Love, within himself, in order to give his Soul her last freedom. The high-road of Love is no Open Road. It is a narrow, tight way, where the soul walks hemmed in between compulsions.

Whitman wanted to take his Soul down the open road. And he failed in so far as he failed to get out of the old rut of Salvation. He forced his Soul to the edge of a cliff, and he looked down into death. And there he camped, powerless. He had carried out his Sympathy as an extension of Love and Charity. And it had brought him almost to madness and soul-death. It gave him his forced, unhealthy, post-mortem quality.

His message was really the opposite of Henley's rant:

> I am the master of my fate,
> I am the captain of my soul.

Whitman's essential message was the Open Road. The leaving of the soul free unto herself, the leaving of his fate to her and to the loom of the open road. Which is the bravest doctrine man has ever proposed to himself.

Alas, he didn't quite carry it out. He couldn't quite break the old maddening bond of the love-compulsion; he couldn't quite get out of the rut of the charity habit—for Love and Charity have degenerated now into habit: a bad habit.

Whitman said Sympathy. If only he had stuck to it! Because Sympathy means feeling with, not feeling for. He kept on having a passionate feeling *for* the Negro slave, or the prostitute, or the syphilitic—which is merging. A sinking of Walt Whitman's soul in the souls of these others.

He wasn't keeping to his open road. He was forcing his soul down an old rut. He wasn't leaving her free. He was forcing her into other people's circumstances.

Supposing he had felt true sympathy with the Negro slave? He would have felt *with* the Negro slave. Sympathy —compassion—which is partaking of the passion which was in the soul of the Negro slave.

What was the feeling in the Negro's soul?

"Ah, I am a slave! Ah, it is bad to be a slave! I must free myself. My soul will die unless she frees herself. My soul says I must free myself."

Whitman came along, and saw the slave, and said to himself: "That Negro slave is a man like myself. We share the same identity. And he is bleeding with wounds. Oh, oh, is it not myself who am also bleeding with wounds?"

This was not *sympathy*. It was merging and self-sacrifice. "Bear ye one another's burdens": "Love thy neighbor as thyself": "Whatsoever ye do unto him, ye do unto me."

If Whitman had truly *sympathized*, he would have said: "That Negro slave suffers from slavery. He wants to free himself. His soul wants to free him. He has wounds, but they are the price of freedom. The soul has a long journey from slavery to freedom. If I can help him I will: I will not take over his wounds and his slavery to myself. But I will help him fight the power that enslaves him when he wants to be free, if he wants my help, since I see in his face that he needs to be free. But even when he is free, his soul has many journeys down the open road, before it is a free soul."

And of the prostitute Whitman would have said:

"Look at that prostitute! Her nature has turned evil under her mental lust for prostitution. She has lost her soul. She knows it herself. She likes to make men lose their souls.

If she tried to make me lose my soul, I would kill her. I wish she may die."

But of another prostitute he would have said:

"Look! She is fascinated by the Priapic mysteries. Look, she will soon be worn to death by the Priapic usage. It is the way of her soul. She wishes it so."

Of the syphilitic he would say:

"Look! She wants to infect all men with syphilis. We ought to kill her."

And of still another syphilitic:

"Look! She has a horror of her syphilis. If she looks my way I will help her to get cured."

This is sympathy. The soul judging for herself, and preserving her own integrity.

But when, in Flaubert, the man takes the leper to his naked body; when Bubi de Montparnasse takes the girl because he knows she's got syphilis; when Whitman embraces an evil prostitute: that is not sympathy. The evil prostitute has no desire to be embraced with love; so if you sympathize with her, you won't try to embrace her with love. The leper loathes his leprosy, so if you sympathize with him, you'll loathe it too. The evil woman who wishes to infect all men with her syphilis hates you if you haven't got syphilis. If you sympathize, you'll feel her hatred, and you'll hate, too, you'll hate her. Her feeling is hate, and you'll share it. Only your soul will choose the direction of its own hatred.

The soul is a very perfect judge of her own motions, if your mind doesn't dictate to her. Because the mind says Charity! Charity! you don't have to force your soul into kissing lepers or embracing syphilitics. Your lips are the lips of your soul, your body is the body of your soul; your own single, individual soul. That is Whitman's message. And your soul hates syphilis and leprosy. Because it *is* a soul, it hates these things, which are against the soul. And therefore to force the body of your soul into contact with uncleanness is a great violation of your soul. The soul wishes to keep clean and whole. The soul's deepest will is to preserve its own integrity, against the mind and the whole mass of disintegrating forces.

Soul sympathizes with soul. And that which tries to kill my soul, my soul hates. My soul and my body are one. Soul and body wish to keep clean and whole. Only the mind is capable of great perversion. Only the mind tries to drive my soul and body into uncleanness and unwholesomeness.

What my soul loves, I love.

What my soul hates, I hate.

When my soul is stirred with compassion, I am compassionate.

What my soul turns away from, I turn away from.

That is the *true* interpretation of Whitman's creed: the true revelation of his Sympathy.

And my soul takes the open road. She meets the souls that are passing, she goes along with the souls that are going her way. And for one and all, she has sympathy. The sympathy of love, the sympathy of hate, the sympathy of simple proximity; all the subtle sympathizings of the incalculable soul, from the bitterest hate to passionate love.

It is not I who guide my soul to heaven. It is I who am guided by my own soul along the open road, where all men tread. Therefore, I must accept her deep motions of love, or hate, or compassion, or dislike, or indifference. And I must go where she takes me, for my feet and my lips and my body are my soul. It is I who must submit to her.

This is Whitman's message of American democracy.

The true democracy, where soul meets soul, in the open road. Democracy. American democracy where all journey down the open road, and where a soul is known at once in its going. Not by its clothes or appearance. Whitman did away with that. Not by its family name. Not even by its reputation. Whitman and Melville both discounted that. Not by a progression of piety, or by works of Charity. Not by works at all. Not by anything, but just itself. The soul passing unenhanced, passing on foot and being no more than itself. And recognized, and passed by or greeted according to the soul's dictate. If it be a great soul, it will be worshiped in the road.

The love of man and woman: a recognition of souls, and a communion of worship. The love of comrades: a recognition of souls, and a communion of worship. Democracy: a recognition of souls, all down the open road, and a great soul seen in its greatness, as it travels on foot among the rest, down the common way of the living. A glad recognition of souls, and a gladder worship of great and greater souls, because they are the only riches.

Love, and Merging, brought Whitman to the Edge of Death! Death! Death!

But the exultance of his message still remains. Purified of MERGING, purified of MYSELF, the exultant message of American Democracy, of souls in the Open Road, full of glad recognition, full of fierce readiness, full of the joy of worship, when one soul sees a greater soul.

The only riches, the great souls.

LOBO, NEW MEXICO.

AMY LOWELL (1874–1925) was a descendant of John Lowell, a Massachusetts lawyer and judge who was active in the Revolutionary cause in the last half of the eighteenth century. He had a son by each of three wives and founded three lines of Lowells. James Russell Lowell was John Lowell's grandson in one of these branches; and Amy Lowell his great-great-granddaughter in another. Miss Lowell published her first book of verse in 1912, and she became one of the principal promoters of the new poetry movement in America that was getting under way at that time. In 1922, she published *A Critical Fable,* a counterpart to and imitation of J. R. Lowell's *Fable for Critics.*

Miss Lowell falls somewhat below her model. Her versification is even worse than Lowell's, and when she allows herself doggerel digressions, she is even more obscure and far-fetched. But she does show quite vividly the difference between the literary activity of Lowell's time and the poetry boom of her own; and she gives us an interesting glimpse of the way the new poetry looked to a lady in Brookline, Mass., who was herself one of its enthusiastic exponents. Miss Lowell amuses herself by imagining her cousin's horror at learning that Whitman and Poe now outrank the other poets of his era, and that Emily Dickinson is taken seriously; but it is doubtful whether she did much better in distinguishing among her contemporaries the poets that were to emerge from the poets that were to be forgotten. One would say at the present time—at the risk of becoming the butt of some subsequent writer on the subject—that, among the writers mentioned in the *Fable,* Robinson, Eliot, and Miss Millay were the most likely to figure to our grandsons as first-rate poets of the full stature. In a letter of January 1924, Miss Lowell wrote to Sara Teasdale: "The one omission I am sorry for is Elinor Wylie, but at the time I wrote it—three years ago—she was not so prominent as she has since become." E. E. Cummings and Marianne Moore were only just beginning to appear in the *Dial* at the time Miss Lowell wrote.

In any case, she does rather well with her portraits of literary personalities; and there is about the whole performance—it was what Amy Lowell contributed to that literary reawakening—something of Lowell's exhilaration in the exercise of literary talent and perhaps something more than his courage in championing the cause of poetry.

A Critical Fable was published anonymously as *A Fable for Critics* had been, and Miss Lowell played out a long comedy of pretending that it had been written by someone else—first by Louis Untermeyer, then by Leonard Bacon, then by an imaginary poet whom she had invented for the occasion. She followed Lowell in every detail except in rhyming the name and address of the publisher—complaining that for Houghton Mifflin there existed no rhyme except "pifflin'."

When she makes Lowell speak of

escaping the tonic arrears
Of a grief not lived through,

she refers to the death of his first wife. The effect on Lowell's work of this event has been mentioned in the introduction to his essay on Thoreau.

Dear Sir (or Dear Madam) who happen to glance at this

TITLE-PAGE

Printed you'll see to enhance its æsthetic attraction,
Pray buy, if you're able, this excellent bargain:

A CRITICAL FABLE

The book may be read in the light of

A *Sequel* to the "FABLE for CRITICS"

A volume unequaled (or hitherto so) for its quips and digressions on

The Poets of the Day

WITHOUT UNDUE PROFESSIONS, I WOULD SAY THAT THIS TREATISE IS FULLY AS LIGHT AS THE FORMER, ITS JUDGMENTS AS CERTAINLY RIGHT AS NEED BE.

A HODGE-PODGE

Delivered primarily in the hope of instilling instruction so airily that readers may see, in the persons on view, a peripatetic, poetic *Who's Who.*

An Account of the Times

BY

A POKER OF FUN, WITT D., O.S., A.I.

Gentle Reader,

The book you're about to peruse has only one object, which is to amuse. If, as over its pages you may chance to potter, you discover it's rather more pungent and hotter than this simple pretension might lead one to think, recollect, if you please, there's a devil in ink; and a critic who starts without any intention to do more than recount will find his apprehension of the poets running on to minutely-limned pictures of the men as he sees them. Neither praises nor strictures were in my design for I tried to elude them; but a man, plus his writings, must always include them inferentially, even if nothing be stated. As the picture emerges, the sitter stands rated.

But who would be backward when others have done the very same thing in a search of pure fun? Sixty-odd years ago a volume appeared called *A Fable for Critics,* wherein were ensphered eighteen authors of merit. The poet who selected them dared many sly prods just because he respected them. What a serious analysis may fail to discover is often revealed to a funloving lover.

In the volume before you, you will find twenty-one

modern poets popped off 'twixt a laugh and a pun. I have spared them no squib and no palm, what I give is a cursory view of them run through a sieve. As I rattle my poets about faster and faster, each man shakes more certainly into a master; to my thinking, at least, for their rich native flavor gives them all so abundant a claim on my favor that I'm willing to leave them for sixty-odd years and let my great-grandchildren foot the arrears.

With the poets I've not noticed, there's a chance for a sequel, and some other critic who thinks himself equal to the writing may build on my scaffolding gratis; and for readers, I really cannot calculate his—with his hundreds of victims he'll sell each edition as fast as it's printed—I'm no mathematician. Take the Poetry Society's roster of members, brush away all the laymen and leave just the embers which spark into verse now and then; for equations, let A. equal the poet and B. his relations; then his wife and her friends with their "circles" and "clubs"; and the cultural ladies, impervious to snubs, who get out long programs of up-to-date readings which are called "very helpful" in the printed proceedings of some Woman's Club's "most remarkable year" (one wonders sometimes what the poor creatures hear, for of course they don't read now books are so dear), and someone's geometry's needed, it's clear, to post up the total. I'll not volunteer for a task which requires an expert cashier. For the ladies I've mentioned, who take what they're told as immaculate gospel in letters of gold, and rather than buy prefer to be sold, they'll be moved, I believe, to purchase his anthology which, like Poe, he might call *A Hand-Book of Conchology*. Since I've got the pearls, he must e'en take the shells, but the public at large has no knowledge of sells —see them gape at the lies which every quack tells—and, as I said before, on the question of vails, if I collar the kudos, why he'll gorge the sales.

For I really don't think there's one person in ten who can tell the first-class from the second-class men. If I've twenty-one poets and he sixty-four, how many will stop to consider that more of the very same thing means a well-watered article? In my book, you'll perceive, there isn't a particle of stuffing or layers of lath to increase the absolute weight of my poets, piece by piece. Each is wrapped in tinfoil and set round the core of a box that I've softened with excelsior which, as everyone knows, is the lightest of packing and exceedingly cheap; so, if money be lacking, you have only to take a few useless trees, such as laurel, or willow, or bay, and with these make a bundle of shavings as thick as you please. The foil, I admit, is a good deal more trouble. To wrap poets round with tin is like hoisting a bubble with grapples and rope. Do you notice my drift? You can't pull at your bubbles or teach your poets thrift. Having done what you can to arrange them precisely—and, considering their angles, this is hard to do nicely—you should view them a moment to be sure that no jutting or oversized head will prevent the box shutting; then, just at the last, right under the cover, to offset any jars, put a thick wad of clover. A few little holes may be left here and there for the egress of words and the ingress of air, and your poets are quite ready for nailing and mailing. If you're sure of your press, the rest is plain sailing.

Having read me so far, you will ask, I am certain, for just a stray peep round the edge of the curtain I have carefully hung up between us, but this is, Gentle Reader, the one of all my prejudices I would not depart from by even a tittle. Suppose, for a moment, the author's a little just-out-of-the-egg sort of fellow—why then, would you care half a jot what fell from his pen? Supposing, for naturally you must suppose at least something or other, he's (under the rose) a personage proper, whose judgments are wont to sway many opinions, would you dare to confront so seasoned a reasoning with your own reflections?

Where's the fun of a book if you can't take objections to this and to that, call the author a zany, and in doing so prove to yourself what a brainy person you are, with a tribe of convictions which only malicious folk speak of as fictions?

Have I labored my point? You'll enjoy me the more if you hazard a guess between every score or so lines. Why, it's endless; you'll see in a twinkling how exciting a book can be when you've no inkling as to who, or to why, or to whether, or what, the author may be. If it fall to your lot to unmask him, how deeply you'll relish the jest. No, Kind Reader, I cannot fulfill your request.

Think again of my poets, each one will be lying in wait with some sharp, eager weapon. For dying—why, all in good time, but not plunked on the head by a furious poet who's disliked what I said. They're all sure to dislike the particular parts which deal with their own books, own heads, and own hearts. All poets are the same in one singular trait: whatever is said of them, that thing they hate. As I wish to enjoy a life of some quiet, I refuse to be pestered by poets on the riot. Having opened my heart, I must seek to preserve it from every result, even though it deserve it.

Then, like most other writers, I've a scant equanimity and scarcely can hope to retain my sublimity, in spite of all efforts to show magnanimity, if anyone penetrates my anonymity.

One word more, and I'm silent in *propria persona:* If you, who are reading, should chance to be owner of the volume in hand and a poet comes to call, fling it into the fire or over the wall, put it into your work-basket, under your seat; but, whatever you do, don't permit him to see it.

With which parting remark, I close my introduction and leave you the book without farther obstruction, only wishing you joy of my modest production.

A CRITICAL FABLE

There are few things so futile, and few so amusing,
As a peaceful and purposeless sort of perusing
Of old random jottings set down in a blank-book
You've unearthed from a drawer as you looked for your
    bank-book,
Or a knife, or a paper of pins, or some string.
The truth is, of course, you'd forgotten the thing,
And all those most vitally important matters
You'd preserved in its pages, just so many spatters
The wheel of your life kicked up in its going

Now hard as caked clay which nothing can grow in.
You raved over Browning, you discovered Euripides,
You devoured all volumes from which you could snip idees
(No one need be surprised if I use the vernacular
Whenever it fits with my text. It's spectacular.
And what smacks of the soil is always tentacular.)—
Astronomy, botany, paleontology—
At least you acquired their strange phraseology
And sprinkled it over your pages in splendid
Profusion because that was what learned men did.
Having one day observed daffodils in a breeze,
You remarked as a brand-new impression that these
Were beautiful objects; you filled quite two pages
With extracts from all those esteemed personages
Whose sayings are found to their last adumbrations
In any respectable book of quotations.
You heard *Pelléas* and returned in a stutter
Of rainbows, and bomb-shells, and thin bread and butter;
And once every twenty-odd entries or so
You recorded a fact it was worth while to know.
At least that was my blank-book, but one of the "odds"
Gave my memory two or three violent prods.
All it said was, "A gentleman taking a walk
Joined me, and we had a most interesting talk."
We certainly did, that day is as clear
As though the whole circumstance happened this year.
But when it did happen I really can't say,
The note is undated, except it says "May."
Put it, then, when you please, whether last year or next
Doesn't matter a rap, and I shall not be vext
If you think I just dreamt it, it swings in my mind
Without root or grapple, a silvery kind
Of antique recollection, that's all I can say.
The sun shone—I remember the scattering way
It shot over the water. I stood by the river.
The plane-trees were just leaving out, and a shiver
Of sunshine and shadow twitched over the grass.
I was poking at something which glittered like glass
With my stick when he joined me and stopped, and his stick

Helped mine to dig up a long bottle-neck, thick,
Brown, and unctuous with memories of cool yellow wine
From some pre-bellum vineyard on the banks of the Rhine:
Berncastler Doctor, perhaps, or *Rüdesheimer,*
Liebfraumilch—could nomenclature ere be sublimer?
Our dear cousins German are so deftly romantic!
Where else in the world could you meet such an antic
Idea, such a sentiment oily to dripping?
The pot-bellied humbugs deserved a good whipping,
With their hands dropping blood and their noses a-sniffle
At some beautiful thought which burns down to mere piffle.
As I rubbed off the dirt (with my handkerchief mainly)
I may have said this, for he answered profanely,
"But their wine was damned good!" I dispensed from replying,
His remark held a truth I was far from denying.
The gentleman seemed not to notice my silence.
"Could you tell me," said he, "if that place a short mile hence
Is really Mt. Auburn?" I said that it was,
And went on to observe I had never had cause
To enter its precincts. "Why should you?" he said.
"The living have nothing to say to the dead.
The fact is entirely the other way round,
The dead do the speaking, the living are wound
In the coil of their words." Here I greatly demurred.
His expression provoked me to utter absurd
Refutations. "In America," I began, with bombast—
"Tut! Tut!" the old gentleman smiled, "not so fast.
Fold your wings, young spread-eagle, I merely have stated
That the worth of the living is much overrated.
I was young once myself some few decades ago,
And I lived hereabouts, so I really should know.
This parkway, for instance, is simply man's cheating
Himself to believe he is once more repeating
A loveliness ruthlessly uptorn and lost.
Those motor-horns, now, do you really dare boast
That they please you as marsh-larks' and bobolinks' songs would?

That shaven grass shore, is it really so good
As the meadows which used to be here, and these plane-
trees,
Are they half as delightful as those weather-vane trees,
The poplars? I grant you they're quaint, and can please
Like an old gouache picture of some Genevese
Lake-bordering highway; but it is just these
Trans-Atlantic urbanities which crowd out the flavor,
The old native lushness and running-wild savor,
Of mulleins, and choke-cherries in a confusion
So dire that only small boys dared intrusion;
Beyond, where there certainly wasn't a shore,
Just tufted marsh grass for an acre or more
Treading shiftily into the river and drowned
When the high Spring tides turned inconveniently round,
And on the tall grass-sprays, as likely as not,
Red-winged blackbirds, a score of them, all in one spot.
This place had the taste which a boy feels who grapples
With the season's first puckery, bitter-green apples.
Regardless of consequence, he devours and crams on.
Does maturity get the same joy from a damson?
But we, with our marshes, were more certainly urban
Than you with your brummagem, gilded suburban,
Which you wear like a hired theatrical turban.
You move and you act like folk in a play
All carefully drilled to walk the same way.
Just look at this bottle, we were free in my time,
But I think you are free of nothing but rhyme."
Now here was a thing which was not to be stood,
Poking fun at a soul just escaped from the wood
Like a leaf freshly burst from the bark of its twig.
"At least," I said hotly, "we are not a mere sprig
From an overseas' bush, and we don't care a fig
For a dozen dead worthies of classic humdrum,
And each one no bigger than Hop-o'-my-thumb
To our eyes. Why, the curse of their damned rhetoric
Hangs over our writers like a schoolmaster's stick."
Here I caught a few words like "the dead and the quick."
I admit I was stung by his imperturbability

And the hint in his eyes of suppressed risibility.
"We are breaking away..." Here he tossed up the bottle,
Or the poor jagged neck which was left of the hot Hell
Container, as I think Mr. Volstead might say.
How thankful I am I preceded his day
And remember the lovely, suave lines of these flasks.
To piece them together will be one of the tasks
Of thirty-third century museum curators,
Subsidized and applauded by keen legislators.
It flashed in the sun for an instant or two,
And we watched it in silence as men always do
Things that soar, then it turned and fell in chaotic
Uprisings of spray from a sudden aquatic
Suppression beneath the waves of the Charles.
"Yet that, like so much, is but one of the snarls,"
He dusted his fingers. "And if a man flings
His tangles in air, there are so many strings
To a single cat's-cradle of impulse, who knows
When you pull at one end where the other end goes.
We were worthy, respectable, humdrum, quite so,
An admirable portrait of one Edgar Poe."
"Oh, Poe was a bird of a different feather,
We always rank him and Walt Whitman together."
"You do?" The old gentleman tugged at his whisker.
"I could scarcely myself have imagined a brisker
Sarcasm than that to set down in my *Fable*.
I did what I could, but I scarcely was able
To throw leaves of grass to Poe's raven as sops
For his Cerberus master, who would be mad as hops
At a hint of your excellent juxtaposition,
Since that book was not yet in its first slim edition.
You remember I said that Poe was three parts genius.
As to Whitman, can you think of an action more heinous
Than to write the same book every two or three years?
It's enough to reduce any author to tears
At the thought of this crime to the writing fraternity.
A monstrous, continual, delaying paternity.
But I wax somewhat hot, let's have done with the fellows.
Your strange estimation has made me quite jealous

For those of my time whose secure reputations
Gave us no concern. These are trifling vexations,
But they itch my esteem. Is there really not one
You sincerely admire?" "Yes, Miss Dickinson,"
I hastily answered. At this he stopped dead
In his walk and his eyes seemed to pop from his head.
"What," he thundered, "that prim and perverse little person
Without an idea you could hang up a verse on!
Wentworth Higginson did what he could, his tuition
Was ardent, unwearied, but bore no fruition.
You amaze me, young man, where are Longfellow, Lowell,
With Whittier, Bryant, and Holmes? Do you know well
The works of these men? What of Washington Irving,
And Emerson and Hawthorne, are they not deserving
A tithe of your upstart, unfledged admiration?
In the name of the Furies, what's come to the nation!"
Here I thought it was prudent to say, as to prose
I was perfectly willing to hand him the rose.
But I could not admit that our poets were so backward.
I thought, if he knew them, he'd see they'd a knack would
Command his respect. For the matter of liking,
The men he had mentioned might be each a Viking,
While we, very probably, were merely the skippers
Of some rather lively and smartish tea-clippers;
Or, to put it in terms somewhat more up to date,
Our steamers and aeroplanes might be first-rate
As carriers for a particular freight.
Each time for its heroes, and he must excuse
The terms I employed, I'd not meant to abuse
Our forerunners, but only to speak of a preference—
Anno Domini merely. So classic a reference
Should cool him, I thought. Here I went on to better a
Most happy allusion, and continued—*et cætera.*
I will not repeat all the soothing remarks
With which I endeavored to smother the sparks
Of his anger. Suffice it to say I succeeded
In clouding the issue of what had preceded.
I enjoyed it myself and I almost think he did.
I admit there was something a trifle pragmatical

In my method, but who wants the truth mathematical?
It sours good talk as thunder does cream.
I ignore, for the nonce, a disquieting gleam
In his eye. "But your critics," he answered demurely,
"For your poets, by and by; with your critics you surely
Surpass what we did. I was not fond of critics;
If I rightly remember, I gave them some sly ticks.
I called them, I think, poor broken-kneed hacks."
"We've advanced," I replied, "to the office boot-blacks.
We are quite democratic, and the newspapers think
One man is as good as another in ink.
The fluid that's paid for at so much a sprinkling
Is a guaranteed product, quite free of all inkling
That standardized morals, and standardized criticisms,
And a standardized series of cut-and-dried witticisms,
Are poor stuff to purvey as a full reading ration,
Though they suit to a T the views of a nation
Which fears nothing so much as a personal equation.
Subscribers demand that their thoughts be retailed to them
So often and plenteously that they become nailed to them
And when traveling are lost if their journal's not mailed
to them.
By this safe and sane rule our newspapers get on
Without any gambling, since there's nothing to bet on.
Of course I refer to things of import
Such as stock-exchange news, murders, fashions, and sport,
With a smattering of politics, garbled to fit
Editorial policy; if they admit
Puerilities like music and art, these are extras
Put in to augment, by means of a dexterous
Metropolitan appearance, their own circulation,
For a paper's first duty is self-preservation.
If they will run book columns, why someone must feed
them,
And, after all, few take the trouble to read them.
With a pastepot and scissors to cut up his betters
And any young numskull is equal to letters.
He scans what the publisher says on the jacket,
Then the first paragraph and the last, and the packet

Goes off to the second-hand bookshop, the bunch
Polished off in the minutes he's waiting for lunch.
I believe there's no record of anyone feeling
As he pockets his pay that he may have been stealing.
The thing would be murder, but that time has gone by
When an author can be made or marred by such fry.
Some good paper is spoiled, that's the long and the short
of it."
Here I watched the old gentleman to see what he thought
of it.
"These reviews which you speak of have one great ad-
vantage,"
He remarked, "they are brief. In our less petulant age
They had not that merit. But I see we agree
On essentials. Yet we had a very few men
Who wielded a passably powerful pen."
"And one woman," I slyly put in. He grimaced.
"That's the second you've dug up and greatly displaced.
Since you criticize thus, do I err if I doubt
Whether you are the boot-black on his afternoon out?"
Fairly touched and I owned it, and let Margaret Fuller
Slide softly to limbo. 'Twas unmanly to rule her
Out of count in this way, but the fish I must fry
Required considerable diplomacy
To keep in the pan and not drop in the fire.
'Twas an expert affair, and might shortly require
I knew not what effort to induce him to grant
That whatever we are is worth more than we aren't.
So I instantly seized on his "very few men"
And assured him that we also, now and again,
Found a youth who was willing to write good reviews
While learning to tickle the publishers' views
And make them believe he was worth-while to back.
"The thing after all is a question of knack,
Ten to one if you have it you turn out a quack;
If you don't, and win through, you've arrived without doubt,
But the luck's on your side if you're not quite worn out."
"Good old world," he remarked, as he prodded the ground
With the point of his cane, "I observe it goes round

In the same soothing, punctual way. This pastiche
Of the quite unfamiliar is merely a bleach,
A veneer, acid-bitten, on a color we knew.
By the way, when it's finished, who reads your review?"
"The fellow who wrote it, on all those occasions
When his fine self-esteem has received some abrasions.
Then the fellow who's written about cons the thing
Over several times in a day till the sting
Of its strictures becomes just the usual pedantic
Outpouring, and its granules of praise grow gigantic.
Once acquire this excellent trick for benumbing
What you don't want to hear by an extra loud strumming
On the things which you do and you fast are becoming
A real going author. Then there are the gentry
Who must read reviews to fill out an entry
In next week's advertisement; and others peruse
The paper with care to note down its abuse
Of their dear brother writer, and suck up each injurious
Phrase to retail with a finely luxurious
Hypocritical pretense of its being unsuitable,
While all the time showing it quite irrefutable.
Then there are the sisters, and cousins, and aunts
Of the writer and wrote about; some sycophants
Who pry into favor by announcing they've read it,
And praise or deride to heighten their credit
With the interested person. There are others who edit
Gossip columns, and who must go through at a deadheat
The news of the day for the spicy tidbits
And who greatly prefer the more virulent hits.
By the time we are through, a fairly large public
Has skimmed through the paper." He gave a quick flick
To a stone which arose with a circular twist
And plopped into the river. "But if I insist
On your people of parts?" "Oh, they do not exist,"
I assured him, "or only as sparsely as daisies
In city back yards. And if one of them raises
His voice it is drowned in the whirligig hazes
Of mob murmurings. If these men hold the key
To the spacious demesne known as posterity

The gate must have shrunk to a postern, I think.
Everyone worth his salt glues his eye to the chink
'Twixt the frame and the door, but it's long to keep looking
With never a chance to get even a hook in
And pull open a door where it's 'Skeletons Only.'
A notice designed to make anyone lonely.
It stares over the gate in huge letters of red:
'No person admitted until he is dead.'
Small wonder if some of them cannot hold out.
As they dwindle away, the watchers, no doubt,
Feel a sort of cold envy creep through their contempt.
Then perhaps the door opens and one is exempt,
Gone over to dust and to fame. As it slams,
The requiem fraternal, a chorus of 'Damns!'
Cracks the silence a moment. More still break away,
But the shriveled remainder waits each one his day.
It takes marvelous force and persistence to tarry on
When your own special corpse may be counted as carrion
And left where it lies to await decomposing
While that devilish door shows no sign of unclosing.
These custodians of keys are ill to rely on
As the last Day of Judgment to the followers of Zion.
There are folk who dress up in the very same guise
And boast of a power that's nothing but lies.
They shout from their chosen, particular steeple
Of some weekly review: 'We are surely the people!
We know what posterity wants, for we know
What other posterities have wanted, and so
We affirm confidently the true cut and fashion
Which the future will certainly dote on with passion.
There is no need at all of making a fuss
For all generations are exactly like us.
We represent that which is known as the *Vox*
Populi, species *Intelligentsia,* or Cocks
Of the Walk on the Dunghill of High Erudition,
Referred to more elegantly as Fields Elysian.'
The matter of clocks may be readily dropped,
Every Ph.D. knows that they long ago stopped.
What are colleges for with their dignified massiveness

But just to reduce all time-pieces to passiveness."
"The picture you draw does not greatly attract
One who seeks for the absolute even in fact.
That fanciful bit you put in about clocks
Borders rather too smartly upon paradox.
We had a few poets, and we had a few colleges,
And something like half of your bundle of knowledges.
We delivered our lectures and wrote our lampoons,
And I venture to say that the fire-balloons
Of our verse made as lively a sputter as yours.
If things are so changed, what, pray, is the cause?"
I groaned. Poor old gentleman, should I be tempted
To tell him the fault was that he had preëmpted,
He and the others, the country's small stock
Of imagination? The real stumbling-block
Was the way they stood up like Blake's angels, a chorus
Of geniuses over our heads, no more porous
Than so much stretched silk; rain, sun, and the stellar
Effulgences balked by our national umbrella
Of perished celebrities. To mention a trifling
Fact, underneath them the air's somewhat stifling.
Youthful lungs need ozone and, considering the tent,
No man can be blamed if he punches a rent
With his fist in the stiff, silken web if he can.
A feat, I assured him, more horrible than
Cataclysmic tidewaters or Vesuvian
Explosions to all those quaint, straitly-laced folk
Who allow a man only the freedom to choke.
"We may buckle the winds and rip open the sea,
But we mayn't poke a finger at authority."
"A nursery game," the old man spoke benignly,
"To all schoolboys, convention's a matter divinely
Ordained, and the youngster who feels himself bold enough
To step out of the ring will soon find himself cold enough.
To be chips from a hardened old tree may be crippling,
But it's nothing compared to the lot of the stripling.
For the sake of the argument, let us agree
That we were the last surge of life which the tree
Could produce, that our heart-wood was long ago rotted,

Our sap-wood decaying, and all our roots spotted
With fungus; the Spring of our flourishing over,
The first Winter storm would most likely have rove a
Great cleft through the trunk, and the next year's outleaving
Would unbalance the whole without hope of retrieving.
The gentlest of breezes would then send it crashing.
Good luck to the striplings if they escape smashing.
When an oak, having lasted its time, is once thrown,
What is left are the acorns it cast, and these grown
Are the forest of saplings in which it lies prone.
But 'twould be a dull acorn who should dare to declare
It was sprung only from earth's connection with air,
The miraculous birth of a marvelous rut.
Such an acorn indeed would be a poor nut."
He quickened his steps and I followed along,
Listening partly to him, and partly to the song
Of the little light leaves in the plane-trees. Said he,
Stopping short quite abruptly, "I think it should be
Somewhere about here that a house I once knew
Used to stand. It was not much to look at, 'tis true,
But its elms were superb and it had a fine view
Of the river. A friend of mine owned it, indeed
He was born here and loved every tree, every weed.
Circumstance loosed his moorings, but he came back to die,
To envisage the past with a chill, older eye,
And dwelt a few years with the bitter-sweet ghosts
Of his earlier dreams, with the shadowless hosts
Of the things he had never brought farther than planning.
How often he wished there were some way of spanning
The past and the present, to go back again
And drink to the dregs the austere cup of pain.
Instead, he allowed the nepenthe of change
To smother that loneliness by which the range
Of his soul might have reached to some highest achievement
Through the vision won out of a grievous bereavement.
He'd a wit and a fancy, a hint of some deepness,
An excellent humor quite unmarred by cheapness,
But somehow his work never got beyond soundings.

I wonder sometimes if it was his surroundings
Or the fact that he fled them. With a grim taciturnity,
He admitted no masterpiece owed its paternity
To him. Now they've pulled down his house, I suppose.
Thistles spring up and die, and the thistledown goes
Anywhere the wind blows it." "Wait," I said, "if you mean
James Lowell's house, 'Elmwood,' you can see it between
That brick porch and that window, and those are its chim-
    neys.
The grounds are cut up and built over, their trimness
Is due to that cluster of very new houses.
In its rather bedraggled condition, it rouses
My ire each time I come anywhere near it.
It deserved better treatment." "I fear it! I fear it!"
He murmured. "Was it lack of success, or those years
I spent in escaping the tonic arrears
Of a grief not lived through. I cannot bear more."
He turned and walked rapidly down to the shore
Of the river and seated himself on the bank.
Many minutes went by, then he asked me point-blank
Who were the young poets of the day. "Since my mood
Will admit no more sorrowful past, be so good
As to marshal your forces, I shall find it quite pleasant
To stroll for a little with you in the present.
So bring them out, lock, stock, and barrel, the whole of
    them,
I'm really most anxious to get a good toll of them.
Recount me their merits, their foibles and absurdities,
Such a tale is too saccharine without some acerbities."
His gesture of challenge was so debonnaire
I could only accept with as devil-may-care
A grace as I could. But our Ostrogothic
Modern manners, I fear, made me seem sans-culottic,
I know that I felt supremely idiotic.
Still "out of the mouths of the babes and the sucklings,"
And I was prepared with some brave ugly ducklings
I was willing to swear would prove to be swans,
Or, to tone up the metaphor, Bellerophons.
At least they'd no fear of a chase round the paddock

After Pegasus, who "might be lamed by a bad hock
And so easily mounted"—I can hear the malicious
Sneers of the critics when one dare be ambitious
And attempt a bold thing, yet it's hard to decry a
Flight its existence when above you the flyer
Is gyrating and plunging on his way to the zenith,
And he grins the best who at the last grinneth.
But my unknown old friend seemed to need no acquainting
With this style of horseflesh, he would notice my painting,
No chance then at all to confuse him by feinting.
I must prove that my horse had his quota of wings,
Was sound wind and limb, that his sidles and swings
Were no circus parade, that the man who would stride him
Knew perfectly well why he wanted to ride him.
That 'twas bareback or die, that the fellow was game
For whichever result was the end of his aim.
As I pondered, I harbored no little aversion
At having embarked on so great an excursion,
Nothing less, be it said, than his total conversion.
"Come, come," he urged quickly, "you're taking some time
To trot out your up-to-date dabblers in rhyme."
I pouted, I think. "Ha! Ha! you're offended!
Because I said 'dabblers' or because I pretended
Not to know that rhyme's lost its erstwhile predominance?"
I assured him at once that we gave no prominence
To rhyme or the lack of it. To which he said "Good!
We've got somewhere at last; now let's have the whole brood
In their rareness and rawness. I am surely no prude,
I shall not be satisfied if you exclude
Any atom of character, any least mood.
Give your men as you see them from their toes to their chin.
Only, for God's sake, my dear fellow, begin."
Since he and I wanted the same thing exactly,
I started to put it quite matter-of-factly.
He had spoken of acorns, so poets in a nutshell
Should please him, I thought, and they're none of them but shell.
To hesitate longer would smack of the boyish,

And a prophet's ill served by an attitude coyish,
Like a diffident girl asked to play the piano.
I detest all such feminine ruses, and so
I hitched up my mind as sailors and whalers
Are reported to do with their trousers (why tailors
Should so fashion these garments that this act must precede
Every truly stupendous and heroic deed
I am quite at a loss to surmise). To continue,
I exerted each muscle and braced every sinew
For the duty in hand. In a fiery burst
Which I hoped might be eloquence, I took up the first
Poet I happened to think of, explaining quite clearly
That my order of precedence meant nothing really.
Number ten might be easily rated as equal
To one or fifteen, if we lived for the sequel.
Here I saw with concern he had fixed both his eyes on
That soothing Nirvana we call the horizon.
There was danger of slumber I felt, so embarking
On my story with gusto, I began by remarking
(And here I must add for my just self-esteem
That the minute I spoke he awoke from his dream
And never thereafter did so much as blink,
Though I thought, once or twice, I detected a wink.)
But I'm straying again. I remarked then succinctly,
Without farther preamble:

"To name them distinctly,
There's Frost with his blueberry pastures and hills
All peopled by folk who have so many ills
'Tis a business to count 'em, their subtle insanities.
One half are sheer mad, and the others inanities.
He'll paint you a phobia quick as a wink
Stuffed into a hay-mow or tied to a sink.
And then he'll deny, with a certain rich rapture,
The very perversion he's set out to capture.
Were it not for his flowers, and orchards, and skies,
One would think the poor fellow was blind of both eyes
Or had never read Freud, but it's only his joke.
If we're looking for cheer, he's a pig in a poke.

But he's such a good chap, he is welcome to say
Tweedledum's Tweedledee if he's feeling that way.
When he calls a thing yellow and you know it is pink,
Why, you've purchased his book and you're welcome to
think.
He's a foggy benignity wandering in space
With a stray wisp of moonlight just touching his face,
Descending to earth when a certain condition
Reminds him that even a poet needs nutrition,
Departing thereafter to rarefied distances
Quite unapproachable to those persistencies,
The lovers of Lions, who shout at his tail—
At least so he says—when he comes within hail.
Majestic, remote, a quite beautiful pose,
(Or escape, or indulgence, or all three, who knows?)
Set solidly up in a niche like an oracle
Dispensing replies which he thinks categorical.
No wonder he cleaves to his leafy seclusion,
Barricading his door to unlawful intrusion,
The goal of the fledgling, a god in a thicket,
To be viewed only Tuesdays and Fridays by ticket.
Yet note, if you please, this is but one degree
Of Frost, there are more as you'll presently see,
And some of them are so vexatiously teasing
All this stored heat is needed to keep him from freezing.
Life is dreadfully hard on a man who can see
A rainbow-clad prophet atop of each tree;
To whom every grass-blade's a telephone wire
With Heaven as central and electrifier.
He has only to ring up the switch-board and hear
A poem lightly pattering into his ear,
But he must be in tune or the thing takes a kink,
An imminent lunch-bell puts it all on the blink.
Someone to be seen in the late afternoon
Throws all his poetical thoughts in a swoon.
He can't walk with one foot on Parnassus, and stutter
Along with the other foot deep in the gutter,
As many poets do, all those who have tamely
Submitted to life as men live it, and lamely

Continue to limp, half man-in-the-street,
Half poet-in-the-air. How often we meet
Such fellows, they throng the bohemian centers,
The 'Blue Cats' and 'Pink Moons' those artistic frequenters
Who eat at the house's expense for the fame
Their presence ensures have conceived as a name
Full of rich innuendo. Though why a strange hue
Connected with something—moons pink or cats blue—
Should make it so vicious, I can't see, can you?
These double-paced bardlings are marvels at talking,
But their writing seems curiously given to balking,
A result, like as not, of their manner of walking.
Not so Frost, he divides his life into two pieces,
Keeping one for himself while the other he leases
To various colleges. He's eclectic in choice
And at least half-a-dozen have cause to rejoice
That he's sojourned among them; for his unique duty,
What they pay him to do and regard as their booty,
Is the odd one of being on hand, nothing more.
He's an unexplored mine you know contains ore;
Or rather, he acts as a landscape may do
Which says one thing to me and another to you,
But which all agree is a very fine view.
Such a sight is experience, a wonderful thing
To have looked at and felt. This establishing
Of a poet in a college like a bird in a cage
Is a happy endowment for art which our age
Is the first to have thought of and made quite the rage.
That the poet cannot function while kept as a zoo,
Does not matter at all to the wiseacres who
Invented the scheme. They secure for the year
That desideratum, a high atmosphere.
If the poet who provides it be drained to the pith,
That is nothing to leaving their college a myth,
A tradition, to hand down to all future classes.
A thing and its shadow are one to the masses.
The man's written his poems, now he can recite them;
As for new ones, he is a great fool to invite them,
Notoriety offers a constant repose,

Like a time-honored rose-bush which now bears no rose.
Instead of one poet, we've a score of poetasters.
Are we wise in our method or ignorant wasters?
Frost suffers himself to be bled for the small fry
While Pegasus, never a quiescent palfrey,
Stamps at the hitching-post. Still, I'm not saying
There is really much harm in this lengthy delaying.
There's the other half-year and his telegraph grasses
And no college thrives on a diet of asses;
A man must be sacrificed now and again
To provide for the next generation of men.
So if, once in a while, a real poet is captured
And bled for the future, we should all be enraptured.
The violence done to his own special nature
Is a thing of no moment if he add to the stature
Of a handful of students, and business is booming
For the troubadour poets in the town he's illuming.
They come, called in shoals by the interest he rouses,
And talk of themselves to preposterous houses.
But who, in the end, has the best of the luck,
The migrating birds or the poor decoy duck?
Small surprise, when Commencement has ended the year,
If our poet's first free action is to disappear.
Chained up on a campus creating diurnal
Poetic fine weather must be an eternal
Annoyance, a horror, growing always more biting.
How pleasant his mountains must look, how exciting
The long leisured moments to think, with no gaping
Importunate youths whose lives he is shaping
Forever observing his least little movement.
Why, a bleak desert island would be an improvement
On such an existence. Though we should be proud
That there is such a man to let loose on a crowd
Of young bears, any one of whom may become President,
We should be even prouder to know him a resident
Of our woods and our hills, a neighbor of neighbors,
A singer of countrysides and country labors,
Like a hermit thrush deep in a wood whose fresh fire
Of song burns the whole air to music, and higher

Upsoars till it seems not one voice but a choir—
The choir of his people whose hearths are the altars
Of that deep race-religion which in him never falters,
His life is its worship, his songs are its psalters.
Prophet, seer, psalmist, is the world so importunate
As to leave you no peace even here? You are fortunate
At least to abide, remote as the fables,
In a place much neglected by railroad time-tables.
I promise, for one, when I turn from the wicket,
That the name of your town will not be on my ticket.
You have as much right to protect your seclusion
As any old monk of the order Carthusian,
Though solitude really is but an illusion
As most men find out to their utter confusion.
To speak of seclusion is to think of a man
Who is built on a toally otherwise plan.
I mean, and I rather imagine you know it,
Edwin Arlington Robinson, excellent poet,
And excellent person, but vague as a wood
Gazed into at dusk. His preponderant mood
Is withdrawal, and why? For a man of his stamp,
So conscious of people, it seems odd to scamp
Experience and contact, to live in a hollow
Between the four winds and perpetually swallow
The back draughts of air from a swift forward motion.
It takes a huge strength to withstand all emotion,
But Robinson stays with his feet planted square
In the middle of nothing, the vacuum where
The world's swinging starts and whirls out, where is left
The dead root of movement, an emptiness cleft
In the heart of an aim, of all aims, peering out
At the dust and the grass-blades that swirl all about.
He notes who is here, who is coming along,
Who has passed by alone, who is one of a throng.
He peers with intentness bent all into seeing,
A critical eye finely pointed on being.
He is cruel with dispassion, as though he most dreaded
Some shiver of feeling might yet be imbedded
Within him. And if this occurrence should happen,

He would probably see himself with a fool's cap on
And feel himself sinking to shipwreck at once;
Of the two, much preferring disaster to dunce.
For the dunce is contingent on a sort of a curse
He thinks he is doomed with. A curious, perverse
Undercutting of Fate which decrees him observer
And hoods him in ice from all possible fervor.
The slightest conceivable hint of a thaw
Wounds his conscience as though he had broken a law
He had sworn to uphold. Are there demons in hiding
Within his ice-mail? Can he feel them abiding
A time to break loose and disrupt into tatters
The scheme of existence he has taught himself matters,
A barrier raised betwixt him and his satyrs?
For he has them; his quaint, artificial control
Is a bandage drawn tightly to hold down his soul.
Should a nail or a thorn tear the least little mesh, it
Would let all his nature go leaping in freshet
Overflowing his banks and engulfing his dams
In a flurry of life. But the desolate calms
He has cherished so long would be lost in the slams,
The torrential vortices of a swift current
Exploding in motion. Some uncouth, deterrent
Complex in his make-up enforces recoil
Before the fatigue and the wrench of turmoil.
He compounds with inertia by calling it Fate,
Deeply dreading the rush of emotion in spate,
Distrusting his power to outwit disaster
In the realization that with him fast means faster,
And refusing to see that a turbulent strife
Is the valuable paradox given to life
Which only the few may possess. With the prize
In his hand, he turns sadly away, crucifies
His manhood each day with the old dog's-eared lies,
The heritage, left by those Puritan heirs.
His bogies and satyrs are grandsons of theirs.
Could he see them as fruit-trees distorted by mist,
He might unknot himself from the terrible twist
He has suffered through fear of them. Now, with vicarious

Experience in verse, he cheats all the various
Impulses within him which make him a poet;
But, try as he will, his poems all show it.
His tight little verses an inch in diameter,
His quatrains and whole-book-long tales in pentameter,
With never a hint of what he'd call a sham meter,
Though some people style his kind *ad nauseam* meter—
With gimlets for eyes and a sensitive heart,
All battened down tight in the box of his art,
And we have his rare merits and his strange deficiencies
Which mix to a porridge of peculiar efficiencies.
Admired by everyone dowered with wit,
He has scarcely the qualifications to hit
The unlettered public, but the fact that his name
Is already spotted with the lichens of fame
Opens up a most fecund and pertinent query
And is one of the pedestals on which my theory
Is based: whether now we have not reached the stage
Of a perfectly genuine coming-of-age.
I am willing to swear that when he has retired
His books will be listed as 'reading required,'
And poor sweltering youths taking examinations
Will crown him with the bays of their wild lamentations.
Our beautiful system is to make every course able
To render delight quite sterile through forcible
Insistence upon it. But these are the laurels
With which no man who's not insane ever quarrels.
Perhaps it's as well not to look at the guerdon
Too closely or no one would shoulder the burden
Of being a poet.

"The next I shall take up
Is a fellow as utterly different in make-up
As you're likely to see if you scour the land
With field-glasses and microscopes. This is Carl Sand-
burg, a strange, gifted creature, as slow as a fog
Just lifting to sunshine, a roughly hewn Gog,
Shorn of his twin Magog, set over the portal
Through which brawls the stream of everything mortal.

Day and night he observes it, this river of men,
With a weary-sweet, unflagging interest, and ten
Times in a day he seeks to detach
Himself from the plinth where he's destined to watch,
And mingle as one of them, mistaking his stature
To be but that generally ordained by nature
For the run of humanity. His miscalculations
Of the possible height to which civilizations
May rightly aspire are constantly leading
Him into positions whence there's no proceeding.
Because he can easily reach to the stars,
He cannot believe that a short arm debars
Any others from doing the same, and declares
His qualifications assuredly theirs.
Endowing each man whom he meets with his own
Stretch and feeling, he takes for the foundation stone
Of his creed the ability to walk cheek by jowl
With the sun, at the same time not losing control
Of feet always set on the earth. It is droll
To hear him announce neither giants nor pigmies
Exist, that there's only onc knowable size,
Which by implication's as tall as the skies.
What he feels about souls, he has brought into speech,
But since perfect English is a hard thing to teach
To those brought up without it, he changes his tactics
And declares correct use the hypochondriactics
Of language too timid for red-blooded slang.
This theory of his is a swift boomerang
Overturning his balance and flooring him pell-mell, he
Presents the strange sight of a man on his belly
Proclaiming that all men walk that way from preference
And the manner, though new, must be treated with deference.
Since his own natural speech is correct to a dot,
His theory, to use the red-blooded, is 'rot,'
And as man does not wiggle along like a jelly
When he walks, to affect that laid flat on the belly
Is the easiest position to attain locomotion
Must surely be called a preposterous notion.

But what's the poor fellow to do? It is plain
He overtops folk if he stands; once again
It's the hill and Mohammed, since he can't raise the others
He must lie if he'd be the same height as his brothers.
It may weary his readers to see a true poet
Who apparently has not the instinct to know it,
And so burdens his beauty with wild propaganda
That much of his work is a hideous slander
Against his remarkable genius, but scratch it
With a prudent pen-knife and there's nothing to match it
Going on in the whole world today. He has sight
Of a loveliness no man has seen, and a might,
A great flowing power of words to express
Its hugeness and littleness. All the excess
Of his passion for living leaps out from his pen
In a gush of fresh imminence; again and again
We read him to fill our soul's withering lungs
With the wind-over-water sweep which is his tongue's
Particular gift—though I should have said 'prairies,'
Not 'water,' he is no result of the seas,
But in every whiff of him, flat and extended,
A man of the plains, whose horizons are ended
By the upreach of earth to that sky which he touches
And carries off great fragments of in his clutches.
Wood-smoke, and water-smoke rising from runnels
At sunrise, long lines of black smoke from the funnels
Of engines and factories, steel of man's forging
And steel he's forged into; the slow, passive gorging
Of earth with mankind, blood of souls, blood of hearts,
Swallowed into the fields where the sprouting grain parts
A right rail from a left rail, and always asunder
Go marching the fields cleft in two by the wonder
Of man gauging distance as magic and burning it
Under boot-heels or car-wheels and all the time earning it
For the silt of his mind from which a new soil
Is gradually risen. This turgescent coil
Is the crawling of glaciers, the upheave of hills,
The process of making and change, the huge spills
Of watersheds seeking their oceans, the miracle

Of creeping continuance. This is the lyrical
Stuff Sandburg works into something as lazy
And deep as geology planting its clays, he
Makes keenly, unhastingly, as evolution,
And yet, poor blind eagle, he dreams revolution.
With the centuries his if he could but decide
To pocket his picayune, popular pride,
Give up his day-dreams and his tin-penny logic,
Be Gog as God made him and not demagogic,
Sit solidly down with his eyes and his heart,
And a file and a chisel, to fashion great art—
If he would, but will he? It really is vexing
To see such a fellow perpetually flexing
His knees to false idols, a mere artisan
When he might be an artist. Some historian
Of the future will round him up in an abstract
By denouncing the times as too matter-of-fact,
Not observing what might well be seen for the looking
That it's simply a case of not quite enough cooking.
An accredited hero or a dream-blinded sloven
Is entirely a matter of stoking the oven.
The material's certainly A number one,
It will be his own fault if he dies underdone.

"The man whom I next shall bring to the fore
Is becoming, I fear, an impossible bore.
Some few years ago, Minerva mislaid
Her glasses, and unable to see in the shade,
Feeling also, quite naturally, rather afraid
To proclaim that she wore them, like any old maid
Teaching school—for a Goddess is loath to parade
Her antiquity, even as others—she said
No word of the matter at home on Olympus.
A pity, because a very bad *impasse*
Might have so been averted. The handmaids and lackeys,
Who are always possessed of both front door and back keys,
Would have hunted the palace from cellar to roof
And most probably found them not very aloof
From the spot where poor Vulcan, in playing Tartuffe,

Had received a convincing and permanent proof
That the lady was chaste. Indeed, however frigid,
No woman of spirit admits to the rigid
Mathematical count of the years after forty,
And even immortals, though reputed quite 'sporty,'
And figuring time by the so many centuries,
Still scarcely desire to add up the entries
And publish the total. Minerva, then, hid
The fact that she could not quite see what she did,
And since it would give things away to inquire, 'Oh,
She could not do that!' And after a *giro*
Which blindly confused every main street and by-row,
In the end she conferred a great book on a tyro.
The author in question, though an excellent notary,
Could scarcely be classed at that time as a votary
Worth Minerva's attention. But, however unsuitable,
The deed, once accomplished, became quite immutable.
No matter how foolish she felt, the poor Goddess
Must carry it through in a pitiless progress.
For be sure, when her family learnt of her blunder,
Which they very soon did, she'd have welcomed Jove's thunder
To be quit of his really abominable quizzing.
His jokes were caught up by Neptune and sent whizzing
For Vulcan to cap them, and as he was still smarting
Beneath the rebuke she'd not spared him at parting,
He gave her good measure now he'd got the upper
Hand. Then the women joined in; what at supper
Was observed was rehashed for breakfast and dinner,
Even Venus said 'Minnie, you *have* picked a winner!
From all that I hear, your man is verbose.
He'll print in ten volumes, a very large dose
For you to inspire.' 'Oh, Minnie is game,'
Cried Mercury, kind-hearted boy. 'All the same,'
Growled Vulcan, 'if Min can hold out, 'twould be speedier
To imbue him at once with an encyclopedia.'
Here Minerva, in tears which begemmed her found glasses,
Declared her relations were all of them asses,
That she cared not a fig for their tuppenny threats

Having settled the book to be done in vignettes.
The Gods broke out laughing. 'Give Minnie the handle
And not one of you is worth even her sandal,'
Shouted Jove, 'she's arranged for a *succès de scandal.*'
Which she had, and her poet, never doubting the giver,
Wrote steadily on without the least quiver,
And at last, in due course, was published *Spoon River.*
Now having explained the volume's true genesis,
Let me say it is not for a party where tennis is
In order, or bridge. If you like porcupining
Your soul with your conscience, here's a chance for refining
On misery, and since Minerva'd a hand in it
No person need doubt that there's plenty of sand in it.
Of course the thing's genius no matter how squint-eyed,
And the reader who never once weeps must be flint-eyed.
But hey, Mr. Masters, how weary and dreary
You make all your folk! How impossibly smeary
And sticky they are with old amorous contacts,
A series of ticketed, sexual facts
Tucked away, all unwashed, in the ground. Who once told you
The great, biological truths with a few
Dirty smudges you've never forgotten, like plasters
Thumbed tight to your mind? They're the trade-mark of 'Masters.'
Whatever he's writing—Minerva-inspired
As this book, *Spoon River;* or, nervous and tired,
Worrying his public as a dog does a bone
As in *Domesday Book,* done, you'll agree, quite alone—
They all have the stamp of back-alley lust
Which you stand as you can, for stand it you must
If you'd read him at all. I've no wish to cloud over
The fame of a book which, from cover to cover,
Shows the trace of Minerva's most helpful collusion.
The hall-marks of genius are here in profusion.
People swarm through its pages like ants in a hill,
No one's like the others, a personal will
Makes each man what he is and his life what it was.
The modern Balzac? Not at all—the new 'Boz!'

Where the Frenchman employed an urbane moderation,
The Englishman gloried in exaggeration.
But, in spite of his gargoyles, his fine gift of humor
Kept even his quaintness from the taint of ill-rumor.
In a grin of delight, he played tricks with his drawing,
And no matter how far from the real he was yawing,
His object was merely a louder guffawing.
He never believed his grotesques were true pictures
Of life, he knew perfectly well men are mixtures
Of rather more this or a little less that;
No man is pure angel and none is sheer brat.
Where he painted them so, it was done to enhance
Some meaning he wished to make clear; circumstance
Induced him to stress both the gall and the honey,
And no one knew better just when to be funny.
Mr. Masters, quite otherwise, thinks his creations
Reveal abstract truth in their vilest relations.
He sees everyone as the suffering prey
Of some low, hidden instinct, his business to flay
The decency off them and show them all naked,
A few of them zanies, the rest downright wicked.
In all his vast gallery there's but one exception,
And that, I hold, is to have wrought with deception.
If some excellent sense of the really amusing
Had led him to practice a little more fusing
Of the good and the bad, his book had succeeded
In being the great masterpiece we have needed
Ever since the beginning. As it is, his caprice
Has given us only a great Masters' piece.
How Minerva deserted him all through the sequel,
We can easily see if we hunt for an equal
Success in the list of his subsequent works.
Each hitches along in a series of jerks.
He tries lyrics, and ballads, and novels in verse,
But lacks always the wit to return to the terse.
In the last, *Domesday Book,* he relied upon Browning
To replace Minerva and keep him from drowning.
Shallow hope! He achieved a self-hitting satire,

Mr. Masters looked so odd in Browning's attire.
The huge bulk of his book brought to mind the old fable
Of the bull-frog who, seeing an ox in the stable,
Puffed up till he burst in a vainglorious trying
To attain the same size. But no magnifying
Can make of unripeness a thing brought to a finish,
For blowing it up only makes it look thinnish.
If asked my opinion, I think that Minerva
Was cruel to abandon the role of preserver.
To lift a man suddenly out of obscurity
And leave him quite solus in his prematurity
Was not, I think, cricket. (I like to imply an
Acquaintance with idioms as remote as the Chian,
They read like a dash of the pepper called Cayenne.)
To conclude, I believe, when the Gods have done chaffing,
Minerva will one morning catch herself laughing,
And, as laughing's a good-natured act to fall into,
I should not be surprised if she found she had been too
High-handed and harsh in her speedy desertion
Of an author who might have become her diversion
Had her relatives not been so prompt with their jeers.
Then, totaling up the count of the years
And the works she'd permitted her erstwhile protégé
To publish without her assistance, 'Heyday!'
I can hear her exclaiming. 'This will scarcely redound
To my credit, and since the world knows that I found
Him and helped him, I really think it would be better
If I helped him again to become the begetter
Of another *Spoon River,* or at least some quite fine thing
Which folk will acknowledge to be a divine thing.'
I should not be astonished if, touched to the marrow,
Minerva set out in her largest Pierce Arrow,
Or else (since I would not pretend to a choice)
Departed in her most expensive Rolls-Royce,
With a dozen or two extremely sharp axes,
Three or four different saws, and various waxes,
A hammer and nails, also scissors and strings,
The whole bundle of tools which a good workman brings

To a job who's no wish to go back for his 'things.'
Arriving *chez* Masters, there'll be a short parley,
And I conjure the world not to miss the finale."

At this point in my tale, there suddenly grew
On my ear a low sound like wind sweeping through
Many acres of pine-trees; but, even as I listened,
It changed into bird-calls which merrily glistened
Like sun-spattered feathers of tone through the glancing
Of leaves over water where shadows are dancing.
Once again was a change, and I heard the low roar
Of surf beating up against a rock shore;
This gave place to the clanging of bells over valleys
And the long monotone of horns blown from Swiss chalets.
I'd scarcely determined that fact when again
It transmuted itself into pattering rain,
Which fused in its turn to harsh drums and to blares
Of tin trumpets, the kind that you meet with at fairs.
But before I'd accustomed myself to the noise,
It rose quiet, single, enduring in poise,
Held high to a balance above growling thunder
As though I were harkening to the world's wonder,
The organ at Harlem, while the *Mourning of Rachel*
Was played—and I knew I was listening to Vachel.
"Who else has, or ever has had, such a voice
As is his, Vachel Lindsay's? Whatever his choice,
Be it singing, exhorting, making fun, prophesying,
It is equally lovely and soul-satisfying.
He's a composite choir, whether shouting or chanting,
Whoever's heard once must admit to a haunting
Nostalgia to hear him again. It's enchanting.
A Sunday-school orator, plus inspiration,
The first ballad-singer, bar none, of the Nation.
When he is performing, I acknowledge to being
More delighted with hearing than I am with seeing.
Perhaps I'm self-conscious, but his postures and poses
Do not strike me as happily chosen for Moses
Bearing down from the mountain his Tables of Stone,
Otherwise the part fits him as though 'twere his own.

When he starts in proclaiming his credo of new laws,
They appear to be vaudeville stunts dashed with blue laws.
He's so desperately earnest there's no modifying him,
And that wonderful voice is forever enskying him.
There's a sober old owl and a bright dragonfly in him,
But clearly there's nothing at all of the dry in him.
An odd, antic fellow, but if you insist
On the unvarnished truth, a sublime egotist
Delighting to cover his titles and fly-leaves
With the personal notes his omnipresent 'I' leaves.
This trait should endear him to every collector
Long after his ego's become a mere specter.
If his writing's so *chic* that you can't read a particle,
Why, all the more grist for a bibliophile's article.
He's a sort of mad xylophone, twinkling his bells
Before all the doors of the thirty-six Hells.
No whirligig dervish gyrating his piety
Can ever be less moved than he with anxiety
Lest his furious rhythms may show impropriety
And injure his creed in the eyes of society.
He knows his own heart and its innate sobriety
And cares nothing for fools who may note with dubiety
A worship which ranges through so much variety.
A mighty jazz dancer before the Lord!—
I can think of no happier term to record
His effect when reciting. He's astoundingly mystic
Even when he purports to be most naturalistic,
A queer ancient trait we may call Judaistic,
Engraft on a style which is pure Methodistic.
He is always attempting to fathom his soul,
But he cannot get hold of a long enough pole.
As he uses an ancient one which he inherited,
Perhaps, after all, his failure is merited.
It's a battered old thing might be John Wesley's staff,
Good enough in its day, but too short by half
To reach to his bottom. Still there's something so stable
In his love for the heirloom, it might pass for a label.
The fellow has scarce an iota of logic
Though he leans rather strongly toward the pedagogic.

These two traits make his teaching less vivid than taking,
He appears as the herald of some proud awaking,
But what it's to be, I dare swear he's no whit
More enlightened than we are, not one little bit.
I like his conceit of the amaranth apples,
(The word is so charming, the look of it dapples
His page with sunshine) and his modern Valkyrie,
A cross between Joan of Arc and a fairy—
I, too, should have relished some good latakia
At a table for two behind clumps of spirea
At the top of his Truth Tower cafeteria
With this twenty-first century wise young Medea.
Who wouldn't, indeed! But the sweepings and shavings
I gather up after her talk seem mere ravings,
The opaline fancies of moonlight and youth.
Among them I scarcely can plot out one truth
Plain enough to be platformed by some voting sleuth
And paraded before the precinct polling-booth.
What's the difference, say I, since the book is as airy
As the dew-dripping song of a young wild canary.
Who dotes on perusing economists' tracts?
There are millions of volumes which deal with mere facts.
I prefer this spiced basket of rose and camellia,
And a populace dancing a gay seguidilla
Under Tajes Mahal, with the star-chimes all ringing.
(That term, by the way, simply does its own singing.)
'Amaranth apple-trees, sandal-wood thickets!'
Bless the man who has shown us the way through the wickets
Which lead to this pleasance, and haply the leaven
Works none the less well because he calls it Heaven.
The book is the whole of him, minus his rhythm.
But the others—how often I pass a day with them,
Boomlaying and shouting, 'creeping through the black,'
With a whole troop of nigger-gods yelling at my back,
And the motors whizzing with their 'crack-crack-crack,'
Till at last I strike the wheat-ridge track
And up along a mulberry lane
I listen to the song of the Rachel-Jane.

And as I listen, perhaps it is absurd,
The singer changes to a small gray bird,
And then I see the purple quiver
Of a rainbow junk on a silver river.
I know that 'Spring comes on forever.'
I know it by heart, I have heard the tale
From Lindsay's jade-gray nightingale.
I shall never forget it, because I know it
By heart. This tribute? Do I not owe it!
Forgive me then, most fanciful poet,
If I find in you rarest, gravest delight
When you would have brought me to Heaven's height.
I am very well off where I am, I think,
Still you certainly write with a golden ink,
But I wish you would give us more of the Chink."

At which juncture, I paused to see if my friend,
Who had not said a word, might have ceased to attend.
Far from it, his eyes were fixed on my face
With an eager insistence as if he would trace
My meaning beyond the mere words. "What you say,"
He broke silence at last in his impassive way,
"Proves your poets to be certainly not of my day.
You put the fact gently, but we are *passé*.
At least that I presume's what you wish to convey."
With a horrified gesture I started to say—
But what? Thank the Lord I had no time to get in
The something I should have wrapt up my regret in,
Like a pill in a sugar-plum, since he went on:
"I should not be surprised, as your judgment anon,
If I heard you correctly, was for Miss Dickinson,
With Whitman and Poe. To throw off constraint,
I will say I consider your pronouncement quaint.
But I'm not so at sea to account for the cause
As before your narration I certainly was.
For the men, I'll admit there is room for dispute;
But the choice of Miss Dickinson I must refute."
Then seeing me shrug, he observed, "I am human,
And hardly can bear to allow that a woman

Is ever quite equal to man in the arts;
The two sexes cannot be ranked counterparts."
"My dear Sir," I exclaimed, "if you'd not been afraid
Of Margaret Fuller's success, you'd have stayed
Your hand in her case and more justly have rated her."
Here he murmured morosely, "My God, how I hated her!
But have you no women whom you must hate too?
I shall think all the better of you if you do,
And of them, I may add." I assured him, "A few.
But I scarcely think man feels the same contradictory
Desire to love them and shear them of victory?"
"You think wrong, my young friend," he declared with a frown,
"Man will always love woman and always pull down
What she does." "Well, of course, if you will hug the cynical,
It is quite your affair, but there is the pinnacle.
She's welcome to climb with man if she wishes."
"And fall with a crash like a trayful of dishes,"
He answered at once, "but if there's no gainsaying her,
There's certainly not the least use in delaying her."
"Very well," I assured him, and quite without mockery,
"But I know several women not yet broken crockery.
Amy Lowell, for instance," I spoke a bit clammily.
"Good Heavens!" he shouted, "not one of the family!
I remember they used to be counted by dozens,
But I never was interested in immature cousins."
"They grow, I believe." The retort was so pat
There was nothing to say, and he pulled down his hat.
I continued: "But since this is not genealogy,
You'll permit me to waive any sort of analogy
Between her and your friend. No one likes to be bound
In a sort of perpetual family pound
Tied by *esprit de corps* to the wheels of the dead.
A poet above all people must have his head.
Indeed it's been whispered the lady sees red
When the subject is broached, she will find her own latitude."
"My friend, were he here, would extol such an attitude,"

He said very gravely. "But proceed, Sir, I pray."
I hastened as fast as I could to obey:
"Conceive, if you can, an electrical storm
Of a swiftness and fury surpassing the norm;
Conceive that this cyclone has caught up the rainbow
And dashed dizzily on with it streaming in tow.
Imagine a sky all split open and scissored
By lightnings, and then you can picture this blizzard.
That is, if you'll also imagine the clashes
Of tropical thunder, the incessant crashes
Which shiver the hearing and leave it in ashes.
Remember, meanwhile, that the sky is prismatic
And outrageous with color. The effect is erratic
And jarring to some, but to others ecstatic,
Depending, of course, on the idiosyncratic
Response of beholders. When you come to think of it,
A good deal is demanded by those on the brink of it.
To be caught in the skirts of a whirling afflatus
One must not suppose is experienced gratis.
Broncho-busting with rainbows is scarcely a game
For middle-aged persons inclined to the tame.
Likewise, who'd enjoy a sunrise from the Matter-
horn—something all travelers agree is the attar
Of distilled perfection—must be ready to reap
The mid-afternoon pangs of too little sleep.
I might go on forever commingling my metaphors,
And verse by this means does undoubtedly get a force,
But persons who so air their fancy are bores,
A thing every bone in my body abhors,
And you'll guess by this time, without farther allusion,
That the lady's unique and surprising profusion
Creates in some minds an unhappy confusion.
No one's to be blamed who's not something and twenty,
But it's lucky for her that young folk are so plenty.
The future's her goose and I daresay she'll wing it,
Though the triumph will need her own power to sing it.
Although I'm no prophet, I'll hazard a guess
She'll be rated by time as more rather than less.
Once accustom yourself to her strange elocution,

And milder verse seems by contrast mere dilution.
Then again (for I've kept back a very great part),
Despite her traducers, there's always a heart
Hid away in her poems for the seeking; impassioned,
Beneath silver surfaces cunningly fashioned
To baffle coarse pryings, it waits for the touch
Of a man who takes surfaces only as such.
Her work's not, if you will, for the glib amateur,
But I wonder, would it be improved if it were?
Must subtlety always be counted a flaw
And poetry not poetry which puzzles the raw?
Let me turn for an instant to note the reverse
Of my poet, who employs many manners of verse
And when not hurricaning's astoundingly terse;
Yet here the poor creature but makes matters worse.
There are plenty of critics who say they can't hear
When she sings *sotto voce,* the sensation's queer
And inspires a species of horrible fear.
To be told there's a sound and catch nothing at all,
Is a circumstance fairly designed to appall
Most casual people, for here is the hitch:
The admission that one's own ears can't grasp a pitch
Clear and lovely to others. Whereupon a bow-wow
Which swells to a perfectly hideous row.
They've accused her of every description of quackery,
Of only concerning herself with knick-knackery,
It has all been enough to set anyone's back awry.
She's a fool to resent it, a man would have grinned?
Quite so, but then poets are created thin-skinned,
And when one is more than a little volcanic,
With a very strong dash of the ultra-tyrannic,
The retort contentious will be simply Titanic.
Behold, then, our poet, by the lash of atrociousness
Goaded into an attitude much like ferociousness.
Every book that she writes has a preface to guard it
Which spits fire and cannon-balls, making each hard hit
Tell, and mow down its swathe of objectors.
But critics have ever been good resurrectors.
Since she keeps the fight going, they rise to do battle,

When the whole mess is only so much tittle-tattle.
So it goes back and forth with the cries and the cheering,
And there's no sign at all of the atmosphere clearing.
Her books follow each other despite all the riot,
For, oddly enough, there's a queer, crumpled quiet
Perpetually round her, a crazy-quilt tent
Dividing her happily from the event.
Armed to the teeth like an old Samurai,
Juggling with jewels like the ancient genii,
Hung all over with mouse-traps of meters, and cages
Of bright-plumaged rhythms, with pages and pages
Of colors slit up into streaming confetti
Which give the appearance of something sunsetty,
And gorgeous, and flowing—a curious sight
She makes in her progress, a modern White Knight,
Forever explaining her latest inventions
And assuring herself of all wandering attentions
By pausing at times to sing, in a duly
Appreciative manner, an aria from Lully.
The horse which she rides will suit any part
Either Peg (with the 'asus') or 'Peg o' my heart.'
To avoid making blunders, he's usually known
Without any suffix as 'Peg' all alone.
This style of address has become a tradition
Most offendingly silly, since no erudition
Unaided can ever produce a magician.
For the magic she has, I see nothing demonic
In the use of free verse (the 'free' is quite comic!)
Or even that mule of the arts, polyphonic.
No matter what pedants may find that's awry in him,
There's plenty of kick and plenty of fly in him.
Taking this thing and that, and considering on it,
I believe there are more guesses under her bonnet
Than in any two hats you are likely to meet
(Straw or felt, take your choice, so the shape be discreet,
Not too flap-brimmed and weird, nor too jaunty and neat)
In any particular city or street
You may happen to pick. Note, I only say questions,
Which leaves the mind open to many suggestions,

Up or down, there's the rub. (The mere matter of hats
Is too nice, by the way, to be dealt with as 'Rats!'
There's a temperature here which the best thermostats
Could not regulate better. We're all diplomats
Now the 'Arrys have ousted the aris-tocrats.)"

I looked at my friend, his face was averted.
"You make it quite clear why we are deserted,
Old men are tough customers. Now, as a foil,
Give me something as smooth and slow-running as oil,
Something clear, uncontentious, it even may be
A bit chilly in beauty perhaps." "There's 'H. D.,'"
I was tempted to shout, she fitted so rightly
His immediate preference: frost falling lightly
In delicate patterns on thin blades of grass.
(Since oil does not fit, I let that figure pass,
Though it did well enough up above where it was.)
"This author's become a species of fable
For she masks her identity under a label.
If others have ancestors, she would forget hers
And appear the spontaneous child of two letters,
The printing of which is the bane of typesetters.
They have called her a dryad just stepped from a bosk,
But I see an ice maiden within an ice kiosk,
With icicle stalactites hanging around her,
And the violets frozen with which they have crowned her—
The man who would filch them would be an icebounder,
Which I surely am not. If each lovely, veined petal
Becomes by the contact a trifle too brittle
And cold to give out its usual warm scent,
They make it up amply by such dazzlement
Of sun-shot-through-ice that the shine of her shrine
Seems the sky-piercing glitter of some Apennine.
I have told you before that my mind teems with similes.
It's a shocking bad habit persists in some families,
I've an uncle—but there, I spread out like a runnel,
When I should flow as straight as though poured through a
    funnel.
So take this digression in the light of an interlude

Leading up to a change which I wish to obtrude
On the form of my speech, for I find I am freezing
Before the remarkably chilly, though pleasing,
Ice image I've painted, and soon shall be sneezing.
My Muse must immediately seek out a clime
Where her trippings and flittings are not above rime,
Or dew that is duly congealed, or hoar-frost.
I'm indifferent to science, so the meaning be tossed
Into some sort of shape which fits well with my pattern,
For, whatever the faults of said Muse, she's no slattern.
My verse, I'll allow, is the species fantastic,
I've been *épris* for years of the style Hudibrastic,
But my rhyming morale is, I trust, inelastic.
Which preamble means I have searched for a week
To rouse neither my Muse's nor heroine's pique
In the matter of climate. I've found it in Greek.
'H. D.' (for it's time we got back to the girl)
Might be some ancient mirror, with mother-of-pearl
Let into its metal, a thing which a nation
Deems well worth the cost of its own exhumation,
A prize to count up to the whole excavation.
This mirror, which carries the breath of the past
On its scarcely stained surface, is no scholiast,
But a living replica of what once was living
At the touch of a rare adoration reviving.
Here youths in scant armor, on the way to the galleys,
Woo maidens in dark ilex-groves; in the valleys,
Anemone-sprinkled, young shepherds guard flocks
Clad in ram's fleeces only; above the sharp rocks
Jutting into the purple Ionian sea
Are the white, fluted columns of—Fiddle-de-dee!
Such lyrical bursts in a mere *jeu d'esprit*
Are like brandy poured into a cup of bohea,
A transaction called 'lacing' in old days, *on dit.*
I can't say for myself, being no devotee
Of either diluted or straight *eau-de-vie,*
And the eighteenth amendment is nothing to me.
Still, I don't like a law couched in hyperbole,
It gets anyone's goat. To return to 'H. D.,'

Whom I've really kept waiting most outrageously,
She's the thing as it was, not the thing we have made it
And with insolent ornament quite overlaid it.
She descends to no commonplace, flock-guarding shepherds.
No pompous Victorian gush ever jeopards
Her reticent, finely drawn line. No Greek marble
Has less of the pueril and less of the garble.
Her sea is the sea of a child or a Neriad,
And yet no false word lifts it out of its period.
Her flowers of shore and of cliff those we seek
On our cliffs and our shores, but hers somehow are Greek.
Her poems are excitement and rest, and the glory
Of living a life and not reading a story.
Archaeology? Yes, in the very same way
That geology's the mountain we climb every day.
The armor she welds, the dyed cloth she weaves,
Are so perfect in artistry, every word cleaves
To the substance as though that would crackle without it
And split. Read her books (there are two) if you doubt it.
Perhaps, after all, this quintessence of Greece
Is the wool on a century-garlanded fleece;
Underneath is, and was, a tough fiber of leather.
Is the Greece she has given us Greece altogether?
As well might one ask if the youth of Praxiteles
Is an everyday chap or a scheme to belittle ease
By exalting the sharp line of young masculinity.
In her method and his is there not some affinity?
Each sheers to the soul, to the base of a nemesis,
And the hard, glancing residue is the ultimate genesis.
For out of the past is the future; a truism,
You must pardon, since man has invented no new 'ism'
Since the days of the cavemen. I wish merely to prove
That this most modern poet runs along an old groove,
That the erudite novelties filling her pages
Are as old as this morning and as new as the ages."

Here a voice interrupted my long peroration,
Speaking, I detected, in some irritation.
"I think," it announced, "though I may be mistaken,

There's a poet whom you've not mentioned yet, Conrad
    Aiken."
Such an ill-governed mind as I've got, and the porter
Never keeps out intruders who call, as he ought to.
(That rhyme will be cursed as "a regular snorter"
By every stand-pat, Tennysonian supporter.
I am sorry myself to be forced to distort a
Fine line unduly, and if I or my thought err
I am willing to own it without the least *hauteur*.
I rhyme as I can, and am never a courter
For all suffrages.) The doorman, I said,
Who, between you and me, is a crass dunderhead,
Had let this extremely irascible gentleman
Pass through the door, and of course he began
At once to upbraid me. It's the method he uses
To force himself into the sight of the Muses.
"Young man," I replied with some heat, "you mistake
My preoccupation. If you wish to make
Your entrance at once with the ladies, I'll see to it,
But I should have supposed you'd immediately veto it."
This was rather a staggerer, to be grouped with the women
Would tax the endurance of any male human;
Yet to wait any longer, when I might be weary
Before his turn came, did not strike him as cheery.
He puffed and he fumed, with pride pulling both ways;
It was pitiable to see the poor fellow's malaise.
But finally, with a great bluffing of chivalry,
He declared he had no sort of feeling of rivalry
Against the fair sex who adorned his profession.
A very neat way, this, to blur a confession,
For the long and the short of it was he'd go on
The carpet at once, if I pleased. Thereupon
I hastily made my excuses to one
Or two ladies I'd meant to have been next presented.
Being sensible persons, they seemed quite contented.
Perhaps 'twas as well, for I'd rather a hunch
The irascible poet might make good with his "Punch"
And land me that terrible "one on the jaw,"
When I'm sure I should "measure my length" in the straw.

It will clearly be seen that my anxious perusal
Of a recent combat has done much to bamboozle
The erstwhile classic grace of my natural diction.
You see I obeyed a strong predilection
In Carpentier's favor to the tune of a tenner
And, with other good sportsmen, I found my Gehenna.
"Mr. Aiken's a poet so cram full of knowledge
He knows all about poetry that's taught in a college.
His versification's as neat as a pin,
His meter so fine it becomes finikin.
I say nothing of rhythm, for he's something fanatical
Anent the advantage of the beat mathematical.
Within his set limits, the pulse of his verse
Is often most subtle, and even his worse
Attempts are by no means either jejune or lacking
In form, one can hardly imagine him slacking
In pains or desire. He's all that a poet
Can make of himself when he sets out to do it
With his heart, and his soul, and his strength, and his mind.
For years now, he's had a most horrible grind
With his work, with the public, but what stands in his way
Is the awkward necessity of something to say.
A man of sensations, of difficult cheerfulness
Which the fog in his brain has tormented to fearfulness,
Possessed of much music and little idea,
Always steeping his soul in the strange undersphere
Of the brain. Since all thought in him tends to grow hazy
When his sentiment's roused, he is lost in a mazy
Vortex where he swings like some pale asteroid.
Seeking orientation, he's stumbled on Freud.
With the Austrian's assistance, he's become neurological,
A terrible fate to befall the illogical.
Being born with an ultra-sensitive cuticle,
We must realize his verse in a sense therapeutical.
If he doesn't quite state any fact, his oblique
Side-glances at subjects are just hide-and-seek
He's playing with all his frustrated ambitions
And gaining, thereby, some vicarious fruitions.
He's so young as to think that he proves his maturity

By boldly colliding with all sorts of impurity.
His ladies are, most of them, a little bit dusty,
But we're learning to think any other kind musty.
The true modern artist would face destitution
Were it not for that universe-wide institution
Plain people frown down on and call prostitution.
No matter how shopworn the plots he has made,
They will always pass muster if he mentions a spade.
At least this is true with that type of Bohemia
Which is not yet aware that such art spells anaemia.
Not so Aiken—his brothels, street-walkers, dope-eaters
Are merely the web he weaves over with meters.
He uses them chiefly because they are easy
And sure to produce an effect on the queasy.
For more than all else he dreads falling flat;
The fear of it teases his brain like a gnat.
He would rather be called wicked, incomprehensible,
Anything, so long as the world's not insensible.
In his anxious desire to escape being tepid,
He makes too great a show of the over-intrepid,
But his real interest lies in quite other directions:
In noting the faintest of fleeting reflections
In tone or in color; in catching the magic
Of words against words; and it simply is tragic
How few apprehend his remarkable quality.
But was ever a public more lost in frivolity
Than ours? It cannot tell feathers from lead
Till you hit it a crack with the last on the head.
His volumes are filled with a sea-green miasma
Shot and sprinkled throughout with the grotesque phantasma
Of an egoist's brain, or a man's when he's sleepy.
They revolve unrelated and sink into creepy
Sight and sound mutterings, yet sometimes so vivid
They are that they seem to stand out in a livid
And flaming protrusion. Take, for instance, the scene
Of his satyrs and mænads, which is white striped on green,
With red, sudden explosions. Sometimes, more surprising,
The fog lifts a moment before a sun rising

As clear and as thin as though painted on china
By some eighteenth-century Dresden designer.
His sordid back rooms disappear and the groans
Of dying dope-fiends, and we hear 'three clear tones,'
The tones of his bird in the china-berry tree.
What a mercy that such a tree happened to be!
Otherwise, I believe, he must have invented it.
Never mind, here it is, and he's simply cemented it
On the botany of poetry forever and ever.
I say that superbly, without the least quiver.
If the rest of his work's neither Saint Paul's nor Kremlin,
He's built a basilica surely in *Senlin.*
At least in that *Morning Song,* which, until lately,
Was the sole, single fragment he'd done adequately.
Till *Punch,* ah! with *Punch* now, he should achieve fame,
But there's nothing so dogging as a once-come-by name.
If this were his first, he'd be up like a rocket,
Now I think he'll burn steadily on in his socket
Making beautiful poems though the public won't stand 'em
Because he can't drive style and tale in a tandem.
Since the books as they are stick so hard in the gizzard,
The sensible thing is to have each one scissored.
Cut out from each volume the one or two scraps
You might like on a third or fourth reading perhaps;
Paste them into a scrap-book, and some rainy day
Just glance over the lot and I think you will say:
'By Jove! What a fellow he is in his way!'
And I'll thank you for that as a true leaf of bay.
If he, the arch-skeptic, finds other folk doubting,
He makes a mistake to be seen always pouting.
He has not his deserts, yet to publish the fact
Is a childish and most unintelligent act,
But everyone knows he's deficient in tact.
A man who can work with such utter devotion
Can afford to wait patiently for his promotion,
And that it will come, I've a very strong notion.
One thing we can say, he will certainly wait
And either get in or turn dust at the gate.
Since Fame is a very good hand at the shears,

I shall not be surprised if he gets his arrears,
For quality counts in the long run of years."
I turned to the shade in my mind, but unused
To listening with patience, the thing had vamoosed

Not so my old friend, he was listening intensely,
And as I stopped speaking, he said, "I'm immensely
Intrigued by that man, he's a curious fellow.
Too bad he's permitted himself to see yellow.
A jaundiced perspective's a great handicap.
Well, what other poets have you got in your lap?
I commend you, young man, as an excellent etcher."
"The next I shall notice will be John Gould Fletcher,"
I answered, "but before I begin my narration
Don't *think;* if you can, *see* an irradiation
Spreading out over roofs, over trees, over sky,
The gold screen of a moment, on which you descry
Such oddments as heaps of 'vermilion pavilions'
And Gabriel's angels all riding on pillions
On the backs of cloud horses, blowing trumpets of thunder,
Above forests of elephant trees standing under
The precipitous cone of some steep afternoon.
The whirling wind 'screams,' the stars 'shrill,' the streets croon.
A cataract of music swirls out of the throats
Of the long scarlet trumpets, the prismatic notes
Sweep over the city like sun spray and laughter,
Embroidered with all colors . . . Then what comes after?
More colors, a rain of them, hanging, delaying,
To sprinkle cool 'jade balustrades' with their staying.
Golden flakes, silver filaments, what pandemonium!
The rainbow joined in wedlock to a bursting harmonium.
Elephantine surrenders, prodigious relapses,
Speech turned to a fire-ball which soars and collapses
And spills down its words like the whole spectrum falling
In a broken excitement: My eye, it's appalling!
Such a chaotic shooting and drifting of particles,
Mere loveliness solus, not stuck tight to articles,
For what it all means does not matter a jot;

You are filled with delight at it, or you are not.
But suppose that you weary of the polychromatic—
Some natures, I realize, are far too lymphatic
To derive any pleasure from what is not static—
There are corners to rest in with fountains, and grass
Streaming up in long slopes, and if you should pass
Just over the hill, there's a house where each column
Is wreathed and entangled with the half-gay, half-solemn
Recollections of childhood. There you can eat luncheon,
And drink slow well-water from some old gray puncheon,
And listen to tales of hobgoblins and genie
Till I venture to say you'll be a bit spleeny
And welcome the rising of white-faced Selene.
(Rather pretty, that last, such touches do garnish
One's writing, I think, and I'm not above varnish.
I like a bright luster in poems or medallions,
The polish one sees in the later Italians.
Here a friend who's dropped in says I've mixed my mythology.
Such a slip, if I've made it, deserves an apology:
Selene, Cybele, Diana—I care
Not at all for mere names. You may take Lemprière
And choose any Goddess you think opportune
So you quite understand I refer to the moon.)
As you sit in the moonlight, the gist of your summary
Will be: Here at last, is a poet without flummery.
A score or two words are his total of plunder,
But the whole is a boyhood imprisoned in wonder.
A boy, and the things all about him—plain stuff,
And not even new, but the measure's enough.
Not the kind which they want for a penny-a-liner;
It's too sharp, and too sheer, but for that all the finer.
Have you ever gone into a dim, disused attic
And poked about there among the erratic
Remains of worn toys, legless soldiers, chipped blocks,
And suddenly come on an old music-box?
As you twist round the handle, the notes seem to squeeze
Through the dust, some are lost and the rest choke and wheeze,

But you make out a tune, and the mere broken hint of it
Is the agonized joy of remembrance, by dint of it
You suffer and love with an ache you'd forgotten.
It were wiser, perhaps, were your ears stuffed with cotton.
So Fletcher's not only the rainbow in spate,
He's the soul of a music-box which can create
All our childhood again. If the tune's a bit scrappy,
What's the odds, just so long as the sound makes us happy?
So far, Mr. Fletcher, for that's only a mood,
We'll not whistle until we are out of the wood.
Were your publishers mad, or why bind together
Your *Old House* and *Symphonies*? One wonders whether
You were bent on emptying out your portfolio.
You created, at any rate, quite an imbroglio.
This break-up of feeling with one or two vile hacks
Of discord is as jarring as gumdrops and smilax
Giving suddenly place to red-peppers and asters.
The symphonies, come on this way, call for plasters.
This arrangement, indeed, was the worst of disasters.
Up bright in the morning, shoes tied and hair brushed,
On a Sunday, maybe, when you're not too much rushed,
You can seek ancient China in Symphony Blue;
Or, if you prefer, you may take a stroll through
Any Spring, in the Green; you may sail over oceans
With the Red glare of stoke-holes to thrill your emotions;
You may fight in the Scarlet, and laugh in the Yellow,
You may do what you please in the Gold. A fine fellow
Whose palette is full if a little bit messy.
But you have a good deal of the world here *in esse*.
At least, you would have, were it not for a doubt
About what any symphony's really about.
He writes, it appears, in a prismatic spasm;
This phase of his work is complete protoplasm.
He is whirling his atoms before quite cohering them,
But there's no doubt at all that he soon will be steering
them.
Yet, hold on a bit, my dear chap, do you think
You can set all America down in cold ink?
Here you are, aeroplaning from Boston to Texas,

And taking snapshots as you fly to perplex us.
If you see a skyscraper, down it goes, and the next
Shot's a square of Chicago—fit it into the text.
Joggle niggers and Mexicans, some of them dead 'uns,
And for spirit, bring in a few battles where reddens
The smoke of proud guns, for your richest of gravies
Is the sauce of Bull Run and the bier of Jeff Davis.
You've done it, my cock, as well as a man
Who is chiefly the slave of his sensations can;
For somehow your genius has a habit of shying
Whenever your heart is involved. It's most trying.
You can work yourself up to a towering passion
Over landscapes and peoples, but when you would fashion
A love lyric—Puff! and the substance dissolves
And melts out of your fingers. A thousand resolves
To break through with yourself, to have done with objectives,
Leave you still where you were, exploring perspectives.
I declare I could weep, did I not know that life
Is only achieved through a vast deal of strife.
You stand in the midst of a cosmic heterogeny,
But I do not despair of your rearing a progeny.
If chaos at last jelled into a man,
What a big chaos did, your small chaos can.
You were built, you perceive, as the first of your clan.
And, whatever you want, you've got what no other
Poet ever has had. So a truce to the pother!
Bless the man, you've done something as new as tomorrow,
And I cannot consider your case with much sorrow.
Just wait" . . . But, most gently, my old friend interrupted,
"Don't go on, Sir, I beg, I am being corrupted.
Your poets are so diverse. One thing I can say,
Good or bad, they're more various than poets were in my day.
If you've more in your bag, produce them, I pray."

Thus adjured, I remembered the one or two ladies
I'd deserted, and mentally crying "Oh, Hades!
Will they be mad as hops or affect a quite staid ease?
Whichever it is, I shall get a good wigging,

To be kept waiting's always a bit *infra dig*ging.
I must cudgel my brain for a really apt whopper,
Women don't pardon blunders when their *amour propre*
Is in question." But all of the chickens I'd counted,
When I'd tallied them up to a total, amounted
To just nothing at all, for your modern Egeria
Is far too advanced to give way to hysteria.
Approaching the first, I said no woman like her
Had yet been considered. She replied "Oh, you piker!
A poet learns to see, and you need not dissemble.
We will go up at once. Grace, here is your thimble."
Then jumping up quickly from where she was sitting
She quite overturned a little girl's knitting
Who was there by some chance, I'll come back to that later.
Said I to myself, no man living can hate her,
She is what I should call a born fascinator.
Upon reaching my friend–and let me explain
That these scenes in the scene all take place in my brain–
I began with a few neatly turned words on love
As the poet's own bourne, and declared that no glove
Ever fitted a hand with less wrinkling and snugger
Than this theme this poet. Here I noticed her shrug her
Shoulders a little, which was rather upsetting.
However, it may have been only coquetting.
Still I thought it was wise to get on with my tale:
"Our love-poet, *par excellence,* Sara Teasdale,"
I said with a flourish. Now that was a whale
Of a compliment, such things deserve an entail,
'Twas so brilliantly super even if it were true,
And I knew very well 'twas but one of a cue.
"This poet," I went on, "is a great niece of Sappho,
I know not how many 'greats' laid in a row
There should be, but her pedigree's perfectly clear;
You can read it in *Magazine Verse* for the year.
She is also a cousin, a few times removed,
Of dear Mrs. Browning, that last can be proved.
The elder poet hid in a shrouding mantilla
Which she called Portuguese. Was ever trick sillier?
Our Sara is bolder, and feels quite at ease

As herself; in her mind there is nothing to tease.
Dale and valley, the country is hers she traverses,
She has mapped it all out in a bushel of verses.
Sara Teasdale she is—was—for our minnesinger,
Behind her front door, is now Mrs. Filsinger.
A hard question this, for a hand-maid of Muses,
When she's once made a name in cold print which she loses
On taking a husband, the law's masculinity
Would seem to demand a perpetual virginity
For all married poets of the downtrodden sex.
To forfeit the sale of a new volume checks
Even marital ardor, to say nothing of checks.
It's just this sort of thing which so frequently wrecks
The artistic composure, and must surely perplex
Any husband who's not in the class of henpecks.
Still I think the poor man should find some consolation
In two or three volumes of sheer adoration.
It's the price he receives for never imposing
Himself on his wife when the lady's composing.
Under whatever name, the world grows awarer
Every year of the prize we have got here in Sara.
She has no colors, no trumpets, no platforms, no skepticisms,
She has no taste for experiments, and joins in no schisms;
She just sings like a bird, and I think you'll agree
This is clearly the place for the china-berry tree—
With a difference, the bird in that pleasant, arboreal
Importation had three tones, while her repertorial
Range is compassed in one, the reflex amatorial.
She loves in a charming, perpetual way,
As thought it just came when she was distrait,
Or quite occupied in affairs of the day.
Or else, and I think the remark's more acute,
She lives as the flower above a deep root.
Like a dedicate nun, she tells bead after bead
At Matins, Tierce, Vespers. You'd think she'd be treed
Just once in a while to find something to say.
Not at all, she's a vast *catalogue raisonnée*
Of the subject. No one's so completely *au fait*.
Her poetry succeeds, in spite of fragility,

Because of her very remarkable agility.
There is no single stunt in the style amatory
Which is not included in her category,
We may as well take that at once *a priori.*
So easy to her seems the work of creation
She might be just jotting down lines from dictation.
There is nothing green here, each poem's of the ripest.
The income tax lists her as Cupid's own typist.
Of course, it is true that she's not intellectual,
But those poets who are, are so apt to subject you all
To theories and treatises, the whole galvanometry
Of the bardling who thinks verse a sort of geometry.
Now Sara's as easy to read as a slip
On a piece of banana, and there's no need to skip,
For each poem's so peculiarly like every other
You may as well stay where you are and not bother.
She's that very rare compost, the dainty erotic;
Such a mixture can't fail to produce a hypnotic
Effect on the reader, whose keenest sensation
Will consist in a perfect identification
Of himself with the poet, and her sorrows and joys
Become his, while he swings to the delicate poise
Of a primitive passion so nicely refined
It could not bring a blush to the most squeamish mind.
Though the poems, I may add, are all interlined
For the ready perusal of those not too blind.
For Sara, if singer, is also a woman,
I know of no creature more thoroughly human.
If woman, she's also a lady who realizes
That a hidden surprise is the best of surprises.
She seems a white statue awaiting unveiling,
But raised on a platform behind a stout railing
Whence she lures and retires, provoking a nearer
Contact which is promised to be even dearer
If we find we have courage enough not to fear her."
I looked at my subject to find she'd departed,
It's a habit of hers when a party's once started
To vanish unnoticed. My poetess had flown.
Seeing which, I remarked that I'd better postpone

The rest of my discourse. "I think you have shown
The outlines at least, my young cicerone,"
Said my friend. "Have you others? I see the sun's setting.
If you have many more, why we must be getting
On faster." I promised to use all despatch
Which I saw was most needed when I took out my watch.

"There's a child here I've not yet had leisure to mention,
Both she and her mother are worth your attention.
And one or two more I can think of, but most of them
Will not take up much time. After that, there's a host of
them
We'll consider, if you are agreeable, *en masse*."
"You spoke of a child, a child in this class!"
He asked me astonished. "I suppose that betrays me
A fogey indeed, but the thing does amaze me."
"No wonder," I answered, "America's youth
Symbolized with a vengeance as plainest of truth.
The poets I've presented may none of them be
Among the top boughs of that flourishing tree,
The *Genus Poeticus, Anglice-folia,*
Whose flowers have rivaled the greater magnolia,
But no shoot we know of has blossomed so early
As ours, and that makes a distinction clearly.
A ten-year-old child, half elf and half sage,
Where else can you find a poet of her age?
This is no little girl, though the critics preëmpt her
As the essence of childhood, but, *caveat emptor;*
It is easy to say, which is all that they care about,
For where is the critic one can see is aware about
Any essence whatever. This child's no more childhood
Than the wolf was the grandmother for donning her mild
hood.
Hilda Conkling (I see I've forgotten to name her)
Is a greater phenomenon than they would proclaim her.
She is poetry itself, for her slight little soul
Is not yet of a size to encompass the whole
She gives out. Without knowing who really is speaking,
She speaks, and her words fall without the least seeking.

There's no need for allowances, the poems that she writes
May be certainly reckoned among the high lights
Of their *genre,* and although I'm no hyperbolist
I say flatly this child is the first Imagist.
But you will remember that Jove sometimes naps,
And the baby in Hilda not seldom entraps
The genius. But what of that! Such handicaps
May be reckoned as *nil* in the total, perhaps.
If she sometimes descends from Parnassus crescendo
To play with her dolls, why, the greatest of men do
The same in their fashion, and no innuendo
Need follow so natural a way of proceeding.
It is merely the little girl in her stampeding.
Since she's neither a freak, nor a ghoul, nor a Houyhnhnm,
We may thank the good fate which has left her a minim
Of usual childhood—but, bless my soul, what
Has become of her now, she was here, was she not?"
"Oh," her mother joined in, "she ran off to catch
A white kitten she saw. There's no fear of a scratch,
She understands kittens." "Did she hear what I'm saying?"
I asked. "I am really afraid she was paying
But little attention, her fingers were drumming
In time to some sort of a tune she was humming.
Now she and the kitten are disposed to agree,
We have lost her, I fear, so you'll have to take me."

Now what can a gallant gentleman do
On receiving a challenge so couched? *"Entre nous,*
I think you're delightful," I said in aside,
"Your verses have made many poets emerald-eyed.
What you seem to do without turning a hair
Is just the one trick makes the less gifted swear.
Who would copy you, digs for himself a fine snare."
But when a man whispers inside of his mind
He can scarcely expect an onlooker to find
His abstraction amusing. My friend woke me smartly
From my silent flirtation by announcing, quite tartly,
"The child, as you've proved, is a *lusus naturæ,*
A verdict I'm sure any qualified jury

Would agree to at once were her case up for trial.
Why even our feminophobe on the *Dial*
Never dared to bring forward young ladies of ten
As serious rivals to middle-aged men.
Poor Margaret Fuller, how she would have doted on
Your remarkable age, and how happily floated on
Its dawn-colored currents and all its forensical
Preoccupations! We were so common-sensical.
Perhaps we were tainted with some sentimentalism,
But your *beau ideal* seems to be elementalism.
I can cap you, however, by mentioning one
Poet who never grew up, your friend, Miss Dickinson."
"The comparison's just," I declared. "As to Hilda,
Your juxtaposition need never bewilder
The admirers of either. One you failed quite to scotch;
The other, I think, you should certainly watch."
"Well, well," he said hastily, "but I protest
At sitting all night with you and your quest.
Who's the next, and be quick." As if riding a race
I dashed at my subject: "Let me introduce Grace
Conkling, no one is so handy at brooks,
They chatter and spatter through all of her books.
And her fish—every angler is on tenterhooks
Lest they should escape him. The same with her birds.
My land, what a fluttering they make! Quite two thirds
Of her work is concerned with them, so that her pages
Present the appearance of so many cages.
Then mountains—yes, mountains—she crams them in too.
The little near-by ones all green, and all blue
The more distant peaks. She is great on perspective.
And whatever her theme, she is always selective.
Take her love-poems, for instance, she serves, piping hot,
A lyric of passion, and chooses the spot
For its setting somewhere where you go in a yacht:
South America, Mexico, wherever not,
So there is a garden with grapefruit, kumquat,
A score or two peach-trees and some apricot.
For her flowers, one should be an encyclopedia.
No less an abundance of knowledge the medea

Could possibly be to surmount and recount 'em.
(Here I've got in a mess. There's no rhyme except 'fount.'
Hem!
Take no notice I beg of the exceedingly thin ice
I'm skating on; if you find my heroine nice,
Which she certainly must be to all masculine eyes,
I care not a whit with what names I am twitted.
On account of my subject, the claim's manumitted.)
Now turn back six lines, so you capture the gist
Of my tale where I left it—I will jot down a list
Of a few of her flowers which must not be missed.
There's magnolia first, of the kind grandiflora,
With its moons of blooms scenting the air where Señora
Jimenez, Alcaro—take your pick, I would banish
Such names if I could, but the Señora's Spanish—
Walks under daturas whose cups of perfume
Hang above her, with jasmine so thick there's scant room
To pass down the path to the beds where the lilies
Are standing together in a stately and still ease.
The dates are in blossom, or is it in fruit?—
One should not make a list unless able to do't,
And this Mexican flora trips anyone's foot—
Never mind, it's enough that the lady's en route
To a clandestine tryst, when a tingling *sol fa*
Shakes the garden to life, for he's brought his guitar.
I acknowledge I've taken a few autocratic
Liberties with my author, who's never dramatic,
But the garden alone seemed to me miasmatic,
With its scents and its sounds, but for the rest solus.
If we must not embroider, why she must parole us.
Since I've given no promise, and the scene, without doubt,
Should have been there although the poet left it out,
It shall stand in my version—and there's a night-piece.
But what of the mornings, as soft as crêpe-lisse
Till the mists burn away with the sun and leave staring
A peacock-hued dome, with gilt cornices, flaring
Above an old market-place crowded with fig trees
And the flame-colored awnings of booths where the big
trees

Make a thunder-cloud shade, and Giuseppe, Felice,
(These Mexican names make our own sound so screechy!)
Are vociferously selling figs, melons, and grapes?
It's the rainbow gone mad in all colors and shapes.
There are smoky blue plums and raw-striped cucumbers,
Red slits of pomegranates, gold loquats, the umbers
Of nuts and the green of almonds not yet husked;
Huge elephant baskets of flowers all betusked
With long sprays of yucca—the poet has attacked us
With all of her armory at once—spears of cactus
Shoot out between passion vines spreading their discus-
Like blooms just above a bouquet of hibiscus.
The trees, I observe, are all festooned with monkeys,
Long necklaces of them, and the square's choked with donkeys.
The bell in the peacock dome clatters and clangs,
Parakeets flash through leaves like so many whiz-bangs
On the fourth of July, there are orchids exploding
New flowers each minute over hand-carts unloading
Bread-fruit and bananas, and the hot, dry sirocco
Tips it all to a sparkle so bright and rococo
The book should be bound in a purple morocco
If the contents and cover were made to agree,
This dismal sage-green is a catastrophe;
But what publisher thinks of aught else but his fee.
I have written my best, but it's so multiplex I can
Never compete with her when she's on Mexican
Horticulture, zoölogy, and I don't know what all,
Unless I've Gray's *Botany* handy, and Nuttall,
With Wilson and Chapman close by on the table;
And as to the speech, it is just so much Babel
To me if each word is not tagged with a label
In good easy English. Well, no matter for that,
I've told you she's got every atmosphere pat.
She's as happy with pine-trees and an orchard of apples
And the clouds which a 'slender sky' scatters and dapples
Over grass-and-stone hillsides, as with lotus-brimmed fountains,
And I'll swear that no poet has done better with mountains.

Her flickers, and veeries, and finches, and thrushes
Are as good as her nightingale hid in a bush is,
And when she would sing of the Old Mohawk Trail
I toss up my hat with a shout of 'All hail!
Troubadour of New England, who knows that white pine is
Her very soul's self,' and I write in gold, 'Finis!' "

"Dear me," said my friend, "so you think she's the laureate
Of poor old New England." "If there's any one bore I hate
More than another," I answered, "it's the man
Who pretends to see farther than anyone can.
Considering we've Robinson, Miss Lowell, and Frost,
Such a statement were rash. I'm afraid you have lost
Just the shade I intended; there's a difference, be sure,
Between a poet laureate and a troubadour."
"The point is well taken," he admitted at once.
"Was I laureate or troubadour? The distinction confronts
Me now rather unpleasantly. For, was I able
To go her one better in my famous *Fable?*
That I loved my New England you'll find by the space
I devoted to her in that book. Face to face
With her new poets, I'm wondering who'll win in the race.
Am I in the lead since they've quickened the pace?
I'm beginning to doubt it as far as mere praise
Counts at least, I was Frost and she mixed, hence my bays,
If I really deserved any. But with this poetess
I find myself back on old ground, none the less
Delightful, be sure, and there is a slight change
In her manner, I do detect that, but her range
Does not carry me out of the depth of my sympathy."
"The next fellow will," was my succinct reply.
"Alfred Kreymborg, deft master of the oddest machine
Made of strings and of gut which I ever have seen.
A hybrid of sorts yclept mandolute.
Queer instrument? Very. His voice is the flute
Playing over the strings, and his songs epigrams
Tinkled up into rhythm. Oh, yes, they're called shams
By the public at large, but who wants a large public?
Kreymborg's manner to his is a kiss and a kick.

He's the monkey of poetry who climbs on a stick,
But that's only his way to conceal by a trick
The real truth he has. Oh, he's impolitic
To a fault, but the fellow is no lunatic,
Nor mountebank either, though some people think
He has squeezed not two drops of his blood in his ink
And regard him as jester with more than suspicion.
The fact is he's an untaught, but natural musician.
His poems and his tunes come straight out of his pestle
And fall as they will. Unbaked clay's not a vessel,
However, and though I believe he has made
Some excellent poems, that's not really his trade,
Which I grieve to admit consists largely of bluffing.
The gems in his books are half smothered in stuffing.
He's an ironist pure, but I can't call him simple;
More than one of his efforts may be classed as a pimple
On the fair face of poetry, but others delight us
As much for their beauty as the first kind affright us
By their horrible ugliness, wry-formed and waxy.
He's a man flinging queer little toys from a taxi.
If you scrabble round fast enough you may pick a good one,
But the chances are ten to one you'll get a wooden
Contraption of rude, creaky springs, badly gilt,
Just words nailed together haphazard, no lilt,
And no sense you can find. It's a real 'hunt the slipper'
To read what he writes, and you may come a tripper
Or you may win a prize, that's the whole proposition.
How does it affect his poetic position?
I tell you quite frankly I feel at a loss
For an answer to give you, we might try a toss
Or leave it in peace on the lap of the Gods.
To put it quite plainly, dear Sir, what's the odds?
When we come to his singing, it's another concern.
However on earth did the chap come to learn
Of those strange sweeping chords and that odd whispered singing
Which cleaves to the heart and sets the nerves stinging,
And where did he find his sawed-off mandolin
Or guitar, or banjo? Good Lord, it's a sin

When there is such an instrument no one else knows it,
But the luckier for him, I say, and therefore—*prosit!*
The poems he writes down never end, scarce begin,
If the truth must be told; in the music, a thin
Silver chord holds a something, a glitter of fable,
And the tale and its moral lie strung on a cable,
Half-music, half-thought, but what we have heard
Is more echo than music, more music than word.
He's a poet in the core of him, a bit of a clown,
And two-thirds of a vagabond drifting round town,
Seeing whimsical nothings at every street corner.
A lover possessed, an inveterate scorner,
Engaged in a pulling of plums like Jack Horner—
There's the man, Alfred Kreymborg." "We had no counter-
part
To your monkey-musician. Do you call the thing art
You've been talking about?" The old gentleman's tone
Betrayed just a trace of annoyance. "I've shown
You a figure, make of him whatever you can,
To tag him as this or that's not in my plan.
You asked me to give you each phase of the time."
"And I could not stand Whitman because he'd no rhyme!"
He gasped. "You may banish all verse that's harmonious,
But it's not so far short of being felonious
When you ask us to substitute for it the simious.
You will find what that means in the pages of Linnæus.
We raised roses, but you seem to cultivate zinnias,
Not to call your verse anything more ignominious."
"You forget," I reminded him, "his mandolute;
To judge him without it is hardly acute."
The old gentleman suddenly turned and snapped "Non-
sense!"
"On the contrary, Sir, it's the *sine quâ non* sense.
We have Lindsay, a voice; and Kreymborg, an instrument."
"Is your poetry a junk-shop? I am now quite convinced
you meant
All this as hoaxing." I tried to protest.
He went on in a stream like a person possessed:
"A junk-shop indeed! There is Frost, a dim Buddha

Set high on a shelf; there is Sandburg, a cruder
Carved god of some sort, neither English nor Gothic—
Assyrian, Egyptian, perhaps—a huge Thothic
Sacerdotal presentment placed over the door;
There are two Chinese vases, a spy-glass, three score
Or so dog's-eared books, flowerpots, and a spinet,
This odd jumble's Miss Lowell; there's a little green linnet
Hung up in a cage, Sara Teasdale, I think;
And a battered old desk all bespattered with ink,
That's Masters; and just up above is a palette
Smudged over with paint, that is Fletcher; a mallet
Thrown down on a heap of new books which it crushes
Is Aiken; and there is a bundle of rushes
Just picked and brought in to the shop to set off
A stone-lantern—'H. D.'; just behind is a trough
To water poor readers, it's not overflowing
But full to the brim and seems always just going
To spill, but that never quite happens, you guess
At once this is Robinson; in a recess
Just under the counter are two or three chromos
Of tropical scenes, Mrs. Conkling is those;
And the blocks which you see have just come from the gilder
I need hardly tell you are your precious Hilda,
They are specially made to build Castles in Spain.
There's your junk-shop of poets, and I tell you again
I don't like to be quizzed." Poor old soul, he was furious,
But when once convinced his suspicions were spurious
He was eager as ever. "For," said I, "there's no quarrel,
The shop sign's a wreath and it's possibly laurel."
"Perhaps I have half a suspicion of that
Myself," he smiled broadly, "now give tit for tat,
And confound all my quondam ridiculous ires
With something so pleasant and . . ."

"The Untermeyers!"

The shout which I gave cut his sentence in two,
And we lost the last part in the hullabaloo
I made as I served up my marital dish.

"Two poets, and between them whatever you wish.
If they haven't the depth, they've more range than the
Brownings,
It runs all the way from complexes to clownings,
With love songs so frank they pursue more than follow man
Being made on the pattern approved by King Soloman.
(My so spelling that name is nothing to look solemn on,
I've a black-letter precedent one might write a column on.
Orthographical pedantry was not in King Solomon.)
At least hers are, a perfectly natural law
Vide Freud, D. H. Lawrence, and George Bernard Shaw.
For woman possesses, it seems, an atomic
Attraction for man, and his serio-comic
Pretense of pursuit is a masculine blind
To keep up his prestige within his own mind.
If the lady appears to be fleeing, the stroke
Is a masterly one and just her little joke.
But when this same woman, in some bright confection
Of boudoir attire, gives herself to reflection
And writes down her heart in a freak of exposure,
The result will most certainly jar the composure
Of elderly persons brought up more demurely,
While youth will retire, with doors locked securely,
And read what to them is a gorgeous display
Of Paradise opened on visiting day.
The best gifts of our time are these pure revelations
Of facts as they are in all human relations
With no understatements or exaggerations.
And the West is the East, with the puritan night
Swallowed up in a gush of approaching daylight—
At least, so our cherished delusion mistakes it,
And since everything is as man's attitude makes it,
What the Orient knew we are learning again
For the next generation to laud with 'Amen!'
In this wise are the poems of Jean Untermeyer,
Though the whole of her output takes less than a quire
Of paper to hold it. Not at all so with Louis,
He's as rich and eclectic as a bowl of chop suey.
If his wife plays a timbrel, he plays a ram's horn,

His ardor for worship is never outworn,
One of Joshua's soldiers, protecting his candle
With thc pitcher he eagerly holds by the handle,
Tramping his turn at a long sentry-go
Round and round the high walls of our new Jericho;
Or, again, on a harp which, if slightly archaic,
Has lost nothing in tone or in timbre since Hebraic
Psalmists once plucked it in stern exhortations
Before kneeling hosts of the wandering nations.
Through the streets of today, with his shoulders set square,
He walks, full of business, and yet one's aware
Of a something he sees which surrounds and encloses
His vision, he might be just gazing on Moses
Descending the mountain, but his tables of stone
Have Marx written on them and Debs, while his own
Name has no place at all, and that's characteristic;
His ego's too eager to be egotistic.
When everything beckons, why sit at home brooding
On the opposite wall; he's no taste for secluding
Himself or his interests, and they're only controlled
By the small slice of time which he happens to hold.
Punctiliously present in this exact moment,
His dates began when he learnt what 'proximo' meant.
No glance of his, scanning the past, finds it prizable,
The only real worth is in the realizable;
Neither history nor legend induce him to vary
His perfect allegiance to the mere temporary.
When he takes on himself the role of appraiser,
His words spout and gush like a Yellowstone geyser,
At least for the poet whose political ways err
From those of society, an apt paraphraser
Of the poems of such men, he becomes a sharp razor
To others, no hint of the sham sentimental
Escapes his smooth blade, and he is not gentle
With the scenes or the poses in which 'temperamental'
Poets indulge, and he's scarcely parental
To persons with leanings toward the transcendental.
His dictums, it's true, are less poignant than plenty,
And do not rank too high among *cognoscenti*,

Who are usually college boys not quite turned twenty.
He has a blind spot: he cannot keep his eye on
A world without man. Why, a fresh dandelion
Is nothing to him without someone to pick it,
Observe it alone and he hands you the ticket
For exit at once, and it's not a return check.
He hopes in this way to act as a stern check
On all those untoward imaginative flights
In which he is sure he descries signal-lights
Of a shower of earth-wrecking meteorites.
Now why should a man who is so pyrotechnical
Find a mere meteoric display apoplectical,
While many consider it a beautiful spectacle?
That's a matter for wonder; but, speaking of rockets,
He carries them round like small change in his pockets.
A touch and they're off, and the whiz and the flare
And the burst of bright balls are quite his affair.
What a crackle of rhymes! They go off like red crackers
Beneath a tin pan. And there are some whackers
Exploding at intervals when you least expect them,
And long trailing assonances set to connect them.
His wit is a pin-wheel which at first jerks and spits
Then whirls suddenly round as though ten thousand fits
Were in it, and all is one sparkling gyration
In every known manner of versification.
But the best of his fire-works comprise his set-pieces
Which are really so many bright-colored *esquisses.*
(Please pardon a liberty in pronunciation.
Le mot juste, I believe, needs no justification,
Even when it involves a slight deviation
From the speech of a friendly but jaw-breaking nation,
Who, I trust, will regard this brief explanation
In the light of a willing, though painful, libation.)
But how I run on! To return to my symbol:
A bare two or three poets have ever been nimble
Enough to depict their confrères and show them
Drawn to scale in each feature as all their friends know
    them.
Just glance at them now, each hung on a hook

Awaiting the match—Ftt! Presto! Now, look—
How they flicker and burn, each one to his trick:
There are Robinson's quatrains, Frost's long, pliant stick
Of blank verse which he carries when taking his walks,
And Sandburg with his suitcase all crammed full of talks
With murderers and hobos and such worth-while gentry;
Here is Lindsay retreating at speed to the entry
To stand on the stair and harangue new arrivals
With the very same stunts they employ at revivals,
While Amy Lowell, close by the library door,
Announces her theories and tries hard to score
More disciples than Lindsay; though, with his and her
    medium,
It's a matter of choice which produces least tedium.
Whoever the poet and whatever his foibles,
Even dull ones like—well, I won't say—are enjoyables
When he touches them up to a glare with his slow-match.
At this sort of thing everyone else is no match
For him, and the best simply rank as '—and Other Poets.'
A terrible fellow with his black line to smother poets,
And that line is become the poetical plank
From which he dives into posterity's tank.
It's a curious conceit, and his one bit of swank,
To flaunt himself under a long line of blank.
But what poet, quick or dead, would dare to decline
An immortal existence conferred by one line.
Take it then, Untermeyer, irrepressible Louis,
And observe, as you touch it, that the leaves are still dewy.
That dew is the proof that it's not bombazine,
One has to be careful with a housewife like Jean.
The lady, you know, is a trifle impulsive,
And I should not like my gift to receive a propulsive
Reception. For fame's rather like millinery,
Today it's a blossom, tomorrow a cherry,
The day after, glass flowers in some cemetery.
But who, even in fame, would remain stationary?
Not you certainly, Louis, your deepest devotion
Is involved in this question, but you have no notion
How nearly you come to perpetual motion."

Here I ended abruptly. When he's carried a man
To the center of movement, the historian
Does well to leave off. I left off therefore.
My old friend somewhat wearily asked, "Is there more?"
"A few odds and ends, but not much you need heed,"
I replied. "Very well, run them over at speed,"
He commanded.

Now if he had wielded a bludgeon
I could not have more quickly obeyed, no curmudgeon
Could have forced my direction more surely than he did.
His imperious courtesy was all that I needed
To start off again with my tale: "The expatriates
Come next," I began, "but the man who expatiates
Upon them must go all yclad in cold steel
Since these young men are both of them most *difficile,*
And each is possessed of a gift for satire.
Their forked barbs would pierce any usual attire.
In order of merit, if not of publicity,
I will take Eliot first, though it smacks of duplicity
To award Ezra Pound the inferior place
As he simply won't run if not first in a race.
Years ago, 'twould have been the other way round,
With Eliot a rather bad second to Pound.
But Pound has been woefully free with the mustard
And so occupied has quite ruined his custard.
No poems from his pen, just spleen on the loose,
And a man who goes on in that way cooks his goose.
T. S. Eliot's a very unlike proposition,
He has simply won through by process of attrition.
Where Pound played the fool, Eliot acted the wiseacre;
Eliot works in his garden, Pound stultifies his acre.
Eliot's always engaged digging fruit out of dust;
Pound was born in an orchard, but his trees have the rust.
Eliot's mind is perpetually fixed and alert;
Pound goes off anywhere, anyhow, like a squirt.
Pound believes he's a thinker, but he's far too romantic;
Eliot's sure he's a poet when he's only pedantic.
But Eliot has raised pedantry to a pitch,

While Pound has upset romance into a ditch.
Eliot fears to abandon an old masquerade;
Pound's one perfect happiness is to parade.
Eliot's learning was won at a very great price;
What Pound calls his learning he got in a trice.
Eliot knows what he knows, though he cannot digest it;
Pound knows nothing at all, but has frequently guessed it.
Eliot builds up his essays by a process of massing;
Pound's are mostly hot air, what the vulgar call 'gassing.'
Eliot lives like a snail in his shell, pen protruding;
Pound struts like a cock, self-adored, self-deluding.
Pound's darling desire is his ego's projection;
Eliot tortures his soul with a dream of perfection.
Pound's an ardent believer in the value of noise;
Eliot strains every nerve to attain a just poise.
Each despises his fellows, for varying reasons;
Each one is a traitor, but with different treasons.
Each has left his own country, but Pound is quite sick of it,
While for Eliot's sojourn, he is just in the nick of it.
Pound went gunning for trouble, and got it, for cause;
Eliot, far more astute, has deserved his applause.
Each has more brain than heart, but while one man's a
critic
The other is more than two-thirds tympanitic.
Both of them are book-men, but where Eliot has found
A horizon in letters, Pound has only found Pound.
Each man feels himself so little complete
That he dreads the least commerce with the man in the
street;
Each imagines the world to be leagued in a dim pact
To destroy his immaculate taste by its impact.
To conceive such a notion, one might point out slyly,
Would scarcely occur to an author more highly
Original; such men seldom bother their wits
With outsiders at all, whether fits or misfits.
Where they are, whom they see, is a matter of sheer
Indifference to a poet with his own atmosphere
To exist in, and such have no need to be preachy
Anent commonplaceness since they can't write a *cliché*—

In toto, at least, and it's *toto* that grounds
All meticulous poets like the Eliots and Pounds.
Taking up Eliot's poetry, it's a blend of intensive
And elegant satire with a would-be offensive
Kind of virulent diatribe, and neither sort's lacking
In the high type of polish we demand of shoe-blacking.
Watteau if you like, arm in arm with Laforgue,
And both of these worthies laid out in a morgue.
The poems are expert even up to a vice,
But they're chilly and dead like corpses on ice.
Now a man who's reluctant to heat his work through,
I submit, is afraid of what that work will do
On its own, with its muscles and sinews unfrozen.
Something, I must think, which he would not have chosen.
Is there barely a clue here that the action of heat
Might reveal him akin to the man in the street?
For his brain—there's no doubt that is up on a steeple,
But his heart might betray him as one of the people.
A fearful dilemma! We can hardly abuse him
For hiding the damaging fact and excuse him
If it really be so, and we've more than a hint of it,
Although I, for one, like him better by dint of it.
Since the poet's not the half of him, we must include
The critical anchorite of his *Sacred Wood.*
'This slim duodecimo you must have your eye on
If you'd be up to date,' say his friends. He's a sly one
To have chosen this format—the book's heavy as iron.
I'm acutely aware that its grave erudition
Is quite in the line of a certain tradition,
That one which is commonly known as tuition.
To read it is much like a lengthy sojourning
In at least two or three institutions of learning.
But, being no schoolboy, I find I'm not burning
For this sort of instruction, and vote for adjourning.
What the fellow's contrived to stuff into his skull
May be certainly classed as a pure miracle,
But the way he imparts it is terribly dull.
This may not be fair, for I've only begun it,
And one should not pronounce on a book till one's done it,

But I've started so often, in so many places,
I think, had there been any livelier spaces
I must have encountered at least one of those
Before falling, I say it with shame, in a doze.
We must take Ezra Pound from a different angle:
He's a belfry of excellent chimes run to jangle
By being too often and hurriedly tugged at,
And even, when more noise was wanted, just slugged at
And hammered with anything there was lying round.
Such delicate bells could not stand so much Pound.
Few men have to their credit more excellent verses
Than he used to write, and even his worse is
Much better than most people's good. He'd a flair
For just the one word indispensably there,
But which few could have hit on. Another distinction
Was the way he preserved fledgeling poets from extinction.
Had he never consented to write when the urge
To produce was not on him, he'd have been on the verge
Of a great reputation by now, but his shoulder
Had always its chip, and Ezra's a scolder.
Off he flew, giving nerves and brain up to the business
In a crowing excitement not unmixed with dizziness,
Whenever he could get any sort of newspaper
To lend him a column and just let him vapor.
But while he was worrying his gift of invention
For adequate means to ensure the prevention
Of anyone's getting what he had not got,
His uncherished talent succumbed to dry rot.
When, after the battle, he would have employed her,
He learnt, to his cost, that he had destroyed her.
Now he does with her ghost, and the ghosts of the hosts
Of troubadours, minstrels, and kings, for he boasts
An acquaintance with persons of whose very names
I am totally ignorant, likewise their fames.
The foremost, of course, is Bertrand de Born,
He's a sort of pervasively huge leprechaun
Popping out from Pound's lines where you never expect
him.
He is our poet's chief lar, so we must not neglect him.

There is Pierre de Maensac, and Pierre won the singing—
Where or how I can't guess, but Pound sets his fame ringing
Because he was *dreitz hom* (whatever that is)
And had De Tierci's wife; what happened to his
We don't know, in fact we know nothing quite clearly,
For Pound always treats his ghosts cavalierly.
There is John Borgia's bath, and be sure that he needed it;
Aurunculeia's shoe, but no one much heeded it.
There's a chap named Navighero and another Barabello,
Who prods a Pope's elephant; and one Mozarello;
Savairic Mauleon—Good Lord, what a dance
Of impossible names! First I think we're in France,
Then he slides in Odysseus, and Eros, and Atthis—
But I'm not to be fooled in my Greek, that's what that is.
Yet, look, there's Italian sticking out in italics
And French in plain type, the foreign vocalics
Do give one the feeling of infinite background,
When it's all just a trick of that consummate quack, Pound,
To cheat us to thinking there's something behind it.
But, when nothing's to find, it's a hard job to find it.
The tragedy lies in the fact that the man
Had a potentiality such as few can
Look back to or forward to; had he but kept it,
There's no bar in all poetry but he might have leapt it.
Even now, I believe, if he'd let himself grow,
He might start again . . ." "We will have no 'although'
In your gamut of poets. Your man is a victim
Of expatriation, and, as usual, it's licked him.
It has happened more times than I care to reflect,
And the general toll is two countries' neglect."
The old gentleman sighed. "I presume that you've finished,"
He went on at last. "The ranks are diminished,"
I answered, "but still there remain one or two
Whose names, at the least, I must pass in review.

"There's William Rose Benét, his poems have no beaters
In their own special *genre;* he's a wonder with meters,
A sleight-of-hand artist, and one of his mysteries
Is his cabinet trick with all the world's histories.

There's Bodenheim, trowel in hand, bent on laying
A tessellate floor with the words he is saying.
Squares of marble, moss-agate, and jade, and carnelian,
Byzantium *in pleno,* never Delphic nor Delian.
A perfect example of contemporaneity,
But with too little force and too much femineity.
The man's a cascade of verbose spontaneity.
Except when he's giving Advice, there he shines
And La Fontaine plays hide and seek in his lines.
As a maker of Fables, no one ever quarrels
With his style, and old Æsop must look to his laurels.
There's another young man who strums a clavier
And prints a new poem every third or fourth year.
Looking back, I don't know that anything since
Has delighted me more than his *Peter Quince.*
He has published no book and adopts this as pose,
But it's rather more likely, I think, to suppose
The particular gift he's received from the Muses
Is a tufted green field under whose grass there oozes
A seeping of poetry, like wind through a cloister;
On occasion it rises, and then the field's moister
And he has a poem if he'll trouble to bale it,
Address it to *Poetry,* and afterwards mail it.
His name, though the odds overbalance the evens
Of those who don't know it as yet's Wallace Stevens,
But it might be John Doe for all he seems to care—
A little fine work scattered into the air
By the wind, it appears, and he quite unaware
Of the fact, since his motto's a cool *'laisser-faire.'*
There's Edna Millay with her *Aria da Cap-*
O'h, she dealt all society a pretty sharp rap
With that bauble of hers, be it drama or fable,
Which I certainly trust won't be laid on the table
In my time. Her *Bean-Stalk* is a nice bit of greenery,
For one of her charms is her most charming scenery,
Few can handle more deftly this sort of machinery.
But I must call a halt, or your brain will be flooded
With big poets, and little poets, and poets not yet budded."
"Have you really so many?" my old friend desired

To know. "If you count all the ones who've aspired,
I could go on all night. You see we have got
A Renaissance on." "Dear me, I forgot,"
He remarked somewhat dryly. "We were not renaissant,
But also I note we were far less complacent
Than you seem to be, and this beggar-my-neighbor
Game you all indulge in was no part of our labor."
"No," I told him, "you played on a pipe and a tabor;
We go girt with a shield and drawing a saber.
And yet you, with Miranda . . ." I talked to the swell
Of the wide-running river, to a clock-striking bell.
There was no one beside me. A wave caught the sedge
Of the bank and went ruffling along its soft edge.
Behind me a motor honked twice, and the bridges
Glared suddenly out of the dusk, twinkling ridges
Notched into the dim river-line. Wind was whirling
The plane-trees about, it sent the waves curling
Across one another in a chuckle of laughter—
And I recollect nothing that happened thereafter.
Who my gentleman was, if you hazard a guess,
I will tell you I know nothing more, nothing less,
Than I here have set forth. For I never have met him
From that day to this, or I should have beset him
With questions, I think. My unique perseverance
Kept me haunting the river for his reappearance,
Armed with two or three books which might serve as a
primer
To point my remarks, for I am no skimmer,
When I push at a wheel it must go or I'll break it,
Once embarked on a mission I never forsake it.
Did he guess my intention and think he'd enough
Of me and my poets, a sufficient rebuff;
But I've never believed he went off in a huff.
Did I dream him perhaps? Was he only a bluff
Of the past making sport with my brain? But that's stuff!
Take it what way you like, if he were a specter
Then the ghosts of old poets have received a correcter
Account than they had of us, and may elect a
Prize winner and vote over post-prandial nectar.

Suppose that, before awarding the prize,
The poets had determined to sift truth from lies
And had sent an ambassador down to enquire
Whose flames were cut tinsel and whose were real fire.
Selecting a man once employed in the trade,
They had only to wait the report that he made
And discuss it at *al fresco* lunch in the shade
Of some cloudy and laurel-embowered arcade.
Supposing it happened that their emissary
Determined to take me as a tutelary
Genius to guide him, and after he'd pumped me
Of all that I knew, quite naturally dumped me
And returned whence he came. You call this bizarre?
But then, after all, so many things are!
If it were so, at least the conclave knows who's who,
And will see there's no reason at all to pooh-pooh.
I, for one, am most eager to know what they'll do.
Aren't you?

H. L. MENCKEN OF BALTIMORE became literary editor of the *Smart Set* in 1908. This monthly magazine was owned by the dubious Colonel Mann of *Town Topics* and had a frivolous cover and cheap paper; but the monthly articles of Mencken and of the dramatic critic, George Jean Nathan, began to attract attention.

The effect of Mencken's criticism was startling to the young people who had been brought up in the Howells era. Howells had tried very hard to be hospitable to new talent from everywhere, but he had himself kept quite close to the genteel tradition. Mencken had the temerity to put his foot through the genteel tradition, and it suddenly turned out that the spell no longer held. The cobwebs dropped away, and we were able to look out across the country and to see what was actually being produced in the way of interesting work—which seemed scarcely at any point to coincide with the kind of thing admired by our most impressive critics, such as W. C. Brownell. There were crude naturalistic novelists writing about the West, like Dreiser and Frank Norris; a romantic of the primitive like Jack London, who wrote about the Yukon and the Klondike and the Oakland water-front; humorists like George Ade, who were turning American slang into a compressed and pungent speech; radical pamphleteers headed by Upton Sinclair, himself as well-informed as a reporter and as passionate as a poet; solitary, gifted Middle Westerners of the type of Ed Howe, who had stuck to their little cities in the role of the local heretic; San Francisco Bohemians like Ambrose Bierce, who shot up the town in the local newspapers; Southerners like Miss Reese and Cabell, who, more or less unnoticed by the North, had quietly been cultivating the literary art in cities like Baltimore and Richmond.

All these people Mencken read and tried to give their due. He had something that perhaps none of our literary men had ever had before him: an appetite for American print that was limitless and omnivorous. He read many books, magazines, newspapers, pamphlets, and manuscripts, as they came in to him from all corners of the country; and he used to say that he even enjoyed reading the prospectuses put out by bond houses, because everything written was an attempt to express the aspirations of some human being. He also had a good prose style of a kind to which we were quite unaccustomed, though it was immediately imitated to nausea: a blend of American colloquial speech with a rakish literary English that sounded as if it had come out of old plays of the period of Congreve and Wycherley; and a tone that was humorous and brutal in the combative Germanic manner. By the beginning of the twenties the Mencken who had begun by merely making a few protests and declaring a few emphatic preferences in a quarter of the journalistic world not much frequented by the literary found himself—now, with Nathan, editor as well as critic of the *Smart Set*—a sort of central bureau to which the young looked for tips to guide them in the cultural confusion and to whom almost everyone who was trying to write anxiously brought his efforts. The *Smart Set* was a raffish magazine; but the old magazines with their editors of the type of Richard Watson Gilder were so paralyzed by their publics and their publishers that they could never have let down the bars and given the new American writers a hearing.

The essays on James Huneker and Theodore Dreiser included in this selection came out in *A Book of Prefaces,* which was published in 1917 and represented Mencken's first attempt—though he had already published books on Shaw and on Nietzsche—to put forward his critical point of view in a book.

The appearance of *A Book of Prefaces* was thus the first explicit vindication of the dignity of certain figures, with the tendencies they represented, who had hitherto been rather ill-regarded.

James Huneker, though he came from Philadelphia, belonged to that Bohemian New York which had rather dropped into obscurity since the days of Pfaff's beer-cellar but had persisted and was now reviving, with Luchow's on Fourteenth Street taking the place of Pfaff's. It was here that Huneker liked to hold the floor, and there grew up about him in New York a whole group of critics who had drunk with him or been nourished by his books. Mencken, Nathan, Carl Van Vechten, Paul Rosenfeld, and Lawrence Gilman—all of them had caught from Huneker something of his crispness and color, something of his special electrical version of the Manhattan cosmopolitanism. All loved music as well as literature, and all knew something of painting, as Huneker did. All liked to go to Europe when they could and to bring back the news of its triumphs of the opera, the gallery, the press, the theater, the music-hall, the table. All contributed to stimulate their readers as the older critics had never done to a sense of the marvelous things that the life of art could give, and they differed from the Howells generation in making one feel that no other kind of life was comparable to this. They not only said that art was great, as Charles Eliot Norton would have done, but they proved that they believed it by being willing to run foul of respectable social prejudice, provincial ignorance, academic usage, and puritanical scruple, in the interests of the claims of good art. Mencken's tribute to Huneker really marks one of the stages of a campaign the first battle of which had already been won and to which new recruits were streaming.

But Huneker was mainly a music-lover and he did not

find much in America. It was Mencken who first had the courage to open the Hunekerian pantheon: Nietzsche, Wagner, Ibsen, Huysmans, Richard Strauss, George Moore, etc., to candidates from the United States. The first of these candidates, Dreiser, was now looming to conventional criticism like Grendel in *Beowulf*: a huge, bristling, destructive, and formless monster that every instinct told it to kill. But Mencken knew perfectly how to handle the matter. He had always had a sort of relish for the squalid, semiliterate writing of which so much has been produced in the United States. He amused himself by analyzing and exhibiting specimens of this kind of thing, as in the little piece here included on the prose style of President Harding; and he liked to explore this medium for a record of the sad realities of that common and obscure American life which tried thus to describe its experience. In Dreiser, wrapped up in an integument that sounded superficially like the *Family Herald* (and which must have served as one of the models for the cabmen's-shelter chapter in *Ulysses*), he found a man of first-rate ability; and he managed to spike the worst guns of the enemy by admitting Dreiser's technical faults and exposing them with amiable drollery instead of with indignation. Mencken's study of Dreiser's style reminds us of Mark Twain on Cooper; and, after all, we ask ourselves, does Dreiser really write worse than Cooper? It has been one of the misfortunes of American fiction that American life itself has not always provided an instrument worthy of the interest of its new material. Yet as Cooper has his all-suffusing poetry, so Dreiser has his solemn rhythms. If we can get used to the imprecise language, we can hear in the heavy German cadences a music of the sense of doom at the mercy of material forces which has been stirred in a sensitive and reflective mind at the beginning of the nineteenth century by our sprawling and unkempt and mechanized American industrial life.

The best of Mencken's work as a critic both of literature and of society was certainly done in the days of the *Smart Set*. When he and Nathan, in 1923, started the *American*

Mercury, more elegant and more pretentious, Mencken seemed to become less open-minded. His own prejudices and mannerisms had hardened, and he tended to try to impose them on other writers in the magazine; and he became a little excessively indulgent to writers like Sinclair Lewis whom he himself had helped to create. Like every other good thing in the period of the Boom—like Florida real estate and Lindbergh—the public overdid him. When he made a trip West in the later twenties, he was given the triumphal progress of a candidate for the presidency; and when the movie star Rudolph Valentino became worried about his personal life, he came to Mencken for words of healing as if to an accredited wise man. Mencken's preachings of an equanimous hedonism which involved playing Brahms and drinking beer were followed by the debaucheries of the twenties; and he must have been disgusted by the liberated broker who read *Jurgen* and the *American Mercury* and had etchings of wild geese on his walls.

At any rate, he finally withdrew from this national apotheosis. He resigned from the *American Mercury* in 1933, and has since published a new edition of his work on *The American Language* and a series of autobiographical memoirs which contain some of his best writing.

The essays on Lardner and on the death of Howells came out in *Prejudices, Fifth Series,* of 1926; *A Short View of Gamalielese* was published in the *Nation* of April 27, 1921, and has never been reprinted by Mr. Mencken.

H. L. MENCKEN

THEODORE DREISER

1917

Out of the desert of American fictioneering, so populous and yet so dreary, Dreiser stands up—a phenomenon unescapably visible, but disconcertingly hard to explain. What forces combined to produce him in the first place, and how has he managed to hold out so long against the prevailing blasts—of disheartening misunderstanding and misrepresentation, of Puritan suspicion and opposition, of artistic isolation, of commercial seduction? There is something downright heroic in the way the man has held his narrow and perilous ground, disdaining all compromise, unmoved by the cheap success that lies so inviting around the corner. He has faced, in his day, almost every form of attack that a serious artist can conceivably encounter, and yet all of them together have scarcely budged him an inch. He still plods along in the laborious, cheerless way he first marked out for himself; he is quite as undaunted by baited praise as by bludgeoning, malignant abuse; his later novels are, if anything, more unyieldingly dreiserian than his earliest. As one who has long sought to entice him in this direction or that, fatuously presuming to instruct him in what would improve him and profit him, I may well bear a reluctant and resigned sort of testimony to his gigantic steadfastness. It is almost as if any change in his manner, any concession to what is usual and esteemed, any amelioration of his blind, relentless exercises of *force majeure,* were a physical impossibility. One feels him at last to be authentically no more than a helpless instrument (or victim) of that inchoate flow of forces which he himself is so fond of depicting as at once the answer to the riddle of life, and a riddle ten times more vexing and accursed.

And his origins, as I say, are quite as mysterious as his motive power. To fit him into the unrolling chart of American or even of English fiction is extremely difficult. Save one thinks of H. B. Fuller (whose *With the Procession* and *The Cliff-Dwellers* are still remembered by Huneker, but by whom else?[1]), he seems to have had no forerunner among us, and for all the discussion of him that goes on, he has few avowed disciples, and none of them gets within miles of him. One catches echoes of him, perhaps, in Willa Sibert Cather, in Mary S. Watts, in David Graham Phillips, in Sherwood Anderson, and in Joseph Medill Patterson, but, after all, they are no more than echoes. In Robert Herrick the thing descends to a feeble parody; in imitators further removed to sheer burlesque. All the latter-day American novelists of consideration are vastly more facile than Dreiser in their philosophy, as they are in their style. In the fact, perhaps, lies the measure of their difference. What they lack, great and small, is the gesture of pity, the note of awe, the profound sense of wonder—in a phrase, that "soberness of mind" which William Lyon Phelps sees as the hallmark of Conrad and Hardy, and which even the most stupid cannot escape in Dreiser. The normal American novel, even in its most serious forms, takes color from the national cocksureness and superficiality. It runs monotonously to ready explanations, a somewhat infantile smug-

[1]Fuller's disappearance is one of the strangest phenomena of American letters. I was astonished some time ago to discover that he was still alive. Back in 1899 he was already so far forgotten that William Archer mistook his name, calling him Henry Y. Puller. *Vide* Archer's pamphlet, *The American Language,* New York, 1899. H. L. M.

ness and hopefulness, a habit of reducing the unknowable to terms of the not worth knowing. What it cannot explain away with ready formulae, as in the later Winston Churchill, it snickers over as scarcely worth explaining at all, as in the later Howells. Such a brave and tragic book as *Ethan Frome* is so rare as to be almost singular, even with Mrs. Wharton. There is, I daresay, not much market for that sort of thing. In the arts, as in the concerns of everyday, the American seeks escape from the insoluble by pretending that it is solved. A comfortable phrase is what he craves beyond all things—and comfortable phrases are surely not to be sought in Dreiser's stock.

I have heard argument that he is a follower of Frank Norris, and two or three facts lend it a specious probability. *McTeague* was printed in 1899; *Sister Carrie* a year later. Moreover, Norris was the first to see the merit of the latter book, and he fought a gallant fight, as literary advisor to Doubleday, Page & Co., against its suppression after it was in type. But this theory runs aground upon two circumstances, the first being that Dreiser did not actually read *McTeague,* nor, indeed, grow aware of Norris, until after *Sister Carrie* was completed, and the other being that his development, once he began to write other books, was along paths far distant from those pursued by Norris himself. Dreiser, in truth, was a bigger man than Norris from the start; it is to the latter's unending honor that he recognized the fact instanter, and yet did all he could to help his rival. It is imaginable, of course, that Norris, living fifteen years longer, might have overtaken Dreiser, and even surpassed him; one finds an arrow pointing that way in *Vandover and the Brute* (not printed until 1914). But it swings sharply around in *The Epic of the Wheat.* In the second volume of that incomplete trilogy, *The Pit,* there is an obvious concession to the popular taste in romance; the thing is so frankly written down, indeed, that a play has been made of it, and Broadway has applauded it. And in *The Octopus,* despite some excellent writing, there is a descent to a mysticism so fantastic and preposterous that it quickly passes beyond serious consideration. Norris, in his day, swung even lower—for example, in *A Man's Woman* and in some of his short stories. He was a pioneer, perhaps only half sure of the way he wanted to go, and the evil lures of popular success lay all about him. It is no wonder that he sometimes seemed to lose his direction.

Emile Zola is another literary father whose paternity grows dubious on examination. I once printed an article exposing what seemed to me to be a Zolaesque attitude of mind, and even some trace of the actual Zola manner, in *Jennie Gerhardt;* there came from Dreiser the news that he had never read a line of Zola, and knew nothing about his novels. Not a complete answer, of course; the influence might have been exerted at second hand. But through whom? I confess that I am unable to name a likely medium. The effects of Zola upon Anglo-Saxon fiction have been almost *nil;* his only avowed disciple, George Moore, has long since recanted and reformed; he has scarcely rippled the prevailing romanticism. . . . Thomas Hardy? Here, I daresay, we strike a better scent. There are many obvious likenesses between *Tess of the D'Urbervilles* and *Jennie Gerhardt* and again between *Jude the Obscure* and *Sister Carrie.* All four stories deal penetratingly and poignantly with the essential tragedy of women; all disdain the petty, specious explanations of popular fiction; in each one finds a poetical and melancholy beauty. Moreover, Dreiser himself confesses to an enchanted discovery of Hardy in 1896, three years before *Sister Carrie* was begun. But it is easy to push such a fact too hard, and to search for likenesses and parallels that are really not there. The truth is that Dreiser's points of contact with Hardy might be easily matched by many striking points of difference, and that the fundamental ideas in their novels, despite a common sympathy, are anything but identical. Nor does one apprehend any ponderable result of Dreiser's youthful enthusiasm for Balzac, which antedated his discovery of Hardy by two years. He got from both men a sense of the scope and dignity of the novel; they taught him that a story might be a good one, and yet considerably more than a story; they showed him the essential drama of the commonplace. But that they had more influence in forming his point of view, or even in shaping his technique, than any one of half-a-dozen other gods of those young days—this I scarcely find. In the structure of his novels, and in their manner of approach to life no less, they call up the work of Dostoevsky and Turgenev far more than the work of either of these men—but of all the Russians save Tolstoy (as of Flaubert) Dreiser himself tells us that he was ignorant until ten years after *Sister Carrie.* In his days of preparation, indeed, his reading was so copious and so disorderly that antagonistic influences must have well-nigh neutralized one another, and so left the curious youngster to work out his own method and his own philosophy. Stevenson went down with Balzac, Poe with Hardy, Dumas *fils* with Tolstoy. There were even months of delight in Sienkiewicz, Lew Wallace, and E. P. Roe! The whole repertory of the pedagogues had been fought through in school and college: Dickens, Thackeray, Hawthorne, Washington Irving, Kingsley, Scott. Only Irving and Hawthorne seem to have made deep impressions. "I used to lie under a tree," says Dreiser, "and read *Twice-Told Tales* by the hour. I thought *The Alhambra* was a perfect creation, and I still have a lingering affection for it." Add Bret Harte, George Ebers, William Dean Howells, Oliver Wendell Holmes, and you have a literary stew indeed! . . . But for all its bubbling I see a far more potent influence in the chance discovery of Spencer and Huxley at twenty-three—the year of choosing! Who, indeed, will ever measure the effect of those two giants upon the young men of that era—Spencer with his inordinate meticulousness, his relentless pursuit of facts, his overpowering syllogisms, and Huxley with his devastating agnosticism, his insatiable questionings of the old axioms, above all, his brilliant style? Huxley, it would appear, has been condemned to the scientific hulks, along with bores innumerable and unspeakable; one looks in vain for any appreciation of him in treatises on beautiful letters.[1] And yet the man was a superb artist in works, a

[1]For example, in *The Cambridge History of English Literature,* which runs to fourteen large volumes and a total of nearly 10,000 pages, Huxley receives but a page and a quarter of notice, and his

master-writer even more than a master-biologist, one of the few truly great stylists that England has produced since the time of Anne. One can easily imagine the effect of two such vigorous and intriguing minds upon a youth groping about for self-understanding and self-expression. They swept him clean, he tells us, of the lingering faith of his boyhood—a mediaeval, Rhenish Catholicism;—more, they filled him with a new and eager curiosity, an intense interest in the life that lay about him, a desire to seek out its hidden workings and underlying causes. A young man set afire by Huxley might perhaps make a very bad novelist, but it is a certainty that he could never make a sentimental and superficial one. There is no need to go further than this single moving adventure to find the genesis of Dreiser's disdain of the current platitudes, his sense of life as a complex biological phenomenon, only dimly comprehended, and his tenacious way of thinking things out, and of holding to what he finds good. Ah, that he had learned from Huxley, not only how to inquire, but also how to report! That he had picked up a talent for that dazzling style, so sweet to the ear, so damnably persuasive, so crystal-clear!

But the more one examines Dreiser, either as writer or as theorist of man, the more his essential isolation becomes apparent. He got a habit of mind from Huxley, but he completely missed Huxley's habit of writing. He got a view of woman from Hardy, but he soon changed it out of all resemblance. He got a certain fine ambition and gusto out of Balzac, but all that was French and characteristic he left behind. So with Zola, Howells, Tolstoy, and the rest. The tracing of likenesses quickly becomes rabbinism, almost cabalism. The differences are huge and sprout up in all directions. Nor do I see anything save a flaming up of colonial passion in the current efforts to fit him into a German frame, and make him an agent of Prussian frightfulness in letters. Such bosh one looks for in the *Nation* and the Boston *Transcript,* and there is where one actually finds

remarkable mastery of English is barely mentioned in passing. His two debates with Gladstone, in which he did some of the best writing of the century, are not noticed at all. H. L. M.

it. Even the *New Republic* has stood clear of it; it is important only as material for that treatise upon the Anglo-Saxon under the terror which remains to be written. The name of the man, true enough, is obviously Germanic, he has told us himself, in *A Traveler at Forty,* how he sought out and found the tombs of his ancestors in some little town of the Rhine country. There are more of these genealogical revelations in *A Hoosier Holiday,* but they show a Rhenish strain that was already running thin in boyhood. No one, indeed, who reads a Dreiser novel can fail to see the gap separating the author from these half-forgotten forbears. He shows even less of German influence than of English influence.

There is, as a matter of fact, little in modern German fiction that is intelligibly comparable to *Jennie Gerhardt* and *The Titan,* either as a study of man or as a work of art. The naturalistic movement of the eighties was launched by men whose eyes were upon the theater, and it is in that field that nine-tenths of its force has been spent. "German naturalism," says George Madison Priest, quoting Gotthold Klee's *Grunzüge der deutschen Literaturgeschichte,* "created a new type only in the drama."[1] True enough, it has also produced occasional novels, and some of them are respectable. Gustav Frenssen's *Jörn Uhl* is a specimen: it has been done into English. Another is Clara Viebig's *Das tägliche Brot,* which Ludwig Lewisohn compares to George Moore's *Esther Waters.* Yet another is Thomas Mann's *Buddenbrooks.* But it would be absurd to cite these works as evidences of a national quality, and doubly absurd to think of them as inspiring such books as *Jennie Gerhardt* and *The Titan,* which excel them in everything save workmanship. The case of Mann reveals a tendency that is visible in nearly all of his contemporaries. Starting out as an agnostic realist not unlike the Arnold Bennett of *The Old Wives' Tale,* he has gradually taken on a hesitating sort of romanticism, and in one of his later books, *Königliche Hoheit* (in English, *Royal Highness*), he ends upon a note of sentimentalism borrowed

[1]*A Brief History of German Literature;* New York, Chas. Scribner's Sons, 1909. H. L. M.

from Wagner's *Ring*. Fräulein Viebig has also succumbed to banal and extra-artistic purposes. Her *Die Wacht am Rheim*, for all its merits in detail, is, at bottom, no more than an eloquent hymn to patriotism—the most doggish and dubious of all the virtues. As for Frenssen, he is a parson by trade, and carries over into the novel a good deal of the windy moralizing of the pulpit. All of these German naturalists—and they are the only German novelists worth considering—share the weakness of Zola, their *Stammvater*. They, too, fall into the morass that engulfed *Fécondité*, and make sentimental propaganda.

I go into this matter in detail, not because it is intrinsically of any moment, but because the effort to depict Dreiser as a secret agent of the Wilhelmstrasse, told off to inject subtle doses of *Kultur* into a naïf and pious people, has taken on the proportions of an organized movement. The same critical imbecility which detects naught save a tom-cat in Frank Cowperwood can find naught save an abhorrent foreigner in Cowperwood's creator. The truth is that the trembling patriots of letters, male and female, are simply at their old game of seeing a man under the bed. Dreiser, in fact, is densely ignorant of German literature, as he is of the better part of French literature, and of much of English literature. He did not even read Hauptmann until after *Jennie Gerhardt* had been written, and such typical German moderns as Ludwig Thoma, Otto Julius Bierbaum, and Richard Dehmel remain as strange to him as Heliogabalus.

II

In his manner, as opposed to his matter, he is more the Teuton, for he shows all of the racial patience and pertinacity and all of the racial lack of humor. Writing a novel is as solemn a business to him as trimming a beard is to a German barber. He blasts his way through his interminable stories by something not unlike main strength; his writing, one feels, often takes on the character of an actual siege operation, with tunnelings, drum-fire, assaults in close order, and hand-to-hand fighting. Once, seeking an analogy, I called him the Hindenburg of the novel. If it holds, then *The "Genius"* is his Poland. The field of action bears the aspect, at the end, of a hostile province meticulously brought under the yoke, with every road and lane explored to its beginning, and every crossroads village laboriously taken, inventoried, and policed. Here is the very negation of Gallic lightness and intuition, and of all other forms of impressionism as well. Here is no series of illuminating flashes, but a gradual bathing of the whole scene with white light, so that every detail stands out.

And many of those details, of course, are trivial; even irritating. They do not help the picture; they muddle and obscure it; one wonders impatiently what their meaning is, and what the purpose may be of revealing them with such a precise, portentous air. . . . Turn to page 703 of *The "Genius."* By the time one gets there, one has hewn and hacked one's way through 702 large pages of fine print—97 long chapters, more than 250,000 words. And yet, at this hurried and impatient point, with the *coda* already begun, Dreiser halts the whole narrative to explain the origin, nature, and inner meaning of Christian Science, and to make us privy to a lot of chatty stuff about Mrs. Althea Jones, a professional healer, and to supply us with detailed plans and specifications of the apartment house in which she lives, works her tawdry miracles, and has her being. Here, in sober summary, are the particulars:

1. That the house is "of conventional design."
2. That there is "a spacious areaway" between its two wings.
3. That these wings are "of cream-colored pressed brick."
4. That the entrance between them is "protected by a handsome wrought-iron door."
5. That to either side of this door is "an electric lamp support of handsome design."
6. That in each of these lamp supports there are "lovely cream-colored globes, shedding a soft luster."
7. That inside is "the usual lobby."
8. That in the lobby is "the usual elevator."
9. That in the elevator is the usual "uniformed Negro elevator man."

10. That this Negro elevator man (name not given) is "indifferent and impertinent."

11. That a telephone switchboard is also in the lobby.

12. That the building is seven stories in height.

In *The Financier* there is the same exasperating rolling up of irrelevant facts. The court proceedings in the trial of Cowperwood are given with all the exactness of a parliamentary report in the London *Times*. The speeches of the opposing counsel are set down nearly in full, and with them the remarks of the judge, and after that the opinion of the Appellate Court on appeal, with the dissenting opinions as a sort of appendix. In *Sister Carrie* the thing is less savagely carried out, but that is not Dreiser's fault, for the manuscript was revised by some anonymous hand, and the printed version is but little more than half the length of the original. In *The Titan* and *Jennie Gerhardt* no such brake upon exuberance is visible; both books are crammed with details that serve no purpose, and are as flat as ditchwater. Even in the two volumes of personal record, *A Traveler at Forty* and *A Hoosier Holiday,* there is the same furious accumulation of trivialities. Consider the former. It is without structure, without selection, without reticence. One arises from it as from a great babbling, half drunken. On the one hand the author fills a long and gloomy chapter with the story of the Borgias, apparently under the impression that it is news, and on the other hand he enters into intimate and inconsequential confidences about all the persons he meets en route, sparing neither the innocent nor the obscure. The children of his English host at Bridgely Level strike him as fantastic little creatures, even as a bit uncanny—and he duly sets it down. He meets an Englishman on a French train who pleases him much, and the two become good friends and see Rome together, but the fellow's wife is "obstreperous" and "haughty in her manner" and so "loud-spoken in her opinions" that she is "really offensive"—and down it goes. He makes an impression on a Mlle. Marcelle in Paris, and she accompanies him from Monte Carlo to Ventimiglia, and there gives him a parting kiss and whispers, *"Avril-Fontainebleau"*—and lo, this sweet one is duly spread upon the minutes. He permits himself to be arrested by a fair privateer in Piccadilly, and goes with her to one of the dens of sin that suffragettes see in their nightmares, and cross-examines her at length regarding her ancestry, her professional ethics and ideals, and her earnings at her dismal craft—and into the book goes a full report of the proceedings. He is entertained by an eminent Dutch jurist in Amsterdam—and upon the pages of the chronicle it appears that the gentleman is "waxy" and "a little pedantic," and that he is probably the sort of "thin, delicate, well-barbered" professor that Ibsen had in mind when he cast about for a husband for the daughter of General Gabler.

Such is the art of writing as Dreiser understands it and practices it—an endless piling up of minutiae, an almost ferocious tracking down of ions, electrons, and molecules, an unshakable determination to tell it all. One is amazed by the molelike diligence of the man, and no less by his exasperating disregard for the ease of his readers. A Dreiser novel, at least of the later canon, cannot be read as other novels are read—on a winter evening or summer afternoon, between meal and meal, traveling from New York to Boston. It demands the attention for almost a week, and uses up the faculties for a month. If, reading *The "Genius,"* one were to become engrossed in the fabulous manner described in the publishers' advertisements, and so find oneself unable to put it down and go to bed before the end, one would get no sleep for three days and three nights.

Worse, there are no charms of style to mitigate the rigors of these vast steppes and pampas of narration. Joseph Joubert's saying that "words should stand out well from the paper" is quite incomprehensible to Dreiser; he never imitates Flaubert by writing for *"la respiration et l'oreille."* There is no painful groping for the inevitable word, or for what Walter Pater called "the gipsy phrase"; the common, even the commonplace, coin of speech is good enough. On the first page of *Jennie Gerhardt* one encounters "frank, open countenance," "diffident manner," "helpless poor," "untutored mind," "honest necessity," and half-a-dozen other stand-bys of the second-rate newspaper reporter. In *Sister Carrie* one finds "high noon," "hurrying throng," "unassuming restaurant," "dainty slippers," "high-strung nature," and "cool, calculating world"—all on a few pages. Carrie's sister, Minnie Hanson, "gets" the supper. Hanson himself is "wrapped up" in his child. Carrie decides to enter Storm and King's office, "no matter what." In *The Titan* the word "trig" is worked to death; it takes on, toward the end, the character of a banal and preposterous refrain. In the other books one encounters mates for it—words made to do duty in as many senses as the American verb "to fix" or the journalistic "to secure." . . .

I often wonder if Dreiser gets anything properly describable as pleasure out of this dogged accumulation of threadbare, undistinguished, uninspiring nouns, adjectives, verbs, adverbs, pronouns, participles, and conjunctions. To the man with an ear for verbal delicacies—the man who searches painfully for the perfect word, and puts the way of saying a thing above the thing said—there is in writing the constant joy of sudden discovery, of happy accident. A phrase springs up full blown, sweet and caressing. But what joy can there be in rolling up sentences that have no more life and beauty in them, intrinsically, than so many election bulletins? Where is the thrill in the manufacture of such a paragraph as that in which Mrs. Althea Jones's sordid habitat is described with such inexorable particularity? Or in the laborious confection of such stuff as this, from Book I, Chapter IV, of *The "Genius"*:

The city of Chicago—who shall portray it! This vast ruck of life that had sprung suddenly into existence upon the dank marshes of a lake shore!

Or this from the epilogue to *The Financier:*

There is a certain fish whose scientific name is *Mycteroperca Bonaci,* and whose common name is Black Grouper, which is of considerable value as an afterthought in this connection, and which deserves much to be better known. It is a healthy creature, growing quite regularly to a weight of two hundred and fifty pounds, and living a comfortable, lengthy existence because of its very remarkable ability to adapt itself to conditions. . . .

Or this from his pamphlet, *Life, Art and America:*[1]

Alas, alas! for art in America. It has a hard stubby row to hoe.

But I offer no more examples. Every reader of the Dreiser novels must cherish astounding specimens—of awkward, platitudinous marginalia, of whole scenes spoiled by bad writing, of phrases as brackish as so many lumps of sodium hyposulphite. Here and there, as in parts of *The Titan* and again in parts of *A Hoosier Holiday,* an evil conscience seems to haunt him and he gives hard striving to his manner, and more than once there emerges something that is almost graceful. But a backsliding always follows this phosphorescence of reform. *The "Genius,"* coming after *The Titan,* marks the high tide of his bad writing. There are passages in it so clumsy, so inept, so irritating that they seem almost unbelievable; nothing worse is to be found in the newspapers. Nor is there any compensatory deftness in structure, or solidity of design, to make up for this carelessness in detail. The well-made novel, of course, can be as hollow as the well-made play of Scribe—but let us at least have a beginning, a middle, and an end! Such a story as *The "Genius"* is as gross and shapeless as Brünnhilde. It billows and bulges out like a cloud of smoke, and its internal organization is almost as vague. There are episodes that, with a few chapters added, would make very respectable novels. There are chapters that need but a touch or two to be excellent short stories. The thing rambles, staggers, trips, heaves, pitches, struggles, totters, wavers, halts, turns aside, trembles on the edge of collapse. More than once it seems to be foundering, both in the equine and in the maritime senses. The tale has been heard of a tree so tall that it took two men to see to the top of it. Here is a novel so brobdingnagian that a single reader can scarcely read his way through it. . . .

[1]New York, 1917; reprinted from *The Seven Arts* for February, 1917. H. L. M.

III

Of the general ideas which lie at the bottom of all of Dreiser's work it is impossible to be in ignorance, for he has exposed them at length in *A Hoosier Holiday* and summarized them in *Life, Art and America.* In their main outlines they are not unlike the fundamental assumptions of Joseph Conrad. Both novelists see human existence as a seeking without a finding; both reject the prevailing interpretations of its meaning and mechanism; both take refuge in "I do not know." Put *A Hoosier Holiday* beside Conrad's *A Personal Record,* and you will come upon parallels from end to end. Or better still, put it beside Hugh Walpole's *Joseph Conrad,* in which the Conradean metaphysic is condensed from the novels even better than Conrad has done it himself: at once you will see how the two novelists, each a worker in the elemental emotions, each a rebel against the current assurance and superficiality, each an alien to his place and time, touch each other in a hundred ways.

"Conrad," says Walpole, "is of the firm and resolute conviction that life is too strong, too clever, and too remorseless for the sons of men." And then, in amplification: "It is as though, from some high window, looking down, he were able to watch some shore, from whose security men were forever launching little cockleshell boats upon a limitless and angry sea. . . . From his height he can follow their fortunes, their brave struggles, their fortitude to the very end. He admires their courage, the simplicity of their faith, but his irony springs from his knowledge of the inevitable end." . . .

Substitute the name of Dreiser for that of Conrad, and you will have to change scarcely a word. Perhaps one, to wit, "clever." I suspect that Dreiser, writing so of his own creed, would be tempted to make it "stupid," or, at all events, "unintelligible." The struggle of man, as he sees it, is more than impotent; it is gratuitous and purposeless. There is, to his eye, no grand ingenuity, no skillful adaptation of means to end, no moral (or even dramatic) plan in the order of the universe. He can get out of it only a sense of profound and inexplicable *dis*order. The waves which batter the cockleshells change their direction at every instant. Their navigation is a vast adventure, but intolerably fortuitous and inept—a voyage without chart, compass, sun, or stars. . . .

So at bottom. But to look into the blackness steadily, of course, is almost beyond the endurance of man. In the very moment that its impenetrability is grasped the imagination begins attacking it with pale beams of false light. All religions, I daresay, are thus projected from the questioning soul of man, and not only all religions, but also all great agnosticisms. Nietzsche, shrinking from the horror of that abyss of negation, revived the Pythagorean concept of *der ewigen Wiederkunft*—a vain and blood-curdling sort of comfort. To it, after a while, he added explanations almost Christian—a whole repertoire of whys and wherefores, aims and goals, aspirations and significances. The late Mark Twain, in an unpublished work, toyed with an equally daring idea: that men are to some unimaginably vast and incomprehensible Being what the unicellular organisms of his body are to man, and so on *ad infinitum*. Dreiser occasionally inclines to much the same hypothesis; he likens the endless reactions going on in the world we know, the myriadal creation, collision, and destruction of entities, to the slow accumulation and organization of cells *in utero*. He would make us specks in the insentient embryo of some gigantic Presence whose form is still unimaginable and whose birth must wait for Eons and Eons. Again, he turns to something not easily distinguishable from philosophical idealism, whether out of Berkeley or Fichte it is hard to make out—that is, he would interpret the whole phenomenon of life as no more than an appearance, a nightmare of some unseen sleeper or of men themselves, an "uncanny blur of nothingness"—in Euripides' phrase, "a song sung by an idiot, dancing down the wind." Yet again, he talks vaguely of the intricate polyphony of a cosmic orchestra, cacophonous to our dull ears. Finally, he puts the observed into the ordered, reading a purpose in the displayed event: "life was intended to sting and hurt" . . . But these are only gropings, and not to be read too critically. From speculations and explanations he always returns, Conrad-like, to the bald fact: to "the spectacle and stress of life." All he can make out clearly is "a vast compulsion which has nothing to do with the individual desires or tastes or impulses of individuals." That compulsion springs "from the settling processes of forces which we do not in the least understand, over which we have no control, and in whose grip we are as grains of dust or sand, blown hither and thither, for what purpose we cannot even suspect."[1] Man is not only doomed to defeat, but denied any glimpse or understanding of his antagonist. Here we come upon an agnosticism that has almost got beyond curiosity. What good would it do us, asks Dreiser, to know? In our ignorance and helplessness, we may at least get a slave's consolation out of cursing the unknown gods. Suppose we saw them striving blindly, too, and pitied them? . . .

But, as I say, this skepticism is often tempered by guesses at a possibly hidden truth, and the confession that this truth may exist reveals the practical unworkableness of the unconditioned system, at least for Dreiser. Conrad is far more resolute, and it is easy to see why. He is, by birth and training, an aristocrat. He has the gift of emotional detachment. The lures of facile doctrine do not move him. In his irony there is a disdain which plays about even the ironist himself. Dreiser is a product of far different forces and traditions, and is capable of no such escapement. Struggle as he may, and fume and protest as he may, he can no more shake off the chains of his intellectual and cultural heritage than he can change the shape of his nose. What that heritage is you may find out in detail by reading *A Hoosier Holiday*, or in summary by glancing at the first few pages of *Life, Art and America*. Briefly described, it is the burden of a believing mind, a moral attitude, a lingering superstition. One half of the man's brain, so to speak, wars with the other half. He is intelligent, he is thoughtful, he is a sound artist —but there come moments when a dead hand falls upon him, and he is once more the Indiana peasant, snuffing

[1]*Life, Art and America*, p. 5. H. L. M.

absurdly over imbecile sentimentalities, giving a grave ear to quackeries, snorting and eye-rolling with the best of them. One generation spans too short a time to free the soul of man. Nietzsche, to the end of his days, remained a Prussian pastor's son, and hence two-thirds a Puritan; he erected his war upon holiness, toward the end, into a sort of holy war. Kipling, the grandson of a Methodist preacher, reveals the tin-pot evangelist with increasing clarity as youth and its ribaldries pass away and he falls back upon his fundamentals. And that other English novelist who springs from the servants' hall—let us not be surprised or blame him if he sometimes writes like a bounder.

The truth about Dreiser is that he is still in the transition stage between Christian Endeavor and civilization, between Warsaw, Indiana, and the Socratic grove, between being a good American and being a free man, and so he sometimes vacillates perilously between a moral sentimentalism and a somewhat extravagant revolt. *The "Genius,"* on the one hand, is almost a tract for rectitude, a Warning to the Young; its motto might be *Scheut die Dirnen!* And on the other hand, it is full of a laborious truculence that can only be explained by imagining the author as heroically determined to prove that he is a plain-spoken fellow and his own man, let the chips fall where they may. So, in spots, in *The Financier* and *The Titan,* both of them far better books. There is an almost moral frenzy to expose and riddle what passes for morality among the stupid. The isolation of irony is never reached; the man is still evangelical; his ideas are still novelties to him; he is as solemnly absurd in some of his floutings of the Code American as he is in his respect for Bouguereau, or in his flirtings with the New Thought, or in his naïf belief in the importance of novel-writing. Somewhere or other I have called all this the Greenwich Village complex. It is not genuine artists, serving beauty reverently and proudly, who herd in those cockroached cellars and bawl for art; it is a mob of half-educated yokels and cockneys to whom the very idea of art is still novel, and intoxicating—and more than a little bawdy.

Not that Dreiser actually belongs to this ragamuffin company. Far from it, indeed. There is in him, hidden deep-down, a great instinctive artist, and hence the makings of an aristocrat. In his muddled way, held back by the manacles of his race and time, and his steps made uncertain by a guiding theory which too often eludes his own comprehension, he yet manages to produce works of art of unquestionable beauty and authority, and to interpret life in a manner that is poignant and illuminating. There is vastly more intuition in him than intellectualism; his talent is essentially feminine, as Conrad's is masculine; his ideas always seem to be deduced from his feelings. The view of life that got into *Sister Carrie,* his first book, was not the product of a conscious thinking out of Carrie's problems. It simply got itself there by the force of the artistic passion behind it; its coherent statement had to wait for other and more reflective days. The thing began as a vision, not as a syllogism. Here the name of Franz Schubert inevitably comes up. Schubert was an ignoramus, even in music; he knew less about polyphony, which is the mother of harmony, which is the mother of music, than the average conservatory professor. But nevertheless he had such a vast instinctive sensitiveness to musical values, such a profound and accurate feeling for beauty in tone, that he not only arrived at the truth in tonal relations, but even went beyond what, in his day, was known to be the truth, and so led an advance. Likewise, Giorgione da Castelfranco and Masaccio come to mind: painters of the first rank, but untutored, unsophisticated, uncouth. Dreiser, within his limits, belongs to this sabot-shod company of the elect. One thinks of Conrad, not as artist first, but as savant. There is something of the icy aloofness of the laboratory in him, even when the images he conjures up pulsate with the very glow of life. He is almost as self-conscious as the Beethoven of the last quartets. In Dreiser the thing is more intimate, more disorderly, more a matter of pure feeling. He gets his effects, one might almost say, not by designing them, but by living them.

But whatever the process, the power of the image evoked is not to be gainsaid. It is not only brilliant on the surface, but mysterious and appealing in its depths. One swiftly forgets his intolerable writing, his mirthless, sedulous, repellent manner, in the face of the Athenian tragedy he instills into his seduced and soul-sick servant-girls, his barbaric pirates of finances, his conquered and hamstrung supermen, his wives who sit and wait. He has, like Conrad, a sure talent for depicting the spirit in disintegration. Old Gerhardt, in *Jennie Gerhardt,* is alone worth all the *dramatis personae* of popular American fiction since the days of *Rob o' the Bowl;* Howells could no more have created him, in his Rodinesque impudence of outline, than he could have created Tartuffe or Gargantua. Such a novel as *Sister Carrie* stands quite outside the brief traffic of the customary stage. It leaves behind it an unescapable impression of bigness, of epic sweep and dignity. It is not a mere story, not a novel in the customary American meaning of the word; it is at once a psalm of life and a criticism of life—and that criticism loses nothing by the fact that its burden is despair. Here, precisely, is the point of Dreiser's departure from his fellows. He puts into his novels a touch of the eternal *Weltschmerz.* They get below the drama that is of the moment and reveal the greater drama that is without end. They arouse those deep and lasting emotions which grow out of the recognition of elemental and universal tragedy. His aim is not merely to tell a tale; his aim is to show the vast ebb and flow of forces which sway and condition human destiny. One cannot imagine him consenting to Conan Doyle's statement of the purpose of fiction, quoted with characteristic approval by the New York *Times:* "to amuse mankind, to help the sick and the dull and the weary." Nor is his purpose to instruct; if he is a pedagogue it is only incidentally and as a weakness. The thing he seeks to do is to stir, to awaken, to move. One does not arise from such a book as *Sister Carrie* with a smirk of satisfaction; one leaves it infinitely touched.

IV

It is, indeed, a truly amazing first book, and one marvels to hear that it was begun lightly. Dreiser in those days (*circa* 1899) had seven or eight years of newspaper work behind him, in Chicago, St. Louis, Toledo, Cleveland, Buffalo, Pittsburgh, and New York, and was beginning to feel that reaction of disgust which attacks all newspaper-men when the enthusiasm of youth wears out. He had been successful, but he saw how hollow that success was, and how little surety it held out for the future. The theater was what chiefly lured him; he had written plays in his nonage, and he now proposed to do them on a large scale, and so get some of the easy dollars of Broadway. It was an old friend from Toledo, Arthur Henry, who turned him toward story writing. The two had met while Henry was city editor of the *Blade* and Dreiser a reporter looking for a job.[1] A firm friendship sprang up, and Henry conceived a high opinion of Dreiser's ability, and urged him to try a short story. Dreiser was distrustful of his own skill, but Henry kept at him, and finally, during a holiday the two spent together at Maumee, Ohio, he made the attempt. Henry had the manuscript typewritten and sent it to *Ainslee's Magazine.* A week or so later there came a check for $75.

This was in 1898. Dreiser wrote four more stories during the year following, and sold them all. Henry now urged him to attempt a novel, but again his distrust of himself held him back. Henry finally tried a rather unusual argument: he had a novel of his own on the stocks,[2] and he represented that he was in difficulties with it and in need of company. One day, in September 1899, Dreiser took a sheet of yellow paper and wrote a title at random. That title was *Sister Carrie,* and with no more definite plan than the mere name offered the book began. It went ahead steadily enough until the middle of October, and had come by then to the place where Carrie meets Hurstwood. At that point Dreiser left it in disgust. It seemed pitifully dull and inconsequential, and for two months he put the manuscript away. Then, under renewed urgings by Henry, he resumed the writing, and kept on to the place where Hurstwood steals the money. Here he went aground upon a comparatively simple prob-

[1]The episode is related in *A Hoosier Holiday*. H. L. M.

[2]*A Princess of Arcady,* published in 1900. H. L. M.

lem; he couldn't devise a way to manage the robbery. Late in January he gave it up. But the faithful Henry kept urging him, and in March he resumed work, and soon had the story finished. The latter part, despite many distractions, went quickly. Once the manuscript was complete, Henry suggested various cuts, and in all about 40,000 words came out. The fair copy went to the Harpers. They refused it without ceremony and soon afterward Dreiser carried the manuscript to Doubleday, Page & Co. He left it with Frank Doubleday, and before long there came notice of its acceptance, and, what is more, a contract. But after the story was in type it fell into the hands of the wife of one of the members of the firm, and she conceived so strong a notion of its immorality that she soon convinced her husband and his associates. There followed a series of acrimonious negotiation, with Dreiser holding resolutely to the letter of his contract. It was at this point that Frank Norris entered the combat—bravely but in vain. The pious Barabbases, confronted by their signature, found it impossible to throw up the book entirely, but there was no nomination in the bond regarding either the style of binding or the number of copies to be issued, and so they evaded further dispute by bringing out the book in a very small edition and with modest unstamped covers. Copies of this edition are now eagerly sought by book-collectors, and one in good condition fetches $25 or more in the auction rooms. Even the second edition (1907), bearing the imprint of B. W. Dodge & Co., carries an increasing premium.

The passing years work strange farces. The Harpers, who had refused *Sister Carrie* with a spirit bordering upon indignation in 1900, took over the rights of publication from B. W. Dodge & Co., in 1912, and reissued the book in a new (and extremely hideous) format, with a publisher's note containing smug quotations from the encomiums of the *Fortnightly Review,* the *Athenaeum,* the *Spectator,* the *Academy* and other London critical journals. More, they contrived humorously to push the date of their copyright back to 1900. But this new enthusiasm for artistic freedom did not last long. They had published *Jennie Gerhardt* in

1911 and they did *The Financier* in 1912, but when *The Titan* followed, in 1914, they were seized with qualms, and suppressed the book after it had got into type. In this emergency the English firm of John Lane came to the rescue, only to seek cover itself when the Comstocks attacked *The "Genius"* two years later. . . . For his high services to American letters, Walter H. Page, of Doubleday, Page & Co., was made ambassador to England, where *Sister Carrie* is regarded (according to the Harpers) as "the best story, on the whole, that has yet come out of America." A curious series of episodes. Another proof, perhaps, of that cosmic imbecility upon which Dreiser is so fond of discoursing. . . .

But of all this I shall say more later on, when I come to discuss the critical reception of the Dreiser novels, and the efforts made by the New York Society for the Suppression of Vice to stop their sale. The thing to notice here is that the author's difficulties with *Sister Carrie* came within an ace of turning him from novel-writing completely. Stray copies of the suppressed first edition, true enough, fell into the hands of critics who saw the story's value, and during the first year or two of the century it enjoyed a sort of esoteric vogue, and encouragement came from unexpected sources. Moreover, a somewhat bowdlerized English edition, published by William Heinemann in 1901, made a fair success, and even provoked a certain mild controversy. But the author's income from the book remained almost *nil,* and so he was forced to seek a livelihood in other directions. His history during the next ten years belongs to the tragi-comedy of letters. For five of them he was a Grub Street hack, turning his hand to any literary job that offered. He wrote short stories for the popular magazines, or special articles, or poems, according as their needs varied. He concocted fabulous tales for the illustrated supplements of the Sunday newspapers. He rewrote the bad stuff of other men. He returned to reporting. He did odd pieces of editing. He tried his hand at one-act plays. He even ventured upon advertisement writing. And all the while, the best that he could get out of his industry was a meager living.

In 1905, tiring of the uncertainties of this life, he accepted a post on the staff of Street & Smith, the millionaire publishers of cheap magazines, servant-girl romances, and dime-novels, and here, in the very slums of letters, he labored with tongue in cheek until the next year. The tale of his duties will fill, I daresay, a volume or two in the autobiography on which he is said to be working; it is a chronicle full of achieved impossibilities. One of his jobs, for example, was to reduce a whole series of dime-novels, each 60,000 words in length, to 30,000 words apiece. He accomplished it by cutting each one into halves, and writing a new ending for the first half and a new beginning for the second, with new titles for both. This doubling of their property aroused the admiration of his employers; they promised him an assured and easy future in the dime-novel business. But he tired of it, despite this revelation of a gift for it, and in 1906 he became managing editor of the *Broadway Magazine,* then struggling into public notice. A year later he transferred his flag to the Butterick Building, and became chief editor of the *Delineator,* the *Designer,* and other such gospels for the fair. Here, of course, he was as much out of water as in the dime-novel foundry of Street & Smith, but at all events the pay was good, and there was a certain leisure at the end of the day's work. In 1907, as part of his duties, he organized the National Child Rescue Campaign, which still rages as the *Delineator's* contribution to the Uplift. At about the same time he began *Jennie Gerhardt.* It is curious to note that, during these same years, Arnold Bennett was slaving in London as the editor of *Woman.*

Dreiser left the *Delineator* in 1910, and for the next half year or so endeavored to pump vitality into the *Bohemian Magazine,* in which he had acquired a proprietary interest. But the *Bohemian* soon departed this life, carrying some of his savings with it, and he gave over his enforced leisure to *Jennie Gerhardt,* completing the book in 1911. Its publication by the Harpers during the same year worked his final emancipation from the editorial desk. It was praised, and, what is more, it sold, and royalties began to come in. A new edition of *Sister Carrie* followed in 1912, with *The Financier* hard upon its heels. Since then Dreiser has devoted himself wholly to serious work. *The Financier* was put forth as the first volume of "a trilogy of desire"; the second volume, *The Titan,* was published in 1914; the third is yet to come. *The "Genius"* appeared in 1915; *The Bulwark* is just announced. In 1912, accompanied by Grant Richards, the London publisher, Dreiser made his first trip abroad, visiting England, France, Italy, and Germany. His impressions were recorded in *A Traveler at Forty,* published in 1913. In the summer of 1915, accompanied by Franklin Booth, the illustrator, he made an automobile journey to his old haunts in Indiana, and the record is in *A Hoosier Holiday,* published in 1916. His other writings include a volume of *Plays of the Natural and the Supernatural* (1916); *Life, Art and America,* a pamphlet against Puritanism in letters (1917); a dozen or more short stories and novelettes, a few poems, and a three-act drama, *The Hand of the Potter.*

Dreiser was born at Terre Haute, Indiana, on August 27, 1871, and, like most of us, is of mongrel blood, with the German, perhaps, predominating. He is a tall man, awkward in movement and nervous in habit; the boon of beauty has been denied him. The history of his youth is set forth in full in *A Hoosier Holiday.* It is curious to note that he is a brother to the late Paul Dresser, author of *The Banks of the Wabash* and other popular songs, and that he himself, helping Paul over a hard place, wrote the affecting chorus:

Oh, the moon is fair tonight along the Wabash,
From the fields there comes the breath of new-mown hay;
Through the sycamores the candle lights are gleaming . . .

But no doubt you know it.

V

The work of Dreiser, considered as craftsmanship pure and simple, is extremely uneven, and the distance separating his best from his worst is almost infinite. It is difficult to believe that the novelist who wrote certain extraordinarily vivid chapters in *Jennie Gerhardt,* and *A Hoosier Holiday,* and, above all, in *The Titan,* is the same who achieved the unescapable dullness of parts of *The Financier* and the general stupidity and stodginess of *The "Genius."* Moreover, the tide of his writing does not rise or fall with any regularity; he neither improves steadily nor grows worse steadily. Only half an eye is needed to see the superiority of *Jennie Gerhardt,* as a sheer piece of writing, to *Sister Carrie,* but on turning to *The Financier,* which followed *Jennie Gerhardt* by an interval of but one year, one observes a falling off which, at its greatest, is almost indistinguishable from a collapse. *Jennie Gerhardt* is suave, persuasive, well-ordered, solid in structure, instinct with life. *The Financier,* for all its merits in detail, is loose, tedious, vapid, exasperating. But had any critic, in the autumn of 1912, argued thereby that Dreiser was finished, that he had shot his bolt, his discomfiture would have come swiftly, for *The Titan,* which followed in 1914, was almost as well done as *The Financier* had been ill done, and there are parts of it which remain, to this day, the very best writing that Dreiser has ever achieved. But *The "Genius"*? Aye, in *The "Genius"* the pendulum swings back again! It is flaccid, elephantine, doltish, coarse, dismal, flatulent, sophomoric, ignorant, unconvincing, wearisome. One pities the jurisconsult who is condemned, by Comstockian clamor, to plow through such a novel. In it there is a sort of humorless *reductio ad absurdum,* not only of the Dreiser manner, but even of certain salient tenets of the Dreiser philosophy. At its best it has a moral flavor. At its worst it is almost maudlin. . . .

The most successful of the Dreiser novels, judged by sales, is *Sister Carrie,* and the causes thereof are not far to seek. On the one hand, its suppression in 1900 gave it a whispered fame that was converted into a public celebrity when it was republished in 1907, and on the other hand, it shares with *Jennie Gerhardt* the capital advantage of having a young and appealing woman for its chief figure. The sentimentalists thus have a heroine to cry over, and to put into a familiar pigeonhole; Carrie becomes a sort of Pollyanna. More, it is, at bottom, a tale of love—the one theme of permanent interest to the average American novel reader, the chief stuffing of all our best-selling romances. True enough, it is vastly more than this—there is in it, for example, the astounding portrait of Hurstwood; but it seems to me plain that its relative popularity is by no means a test of its relative merit, and that the causes of that popularity must be sought in other directions. Its defect, as a work of art, is a defect of structure. Like Norris' *McTeague* it has a broken back. In the midst of the story of Carrie, Dreiser pauses to tell the story of Hurstwood—a memorably vivid and tragic story, to be sure, but still one that, considering artistic form and organization, does damage to the main business of the book. Its outstanding merit is its simplicity, its unaffected seriousness and fervor, the spirit of youth that is in it. One feels that it was written, not by a novelist conscious of his tricks, but by a novice carried away by his own flaming eagerness, his own high sense of the interest of what he was doing. In this aspect, it is perhaps more typically Dreiserian than any of its successors. And maybe we may seek here for a good deal of its popular appeal, for there is a contagion in naïveté as in enthusiasm, and the simple novel-reader may recognize the kinship of a simple mind in the novelist.

But it is in *Jennie Gerhardt* that Dreiser first shows his true mettle. . . . "The power to tell the same story in two forms," said George Moore, "is the sign of the true artist." Here Dreiser sets himself that difficult task, and here he carries it off with almost complete success. Reduce the story to a hundred words, and the same words would also describe *Sister Carrie*. Jennie, like Carrie, is a rose grown from turnipseed. Over each, at the start, hangs poverty, ignorance, the dumb helplessness of the Shudra, and yet in each there is that indescribable something, that element of essential gentleness, that innate inward beauty which levels all barriers of caste, and makes Esther a fit queen for Ahasuerus. Some Frenchman has put it into a phrase: *"une âme grande dans un petit destin"*—a great soul in a small destiny. Jennie has some touch of that greatness; Dreiser is forever calling her "a big woman"; it is a refrain almost as irritating as the "trig" of *The Titan*. Carrie, one feels, is of baser metal; her dignity never rises to anything approaching nobility. But the history of each is the history of the other. Jennie, like Carrie, escapes from the physical miseries of the struggle for existence only to taste the worse miseries of the struggle for happiness. Don't mistake me; we have here no maudlin tales of seduced maidens. Seduction, in truth, is far from tragedy for either Jennie or Carrie. The gain of each, until the actual event has been left behind and obliterated by experiences more salient and poignant, is greater than her loss, and that gain is to the soul as well as to the creature. With the rise from want to security, from fear to ease, comes an awakening of the finer perceptions, a widening of the sympathies, a gradual unfolding of the delicate flower called personality, an increased capacity for loving and living. But with all this, and as a part of it, there comes, too, an increased capacity for suffering—and so in the end, when love slips away and the empty years stretch before, it is the awakened and supersentient woman that pays for the folly of the groping, bewildered girl. The tragedy of Carrie and Jennie, in brief, is not that they are degraded, but that they are lifted up, not that they go to the gutter, but that they escape the gutter and glimpse the stars.

But if the two stories are thus variations upon the same somber theme, if each starts from the same place and arrives at the same dark goal, if each shows a woman heartened by the same hopes and tortured by the same agonies, there is still a vast difference between them, and that difference is the measure of the author's progress in his craft during the eleven years between 1900 and 1911. *Sister Carrie,* at bottom, is no more than a first sketch, a rough piling up of observations and ideas, disordered and often incoherent. In the midst of the story, as I have said, the author forgets it, and starts off upon another. In *Jennie Gerhardt* there is no such flaccidity of structure, no such vacillation in aim, no such proliferation of episode. Considering that it is by Dreiser, it is extraordinarily adept and intelligent in design; only in *The Titan* has he ever done so well. From beginning to end the narrative flows logically, steadily, congruously. Episodes there are, of course, but they keep their proper place and bulk. It is always Jennie that stands at the center of the traffic; it is in Jennie's soul that every scene is ultimately played out. Her father and mother; Senator Brander, the god of her first worship; her daughter Vesta, and Lester Kane, the man who makes and mars her—all these are drawn with infinite painstaking, and in every one of them there is the blood of life. But it is Jennie that dominates the drama from curtain to curtain. Not an event is unrelated to her; not a climax fails to make clearer the struggles going on in her mind and heart.

It is in *Jennie Gerhardt* that Dreiser's view of life begins to take on coherence and to show a general tendency. In *Sister Carrie* the thing is still chiefly representation and no more; the image is undoubtedly vivid, but its significance, in the main, is left undisplayed. In *Jennie Gerhardt* this pictorial achievement is reinforced by interpretation; one carries away an impression that something has been said; it is not so much a visual image of Jennie that remains as a sense of the implacable tragedy that engulfs her. The book is full of artistic passion. It lives and glows. It awakens recognition and feeling. Its lucid ideational structure, even more than the artless gusto of *Sister Carrie,* produces a penetrating and powerful effect. Jennie is no mere individual; she is a type of the national character, almost the archetype of the muddled, aspiring, tragic, fate-flogged mass. And the scene in which she is set is brilliantly national too. The Chicago of those great days of feverish money-grabbing and crazy aspiration may well stand as the epitome of America, and it is made clearer here than in any other American novel—clearer than in *The Pit* or *The Cliff-Dwellers*—clearer than in any book by an Easterner—almost as clear as the Paris of Balzac and Zola. Finally, the style of the story is indissolubly wedded to its matter. The narrative, in places, has an almost scriptural solemnity; in its very harshness and baldness there is something subtly meet and fitting. One cannot imagine such a history done in the strained phrases of Meredith or the fugal manner of Henry James. One cannot imagine that stark, stenographic dialogue adorned with the tinsel of pretty words. The thing, to reach the heights it touches, could have been done only in the way it has been done. As it stands, I would not take anything away from it, not even its journalistic banalities, its lack of humor, its incessant returns to C major. A primitive and touching poetry is in it. It is a novel, I am convinced, of the first consideration. . . .

In *The Financier* this poetry is almost wholly absent, and fact is largely to blame for the book's lack of charm. By the time we see him in *The Titan* Frank Cowperwood has taken on heroic proportions and the romance of great adventure is in him, but in *The Financier* he is still little more than an extra-pertinacious money-grubber, and not unrelated to the average stockbroker or corner grocer. True enough, Dreiser says specifically that he is more, that the thing he craves is not money but power—power to force lesser men to execute his commands, power to surround himself with beautiful and splendid things, power to amuse himself with women, power to defy and nullify the laws made for the timorous and unimaginative. But the intent of the author never really gets into his picture. His Cowperwood in this first stage is hard, commonplace, unimaginative. In *The Titan* he flowers out as a blend of revolutionist and voluptuary, a highly civilized Lorenzo the Magnificent, an immoralist who would not hesitate two minutes about seducing a saint, but would turn sick at the thought of harming a child. But in *The Financier* he is still in the larval state, and a repellent sordidness hangs about him.

Moreover, the story of his rise is burdened by two defects which still further corrupt its effect. One lies in the fact that Dreiser is quite unable to get the feel, so to speak, of Philadelphia, just as he is unable to get the feel of New York in *The "Genius."* The other is that the style of the writing in the book reduces the dreiserian manner to absurdity, and almost to impossibility. The incredibly lazy, involved, and unintelligent description of the trial of Cowperwood I have already mentioned. We get, in this lumbering chronicle, not a cohesive and luminous picture, but a dull, photographic representation of the whole tedious process, beginning with an account of the political obligations of the judge and district attorney, proceeding to a consideration of the habits of mind of each of the twelve jurymen, and ending with a summary of the majority and minority opinions of the court of appeals, and a discussion of the motives, ideals, traditions, prejudices, sympathies, and chicaneries behind them, each and severally. When Cowperwood goes into the market, his operations are set forth in their last detail; we are told how many shares he buys, how much he pays for them, what the commission is, what his profit comes to. When he comes into chance contact with a politician, we hear all about that politician, including his family affairs. When he builds and furnishes a house, the chief rooms in it are inventoried with such care that not a chair or a rug or a picture on the wall is overlooked. The endless piling up of such nonessentials cripples and incommodes the story; its drama is too copiously swathed in words to achieve a sting; the Dreiser manner devours and defeats itself.

But nonetheless the book has compensatory merits. Its character sketches, for all the cloud of words, are lucid and vigorous. Out of that enormous complex of crooked politics and crookeder finance, Cowperwood himself stands out in the round, comprehensible and alive. And all the others, in their lesser measures, are done almost as well—Cowperwood's pale wife, whimpering in her empty house; Aileen Butler, his mistress; his doddering and eternally amazed old father; his old-fashioned, stupid, sentimental mother; Stener, the City Treasurer, a dish-rag in the face of danger; old Edward Malia Butler, that barbarian in a boiled shirt, with his Homeric hatred and his broken heart. Particularly old Butler. The years pass and he must be killed and put away, but not many readers of the book, I take it, will soon forget him. Dreiser is at his best, indeed, when he deals with old men. In their tragic helplessness they stand as symbols of that unfathomable cosmic cruelty which he sees as the motive power of life itself. More, even, than his women, he makes them poignant, vivid, memorable. The picture of old Gerhardt is full of a subtle brightness, though he is always in the background, as cautious and penny-wise as an ancient crow, trotting to his Lutheran church, pathetically ill-used by the world he never understands. Butler is another such, different in externals, but at bottom the same dismayed, questioning, pathetic old man. . . .

In *The Titan* there is a tightening of the screws, a clarifying of the action, an infinite improvement in the manner. The book, in truth, has the air of a new and clearer thinking out of *The Financier,* as *Jennie Gerhardt* is a new thinking out of *Sister Carrie.* With almost the same materials, the thing is given a new harmony and unity, a new plausibility, a new passion and purpose. In *The Financier* the artistic voluptuary is almost completely overshadowed by the dollar-chaser; in *The Titan* we begin to see clearly that grand battle between artist and man of money, idealist and materialist, spirit and flesh, which is the informing theme of the whole trilogy. The conflict that makes the drama, once chiefly external, now becomes more and more internal; it is played out within the soul of the man himself. The result is a character sketch of the highest color and brilliance, a superb portrait of a complex and extremely fascinating man. Of all the personages in the Dreiser books, the Cowperwood of *The Titan* is perhaps the most radiantly real. He is accounted for in every detail, and yet, in the end, he is not accounted for at all; there hangs about him, to the last, that baffling mysteriousness which hangs about those we know most intimately. There is in him a complete and indubitable masculinity, as the eternal feminine is in Jennie. His struggle with the inexorable forces that urge him on as with whips, and lure him with false lights, and bring him to disillusion and dismay, is as typical as hers is, and as tragic. In his ultimate disaster, so plainly foreshadowed at the close, there is the clearest of all projections of the ideas that lie at the bottom of all Dreiser's work. Cowperwood, above any of them, is his protagonist.

The story, in its plan, is as transparent as in its burden. It has an austere simplicity in the telling that fits the directness of the thing told. Dreiser, as if to clear decks, throws over all the immemorial baggage of the novelist, making short shrift of "heart interest," conventional "sympathy," and even what ordinarily passes for romance. In *Sister Carrie,* as I have pointed out, there is still a sweet dish for the sen timentalists; if they don't like the history of Carrie as a work of art they may still wallow in it as a sad, sad love story. Carrie is appealing, melting; she moves, like Marguerite Gautier, in an atmosphere of romantic depression. And Jennie Gerhardt, in this aspect, is merely Carrie done over—a Carrie more carefully and objectively drawn, perhaps, but still conceivably to be mistaken for a "sympathetic" heroine in a best-seller. A lady eating chocolates might jump from *Laddie* to *Jennie Gerhardt* without knowing that she was jumping ten thousand miles. The tear jugs are there to cry into. Even in *The Financier* there is still a hint of familiar things. The first Mrs. Cowperwood is sorely put upon; old Butler has the markings of an irate father; Cowperwood himself suffers the orthodox injustice and languishes in a cell. But no one, I venture, will ever fall into any such mistake in identity in approaching *The Titan.* Not a single appeal to facile sentiment is in it. It proceeds from beginning to end in a forthright, uncompromising, confident manner. It is an almost purely objective account, as devoid of cheap heroics as a death certificate, of a strong man's contest with incontestable powers without and no less incontestable powers within. There is nothing of the conventional outlaw about him; he does not wear a red sash and bellow for liberty; fate wrings from him no melodramatic defiances. In the midst of the battle he views it with a sort of ironical detachment, as if lifted above himself by the sheer aesthetic spectacle. Even in disaster he asks for no quarter, no generosity, no compassion. Up or down, he keeps his zest for the game that is being played, and is sufficient unto himself.

Such a man as this Cowperwood of the Chicago days, described romantically, would be indistinguishable from the wicked earls and seven-foot guardsmen of Ouida, Robert W. Chambers, and The Duchess. But described realistically and cold-bloodedly, with all that wealth of minute and apparently inconsequential detail which Dreiser piles up so amazingly, he becomes a figure astonishingly vivid, lifelike, and engrossing. He fits into no *a priori* theory of conduct or scheme of rewards and punishments; he proves nothing and teaches nothing; the forces which move him are never obvious and frequently unintelligible. But in the end he seems genuinely a man—a man of the sort we see about us in the real world—not a patent and automatic fellow, reacting docilely and according to a formula, but a bundle of complexities and contradictions, a creature oscillating between the light and the shadow—at bottom, for all his typical representation of a race and a civilization, a unique and inexplicable personality. More, he is a man of the first class, an Achilles of his world; and here the achievement of Dreiser is most striking, for he succeeds where all forerunners failed. It is easy enough to explain how John Smith courted his wife, and even how William Brown fought and died for his country, but it is inordinately difficult to give plausibility to the motives, feelings, and processes of mind of a man whose salient character is that they transcend all ordinary experience. Too often, even when made by the highest creative and interpretative talent, the effort has resolved itself into a begging of the question. Shakespeare made Hamlet comprehensible to the groundlings by diluting that half of him which was Shakespeare with a half which was a college sophomore. In the same way he saved Lear by making him, in large part, a tedious and obscene old donkey—the blood brother of any average ancient of any average English taproom. Tackling Caesar, he was rescued by Brutus' knife. George Bernard Shaw, facing the same difficulty, resolved it by drawing a composite portrait of two or three London actor-managers and a half-a-dozen English politicians. But Dreiser makes no such compromise. He bangs into the difficulties of his problem head on, and if he does not solve it absolutely, he at least makes an extraordinarily close approach to a solution. In *The Financier* a certain incredulity still hangs about Cowperwood; in *The Titan* he suddenly comes unquestionably real. If you want to get the true measure of this feat, put it beside the failure of Frank Norris with Curtis Jadwin in *The Pit*. . . .

The "Genius," which interrupted the "trilogy of desire," marks the nadir of Dreiser's accomplishment, as *The Titan* marks its apogee. The plan of it, of course, is simple enough, and it is one that Dreiser, at his best, might have carried out with undoubted success. What he is trying to show, in brief, is the battle that goes on in the soul of every man of active mind between the desire for self-expression and the desire for safety, for public respect, for emotional equanimity. It is, in a sense, the story of Cowperwood told over again, but with an important difference, for Eugene Witla is a much less self-reliant and powerful fellow than Cowperwood, and so he is unable to muster up the vast resolution of spirits that he needs to attain happiness. *The Titan* is the history of a strong man. *The "Genius"* is the history of a man essentially weak. Eugene Witla can never quite choose his route in life. He goes on sacrificing ease to aspiration and aspiration to ease to the end of the chapter. He vacillates abominably and forever between two irreconcilable desires. Even when, at the close, he sinks into a whining sort of resignation, the proud courage of Cowperwood is not in him; he is always a bit despicable in his pathos.

As I say, a story of simple outlines, and well adapted to the dreiserian pen. But it is spoiled and made a mock of by a donkeyish solemnity of attack which leaves it, on the one hand, diffuse, spineless, and shapeless, and, on the other hand, a compendium of platitudes. It is as if Dreiser, suddenly discovering himself a sage, put off the high passion of the artist and took to pounding a pulpit. It is almost as if he deliberately essayed upon a burlesque of himself. The book is an endless emission of the obvious, with touches of the scandalous to light up its killing monotony. It runs to 736 pages of small type; its reading is an unbearable weariness to the flesh; in the midst of it one has forgotten the beginning and is unconcerned about the end. Mingled with all the folderol, of course, there is stuff of nobler quality. Certain chapters stick in the memory; whole episodes lift themselves to the fervid luminosity of *Jennie Gerhardt;* there are character sketches that deserve all praise; one often pulls up with a reminder that the thing is the work of a proficient craftsman. But in the main it lumbers and jolts, wabbles and bores. A sort of ponderous imbecility gets into it. Both in its elaborate devices to shake up the pious and its imposing demonstrations of what everyone knows, it somehow suggests the advanced thinking of Greenwich Village. I suspect, indeed, that the *vin rouge* was in Dreiser's arteries as he concocted it. He was at the intellectual menopause, and looking back somewhat wistfully and attitudinizingly toward the goatish days that were no more.

But let it go! A novelist capable of *Jennie Gerhardt* has rights, privileges, prerogatives. He may, if he will, go on a spiritual drunk now and then, and empty the stale bilges of his soul. Thackeray, having finished *Vanity Fair* and *Pendennis,* bathed himself in the sheep's milk of *The Newcomes,* and after *The Virginians* he did *The Adventures of Philip.* Zola, with *Germinal, La Débâcle* and *La Terre* behind him, re-created himself horribly with *Fécondité.* Tolstoy, after *Anna Karenina,* wrote *What Is Art?* Ibsen, after *Et Dukkehjem* and *Gengangere,* wrote *Vildanden.* The good God himself, after all the magnificence of *Kings* and *Chronicles,* turned Dr. Frank Crane and so botched his Writ with *Proverbs.* . . . A weakness that we must allow for. Whenever Dreiser, abandoning his fundamental skepticism, yields to the irrepressible human (and perhaps also divine) itch to label, to moralize, to teach, he becomes a bit absurd. Observe *The "Genius,"* and parts of *A Hoosier Holiday* and of *A Traveler at Forty,* and of *Plays of the Natural and the Supernatural.* But in this very absurdity, it seems to me, there is a subtle proof that his fundamental skepticism is sound. . . .

I mention the *Plays of the Natural and the Supernatural.* They are ingenious and sometimes extremely effective, but their significance is not great. The two that are "of the natural" are *The Girl in the Coffin* and *Old Ragpicker,* the first a laborious evocation of the gruesome, too long by half, and the other an experiment in photographic realism, with a pair of policemen as its protagonists. All five plays "of the supernatural" follow a single plan. In the foreground, as it were, we see a sordid drama played out on the human plane, and in the background (or in the empyrean above, as you choose) we see the operation of the godlike imbecilities which sway and flay us all. The technical trick is well managed. It would be easy for such four-dimensional pieces to fall into burlesque, but in at least two cases, to wit, in *The Blue Sphere* and *In the Dark,* they go off with an air. Superficially, these plays "of the supernatural" seem to show an abandonment to the wheezy, black bombazine mysticism which crops up toward the end of *The "Genius."* But that mysticism, at bottom, is no more than the dreiserian skepticism made visible. "For myself," says Dreiser somewhere, "I do not know what truth is, what beauty is, what love is, what hope is." And in another place: "I admit a vast compulsion which has nothing to do with the individual desires or tastes or impulses." The jokers behind the arras pull the strings. It is pretty, but what is it all about? . . . The criticism which deals only with externals sees *Sister Carrie* as no more than a deft adventure into realism. Dreiser is praised, when he is praised at all, for making Carrie so clear, for understanding her so well. But the truth is, of course, that his achievement consists precisely in making patent the impenetrable mystery of her, and of the tangled complex of striving and aspiration of which she is so helplessly a part. It is in this sense that *Sister Carrie* is a profound work. It is not a book of glib explanations, of ready formulae; it is, above all else, a book of wonder. . . .

Of *A Traveler at Forty* I have spoken briefly. It is heavy with the obvious; the most interesting thing in it is the fact that Dreiser had never seen St. Peter's or Piccadilly Circus until he was too old for either reverence or romance. *A Hoosier Holiday* is far more illuminating, despite its platitudinizing. Slow in tempo, discursive, reflective, intimate, the book covers a vast territory, and lingers in pleasant fields. One finds in it an almost complete confession of faith, artistic, religious, even political. And not infrequently that confession takes the form of ingenuous confidences—about the fortunes of the house of Dreiser, the dispersed Dreiser clan, the old neighbors in Indiana, new friends made along the way. In *A Traveler at Forty* Dreiser is surely frank enough in his vivisections; he seldom forgets a vanity or a wart. In *A Hoosier Holiday* he goes even further; he speculates heavily about all his *dramatis personae,* prodding into the motives behind their acts, wondering what they would do in this or that situation, forcing them painfully into laboratory jars. They become, in the end, not unlike characters in a novel; one misses only the neatness of a plot. Strangely enough, the one personage of the chronicle who remains dim throughout is the artist, Franklin Booth, Dreiser's host and companion on the long motor ride from New York to Indiana, and the maker of the book's excellent pictures. One gets a brilliant etching of Booth's father, and scarcely less vivid portraits of Speed, the chauffeur; of various persons encountered on the way, and of friends and relatives dredged up out of the abyss of the past. But of Booth one learns little save that he is a Christian Scientist and a fine figure of a man. There must have been much talk during those two weeks of careening along the high-road, and Booth must have borne some part in it, but what he said is very meagerly reported, and so he is still somewhat vague at the end—a personality sensed but scarcely apprehended.

However, it is Dreiser himself who is the chief character of the story, and who stands out from it most brilliantly. One sees in the man all the special marks of the novelist: his capacity for photographic and relentless observation, his insatiable curiosity, his keen zest in life as a spectacle, his comprehension of and sympathy for the poor striving of humble folks, his endless mulling of insoluble problems, his recurrent Philistinism, his impatience of restraints, his fascinated suspicion of messiahs, his passion for physical beauty, his relish for the gaudy drama of big cities; his incurable Americanism. The panorama that he enrolls runs the whole scale of the colors; it is a series of extraordinarily vivid pictures. The somber gloom of the Pennsylvania hills, with Wilkes-Barre lying among them like a gem; the procession of little country towns, sleepy and a bit hoggish; the flash of Buffalo, Cleveland, Indianapolis; the gargantuan coal-pockets and ore-docks along the Erie shore; the tinsel summer resorts; the lush Indiana farmlands, with their stodgy, bovine people—all of these things are sketched in simply, and yet almost magnificently. I know, indeed, of no book which better describes the American hinterland. Here we have no idle spying by a stranger, but a full-length representation by one who knows the thing he describes intimately, and is himself a part of it. Almost every mile of the road traveled has been Dreiser's own road in life. He knew those unkempt Indiana towns in boyhood; he wandered in the Indiana woods; he came to Toledo, Cleveland, Buffalo as a young man; all the roots of his existence are out there. And so he does his chronicle *con amore,* with many a sentimental dredging up of old memories, old hopes, and old dreams.

Save for passages in *The Titan, A Hoosier Holiday* marks the high tide of Dreiser's writing—that is, as sheer writing. His old faults are in it, and plentifully. There are empty, brackish phrases enough, God knows—"high noon" among them. But for all that, there is an undeniable glow in it; it shows, in more than one place, an approach to style; the mere wholesaler of words has become, in some sense a connoisseur, even a voluptuary. The picture of Wilkes-Barre girt in by her hills is simply done, and yet there is imagination in it, and touches of brilliance. The somber beauty of the Pennsylvania mountains is vividly transferred to the page. The towns by the wayside are differentiated, swiftly drawn, made to live. There are excellent sketches of people—a courtly hotelkeeper in some godforsaken hamlet, his self-respect triumphing over his wallow; a group of babbling Civil War veterans, endlessly mouthing incomprehensible jests; the half-grown beaux and belles of the summer resorts, enchanted and yet a bit staggered by the awakening of sex; Booth *père* and his sinister politics; broken and forgotten men in the Indiana towns; policemen, waitresses, farmers, country characters; Dreiser's own people—the boys and girls of his youth; his brother Paul, the Indiana Schneckenburger and Francis Scott Key; his sisters and brothers; his beaten, hopeless, pious father; his brave and noble mother. The book is dedicated to this mother, now long dead, and in a way it is a memorial to her, a monument to affection. Life bore upon her cruelly; she knew poverty at its lowest ebb and despair at its bitterest; and yet there was in her a touch of fineness that never yielded, a gallant spirit that faced and fought things through. One thinks, somehow, of the mother of Gounod. . . . Her son has not forgotten her. His book is her epitaph. He enters into her presence with love and with reverence and with something not far from awe. . . .

As for the rest of the Dreiser compositions, I leave them to your curiosity.

VI

Dr. William Lyon Phelps, the Lampson professor of English language and literature at Yale, opens his chapter on Mark Twain in his *Essays on Modern Novelists* with a humorous account of the critical imbecility which pursued Mark in his own country down to his last years. The favorite national critics of that era (and it extended to 1895, at the least) were wholly blind to the fact that he was a great artist. They admitted him, somewhat grudgingly, a certain low dexterity as a clown, but that he was an imaginative writer of the first rank, or even of the fifth rank, was something that, in their insanest moments, never so much as occurred to them. Phelps cites, in particular, an ass named Professor Richardson, whose *American Literature,* it appears, "is still a standard work" and "a deservedly high authority"—apparently in colleges. In the 1892 edition of this *magnum opus,* Mark is dismissed with less than four lines, and ranked below Irving, Holmes, and Lowell—nay, actually below Artemus Ward, Josh Billings, and Petroleum V. Nasby! The thing is fabulous, fantastic, *unglaublich*—but nevertheless true. Lacking the "higher artistic or moral purpose of the greater humorists" (*exempli gratia,* Rabelais, Molière, Aristophanes!!), Mark is dismissed by this Professor Balderdash as a hollow buffoon. . . . But stay! Do not laugh yet! Phelps himself, indignant at the stupidity, now proceeds to credit Mark with a moral purpose! . . . Turn to *The Mysterious Stranger,* or *What Is Man?* . . .

College professors, alas, never learn anything. The identical gentleman who achieved this discovery about old Mark in 1910 now seeks to dispose of Dreiser in the exact manner of Richardson. That is to say, he essays to finish him by putting him into Coventry, by loftily passing over him. "Do not speak of him," said Kingsley of Heine; "he was a wicked man!" Search the latest volume of the Phelps revelation, *The Advance of the English Novel,* and you will find that Dreiser is not once mentioned in it. The late O. Henry is hailed as a genius who will have "abiding fame"; Henry Sydnor Harrison is hymned as "more than a clever novelist," nay, "a valuable ally of the angels" (the right-thinker complex! art as a form of snuffling!), and an obscure Pagliaccio named Charles D. Stewart is brought forward as "the American novelist most worthy to fill the particular vacancy caused by the death of Mark Twain"—but Dreiser is not even listed in the index. And where Phelps leads with his baton of birch most of the other drovers of rah-rah boys follow. I turn, for example, to *An Introduction to American Literature,* by Henry S. Pancoast, A.M., L.H.D., dated 1912. There are kind words for Richard Harding Davis, for Amélie Rives, and even for Will N. Harben, but not a syllable for Dreiser. Again, there is *A History of American Literature,* by Reuben Post Halleck, A.M., LL.D., dated 1911. Lew Wallace, Marietta Holley, Owen Wister, and Augusta Evans Wilson have their hearings, but not Dreiser. Yet again, there is *A History of American Literature Since 1870,* by Prof. Fred Lewis Pattee,[1] instructor in "the English language and literature" somewhere in Pennsylvania. Pattee has praises for Marion Crawford, Margaret Deland, and F. Hopkinson Smith, and polite bows for Richard Harding Davis and Robert W. Chambers, but from end to end of his fat tome I am unable to find the slightest mention of Dreiser.

So much for one group of heroes of the new *Dunciad.* That it includes most of the acknowledged heavyweights of the craft—the Babbitts, Mores, Brownells, and so on—goes without saying; as Van Wyck Brooks has pointed out,[2] these magnificoes are austerely above any consideration of the literature that is in being. The other group, more courageous and more honest, proceeds by direct attack; Dreiser is to be

[1]New York, The Century Co., 1916. H. L. M.

[2]In *The Seven Arts,* May 1917. H. L. M.

disposed of by a moral *attentat*. Its leaders are two more professors, Stuart P. Sherman and H. W. Boynton, and in its ranks march the lady critics of the newspapers, with much shrill, falsetto clamor. Sherman is the only one of them who shows any intelligible reasoning. Boynton, as always, is a mere parroter of conventional phrases, and the objections of the ladies fade imperceptibly into a pious indignation which is indistinguishable from that of the professional suppressors of vice.

What, then, is Sherman's complaint? In brief, that Dreiser is a liar when he calls himself a realist; that he is actually a naturalist, and hence accursed. That "he has evaded the enterprise of representing human conduct, and confined himself to a representation of animal behavior." That he "imposes his own naturalistic philosophy" upon his characters, making them do what they ought not to do, and think what they ought not to think. That "he has just two things to tell us about Frank Cowperwood: that he has a rapacious appetite for money, and a rapacious appetite for women." That this alleged "theory of animal behavior" is not only incorrect but downright immoral, and that "when one half the world attempts to assert it, the other half rises in battle."[1]

Only a glance is needed to show the vacuity of all this *brutum fulmen*. Dreiser, in point of fact, is scarcely more the realist or the naturalist, in any true sense, than H. G. Wells or the later George Moore, nor has he ever announced himself in either the one character or the other—if there be, in fact, any difference between them that anyone save a pigeonholing pedagogue can discern. He is really something quite different, and, in his moments, something far more stately. His aim is not merely to record, but to translate and understand; the thing he exposes is not the empty event and act, but the endless mystery out of which it springs; his pictures have a passionate compassion in them that it is hard to separate from poetry. If this sense of the universal and inexplicable tragedy, if this vision of life as a seeking without a finding, if this adept summoning up of moving images, is mistaken by college professors for the empty, meticulous

[1]The *Nation*, December 2, 1915. H. L. M.

nastiness of Zola in *Pot-Bouille*—in Nietzsche's phrase, for "the delight to stink"—then surely the folly of college professors, as vast as it seems, has been underestimated. What is the fact? The fact is that Dreiser's attitude of mind, his manner of reaction to the phenomena he represents, the whole of his alleged "naturalistic philosophy," stems directly, not from Zola, Flaubert, Augier, and the younger Dumas, but from the Greeks. In the midst of democratic cocksureness and Christian sentimentalism, of doctrinaire shallowness and professorial smugness, he stands for a point of view which at least has something honest and courageous about it; here, at all events, he is a realist. Let him put a motto to his books, and it might be:

Ἰὼ γενεαὶ βροτῶν,
Ὡς ὑμᾶς ἴσα καὶ τὸ μηδὲν ζώσας ἐναριθμῶ.

If you protest against that as too harsh for Christians and college professors, right thinkers and forward lookers, then you protest against *Oedipus Rex*.[1]

As for the animal behavior prattle of the learned headmaster, it reveals, on the one hand, only the academic fondness for seizing upon high-sounding but empty phrases and using them to alarm the populace, and, on the other hand, only the academic incapacity for observing facts correctly and reporting them honestly. The truth is, of course, that the behavior of such men as Cowperwood and Witla and of such women as Carrie and Jennie, as Dreiser describes it, is no more merely animal than the behavior of such acknowledged and undoubted beings as Dr. Woodrow Wilson and Dr. Jane Addams. The whole point of the story of Witla, to take the example which seems to concern the horrified watchmen most, is this: that his life is a bitter conflict between the animal in him and the aspiring soul, between the flesh and the spirit, between what is weak in him and what is strong, between what is base and what is noble. Moreover,

[1] 1186–1189. So translated by Floyd Dell: "O ye deathward-going tribes of man, what do your lives mean except that they go to nothingness?" H. L. M.

the good, in the end, gets its hooks into the bad: as we part from Witla he is actually bathed in the tears of remorse, and resolved to be a correct and godfearing man. And what have we in *The Financier* and *The Titan?* A conflict, in the ego of Cowperwood, between aspiration and ambition, between the passion for beauty and the passion for power. Is either passion animal? To ask the question is to answer it.

I single out Dr. Sherman, not because his pompous syllogisms have any plausibility in fact or logic, but simply because he may well stand as archetype of the booming, indignant corrupter of criteria, the moralist turned critic. A glance at his paean to Arnold Bennett[1] at once reveals the true gravamen of his objection to Dreiser. What offends him is not actually Dreiser's shortcoming as an artist, but Dreiser's shortcoming as a Christian and an American. In Bennett's volumes of pseudo-philosophy—*e.g., The Plain Man and His Wife* and *The Feast of St. Friend*—he finds the intellectual victuals that are to his taste. Here we have a sweet commingling of virtuous conformity and complacent optimism, of sonorous platitude and easy certainty—here, in brief, we have the philosophy of the English middle classes—and here, by the same token, we have the sort of guff that the half-educated of our own country can understand. It is the calm, superior numskullery that was Victorian; it is by Samuel Smiles out of Hannah More. The offense of Dreiser is that he has disdained this revelation and gone back to the Greeks. Lo, he reads poetry into "the appetite for women"—he rejects the Pauline doctrine that all love is below the diaphragm! He thinks of Ulysses, not as a mere heretic and criminal, but as a great artist. He sees the life of man, not as a simple theorem in Calvinism, but as a vast adventure, an enchantment, a mystery. It is no wonder that respectable schoolteachers are against him. . . .

The comstockian attack upon *The "Genius"* seems to have sprung out of the same muddled sense of Dreiser's essential hostility to all that is safe and regular—of the danger in him to that mellowed Methodism which has become the national ethic. The book, in a way, was a direct challenge, for though

[1]The New York *Evening Post,* December 31, 1915. H. L. M.

it came to an end upon a note which even a Methodist might hear as sweet, there were undoubted provocations in detail. Dreiser, in fact, allowed his scorn to make off with his taste—and *es ist nichts fürchtlicher als Einbildungskraft ohne Geschmack.* The Comstocks arose to the bait a bit slowly, but nonetheless surely. Going through the volume with the terrible industry of a Sunday-school boy dredging up pearls of smut from the Old Testament, they achieved a list of no less than 89 alleged floutings of the code—75 described as lewd and 14 as profane. An inspection of these specifications affords mirth of a rare and lofty variety; nothing could more cruelly expose the inner chambers of the moral mind. When young Witla, fastening his best girl's skate, is so overcome by the carnality of youth that he hugs her, it is set down as lewd. On page 51, having become an art student, he is fired by "a great, warm-tinted nude of Bouguereau"—lewd again. On page 70 he begins to draw from the figure, and his instructor cautions him that the female breast is round, not square—more lewdness. On page 151 he kisses a girl on mouth and neck and she cautions him: "Be careful! Mamma may come in"—still more. On page 161, having got rid of mamma, she yields "herself to him gladly, joyously" and he is greatly shocked when she argues that an artist (she is by way of being a singer) had better not marry—lewdness doubly damned. On page 245 he and his bride, being ignorant, neglect the principles laid down by Dr. Sylvanus Stall in his great works on sex hygiene—lewdness most horrible! But there is no need to proceed further. Every kiss, hug, and tickle of the chin in the chronicle is laboriously snouted out, empaneled, exhibited. Every hint that Witla is no vestal, that he indulges his unchristian fleshliness, that he burns in the manner of *I Corinthians,* VII, 9, is uncovered to the moral inquisition.

On the side of profanity there is a less ardent pursuit of evidences, chiefly, I daresay, because their unearthing is less stimulating. (Beside, there is no law prohibiting profanity in books: the whole inquiry here is but so much *lagniappe.*) On page 408, in describing a character called Daniel C. Summerfield, Dreiser says that the fellow is "very much given to swearing, more as a matter of habit than of foul intention," and then goes on to explain somewhat lamely that "no picture of him would be complete without the interpolation of his various expressions." They turn out to be *God damn* and *Jesus Christ*—three of the latter and five or six of the former. All go down; the pure in heart must be shielded from the knowledge of them. (But what of the immoral French? They call the English *Goddams.*) Also, three plain *damns,* eight *hells,* one *my God,* five *by Gods,* one *go to the devil,* one *God Almighty,* and one plain *God.* Altogether, 31 specimens are listed. *The "Genius"* runs to 350,000 words. The profanity thus works out to somewhat less than one word in 10,000. . . . Alas, the comstockian proboscis, feeling for such offendings, is not as alert as when uncovering more savory delicacies. On page 191 I find an overlooked *by God.* On page 372 there are *Oh God, God curse her,* and *God strike her dead.* On page 373 there are *Ah God, Oh God,* and three other invocations of God. On page 617 there is *God help me.* On page 720 there is *as God is my judge.* On page 723 there is *I'm no damned good.* . . . But I begin to blush.

When the Comstock Society began proceedings against *The "Genius,"* a group of English novelists, including Arnold Bennett, H. G. Wells, W. L. George, and Hugh Walpole, cabled an indignant caveat. This bestirred the Author's League of America to activity, and its executive committee issued a minute denouncing the business. Later on a protest of American *literati* was circulated, and more than 400 signed, including such highly respectable authors as Winston Churchill, Percy MacKaye, Booth Tarkington, and James Lane Allen, and such critics as Lawrence Gilman, Clayton Hamilton, and James Huneker, and the editors of such journals as the *Century,* the *Atlantic Monthly,* and the *New Republic.* Among my literary lumber is all the correspondence relating to this protest, not forgetting the letters of those who refused to sign, and someday I hope to publish it, that posterity may not lose the joy of an extremely diverting episode. Meanwhile, the case moves with stately dignity through the interminable corridors of jurisprudence, and the bulk of the briefs and exhibits that it throws off begins to rival the staggering bulk of *The "Genius"* itself.[1]

[1]Despite the comstockian attack, Dreiser is still fairly well represented on the shelves of American public libraries. A canvass of the libraries of the 25 principal cities gives the following result, an × indicating that the corresponding book is catalogued, and a – that it is not:

	Sister Carrie	*Jennie Gerhardt*	*The Financier*	*The Titan*	*A Traveler at Forty*	*The "Genius"*	*Plays of the Natural*	*A Hoosier Holiday*
New York	×	—	—	×	×	×	×	×
Boston	—	—	—	—	×	—	×	—
Chicago	×	×	×	×	×	×	×	×
Philadelphia	×	×	×	×	×	×	×	×
Washington	—	—	—	—	×	—	×	—
Baltimore	—	—	—	—	×	—	—	—
Pittsburgh	—	—	×	×	×	×	—	×
New Orleans	—	—	—	—	—	—	—	—
Denver	×	×	×	×	×	×	×	×
San Francisco	×	×	×	×	×	—	—	×
St. Louis	×	×	×	×	×	—	×	—
Cleveland	×	×	×	×	—	×	×	—
Providence	—	—	—	—	—	—	—	—
Los Angeles	×	×	×	×	×	×	×	×
Indianapolis	×	×	×	—	×	—	×	×
Louisville	×	×	—	×	×	×	×	×
St. Paul	×	×	—	—	×	—	×	×
Minneapolis	×	×	×	—	×	—	×	—
Cincinnati	×	×	×	—	×	—	×	×
Kansas City	×	×	×	×	×	×	×	×
Milwaukee	—	—	—	—	×	—	×	×
Newark	×	×	×	×	×	×	×	×
Detroit	×	×	×	—	×	×	×	×
Seattle	×	×	—	—	×	—	×	×
Hartford	—	—	—	—	—	—	—	×

This table shows that but two libraries, those of Providence and New Orleans, bar Dreiser altogether. The effect of alarms from newspaper reviewers is indicated by the scant distribution of the *The "Genius,"* which is barred by 14 of the 25. It should be noted that some of these libraries issue certain of the books only under restrictions. This I know to be the case in Louisville, Los Angeles, Newark, and Cleveland. The Newark librarian informs me that *Jennie Gerhardt* is to be removed altogether, presumably in response to some protest from local Comstocks. In Chicago *The "Genius"* has been stolen, and on account of the withdrawal of the book the Public Library has been unable to get another copy. H. L. M.

VII

Dreiser, like Mark Twain and Emerson before him, has been far more hospitably greeted in his first stage, now drawing to a close, in England than in his own country. The cause of this, I daresay, lies partly in the fact that *Sister Carrie* was in general circulation over there during the seven years that it remained suppressed on this side. It was during these years that such men as Arnold Bennett, Theodore Watts-Dunton, Frank Harris, and H. G. Wells, and such critical journals as the *Spectator*, the *Saturday Review*, and the *Athenaeum* became aware of him, and so laid the foundations of a sound appreciation of his subsequent work. Since the beginning of the war, certain English newspapers have echoed the alarmed American discovery that he is a literary agent of the Wilhelmstrasse, but it is to the honor of the English that this imbecility has got no countenance from reputable authority and has not injured his position.

At home, as I have shown, he is less fortunate. When criticism is not merely an absurd effort to chase him out of court because his ideas are not orthodox, as the Victorians tried to chase out Darwin and Swinburne, and their predecessors pursued Shelley and Byron, it is too often designed to identify him with some branch or other of "radical" poppycock, and so credit him with purposes he has never imagined. Thus Chautauqua pulls and Greenwich Village pushes. In the middle ground there proceeds the pedantic effort to dispose of him by labeling him. One faction maintains that he is a realist; another calls him a naturalist; a third argues that he is really a disguised romanticist. This debate is all sound and fury, signifying nothing, but out of it has come a valuation by Lawrence Gilman[1] which perhaps strikes very close to the truth. He is, says Mr. Gilman, "a sentimental mystic who employs the mimetic gestures of the realist." This judgment is apt in particular and sound in general. No such thing as a pure method is possible in the novel. Plain realism, as in Gorky's *Nachtasyl* and the war stories of Ambrose Bierce, simply wearies us by its vacuity; plain romance, if we ever

[1]The *North American Review*, February 1916. H. L. M.

get beyond our nonage, makes us laugh. It is their artistic combination, as in life itself, that fetches us—the subtle projection of the concrete muddle that is living against the ideal orderliness that we reach out for—the eternal war of experience and aspiration—the contrast between the world as it is and the world as it might be or ought to be. Dreiser describes the thing that he sees, laboriously and relentlessly, but he never forgets the dream that is behind it. "He gives you," continues Mr. Gilman, "a sense of actuality; but he gives you more than that: out of the vast welter and surge, the plethoric irrelevancies, . . . emerges a sense of the infinite sadness and mystery of human life." . . .[1]

"To see truly," said Renan, "is to see dimly." Dimness or mystery, call it what you will: it is in all these overgrown and formless, but profoundly moving books. Just what do they mean? Just what is Dreiser driving at? That such questions should be asked is only a proof of the straits to which pedagogy has brought criticism. The answer is simple: he is driving at nothing, he is merely trying to represent what he sees and feels. His moving impulse is no flabby yearning to teach, to expound, to make simple; it is that "obscure inner necessity" of which Conrad tells us, the irresistible creative passion of a genuine artist, standing spellbound before the impenetrable enigma that is life, enamored by the strange beauty that plays over its sordidness, challenged to a wondering and half-terrified sort of representation of what passes understanding. And *jenseits von Gut und Böse*. "For myself," says Dreiser, "I do not know what truth is, what beauty is, what love is, what hope is. I do not believe anyone absolutely and I do not doubt anyone absolutely. I think people are both evil and well-intentioned." The hatching of the Dreiser bugaboo is here; it is the flat rejection of the rubber-stamp formulae that outrages petty minds; not being "good," he must be "evil"—as William Blake said of Milton, a true poet is always "of the devil's party." But in that very groping toward a light but dimly seen there is a measure, it seems to me, of Dreiser's rank and consideration as an artist. "Now

[1]Another competent valuation, by Randolph Bourne, is in *The Dial,* June 14, 1917. H. L. M.

comes the public," says Hermann Bahr, "and demands that we explain what the poet is trying to say. The answer is this: If we knew exactly he would not be a poet. . . ."

JAMES HUNEKER

1917

EDGAR ALLAN POE, I am fond of believing, earned as a critic a good deal of the excess of praise that he gets as a romancer and a poet, and another overestimated American dithyrambist, Sidney Lanier, wrote the best textbook of prosody in English;[1] but in general the critical writing done in the United States has been of a low order, and most American writers of any genuine distinction, like most American painters and musicians, have had to wait for understanding until it appeared abroad. The case of Emerson is typical. At thirty, he was known in New England as a heretical young clergyman and no more, and his fame threatened to halt at the tea-tables of the Boston Brahmins. It remained for Landor and Carlyle, in a strange land, to discern his higher potentialities, and to encourage him to his real life-work. Mark Twain, as I have hitherto shown, suffered from the same lack of critical perception at home. He was quickly recognized as a funny fellow, true enough, but his actual stature was not even faintly apprehended, and even after *Huckleberry Finn* he was still bracketed with such laborious farceurs as Artemus Ward. It was Sir Walter Besant, an Englishman, who first ventured to put him on his right shelf, along with Swift, Cervantes, and Molière. As for Poe and Whitman, the native recognition of their genius was so greatly conditioned by a characteristic horror of their immorality that it would be absurd to say that their own country understood them. Both were better and more quickly apprehended in France, and it was in France, not in Amer-

[1] *The Science of English Verse;* New York, Scribner, 1880. H. L. M.

ica, that each founded a school. What they had to teach we have since got back at second-hand—the tale of mystery, which was Poe's contribution, through Gaboriau and Boisgobey; and *vers libre,* which was Whitman's, through the French *imagistes.*

The cause of this profound and almost unbroken lack of critical insight and enterprise, this puerile Philistinism and distrust of ideas among us, is partly to be found, it seems to me, in the fact that the typical American critic is quite without any adequate cultural equipment for the office he presumes to fill. Dr. John Dewey, in some late remarks upon the American universities, has perhaps shown the cause thereof. The trouble with our educational method, he argues, is that it falls between the two stools of English humanism and German relentlessness—that it produces neither a man who intelligently feels nor a man who thoroughly knows. Criticism, in America, is a function of this half-educated and conceited class; it is not a popular art, but an esoteric one; even in its crassest journalistic manifestations it presumes to a certain academic remoteness from the concerns and carnalities of everyday. In every aspect it shows the defects of its practitioners. The American critic of beautiful letters, in his common incarnation, is no more than a talented sophomore, or, at best, a somewhat absurd professor. He suffers from a palpable lack of solid preparation; he has no background of moving and illuminating experience behind him; his soul has not sufficiently adventured among masterpieces, nor among men. Imagine a Taine or a Sainte-Beuve or a Macaulay—man of the world, veteran of philosophies, "lord of life"—and you imagine his complete antithesis. Even on the side of mere professional knowledge, the primary material of his craft, he always appears incompletely outfitted. The grand sweep and direction of the literary currents elude him; he is eternally on the surface, chasing bits of driftwood. The literature he knows is the fossil literature taught in colleges—worse, in high schools. It must be dead before he is aware of it. And in particular he appears ignorant of what is going forward in other lands. An exotic idea, to penetrate his consciousness, must first become stale, and even then he is apt to purge it of all its remaining validity and significance before adopting it.

This has been true since the earliest days. Emerson himself, though a man of unusual discernment and a diligent drinker from German spigots, nevertheless remained a *dilettante* in both aesthetics and metaphysics to the end of his days, and the incompleteness of his equipment never showed more plainly than in his criticism of books. Lowell, if anything, was even worse; his aesthetic theory, first and last, was nebulous and superficial, and all that remains of his pleasant essays today is their somewhat smoky pleasantness. He was a Charles Dudley Warner in nobler trappings, but still, at bottom, a Charles Dudley Warner. As for Poe, though he was by nature a far more original and penetrating critic than either Emerson or Lowell, he was enormously ignorant of good books, and, moreover, he could never quite throw off a congenital vulgarity of taste, so painfully visible in the strutting of his style. The man, for all his grand dreams, had a shoddy soul; he belonged authentically to the era of cuspidors, "females," and Sons of Temperance. His occasional affectation of scholarship has deceived no one. It was no more than Yankee bluster; he constantly referred to books that he had never read. Beside, the typical American critic of those days was not Poe, but his arch-enemy, Rufus Wilmot Griswold, that almost fabulous ass—a Baptist preacher turned taster of the beautiful. Imagine a Baptist valuing Balzac, or Molière, or Shakespeare, or Goethe—or Rabelais!

Coming down to our own time, one finds the same endless amateurishness, so characteristic of everything American, from politics to cookery—the same astounding lack of training and vocation. Consider the solemn ponderosities of the pious old maids, male and female, who write book reviews for the newspapers. Here we have a heavy pretension to culture, a campus cocksureness, a laborious righteousness—but of sound aesthetic understanding, of alertness and hospitality to ideas, not a trace. The normal American book reviewer, indeed, is an elderly virgin, a superstitious bluestocking, an apostle of Vassar *Kultur;* and her customary attitude of mind is one of fascinated horror. (The Hamilton Wright Mabie complex! The "white list" of novels!) William Dean Howells, despite a certain jauntiness and even kittenishness of manner, is spiritually of that company. For all his phosphorescent heresies, he is what the uplifters call a right-thinker at heart, and soaked in the national tradition. He is easiest intrigued, not by force and originality, but by a sickly, *Ladies' Home Journal* sort of piquancy; it was this that made him see a genius in the Philadelphia Zola, W. B. Trites, and that led him to hymn an abusive business letter by Frank A. Munsey, author of *The Boy Broker* and *Afloat in a Great City,* as a significant human document. Moreover, Howells runs true to type in another way, for he long reigned as the leading Anglo-Saxon authority on the Russian novelists without knowing, so far as I can make out, more than ten words of Russian. In the same manner, we have had enthusiasts for D'Annunzio and Mathilde Serao who knew no Italian, and celebrants of Maeterlinck and Verhaeren whose French was of the finishing school, and Ibsen authorities without a single word of Dano-Norwegian—I met one once who failed to recognize *Et Dukkehjem* as the original title of *A Doll's House,*—and performers upon Hauptmann who could no more read *Die Weber* than they could decipher a tablet of Tiglath-Pileser III.

Here and there, of course, a more competent critic of beautiful letters flings out his banner—for example, John Macy, Ludwig Lewisohn, André Tridon (it is a pity Tridon writes so little: his slaughter of Maeterlinck was extraordinarily well performed), Otto Heller, J. E. Spingarn, Willard Huntington Wright, the late Percival Pollard. Well-informed, intelligent, wide-eyed men—but only two of them even Americans, and not one of them with a wide audience, or any appreciable influence upon the main stream of American criticism. Pollard's best work is buried in the perfumed pages of *Town Topics;* his book on the Munich wits and dramatists[1] is almost unknown. Heller and Lewisohn make their way slowly; a patriotic wariness, I daresay, mixes itself

[1] *Masks and Minstrels of New Germany;* Boston, John W. Luce & Co., 1911. H. L. M.

up with their acceptance. Wright turns to journalism and to theoretical aesthetics—a colossal dispersal indeed. As for Macy, I recently found his *The Spirit of American Literature*[1] by long odds the soundest, wisest book on its subject, selling for fifty cents on a Fifth Avenue remainder counter.

How many remain? A few competent reviewers who are primarily something else—Gilman, Bourne, Untermeyer and company. A few youngsters on the newspapers, struggling against the business office. And then a leap to the Victorians, the crêpe-clad pundits, the bombastic word-mongers of the *Nation* school—H. W. Boynton, W. C. Brownell, Paul Elmer More, William Lyon Phelps, Frederick Taber Copper, *et al.* Here, undoubtedly, we have learning of a sort. More, it appears, once taught Sanskrit to the adolescent suffragettes of Bryn Mawr—an enterprise as stimulating (and as intelligible) as that of setting off fireworks in a blind asylum. Phelps sits in a chair at Yale. Boynton is a master of arts in English literature, whatever that may mean. Brownell is both L.H.D. and Litt.D., thus surpassing Samuel Johnson by one point, and Hazlitt, Coleridge, and Malone by two. But the learning of these august *umbilicarii*, for all its pretensions, is precisely the sterile, foppish sort one looks for in second-rate college professors. Thc appearance is there, but not the substance. One ingests a horse doctor's dose of words, but fails to acquire any illumination. Read More on Nietzsche[2] if you want to find out just how stupid criticism can be and yet show the outward forms of sense. Read Phelps's *The Advance of the English Novel*[3] if you would see a fine art treated as a moral matter, and great works tested by the criteria of a small-town Sunday school, and all sorts of childish sentimentality whooped up. And plow through Brownell's *Standards*,[4] if you have the patience, and then try to reduce its sonorous platitudes to straightforward and defensible propositions.

[1]New York, Doubleday, Page & Co., 1913. H. L. M.

[2]*The Drift of Romanticism;* Boston, Houghton Mifflin Co., 1913. H. L. M.

[3]New York, Dodd, Mead & Co., 1916. H. L. M.

[4]New York, Charles Scribner's Sons, 1917. H. L. M.

II

Now for the exception. He is, of course, James Gibbons Huneker, the solitary Iokanaan in this tragic aesthetic wilderness, the only critic among us whose vision sweeps the whole field of beauty, and whose reports of what he sees there show any genuine gusto. That gusto of his, I fancy, is two-thirds of his story. It is unquenchable, contagious, inflammatory; he is the only performer in the commissioned troupe who knows how to arouse his audience to anything approaching enthusiasm. The rest, even including Howells, are pedants lecturing to the pure in heart, but Huneker makes a joyous story of it; his exposition, transcending the merely expository, takes on the quality of an adventure hospitably shared. One feels, reading him, that he is charmed by the men and women he writes about, and that their ideas, even when he rejects them, give him an agreeable stimulation. And to the charm that he thus finds and exhibits in others, he adds the very positive charm of his own personality. He seems a man who has found the world fascinating, if perhaps not perfect; a friendly and good-humored fellow; no frigid scholiast, but something of an epicure; in brief, the reverse of the customary maker of books about books. Compare his two essays on Ibsen, in *Egoists* and *Iconoclasts,* to the general body of American writing upon the great Norwegian. The difference is that between a portrait and a Bertillon photograph, Richard Strauss and Czerny, a wedding and an autopsy. Huneker displays Ibsen, not as a petty mystifier of the women's clubs, but as a literary artist of large skill and exalted passion, and withal a quite human and understandable man. These essays were written at the height of the symbolism madness; in their own way, they even show some reflection of it; but taking them in their entirety, how clearly they stand above the ignorant obscurantism of the prevailing criticism of the time—how immeasurably superior they are, for example, to that favorite hymn-book of the Ibsenites, *The Ibsen Secret* by Jennette Lee! For the causes of this difference one need not seek far. They are to be found in the difference between the bombastic half-knowledge of a schoolteacher and the discreet and complete knowledge of a man of culture. Huneker is that man of culture. He has reported more of interest and value than any other American critic, living or dead, but the essence of his criticism does not lie so much in what he specifically reports as in the civilized point of view from which he reports it. He is a true cosmopolitan, not only in the actual range of his adventurings, but also and more especially in his attitude of mind. His world is not America, nor Europe, nor Christendom, but the whole universe of beauty. As Jules Simon said of Taine: *Aucun écrivain de nos jours n'a . . . découvert plus d'horizons variés et immenses."*

Need anything else be said in praise of a critic? And does an extravagance or an error here and there lie validly against the saying of it? I think not. I could be a professor if I would and show you slips enough—certain ponderous nothings in the Ibsen essays, already mentioned; a too easy bemusement at the hands of Shaw; a vacillating over Wagner; a habit of yielding to the hocus-pocus of the mystics, particularly Maeterlinck. On the side of painting, I am told, there are even worse aberrations; I know too little about painting to judge for myself. But the list, made complete, would still not be overlong, and few of its items would be important. Huneker, like the rest of us, has sinned his sins, but his judgments, in the overwhelming main, hold water. He has resisted the lure of all the wild movements of the generation; the tornadoes of doctrine have never knocked him over. Nine times out of ten, in estimating a new man in music or letters, he has come curiously close to the truth at the first attempt. And he has always announced it in good time; his solo has always preceded the chorus. He was, I believe, the first American (not forgetting William Morton Payne and Hjalmar Hjorth Boyesen, the pioneers) to write about Ibsen with any understanding of the artist behind the prophet's mask; he was the first to see the rising star of Nietzsche (this was back in 1888); he was beating a drum for Shaw the critic before ever Shaw the dramatist and mob philosopher was born (*circa* 1886–90); he was writing about Hauptmann and Maeterlinck before they had got well set on their legs in their own countries; his estimate of Sudermann, bearing date of 1905, may stand with scarcely the change of a word today; he did a lot of valiant pioneering for Strindberg, Hervieu, Stirner, and Gorki, and later on helped in the pioneering for Conrad; he was in the van of the MacDowell enthusiasts; he fought for the ideas of such painters as Davies, Lawson, Luks, Sloan, and Prendergast (Americans all, by the way: an answer to the hollow charge of exotic obsession) at a time when even Manet, Monet, and Degas were laughed at; he was among the first to give a hand to Frank Norris, Theodore Dreiser, Stephen Crane, and H. B. Fuller. In sum, he gave some semblance of reality in the United States, after other men had tried and failed, to that great but ill-starred revolt against Victorian pedantry, formalism, and sentimentality which began in the early nineties. It would be difficult, indeed, to overestimate the practical value to all the arts in America of his intellectual alertness, his catholic hospitality to ideas, his artistic courage, and, above all, his powers of persuasion. It was not alone that he saw clearly what was sound and significant; it was that he managed, by the sheer charm of his writings, to make a few others see and understand it. If the United States is in any sort of contact today, however remotely, with what is aesthetically going on in the more civilized countries—if the Puritan tradition, for all its firm entrenchment, has eager and resourceful enemies besetting it—if the pall of Harvard quasi-culture, by the Oxford manner out of Calvinism, has been lifted ever so little—there is surely no man who can claim a larger share of credit for preparing the way. . . .

III

Huneker comes out of Philadelphia, that depressing intellectual slum, and his first writing was for the Philadelphia *Evening Bulletin.* He is purely Irish in blood, and is of very respectable ancestry, his maternal grandfather and godfather having been James Gibbons, the Irish poet and patriot, and president of the Fenian Brotherhood in America. Once, in a review of *The Pathos of Distance*, I ventured the guess that there was a German strain in him somewhere, and based it upon the beery melancholy visible in parts of that book. Who but a German sheds tears over the empty bottles of day before yesterday, the Adelaide Neilson of 1877? Who but a German goes into woolen undershirts at forty-five, and makes his will, and begins to call his wife "Mamma"? The green-sickness of youth is endemic from pole to pole, as much so as measles; but what race save the wicked one is floored by a blue distemper in middle age, with sentimental burblings *a cappella,* hallucinations of lost loves, and an unquenchable lacrymorrhea? . . . I made out a good case, but I was wrong, and the penalty came swiftly and doubly, for on the one hand the Boston *Transcript* sounded an alarm against both Huneker and me as German spies, and on the other hand Huneker himself proclaimed that, even spiritually, he was less German than Magyar, less "Hun" than Hun. "I am," he said, "a Celto-Magyar: Pilsener at Donneybrook Fair. Even the German beer and cuisine are not in it with the Austro-Hungarian." Here, I suspect, he meant to say Czech instead of Magyar, for isn't Pilsen in Bohemia? Moreover, turn to the chapter on Prague in *New Cosmopolis,* and you will find out in what highland his heart really is. In this book, indeed, is a vast hymn to all things Czechic—the Pilsen *Urquell,* the muffins stuffed with poppy-seed jam, the spiced chicken liver *en casserole,* the pretty Bohemian girls, the rose and golden glory of Hradčany Hill. . . . One thinks of other strange infatuations: the Polish Conrad's for England, the Scotch Mackay's for Germany, the Low German Brahms's for Italy. Huneker, I daresay, is the first Celto-Czech—or Celto-Magyar, as you choose. (Maybe the name suggests something. It is not to be debased to *Hoon*-eker, remember, but kept at *Hun*-eker, rhyming initially with *nun* and *gun.*) An unearthly marriage of elements, by all the gods! but there are pretty children of it. . . .

Philadelphia humanely disgorged Huneker in 1878. His father designed him for the law, and he studied the institutes at the Philadelphia Law Academy, but, like Schumann, he was spoiled for briefs by the stronger pull of music and the *cacoëthes scribendi.* (Grandpa John Huneker had been a composer of church music, and organist at St. Mary's.) In the year mentioned he set out for Paris to see Liszt; his aim was to make himself a piano virtuoso. His name does not appear on his own exhaustive list of Liszt pupils, but he managed to quaff of the Pierian spring at second hand, for he had lessons from Theodore Ritter (*né* Bennet), a genuine pupil of the old walrus, and he was also taught by the venerable Georges Mathias, a pupil of Chopin. These days laid the foundations for two subsequent books, the *Chopin: the Man and His Music* of 1900, and the *Franz Liszt* of 1911. More, they prepared the excavations for all of the others, for Huneker began sending home letters to the Philadelphia *Bulletin* on the pictures that he saw, the books that he read, and the music that he heard in Paris, and out of them gradually grew a body of doctrine that was to be developed into full-length criticism on his return to the United States. He stayed in Paris until the middle eighties, and then settled in New York.

All the while his piano studies continued, and in New York he became a pupil of Rafael Joseffy. He even became a teacher himself and was for ten years on the staff of the National Conservatory, and showed himself at all the annual meetings of the Music Teachers' Association. But bit by bit criticism elbowed out music-making, as music-making had elbowed out criticism with Schumann and Berlioz. In 1886 or thereabout he joined the *Musical Courier;* then he went, in succession, to the old *Recorder,* to the *Morning Advertiser,* to the *Sun,* to the *Times,* and finally back to the *Sun,* in whose columns he still occasionally holds forth. Various weeklies and monthlies have also enlisted him: *Mlle. New York,* the *Atlantic Monthly,* the *Smart Set,* the *North American Review,* and *Scribner's.* He has even stooped to *Puck,* vainly trying to make an American *Simplicissimus* of that dull offspring of synagogue and barbershop. He has been, in brief, an extremely busy and not too fastidious journalist, writing first about one of the arts, and then about another, and then about all seven together. But music has been the steadiest of all his loves; his first three books dealt almost wholly with it; of his complete canon more than half have to do with it.

IV

His first book, *Mezzotints in Modern Music,* published in 1899, revealed his predilections clearly, and, what is more, his critical insight and sagacity. One reads it today without the slightest feeling that it is an old story; some of the chapters, obviously reworkings of articles for the papers, must go back to the middle nineties, and yet the judgments they proclaim scarcely call for the change of a word. The single noticeable weakness is a too easy acquiescence in the empty showiness of Saint-Saëns, a tendency to bow to the celebrated French parlor magician too often. Here, I dare-say, is an echo of old Paris days, for Camille was a hero on the Seine in 1880, and there was even talk of pitting him against Wagner. The estimates of other men are judiciously arrived at and persuasively stated. Tschaikowsky is correctly put down as a highly talented but essentially shallow fel-low—a blubberer in the regalia of a philosopher. Brahms, then still under attack by Henry T. Finck, of the *Evening Post* (the press-agent of Massenet: ye gods, what Harvard can do, even to a Württemberger!) is subjected to a long, an intelligent, and an extremely friendly analysis; no better has got into English since, despite too much stress on the piano music. And Richard Strauss, yet a nine days' wonder, is described clearly and accurately, and his true stature indicated. The rest of the book is less noteworthy; Huneker says the proper things about Chopin, Liszt, and Wagner, and adds a chapter on piano methods, the plain fruit of his late pedagogy. But the three chapters I have mentioned are enough; they fell, in their time, into a desert of stupidity; they set a standard in musical criticism in America that only Huneker himself has ever exceeded.

The most popular of his music books, of course, is the *Chopin* (1900). Next to *Iconoclasts,* it is the best seller of them all. More, it has been done into German, French, and

Italian, and is chiefly responsible for Huneker's celebrity abroad as the only critic of music that America has ever produced. Superficially, it seems to be a monument of pedantry, a meticulous piling up of learning, but a study of it shows that it is very much more than that. Compare it to Sir George Grove's staggering tome on the Beethoven symphonies if you want to understand the difference between mere scholastic diligence and authentic criticism. The one is simply a top-heavy mass of disorderly facts and worshiping enthusiasm; the other is an analysis that searches out every nook and corner of the subject, and brings it into coherence and intelligibility. The Chopin rhapsodist is always held in check by the sound musician; there is a snouting into dark places as well as a touching up of high lights. I myself am surely no disciple of the Polish tuberose—his sweetness, in fact, gags me, and I turn even to Moszkowski for relief—but I have read and reread this volume with endless interest, and I find it more bethumbed than any other Huneker book in my library, saving only *Iconoclasts* and *Old Fogy*. Here, indeed, Huneker is on his own ground. One often feels, in his discussions of orchestral music, that he only thinks orchestrally, like Schumann, with an effort —that all music, in his mind, gets itself translated into terms of piano music. In dealing with Chopin no such transvaluation of values is necessary; the raw materials are ready for his uses without preparation; he is wholly at home among the black keys and white.

His *Liszt* is a far less noteworthy book. It is, in truth, scarcely a book at all, but merely a collection of notes for a book, some of them considerably elaborated, but others set down in the altogether. One reads it because it is about Liszt, the most fantastic figure that ever came out of Hungary, half devil and half clown; not because there is any conflagration of ideas in it. The chapter that reveals most of Huneker is the appendix on latter-day piano virtuosi, with its estimates of such men as de Pachmann, Rosenthal, Paderewski, and Hofmann. Much better stuff is to be found in *Overtones, The Pathos of Distance* and *Ivory, Apes and Peacocks*—brilliant, if not always profound studies of Strauss,

Wagner, Schoenberg, Moussorgsky, and even Verdi. But if I had my choice of the whole shelf, it would rest, barring the *Chopin*, on *Old Fogy*—the *scherzo* of the Hunekerian symphony, the critic taking a holiday, the Devil's Mass in the tonal sanctuary. In it Huneker is at his very choicest, making high-jinks with his Davidsbund of one, rattling the skeletons in all the musical closets of the world. Here, throwing off his critic's black gown, he lays about him right and left, knocking the reigning idols off their perches; resurrecting the old, old dead and trying to pump the breath into them; lambasting on one page and lauding on the next; lampooning his fellow critics and burlesquing their rubber-stamp fustian; extolling Dussek and damning Wagner; swearing mighty oaths by Mozart, and after him, Strauss—not Richard, but Johann! The Old Fogy, of course, is the thinnest of disguises, a mere veil of gossamer for "Editor" Huneker. That Huneker in false whiskers is inimitable, incomparable, almost indescribable. On the one hand, he is a prodigy of learning, a veritable warehouse of musical information, true, half-true, and apocryphal; on the other hand, he is a jester who delights in reducing all learning to absurdity. Reading him somehow suggests hearing a Bach mass rescored for two fifes, a tambourine in B, a wind machine, two tenor harps, a contrabass oboe, two banjos, eight tubas, and the usual clergy and strings. The substance is there; every note is struck exactly in the middle—but what outlandish tone colors, what strange, unearthly sounds! It is not Bach, however, who first comes to mind when Huneker is at his tricks, but Papa Haydn—the Haydn of the Surprise symphony and the Farewell. There is the same gargantuan gaiety, the same magnificent irreverence. Haydn did more for the symphony than any other man, but he also got more fun out of it than any other man.

Old Fogy, of course, is not to be taken seriously: it is frankly a piece of fooling. But all the same a serious idea runs through the book from end to end, and that is the idea that music is getting too subjective to be comfortable. The makers of symphonies tend to forget beauty altogether; their one effort is to put all their own petty trials and tribulations, their empty theories and speculations into cacophony. Even so far back as Beethoven's day that autobiographical habit had begun. "Beethoven," says Old Fogy, is "dramatic, powerful, a maker of storms, a subduer of tempests; but his speech is the speech of a self-centered egotist. He is the father of all the modern melomaniacs, who, looking into their own souls, write what they see therein—misery, corruption, slighting selfishness, and ugliness." Old Ludwig's groans, of course, we can stand. He was not only a great musician, but also a great man. It is just as interesting to hear him sigh and complain as it would be to hear the private prayers of Julius Caesar. But what of Tschaikowsky, with his childish Slavic whining? What of Liszt, with his cheap playacting, his incurable lasciviousness, his plebeian warts? What of Wagner, with his delight in imbecile fables, his popinjay vanity, his soul of a *Schnorrer*? What of Richard Strauss, with his warmed-over Nietzscheism, his flair for the merely horrible? Old Fogy sweeps them all into his rag-bag. If art is to be defined as beauty seen through a temperament, then give us more beauty and cleaner temperaments! Back to the old gods, Mozart and Bach, with a polite bow to Brahms and a sentimental tear for Chopin! Beethoven tried to tell his troubles in his music; Mozart was content to ravish the angels of their harps. And as for Johann Sebastian, "there was more real musical feeling, uplifting, and sincerity in the old Thomaskirche in Leipzig . . . than in all your modern symphony and oratorio machine-made concerts put together."

All this is argued, to be sure, in extravagant terms. Wagner is a mere ghoul and impostor: *The Flying Dutchman* is no more than a parody on Weber, and *Parsifal* is "an outrage against religion, morals, and music." Daddy Liszt is "the inventor of the Liszt pupil, a bad piano player, a venerable man with a purple nose—a Cyrano de Cognac nose." Tschaikowsky is the Slav gone crazy on vodka. He transformed Hamlet into "a yelling man" and Romeo and Juliet into "two monstrous Cossacks, who gibber and squeak at each other while reading some obscene volume." "His Manfred is a libel on Byron, who was a libel on God."

And even Schumann is a vanishing star, a literary man turned composer, a pathological case. But, as I have said, a serious idea runs through all this concerto for slapstick and seltzer siphon, and to me, at least, that idea has a plentiful reasonableness. We are getting too much melodrama, too much vivisection, too much rebellion—and too little music. Turn from Tschaikowsky's *Pathétique* or from any of his wailing tone-poems to Schubert's C major, or to Mozart's *Jupiter,* or to Beethoven's *kleine Sinfonie in F dur:* it is like coming out of a *Kaffeeklatsch* into the open air, almost like escaping from a lunatic asylum. The one unmistakable emotion that much of this modern music from the steppes and morgues and *Biertische* engenders is a longing for form, clarity, coherence, a self-respecting tune. The snorts and moans of the pothouse Werthers are as irritating, in the long run, as the bawling of a child, the squeak of a pig under a gate. One yearns unspeakably for a composer who gives out his pair of honest themes, and then develops them with both ears open, and then recapitulates them unashamed, and then hangs a brisk coda to them, and then shuts up.

V

So much for *Old Fogy* and the musical books. They constitute, not only the best body of work that Huneker himself has done, but the best body of musical criticism that any American has done. Musical criticism, in our great Calvinist republic, confines itself almost entirely to transient reviewing, and even when it gets between covers, it keeps its trivial quality. Consider, for example, the published work of Henry Edward Krehbiel, for long the *doyen* of the New York critics. I pick up his latest book, *A Second Book of Operas,*[1] open it at random, and find this:

> On January 31, 1893, the Philadelphia singers, aided by the New York Symphony Society, gave a performance of the opera, under the auspices of the Young Men's Hebrew Association, for the benefit of its charities, at the Carnegie Music Hall, New

[1]New York, The Macmillan Company, 1917. H. L. M.

York. Mr. Walter Damrosch was to have conducted, but was detained in Washington by the funeral of Mr. Blaine, and Mr. Hinrichs took his place.

O Doctor *admirabilis, acutus et illuminatissimus!* Needless to say the universities have not overlooked this geyser of buttermilk: he is an honorary A.M. of Yale. His most respectable volume, that on Negro folksong, impresses one principally by its incompleteness. It may be praised as a sketch, but surely not as a book. The trouble with Krehbiel, of course, is that he mistakes a newspaper morgue for Parnassus. He has all of the third-rate German's capacity for unearthing facts, but he doesn't know how either to think or to write, and so his criticism is mere pretense and pishposh. W. J. Henderson, of the *Sun,* doesn't carry that handicap. He is as full of learning as Krehbiel, as his books on singing and on the early Italian opera show, but he also wields a slippery and intriguing pen, and he could be hugely entertaining if he would. Instead, he devotes himself to manufacturing primers for the newly intellectual. I can find little of the charm of his *Sun* articles in his books. Lawrence Gilman? A sound musician but one who of late years has often neglected music for the other arts. Philip H. Goepp? His three volumes on the symphonic repertoire leave twice as much to be said as they say. Carl Van Vechten? A very promising novice, but not yet at full growth. Philip Hale? His gigantic annotations scarcely belong to criticism at all; they are musical talmudism. Beside, they are buried in the program books of the Boston Symphony Orchestra, and might as well be inscribed on the temple walls of Baalbec. As for Upton and other such fellows, they are merely musical chautauquans, and their tedious commentaries have little more value than the literary criticisms in the religious weeklies. One of them, a Harvard *maestro,* has published a book on the orchestra in which, on separate pages, the reader is solemnly presented with pictures of first and second violins!

It seems to me that Huneker stands on a higher level than any of these industrious gentlemen, and that his writings on music are of much more value, despite his divided allegiance among the *beaux arts*. Whatever may be said against him, it must at least be admitted that he knows Chopin, and that he has written the best volumes upon the tuberculous Pole in English. Vladimir de Pachmann, that king of all Chopin players, once bore characteristic testimony to the fact—I think it was in London. The program was heavy with the études and ballades, and Huneker sat in the front row of fanatics. After a storm of applause de Pachmann rose from the piano stool, levelled a bony claw at Huneker, and pronounced his dictum: "*He* knows more than *all* of you." Joseffy seems to have had the same opinion, for he sought the aid of his old pupil in preparing his new edition of Chopin, the first volume of which is all he lived to see in print. . . . And, beyond all the others, Huneker disdains writing for the kindergarten. There is no stooping in his discourse; he frankly addresses himself to an audience that has gone through the forms, and so he avoids the tediousness of the A B C expositors. He is the only American musical critic, save Van Vechten, who thus assumes invariably that a musical audience exists, and the only one who constantly measures up to its probable interests, supposing it to be there. Such a book as *Old Fogy*, for all its buffoonery, is conceivable only as the work of a sound musician. Its background is one of the utmost sophistication; in the midst of its wildest extravagances there is always a profound knowledge of music on tap, and a profound love of it to boot. Here, perhaps, more than anywhere else, Huneker's delight in the things he deals with is obvious. It is not a seminary that he keeps, but a sort of club of tone enthusiasts, and membership in it is infinitely charming.

VI

This capacity for making the thing described seem important and delightful, this quality of infectious gusto, this father-talent of all the talents that a critic needs, sets off his literary criticism no less than his discourse on music and musicians. Such a book as *Iconoclasts* or *Egoists* is full of useful information, but it is even more full of agreeable adventure. The style is the book, as it is the man. It is arch, staccato, ironical, witty, galloping, playful, polyglot, allusive —sometimes, alas, so allusive as to reduce the Drama Leaguer and women's clubber to wonderment and ire. In writing of plays or of books, as in writing of cities, tone-poems or philosophies, Huneker always assumes that the elements are already well-grounded, that he is dealing with the initiated, that a pause to explain would be an affront. Sad work for the Philistines—but a joy to the elect! All this polyphonic allusiveness, this intricate fuguing of ideas, is not to be confused, remember, with the hollow showiness of the academic soothsayer. It is as natural to the man, as much a part of him, as the clanging Latin of Johnson, or, to leap from art to art Huneker-wise, the damnable cross-rhythms of Brahms. He could no more write without his stock company of heretic sages than he could write without his ration of malt. And, on examination, all of them turned out to be real. They are far up dark alleys, but they are there! . . . And one finds them, at last, to be as pleasant company as the multilingual puns of Nietzsche or Debussy's chords of the second.

As for the origin of that style, it seems to have a complex ancestry. Huneker's first love was Poe, and even today he still casts affectionate glances in that direction, but there is surely nothing of Poe's elephantine laboring in his skipping, *pizzicato* sentences. Then came Carlyle—the Carlyle of *Sartor Resartus*—a god long forgotten. Huneker's mother was a woman of taste; on reading his first scribblings, she gave him Cardinal Newman, and bade him consider the Queen's English. Newman achieved a useful purging; the style that remained was ready for Flaubert. From the author of *L'Education Sentimentale*, I daresay, came the deciding influence, with Nietzsche's staggering brilliance offering suggestions later on. Thus Huneker, as stylist, owes nearly all to France, for Nietzsche, too, learned how to write there, and to the end of his days he always wrote more like a Frenchman than a German. His greatest service to his own country, indeed, was not as anarch, but as teacher of writing. He taught the Germans that their language had a snap in it as well as sighs and gargles—that it was possible to write German and yet not wander in a wood. There are whole pages of Nietzsche that suggest such things, say, as the essay on Maurice Barrès in *Egoists,* with its bold tropes, its rapid gait, its sharp *sforzandos.* And you will find old Friedrich at his tricks from end to end of *Old Fogy.*

Of the actual contents of such books as *Egoists* and *Iconoclasts* it is unnecessary to say anything. One no longer reads them for their matter, but for their manner. Every flapper now knows all that is worth knowing about Ibsen, Strindberg, Maeterlinck, and Shaw, and a great deal that is not worth knowing. We have disentangled Hauptmann from Sudermann, and, thanks to Dr. Lewisohn, may read all his plays in English. Even Henri Becque has got into the vulgate and is familiar to the Drama League. As for Anatole France, his *Revolt of the Angels* is on the shelves of the Carnegie Libraries, and the Comstocks have let it pass. New gods whoop and rage in Valhalla: Verhaeren, Artzibashef, Przhevalski. Huneker, alas, seems to drop behind the procession. He writes nothing about these second-hand third-raters. He has come to Wedekind, Schnitzler, Schoenberg, Korngold, and Moussorgsky, and he has discharged a few rounds of shrapnel at the Gallo-Asiatic petticoat philosopher, Henri Bergson, but here he has stopped, as he has stopped at Matisse, Picasso, Epstein, and Augustus John in painting. As he says himself, "one must get off somewhere." . . .

Particularly if one grows weary of criticism—and in Huneker, of late, I detect more than one sign of weariness. Youth is behind him, and with it some of its zest for exploration and combat. "The pathos of distance" is a phrase that haunts him as poignantly as it haunted Nietzsche, its maker. Not so long ago I tried to induce him to write some new Old Fogy sketches, nominating Puccini, Stravinsky, Schoenberg, Korngold, Elgar. He protested that the mood was gone from him forever, that he could not turn the clock back twenty years. His late work in *Puck,* the *Times,* and the *Sun,* shows an unaccustomed acquiescence in current valuations. He praises such one-day masterpieces as McFee's *Casuals of the Sea;* he is polite to the kept idealists of the *New Republic;* he gags a bit at Wright's *Modern Painting;* he actually makes a gingery curtsy to Frank Jewett Mather, a Princeton professor. . . . The pressure in the gauges can't keep up to 250 pounds forever. Man must tire of fighting after awhile, and seek his ease in his inn. . . .

Perhaps the post-bellum transvaluation of all values will bring Huneker to his feet again, and with something of the old glow and gusto in him. And if the new men do not stir up, then assuredly the wrecks of the ancient cities will: the Paris of his youth; Munich, Dresden, Vienna, Brussels, London; above all, Prague. Go to *New Cosmopolis* and you will find where his heart lies, or, if not his heart, then at all events his oesophagus and pylorus. . . . Here, indeed the thread of his meditations is a thread of nutriment. However diverted by the fragrance of the Dutch woods, the church bells of Belgium, the music of Stuttgart, the bad pictures of Dublin, the plays of Paris, the musty romance of old Wien, he always comes back anon to such ease as a man may find in his inn. "The stomach of Vienna," he says, "first interested me, not its soul." And so, after a dutiful genuflexion to St. Stephen's ("Old Steffel," as the Viennese call it), he proceeds to investigate the paprika-chicken, the *Gulyas,* the *Risi-bisi,* the *Apfelstrudel,* the *Kaiserchmarn,* and the native and authentic *Wienerschnitzel.* And from food to drink—specifically, to the haunts of Pilsener, to "certain semi-sacred houses where the ritual of beer-drinking is observed," to the shrines at which beer maniacs meet, to "a little old house near a Greek church" where "the best-kept Pilsener in Vienna may be found."

The best-kept Pilsener in Vienna! The phrase enchants like an entrance of the horns. The best caviare in Russia, the worst actor on Broadway, the most virtuous angel in Heaven! Such superlatives are transcendental. And yet,—so rare is perfection in this world!—the news swiftly follows, unexpected, disconcerting, that the best Pilsener in Vienna is far short of the ideal. For some undetermined reason—the influence of the American tourist? the decay of the

Austrian national character?—the Vienna *Bierwirte* freeze and paralyze it with too much ice, so that it chills the nerves it should caress, and fills the heart below with heaviness and repining. Avoid Vienna, says Huneker, if you are one who understands and venerates the great Bohemian brew! And if, deluded, you find yourself there, take the first *D-zug* for Prague, that lovely city, for in it you will find the Pilsen *Urquell,* and in the Pilsen *Urquell* you will find the best Pilsener in Christendom—its color a phosphorescent, translucent, golden yellow, its foam like whipped cream, its temperature exactly and invariably right. Not even at Pilsen itself (which the Bohemians call Plzeň) is the emperor of malt liquors more stupendously grateful to the palate. Write it down before you forget: the Pilsen *Urquell,* Prague, Bohemia, 120 miles S. S. E. of Dresden, on the river Moldau (which the natives call the Vltava). Ask for Fräulein Ottilie. Mention the name of Herr Huneker, the American *Schriftsteller.*

Of all the eminent and noble cities between the Alleghenies and the Balkans, Prague seems to be Huneker's favorite. He calls it poetic, precious, delectable, original, dramatic—a long string of adjectives, each argued for with eloquence that is unmistakably sincere. He stands fascinated before the towers and pinnacles of the Hradčany, "a miracle of tender rose and marble white with golden spots of sunshine that would have made Claude Monet envious." He pays his devotions to the Chapel of St. Wenceslaus, "crammed with the bones of buried kings," or, at any rate, to the shrine of St. John Nepomucane, "composed of nearly two tons of silver." He is charmed by the beauty of the stout, black-haired, red-cheeked Bohemian girls, and hopes that enough of them will emigrate to the United States to improve the fading pulchritude of our own houris. But most of all, he has praises for the Bohemian cuisine, with its incomparable apple tarts and its dumplings of cream cheese, and for the magnificent, the overpowering, the ineffable Pilsener of Prague. This Pilsener motive runs through the book from cover to cover. In the midst of Dutch tulip-beds, Dublin cobblestones, Madrid sunlight, and Atlantic City leg-shows, one hears it insistently, deep down in the orchestra. The cellos weave it into the polyphony, sometimes clearly, sometimes in scarcely recognizable augmentation. It is heard again in the wood-wind; the bassoons grunt it thirstily; it slides around in the violas; it rises to a stately choral in the brass. And chiefly it is in minor. Chiefly it is sounded by one who longs for the Pilsen *Urquell* in a far land, and among a barbarous and teetotaling people, and in an atmosphere as hostile to the recreations of the palate as it is to the recreations of the intellect.

As I say, this Huneker is a foreigner and hence accursed. There is something about him as exotic as a samovar, as essentially un-American as a bashi-bazouk, a nose-ring, or a fugue. He is filled to the throttle with strange and unpatriotic heresies. He ranks Beethoven miles above the national gods, and not only Beethoven, but also Bach and Brahms, and not only Bach and Brahms, but also Berlioz, Bizet, Bruch, and Bülow and perhaps even Balakirev, Bellini, Balfe, Borodin, and Boïeldieu. He regards Budapest as a more civilized city than his native Philadelphia, Stendhal as a greater literary artist than Washington Irving, *Künstler Leben* as better music than *There Is Sunlight in My Soul.* Irish? I still doubt it, despite the *Stammbaum.* Who ever heard of an Irish epicure, an Irish *flâneur,* or, for that matter, an Irish contrapuntist? The arts of the voluptuous category are unknown west of Cherbourg; one leaves them behind with the French pilot. Even the Czech-Irish hypothesis (or is it Magyar-Irish?) has a smell of the lamp. Perhaps it should be Irish-Czech. . . .

VII

There remain the books of stories, *Visionaries* and *Melomaniacs.* It is not surprising to hear that both are better liked in France and Germany than in England and the United States. (*Visionaries* has even appeared in Bohemian.) Both are made up of what the Germans call *Kultur-Novellen*—that is, stories dealing, not with the emotions common to all men, but with the clash of ideas among the civilized and godless minority. In some of them, *e.g.*, *Rebels of the Moon*, what one finds is really not a story at all, but a static discussion, half aesthetic and half lunatic. In others, *e.g.*, *Isolde's Mother*, the whole action revolves around an assumption incomprehensible to the general. One can scarcely imagine most of these tales in the magazines. They would puzzle and outrage the readers of Gouverneur Morris and Gertrude Atherton, and the readers of Howells and Mrs. Wharton no less. Their point of view is essentially the aesthetic one; the overwhelming importance of beauty is never in any doubt. And the beauty thus vivisected and fashioned into new designs is never the simple Wordsworthian article, of fleecy clouds and primroses all compact; on the contrary, it is the highly artificial beauty of pigments and tone-colors, of Cézanne landscapes and the second act of *Tristan und Isolde*, of Dunsanyan dragons and Paracelsian mysteries. Here, indeed, Huneker riots in the aesthetic occultism that he loves. Music slides over into diabolism; the Pobloff symphony rends the firmament of Heaven; the ghost of Chopin drives Mychowski to drink; a single drum-beat finishes the estimable consort of the composer of the Tympani symphony. In *The Eighth Deadly Sin* we have a paean to perfume—the only one, so far as I know, in English. In *The Hall of the Missing Footsteps* we behold the reaction of hasheesh upon Chopin's ballads in F major. . . . Strangely-flavored, unearthly, perhaps unhealthy stuff. I doubt that it will ever be studied for its style in our new Schools of Literature; a devilish cunning is often there, but it leaves a smack of the pharmacopoeia. However, as George Gissing used to say, "the artist should be free from everything like moral prepossession." This lets in the Antichrist. . . .

Huneker himself seems to esteem these fantastic tales above all his other work. Story-writing, indeed, was his first love, and his Opus 1, a bad imitation of Poe, by name *The Comet*, was done in Philadelphia so long ago as July 4, 1876. (Temperature, 105 degrees Fahrenheit.) One rather marvels that he has never attempted a novel. It would have been as bad, perhaps, as *Love Among the Artists*, but certainly no bore. He might have given George Moore useful help with *Evelyn Innes* and *Sister Teresa:* they are about music, but not by a musician. As for me, I see no great talent for fiction *qua* fiction in these two volumes of exotic tales. They are interesting simply because Huneker the story teller so often yields place to Huneker the playboy of the arts. Such things as *Antichrist* and *The Woman Who Loved Chopin* are no more, at bottom, than second-rate anecdotes; it is the filling, the sauce, the embroidery that counts. But what filling! What sauce! What embroidery! . . . One never sees more of Huneker. . . .

VIII

He must stand or fall, however, as critic. It is what he has written about other men, not what he has concocted himself, that makes a figure of him, and gives him his unique place in the sterile literature of the republic's second century. He stands for a *Weltanschauung* that is not only unnational, but anti-national; he is the chief of all the curbers and correctors of the American Philistine; in praising the arts he has also criticized a civilization. In the large sense, of course, he has had but small influence. After twenty years of earnest labor he finds himself almost as alone as a Methodist in Bavaria. The body of native criticism remains as I have described it; an endless piling up of platitudes, an homeric mass of false assumptions and jejune conclusions, an insane madness to reduce beauty to terms of a petty and pornographic morality. One might throw a thousand bricks in any American city without striking a single man who could give an intelligible account of either Hauptmann or Cézanne, or of the reasons for holding Schumann to have been a better composer than Mendelssohn. The boys in our colleges are still taught that Whittier was a great poet and Fenimore Cooper a great novelist. Nine-tenths of our people—perhaps ninety-nine hundredths of our native-born—have yet to see their first good picture, or to hear their first symphony. Our Chamberses and Richard Harding Davises are national figures; our Norrises and Dreisers are scarcely tolerated. Of the two undoubted world figures that we have contributed to letters, one was allowed to die like a stray cat up an alley and the other was mistaken for a cheap buffoon. Criticism, as the average American "intellectual" understands it, is what a Frenchman, a German, or a Russian would call donkeyism. In all the arts we still cling to the ideals of the dissenting pulpit, the public cemetery, the electric sign, the bordello parlor.

But for all that, I hang to a somewhat battered optimism, and one of the chief causes of that optimism is the fact that Huneker, after all these years, yet remains unhanged. A picturesque and rakish fellow, a believer in joy and beauty, a disdainer of petty bombast and moralizing, a sworn friend of all honest purpose and earnest striving, he has given his life to a work that must needs bear fruit hereafter. While the college pedagogues of the Brander Matthews type still worshiped the dead bones of Scribe and Sardou, Robertson and Bulwer-Lytton, he preached the new and revolutionary gospel of Ibsen. In the golden age of Rosa Bonheur's *The Horse Fair* he was expounding the principles of the post-impressionists. In the midst of the Sousa marches he whooped for Richard Strauss. Before the rev. professors had come to Schopenhauer, or even to Spencer, he was hauling ashore the devil-fish, Nietzsche. No stranger poisons have ever passed through the customs than those he has brought in his baggage. No man among us has ever urged more ardently, or with sounder knowledge or greater persuasiveness, that catholicity of taste and sympathy which stands in such direct opposition to the booming certainty and snarling narrowness of Little Bethel.

If he bears a simple label, indeed, it is that of anti-Philistine. And the Philistine he attacks is not so much the vacant and harmless fellow who belongs to the Odd Fellows and recreates himself with *Life* and *Leslie's Weekly* in the barber-shop, as that more belligerent and pretentious donkey who presumes to do battle for "honest" thought and a "sound" ethic—the "forward-looking" man, the university ignoramus, the conservator of orthodoxy, the rattler of ancient phrases—what Nietzsche called "the Philistine of culture." It is against this fat milch cow of wisdom that Huneker has brandished a spear since first there was a Huneker. He is a sworn foe to "the traps that snare the attention from poor or mediocre workmanship—the traps of sentimentalism, of false feeling, of cheap pathos, of the cheap moral." He is on the trail of those pious mountebanks who "clutter the market places with their booths, mischievous half-art and tubs of tripe and soft soap." Superficially, as I say, he seems to have made little progress in this benign *pogrom*. But under the surface, concealed from a first glance, he has undoubtedly left a mark—faint, perhaps, but still a mark. To be a civilized man in America is measurably less difficult, despite the war, than it used to be, say, in 1890. One may at least speak of *Die Walküre* without being laughed at as a half-wit, and read Stirner without being confused with Castro and Rasuili, and argue that Huxley got the better of Gladstone without being challenged at the polls. I know of no man who pushed in that direction harder than James Huneker.

A SHORT VIEW OF GAMALIELESE[1]

1921

In the first sentence of the historic address from the east front of the Capitol, glowing there like a gem, was that piquant miscegenation of pronouns, the *one-he* combination, for years a favorite of bad newspaper reporters and the inferior clergy. In the fourth sentence of the first message to Congress is *illy*, the passion of rural grammar-teachers and professors of rhetoric in one-building universities. We are, as they say, getting warm. The next great state paper—who knows?—may caress and enchant us with "*Whom* can

[1]This article deals with the inaugural address on March 4, 1921, by Warren Gamaliel Harding, twenty-ninth President of the United States. E. W.

deny?" And the next with "I would *have had* to *have had*." And the next with "between you and *I*." And the next, going the whole hog, with *alright*, to date the gaudiest, loveliest, darnedest flower of the American language, which God preserve!

Hog: flower? Perhaps the distemper is contagious. But certainly not uninteresting to study and snuffle over—certainly no dull thing to the specialist in morbid philology. In the style of the late Woodrow there was nothing, after all, very remarkable, despite the orgiastic praises of Adolph Ochs, the Hon. Josephus Daniels, and other such fanatics. It was simply the style of a somewhat literary and sentimental curate, with borrowings from Moody and Sankey and Dr. Berthold Baer. Its phrases lisped and cooed; there was a velvety and funereal gurgling in them; they were made to be intoned between the second and third lessons by fashionable rectors; aided by fifes and drums, or even by cost-plus contracts, they were competent to vamp the intellect. But intrinsically they were hollow. No heart's blood was in them; no gobs of raw flesh. There was no passion there, hot, exigent, and challenging. They could not make one puff and pant. . . . One had to wait for Dr. Harding for that. In his style there is pressure, ardency, effortcy, gasping, a high grunting, Cheyne-Stokes breathing. It is a style that rolls and groans, struggles and complains. It is the style of a rhinoceros liberating himself by main strength from a lake of boiling molasses.

In the doctrine that it is obscure I take no stock whatever. Not a single sentence in the two great papers is incomprehensible to me, even after I have dined. I exhume a sample strophe from the canto on the budget system in the message: "It will be a very great satisfaction to know of its early enactment, so it may be employed in establishing the economies and business methods so necessary in the minimum of expenditure." This is awful stuff, I grant you, but is it actually unintelligible? Surely not. Read it slowly and critically, and it may boggle you, but read it at one flash, and the meaning will be clear enough. Its method is that of *pointillisme*. The blotches of color are violent, and, seen too closely, they appear insane, but stand off a bit and a quite simple and even austere design is at once discerned. "I hope it is adopted soon, so that we may employ the economies and business methods needed to hold down expenses": this is the kernel. What else is there is the style. It is the style of what the textbooks of rhetoric call "elevated" discourse. Its aim is to lend force to a simple hope or plea or asseveration by giving it the dynamic whoop and hoopla of a revival sermon, an auction sale, or a college yell. The nuclear thought is not smothered in the process, as Democratic aesthetes argue, nor is it true that there is sometimes no nuclear thought at all. It is always present, and nine times out of ten it is simple, obvious, and highly respectable. But it lacks punch; it is devoid of any capacity to startle and scorch. To give it the vigor and dignity that a great occasion demands it is carefully encased in those swathings of sonorous polysyllables, and then, the charge being rammed home, it is discharged point-blank into the ears and cerebrums of Christendom.

Such is the Gamalian manner, the secret of the Gamalian style. That style had its origin under circumstances that are surely not unknown to experts in politico-agrarian oratory. It came to birth on the rustic stump, it developed to full growth among the chautauquas, and it got its final polishing in a small-town newspaper office. In brief, it reflects admirably the tastes and traditions of the sort of audience at which it was first aimed, to wit, the yokelry of the hinterland, naïve, agape, thirsty for the prodigious, and eager to yell. Such an audience has no fancy for a well-knit and succinct argument, packed with ideas. Of all ideas, indeed, it is suspicious, but it will at least tolerate those that it knows by long hearing, those that have come to the estate of platitudes, those that fall readily into gallant and highfalutin phrases. Above all, it distrusts perspicuity, for perspicuity is challenging and forces one to think, and hence lays a burden on the mind. What it likes most of all is the roll of incomprehensible polysyllables—the more incomprehensible the better. It wants to be bombarded, bawled at, overwhelmed by mad gusts of the parts of speech. It wants to be entertained by orators who are manifestly superior—fellows whose discourse is so all-fired learned and unintelligible, so brilliant with hard words and trombone phrases, that it leaves them gasping. Let the thunder sound, and it takes all else on trust. If a sentence ends with a roar, it does not stop to inquire how it began. If a phrase has punch, it does not ask that it also have a meaning. If a word stings, that is enough.

Trained to the service of such connoisseurs, Dr. Harding carries over the style that they admire into his traffic with the Congress, the effete *intelligentsia,* and the powers and principalities of Europe. That style is based upon the simplest of principles. For every idea there is what may be called a maximum investiture—a garb of words beyond which it is a sheer impossibility to go in gaudiness. For every plain word there is a word four times as big. The problem is to think the thing out in terms of harmless banality, to arrance a series of obvious and familiar ideas in a logical sequence, and then to translate them, one by one, into nouns, verbs, adjectives, adverbs, and pronouns of the highest conceivable horse-power—to lift the whole discourse to the plane of artillery practice—to dignify the sense by all the arts of sorcery. Turn to the two immortal documents. The word *citizen* is plainly banal; even a Congressman can understand it. Very well, then, let us make it *citizenship*—and *citizenship* it becomes every time. But even that is not enough. There comes a high point in the argument; a few more pounds of steam must be found. *Citizen* now undergoes a second proliferation; it becomes *factor in our citizenship.* "We must invite . . . every factor in our citizenship to join in the effort"—to restore normalcy. So with *women.* It is a word in common use, a vulgar word, a word unfit for the occasion of statecraft. *Also,* it becomes *womanhood.* Again, there is *reference;* it swells up a bit and becomes *referendum.* Yet again, *civil* becomes *civic*—more scholarly, more tasty, more nobby. Yet again, *interference* has a low smack; it suggests plow-horses that interfere. *En avant!* there is *intermediation!* And so with whole phrases. "The views of the world" gives way to "the expressed views of world opinion." "Heedless of cost" becomes "in heedlessness of cost." "Public conscience" becomes "the expressed conscience of progress." The "uplift," now ancient and a trifle obscene, is triumphantly reincarnated in "our manifestation of human interest." "The Government's duty to develop good citizens" shrieks upward like a rocket and bursts magnificently into "the Government's obligation affirmatively to encourage the development of the highest and most efficient type of citizenship." And so on and on.

Naturally enough, this style has its perils, no less hellish than war's. A man, so blowing up the parts of speech, may have one burst in his face. I discern something of the sort, alas, in "Congress might speed the price readjustment to normal relationship, with helpfulness of both producer and consumer." Here there has been an accident, just what I do not know. I suspect that "normal relationship" was substituted for *normalcy,* and that *normalcy* somehow got its revenge. Or maybe *helpfulness* came to its rescue and did the dirty work. Furthermore, the little word *of* has a suspicious look. I let the problem go. It is not one that a literary man engages with much gusto. He knows by harsh experience that words have a way of playing tricks—that they run amok at times, and toss him in the air, or stand him on his head—that fooling with them is like training leopards and panthers to leap through hoops and play the violoncello. There is, I have a notion, a foul conspiracy among words to pull Dr. Harding's legs from under him. He has tortured them for years—on the stump, in the chautauquas, beside the felled and smoking ox, at the annual banquets of the Chamber of Commerce, the Knights of Pythias, the Rotary Club, the Moose; above all, on the floors of legislative halls and in the columns of the Marion *Star*. He has forced them into strange and abhorrent marriages. He has stretched them as if they were chewing-gum. He has introduced pipes into them and pumped them until they screamed. He has put them to cruel and unusual uses. He has shown them no mercy. . . . Now, at last, they have him before a crowd that loves mirth, and make ready to get their *revanche*. Now they prepare to put the skids under him.

WANT AD

1926

THE DEATH of William Dean Howells in 1920 brought to an end a decorous and orderly era in American letters, and issued in a sort of anarchy. One may best describe the change, perhaps, by throwing it into dramatic form. Suppose Joseph Conrad and Anatole France were still alive and on their way to the United States on a lecture tour, or to study Prohibition or sex hygiene, or to pay their respects to Henry Ford. Suppose they were to arrive in New York at 2 P.M. today. Who would go down the bay on a revenue-cutter to meet them—that is, who in addition to the newspaper reporters and baggage-searchers—who to represent American Literature? I can't think of a single fit candidate. So long as Howells kept to his legs he was chosen almost automatically for all such jobs, for he was the dean of the national letters, and acknowledged to be such by everyone. Moreover, he had experience at the work and a natural gift for it. He looked well in funeral garments. He had a noble and ancient head. He made a neat and caressing speech. He understood etiquette. And before he came to his growth, stretching back into the past, there was a long line precisely like him —Mark Twain, General Lew Wallace, James Russell Lowell, Edmund Clarence Stedman, Richard Watson Gilder, Bryant, Emerson, Irving, Cooper, and so on back to the dark abysm of time.

Such men performed a useful and highly onerous function. They represented letters in all public and official ways. When there was a grand celebration at one of the older universities they were present in their robes, freely visible to the lowliest sophomore. When there was a great banquet, they sat between generals in the Army and members of the firm of J. P. Morgan & Company. When there was a solemn petition or protest to sign—against fiat money, the massacres in Armenia, municipal corruption, or the lack of international copyright—they signed in fine round hands, not for themselves alone, but for the whole fraternity of American literati. Most important of all, when a literary whale from foreign parts was sighted off Fire Island, they jumped into their frock coats, clapped on their plug-hats, and made the damp, windy trip through the Narrows on the revenue-cutter, to give the visitor welcome in the name of the eminent living and the illustrious dead. It was by such men that Dickens was greeted, and Thackeray, and Herbert Spencer, and Max O'Rell, and Blasco Ibáñez, and Matthew Arnold, and James M. Barrie, and Kipling, and (until they found his bootleg wife under his bed) Maxim Gorky. I name names at random. No worthy visitor was overlooked. Always there was the stately committee on the revenue-cutter, always there was the series of polite speeches, and always there was the general feeling that the right thing had been done in the right way—that American literature had been represented in a tasteful and resounding manner.

Who is to represent it today? I search the country without finding a single suitable candidate, to say nothing of a whole posse. Turn, for example, to the mystic nobles of the American Academy of Arts and Letters. I pick out five at random: William C. Brownell, Augustus Thomas, Hamlin Garland, Owen Wister, and Henry van Dyke. What is wrong with them? The plain but dreadful fact that no literary foreigner has even heard of them—that their appearance on the deck of his incoming barge would puzzle and alarm him, and probably cause him to call for the police. These men do not lack the homely virtues. They spell correctly, write neatly, and print nothing that is not constructive. In the five of them there is not enough sin to raise a congressman's temperature one-hundredth of a degree. But they are completely devoid of what is absolutely essential to the official life: they have, so to speak, no stage presence. There is nothing rotund and gaudy about them. No public and unanimous reverence bathes them. What they write or say never causes any talk. To be welcomed by them, jointly or severally, would appear to Thomas Hardy or Gabriel D'Annunzio as equal to being welcomed by representatives of the St. Joe, Mo., Rotary Club. Nor do I find any better stock among their heirs and apprentices in the National Institute. Put Henry Sydnor Harrison, say, against Howells: it is a wart succeeding Ossa. Match Clayton Hamilton with Edmund Clarence Stedman: Broadway against Wall Street. Shove Robert W. Chambers or Herman Hagedorn into the coat of Lowell: he would rattle in one of its pockets.

Worse, there are no better candidates outside the academic cloister. I daresay that most literate foreigners, asked to name the principal American novelist in practice today, would nominate Theodore Dreiser. He would get probably 75 per cent of the votes, with the rest scattered among Upton Sinclair, Sinclair Lewis, Cabell, Hergesheimer, and Sherwood Anderson. But try to imagine any of these gentlemen togged out in a long-tailed coat, shivering on the deck of a revenue-cutter while Gerhart Hauptmann got a grip on himself aboard the *Majestic!* Try to imagine Cabell presiding at a banquet to Knut Hamsun, with Dr. A. Lawrence Lowell to one side of him and Otto Kahn to the other! Try to picture Sinclair handing James Joyce a wreath to put upon the grave of James Whitcomb Riley! The vision, indeed, is more dismal than ludicrous. Howells, the last of his lordly line, is missed tremendously; there is something grievously lacking in the official hospitality of the country. The lack showed itself the instant he was called away. A few weeks later Columbia University gave a soirée in honor of the centenary of Lowell. The president of Columbia, Dr. Nicholas Murray Butler, is a realist. Moreover, he is a member of the American Academy himself, elected as a wet to succeed Edgar Allan Poe. He was thus privy to the deficiencies of his colleagues. To conceal the flabbiness of the evening he shoved them into back seats—and invited John D. Rockefeller, Jr., Tex Rickard, General Pershing, and the board of governors of the New York Stock Exchange to the platform!

I believe that, of living masters of letters, H. G. Wells was the first to feel the new chill. When he last visited the republic he was made welcome by a committee of ship-news reporters. It was as if one of the justices of the King's

Bench, landing in America, had been received by a committee of police-court lawyers from Gary, Ind. Later on American literature bestirred itself and gave Wells a banquet in New York. I was present at this feast, and a singular one it was. Not a single author read in Iowa or taught at Harvard was present. The principal literatus at the board was the late Frank A. Munsey, author of *Derringforth* and *The Boy Broker,* and the principal address was made by Max Eastman, formerly editor of the *Masses!* . . .

I come to a constructive suggestion. Let the literati of America meet in their respective places of social relaxation, each gang determining the credentials of its own members, and elect delegates to a national convention. Then let the national convention, by open ballot, choose ten spokesmen and ten alternates to represent the national letters on all formal occasions—not only when an eminent foreigner is to be made welcome, but also when Columbia University holds memorial services, when a President is inaugurated, when Harvard meets Yale, when monuments are unveiled—in brief, at all times of solemn public ceremonial. Let these representatives practice deportment and elocution. Let them employ good tailors and trustworthy bootleggers. I have, alas, no candidates for the committee. As I have said, there is a dreadful dearth of them. Does Dr. Frank Crane wear whiskers? If so, I nominate him.

RING LARDNER

1926

A FEW YEARS AGO a young college professor, eager to make a name for himself, brought out a laborious "critical" edition of *Sam Slick,* by Judge Thomas C. Haliburton, eighty-seven years after its first publication. It turned out to be quite unreadable—a dreadful series of archaic jocosities about varieties of *Homo americanus* long perished and forgotten, in a dialect now intelligible only to paleophilologists. Sometimes I have a fear that the same fate awaits Ring Lardner. The professors of his own day, of course, are quite unaware of him, save perhaps as a low zany to be enjoyed behind the door. They would no more venture to whoop him up publicly and officially than their predecessors of 1880 would have ventured to whoop up Mark Twain, or their remoter predecessors of 1837 would have dared to say anything for Haliburton. In such matters the academic mind, being chiefly animated by a fear of sneers, works very slowly. So slowly, indeed, does it work that it usually works too late. By the time Mark Twain got into the textbooks for sophomores two-thirds of his compositions, as the Young Intellectuals say, had already begun to date; by the time Haliburton was served up as a sandwich between introduction and notes he was already dead. As I say, I suspect sadly that Lardner is doomed to go the same route. His stories, it seems to me, are superbly adroit and amusing; no other contemporary American, sober or gay, writes better. But I doubt that they last: our grandchildren will wonder what they are about. It is not only, or even mainly, that the dialect that fills them will pass, though that fact is obviously a serious handicap in itself. It is principally that the people they depict will pass, that Lardner's Low-Down Americans—his incomparable baseball players, pugs, song-writers, Elks, small-town Rotarians, and golf caddies—are flitting figures of a transient civilization, and doomed to be as puzzling and soporific, in the year 2000, as Haliburton's Yankee clock peddler is today.

The fact—if I may assume it to be a fact—is certainly not to be set against Lardner's account; on the contrary, it is, in its way, highly complimentary to him. For he has deliberately applied himself, not to the anatomizing of the general human soul, but to the meticulous histological study of a few salient individuals of his time and nation, and he has done it with such subtle and penetrating skill that one must belong to his time and nation to follow him. I doubt that anyone who is not familiar with professional ball-players, intimately and at first hand, will ever comprehend the full merit of the amazing sketches in *You Know Me, Al;* I doubt that anyone who has not given close and deliberate attention to the American vulgate will ever realize how magnificently Lardner handles it. He has had more imitators, I suppose, than any other living American writer, but has he any actual rivals? If so, I have yet to hear of them. They all try to write the speech of the streets as adeptly and as amusingly as he writes it, and they all fall short of him; the next best is miles and miles behind him. And they are all inferior in observation, in sense of character, in shrewdness and insight. His studies, to be sure, are never very profound; he makes no attempt to get at the primary springs of human motive; all his people share the same amiable stupidity, the same transparent vanity, the same shallow swinishness; they are all human Fords in bad repair, and alike at bottom. But if he thus confines himself to the surface, it yet remains a fact that his investigations on that surface are extraordinarily alert, ingenious, and brilliant—that the character he finally sets before us, however roughly articulated as to bones, is so astoundingly realistic as to epidermis that the effect is indistinguishable from that of life itself. The old man in *The Golden Honeymoon* is not merely well done; he is perfect. And so is the girl in *Some Like Them Cold.* And so, even, is the idiotic Frank X. Farrell in *Alibi Ike*—an extravagant grotesque and yet quite real from glabella to calcaneum.

Lardner knows more about the management of the short story than all of its professors. His stories are built very carefully, and yet they seem to be wholly spontaneous, and even formless. He has grasped the primary fact that no conceivable ingenuity can save a story that fails to show a recognizable and interesting character; he knows that a good character sketch is always a good story, no matter what its structure. Perhaps he gets less attention than he ought to get, even among the anti-academic critics, because his people are all lowly boors. For your reviewer of books, like every other sort of American, is always vastly impressed by fashionable pretensions. He belongs to the white-collar class of labor, and shares its prejudices. He praises F. Scott Fitzgerald's stories of country-club flappers eloquently, and overlooks Fitzgerald's other stories, most of which are much better. He can't rid himself of the feeling that Edith Wharton, whose people have butlers, is a better novelist than Willa Cather, whose people, in the main, dine in their kitchens. He lingers under the spell of Henry James, whose most humble character, at any rate of the later years, was at least an Englishman, and hence superior. Lardner, so to speak, hits such critics under the belt. He not only fills his stories with people who read the tabloids, say "Shake hands with my friend," and buy diamond rings on the instalment plan; he also shows them having a good time in the world, and quite devoid of inferiority complexes. They amuse him sardonically, but he does not pity them. A fatal error! The moron, perhaps, has a place in fiction, as in life, but he is not to be treated too easily and casually. It must be shown that he suffers tragically because he cannot abandon the plow to write poetry, or the sample-case to study for opera. Lardner is more realistic. If his typical hero has a secret sorrow it is that he is too old to take up osteopathy and too much in dread of his wife to venture into bootlegging.

Of late a sharply acrid flavor has got into Lardner's buffoonery. His baseball players and fifth-rate pugilists, beginning in his first stories as harmless jackasses, gradually convert themselves into loathsome scoundrels. The same change shows itself in Sinclair Lewis; it is difficult, even for an American, to contemplate the American without yielding to something hard to distinguish from moral indignation. Turn, for example, to the sketches in the volume called *The Love Nest.* The first tells the story of a cinema queen married to a magnate of the films. On the surface she seems to be nothing but a noodle, but underneath there is a sewer; the woman is such a pig that she makes one shudder. Again, he investigates another familiar type: the village practical joker. The fellow, in one form or other, has been laughed at since the days of Aristophanes. But here is a mercilessly realistic examination of his dung-hill humor, and of its effects upon decent people. A third figure is a successful theatrical manager: he turns out to have the professional competence of a chiropractor and the honor of a Prohibition agent. A fourth is a writer of popular songs: stealing other men's ideas has become so fixed a habit with him that he comes to believe that he has an actual right to them. A fifth is a trained nurse—but I spare you this dreadful nurse. The rest are bores of the homicidal type. One gets the effect, communing with the whole gang, of visiting a museum of anatomy. They are as shocking as what one encounters there—but in every detail they are as unmistakably real.

Lardner conceals his new savagery, of course, beneath his old humor. It does not flag. No man writing among us has greater skill at the more extravagant varieties of jocosity. He sees startling and revelatory likeness between immensely disparate things, and he is full of pawky observations and bizarre comments. Two baseball-players are palavering, and one of them, Young Jake, is boasting of his conquests during spring practice below the Potomac. "Down South ain't here!" replies the other. "Those dames in some of those swamps, they lose their head when they see a man with shoes on!" The two proceed to the discussion of a third imbecile, guilty of some obscure tort. "Why," inquires Young Jake, "didn't you break his nose or bust him in the chin?" "His nose was already broke," replied the other, "and he didn't have no chin." Such wisecracks seem easy to devise. Broadway diverts itself by manufacturing them. They constitute the substance of half the town shows. But in those made by Lardner there is something far more than mere facile humor: they are all rigidly in character, and they illuminate that character. Few American novelists, great or small, have character more firmly in hand. Lardner does not see situations; he sees people. And what people! They are all as revolting as so many Methodist evangelists, and they are all as thoroughly American.

ONE of the most important elements in the literary activity that followed the War was the return from military service of a number of first-rate young writers: John Dos Passos, William Faulkner, Ernest Hemingway, E. E. Cummings. These men had had a deeper experience than Stephen Crane and Sherwood Anderson had had in the Spanish War: they had been involved in a world crisis, and they had seen what it meant at first hand. They had come back with a vivid memory of what human society looks like when the laws and the conventions are suspended, and with a conviction that they knew the reality which the civilians at home could not imagine.

This review by Dos Passos of Cummings' book appeared in *The Dial* of July 1922. Cummings had enlisted, during the War, in the Norton Harjes Ambulance Corps, but his unconstrained letters and talk had aroused the suspicions of the French authorities, who charged him with treasonable activity and sent him to a concentration camp. *The Enormous Room* (1922) is the story of the three months he spent there. Dos Passos had published the year before a novel about the War: *Three Soldiers*. Dos Passos at this time was twenty-six; Cummings twenty-seven.

JOHN DOS PASSOS

OFF THE SHOALS: *THE ENORMOUS ROOM* BY E. E. CUMMINGS

When the American Chicle Company brings out gum of a new shape and unfamiliar flavor gumchewers are delighted and miss their subway trains in rush hour and step on each other's heels crowding round slot machines in their haste to submit to a new sensation. Frequenters of cabarets and jazz palaces shimmy themselves into St. Vitus's dance with delight over a new noise in the band or a novel squirm in the rhythm. People mortgage their houses to be seen in the newest and most bizarre models of autos. Women hock their jewels and their husbands' insurance policies to acquire an unaccustomed shade in hair or *crêpe de chine.* Why, then, is it that when anyone commits anything novel in the arts he should be always greeted by this same peevish howl of pain and surprise? One is led to suspect that the interest people show in these much-talked-of commodities, painting, music, and writing, cannot be very deep or very genuine when they wince so under any unexpected impact.

The man who invented Eskimo Pie made a million dollars, so one is told, but E. E. Cummings, whose verse has been appearing off and on for three years now, and whose experiments should not be more appalling to those interested in poetry than the experiment of surrounding ice-cream with a layer of chocolate was to those interested in soda fountains, has hardly made a dent in the doughy minds of our so-called poetry-lovers. Yet one might have thought that the cadences of

> Or with thy mind against my mind, to hear
> nearing our hearts' irrevocable play—
> through the mysterious high futile day
> an enormous stride
>   (and drawing thy mouth toward
> my mouth, steer our lost bodies carefully downward)

would have melted with as brittle freshness on the senses of the readers of the *Dial* as melted the brown-encrusted oblongs of ice cream in the mouths of tired stenographers and their beaux. Can it be that people like ice-cream and only pretend to like poetry?

Therefore it is very fortunate that this book of E. E. Cummings has come out under the disguise of prose. The average reader is less self-conscious and more open to direct impressions when reading prose than verse; the idea that prose is ART will have closed the minds of only a few overeducated people. Here at last is an opportunity to taste without overmuch prejudice a form, an individual's focus on existence, a gesture unforeseen in American writing. The attempt to obscure the issue, on the paper-cover blurb and in the preface, will fool no one who reads beyond the first page. It's not as an account of a war atrocity or as an attack on France or the holy Allies timely to the Genoa Conference that *The Enormous Room* is important, but as a distinct conscious creation separate from anything else under heaven.

Here's a book that has been conceived unashamedly and directly without a thought either of the columnists or the book trade or Mr. Sumner, or of fitting into any one of the neatly labeled pigeonholes of novel, play, essay, history, travel book, a book that exists because the author was so moved, excited, amused by a certain slice of his existence that things happened freely and cantankerously on paper. And he had the nerve to let things happen. In this pattern-cut generation, most writers are too afraid of losing their private reputations as red-blooded, clear-eyed, hundred-percenters, well-dressed, well-mannered, and thoroughly disinfected fashion plates, to make any attempt to feel and express directly the life about them and in them. They walk in daily fear that someone will call them morbid, and insulate themselves from their work with the rubber raincoat of fiction. *The Enormous Room* seems to me to be the book that has nearest approached the mood of reckless adventure in which men will reach the white heat of imagination needed to fuse the soggy, disjointed complexity of the industrial life about us into seething fluid of creation. There can be no more playing safe. Like the old steamboat captains on the Mississippi we'll have to forget the hissing of the safety-valve and stoke like beavers if we are to get off the sticky shoals into the deeper reaches beyond. And many an old tub will blow sky high with all hands before someone makes the course. *The Enormous Room* for one seems to me at least to have cleared the shoals.

Along with Sandburg and Sherwood Anderson, E. E. Cummings takes the rhythms of our American speech as the material of his prose as of his verse. It is writing created in the ear and lips and jotted down. For accuracy in noting the halting cadences of talk and making music of it, I don't know anything that comes up to these two passages. This is a poem that came out in *The Dial:*

Buffalo Bill's
defunct
        who used to
        ride a watersmooth-silver
                                        stallion
and break onetwothreefourfive pigeonsjustlikethat
                                                                Jesus
he was a handsome man
                                    and what i want to know is
how do you like your blueeyed boy
Mister Death

This from *The Enormous Room:*

Sunday: green murmurs in coldness. Surplice fiercely fearful, praying on his bony both knees, crossing himself. . . . The

Fake French Soldier, alias Garibaldi, beside him, a little face filled with terror . . . the Bell cranks the sharp-nosed priest on his knees . . . titter from bench of whores—

And that reminds me of a Sunday afternoon on our backs spent with the wholeness of a hill in Chevancourt, discovering a great apple pie, B. and Jean Stahl and Maurice le Menusier and myself; and the sun falling roundly before us.

—And then one *Dimanche* a new high old man with a sharp violet face and green hair—"You are free, my children, to achieve immortality—*Songez, songez, donc—L'Eternité est une existence sans durée—Toujours le Paradis, toujours l'Enfer*" (to the silently roaring whores) "Heaven is made for you"—and the Belgian ten-foot farmer spat three times and wiped them with his foot, his nose dripping; and the nigger shot a white oyster into a far-off scarlet handkerchief—and the priest's strings came untied and he sidled crablike down the steps—the two candles wiggle a strenuous softness . . .

In another chapter I will tell you about the nigger.

And another Sunday I saw three tiny old females stumble forward, three very formerly and even once bonnets perched upon three wizened skulls, and flop clumsily before the priest, and take the wafer hungrily into their leathery faces.

This sort of thing knocks literature into a cocked hat. It has the raucous directness of a song-and-dance act in cheap vaudeville, the willingness to go the limit in expression and emotion of a Negro dancing. And in this mode, nearer the conventions of speech than those of books, in a style infinitely swift and crisply flexible, an individual not ashamed of his loves and hates, great or trivial, has expressed a bit of the underside of History with indelible vividness.

The material itself, of course, is superb. The Concentration Camp at La Ferté-Macé was one of those many fantastic crossroads of men's lives where one lingered for unforgettable moments, reaching them one hardly knew how, shoved away from them as mysteriously by some movement of the pawns on the chessboard, during the fearfully actual nightmare of war. A desperate recklessness in the air made every moment, every intonation snatched from the fates of absolute importance. In The Wanderer and Jean le Nègre and Surplice and Mexique and Apollyon and the Machine Fixer and in those grotesque incidents of the fight with the stovepipes and Celina's defiance we have that intense momentary flare in which lifetimes, generations are made manifest. To have made those moments permanent on a printed page is no common achievement.

For some reason there is a crispness and accuracy about these transcripts of the smell and taste and shiver of that great room full of huddled prisoners that makes me think of Defoe. In *The Journal of the Plague Year* or in the description of a night spent among enormous bones and skeletons in the desert journey in *Captain Singleton* one finds passages of a dry definiteness that somehow give the sort of impression that gives this hotly imaged picture of a roadside crucifix:

> I banged forward with bigger and bigger feet. A bird, scared, swooped almost into my face. Occasionally some night noise pricked a futile, minute hole in the enormous curtain of soggy darkness. Uphill now. Every muscle thoroughly aching, head spinning, I half-straightened my no longer obedient body; and jumped: face to face with a little wooden man hanging all by itself in a grove of low trees.
>
> —The wooden body, clumsy with pain, burst into fragile legs with absurdly large feet and funny writhing toes; its little stiff arms made abrupt cruel equal angles with the road. About its stunted loins clung a ponderous and jocular fragment of drapery. On one terribly brittle shoulder the droll lump of its neckless head ridiculously lived. There was in this complete silent doll a gruesome truth of instinct, a success of uncanny poignancy, an unearthly ferocity of rectangular emotion.
>
> For perhaps a minute the almost obliterated face and mine eyed one another in the silence of intolerable autumn.

Perhaps one thinks of Defoe because of the unashamed directness with which every twitch of the individual's fibers, stung or caressed by the world's flowing past outside, is noted down. There is no straining through the standard literary sieve.

Of the English eighteenth century, too, is the fine tang of

high adventure along roads among grotesque companions that comes to the surface in passages like this:

The high-road won, all of us relaxed considerably. The *sac* full of suspicious letters which I bore on my shoulder was not so light as I had thought, but the kick of the Briouse *pinard* thrust me forward at a good clip. The road was absolutely deserted; the night hung loosely around it, here and there tattered by attempting moonbeams. I was somewhat sorry to find the way hilly, and in places bad underfoot; yet the unknown adventure lying before me, and the delicious silence of the night (in which our words rattled queerly like tin soldiers in a plush-lined box) boosted me into a condition of mysterious happiness. We talked, the older and I, of strange subjects. As I suspected he had not always been a *gendarme*. He had seen service among the Arabs.

and the first description of The Wanderer:

B. called my attention to a figure squatting in the middle of the *cour* with his broad back against one of the more miserable trees. This figure was clothed in a remarkably picturesque manner; it wore a dark sombrerolike hat with a large drooping brim, a bright red gipsy shirt of some remarkably fine material with huge sleeves loosely falling, and baggy corduroy trousers whence escaped two brown, shapely, naked feet. On moving a little I discovered a face—perhaps the handsomest face that I have ever seen, of a gold-brown color, framed in an amazingly large and beautiful black beard. The features were finely formed and almost fluent, the eyes soft and extraordinarily sensitive, the mouth delicate and firm beneath a black mustache which fused with the silky and wonderful darkness falling upon the breast. The face contained a beauty and dignity which, as I first saw it, annihilated the surrounding tumult without an effort. Around the carefully formed nostrils there was something almost of contempt. The cheeks had known suns of which I might not think. The feet had traveled nakedly in countries not easily imagined. Seated gravely in the mud and noise of the *cour* under the pitiful and scraggly *pommier* . . . behind the eyes lived a world of complete strangeness and silence. The composure of the body was graceful and Jovelike. This being might have been a prophet come out of a country nearer to the sun. Perhaps a god who had lost his road and allowed himself to be taken prisoner by *le gouvernement français*. At least a prince of a dark and desirable country, a king over a gold-skinned people who would return when he wished to his fountains and his houris. I learned upon inquiry that he traveled in various countries with a horse and cart and his wife and children, selling bright colors to the women and men of these countries. As it turned out he was one of the Delectable Mountains; to discover which I had come a long and difficult way. Wherefore I shall tell you no more about him for the present, except that his name was Joseph Demestre.

We called him The Wanderer.

There is about this sort of writing a gusto, an intense sensitiveness to men and women and colors and stenches and anger and love that, like the face of Joseph Demestre, "annihilates the surrounding tumult without an effort." When a book like *The Enormous Room* manages to emerge from the morass of print that we flounder in, it is time to take off your new straw hat and jump on it.

SHERWOOD ANDERSON died suddenly, March 8, 1941, on a trip to South America, where he had intended to stay six months, visiting small towns of the kind that particularly interested him, and acquainting himself with the literary world. The effect of the second world war had been to make the United States feel the need of establishing a livelier interchange between the two Americas.

This group of letters to Van Wyck Brooks first appeared in *Story* magazine of September–October 1941—a special number devoted to Anderson. They are interesting because they show that Anderson was conscious of a literary tradition based on Lincoln, Mark Twain, and Whitman, and thought of himself as belonging to it. Brooks's "essay on *Highbrows and Lowbrows*" of which Anderson speaks, is the first chapter of Brooks's book, *America's Coming of Age,* published in 1915. In this chapter Brooks pointed out that there were "two main currents in the American mind running side by side but rarely mingling." On the one hand, you had "the current of Transcendentalism, originating in the piety of the Puritans, becoming a philosophy in Jonathan Edwards, passing through Emerson, producing the fastidious refinement and aloofness of the chief American writers, and, as the coherent ideals and beliefs of Transcendentalism gradually faded out, resulting in the final unreality of most contemporary American culture; and, on the other hand, the current of catchpenny opportunism, originating in the practical shifts of Puritan life, becoming a philosophy in Franklin, passing through the American humorists, and resulting in the atmosphere of contemporary business life."

Brooks regarded these currents as "both equally unsocial." In his time they were beginning to flow together. The moment of his describing the situation, the moment of our feeling it as uncomfortable, was the moment when it was coming to an end. Brooks himself was one of the writers who was helping to bring this about. And yet one still hears in these letters an echo of the imperfect understanding between Walt Whitman and Emerson.

SHERWOOD ANDERSON

LETTERS TO VAN WYCK BROOKS

Introductory Note by Van Wyck Brooks

I FIRST MET Sherwood Anderson in the late winter of 1917 at the office of *The Seven Arts* in New York. I think it was Waldo Frank who brought him into the magazine, of which Frank and I and James Oppenheim were editors. Paul Rosenfeld and Randolph Bourne were also of the circle, and we all became good friends; and I believe that *The Seven Arts* published the first of the Winesburg stories. Sherwood was still at that time in business, but he had written several novels, along with a great number of short stories; and he was eager to break his connection with business and establish himself as a writer. As he said in one of his letters, "I want to quit working for a living and go wander for five years in our towns." I can remember how struck I was by his fresh healthy mind and his true Whitmanian feeling for comradeship, his beautiful humility, his lovely generosity, and the "proud, conscious innocence" of his nature. This was his own phrase for Mark Twain's mind at the time when he was writing *Huckleberry Finn,* and it goes for Sherwood also. He was the most natural of men, as innocent as any animal or flowering tree.

For six or seven years we saw much of each other, and

these letters are the record of our friendship. They are especially interesting because these were the years during which he was discovering himself and his world. He was, as he says, "setting out on new roads," tasting the "Mid-America" that was his land, "the place between mountain and mountain"—touching it, catching its scent, listening, seeing; and his letters bring back the feeling of that time, when we were all of us groping and lonely. We were all trying to understand the nature of America, turning away from "European culture," and we all felt, as Sherwood says, that we were "struggling in a vacuum"—we had that "queer sense of carving a stone" that would be "cast into a stagnant sea." Well I remember these feelings, which Sherwood expresses; and I remember, too, what a boon it was to have a meeting-place at *The Seven Arts.* While most of us were Easterners, we felt that the heart of America lay in the West; and Sherwood was the essence of his West. He was full of Lincoln and especially of Mark Twain, and he wanted to sell me Twain, as he said in a letter. I was writing *The Ordeal of Mark Twain,* and he was anxious for me to understand him; and after I published the book he showed me clearly where my study had fallen short. I had failed to write the most important chapter, in which I should have praised *Huckleberry Finn.* I was too much concerned with the psychological problem, and the psychologist inhibited the poet in me. I regretted this as much as Sherwood, who loved Mark Twain above all writers. The last time I saw Sherwood, about 1939, we were dining in New York in a semipublic room. On the wall hung a life-sized photograph of Mark Twain, sitting in his rocking chair on the piazza at Redding. Sherwood looked up at it and smiled as he said, "There was a lovely man."

Sherwood bewailed Mark Twain's going East, among men from "barren hills and barren towns"; and he wrote to me, "A man cannot be a pessimist who lives near a brook or a cornfield." He never lost his happiness or his faith, for he knew where he belonged and he loved it. He brooded over his own country and sang it. He sang it least well perhaps in the *Mid-American Chants,* which was rather a matrix of poetry than poetry proper. But his short stories were poems.

They were certainly acrid at moments, but there he was always the poet. He suggests in these letters that I questioned his quality now and then, though he said that I was entitled to my personal taste. Well, the only question I felt regarded his novels, and I may have been quite mistaken. I only regretted that he wrote novels when he had a gift for storytelling that was, in its different way, like Chekhov's; for I never could feel that his novels were as good as his stories, and he was the most enthralling teller of tales. Never can I forget an evening, in 1937, which he spent at my house in Westport. For two hours he told stories about the folks at Marion, while we all listened like a three years' child.

CHICAGO—*1918?–19?*

BROOKS:

I cannot resist the temptation to write you a letter induced by a talk Waldo Frank and I had last evening. The talk drifted to Mark Twain and your attitude toward him. Something Waldo said gave me the notion that your digging into his work had made you a little ill—that you had seen, perhaps too clearly, his dreadful vulgarity and cheapness.

Of course your book cannot be written in a cheerful spirit. In facing Twain's life you face a tragedy. How could the man mean what he does to us if it were not a tragedy. Had the man succeeded in breaking through he would not have been a part of us. Can't you take it that way?

America a land of children—broken off from the culture of the world. Twain there—a part of that. Then the coming of industrialism. The putting of the child into the factory.

Mark Twain was a factory child. I am that. I can however stand off and look at him. When it would be second rate and unmanly to weep concerning myself I can think of him. For his very failure I love him. He was maimed, hurt, broken. In some way he got caught up by the dreadful cheap smartness, the shrillness that was a part of the life of the country, that is still its dominant note.

I don't want you to get off Twain. I want your mind on it. Please do not lose courage, do not be frightened away by the muck and ugliness of it.

For the Americans of the future there can be no escape. They have got to, in some way, face themselves. Your book, about the man they love and in a dumb way understand, will help mightily. I do want you to write that book.

SHERWOOD ANDERSON

VAN WYCK BROOKS

DEAR BROOKS:

I am glad you are going to get at Twain. It is absurd that he should have been translated as an artist by a man like Howells or that fellow Paine. There is something about him no one has got hold of. He belonged out here in the Middle West and was only incidentally a writer.

I've a notion that after Twain passed under the influence of Howells and others of the East he began to think of himself as a writer and lost something of his innocence. Should not one go to Huck Finn for the real man, working out of a real people?

Several years ago I tried to write a story concerning Twain. It never got to anything but I have a copy of the attempt in my desk. There is a character in the story—the old cheese maker from Indiana that I will sometime make the central figure in a real story. He is Twain's type of man.

It is odd what literary connections one makes. In my own mind I have always coupled Mark Twain with George Borrow. I get the same quality of honesty in them, the same wholesome disregard of literary precedent.

Lane's[1] have decided to go ahead with my cornfield songs. I call them Mid-American chants. Then I am going to publish the Winesburg tales—some two dozen of them in a book under the title *Winesburg*. When I came to look at my novel *Mary Cochran*—written several years ago—it didn't suit me. I shall hold it back for more work.

[1]John Lane published several of Anderson's books. V. W. B.

One has to realize that although there is truth in the Winesburg things there is another big story to be done. We are no longer the old America. Those are tales of farming people. We've got a new people now. We are a growing, shifting, changing thing. Our life in our factory towns intensifies. It becomes at the same time more ugly and more intense.

God damn it, Brooks, I wish my books would sell for one reason. I want to quit working for a living and go wander for five years in our towns. I want to be a factory hand again and wander from place to place. I want my frame to unbend from the desk and to go look and listen to this new thing.

My songs are going to be widely abused and perhaps rightly. I'm a poor enough singer. But there is a song here and it has been muffed. Masters might get it but he has too keen a quality of hate.

It makes me ill when I think how little I get done and the years hurrying along but I suppose we all know that sickness. I would like you to know I appreciate your interest in my efforts. The fact that you are interested is one of the bright spots. The quality of your mind I have always thought one of the really bully things of my generation.

I'll get to New York again some time. When I do I hope to see and talk with you.

SHERWOOD ANDERSON

59 W. Schiller St.

I'll send you the Twain thing to read, if I can find it, foı the sake of the cheese maker.

1918

DEAR BROOKS:

Waldo Frank gave me Charnwood's *Lincoln* when he was out here. Today there came from my bookseller your *America's Coming of Age*—I had not read it.

You and Charnwood are so oddly in the same spirit that I have been thinking of you. At lunch I read your essay on *Highbrows and Lowbrows.*

The conviction grows in me that you are seeing and think ing with extraordinary clearness but I am constantly puzzled by something.

I get in some odd way a sense of the fact that you want constantly to write of men like Twain and Whitman but draw back from their imperfections, their looseness of thought, their vulgarities.

The thought that was in my mind at lunch and that I want to put over to you may have no essential value as it may be an old thought to you.

Is not the tendency to dislike these men's imperfections—if you have it—an inclination in you to drift toward your own Highbrow classification?

I ask hesitatingly. I do not of course know.

I want you to write of Twain. I want to see that book come from you.

Surely the thing has to be undertaken as a labor of love and love should stomach imperfections.

I dare say that as you work you see little result from your work. You can't of course be popular. I believe however that you by some odd chance see the difficulties of the artistic tendency in the midst of American life more clearly than anyone else.

It is always and more than you realize worth while to men deeply involved and perhaps muddied by the looseness and vulgarity of life that you keep going ahead.

Your book is helpful to me as everything of yours I have ever seen is helpful.

S. Anderson

May 23rd, 1918

Dear Brooks:

I cannot resist an impulse I have to write to you again concerning your book—*America's Coming of Age.* Are there any others of your books in which you also develop the theme you have here taken hold of so firmly?

The amazing thing to me about your mind, Brooks, is that

you see so clearly what I did not suppose any man with a background such as I had thought of you as having could see.

I have myself understood the trenchant sadness of Lincoln, the rather childlike pessimism of Twain, the half sullen and dogmatic insistence on the part of Dreiser on the fight with Puritanism and Whitman's windy insistence on America. I thought I understood these things because I have lived in such a barren place, felt myself so futile, because I have really always felt a lack of strength to continue struggling in a vacuum and looked forward hopelessly to the time when some quirk of the mind would lead me to adopt finally some grotesque sectional attitude and spend myself uselessly on that.

When I talked to Waldo out here I felt in him a sense of background I have never had. I wondered if he knew the utter lack of background. It means so very much that you know and of course he must know also.

One works in an oddly futile way. This year, because I have been very tired after ten years of trying to stay among the men about me, to be part and parcel of them, and at the same time to build something a little permanent at odd moments.

One cannot surrender to the cheaper inclinations in writing, to miss perhaps the secondary approval of an ass like Mencken as his reward.

But then one gets this queer sense of carving a stone that will presently be cast into a stagnant sea, into the Sargasso Sea as you suggest.

I am very sure, after reading this book, that you must be sad also, that you also must feel deeply the futility of things.

What I want to ask you is why you do not sympathize with me in such expressions as my essay, *An Apology for Crudity,* or my *Chants?* Where do I hit wrong?

In the chants I reached into my own personal mutterings, half insane and disordered, and tried to take out of them a little something ordered. You should see how I clutched at the ordered cornfields, insisted on them to myself, took them as about the only thing I could see.

I haven't the right to expect much from such mutterings but I have the right to expect that, having written this book I have just read, you would know what I was at.

Forgive me if I sink to the triviality of explanation. Your mind has won my honest respect. I do not so much seek your approval as I do your brotherhood.

May I say that for me yours is the first, the only note in American criticism that I have ever thought worth a damn. It is really and deeply understanding.

SHERWOOD ANDERSON

Do try to form the habit of writing me some of your thoughts occasionally. It is lonely out here.

MY DEAR BROOKS:

Your letter has stirred up a world of thought in me. It isn't Twain I'm thinking of but the profound truth of some of your own observations.

As far as Twain is concerned, we have to remember the influences about him. Remember how he came into literature —the crude buffoon of the early days in the mining camps—the terrible cheap and second-rate humor of much of *Innocents Abroad.* It seems to me that when he began he addressed an audience that gets a big laugh out of the braying of a jackass and without a doubt Mark often brayed at them. He knew that later. There was tenderness and subtility in Mark when he grew older.

You get the picture of him, Brooks—the river man who could write going East and getting in with that New England crowd—the fellows from barren hills and barren towns. The best he got out of the bunch was Howells and Howells did Twain no good.

There's another point, Brooks. I can't help wishing Twain hadn't married such a good woman. There was such a universal inclination to tame the man—to save his soul as it were. Left alone, I fancy Mark might have been willing to throw his soul overboard and then—ye gods what a fellow he might have been, what poetry might have come from him.

The big point is—it seems to me that this salvation of the soul business gets under everybody's skin. With artists it takes the form of being concerned with their occupation as writers. A struggle constantly goes on. Call the poet a poet and he is no longer the poet. You see what I mean.

There is a fellow like X. for example. He writes me long letters. His days are often made happy or miserable according to whether or not he is writing well.

Is it so important? What star dust we are. What does it matter?

The point is that I catch X. so often striving to say things in an unusual way. It makes me cringe. I want to beat him with my fists.

I pick on X. as an example because I love him and I know he feels deeply. He should write with a swing—weeping, praying and crying to the gods on paper instead of making sentences as he so often does.

Well now you see I'm coming around. The cultural fellows got hold of Mark. They couldn't hold him. He was too big and too strong. He brushed their hands aside.

But their words got into his mind. In the effort to get out beyond that he became a pessimist.

Now, Brooks, you know a man cannot be a pessimist who lives near a brook or a cornfield. When the brook chatters or at night when the moon comes up and the wind plays in the corn, a man hears the whispering of the gods.

Mark got to that once—when he wrote *Huck Finn*. He forgot Howells and the good wife and everyone. Again he was the half savage, tender, god-worshiping, believing boy. He had proud conscious innocence.

I believe he wrote that book in a little hut on a hill on his farm. It poured out of him. I fancy that at night he came down from his hill stepping like a king—a splendid playboy, playing with rivers and men, ending on the Mississippi, on the broad river that is the great artery flowing out of the heart of the land.

Well, Brooks, I'm alone in a boat on that stream sometimes. The rhythm and swing of it is in some of my songs that are to be published next month. It sometimes gets into some of the Winesburg things. I'll ride it some more perhaps. It depends on whether or not I can avoid taking myself seriously. Whom the gods wish to destroy they first make dumb with the notion of being a writer.

Waldo is coming out to spend a month with me.

Wish I could see you sometime this summer. I'll be in the East for a month or more in June or July. Why couldn't you come to the mountains and have a few days walk with me?

SHERWOOD ANDERSON

May 31, 1918

DEAR BROOKS:

I know of course what you mean and it is because you have the clearsightedness to see that you are of such very great value. American writers have a trick of doing something it is difficult at first to understand. They harden, ripen out of time. Your notion of the stony field has significance. In such a field corn would come too soon to tassel. It would turn yellow and produce no grain.

You can see for yourself how our critics produce that peculiarly shallow effect. Dell goes that way, Mencken, Hackett, and our newspaper men out here are peculiarly so. Waldo can tell you of them.

It is probably true that the reason our men who are of importance, Lincoln, Whitman, Twain, Dreiser etc., all begin when they are almost old men is that they have to spend so much of their lives putting down roots. The strength goes into that. We have, you see, Lincoln producing a few notable utterances, Whitman some clear stuff out of much windiness; Twain, *Huck Finn;* Dreiser, *Sister Carrie,* etc.

Oddly enough you are the first man I have seen stoutly at it trying to take the stones out of the field—to give the roots a chance.

If you could get at Twain sympathetically and show how

and why he failed it would be lifting a great stone. He, now, you see, is just about to be accepted by the smart alecks as the great man. We shall be clubbed with his failures and the cheap things he did. His bad work will be glorified as it has been by Howells and others.

As for myself, I think there is soil for the raising of a crop if the stones can be taken away. . . .

Your attitude toward my own efforts is generous and helpful. What I am trying to say to you in all this letter writing is aside from that but connected with it too.

Any work accomplished is a thing already half dead. It may concern others but it cannot deeply concern the workman. He has to look ahead to new difficulties, to wading through new times of disillusionment and weariness.

In my own place here, in the distracted crowds and in the midst of distracting things, I have often lived on little protective sayings muttered to myself. "Do not lose the fine edge of your contempt," I say to myself. Other such smart sayings come to my lips. I find myself living on them.

Of the newer men I have met you and Waldo give me something else. What friendship you give strengthens. It is a thing that cuts across the darkness and the mist.

I would not be hurt by any criticism of my efforts coming from either of you. I would like to have you both feel brotherhood for me and give me as much as you can out of your thoughts.

Is it not probably true that men like Z. lose their grip because they do not stay among workers? They cannot stand the brusqueness and hardness with which men speak who have much to do. They go among idlers where soft meaningless flattery takes the place of truth.

Well if you see things in me give me your friendship as Waldo has done. Let me see your mind at work as often as you can.

I go back to your figure of the stony field. Corn is planted there. You go about trying to cultivate, throwing stones aside. Much of the corn will be destroyed. That may be my fate. It matters so damn little.

What would matter is that one should grow into a yellow rare ripe thing, that one should quit striving to put down roots. You get the sense of what I drive at.

SHERWOOD ANDERSON

I take the liberty of sending your note on to Frank. I will get and read the book you mention.

CHICAGO, ILL., *June seventh, Nineteen eighteen.*

DEAR BROOKS:

If I can fix one thought in your mind I will feel more free in approaching you. When I write to men like you and Frank I do it to cut the fog of my own loneliness. If I can make you feel that no letter of mine demands answering I shall feel more freedom.

I have had an experience lately that will be of interest to you. I got suddenly an impulse to read everything I could get hold of on Lincoln. Waldo stirred up the impulse in me by giving me Charnwood's life. I read others.

I am wondering if you might not profitably go to Lincoln for a greater understanding of Twain and Whitman. There is something—a quality there—common to the three men. In Lincoln it is perhaps more out in front of you.

I got a sense of three very honest boys brought suddenly to face the complex and intricate world. There is a stare in their eyes. They are puzzled and confused. You will be inclined to think Whitman the greater man perhaps. He came closer to understanding. He lacked Lincoln's very great honesty of soul.

Twain's way lies somewhere between the roads taken by the other two men.

I am struck with the thought that I would like to have you believe that Twain's cheapness was not really a part of him. It was a thing out of the civilization in which he lived that crept in and invaded him.

Lincoln let it creep in less, because he was less warm and human. He did not love and hate. In a simple solid way he stuck to abstract principles. He squares up to those principles. That's what makes him seem so big.

There is a kind of unconscious dodging in that—the country girl who died—I mean Ann—left Lincoln a thing to love that wasn't living and about. He could reach out his hand to that shadowy thing when he was lonely. It was all very fine for the making of the big stony thing that stood up sometimes before the world.

Twain got more deeply into the complex matter of living. He was more like you and me, facing more nearly our kind of problems.

Here I am going to confess something to you. Whitman does not mean as much to me as do the other two. There is somewhere a pretense about him, even trickiness. When I was a boy and another boy caught me fairly—doing some second-rate thing—I was supposed to do what we called "acknowledge the corn."

Lincoln wouldn't have done the second-rate thing.

Twain would and would have acknowledged the corn.

Whitman wouldn't have owned up.

Well there you are. I am putting Whitman below where he stands in my mind.

It is unfair. It springs from a growing desire I have to sell you Twain.

SHERWOOD ANDERSON

DEAR BROOKS:

I have been back in the grind for two weeks now and am looking forward with joy to the notion of wiping the dust of business off my feet for at least a time. I'll come down to New York this fall and stay two or three months. I want to wander about, readjust myself, get the weariness out of me and see if I cannot face life anew.

One of the things I look forward to most is the chance of seeing more of you fellows and feeding an insistent hunger in me for companionship.

You will be amused by my memorandum of resignation to my general manager here.

SHERWOOD ANDERSON

Chicago, June 25, 1918

To: Mr. Barton
Dear Barton:

You have a man in your employ that I have thought for a long time should be fired. I refer to Sherwood Anderson. He is a fellow of a good deal of ability but for a long time I have been convinced that his heart is not in his work.

There is no question but that this man Anderson has in some ways been an ornament to our organization. His hair, for one thing, being long and mussy, gives an artistic carelessness to his personal appearance that somewhat impresses such men as Frank Lloyd Wright and Mr. Curtenius of Kalamazoo when they come into the office.

But Anderson is not really productive. As I have said his heart is not in his work. I think he should be fired and if you will not do the job I should like permission to fire him myself.

I therefore suggest that Anderson be asked to sever his connections with the Company on August 1st. He is a nice fellow. We will let him down easy but let's can him.

Respectfully Submitted
Sherwood Anderson

New York, *August 3, 1918*

Dear Brooks:

Just got into town and am going into the country. I will be back here on Monday and will call you up. I want to find a hole in which to work and perhaps you can advise me. It will be good to see and talk with you.

Sherwood Anderson

Dear Brooks:

I have got settled in my own hole—427 W. 22nd St. Phone Chelsea 6140. I expect to write here every day until noon so you can reach me any morning. I have two cots so any time you will stay in town overnight I have a bed for you.

SHERWOOD ANDERSON

NEW YORK, *Sept. 9, 1918*

DEAR BROOKS:

I think I have got into a vein that may interest you and may suggest some things to your mind in connection with your thoughts of Mark Twain. I wrote a story called *The Dancer* which has nothing to do with what I have in mind. Then I began writing a story about a figure called Hugh McVey, a Lincolnian type from Missouri. The story is very definite in my mind, in fact is definitely outlined. Perhaps our talk of these men led me to take one of these men up, live with him in his impulses and among his people and show if possible what influences have led him to be the kind of man we are puzzling about. I have written ten or fifteen thousand words of the tale. For the moment I have laid aside the other thing I call *The Romanticist.* This new tale I call *The Poor White.* I shall be glad to show you the outline of it. Tennessee is here and will be for two or three weeks. I want her to know you and Mrs. Brooks. Let's try to get together.

With love,
SHERWOOD ANDERSON

OWENSBORO, KY.,
June 24

DEAR BROOKS:

I have been rereading *Letters and Leadership* on a hot day in the Ohio River Valley and that has reminded me I have not sent on your copy of *Winesburg.* I will send it as soon as I get home.

My mind is a little hopeful that in *Winesburg* and in future novels that come from my hand you will find a real refusal to accept life on the terms it is usually presented. If that is true the result is not a conscious effort on my part but is in fact the way life has come to look to me.

The growth of that point of view is I take it what you were seeking when you wrote those remarkable papers. I do hope you will find some realization in *Winesburg.*

SHERWOOD ANDERSON

On train in Kentucky, Wednesday.

DEAR BROOKS:

Beside my own recurring thoughts of you I keep crossing your trail from time to time. The other day I went into a hospital to see the wife of a Chicago judge who is Tennessee's friend and who has been ill for a long time. She was reading your *Letters and Leadership* and said at once your mind had helped her understand the difficulties of American writing as nothing else had.

"I have so often not seen what you were driving at, everything you wrote seemed so incomplete. Now I see that you stand on nothing," she said. I sent her your *America's Coming of Age.*

In a book store I saw a Jew named Larson[1] who is a friend of yours. We talked of you. It was his notion you were almost too prolific, wrote too easily.

I hadn't that angle on you. "I thought he was painfully careful, almost to the point of being constipated sometimes," I said.

We discussed the matter but a few minutes. I liked the looks of him and didn't want to dispute and then I felt that he might as well as not be right and I wrong. "Everything you say shows you don't know Brooks," he declared and I took his word for it.

I have been reading *The Education of Henry Adams* and feel tremendously its importance as a piece of American writing. New England can scarcely go further than that. It must be in its way very complete. We do I am sure both

[1]Properly Max Lippitt Larkin, a Russian. V. W. B.

live and die rather better in the Middle West. Nothing about us is as yet so completely and racially tired.

When you get at your Mark Twain (I suppose you already have) you must do a chapter on the American going East into that tired, thin New England atmosphere and being conquered by its feminine force.

I came West with my new book *Poor White* about laid by—as we out here say of the corn crop in early October. It is in shocks and stood up in the field. The husking is yet to do. I will not attempt it for a time as the proof on *Winesburg* should be along most any time. . . .

I am back at the old place in the advertising office. The moving picture dependence became impossible. That isn't my road out.

Back here I almost feel able to say that I don't care if I never travel again. The place between mountain and mountain I call Mid-America is my land. Good or bad, it's all I'll ever have.

What I want now is to see a magazine started here in the heart of America. I want you fellows from the coast to come here. We have always been going to you. I want it changed if possible.

It isn't impossible. I will get money for the purpose. I have two or three leads that may lead to money. I shall try it out thoroughly.

Do write me the news of yourself. Give my love to Mrs. Brooks. If I were at home Tennessee would want me to wish you a happy year.

SHERWOOD

10th Floor, Brooks Bldg.,
Chicago

HARRODSBURG, KENTUCKY,
Jan. 8, 1919

DEAR VAN WYCK:

I wonder if I hurt you by my letter. I can't quite presume to think so. It would be too absurd.

However I am writing after reading you in Sept. *Dial.* O, what a relief after so much of the New York smart befuddled writing. Those clear crisp sentences, clear crisp thoughts. It is truly the writing, Brooks, I so utterly admire writing here.

SHERWOOD ANDERSON

I am still planning to hold you to your promise to read my book.

March 31, 1919

DEAR BROTHER BROOKS:

I am so glad to hear from you that I gladly forgive you the long silence. The winter has slipped away for me. I went through *Poor White* for the first writing and then put it away to ripen a bit. In the meantime I am doing some experiments.

First, a new book of *Tales* made up of some already written and others that are on the fire.

Second—a purely insane, experimental thing I call *A New Testament.* It is an attempt to express, largely by indirection, the purely fanciful side of a man's life, the odds and ends of thought, the little pockets of thoughts and emotions that are so seldom touched.

I've a fancy this last experiment would make your hair stand on end. It is infinitely more difficult than the chants.

Why do I insist on looking upon you as the apostle of clearness? For some reason you stand in my mind as the supersensitive of all that is best in what is orthodox and certain.

I am myself as uncertain as a weathercock. It seems to me that anything approaching accomplishment grows wearisome.

I want constantly to push out into experimental fields. "What can be done in prose that has not been done?" I keep asking myself.

And so I constantly set out on new roads.

What is gained—perhaps nothing but a little colorful strength in my everyday writing. I push on knowing that none will perhaps care in the least for these experiments into which I put so much emotional force.

It is at least the adventure. How I wish I could sit with you for an hour and talk of what I mean.

About Twain. I have still the hunch. Do not look too much to him for an explanation of what is not understandable in him. Think of him as a boy whipped and blown about by the winds of his times.

Look to his times, to the men and the emotions of his times. He wanted very much to be respectable. I wonder if there wasn't a touch of the inferiority complex in him. That would explain much.

He never gave himself to a great or a deep emotion, didn't dare, didn't trust himself. Whitman must have seemed a monster to him.

He stood on the doorstep of New England. It's a ridiculous notion but it's a fact. Twain with hat in hand and an apologetic air on New England's doorstep.

Good luck to you and Mrs. Brooks. I could write many pages and not say what I would like to you.

SHERWOOD

December 15, 1919

DEAR BROTHER:

It is a good morning when I have letters from you and Paul,[1] both of you have been silent so long. Well I have thought of you daily and in a way have altogether understood that your not writing was something that had nothing to do with our established feeling for each other. I am so glad about the Twain book and I do like the title. Waldo's book[2] came to me as an amazing, splashing, living, colorful thing. It will do something for him too, to have done this job. It will be good ground under his feet.

I put the *Poor White* book away when I left New York and for a long time after I came back here I was pretty much a blank dumb thing. I had you see to reestablish myself in

[1]Paul Rosenfeld.

[2]*Our America.*

this grim business of making a living in business. It grows constantly more like eating my own vomit.

However I have gone quite a long way with my New Testament book. I am going to print some of it in the *Little Review.* It is a thing without beginning or end—something that in the end I hope will express something of what you and Waldo are driving at in a semi-poetic vein.

I have up also an old book of mine called *Mary Cochran* which I am trying to get ready for publishing. Can't tell when it will be ready. I have little time for sustained work. How eagerly I look forward to seeing your Twain book. You will never know, Brooks, what your mind has meant to me, how many dark paths it has illuminated.

It is good, too, to feel that the blow that fell when *Seven Arts* went down did not destroy; that you, Waldo and sometimes myself too have been swimming.

Paul has his book[1] in the publisher's hands. I had a fine letter from him today.

Waldo is out in Nebraska. There is something quiet and fine growing up in him that was always there but often out of control.

I am going to try to get to New York between Christmas and New Year's for a short stay. A letter from there tells me the *Dial* is going to attempt being artistic and literary and is to throw politics away. Scofield Thayer and J. S. Watson, Jr. have taken over control. Stewart Mitchell is managing editor. I do not know any of them.

Tennessee was ill for a long time but is now well and strong again. If you do come east in the Spring stop for a few days and look about here.

And give my love to Mrs. Brooks.

Write me when you can.

SHERWOOD

DEAR BROOKS:

I've been thinking about your letter of the other day and my answer that didn't say what I wanted it to say. Your

[1]*Musical Portraits.*

not writing letters doesn't bother me. I have no special feeling about it at all.

I would in some way like to know how I feel in another respect.

I dare say your book when it comes will not have the passionate flaming thing in it that Waldo's book often has. But, Brooks, you must realize what an inciter to flame in others you are.

I have a hunch you are doomed to be a man whose voice will not be heard by many here for a long time but you should realize what it means to those who do hear it.

When in speaking of *Winesburg* you used the word adolescence you struck more nearly than you know on the whole note of me. I am immature, will live and die immature. A quite terrible confession that would be if I did not represent so much.

I am conscious I do represent much and often I feel like a very small boy in the presence of your mind and of Waldo's too.

What is true of me is true of Sandburg, but we are different. He is submerged in adolescence. I am in it and of it but I look out. Give Sandburg a mind and you perhaps destroy him. I don't know whether that would be true of me or not.

Be sure of this, Brooks. No matter how much you may seem to yourself to work in isolation, it is not true. Your voice always comes clear to me and will to some others. You have been the bearer of a lamp that has illuminated many a dark place for me.

Nothing that is going to happen next year will mean as much to me as getting my hand on your new book.

You, Waldo and me—could three men be more unlike. How truly I love you two men.

SHERWOOD

I think of my Testament as a passionate attempt to get poetry into the thing you have expressed time and again and that you and Waldo have together made me a little conscious of. I want to have it be a distillation. God knows how far I shall succeed.

Sunday
August 24

DEAR VAN WYCK:

A clear beautiful Sunday morning. What a stir I made within myself by writing you that letter. It was written at a time when the engine that is myself was running wildly, grinding no grain.

Someone had told me that your attitude toward my work was that it was not sound, wholesome. In myself—in my right mind—I should have paid no attention. It happened I was spiritually very tired.

There came and still come odd, hurtful reactions from some things I write—a woman I have once known—strange men and women I have never seen, write me queer abusive letters. "Why do you wallow in ugly lies about life?" they ask. I have got a dozen such letters in a week.

I put them aside—the thought of them. There were certain minds I did not expect to approve what I do. I did expect they would feel sure I was going on at my work honestly, with an intent of spiritual integrity.

You must know, must have felt how much I counted on your mind there.

The slipshod gossip that you had another attitude, joined these others in the wallowing theory, would, had I not been spiritually weary, have made no impression on my mind. I did harbor it a little and am ashamed. After I had written you the letter I woke at night sick with shame. I couldn't work because of it.

I won't say I won't do the same again. When I'm tired I'm no good, a yellow dog sometimes.

As for your not knowing sometimes what I'm driving at, I don't always myself. God knows too many of my things don't fully register.

Perhaps I don't care enough. I feel myself often an instrument to adventure in flights along strange paths. Why should you ever under any circumstances feel any obligation to say anything about my work—to approve of it I mean.

A nasty, tired building up of substantiating proofs that the gossip I had heard was true must have gone on within me.

O brother Brooks, please forget my silly letter.

There are lots of sweeter, finer things I can quarrel with you about at the Pittsburg meeting. I could quarrel with you indefinitely as to the value of the whole lot of political-minded magazines.

I am writing a new book I'm sure you are going to love. It really does I feel get hold of a man and woman in American life intimately, intensely. Am I not a lucky dog to have this time to work undisturbed? If my damned books would only sell a little better. Is the *Ordeal* going to sell? I want that book to sell for other reasons than your own interest. I wish to God I could make all Americans read it.

SHERWOOD

FAIRHOPE, ALA., *May 15th*

DEAR BROTHER:

It was a big moment for me when I got your note and found you liked *Poor White*. When the novel was finished some weeks ago I said to Tennessee, "There is one man's mind I would like to have on that book—it's Brooks." I thought of sending it on and asking you to read it but know yours is a busy life and hadn't the nerve. Then Huebsch did it for me and now I have what I want. The gods are good to me. I am also happy about two other things—that your book is at last on the way to me and that you saw what I wanted someone to see in the *Dial* story—*The Triumph of the Egg*. To my mind it was one of the very best things I had ever done but when I showed it to Paul and Waldo they did not seem much impressed. O, Brooks, if you but knew what your own clear fine mind has meant to me these last two or three years. Well, there's no use trying to tell you.

It has been a wonderful time for me here these three months. In the first place I persuaded Tennessee to be utterly reckless, chuck her job and income and run off here with me. That has worked out. She is getting well and is happier than I have ever seen her. What a tremendous thing life is. For several years she has been a tired woman. Here she rested and then suddenly began to play. There are great quantities of red, yellow and blue clay here—very fine and plastic—Tennessee suddenly began working in it and already she does really remarkable things. What new joy in life that approach towards beauty coming in a definite form out of herself has given her. I go about whispering to myself, "She is going to be well. She is going to be well." O, for a world of people not tired. What things could come out of them.

X. has been for a long time silent. Knowing nothing, I still feel I do know there is something the matter. I am sure it is about the novel. It is not getting across with people who have read it and away down underneath has not got across with him but he is fighting that thought insisting. Is my hunch at all correct? If it is I am unspeakably sorry. I love X. very deeply and the deep-seated desire in him to be a great man hurts me at times like an open wound.

We will be leaving here in about a week and after that address me at—Critchfield & Company, 10th Floor, Brooks Bldg., Chicago. I hope to be in New York for a short stay early in June and trust I shall see you then. There are many things I want to talk to you about. Have begun a rollicking, Rabelaisian book called *Many Marriages,* a thing I have long hungered to do. It will take marvelous good health and spirits to carry the thing off but I may never be in better shape to begin it.

Also I am painting and doing my own kind of poetry. The two things are much alike in me—mystic, vague impulses. There is a painter here who looks at my things, shakes his head and goes home and takes Epsom salts. It is perhaps the best way to take the two sides of me.

Tennessee sends love to you. Please bear our love to Mrs.

Brooks. Is there any chance I may sell serial rights for *Poor White* to *Freeman* or *Dial?* It would give me some more freedom if I could achieve some money in this way.

With love,
SHERWOOD

EPHRAIM, WIS.—*Tuesday*

DEAR BROOKS:

This is the sort of thing that I thought might go well in the *Freeman.* I would not want however to sell these things at 2c per word. In a way I should rather keep them for a book I hope some day to print than to send them out at such a low price. I should be asking *Dial* $25 for these things. Would that be impossible for you?

Am back in the woods again and happy here. I hope to be writing pretty steadily this summer.

SHERWOOD

Sunday morning

DEAR BROOKS:

There are two reasons why *Freeman* can't use such things as *The Man in the Brown Coat.* First because it isn't any good. That reason don't go. It is. Second because *Freeman* is a political magazine. *New Republic, Nation, Freeman.* None of them give a damn for literature really. They seem to feel that creative writing has nothing to do with revolution. They want to put a new sort of government in at Washington. Well, the *Freeman* permits you. That's a long step.

There remains *Little Review* and *Dial* as voices for what artistic urge there may be in the country. The gods protect and nourish us. Scattered, immature, undignified, pretentious asinine things. I don't look at *Little Review* at all. I throw such things as *Man in the Brown Coat* into it.

Have just looked at the last *Dial.* It's spoiled eggs. Some old castrated babbler named Hueffer—or Heifer—name don't matter—a lot of other half-baked stuff—no editing—no purpose—hell.

I don't know why I should swear to you about all this—most of the time I don't think about it but go on working. It did hurt though when I found you also rather taking *Winesburg* for example as a sex book. It got under my hide a bit. I'm usually thick-skinned.

To me it seems a little as though one were permitted to talk abstractly of things, to use scientific terms regarding them—in the new dispensation—but when one attempts to dip down into the living stuff the same old formula holds. A really beautiful story like *Hands* for example is—well, nasty. God help us. Dozens of men have told me privately they knew Wing Biddlebaum. I tried to present him sympathetically—taboo.

I get so much force and reality in your *Ordeal*. I read it over and over like a Bible or Shakespeare's *Sonnets*. Twain is dead—he paid the price of caving in—but I wonder if I make you feel what I'm talking about.

In the first place I wish you could know how much I have loved—do love—your mind. I've frankly banked on it more than the mind of any other American. Am I right in my secret belief that you, down at bottom, believe me, in my reactions to life—well, not nice?[1] Can I—have I the privilege of caressing your mind so?

I'm settled down to a quite new novel—a tale of country life in Ohio. It has marched steadily along—a living tale I believe full of winds and farm yards and people. I paint too quite a lot. Your *Ordeal* has struck deep. It sets people talking and wondering.

SHERWOOD

Does Twain's formula "Freedom and the other precious things"—still hold?

What a God damn letter. Well, it's off my chest. It's glorious to have a few more months out of doors—steadily at work.

[1]No, he was wrong here. I had no such thought. V. W. B.

OXFORD, *July 26*

DEAR BROOKS:

I have written a note to Miss Alice Chown[1] and perhaps will see her in London. We will be here all this week, then back to London until sailing time.

The trip has been really wonderful and I for one am bursting full of new impressions. As for Oxford—well you know how unbelievably lovely it is. Saw Stearns in London and he told me of the book by the American intellectual K of Ps.[2] It should be quite a back-breaker.

Will be in New York a few days on my way home and hope I shall see you.

With love,
SHERWOOD

DEAR VAN WYCK:

I think also that *I'm a Fool* is a piece of work that holds water, but do you not think its wide acceptance is largely due to the fact that it is a story of immaturity and poses no problem? After all isn't it, say, Mark Twain at his best, the *Huckleberry Finn* Mark Twain?

In the same book there is a story *There She Is—She Is Taking Her Bath* I would like you to read. And then the story called *The Man Who Became a Woman* and *The Man's Story.*

One doesn't want to go on always with the childlike feeling for surface—not just that. I suppose this is my quarrel with you—which isn't a quarrel because I love you and you have done so much for me, cleared so many paths for me. I mean, I presume that I do not want you to like best of my things the things easiest to like.

I am happy that you are working again and that Paul is working. For a long time after I came out here I was uncomfortable about him, feeling that he was not at work and

[1]An English friend of Randolph Bourne's. V. W. B.

[2]A reference to Harold Stearn's symposium, *Civilization in the United States.* "K of Ps" stands for Knight of Pythias.

was disturbed for some reason. Then at last the beast wrote me and reported himself at work and all right.

You have a kind of power over my mind, Van Wyck, of making me think of what you are thinking and so I got James on my mind after you got to work at him. You may be interested to know my reactions to some solid weeks of James reading—the feeling of him as a man who never found anyone to love—who did not dare love. I really can't care much for any character after he gets through with it—he, in short, takes my love from me too.

I've a fancy—can it be true that he is the novelist of the haters? Oh, the thing infinitely refined and carried far into the field of intellectuality as skillful haters find out how to do.

It is you see but a notion but I thought it might interest you.

I am enthusiastic about Paul's theme—*The Port of New York*—the title is inspired.

Your garden does sound inviting. When will I be where I may talk now and then with the few men who give me most?

I'm working steadily on the book *Straws* and have a new novel stirring and alive in me. I hope strongly I shall be able to get into it this fall and winter.

My regards to Mrs. Brooks. If you get a chance please insult Paul now and then because he does not write to me oftener.

SHERWOOD

33 *East Liberty Street,* RENO,
July

DEAR VAN WYCK:

I got hold of *Dial* with your first paper on James and it fascinated me. It was so good to find you writing again—with that clear flowing style that so got me when I first came to it.

A strange lad—that Henry—and you make one feel the strangeness and reality of him. For a time—when you were working so steadily—doing the *Freeman* things—I thought something in you had got pretty tired but this seems crisp and alive.

I'm sure it is going to be a fine book and only wish I could read all of it now.

Am working pretty steadily and enjoying the fact of life immensely. Last winter in New York I was tired and petulant and that has pretty much passed. I am out on the desert —plenty of sun and wind and a nice large sense of leisure.

This is another world—very distinct from the East and quite as distinct I fancy from the Pacific coast. At first the land seems dead, an endless sea of sagebrush but as you walk and ride over it the under delicacy of color, plant and flower life comes forth and sometimes—to your amazement—all flames into color.

Love and good wishes,
SHERWOOD

RENO, NEVADA, *July 30, 1923*

DEAR VAN WYCK:

After all, Van Wyck, the danger is not imminent. The book is one that spreads out and out. I have to confine it. Get and keep it within a channel if I can.

Do I not know there has always been some of my work you do not like? But how could it be otherwise. I dare say if you and I were to see each other more closely, become really personally acquainted—which we never have quite—there would remain a difficulty.

As for myself, Van Wyck—I have seen so much of ugly meaningless, drifting men that I have come to love the men I feel definitely at work and when you write me of your feeling of being crowded inside I am made happy by your letter. The feeling spreads a sense of richness, of fecundity over my consciousness of you just now and I like that.

I want to settle down really and make myself a home

somewhere soon but Westport has its difficulties. Cost for one thing. You see I can live more economically any number of other places. I have to consider that.[1]

There are a lot of things I would like to talk with you about—the attitude of the artist, for one thing. In your Twain you come so near getting what I feel about the man but you did miss an essential thing some way.

Do you know I had, Van Wyck, a feeling that it was just the artist in Twain you in some way resented. There was somewhat the sense of a just judge trying a criminal rather than the sympathetic friend or lover.[2]

Can we understand at all, ever, where we do not love?

Perhaps all that struggling side of James you will feel more fully. He is more of your own world, isn't he? Twain was more of my world.

You see in my book—which after all I think I shall not call *Straws*—but *A Modernist Notebook*—I am frankly daring to proclaim myself the American Man.

I mean by that to take all into myself if I can, the salesmen, business men, laborers, all among whom I have lived. I do get the feeling that I, in a peculiar way and because of the accident of my position in letters, am a kind of composite essence of it all.

And actually there are days when people by thousands drift in and out of me. On a recent day here when I walked in the streets this natural physical feeling of being completely in rapport with every man, woman and child along a street wherein I walked became so intense that I had to go hide myself—to rest a little.

I speak of this because, when the feeling has leaked over into expression in my work you have so often said you didn't understand what I was talking about.

I want you to understand more than I can say.

And God knows I don't say this as an apology for what is

[1]He thought for a long time of living in Westport, Connecticut, where his brother Karl had long been settled and Paul Rosenfeld and I also lived. But these were his roaming years. Karl spoke to me once of Sherwood's liking "to be alone in strange places." V. W. B.

[2]He was right. It was partly the fault of my method. V. W. B.

not fully fruitioned in my work. No one can be more conscious of the failure of the greater part of it than I am.

But I do want you, Van Wyck, to feel for James and his difficulties, give yourself wholly to James. I can't help asking that you do it more fully than you did when you wrote of Twain.

With love,
SHERWOOD A.

Sunday, RENO

DEAR BROOKS:

When, some time ago, I asked you to take a look at this new book of mine I did not realize what a whale it was going to be. There are almost 150,000 words of it and I could not ask you to wade through any such pile. You have enough on your hands as things stand, and an unfinished book waiting. I should so much rather have you spend your time writing so that I may later read. I'll send it along to Otto Liveright, who is to show it to Harpers. They may want a part of it for the magazine.

The book has you in it with many others. It contains no criticism of you but expresses the regret of a middle western workman that you seemed unwilling or unable to respond to his hunger for more intimate contact, as fellow workmen, with some of the more cultured men of the East.

As for the woman's article in *Dial* I did not in any way connect you with it and did not take her quotation of you as intended to suggest you had said that particular thing of me. I do know of course that you have been out of sympathy with some of my work that has meant most to me and that after some years I still think first-rate work, but I can't very well blame you for that.

I might quarrel with such a statement as applied to Lawrence if I had you here to state at length my point of view—which is that no man can be bogged in immaturity who has done as much good work as Mr. Lawrence.

My dear Brooks, isn't there at least a chance that the fear of emotional response to life may be as much a sign of immaturity as anything else? It does seem so to me.

I really think the article in *Dial* was ill-natured and ill-mannered and largely made up of the fragments of ill-natured things that have been said of me ever since I began working. What puzzles me is the *Dial.* The article is so evidently incompetent. Lord, I could have written so much sharper and clearer criticism of myself. What the *Dial* is up to I can't quite make out. They give me their praise and buy my novel and publish it and then seem to devote themselves to a kind of apology to the public for me.

Of course I want more than anything else freedom for you or any other workman who really wants to work. It has been an odd year for me. I have been more or less separated from all the workmen I know except Stieglitz who has written me often and some very beautiful and helpful letters this year. Poor man, he has had a year of suffering, a part of the time being unable to lift his arms because of pain.

I myself have had an unhappy year. I think often that a good many people, perhaps, you dear Brooks, among them, think of me as a mere reckless adventurer but I have been up to something with my life and work. I am not a mere rudderless ship and now and then I do make a port.

Well, I do know that you have and always have had much to give me and I've got some of it. I'll be glad of more. There are not many sincere workmen in the country and in New York in particular there is so often just a superficial slinging of some smart saying at the head of a man, when understanding or the inclination to try to understand fails. But you know these things as well as I do and I dare say have suffered from them as much. It is a part of the artist's life and I escape a good deal by not seeing the more ill-natured and superficial slings.

For me, anyway, work looms ahead, plenty of it. I really do begin to see a great many of my own failings and shortcomings as a workman and am at least trying all the time to shake them off. And I'll be glad when I can be again where I can see and talk to men whose aims are somewhat like my own.

The book is done for better or worse and will be going off to Liveright I think some time next week.

With love,
SHERWOOD

DEAR VAN WYCK:

I am writing to ask something of you. When I have finished my *Straws,* which is a kind of attempt to picture the artist in our American life, I am wondering if it would be too much trouble for you to read it.

I shall be pretty close to it and perhaps cannot judge it. It will be more or less broken and fragmentary but it is all written on a theme that has occupied your own thoughts all your life.

It is just your mind I would like on it. Will you do it?

SHERWOOD

The disaster would not be immediately impending.

DEAR VAN WYCK:

Well, I shall live more like a monk after this I hope. Have got a little farm in the mountains of Virginia. We go there in the spring. Wish you could come there some time for that real getting acquainted.

Your letter only got to me after I had got back here to New Orleans. There would have been no use seeing each other in New York this trip. I saw no one—not really.

God help me, I've been lecturing to help pay for the farm. Paul said he might try it. Tell him—"No."

It's no go.

I saw young Holt[1] and he talked of a book on me in the McBride books. I had the temerity to suggest you. It was nervy of me. He said something had been said to you and you couldn't do it.

[1]Guy Holt.

I was glad. Had I been able to saddle you with it, I would have been ashamed.

Lordy, how many people are vulgar.

You find out when you go lecturing.

I hope you will really give me a chance to know you sometime.

The years fly so. There is so little done.

I am venturing a book of notes, comments, etc., this spring. I hope it may have some life in it.

Love to all in your house. We shall have a quiet house in the country soon.

Come sometime—when you want a quiet place to work—both of you.

Sherwood

I am consumed with curiosity. When shall we have a new book by you?

November 14, 1925,
Zorle, Penna.

Dear Van Wyck:

How belated I am. I have just got to your James. One reason is that the bookstores where I have been handle no books.

And what a keen delightful book this is—the same clear beautiful prose and—will you forgive my saying so—much more real sympathy with and understanding of your man than in the Twain.

The book is one I shall want to read again and again.

As ever,
Sherwood Anderson

We have bought a little farm down in Virginia and will go there to live in the Spring. New Orleans, for all its charm, is too hot for too many months. My new book seems to be selling. Now I am lecturing to pay for the farm and build a house on it. My regards to Mrs. Brooks.

S. A.

[after a long silence]

MARION, VIRGINIA,
August Sixth,
1938

DEAR VAN WYCK BROOKS:

I am fixing up a room in my house with framed pictures of my friends and men I admire. I spend a great deal of time alone in the country and most of you I often want to see I seldom do see. You may think it a poor substitute but a picture framed and hung up in a room I am in and out of every day does seem to bring my friends closer.

Will you please send me a picture of yourself for framing? I will be grateful.

Sincerely,
(signed) SHERWOOD ANDERSON